The Who's Who of

OLDHAM ATHLETIC

1907-2008

The Who's Who of
OLDHAM ATHLETIC
1907-2008

Garth Dykes

DB PUBLISHING

Pirst published in Great Britain in 2008 by
The Breedon Books Publishing Company Limited
Breedon House, 3 The Parker Centre,
Derby, DE21 4SZ.

This paperback edition published in Great
Britain in 2013 by DB Publishing, an imprint of
JMD Media Ltd

A catalogue record for this book is available from the
British Library.

ISBN 978-1-78091-300-1

Printed and bound in the UK by Copytech (UK)
Ltd Peterborough

Contents

DEDICATION

To my dear sister Hilary
and
To Harry Collins and Zac Taylor
with love from Grandpa

Introduction

As I boarded a number-eight Oldham Corporation double-decker bus at Hollinwood on a snowy late-Saturday afternoon in January 1952, after one of my infrequent playing appearances for Chadderton Grammar School Old Boys FC, a sequence of events unfolded that has remained with me very clearly ever since. 'Hold tight please,' intoned the conductor, whose rather fractured vowels I immediately took to be of East European origin. While still on the platform I noticed that the conductor had a copy of the *Green Final* poking out of the cubby-hole beneath the stairs of the bus. 'How did the Latics get on?' I enquired. 'Won 11–2,' came the swift reply. 'No,' I replied, wondering whether he had misunderstood the question, 'I meant the Latics, not Oldham Rugby!' At this point the *Green Final* was produced with a flourish and my heart sank – my favourite team had in fact won 11–2, Eric Gemmell had scored seven, and I hadn't been there to see it happen. It didn't really help that when I arrived home, my father's ear-to-ear grin confirmed that I had missed the Latics best result bar none. It is ironic that I should so clearly recall a match that I hadn't attended, rather than the many hundreds, and maybe thousands that I have. With odd notable exceptions – 11–0 versus Southport on Boxing Day 1962 for example – I believe that it is the individual players, rather than the matches, that come most readily to mind. Personal memories from school days include Ray Haddington's whiz-bang shooting and one particular penalty-kick against Stockport County in a 3–3 draw at Boundary Park in October 1949. Placing the ball on the spot, Haddington obligingly pointed to the goalkeeper's right, where he intended to place his shot. Whether 'Tiger' Bowles, County's custodian, believed him or not, he hardly had a chance to move a muscle when a typical Haddington thunderbolt shook the rigging at the indicated spot, and the shell-shocked goalkeeper was then treated to a cheeky V-sign to go with the equalising goal! In recalling individual players, it is hoped that a book devoted to every single one of the 900-plus to have represented the club since 1907 – and 1905 for those who played in the earliest FA Cup ties – will have done justice to your particular favourites. Hopefully, also, I may be back in favour with two gentlemen who expressed their amazement at my omission of Simon Stainrod and Paul Warhurst from my last title *The Legends of Oldham Athletic*. Perhaps a view of the full palette of players spanning over 100 years will give some idea of the difficulties encountered in selecting a mere 100! Here, then, follows a biography of every player to pull on a shirt in a Latics first-team game. I appreciate that, like all sporting organisations, Oldham Athletic AFC has to look to the future, but it must also never forget its past and the traditions built by yesterday's heroes. I hope what follows will evoke many happy memories for Latics supporters, whether young or old. As a journey of nostalgia, it has been a pleasure to write, and I do hope that readers will enjoy it as much as I have.

Garth Dykes
Leicester
May 2008

Acknowledgements

Given the number of years that I have spent accumulating the necessary facts for this book, I have a great many people to thank for their input, encouragement and support. As ever, my first debt of gratitude is to my dear partner Ann, to whom the Latics remain runners-up.

A special thank you to my good friends and fellow football historians Jim Creasy, Mike Jackman, Mike Davage, Michael Braham and Barry J. Hugman, truly a Premier League line up of English soccer's foremost researchers!

My dear sister Hilary, to whom this book is dedicated, has once again been a wonderful helpmate, as have her good friends and neighbours Doreen and David Orchard.

Many club and general statisticians, former players and their dependants have added greatly to the content of this book. They are: Stewart Beckett, Bill Cook, John D. Cross, K. Fowweather, Harry Greenmon, Alan Hardy, Alma Haslam, Anne Hemsley, Brian Hobbs, Steve Hobin, Peter Holme (Research Officer of the National Football Museum at Preston), Bryan Horsnell, Gordon Lawton, John Litster (editor of *The Scottish Football Historian*), Wade Martin, Martin Nuttall, Robert W. Reid (Partick Thistle FC), Roy K. Shoesmith, Ray Spiller, David Sullivan (Millwall FC Museum), Doreen Williamson. The late Geoffrey T. Butterworth, H.B. Church, Peter Haslam, Charles J. Hemsley, George C. King, Jim Kirton, Douglas Lamming, George H. Milligan, Jimmy and Florrie Naylor, Beaumont Ratcliffe, Austin W. Trippier, Albert F. Valentine, Tommy Williamson, Peter Windle and Alex O. Wilson.

Finally, sincere thanks once again to my friend Rajesh 'Raj' Jobanputra, whose computing expertise has helped me out on numerous occasions.

Photographs

Most photographs in this book are courtesy of the *Oldham Evening Chronicle*. Copies can be obtained from the *Chronicle* at 172 Union Street, Oldham OL1 1EQ (0161 633 2121).

Additional photographs are from the author's collection, and those kindly loaned by Steve Hobin and Gordon Lawton.

Players

ACKERLEY, Stanley

Full-back

Born: Manchester, 12 July 1942.
Career: Manchester United amateur July 1957, professional November 1959. OLDHAM ATHLETIC June 1961. Kidderminster Harriers August 1962. Altrincham February 1963. Slav Port Villa, Melbourne, Australia, March 1963. APIA, Sydney, Australia c.1964.

■ Two League appearances within the space of two days over the Easter period in 1962 constituted Stan Ackerley's only senior involvement with the Latics. He subsequently won 28 international caps during an illustrious career in Australian football. He represented New South Wales and Victoria and coached five different clubs, winning a distinction award for his services to Australian football. Stan's elder brother, Ernie, played in Division Four football with Barrow, scoring 12 League goals in 53 appearances in the early 1960s.

ADAMS, Neil James

Winger/Midfield

Born: Stoke-on-Trent, 23 November 1965.
Career: Stoke-on-Trent Schoolboys. Stoke City July 1985. Everton July 1986. OLDHAM ATHLETIC loan January to March 1989, permanent August 1989, fee £100,000. Norwich City February 1994, fee £225,000. OLDHAM ATHLETIC July 1999 to May 2001. Norwich City Academy coach July 2001.

■ Neil Adams's first spell at Boundary

Park spanned momentous times for the Latics, including promotion to the top flight and Wembley appearances in the Littlewoods Cup Final and the FA Cup semi-final. His nine goals in 1992–93 did much to keep the side in the Premier League, but his departure the following term coincided with relegation from the top flight. Returning to Boundary Park on a free transfer some five years later, he joined a side who, in the previous season, had narrowly avoided relegation to Division Three. Sadly, in his final season he damaged cruciate ligaments at Stoke City and was sidelined for five months.

ADAMS, Rex Malcolm

Outside-right

Born: Oxford, 13 February 1928.
Career: Oxford City. Blackpool June 1948. Worcester City July 1952. OLDHAM ATHLETIC June 1953. Northwich Victoria 1954. Mossley 1956. Northwich Victoria December 1956 to 1957.

■ A compactly built and speedy outside-right, blond-haired Rex Adams joined Athletic shortly after they had clinched promotion to Division Two. In what proved to be a solitary season at this level, Adams appeared on both extreme wings before losing his place in February when two new wingers, Harry McShane and

Tommy Walker, were signed in an unavailing attempt to ward off relegation.

ADEBOLA, Bamberdele 'Dele'

Forward

Born: Lagos, Nigeria, 23 June 1975.
Career: Liverpool Schoolboys. Crewe Alexandra associate schoolboy January 1990, trainee August 1991, professional June 1993. Birmingham City February 1998, fee £1 million. OLDHAM ATHLETIC loan March–April 2002. Crystal Palace August 2002. Coventry City July 2003. Burnley loan March 2004. Bradford City loan August 2004. Bristol City January 2008.

■ One of seven loan signings fielded by Athletic in 2001–02, the tall and muscular Dele Adebola was recovering from a lengthy spell of injury, and a lack of match fitness was apparent as he was substituted in four of his five appearances. Despite an excellent away point at top-of-the-table Reading on his debut, Athletic's Play-off hopes ended in disappointment and a ninth place finish in Division Two.

ADLAM, Leslie William

Wing-half

Born: Guildford, 24 June 1897.
Died: Guildford, October 1968.
Career: Stoke Athletic, Guildford, 1911. Farnham United Breweries 1920. Grimsby Town trial. Guildford United August 1922. OLDHAM ATHLETIC March 1923, fee £300. Queen's Park Rangers November 1931, with Ted Goodier for a combined fee of £1,500. Cardiff City December 1933 to January 1934, fee £100. French coaching appointment later in 1934. Guildford Post Office, reinstated amateur February 1936.

■ In the season of his transfer to Boundary Park, Leslie Adlam had scored 27 goals in 19 outings for Guildford United. Despite his early promise as a goalscoring forward, it was not until his conversion to wing-half in 1924–25 that he established himself as a regular first-team player. A cool, scheming member of

the middle line, his benefit match against Bristol City in April 1930 marked seven years at Boundary Park and coincided with his 224th Football League outing. During World War One, Adlam served with the Royal Engineers in Greece and Salonika and was demobilised in February 1920, having reached the rank of Company Quartermaster Sergeant.

AGAR, Alfred

Outside-right

Born: Esh Winning, 28 August 1904.
Died: Carlisle, 23 March 1989.
Career: Esh Winning. Shildon. West Stanley August 1925. Dundee August 1926. Barrow July 1927. Carlisle United June 1928. Accrington Stanley June 1930. OLDHAM ATHLETIC May 1932, fee

£200. York City June 1936. Scarborough July 1937 to 1939.

■ Goalscoring wingman Alf Agar gave defenders a great deal of trouble with his speed off the mark and his very useful aptitude for doing the unexpected. He was particularly successful in his first season at Boundary Park, netting 11 goals from the right wing in 32 League matches. On the opposite flank, another former Accrington Stanley recruit, Jack Pears, led the scoring lists with 13 goals in 32 matches. An operation for appendicitis restricted Agar to just 14 League appearances in his final season, 1935–36, which was Athletic's first in the Third Division North.

AGOGO, Manuel 'Junior'

Forward

Born: Accra, Ghana, 1 August 1979.
Career: Willesden Constantine. Sheffield Wednesday October 1996. OLDHAM ATHLETIC loan July–August 1999. Chester City loan September 1999. Chesterfield loan November 1999. Lincoln City loan December 1999. Chigaco Fire, US, February 2000. Colorado Rapids, US, April 2000. San Jose Earthquakes, US, June 2001. Queen's Park Rangers non-contract March 2002. Barnet June 2002, fee £100,000. Bristol Rovers July 2003, fee £110,000. Nottingham Forest August 2006.

■ The first Ghanaian to represent the Latics, Junior Agogo began with Sheffield Wednesday after being invited to Hillsborough for a trial at the age of 16. After failing to impress at Boundary Park in his month-long loan, the speedy striker did much better in a two-month loan with Chester City, netting six goals in 10 matches. A loan spell spanning three matches with Lincoln City, where he scored on his debut, preceded his move to America. Since returning to England in 2002, his value has escalated in a succession of moves, resulting in a call-up for international duty by Ghana. In January 2008 he netted the winning goal against Nigeria to take his country into the Africa Cup of Nations semi-final.

AITKEN, William Robert Crawford

Inside-forward

Born: Dumfries, 11 January 1951.

Career: Castle Douglas High School. South of Scotland Schoolboys. OLDHAM ATHLETIC apprentice August 1966, professional January 1968 to January 1969.

■ The son of a former Motherwell player, diminutive Billy Aitken appeared in final trials for Scotland Schoolboys. A cocky and adroit inside-forward, he made his League bow against newly promoted Luton Town in the opening fixture of the 1968–69 campaign, but a second senior appearance from the bench against Preston North End in the Football League Cup proved to be his last. Probably the smallest player ever to represent Athletic – measuring just 5ft 2in – his lack of physical presence proved unsuited to life in the lower divisions.

ALDEN, Norman Ernest 'Norrie'

Inside-forward

Born: Caerphilly, 3 November 1909.
Died: Hereford, 22 December 1980.

Career: Llanbradach Colliery. Mount Carmel Juniors 1930. Merthyr Town 1931. Liverpool December 1933. OLDHAM ATHLETIC May 1935, fee £100. Southport July 1936. Hereford United July 1937 to April 1938.

■ Norrie Alden made his debut for Athletic in their first ever game in the Third Division North, following their relegation from Division Two, in 1934–35. It proved to be his only senior outing and he faired only slightly better with Southport, for whom he scored twice in seven matches. He retired from the game after a season with Hereford United and subsequently worked for Bulmers, the cider manufacturers.

ALESSANDRA, Lewis

Forward

Born: Heywood, 8 February 1989.
Career: St Joseph's School. Rochdale Centre of Excellence. OLDHAM ATHLETIC trainee July 2005, professional June 2007.

■ One of four Athletic youngsters who signed their first professional contracts in June 2007, Lewis Alessandra suffered a fractured metatarsal in pre-season but recovered to make his first senior appearance, from the bench, against Huddersfield Town on 20 October. His first League goal, against Tranmere Rovers in March, came in his ninth starting appearance. An Achilles injury, suffered in training, kept the young striker out for six matches, but in a season that had seen the introdution of a number of home-produced players, Alessandra was deservedly awarded Athletic's Young Player of the Year trophy.

ALJOFREE, Hasney

Defender

Born: Manchester, 11 July 1978.
Career: Bolton Wanderers trainee, professional July 1996. Dundee United June 2000. Plymouth Argyle August 2002. Sheffield Wednesday loan September 2004. OLDHAM ATHLETIC March 2007. Swindon Town June 2007.

■ Versatile defender Hasney Aljofree joined Athletic on loan in the late stages of a nervy run-in to 2006–07 that ultimately ended in Play-off defeat by Blackpool. As cover for the injured Simon Charlton at

left full-back, Aljofree featured in five matches, shouldering his responsibilities well during Charlton's enforced absence. The former England Youth international was a Division Two Championship winner with Plymouth Argyle in 2004, and made 29 appearances for the Pilgrims in 2006–07 before dropping out in January due to suspension. He then failed to win back his place as Plymouth enjoyed a run to the FA Cup semi-finals.

ALLOTT, Mark Stephen

Striker/Midfield

Born: Middleton, 16 March 1978.
Career: Boundary Park Juniors. OLDHAM ATHLETIC associate schoolboy November 1991, trainee August 1994, professional October 1995. Chesterfield loan December 2001, permanent February 2002. OLDHAM ATHLETIC July 2007.

■ A goal within 10 minutes of his first appearance at Bolton Wanderers launched Mark Allott's League career, but it was a further two years before the locally-born striker established himself at senior level.

In his first full season, 1998–99, a modest return of eight goals was nevertheless sufficient to place him at the head of the scoring list. A more productive season followed when, in tandem with Steve Whitehall, they headed the scoring lists with 11 goals each. Rather surprisingly made available for transfer in a cost-cutting move in December 2001, Allott was quickly fixed up with Chesterfield. Operating as a midfielder in recent times, he was welcomed back to Boundary Park for a second spell in July 2007. An excellent season in 2007–08, spanning 49 League and Cup appearances, saw the experienced midfielder make a clean sweep of all five of the Player of the Year trophies, awarded at Athletic's end-of-season awards ceremony.

ANDERSON, Douglas Eric

Midfield

Born: Hong Kong, 29 August 1963.
Career: Port Glasgow Rangers. OLDHAM ATHLETIC September 1980. Tranmere Rovers August 1984. Plymouth Argyle August 1987. Cambridge United loan September to November 1988. Northampton Town loan December 1988 to January 1989. Double Flower, Hong Kong, March 1989.

■ Blond-haired and of willowy build, Dougie Anderson spent three years at Boundary Park but failed to graduate beyond reserve team football. In a similar spell with Tranmere Rovers, however, he was rarely absent, totalling 126 League appearances and 15 goals. After a less rewarding spell with Plymouth Argyle he was released in March 1989 and returned to his birthplace, Hong Kong.

ANDERSON, Samuel

Full-back

Born: Newton Heath, Manchester, 11 January 1936.
Career: North Manchester Grammar School. Oldham Amateurs. Ferranti FC. OLDHAM ATHLETIC August 1954 to June 1959. Rossendale United.

■ Sammy Anderson was serving an engineering apprenticeship at Ferranti's Moston works when he was recommended to the Latics. Some fine performances with the Reserves led to a promising League debut at Southport, but the youngster failed to establish himself at a time when a wealth of experienced backs were at the club's disposal, including player-manager George Hardwick, Lewis Brook and Bill Naylor.

ANDREWS, Wayne Michael Hill

Forward

Born: Paddington, London, 25 November 1977.
Career: Oratory School. Watford associate schoolboy October 1992, trainee July 1994, professional July 1996. Cambridge United loan October 1998. Peterborough United loan February 1999. St Albans City 1999. Aldershot Town. Chesham United July 2001, fee £3,000. OLDHAM ATHLETIC May 2002. Colchester United July 2003. Crystal Palace September 2004. Coventry City June 2006. Sheffield Wednesday loan November-December 2006. Bristol City loan January 2007. Leeds United loan October 2007. Bristol Rovers loan March 2008.

■ Speedy striker Wayne Andrews was the second player to be recruited from Chesham United, following Fitz Hall from the Ryman League club. Andrews was second-top scorer with 26 goals in the Ryman League in season 2001–02, and his return of 12 goals for Athletic was an important contribution in 2002–03. Sadly, with the club in crisis as the controversial reign of chairman Chris Moore was set to end, Andrews was one of the first to leave Boundary Park, signing a two-year contract with Colchester United in July 2003. He has subsequently linked with ex-Athletic boss Ian Dowie at both QPR and Coventry City.

ANDREWS, William

Inside-forward

Born: Kansas City, US, c.1886.
Career: Stanmills FC Distillery 1905. Glentoran 1906. OLDHAM ATHLETIC

May 1908. Stockport County February 1909, in exchange for W.T.J. Martin. Glentoran June 1910. Grimsby Town August 1912. Distillery 1916. Belfast United 1917. Darlington 1919. Leadgate Park 1920. Belfast Bohemians January 1922 to May 1923.

■ Despite having scored 36 goals for Glentoran in the season prior to his move to Athletic, Irish international Bill Andrews found stiff competition for a first-team berth. Although his opportunities were limited he displayed a good command of the ball, and in seven of his nine first team outings he collected a winning bonus. Nevertheless, his talents were largely unappreciated and he was allowed to join Stockport County. In a second, and altogether more successful, spell in English football he was a regular in Grimsby Town's Second Division side in the three seasons leading up to World War One.

ANTOINE-CURIER, Mickael

Forward

Born: Orsay, France, 5 March 1983.
Career: Nice. Paris St Germain. Nancy FC. Preston North End November 2000. Nottingham Forest June 2001. Mansfield Town trial February 2003. Brentford loan March 2003. Burnley, non-contract, July 2003. OLDHAM ATHLETIC non-contract August 2003. Kidderminster Harriers, non-contract, 19 September 2003. Rochdale, non-contract, 23 September to October 2003. Sheffield Wednesday, non-contract, November 2003. Lillestroem (Norway) trial January 2004. Notts County February 2004. Grimsby Town March to June 2004. SK Vard Haugesund (Norway) July 2004. Hibernian August 2007. Dundee loan January 2008.

■ Associated with 11 Football League clubs, including a staggering six in season 2003–04, Antoine-Curier began his season's wanderings at Boundary Park. The tall and speedy striker began well enough in Athletic's depleted ranks, stripped bare by the financial restraints in the wake of chairman Chris Moore's departure. Despite a return of three goals in six starts and three appearances from the bench, the young Frenchman was not a universally popular squad member. The arrival of Calvin Zola from Newcastle

United and the return to fitness of Chris Killen were doubtless factors that influenced manager Dowie's decision to release the French Under-18 striker.

APPLEBY, Matthew Wilfred

Midfield

Born: Middlesbrough, 16 April 1972.
Career: Nunthorpe. Newcastle United apprentice July 1988, professional May 1990. Darlington loan November 1993, permanent June 1994. Barnsley July 1996, fee £200,000. OLDHAM ATHLETIC loan January 2002, permanent February 2002. Darlington March 2005. Whitby Town June 2006.

■ Matty Appleby assisted Darlington to the Wembley Play-off Final in season 1995–96, and helped Barnsley win promotion to the Premier League in his first season at Oakwell. He joined Athletic on a free transfer at the conclusion of a month's loan and scored twice in 16/1 appearances in 2001–02. Handed the captain's armband at the start of the following season, the experienced midfielder was injured in September and sidelined until February. Sadly, his come back lasted for only three matches. His injury-plagued career at Boundary Park ended in March 2005 when he rejoined one of his former clubs, Darlington.

APPLEYARD, Willie

Centre-forward

Born: Caistor, near Cleethorpes, 1878.
Died: Newcastle upon Tyne, 14 January 1958.
Career: Cleethorpes Town. Grimsby Tradesmen. Grimsby Town July 1901. Newcastle United April 1903, fee £700. OLDHAM ATHLETIC May 1908, together with Finlay Speedie for a combined fee of £400. Grimsby Town October 1908, in exchange for Patrick Stokes. Mansfield Mechanics 1909.

■ A burly and resolute centre-forward whose goals did much to bring the top honours to Tyneside in Newcastle United's dominance of the Edwardian era. The former North Sea fisherman, appropriately nicknamed 'Cockles', scored 87 League and Cup goals in 145 appearances for the Magpies. He was seemingly at the height of his powers when he transferred to Athletic but his form proved extremely disappointing. After just four matches he lost his place to Frank Newton and in the second month of the season was transferred to Grimsby Town.

ARBER, Mark Andrew

Central-defender

Born: Johannesburg, South Africa, 9 October 1977.
Career: Tottenham Hotspur trainee, professional March 1996. Barnet September 1998, fee £75,000. Peterborough United December 2002. OLDHAM ATHLETIC July 2004. Peterborough United loan

December 2004, permanent January 2005. Dagenham & Redbridge loan March 2007. Stevenage Borough June 2007. Dagenham & Redbridge loan February 2008.

■ Signed by manager Brian Talbot with a view to providing competition for youthful centre-backs Will Haining and Danny Hall, the South African international was slow to settle at Boundary Park. He lost his first-team spot after 12 League appearances, at which time the club occupied 20th position in Football League One. Loaned to Peterborough United in mid-season, the move was quickly made permanent but his unhappy season concluded in relegation, the Posh finishing in 23rd place in League One.

ARMITAGE, John Henry

Centre-half

Born: Chapeltown, Sheffield, 21 August 1896.
CAREER: Thorncliffe Works. Mexborough Town April 1921. Burnley May 1924. OLDHAM ATHLETIC May 1926. Southend United June 1929. Northampton Town May 1930. Wombwell FC August 1931.

■ Former miner Jack Armitage had the benefit of two seasons' First Division experience with Burnley prior to joining the Latics in May 1926. Aside from a lengthy absence in 1927–28 following an injury sustained at White Hart Lane in a

fourth-round FA Cup tie, Armitage dominated the pivotal position during his three years at Boundary Park. A big-hearted and tireless worker, he tackled well and was a commanding figure in the centre of defence.

ARMITAGE, Kenneth Joseph

Centre-half

Born: Sheffield, 23 October 1920.
Died: Sheffield, 1952.
Career: Barnsley amateur December 1937. Gainsborough Trinity 1939. Wartime guest with Tottenham Hotspur & Portsmouth. Leyton Orient April 1946. OLDHAM ATHLETIC July 1947. Ashton United March 1948.

■ Signed with a view to replacing long-serving stalwart Tommy Williamson, who had departed to Fleetwood in the close season, Ken Armitage was unfortunate to sustain a serious injury at Mansfield Town in the first month of the new season. His place at centre-half was so successfully filled by Bill Hayes that Armitage was unable to regain the position when restored to fitness.

ARMSTRONG, Christopher

Left-back

Born: Newcastle upon Tyne, 5 August 1982. Career: Sunderland Academy. Bury trainee July 1998, professional March 2001. OLDHAM ATHLETIC October 2001, fee £200,000. Sheffield United July 2003, fee £100,000. Blackpool loan October 2005.

■ Chris Armstrong was one of many players sold by Athletic in the summer of 2003 as the club faced a cash crisis and the very real possibility of liquidation. Manager Dowie described the transfer fee as 'a pittance', and the £100,000 fee certainly fell well below market value for the talented England Under-20 wing-back. The early promise shown by the teenage defender has since been fully realised, despite a career-threatening knee injury that sidelined him for the best part of 18 months. Returning in mid-season 2005–06, Armstrong assisted the Blades to promotion to the Premier League.

ASPDEN, Thomas Eccles

Winger

Born: Liverpool, 1881. Career: Preston North End September 1901. Kettering Town June 1902. Burnley August 1903. Brighton & Hove Albion May 1904. OLDHAM ATHLETIC October 1905 to February 1906.

■ In the Latics' second season in the Lancashire Combination, Tommy Aspden made his debut at outside-left against Liverpool Reserves in a 2–1 victory at Anfield on 14 October 1905. A fortnight later, he was at outside-right in the second qualifying round of the FA Cup, when modest opponents Fairfield were despatched 8–0.

ASPINALL, John

Centre-half

Born: Ashton-under-Lyne, 27 April 1916. Died: Ashton-under-Lyne, September 1996. Career: Lancashire Schoolboys. Mottram Central. Bradford City amateur December 1934. Stalybridge Celtic. OLDHAM ATHLETIC May 1936. Ashton National May 1939. Wartime guest with Southport & Bolton Wanderers. Bolton Wanderers permanent September 1945. Horwich RMI coach 1950.

■ An ideally built centre-half, six-footer Jack Aspinall met opponents squarely and was fearless in the tackle. As understudy to club skipper Beaumont Ratcliffe, his first team opportunities were infrequent, but in the opening weeks of the 1938–39 season, six consecutive appearances at left-half produced four wins and one draw and

got the campaign off to a flying start. Transfer listed in May 1939, he moved into non-League soccer but subsequently joined Bolton Wanderers, for whom he appeared in 14 First Division matches.

ASPREY, William

Defender

Born: Wolverhampton, 11 September 1936.
Career: Wolverhampton Schoolboys. Wolverhampton Wanderers amateur. Stoke City amateur May, professional September 1953. OLDHAM ATHLETIC January 1966. Port Vale December 1967. Sheffield Wednesday coach December 1968. Coventry City assistant manager February 1970. Wolverhampton Wanderers coach. West Bromwich Albion coach. Rhodesia national director of coaching 1975. Oxford United coach May 1978, manager July 1979 to December 1980. Stoke City assistant manager February 1982, manager January 1984 to May 1985.

■ Bill Asprey was a versatile defender who was aided by a powerful physique. He clocked up 303 Football League appearances for Stoke City, assisting them to the Championship of Division Two in 1963 and an appearance in the Football League Cup Final of 1964. One of a number of ex-Stoke City players at Boundary Park during the Jimmy McIlroy era, Asprey was appointed club captain in the summer of 1966, and at either centre-half or full-back he was a

commanding presence who led by example. He actually made his League debut for Stoke City against the Latics as a 17-year-old in March 1954.

ASTON, Vivien Walter

Defender

Born: Coseley, 16 October 1918.
Died: Bury, March 1999.
Career: Bury trial July 1936, professional December 1936. Glentoran December 1941. OLDHAM ATHLETIC July 1948. Chester January 1952 to June 1953.

■ Viv Aston joined Bury at 18 years of age and was unfortunate to have his progress curtailed by the outbreak of World War Two. Resuming at Gigg Lane after the war, he found the Griffiths brothers firmly established in the full-back berths, and was allowed to join Athletic in the summer of 1948. In four seasons at Boundary Park he was never a regular first-team man, but proved to be a loyal and versatile servant who appeared in both full-back roles and all half-back positions.

ATKINSON, Paul Graham

Midfield

Born: Pudsey, 14 August 1961.
Career: Yorkshire Schoolboys. OLDHAM ATHLETIC apprentice August 1977, professional August 1979. Watford July 1983, fee £175,000. OLDHAM

ATHLETIC August 1985 to April 1988, fee £30,000. Swansea City loan December 1986. Bolton Wanderers loan February 1987. Swansea City loan March 1987. Burnley July 1988 to May 1990. Northwich Victoria March 1991. RUS Binchoise, Belgium, until December 1992. Frickley Athletic. Altrincham. Glass Houghton Welfare, Castleford 1993–94.

■ Paul Atkinson was a regular on the left side of Athletic's midfield for four seasons, his partnership with wing-back John Ryan being a particularly effective attacking element in the two seasons preceding his transfer to Watford. Despite a substitute appearance in the 1984 FA Cup Final, his time at Vicarage Road was disappointing. He suffered a broken ankle in pre-season training and made infrequent first-team appearances. A return to Boundary Park at a cut-price £30,000 appeared to be good business, but sadly he failed to recapture his earlier form, appearing only once at senior level in his final season.

BAILEY, Anthony David

Defender

Born: Burton upon Trent, 23 September 1946.
Career: Burton Albion June 1966. Derby County September 1970. OLDHAM ATHLETIC loan January 1974, permanent March 1974, fee £8,000. Bury December 1974. Mossley November 1980.

■ Tony Bailey made only one League appearance for Derby County, this

coming in the 1971–72 season when the Rams won the Championship of the Football League. Moving to Boundary Park, he was more involved in the Latics' Championship of Division Three, making 14 appearances and scoring one goal. A move to Bury in the following term brought his replacement in the number-six jersey, David Holt, to Boundary Park, Athletic paying £25,000 in addition to the player exchange element. Bailey enjoyed a lengthy spell at Gigg Lane, recording 154 League and Cup appearances.

BAILEY, Arthur

Inside-forward

Born: Ancoats, Manchester, 11 January 1911.
Died: 20 April 2006.

Career: Chapel-en-le-Frith. Manchester North End 1932. OLDHAM ATHLETIC May 1933. Stalybridge Celtic February 1937. OLDHAM ATHLETIC July 1939. Wartime guest with Droylsden, Wolverhampton Wanderers, Manchester United, Crewe Alexandra, Blackpool, Port Vale, Rochdale. Shrewsbury Town August 1945.

■ Forty goals for Chapel-en-le-Frith in 1931–32 and 25 in the following season for Manchester North End paved the way for Arthur Bailey's entry into League football, and he made a promising start in his first season with Athletic, scoring 10 League and Cup goals in 30 appearances. Following relegation from Division Two in 1934–35, he made largely reserve team appearances before being transferred to Stalybridge Celtic. Returning to Boundary Park for a second spell in July 1939, Bailey played regularly in wartime football, scoring 52 goals in 137 matches. He also assisted numerous other clubs during the course of his wartime RAF service.

BAKER, Benjamin Howard

Goalkeeper

Born: Liverpool, 13 February 1892.
Died: Warminster, 10 September 1987.
Career: An amateur throughout with Old Malburnians. Lancashire County. Liverpool Balmoral. Preston North End December 1919. Northern Nomads. Blackburn Rovers A Team. Corinthians 1920. Liverpool March 1920. Everton November 1920. Chelsea October 1921.

Corinthians. Everton August 1926. OLDHAM ATHLETIC March 1929.

■ One of the great all-round athletes of his day, Howard Baker won two full England caps in addition to his 10 amateur awards. A British high-jump champion, he represented England in the 1912 and 1920 Olympic Games. In the latter year he recorded a jump of six feet three and a quarter inches in the AAA Open Championships. It was not unknown for youngsters standing behind his goal to request an attempt to jump over the crossbar! In November 1921, to the great delight of the Stamford Bridge faithful, he scored from a penalty-kick in the 1–0 victory against Bradford City in a First Division match. His single appearance for Athletic came when regular custodian, Jack Hacking, was on international duty with England.

BALDWIN, William

Centre-forward

Born: Leigh, 31 January 1907.
Died: Coventry, 1 November 1982.
Career: Abram Wanderers. Leigh FC. Scunthorpe United December 1929. Chesterfield May 1930. Barrow June 1931. OLDHAM ATHLETIC May 1932. Southport June 1933. Gillingham June 1934. Crewe Alexandra June 1936.

■ Bill Baldwin's solitary appearance for Athletic coincided with his 26th birthday, but he had little cause to celebrate as Stoke won 4–0 on their way to the Championship of the Second Division.

At the outset of his career, Baldwin scored 24 Midland League goals in five months for Scunthorpe United but failed to establish himself at League level until he joined Southport, where he was second-highest marksman with 13 goals in 23 matches. With Gillingham he recorded 23 goals in 61 games. A keen and talented bowler in his later years, Baldwin won the All England Cup in 1965.

BALL, James Alan

Inside-forward

Born: Farnworth, Bolton, 23 September 1924.
Died: Nicosia, Cyprus, 2 January 1982.
Career: Bolton Boys' Federation. Southport amateur August 1942, professional March 1946. Birmingham City May 1947. Southport January 1948, fee £500. OLDHAM ATHLETIC July 1950. Rochdale February 1952. Ashton United 1952. Oswestry Town 1952, player-manager 1953–55. Borough United January 1958. Ashton United manager 1959–60. Nantwich manager August 1962. Stoke City coach. Manchester City coach. Cork Celtic coach 1967. Halifax Town manager December 1967. Preston North End manager 1970 to February 1973. Southport manager January 1974 to July 1975. Halifax Town manager February 1976 to November 1977. Blackpool scout 1980–81. Held managerial appointments with five clubs in Sweden, and was in Cyprus to take up a short-term coaching appointment at the time of his death in a motoring accident.

■ Copper-haired Alan Ball began in wartime football with Southport and was transferred to Birmingham City shortly after demobilisation from the Army. A return to Southport preceded his transfer to the Latics. After appearing in seven matches in 1950–51 he did not feature at senior level again before joining Rochdale in February 1952. Following a brief stay at Spotland, Ball moved into non-League circles, where his managerial skills were honed. His subsequent successes included taking Halifax Town out of Division Four in season 1968–69 and winning the Third Division Championship with Preston North End in 1970–71. Father of Alan Ball, the England International and World Cup winner in 1966.

BALMER, Stuart Murray

Central-defender

Born: Falkirk, 20 September 1969.
Career: Celtic Boys' Club 1984. Celtic 1987. Charlton Athletic August 1990, fee £120,000. Wigan Athletic September 1998, fee £200,000. OLDHAM ATHLETIC July 2001. Scunthorpe United loan October 2002. Boston United December 2002. Clyde assistant manager June 2004. Hamilton Academical July 2005. St Mirren player-coach June 2006.

■ Despite an inauspicious start to his League career when he scored two own-goals within the space of his first six matches for Charlton Athletic, Stuart Balmer remained at the Valley for eight years and totalled 225/27 League and Cup appearances. One of 10 players released by Wigan Athletic in the summer of 2001, he was quickly snapped up by Athletic on a free transfer. Until being replaced by new signing Fitz Hall in the final month of 2001–02, Balmer's experience brought stability to the heart of Athletic's defence. His attacking forays at the other end of the pitch additionally resulted in a useful return of six League goals.

BANGER, Nicholas Lee 'Nicky'

Forward

Born: Southampton, 25 February 1971.
Career: Bassett Comets. Southampton trainee July 1987, professional April 1989. OLDHAM ATHLETIC October 1994, fee £250,000. Oxford United July 1997. Dundee October 1999. Plymouth Argyle August 2001. Merthyr Tydfil November 2001. Torquay United March 2002. Woking August 2002. Eastleigh February 2003. AFC Newbury August 2005. Brockenhurst player-coach November

2005. Lymington & New Milton player-coach later in November 2005 to June 2006.

■ Associated with Southampton from the age of 12 but never a regular at The Dell, Nicky Banger's £250,000 move to Boundary Park gave him his first experience of regular first-team football. In sharp contrast to his senior debut for Southampton, when he scored a hat-trick in a Football League Cup tie against Rochdale, it took Banger over five months and 21 matches to open his goalscoring account for the Latics. Adroit in approach play, he nevertheless lacked the physical presence to complement his industry and persistence, and his overall scoring record was disappointing.

BARLOW, Andrew John

Left-back

Born: Oldham, 24 November 1965.
Career: Hulme Grammar School. OLDHAM ATHLETIC associate schoolboy November 1982. Briefly on schoolboy forms with Nottingham Forest. OLDHAM ATHLETIC professional July 1984. Bradford City loan November 1993. Blackpool July 1995. Rochdale July 1997. Ramsbottom United June 1999.

■ Popular, locally-born defender Andy Barlow appeared in 11 seasons of first-team football for the Latics. A hard–working, model professional with great stamina, Barlow was a brainy back, obtaining his effects by sheer skill and judgement. In addition to defensive duties, his rapid incursions down the left flank often provided the springboard for many successful attacks. Sadly, his last three seasons at Boundary Park were blighted by a succession of knee injuries,

restricting his appearances in the heady days of Premier League football. After retiring from the game, Barlow worked as a regional coach for the Professional Footballers' Association.

BARLOW, Colin James

Forward

Born: Collyhurst, Manchester, 14 November 1935.
Career: Xaverian College. Manchester City amateur, signing professional December 1956. OLDHAM ATHLETIC August 1963, fee £1,250. Doncaster Rovers August 1964, retired June 1965.

■ Colin Barlow began as an amateur with Manchester City, initially training two evenings a week at Maine Road. He developed into a lively utility forward, fleet of foot and a good marksman, assets illustrated by his outstanding return of 80 League and Cup goals in 189 matches. Despite a scoring debut for Athletic, he was unable to command a regular place in the side. Subsequently a very successful businessman, in 1994 he was part of a consortium that took over at Manchester City. His late father-in-law, Les McDowall, managed Athletic for two years from 1963.

BARLOW, Matthew John 'Matty'

Forward

Born: Oldham, 25 June 1987.
Career: OLDHAM ATHLETIC trainee July 2003, professional July 2006. Stafford Rangers loan November 2006 to January

2007. Stalybridge Celtic loan January 2007, permanent July 2007.

■ Despite an outstanding record at youth team level, a lack of first-team opportunities saw Athletic's prolific young striker undertake two separate loan spells in 2006–07. After just one start and one appearance from the bench for Stafford Rangers he was recalled two weeks ahead of schedule. A second loan to Stalybridge Celtic proved highly successful and resulted in his permanent move to Bower Fold following his release from Athletic.

BARLOW, Stuart

Forward

Born: Liverpool, 16 July 1968.
Career: Sherwood Park. Everton non-contract 1988, professional June 1990. Rotherham United loan January 1992. OLDHAM ATHLETIC November 1995, fee £450,000. Wigan Athletic March 1998, fee £45,000. Tranmere Rovers July 2000. Stockport County August 2003. Bury July 2005. Morecambe January 2006. Southport trial August 2006. Fleetwood Town August 2006. Skelmersdale United loan January–February 2007.

■ A relative late-comer to professional football at 22 years old, Stuart Barlow

was spotted by Everton in Sunday League football. At Boundary Park he teamed up with ex-Everton colleagues Graeme Sharp, Colin Harvey and Ian Snodin. After a disappointing first season, Barlow headed the scoring charts in 1996–97 and 1997–98. He subsequently registered his 100th League goal for Tranmere Rovers, and his final career aggregate totals amounted to 111 League goals in 262/140 appearances.

BARLOW, Thomas Henry

Wing-half

Born: Bolton, 1875.
Died: Bolton, 25 November 1944.
Career: Halliwell Rovers May 1897. Bolton Wanderers May 1898. Southampton May 1902. Bolton Wanderers May 1903. Millwall Athletic August 1904. Atherton Church House June 1905. OLDHAM ATHLETIC September 1906 to 1907.

■ Despite a successful career that included an international trial match during his Southampton spell, Tom Barlow was unable to break into a very settled and successful Athletic side. In the season prior to the club's entry into the Football League, Barlow played in only three Lancashire Combination matches and three FA Cup ties.

BARNES, Horace

Inside-forward

Born: Wadsley Bridge, Sheffield, 3 January 1891.
Died: Manchester 12 September 1961.

Career: Wadsley Bridge. Derby County amateur 23 October, professional 31 October 1908. Manchester City May 1914, fee £2,500. Wartime guest with Ashton National. Preston North End November 1924, fee £2,750. OLDHAM ATHLETIC November 1925, fee £1,250. Ashton National June 1927, retired due to injury June 1931.

■ Horace Barnes began in first-class football at the age of 17. One week after playing in junior football, he scored on his debut for Derby County at Blackpool. Noted for his fierce left-foot shot, he netted 78 goals in 167 appearances for Derby County. He joined Manchester City for a then record fee in May 1914 and scored 125 goals in 235 appearances, plus 56 in 57 in wartime matches. Briefly with Preston North End before joining Athletic, he showed glimpses of his finishing ability with 10 goals in 22 appearances in his first season, but was transfer listed the following term when, at 36 years of age, his powers appeared to be declining. Nevertheless, in four seasons with Ashton National, before injury compelled his retirement at 40 years of age, Barnes recorded no less than 240 goals, a total that included six in his last match!

BARRETT, Earl Delisser

Defender

Born: Rochdale 28 April 1967.
Career: Manchester City trainee April 1984, professional April 1985. Chester City loan February–April 1986. OLDHAM ATHLETIC November 1987, fee £35,000. Aston Villa February 1992, fee £1.7million. Everton January 1995, fee £1.7million. Sheffield United loan January 1998. Sheffield Wednesday February 1998 to June 1999. Retired due to knee injury December 1999.

■ Despite a lengthy spell on the sidelines during his first season at Boundary Park, Earl Barrett's worth was quickly apparent. Lightning quick, enthusiastic, and able to fit into any pattern of play, he soon caught the eye of international selectors, appearing for England at Under-21 and B levels. He captained the outstanding 1990–91 Division Two Championship side, leading the Latics back into the top flight after an interval

of 68 years. Barrett never failed to lead by example, and had an immense value as a jack of all trades, and was able to fill roles as diverse as full-back and striker. Called up for England's summer tour of the Far East and Australia in 1991, he won the first of his three full caps against New Zealand in Auckland. In his first full season with Aston Villa, he appeared in all 42 League matches, helping his team to second place in the Premier League. Reunited with manager Joe Royle at Everton in January 1995 he was unfortunate to miss out on a Wembley appearance in his first season at Goodison Park. The Toffees beat Manchester United in the FA Cup Final but Barrett was ineligible having played for Aston Villa in an earlier round. Knee injuries blighted him for much of season 1995–96 and eventually ended his career. Just prior to Christmas 1999 it was announced that his serious knee condition had failed to respond sufficiently to allow him to continue in top-flight football. Following his retirement, he was closely associated with a number of campaigns against racism in football, and in November 2006 Barrett came full circle when he returned to Manchester City to work in their Football in the Community scheme.

BARTLEY, Anthony

Winger

Born: Stalybridge, 8 March 1938.
Career: Ashton Schoolboys. Everton amateur. Stalybridge Celtic. Bolton Wanderers September 1956. Stalybridge

BAZLEY, John Alfred

Winger

Born: Runcorn, 4 October 1936.
Career: Runcorn Athletic. Bangor University. Bangor City. OLDHAM ATHLETIC October 1956. Worcester City July 1962. Macclesfield Town July 1963. Mossley August 1964. Stafford Rangers March 1966. Mossley January 1967. Boston FC 1968.

Celtic. Bury November 1958. OLDHAM ATHLETIC September 1964, fee £3,000. Chesterfield July 1966. Sligo Rovers, Ireland, player-manager June 1967. Limerick. Dundalk 1969.

■ Tony Bartley was a traditional wingman with all the necessary qualities of speed, ball control, and more than one way of beating an opponent. He spent three years as an amateur on Everton's books while working as a trainee clerk, but made his debut in League football with Bury. To follow the hugely popular Colin Whitaker in the number-11 jersey at Boundary Park was an unenviable task, but in his first season Bartley rose splendidly to the challenge with 10 goals in 34 League and Cup appearances.

BASSINDALE, Isaac Bradley

Half-back

Born: Harrington, Cumberland, 26 January 1896.
Died: Stockton-on-Tees, 11 June 1985.
Career: Loftus Albion. Hartlepools United (one appearance) December 1920. OLDHAM ATHLETIC amateur February, professional March 1921, fee £50. Mossley 1926. Ashton National October 1926.

■ Fair-haired Ike Bassindale was a cool, calculating player, who always used the ball to advantage. He was also a valuable utility player throughout his six seasons with Athletic. He first appeared regularly in 1922–23, the season in which Athletic suffered relegation from the top flight. In the following term he was switched from inside-forward to right-half, and this proved to be his best position. A part-time professional throughout his career, Bassindale worked as a draughtsman at Platt Brothers, the local textile machinery manufacturers.

BAUDET, Julien

Central-defender

Born: Grenoble, France, 13 January 1979.
Career: Toulouse, France. Boston United trial February 2001. OLDHAM ATHLETIC non-contract October, professional November 2001. Rotherham United August 2003. Notts County July 2004. Crewe Alexandra June 2006.

■ Julien Baudet first tasted League football with Athletic, who signed him on a free transfer after his club Toulouse were relegated and further demoted due to financial irregularities. A combination of strength, athleticism and aerial ability, well abetted by natural physical attributes, served Athletic well for two seasons before his departure to Rotherham United.

■ John Bazley was a nimble-footed outside-right with the ability to swerve past an opponent and deliver an inviting centre. Three years prior to joining Athletic he had represented the Rest of England versus England at Leicester in an Under-18 amateur international trial. During the course of his six years with Athletic, Bazley spent his two years of National Service as a sergeant in the Education Corps, and subsequently worked as a lecturer at Lincoln College of Technology.

BEARDALL, James Thomas

Forward

Born: Salford, 18 October 1946.
Career: Bury apprentice January 1962 to December 1963, signing again on amateur forms August 1964. Blackburn Rovers amateur May 1967, professional March 1968. OLDHAM ATHLETIC May 1969. Great Harwood February 1970. Radcliffe Borough August 1973. Great Harwood until May 1976.

■ Darkly handsome centre-forward Jim Beardall made the best possible start to his Athletic career. The former Blackburn Rovers forward scored six League goals in his first seven outings. By the end of November, however, with the team languishing at the foot of Division Four, Beardall was dropped and subsequently appeared in only three more League matches. While his goalscoring record

was by no means unsatisfactory, his replacement Jim Fryatt was an altogether more potent force, and did much to steer the team clear of a re-election application. Beardall subsequently worked in the printing trade, running his own business in Salford.

BEAVERS, Paul Mark

Forward

Born: Blackpool, 2 October 1978.
Career: Sunderland trainee, professional April 1997. Shrewsbury Town loan December 1998. Ethnikos Piraeus, Greece, loan February 1999. OLDHAM ATHLETIC loan March 1999, permanent August 1999. Hartlepool United loan March 2000. Darlington September 2000. Coleraine loan December 2000 to February 2001.

■ Loaned to Athletic late in the 1998–99 season, Paul Beavers added extra physical presence to a lightweight attack. His close-range header against Stoke City in the penultimate match of the season proved to be a priceless match-winner in the Latics' successful battle to avoid relegation. Sadly, in the season following his recruitment on a free transfer, his form suffered to such an extent that he made only four first-team appearances. These all came within the opening five matches of the campaign, which resulted in successive defeats, and only one goal scored.

BEBBINGTON, Richard Keith

Winger/Midfield

Born: Cuddington near Nantwich, 4 August 1943.
Career: Mid Cheshire Schoolboys. Cuddington FC. Stoke City amateur 1958. Northwich Victoria trial 1960. Stoke City professional August 1960. OLDHAM ATHLETIC August 1966, together with George Kinnell for a combined fee of £25,000. Rochdale July 1972. Winsford United 1973 to 1975.

■ Keith Bebbington made his League debut with Stoke City at 19 years of age and remained with the Potters for almost eight years before joining Athletic. Versatile and mobile, he was also a model of consistency, averaging 42 matches per season during his six years at Boundary Park. He netted 10 League goals in 43 matches in the 1970–71 promotion campaign, but overall Bebbington will be best remembered as a provider of openings, subtly engineered by artistic footwork on either flank or, later, from the right side of midfield.

BECKETT, Luke John

Striker

Born: Sheffield, 25 November 1976.
Career: Barnsley trainee, professional June 1995. Chester City June 1998. Chesterfield July 2000, fee £75,000. Stockport County December 2001, fee £100,000. Sheffield United November 2004, fee £50,000.

Huddersfield Town Loan January 2005. OLDHAM ATHLETIC loan March–May 2005, and July 2005 to May 2006. Huddersfield Town July 2006.

■ It was not until mid-season 2005–06 that prolific marksman Luke Beckett discovered his shooting boots. His winning goal against Bradford City on Boxing Day was only his second of the season, but thereafter his form and confidence soared and he ended the season with 18 League goals to his credit. Sadly, he lacked meaningful support in attack and Athletic's Play-off hopes ended in disappointment. Although Beckett was available following his season-long loan from Sheffield United, a combination of the required fee of £85,000 and the player's wage demands priced Athletic out of a deal to make his move a permanent one.

BECKFORD, Darren Richard Lorenzo

Centre-forward

Born: Ancoats, Manchester, 12 May 1967.
Career: Manchester Schoolboys. Manchester City associate schoolboy November 1981, apprentice April 1984, professional August 1984. Bury loan October 1985. Port Vale loan March 1987, permanent June 1987, fee £15,000. Norwich City June 1991, fee £925,000. OLDHAM ATHLETIC March 1993, fee £300,000. Heart of Midlothian August 1996. Preston North End trial January

1997. Fulham trial February 1997. Walsall March 1997. Rushden & Diamonds trial September 1997. Southport trial October 1997. Llansantffraid (League of Wales) November 1997. Bury non-contract December 1997 to January 1998.

■ Darren Beckford's impressive scoring record with Port Vale – 71 goals in 169/9 League appearances – attracted wide interest and he was transferred to Norwich City for a tribunal-set fee of £925,000 – a club record for the Canaries. In his second season at Carrow Road he suffered a catalogue of injuries, and sadly this continued throughout his spell at Boundary Park and beyond. Glimpses of his speed and bustling qualities were seen to best effect in season 1994–95, when his goals against Derby County, Stoke City and Bolton Wanderers helped Athletic to reach the semi-final of the FA Cup.

BEHARALL, David

Central-defender

Born: Wallsend, 8 March 1979.
Career: Newcastle United School of Excellence, professional July 1997. Grimsby Town loan August 2001. OLDHAM ATHLETIC loan November 2001, permanent March 2002, fee £150,000. Port Vale trial January 2005. Carlisle United February 2005. Stockport County February–May 2006. Retired June 2006.

■ The first player signed by Athletic's new head coach Mick Wadsworth, Dave Beharall's spell at Boundary Park was dogged by injury problems. Aside from an excellent season in 2002–03, when he made the bulk of his first-team appearances, the tall and slim centre-half

endured a frustrating spell with Athletic. With a total of just seven League appearances in 2003–04, he nevertheless enjoyed an isolated success in a bruising encounter at Home Park on 1 November, scoring both of Athletic's goals in the 2–2 draw against Plymouth Argyle.

BELL, Graham Thomas

Midfield

Born: Middleton, 30 March 1955.
Career: Chadderton FC. OLDHAM ATHLETIC amateur June 1972, professional December 1973. Preston North End March 1979, fee £80,000. Huddersfield Town loan November 1981. Carlisle United August 1983. Bolton Wanderers February 1984. Tranmere Rovers August 1986. Hyde United August 1987. Mossley January 1988. Hyde United player-manager January 1991. Mossley July 1991 to January 1992. Horwich R.M.I. February 1992.

■ A lightly-built midfielder with seemingly inexhaustible stamina, flame-haired Graham Bell was working as an apprentice coach builder when he joined the Latics on amateur forms as a 17-year-old. He progressed swiftly through Athletic's junior sides to make his League debut in 1974–75, the season that marked the return to Division Two after an interval of 40 years. His outstanding early progress attracted wide attention, including that of Don Revie, the then England manager. Graham's League career spanned six League clubs, and he appeared in 446/17 matches, scoring 25 goals. His father, Tommy Bell, was a popular Athletic player in the immediate post-war era.

BELL, Peter

Inside-forward

Born: Ferryhill, Co. Durham, 3 March 1895.
Died: Bishop Auckland, 16 May 1965.
Career: Chilton United. Durham City 1919. Willington Athletic. Wartime guest with Chilton United. OLDHAM ATHLETIC January 1920, fee £150. Darlington May 1922. Raith Rovers December 1922, fee £800. Manchester City September 1926, fee £820. Falkirk July 1928. Burton Town August 1929. Darlington September 1930 to January 1931.

■ Signed from Northern League football, Peter Bell did not realise his full potential at Boundary Park. Released on a free transfer, he signed for Darlington, who soon received a useful fee from Raith Rovers for his services. At this stage, operating at outside-right, he was a member of the famous forward line comprising Bell, Miller, Jennings, James and Archibald – which Millwall attempted to buy *en bloc*. In season 1927–28 he was one of a pair of former Athletic players – goalkeeper Albert Gray was the other – who assisted Manchester City to win the Championship of Division Two.

BELL, Thomas Anthony

Full-back

Born: Heyside, 30 December 1923.
Died: Oldham, 21 November 1988.
Career: Mossley. OLDHAM ATHLETIC December 1946, fee £500. Stockport County August 1952. Halifax Town July 1953 to June 1956. Mossley 1958–59. Ashton United 1959–60.

■ A determined full-back with excellent mobility and a sure kick, Tommy Bell

remained at Boundary Park long enough to qualify for a well-deserved benefit in 1952. His entire League career was spent in the Northern Section of Division Three, and he appeared in 318 League games for his three clubs. Aside from football, Bell was a talented amateur batsman with Crompton CC in the Central Lancashire League. Tommy's son, Graham, also played for the Latics and, coincidentally, made exactly the same number of League appearances as his father.

BERESFORD, David

Winger/Midfield

Born: Middleton, 11 November 1976.
Career: Bluecoat School, Oldham. OLDHAM ATHLETIC associate schoolboy January 1991, professional July 1994. Swansea City loan August 1995. Huddersfield Town March 1997, fee £350,000. Preston North End loan December 1999. Port Vale loan September 2000. Hull City July 2001. Plymouth Argyle July 2002. Macclesfield Town loan October 2003. Tranmere Rovers November 2003. Macclesfield Town July 2005. Retired March 2006.

■ England Schools and Youth international David Beresford attended Athletic's School of Excellence at 11 years of age, and spent two years at the FA National School at Lilleshall from the age of 14. After making an early Premier League debut at 17 years of age, he suffered back and hamstring injuries, but a loan spell with Swansea City helped recover his form and confidence. Increasingly involved as a starter or from the bench, his fleet-footed displays on either wing made him a prominent figure in the two seasons preceding his 'deadline' transfer to Huddersfield Town.

BERESFORD, Marlon

Goalkeeper

Born: Lincoln, 2 September 1969.
Career: Sheffield Wednesday trainee, professional September 1987. Bury loan August 1989. Ipswich Town loan September 1989. Northampton Town loan September 1990. Crewe Alexandra loan March 1991. Northampton Town August 1991. Burnley August 1992, fee £95,000. Middlesbrough March 1998, fee £500,000. Sheffield Wednesday loan January 2001. Wolverhampton Wanderers loan August 2001. Burnley loan January 2002. York City August 2002. Burnley October 2002. Bradford City September 2003. Luton Town October 2003. Barnsley January 2004. Luton Town July 2004. OLDHAM ATHLETIC loan October–November 2007.

■ Athletic replaced one 38-year-old goalkeeper with another when they took veteran Marlon Beresford on loan from Luton Town, to replace the injured Mark Crossley. With the experience of 500-plus senior appearances, Beresford proved a more than capable deputy, conceding just one goal in his final three matches. These were all away fixtures and contested within the space of one week. Sadly a torn hamstring cut short Beresford's impressive month's loan.

BERNARD, Michael Peter

Midfield

Born: Shrewsbury, 10 January 1948.
Career: Shrewsbury Town Juniors. Stoke City apprentice April 1963, professional January 1965. Everton April 1972, fee

£140,000. OLDHAM ATHLETIC July 1977 to January 1979.

■ Injuries blighted Mike Bernard's career with Athletic. He appeared in only four first-team outings in his first season at Boundary Park following a pre-season injury and a severe calf muscle tear in mid-term. He was released early from his contract the following season, a disappointing end to an otherwise first-class career. Earlier, Bernard had starred with both Stoke City and Everton, as a quick and forceful tackler, able to operate with equal faculty in midfield or at full-back. On leaving Boundary Park he became a publican in Chester, later working in football commerce with Crewe Alexandra and Stoke City.

BERNARD, Paul Robert James

Midfield

Born: Edinburgh, 30 December 1972.
Career: Stockport Schoolboys. OLDHAM ATHLETIC associate schoolboy January 1987, trainee November 1989, professional July 1991. Aberdeen September 1995, fee £850,000. Preston North End trial January 2001. Burnley trial February 2001. Barnsley trial April 2001, professional July 2001. Plymouth Argyle December 2002. St Johnstone July 2003 to June 2005. Drogheda United 2005.

■ Left-sided midfielder Paul Bernard first attended Athletic's School of Excellence at the age of 11. His League career began late

in season 1990–91 and he was a scorer in the final fixture of the campaign against Sheffield Wednesday. The 3–2 victory secured the Championship and a return to the top flight after an interval of 68 years. Firmly established the following season, he won the first of his 15 Scotland Under-21 caps against Romania, scoring one of Scotland's goals in a 3–1 win. Four months after winning full international recognition in matches against Japan and Ecuador in May 1995, Aberdeen paid a club record for Bernard and he was a Scottish League Cup winner in his first season at Pittodrie.

BERTRAND, Ryan Dominic

Full-back

Born: Bermondsey, 5 August 1989.
Career: Gillingham Centre of Excellence. Chelsea trainee, professional August 2006. AFC Bournemouth loan November 2006. OLDHAM ATHLETIC loan August 2007. Norwich City loan January 2008.

■ Born a stone's throw from Millwall's New Den, Ryan Bertrand was nevertheless an Arsenal supporter. He moved with his family to Kent at an early age and was first spotted by Gillingham, whose Centre of Excellence he attended before being snapped up by Chelsea. With little chance of immediate enhancement at Stamford Bridge, the developing England Under-19 defender was happy to go out on loan for the opportunity to play first-team football. A positive and confident defender with excellent ball control, Athletic would have been more than happy to extend his loan spell, but Chelsea recalled him. Almost immediately, they farmed him out to Championship club Norwich City.

BEST, David

Goalkeeper

Born: Wareham, Dorset, 6 September 1943.
Career: Dorset Schoolboys. Wareham FC. Bournemouth & Boscombe Athletic amateur October 1959, professional October 1960. OLDHAM ATHLETIC September 1966, fee £15,000. Ipswich Town October 1968, fee £25,000. Portsmouth February 1974. AFC Bournemouth July 1975. Dorchester Town 1976–77.

■ A faltering start to season 1966–67 was quickly turned around following the signing of David Best, whose introduction brought an immediate upturn. His sure handling and calm domination of the penalty area inspired a general air of confidence, and a run of improved results ensued. Voted Player of the Year in 1967–68, he was rarely absent during his two years at Boundary Park, with 80 of his 98 League appearances made consecutively. One of Athletic's best post-war goalkeepers, he proved wonderfully consistent throughout his long career, totalling 551 League appearances.

BESWICK, Ivan

Full-back

Born: Manchester, 2 January 1936.
Career: Manchester United amateur May 1954, professional October 1954. Nantile Vale. OLDHAM ATHLETIC August 1958. Stalybridge Celtic season 1961–62.

■ Former FA Youth Cup winner Ivan Beswick left Manchester United on medical advice at the end of the 1956–57 season. Attempting to resurrect his career he signed with Nantile Vale, but never actually played for them. With the Welsh club's blessing he took up the offer of a trial period with Athletic, which resulted in the offer of professional terms in August 1958. Usually in a full-back partnership with Ted West, Beswick enjoyed a lengthy spell of first-team action in his first season. His excellent mobility often caught wingmen by surprise, but he was somewhat lacking in physique for the rigours of Division Four football. Outside of the game he became an extremely successful businessman and lives in retirement in Guernsey.

BETSY, Kevin Eddie Lewis

Midfield

Born: Seychelles, 20 March 1978.
Career: Farnborough Town. Woking July 1996. Fleet Town loan August 1996. Bognor Regis Town loan March 1997. Fulham trial February 1998, professional September 1998, fee £100,000. AFC Bournemouth loan September 1999. Hull City loan November 1999. Barnsley loan February 2002, permanent March 2002, fee £200,000. Hartlepool United loan August 2004. OLDHAM ATHLETIC September 2004. Wycombe Wanderers July 2005. Bristol City January 2007. Yeovil Town loan October 2007. Walsall loan January 2008.

■ Capped by England at Semi-professional level while with Woking, right-sided midfielder or striker Kevin Betsy had his first run of regular first-team football with Barnsley before joining Athletic on a free transfer. He immediately announced his arrival by scoring on his debut against Hartlepool United in a 3–2 win. In a season when Ronnie Moore replaced Brian Talbot as manager, Athletic narrowly avoided relegation from League One. Betsy missed only a handful of matches during the campaign but was allowed to leave as manager Moore reshaped his squad for the new season.

BETTS, Eric

Outside-left

Born: Coventry 27 July 1925.
Died: Rochdale 16 March 1990.
Career: Mansfield Villa. Nottingham Forest amateur July 1943. Crystal Palace March 1945. Mansfield Villa. Mansfield Town February 1946. Coventry City August 1947. Nuneaton Borough 1948. Walsall May 1949. West Ham United April 1950. Nuneaton Borough August 1951. Rochdale October 1951. Crewe Alexandra February 1953. Wrexham October 1953. OLDHAM ATHLETIC February 1956. Bangor City July 1957 to August 1960.

■ Eric Betts was a fast-moving winger who favoured a direct approach. He was unfortunately injured on his debut and played only twice in 1955–56. Under new manager Goodier he appeared in 24 of the season's League matches and scored five goals. In a nomadic career, Betts scored 48 League goals in 209 appearances, a creditable return for a wide player.

BINGHAM, John George

Winger

Born: Ripley, Derbyshire, 23 September 1949.
Career: Charlton Athletic apprentice 1966. Manchester City October 1967. OLDHAM ATHLETIC July 1969. Mansfield Town August 1970. Chester loan March 1972. Stockport County July 1972.

■ Former England Youth international John Bingham was without League experience when he arrived at Boundary Park. He made his senior debut with Athletic at outside-right and subsequently switched flanks following Les Chapman's transfer to Huddersfield Town. Bingham faded from the first-team picture in mid-season and departed to Mansfield Town in the summer. Despite playing little first-team football with his subsequent clubs, he was a member of Australia's World Cup squad in 1984.

BIRCH, Brian

Inside-forward

Born: Salford, 18 November 1931.
Career: Salford Schoolboys. Manchester United amateur May 1946, professional May 1948. Wolverhampton Wanderers March 1952, fee £11,000. Lincoln City December 1952, fee £5,000. Boston United. Barrow June 1956, fee £2,500. Exeter City September 1958, fee £2,000. OLDHAM ATHLETIC January 1960, fee £800. Rochdale March 1961, fee £750.

■ As a 17-year-old inside-forward prodigy who won England Youth honours, Brian Birch made his debut in the First Division with Manchester United, scoring four goals in only eight

appearances in 1950–51, as United finished runners-up to Tottenham Hotspur for the League Championship. A five-figure fee took him to Wolverhampton Wanderers but less than a year later he was with Lincoln City. In a 12-year career he served seven League clubs, totalling 194 appearances and 59 goals. Signed for Athletic by Norman Dodgin, who had previously managed him at Barrow, Brian Birch proved a valuable acquisition, and his fine ball skills and opportunism were used in a variety of forward positions. After retiring as a player he then became one of the game's most persistent globe-trotters in the course of his coaching appointments.

BIRKETT, Ronald

Outside-left

Born: Warrington, 21 July 1927.
Died: Salford, December 1992.
Career: Garswood St Andrew's. Crompton's Recs. Manchester City amateur May 1945, professional January 1946. New Brighton January 1947. OLDHAM ATHLETIC August 1948. Accrington Stanley July 1949. New Brighton 1951–52.

■ Ronnie Birkett could show a clean pair of heels to most full-backs, but his ball control and crossing were rather less impressive. After a year with Manchester City, he made his League debut with New Brighton, at that time a Third Division North club. His debut with Athletic came in a 6–0 defeat at Hull City and he lost his first-team place in the midst of a dreadful opening to the 1948–49 season, which saw one point gathered from the

opening eight League fixtures. Two brothers also played in League football. Goalkeeper Wilf made 177 League appearances for Southport and 20 for Shrewsbury Town between 1946–53. Cliff, the youngest brother, was capped eight times by England schoolboys but failed to build on his early promise, subsequently having a very modest League career of 23 matches and six goals with Manchester United and Southport.

BLACK, Paul Michael

Left-back

Born: Rochdale, 18 May 1990.
Career: Manchester City juniors. OLDHAM ATHLETIC Centre of Excellence 2003, apprentice July 2006, professional January 2008.

■ Highly rated full-back Paul Black captained Athletic youth while studying GSEs at Crompton House School. He was first called into the senior squad for the FA Cup tie against Doncaster Rovers in November 2007 when he was an unused substitute. His senior debut, from the bench, came in the 4–1 win against Huddersfield Town on 29 March 2008. The 18-year-old defender was initially associated with Manchester City but moved to Boundary Park at the age of 13. He was given a two-and-a-half-year contract in the month of his 18th birthday.

BLACKSHAW, Herbert Kitchener

Forward

Born: Altrincham, 8 June 1916.
Died: Wisbech, 18 February 1999.
Career: Altrincham FC. Notts County trial

September 1934. Manchester City trial August 1935. Sheffield United trial July–August 1936. OLDHAM ATHLETIC October 1936. Wartime guest with Carlisle United and Luton Town. Wisbech Town player-manager January 1946, retired following a broken leg in April 1949.

■ Bert Blackshaw had to wait patiently for a first team call-up, spending almost a year in Athletic's reserve team. He nevertheless seized his opportunity when finally selected, scoring in each of his first three senior outings. In 1938–39, he was switched to inside-left to accommodate the newly signed wingman David Halford. Blackshaw proved himself to be a lively attacking force in his new role, possessing forceful qualities and the requisite dash for the position. Appointed player-manager of Wisbech Town after World War Two, he combined football with his work as a hospital physiotherapist in the town.

BLACKSHAW, William

Forward

Born: Ashton-under-Lyne, 6 September 1920.
Died: Ashton-under-Lyne, 17 June 1994.
Career: Audenshaw United. Ashton National. Manchester City amateur May, professional September 1937. OLDHAM ATHLETIC July 1946. Crystal Palace July 1949. Rochdale February to July 1951. Stalybridge Celtic August 1951.

■ A strong-running wingman with few frills, Bill Blackshaw believed in taking the direct route to goal and was a dangerous marksman. His 17 League goals in 1947–48 included four scored in one match at Halifax Town, as the Latics rounded off the season with an emphatic

5–1 win at The Shay. In his first season with Crystal Palace he scored five goals in 28 appearances, but he did not appear at League level with Rochdale.

BLAIR, John Elliott

Centre-forward

Born: Liverpool, 21 October 1898.
Died: Stafford, 1974.
Career: Liverpool University. Northern Nomads. Everton March 1920. Congleton Town January 1922. OLDHAM ATHLETIC August 1922. Mold FC November 1923. Northern Nomads 1925. Arsenal April 1926. Ilford FC October 1926. Northern Nomads 1927–28.

■ A well-built amateur international centre-forward with a bustling, all-action style, whose spell with Athletic was cruelly curtailed by injuries. John Blair made an outstanding individual contribution in 1923–24, scoring 15 League and Cup goals in 19 matches before a leg injury curtailed his season. After just four matches at the start of season 1924–25, he fractured an ankle at Clapton Orient, and this proved to be his final outing as a Latics player. An FA Amateur Cup winner with Northern Nomads in 1926, Blair's England Amateur International cap was awarded for the match versus Wales in 1921.

BLAIR, Ronald Victor

Midfield/Defender

Born: Coleraine, Northern Ireland, 26 September 1949.

Career: Coleraine amateur June 1965. OLDHAM ATHLETIC amateur July, professional October 1966. Rochdale April 1970, fee £1,300. OLDHAM ATHLETIC August 1972, in exchange for Keith Bebbington. Caribous FC (US) May to August 1978. Blackpool August 1981. Rochdale August 1982, re-registering as a non-contract player September 1982. Milton FC. Castleton Gabriels coach, appointed manager midway through season 1990–91, resigned March 1992. Bacup Borough manager June to December 1992.

■ A versatile and accomplished performer in a variety of roles, Ronnie Blair was a great crowd favourite during his two spells at Boundary Park. His return from Rochdale in 1972 spanned a successful era, highlighted by the 1973–74 Third Division Championship season, in which he scored 11 goals in 41 matches. His breakthrough into full international football came in October 1974 and he went on to win five caps, his final one coming in March 1976 against Israel in Tel Aviv. Finally departing Athletic after a combined stay of some 13 years, he spent a good season with Blackpool, but increasing business commitments as a director of a printing company hastened his retirement from senior football.

BLANEY, Alan

Goalkeeper

Born: Belfast, 9 October 1981.
Career: Southampton trainee, professional July 2001. Stockport County loan October 2002. AFC Bournemouth loan December 2002. Rushden & Diamonds loan January 2005. Brighton & Hove Albion loan March 2005 and again September 2005.

Doncaster Rovers January 2006, fee £50,000. OLDHAM ATHLETIC February–May 2007.

■ Three starts and two substitute appearances by Northern Ireland international goalkeeper Alan Blaney included both of Athletic's unsuccessful Play-off semi-final matches against Blackpool. Recruited as a free agent following his release by Doncaster Rovers, Blaney impressed during a brief spell on trial but subsequently failed to capitalise on his opportunities as deputy to Les Pogliacomi. Capped by Northern Ireland at Under-19 and Under-21 levels, Blaney won his first full cap against Romania in Chicago in May 2006.

BLORE, Reginald

Forward

Born: Sesswick, near Wrexham, 18 March 1942.
Career: Liverpool Schoolboys. Liverpool amateur May 1957, professional May 1959. Southport July 1960. Blackburn Rovers November 1963, fee £6,000. OLDHAM ATHLETIC December 1965, fee £8,000. Bangor City 1970. Ellesmere Port Town 1971–72.

■ Born in Wales but raised on Merseyside, Reg Blore joined Liverpool's ground staff straight from school and became a professional two years later. A speedy and accomplished forward with a taste for goals, Blore won the first of his four Wales Under-23 caps while playing in Division Four with Southport, for whom he scored 55 League goals in 139 appearances.

Finding few opportunities in his two years with Blackburn Rovers, he joined the Latics on Christmas Eve 1965. Three years earlier, on Boxing Day 1962, he was Southport's centre-forward at Boundary Park when Athletic won 11–0. In 1968 Blore was the winner of the Professional Footballer's Golf Championship.

BLUNDELL, Christopher Keith

Defender

Born: Billinge, near Wigan, 7 December 1969.
Career: Cheshire Schoolboys. OLDHAM ATHLETIC trainee July 1986, professional June 1987. Waikato United, New Zealand, loan April 1989. Rochdale loan September 1990, permanent December 1990. Northwich Victoria August 1991.

Stalybridge Celtic June 1993. Winsford United August 1993.

■ Reserve full-back Chris Blundell's League debut lasted for approximately four minutes, when he was called on as a very late substitute in the final fixture of season 1987–88 against AFC Bournemouth. His brief appearance coincided with Athletic's 3,000th Football League fixture, and he became the 685th player to represent the club in League football. In the following season he was sent on loan to a club in New Zealand, where he supplemented his earnings by working for the Hamilton Aerospace Corporation.

BOLLANDS, John Frederick

Goalkeeper

Born: Middlesbrough, 11 July 1935.
Career: South Bank Rangers. OLDHAM ATHLETIC March 1953. Sunderland March 1956, fee £2,500. Bolton Wanderers February 1960, fee £7,500. OLDHAM ATHLETIC September 1961 to June 1966, fee £2,500.

■ Johnny Bollands was recommended to the Latics while playing with South Bank Rangers and serving an apprenticeship as a welder. A daring and often brilliant goalkeeper, he was on the small side for his position but agile enough to deal with both high and low shots. His first spell at Boundary Park was restricted by the calls of National Service, but Sunderland were sufficiently impressed by his potential to pay £2,500 for his transfer. He won England Under-23 honours at Roker Park, but had the cruel misfortune to miss a full England cap after breaking his leg in a collision with the late Tommy Taylor of Manchester United. While in a Middlesbrough hospital that same weekend he learned of his selection for the England party. During his Sunderland days he was much admired by schoolboy Jim Montgomery, who subsequently became the club's record-breaking goalkeeper with 623 senior appearances.

BONNER, Mark

Midfield

Born: Ormskirk, 7 June 1974.
Career: Blackpool trainee, professional June 1992. Cardiff City July 1998. Hull City loan January 1999. OLDHAM ATHLETIC March 2004 to December 2005, retired January 2006.

■ Athletic beat the transfer deadline in March 2004 to sign experienced midfielder Mark Bonner, who had played in 169 first-team matches for Cardiff City and 220 for Blackpool. Despite a shaky start with Athletic – he had not played any first-team football for three months – he improved sufficiently to be offered a two-year

contract in July 2004. Hard working and with a good passing range, he nevertheless endured a frustrating first full campaign in 2004–05, with injuries restricting him to just 19 League matches, four coming from the bench. In January of the following term, after he had been out for three months because of a broken arm at Port Vale, agreement was reached to cancel his contract, and the unfortunate midfielder accepted medical advice to retire from the game.

BOOTHMAN, James 'Jerry'

Full-back

Born: Great Harwood, 2 December 1920.
Died: Keighley, Yorkshire, 1980.
Career: Services Football. OLDHAM ATHLETIC January 1946 to April 1949.

■ The son of a former Blackburn Rovers full-back, Jerry Boothman joined the Latics following six years of wartime service in the Fleet Air Arm, which included two and a half years spent in India. A firm tackler who always used the ball constructively, Boothman was Athletic's first-choice at right-back when normal peacetime football resumed in 1946–47. Having appeared in approximately half of the League matches in his first two seasons, he was exclusively a reserve-team player in 1948–49, when Tommy Bell and Bill Pickering dominated the full-back berths.

BOSHELL, Daniel Kevin

Midfield

Born: Bradford, 30 May 1981.
Career: Queensbury Celtic. OLDHAM ATHLETIC associate schoolboy July 1995, trainee July 1997, professional July 1998. Scunthorpe United trial October 2002. Bury loan March 2005. Stockport County August 2005. Grimsby Town trial July, professional August 2006.

■ A ball-playing, cultured midfielder with good, constructive ideas, fair-haired Danny Boshell was associated with Athletic from the tender age of nine, when he first attended the club's Centre of Excellence. Despite a first-team debut at the age of 18, Boshell found senior opportunities at a premium in his eight-year stint as a professional at Boundary Park, totalling 85 first-team matches, 28 coming from the bench. In March 2008 Boshell played at Wembley in the Johnstone's Paint Trophy Final. Sadly he finished on the losing side, after having a first-half penalty saved, MK Dons winning 2–0.

BOSWELL, William

Centre-forward

Born: Cradley Heath, 5 August 1902.
Died: Kidderminster, 1977.
Career: Tansley Green Rovers. Coombs Wood Colliery. Walsall December 1924. Wolverhampton Wanderers May 1925. Gillingham November 1927. Worcester City July 1928. Burton Town December 1930. OLDHAM ATHLETIC January 1932, fee £275. Burton Town April 1932.

Kidderminster Harriers June 1934. Shirley Town August 1937. Solihull Town 1938.

■ Billy Boswell began as a centre-half but made his name as a strong running centre-forward, who was particularly powerful in the air. In a little over two seasons with Worcester City he scored 92 goals in 91 matches, winning successive Birmingham League Championships. He had scored 31 goals for Burton Town at the time of joining Athletic, but despite his immediate scoring debut against Bury on 16 January he returned to non-League football after an otherwise unrewarding three months at Boundary Park.

BOTTOMLEY, William

Half-back

Born: Mossley, 1886.
Career: Mossley Britannia. Failsworth July

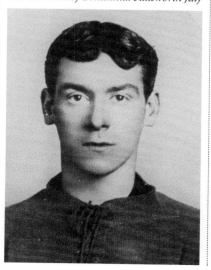

1905. OLDHAM ATHLETIC trial February 1906, professional October 1907. Manchester City May 1908 to September 1919.

■ Billy Bottomley lacked physical advantage at 5ft 8in and 10st 7lb, but the flame-haired defender's best position was centre-half, where his clever and purposeful displays earned him a place in the North versus South international trial match in 1908. Transferred to Manchester City in May 1908, he made 103 League and Cup appearances and won a Second Division Championship medal in season 1909–10.

BOURNE, Albert

Inside-forward

Born: Golborne, 30 September 1934.
Career: Manchester Schoolboys. Manchester City amateur May, professional August 1952. OLDHAM ATHLETIC June 1958 to June 1960, fee £250.

■ Albert Bourne had a six-year association with Manchester City but failed to graduate to senior level. A bustling and persistent forward, he began alongside Gerry Duffy in the opening months of season 1958–59 but by mid-term had lost his place, his return of four goals in 20 League outings proving a disappointment. In 1959–60, when a second consecutive re-election application had to be made, he again failed to improve in front of goal, registering a modest return of four strikes in 17 League matches.

BOWDEN, Jack

Half-back

Born: Manchester, 25 August 1921.
Died: Failsworth, 15 July 1981.
Career: Chadderton Grammar School. Royton Amateurs. OLDHAM ATHLETIC amateur May 1938. Wartime guest with Arsenal. Manchester United amateur June to September 1945. OLDHAM ATHLETIC professional September 1945. Witton Albion June 1949.

■ Jack Bowden began in wartime football with the Latics, while serving in the RAF. In his early days as an inside-forward he scored six goals in eight matches in 1944–45, but it was at wing half-back that he made his mark in League football. After trials with Manchester United he joined Athletic as a professional in September 1945. A gentlemanly, constructive wing-half who distributed the ball to good effect, Bowden was at his best during season 1947–48, when he appeared in 39 matches. A qualified accountant, at various times he worked as deputy treasurer to Failsworth Council, and also in the treasurer's department of Oldham Council from 1958 to 1976.

BOWDEN, Jonathan Lee

Forward/Midfield

Born: Stockport, 21 January 1963.
Career: Grove United, Hazel Grove. OLDHAM ATHLETIC amateur, professional January 1980. Port Vale September 1985, fee £5,000. Wrexham August 1987, fee £12,500. Rochdale September 1991, fee £10,000. OLDHAM ATHLETIC assistant physiotherapist and kit manager July 1995 until May 1997. Doncaster Rovers physiotherapist July 1998.

■ Fair-haired Jon Bowden, a ball-winning central midfielder with a whole-hearted approach, was a versatile performer throughout his career, with extended spells as a forward, midfielder and central-defender. In his first season with Port Vale he assisted them to promotion from Division Four. During his Wrexham spell, the club appeared in three Welsh Cup Finals, bringing a brief taste of European football. A final spell with Rochdale was ended by an Achilles injury.

BOWIE, James McAvoy

Inside-forward/Half-back

Born: Howwood, Renfrewshire, 11 October 1941.
Career: Neilston Waverley. Third Lanark

amateur 1958. Arthurlie Juniors 1960. OLDHAM ATHLETIC July 1962. Rochdale October–November 1972.

■ Jim Bowie was working as a Glasgow insurance clerk when first spotted by the Latics when playing in a Scottish Junior Cup tie with Arthurlie Juniors. Tall and slim at 6ft 3in and 11st 7lb, the young Scot had a deceptively languid style, his ability to find the open space enabling him to use the ball constructively. In his debut season Athletic won promotion from Division Four. During the course of 10 excellent seasons at Boundary Park, he was successfully switched from inside-forward to wing-half in the mid-1960s. Before leaving to join Rochdale he assisted the Latics in a second promotion campaign in season 1970–71.

BOXALL, Daniel James

Defender

Born: Croydon, 24 August 1977.
Career: Tottenham Hotspur associate schoolboy. Crystal Palace associate schoolboy and trainee, professional April 1995. OLDHAM ATHLETIC loan November 1997 and again February 1998. Brentford July 1998. Bristol Rovers July 2002. Dublin City June 2004.

■ Danny Boxall had two separate loan spells with the Latics in season 1997–98, initially as cover in central defence, which was depleted due to injuries and suspensions. During his second spell at Boundary Park he was called up to play for the Republic of Ireland Under-21s against Czechoslovakia. This was his international debut, qualification coming thanks to an Irish great-grandmother. In 1999 he assisted Brentford to the Championship of Division Three.

BRADBURY, William Henry

Inside-forward/Half-back

Born: Longton, Staffordshire, 1883.
Died: Stoke-on-Trent, 30 September 1966.
Career: Newcastle Swifts. Burslem Port Vale May 1903. Fegg Hayes August 1907. Stoke May 1910. Aberdare 1911. OLDHAM ATHLETIC December 1911, fee £200. Scunthorpe & Lindsay United June 1913. OLDHAM ATHLETIC May 1919, (following guest appearances during World War One). Rochdale May 1922.

Burton All Saints amateur 1924. Bass & Company, amateur May 1925.

■ In the final month of season 1911–12, reserve inside-forward Bill Bradbury scored in consecutive First Division matches against Notts County and Aston Villa. Recruited for a second spell after World War One, in which he was awarded the Military Medal, he was a prominent member of the team's defence. At either wing-half or full-back, his game featured robust tackling and an immense capacity for work. After retiring from the game Bradbury became a licensee in Burton upon Trent. His son, Tom, joined Derby County in 1937 but did not graduate to senior level.

BRADSHAW, George Frederick

Goalkeeper

Born: High Park, Southport, 10 March 1913.
Died: Southport, 28 August 1989.
Career: High Park Villa. New Brighton amateur August 1932, professional September 1933. Everton November 1934, fee £500. Arsenal March 1935, fee £2,000. Doncaster Rovers May 1936. Bury June 1938. Wartime guest with OLDHAM ATHLETIC, Bristol City, Cardiff City & Preston North End. OLDHAM ATHLETIC July 1950 to May 1951.

■ Although very slim and slightly built, George Bradshaw lacked nothing in agility and courage. He began in the Third Division North with New Brighton and after 83 League appearances was signed by Everton. He had made only three appearances for them before Arsenal

signed him, just prior to the transfer deadline in March 1935. Two seasons with Doncaster Rovers preceded his move to Bury, where a long spell of service included the World War Two years. Despite suffering a fractured leg in a game against Newcastle United in October 1947, Bradshaw completed over a century of League appearances for the Shakers before his final move to Boundary Park. The son of a Southport grocer, Bradshaw ran a newsagents and off-licence in the town following his retirement from the game.

BRAIDWOOD, Ernest

Centre-half

Born: Heywood, 14 April 1895.
Died: Heywood, 16 July 1968.
Career: Chesterfield Municipal February 1920. OLDHAM ATHLETIC amateur June, professional August 1920. Nelson May 1922. Rochdale March 1926. Great Harwood February 1930. New Mills September 1930.

■ Ideally built at 6ft and 12st, centre-half Ernie Braidwood nevertheless spent much of his two seasons at Boundary Park in the reserves, and was selected to represent the Central League versus The Lancashire Combination at Tranmere on 15 January 1921. In search of regular first-team football, he joined forces with former Athletic teammate David Wilson at Nelson. Braidwood enjoyed a successful spell at Seedhill, which included two promotion seasons, both of which he played in every game. He subsequently came close to winning a second Championship medal with Rochdale, who finished as runners-up to Stoke for the Third Division North Championship in 1926–27.

BRAMWELL, Steven

Midfield

Born: Reddish, Stockport, 9 October 1970.
Career: North West Counties Schoolboys. Manchester United associate schoolboy March 1984. OLDHAM ATHLETIC associate schoolboy April 1987, trainee July 1987, professional July 1989. Wigan Athletic loan April 1990. Crewe Alexandra May 1990 to June 1991. Hyde United 1991.

■ Steve Bramwell's solitary League appearance, as a 76th-minute substitute

for Roger Palmer at West Bromwich Albion, marked the end of an unbeaten 10-match run. Not that this was any reflection on the performance of the 17-year-old YTS midfielder. The match also saw the Latics' debut – again from the bench – of a player at the other end of the scale, 38-year-old Asa Hartford. Hartford had been offered a short-term contract by Athletic, following his dismissal as manager of Stockport County.

BRANAGAN, James Patrick Stephen

Full-back

Born: Urmston, 3 July 1955.
Career: Cadishead FC. OLDHAM ATHLETIC associate schoolboy November 1971, professional July 1973. Cape Town, South Africa, May 1977. Huddersfield Town November 1977. Blackburn Rovers

October 1979, fee £20,000. Preston North End June 1987. York City September 1987. Chorley January 1989, retired May 1989.

■ It was through his father Ken, a former player and later coach to the Latics reserves, that Jim Branagan arrived at Boundary Park. Captain of Athletic's reserve team for many seasons, he was unfortunate to be at Boundary Park at the same time as Ian Wood and Maurice Whittle, who dominated the full-back positions. Branagan's career blossomed after he left Athletic, most notably with Blackburn Rovers where, in nine seasons, he recorded 333/40 appearances in all competitions. After retiring from the game he worked in the insurance and finance trades.

BRANAGAN, Kenneth

Full-back

Born: Salford, 27 July 1930.
Career: North Salford Boys' Club. Manchester United amateur. Manchester City November 1948. OLDHAM ATHLETIC October 1960 to May 1966, in a joint signing with Bert Lister for a combined fee of £10,000. Irlam Town manager. OLDHAM ATHLETIC reserve team trainer & youth coach August 1973 to 1976.

■ Although approaching the veteran stage when recruited, full-back Ken Branagan gave five and a half years of sterling service

to the Latics. He appeared in every match in the 1962–63 promotion season and in his later role as trainer/coach turned out for the reserves in an emergency in May 1974 in a Cheshire League game. He was 43 years old at the time and played alongside his 18-year-old son, Jim. At the outset of his career Branagan played in 208 League and Cup matches for Manchester City, and was 12th man in their 1955 FA Cup Final against Newcastle United.

BRANSTON, Guy Peter Bromley

Central-defender

Born: Leicester, 9 January 1979.
Career: Leicester City trainee, professional July 1997. Rushden & Diamonds loan November 1997. Colchester United loan February 1998 and August 1998. Plymouth Argyle loan November 1998. Lincoln City loan August 1999. Rotherham United October 1999, fee £50,000. Wycombe Wanderers loan September 2003. Peterborough United loan February 2004. Sheffield Wednesday July 2004. Peterborough United loan December 2004. OLDHAM ATHLETIC February 2005. Peterborough United July 2006. Rochdale loan August–October 2007. Northampton Town loan November 2007. Notts County January 2008. Kettering Town February 2008.

■ In his one full season at Boundary Park, commanding centre-half Guy Branston was handed the captaincy in the later stages. In a season of chop and change, 29 players were used by Athletic in all competitions but Branston featured in 42 matches and was offered terms for 2006–07. With his contract up, no agreement on a new deal was reached and Branston signed for Peterborough United, joining three other ex-Athletic players at London Road: Mark Arber, Dean Holden and Richard Butcher.

BRAZIL, Derek Michael

Central-defender

Born: Dublin, 14 December 1968.
Career: Belvedere FC. Rivermount Boys' Club. Manchester United March 1986. OLDHAM ATHLETIC loan November–December 1990. Swansea City loan September 1991. Cardiff City August 1992 to June 1996, fee £85,000. Haverford West manager October 2006.

■ Derek Brazil began in Gaelic football, but had no shortage of admirers when he turned to soccer. He disappointed several interested parties when he joined Manchester United, but then found opportunities limited with players of the calibre of Steve Bruce and Paul McGrath preventing his advancement. He played only once for the Athletic during his loan spell, a 2–0 defeat at Bristol Rovers that surrendered the Latics' lead in Division Two to West Ham United. Eventually made available for transfer by Manchester United, he joined Cardiff City, who won the Division Three Championship in his first season at Ninian Park. Brazil was capped by the Republic of Ireland at Schools, Youth, Under-21, Under-23 and B levels.

BRELSFORD, Ben

Full-back

Born: Attercliffe, Sheffield, 1896.
Died: Oldham, 1968.
Career: Sheffield Wednesday November 1922. Barrow July 1924, fee £150. OLDHAM ATHLETIC May 1926, fee £50. Watford May 1928. Bray Unknowns May 1930. Shelbourne August 1930. Manchester North End December 1930. Rossendale United September 1931. Larne. Newton Heath Loco reinstated amateur January 1933. New Mills amateur January 1934.

■ After two seasons in reserve with Sheffield Wednesday, burly left full-back Ben Brelsford gained League experience with Barrow, recording 72 League and Cup appearances in two years at Holker Street. Brelsford first appeared in Athletic's team following the sale of Sammy Wynne to Bury, but the full-back berths were subsequently dominated by Harry Grundy and Teddy Ivill. Ben Brelsford's footballing brothers included Tom (Sheffield Wednesday, Barrow and

Rotherham United), William Henry (Doncaster Rovers and Sheffield United) and Charles (South Shields and Mansfield Town).

BRENNAN, Mark Robert

Left midfield

Born: Rossendale, 4 October 1965.
Career: Blackburn Schoolboys. Ipswich Town apprentice, professional April 1983. Middlesbrough July 1988, fee £375,000. Manchester City July 1990, fee £500,000. OLDHAM ATHLETIC November 1992 to June 1996, fee £200,000. Dagenham & Redbridge August 2001. Billericay Town June 2002. Canvey Island. Accrington Stanley until May 2003. Tilbury August 2003.

■ Mark Brennan won five England Under-21 caps while on Ipswich Town's

books, completing over 200 appearances and scoring 25 goals before making big money moves to Middlesbrough and Manchester City. His spell with Athletic was mixed. In his first two seasons, under manager Joe Royle, the emerging talents of Paul Bernard restricted his opportunities. Under new player-manager Graeme Sharp he was more regularly employed, but was handed a free transfer in the summer of 1996.

BRIERLEY, Kenneth

Winger/Half-back

Born: Ashton-under-Lyne, 3 April 1926.
Died: Blackpool, February 2004.
Career: Range Boilers FC. OLDHAM ATHLETIC April 1945. Liverpool February 1948, fee £7,000. OLDHAM ATHLETIC March 1953, fee £2,750. Stalybridge Celtic 1955. Mossley August 1956. Wigan Athletic.

■ Ken Brierley began as a 19-year-old inside-left in wartime football, combining soccer with his National Service as a 'Bevin Boy'. Born within three miles of Boundary Park and recruited from local amateur circles, he was immediately impressive. At either inside-forward or on the wing, his vision, energy and skill eventually earned him an upward move, with Liverpool paying a significant sum for his transfer. He was immediately popular at Anfield as he opened his scoring account for the Reds in his first Merseyside derby, a 4–0 victory against Everton. Returning to the Latics in the late stages of season

1952–53, he appeared in the final 15 matches, operating mainly from left-half, and was a vital element in a successful run-in to the Championship of the Third Division North.

BRIGHT, David

Full-back

Born: Hexham, 24 December 1946.
Career: West Wylam Juniors. Sunderland amateur June, professional August 1965. Preston North End August 1967. OLDHAM ATHLETIC March 1969. Great Harwood March 1970.

■ Signed as cover for the injured Alan Lawson just prior to the transfer deadline in March 1969, David Bright lost his favoured left-back spot the following term to a distinguished close season recruit, England's World Cup-winning defender, Ray Wilson.

BRITTON, Frank

Forward

Born: Bristol, 3 March 1910.
Died: Worcester, 1979.
Career: Bristol St George. Bristol Rovers September 1927. Blackburn Rovers June 1930. OLDHAM ATHLETIC June 1934. Accrington Stanley February 1935. Reading trial August 1935. Aldershot October 1935. Worcester City March 1936. Hereford United August 1936. Cradley Heath August 1937. Stourbridge. Evesham Town March 1938. Worcester City 1944.

■ The younger brother of Cliff Britton, the Everton and England international wing-half, Frank Britton spent a season

THE WHO'S WHO OF OLDHAM ATHLETIC

in Athletic's Reserves. An extremely versatile performer, he appeared at centre-forward, in both inside berths, and at both wing-half positions. His one senior outing was at centre-forward in a season when the Latics were relegated from Division Two. In four seasons with Blackburn Rovers, prior to joining the Latics, he scored nine goals in 48 League and Cup matches. After leaving Boundary Park Britton had a brief but rewarding spell with Accrington Stanley, netting nine goals in just 11 matches.

BROAD, James

Inside-forward

Born: Stalybridge, 10 November 1891.
Died: Chelmsford, 22 August 1963.
Career: St Mark's, West Gorton. Stalybridge Celtic. Manchester City October 1909. Manchester United October 1910. Royal Club, Corunna, Spain, until September 1911. Manchester City

September 1912. OLDHAM ATHLETIC August 1913. Wartime guest with Blackburn Rovers & Greenock Morton. Millwall Athletic April 1919, fee £380. Las Palmas, Spain, coach October 1920. Stoke June 1921, fee £2,000. Barcelona, Spain, coach August 1924. Sittingbourne October 1924. Everton November 1924, fee £1,400. New Brighton December 1925, fee £200. Watford August 1926. Caernarvon Town October 1927. Taunton United September 1928. Geneva, Switzerland, coach 1930. Italian coaching appointment 1931. Fleetwood August 1931. Morecambe September 1931.

■ The younger brother of Thomas (below), Jimmy Broad began with Athletic as a goalkeeper, but switched to inside-forward with great success. A most dangerous and skilful attacker, he played in all four sections of the League and, in addition, sampled Scottish, Welsh and Southern League fare. He scored over 100 League goals, including 32 in 39 matches for Millwall in 1919–20, and 25 in 41 matches for Stoke in season 1921–22. In addition to coaching appointments noted above, Broad additionally held similar positions in Turkey, South America, the Netherlands and Norway.

BROAD, Thomas Higginson

Outside-right

Born: Stalybridge, 31 July 1887.
Died: Barton Irwell, 1966.
Career: Redgate Albion. Denton Wanderers. Manchester City trial 1903. Openshaw Lads' Club. West Bromwich Albion September 1905. Chesterfield Town

February 1908. OLDHAM ATHLETIC May 1909, fee £250. Bristol City May 1912, fee £600. Manchester City March 1919. Stoke May 1921, fee £500. Southampton July 1924, fee £250. Weymouth September 1925. Rhyl Athletic January 1926.

■ Tommy Broad belonged to a family of footballers. His father, James Broad, was Manchester City's trainer, while brothers, Jimmy and Wilf played professionally. When Chesterfield Town failed to gain re-election in 1909, the Latics won the race for Broad's signature. In three seasons at Boundary Park he was rarely absent and his raking stride and sinuous runs down the right touchline were a key element in Athletic's promotion to the top flight in 1909–10. Considered unfortunate to have missed full international honours, Tommy Broad enjoyed a lengthy career in the game before taking over the Dudley Arms Hotel in Rhyl.

BROADBENT, Frederick

Centre-forward

Born: Hollinwood, Oldham, 9 November 1900.
Died: Hollinwood, Oldham, 11 October 1959.
Career: Ferranti FC, Hollinwood. OLDHAM ATHLETIC amateur October 1918, professional February 1920. Southport June 1923, retired due to knee injury January 1924.

■ Blond-haired and broad shouldered, Fred Broadbent was a centre-forward of the bustling type. Wonderfully fast, he had many successes on the racing track, including a famous handicap race against the British champion, W.R. Applegarth. At Broughton Rangers RFC ground, Fred received five yards in a 60-yard dash, and won by three yards. Born at the White Hart Inn, Hollins Road, he entered the licensing trade on retiring from football in 1924.

BROADBENT, William Henry

Inside-forward

Born: Chadderton, 20 November 1901.
Died: Lancaster, 14 February 1979.
Career: Droylsden Rugby Football Club

1917. Wellington Albion FC 1919. OLDHAM ATHLETIC amateur April 1920, professional October 1921. Brentford July 1924. Clapton Orient June 1925. Preston North End June 1925. Manchester North End September 1932 to 1933.

■ At 16 years of age Billy Broadbent began as a Rugby League player but switched codes two years later and was quickly spotted by the Latics, initially joining on amateur forms. Within his handful of League appearances, he played as wingman, inside-forward and wing half-back. It was a pattern repeated throughout his career, during which he appeared in every outfield position. In seven years with Clapton Orient he made exactly 200 League appearances.

BROADLEY, Patrick Joseph

Half-back

Born: Croy, Dumbartonshire, 13 May 1926.
Died: Manchester, June 2005.
Career: Bedlay Juniors. Belfast Distillery January 1948. Sligo Rovers. OLDHAM ATHLETIC June 1951. Northwich Victoria 1953–55.

■ Although born in Scotland, Pat Broadley was recruited from Sligo Rovers, the League of Ireland club. Despite representing the League of Ireland on three occasions, against their counterparts the Football League, Scottish League and Irish League, he spent two years at Boundary Park

without mounting a serious challenge for a first-team place. His four senior appearances all came late in season 1951–52 and resulted in three wins and one defeat. In the promotion season that followed he was exclusively a reserve-team player.

BROMAGE, Russell

Defender/Midfield

Born: Stoke-on-Trent, 9 November 1959.
Career: Port Vale apprentice August 1976, professional November 1977. OLDHAM ATHLETIC loan October 1983. Bristol City August 1987, fee £25,000 plus Lawrie Pearson. Brighton & Hove Albion August 1990. Maidstone United loan January 1991. Southwick FC player-coach 1992, subsequently player-manager. Lancing FC February 1995. Littlehampton Town manager 1995–96. Shoreham FC player-coach 1996, joint manager August 1997.

■ A conspicuous figure in Port Vale's defence for over a decade, Russell Bromage appeared in over 400 matches in all competitions, his total including maximum League appearances during the 1982–83 Division Four promotion campaign. It was felt that his loan move to the Latics might have been made permanent at a time when a successor to the departed John Ryan was sought. In the event, he returned to Vale Park after just two outings, and it was not until the

following season that the position was satisfactorily filled, when Scottish International back Willie Donachie was signed from Burnley.

BROOK, Lewis

Centre-forward/Full-back

Born: Halifax 27 July 1918.
Died: Halifax, July 1996.
Career: Northowram FC. Halifax Town amateur August 1935. Huddersfield Town May 1936. Wartime guest with Aldershot, Bournemouth & Boscombe United, Watford and Halifax Town. OLDHAM ATHLETIC March 1948, retired August 1957.

■ One of a number of Huddersfield Town players who migrated to Boundary Park in the 1940s, Lewis Brook made an excellent start, scoring seven goals in his first 11 outings as attack leader. In subsequent seasons he proved an outstanding utility player, appearing in every outfield position during his long spell with the club. He is probably best remembered as a splendid full-back partner to Athletic's player-manager George Hardwick in the 1952–53 Third Division North Championship side. After just short of 200 senior appearances, Brook announced his retirement from the game, in order to take up a position in Halifax, outside of football.

BROOME, Albert Henry

Inside-forward

Born: Unsworth, 30 May 1900.
Died: Chester, December 1989.
Career: South Salford Lads. Manchester University. Northern Nomads. OLDHAM ATHLETIC amateur October 1921. Manchester United January 1923. OLDHAM ATHLETIC professional July 1924 to April 1925. Welshpool FC December 1925. Stockport County March 1927. Mossley August 1928. Chester July 1929. Altrincham August 1930. Northwich Victoria August 1932 to 1934. Sandbach Ramblers December 1926 to March 1927.

■ An outstanding amateur inside-forward whose play featured many neat and skilful touches, Albert Broome nevertheless failed to shine in League football, making only fleeting appearances for his three senior clubs. During his spell with the Latics, Broome combined football with his employment as a commercial traveller.

BROWN, Alfred

Half-back

Born: Chadderton, 22 February 1907.
Died: Kendal, September 1994.
Career: Chamber Colliery. OLDHAM ATHLETIC March 1927. Northampton Town June 1933. Mansfield Town February 1936 to 1937.

■ Alf Brown was discovered by Athletic scouts when playing for Chamber

Colliery in the Oldham Amateur League. He began at centre-half and was later moved across to right-half, which became his established position. Brown's headwork was a feature of his play, and his physique and energy carried him through the keenest of games. His brother Harold (below) also assisted the Latics as an amateur.

BROWN, Harold

Outside-right

Born: Unconfirmed, but thought to be at Chadderton.
Career: OLDHAM ATHLETIC amateur December 1931 to June 1933. British Dyes, Manchester. OLDHAM ATHLETIC amateur October 1934. Stalybridge Celtic. Mossley August 1946.

■ Despite a scoring debut as a late replacement for regular outside-right Leslie Smalley, amateur wingman Harold Brown was obviously short of experience. Mainly involved in Athletic's Midweek League and reserve sides, he nevertheless had the satisfaction of scoring the Latics' last goal in their 6–1 thrashing of Chesterfield. He is the brother of Alfred Brown (above).

BRUCE, Alexander Stephen

Defender

Born: Norwich, 28 September 1984.
Career: Blackburn Rovers trainee, professional July 2002. OLDHAM ATHLETIC loan December 2004. Birmingham City January 2005. OLDHAM ATHLETIC loan January 2005. Sheffield Wednesday loan March 2005. Tranmere Rovers loan August 2005. Ipswich Town August 2006.

■ Briefly on view with Athletic in two separate loan spells, Alex Bruce appeared in two memorable FA Cup ties in January 2005. Premier League opponents Manchester City were beaten 1–0 at Boundary Park in round three, and Bolton Wanderers were given a severe examination in round four before progressing by the only goal of the game. Capped by the Republic of Ireland at Under-21 level in 2005–06, the son of Wigan Athletic manager Steve Bruce appears set for a rewarding future in the game.

BRUNSKILL, Joseph

Centre-forward

Born: Shildon, 22 April 1932.
Died: County Cleveland, August 1989.
Career: Shildon FC. Grimsby Town amateur. Newcastle United amateur. Sunderland professional April 1950. OLDHAM ATHLETIC June 1954 to June 1955, fee £900. North Eastern League football 1955–56.

■ RAF National Service restricted Joe Brunskill's time with Sunderland, and the England Youth international subsequently became Athletic's second signing in a week in May 1954, along with Dennis King, the Spennymoor United outside-right. Following relegation from Division Two, it was expected that Athletic would mount a serious challenge for promotion. In the event they made a dreadful start, and Joe Brunskill was one of the victims, losing his place as attack leader at the end of September. He failed to regain it, as his replacement at centre-forward, Don Travis, enjoyed great success with 32 League goals in 40 matches.

BRUNSKILL, Norman

Half-back

Born: Dipton, Co. Durham, 14 June 1912.
Died: Boston 28 February 1988.
Career: South Moor Juniors. Newcastle United trial. Lintz Colliery. Huddersfield Town amateur October 1930, professional May 1931. OLDHAM ATHLETIC May 1932. Birmingham October 1936, fee

£1,300. *Barnsley November 1938, fee £1,650. Wartime guest with Consett, Middlesbrough, & Hartlepools United. Workington August 1946.*

■ A former coal miner, Norman Brunskill was a strapping six-footer in the true Latics' tradition of robust and hard-fighting defenders. A worthy successor to Les Adlam at right-half, he missed very few games in his four and a half years at Boundary Park, and his loss in 1936–37 – due to the usual financial pressures – seriously affected the balance of the side and probably cost them promotion. Before the outbreak of World War Two, Brunskill won a Third Division North Championship medal with Barnsley in 1938–39.

BRUNTON, Matthew

Centre-forward

Born: Burnley, 20 April 1878.
Died: Burnley, 29 December 1962.
Career: Army football. Preston North End August 1899. Accrington Stanley August 1900. Burnley July 1901. Accrington Stanley May 1902. Leicester Fosse May 1904. Nelson February 1905. Accrington Stanley September 1905. OLDHAM ATHLETIC May 1906. Southport Central July 1908. Haslingden August 1909. Darwen October 1910. Accrington Stanley November 1910 to February 1911, subsequently club trainer. Burnley assistant-trainer pre World War One. Accrington Stanley trainer-coach July 1921. In 1941 he was reported to be coaching Burnley's A Team.

■ Matt Brunton's career began with Preston North End, who bought his

release from the 40th South Lancashire Regiment. He subsequently became prominent in Lancashire Combination circles, winning two Championships with Accrington Stanley. He repeated the feat with the Latics, his 23 goals in 1906–07 being a major contribution in the season prior to League entry. A direct and forceful attack leader despite his lack of inches, he formed part of a lethal spearhead in 1906–07, when Athletic's three inside men scored a total of 72 goals between them.

BRYAN, Peter Anthony

Defender

Born: Birmingham, 22 June 1943.
Career: Middlesbrough amateur May, professional August 1961. OLDHAM ATHLETIC July 1965 to March 1966. Nuneaton Borough September 1966.

■ Brought to Boundary Park by new manager Gordon Hurst, the tall and slim

defender was injured on his debut at Millwall, and made only a further four starts. Peter Bryan was released shortly after the mid-season appointment of manager Jimmy McIlroy, who almost totally dismantled Gordon Hurst's early-season side.

BRYCELAND, Thomas

Inside-forward

Born: Greenock, 1 March 1939.
Career: Gourock Juniors. St Mirren March 1956. Norwich City September 1962, fee £20,000. OLDHAM ATHLETIC March 1970. St Mirren player-manager January 1972 to 1974.

■ Tommy Bryceland's extensive experience served the Latics well in the promotion season of 1970–71, and 10 goals in 45 League matches during the term were rewarded with the Player of the Year trophy by Athletic's supporters. A Scotland Schoolboy international against Ireland and Wales, he was coveted by several Football League clubs but commenced with St Mirren at 17 years of age. With Norwich City he recorded 281/3 appearances and scored 55 goals.

BUCHAN, Martin McLean

Defender

Born: Aberdeen, 6 March 1949.
Career: Banks O'Dee A. Aberdeen amateur 1965, professional August 1966. Manchester United March 1972, fee £125,000. OLDHAM ATHLETIC August

1983, retired due to injury October 1984. Burnley manager June to October 1985.

■ One of the coolest and classiest defenders of his era, Martin Buchan combined an acute positional sense and simple distribution with a searing turn of pace which gave him excellent powers of recovery. A Scottish international with 34 caps and the experience of 455 matches with Manchester United, he joined the Latics on a free transfer in August 1983. The former United skipper played a vital part in Athletic's successful battle against relegation in his first season, but a persistent thigh strain enforced his retirement after only four matches in 1984–85. After a brief and unhappy spell as manager of Burnley, Buchan worked as an area manager for a large sportswear company, and later as a player's representative for the PFA.

BUCKLEY, Arthur

Outside-left

Born: Greenfield, near Oldham, 3 July 1913.
Died: Oldham, 20 October 1992.
Career: Greenfield. OLDHAM ATHLETIC amateur May, professional October 1932. Leeds United October 1936, fee £2,500. Wartime guest with OLDHAM ATHLETIC and Aldershot.

■ Local product Arthur Buckley had to wait for two years before making his League debut and was offered a free transfer before finally making the grade with Athletic. Once established, however, he was an integral member of the Latics attack. A dashing wingman with fine individualistic qualities, he was outstanding during 1935–36, scoring 11 goals from the wing in 36 League and Cup matches. Early in the following term he joined Leeds United, where he remained first-choice outside-left until the outbreak of World War Two. During the war he was welcomed back to Boundary Park as a guest player.

BUCKLEY, Ian

Winger

Born: Oldham, 8 October 1953.
Career: Chadderton Schoolboys. OLDHAM ATHLETIC apprentice July 1969, professional December 1971. Rochdale loan February 1974. Stockport County August 1975 to May 1977. Durban City, South Africa. Cambridge United November 1977 to January 1981.

■ The first Athletic player to win an England Youth cap, blond-haired wingman Ian Buckley played against Spain in Alicante in February 1972. A traditional outside-left, he played at a time when wingers were out of fashion at Boundary Park, the team at that time mainly operating a 4–3–3 system. After leaving Athletic Buckley made 55/10

appearances in two seasons with Stockport County, and in his first season with Cambridge United assisted them to win promotion from Division Three, as runners-up to Wrexham.

BULLOCK, Steven

Defender

Born: Stockport, 5 October 1966.
Career: OLDHAM ATHLETIC associate schoolboy June 1982, amateur June 1983, professional July 1984. Tranmere Rovers August 1986. Stockport County August 1987. Hyde United August 1991. Brisbane United, Australia, September 1992. Witton Albion August 1993. Caernarfon. Rossendale United November 1994.

■ Steve Bullock was a key member of Athletic's Central League Second

Division Championship side in season 1985–86. Earlier, the youthful centre-back was handed his League debut at 17 years of age, and made 6/3 senior appearances in 1984–85. A move to Tranmere Rovers gave Bullock his first extended run of first-team football and this was followed by a transfer to his home-town club, Stockport County. At Edgeley Park he made a total of 106/14 appearances, assisting County to promotion from Division Four in his final season.

BUNN, Frank Stephen

Centre-forward

Born: Birmingham, 6 November 1962.
Career: Luton Town apprentice April 1979, professional May 1980. Hull City July 1985, fee £40,000. OLDHAM ATHLETIC December 1987 to December 1991, fee £90,000. Stalybridge Celtic August 1992. Wigan Athletic Community Scheme officer later in the same season. Radcliffe Borough December 1994. Manchester City Academy coach 1998, reserve team manager May 2006. Coventry City first-team coach February 2007.

■ Frankie Bunn's superb opportunism and general all-round play were major factors in the turnaround of Athletic's fortunes following his signing in December 1987. The Latics had not scored a League goal in the month prior to Bunn's arrival, but thereafter they hardly knew failure. Had they shown any reasonable form in early season they

would have been prime candidates for promotion. The undoubted highlight of Bunn's career was his stunning double hat-trick against Scarborough in the Football League Cup in October 1989, the first such feat by an Athletic player since Bert Lister's six against Southport on Boxing Day 1962. Sadly, Bunn was forced to retire from first-class football after aggravating a serious knee injury in the Littlewoods Cup Final against Nottingham Forest at Wembley in April 1990.

BUNTING, Benjamin

Left-back

Born: Rochdale, 14 February 1923.
Died: Rochdale, 18 August 2007.
Career: Royal Navy football. OLDHAM ATHLETIC August 1946 to April 1949. Bradford City trial September–October 1951.

■ Burly left-back Ben Bunting appeared to enjoy every minute of every game. He tackled well and cleared promptly and was a popular and reliable defender. After a season spent mainly in reserve, he established himself in 1947–48 and had appeared in 29 consecutive matches when a cartilage injury, sustained at Gateshead in February 1948, effectively terminated his career. One particular incident in his career has remained clearly in the writer's memory for almost 60 years. In the Christmas Day meeting at Crewe Alexandra in 1947 Athletic were awarded a penalty. Bunting took the kick, but at the end of his lengthy run-up

appeared to try to change his stride pattern. Amazingly, the ball finished nearer to the corner flag than the goal! As he ruefully admitted many years later, 'I was never asked to take another!'

BURDESS, John

Forward

Born: East Rainton, Co. Durham, 10 April 1946.
Career: North-Eastern Schoolboys. OLDHAM ATHLETIC apprentice February 1962, professional April 1964. Stalybridge Celtic August 1966. Glossop May 1968.

■ Diminutive John Burdess made his League debut while still a teenager and on apprentice forms. Two outings against Hull City over the Easter period in 1964 earned him a professional contract in the month of his 18th birthday. A clever and elusive inside-forward at reserve level, he was handicapped by his small build and failed to graduate at senior level.

BURGESS, Benjamin Keiron

Forward

Born: Buxton, 9 November 1981.
Career: Blackburn Rovers trainee, professional November 1998. Northern Spirit, Australia, loan October 2000. Brentford season-long loan August 2001. Stockport County August 2002, fee £450,000. OLDHAM ATHLETIC loan January 2003. Hull City March 2003, fee £100,000. Blackpool August 2006, fee £25,000.

■ Athletic's manager Ian Dowie revealed that he had been a long-time admirer of the hefty 21-year-old striker signed on a three-month loan from Stockport County, who made his name in a season-long loan with Brentford. His 17 League goals helped take the Bees to within a whisker of promotion and an appearance in the Division Two Play-off Final at the Millennium Stadium. Having fallen out of favour despite a return of six goals for Stockport County, Burgess made an excellent start at Boundary Park, ironically against Brentford. A bruising encounter finished 2–1 to Athletic, with Burgess linking well with Chris Killen in attack. Overall, however, the Irish Under-21 international failed to impress, and did not score in his seven outings. Recalled early by Stockport County to enable a £100,000 transfer to Hull City, he quickly entered the record books as the first Hull City player to register a hat-trick in the new Kingston Communications Stadium, in a 4–1 win against Kidderminster Harriers on 26 April 2003.

BURKE, Peter Joseph

Centre-half

Born: Aintree, Liverpool, 1 February 1912. Died: Walton, Liverpool, 18 November 1979.
Career: ROF Fazakerley. Liverpool amateur October 1929. Prescot Cables May 1930. Liverpool amateur June 1931. OLDHAM ATHLETIC May 1933, fee £100. Norwich City December 1935, fee £2,610. Luton Town June 1939. Wartime guest with Brighton & Hove Albion. Southport July 1946. Prescot Cables November 1946.

■ A product of Lancashire Combination football, Peter Burke immediately made the centre-half position his own and was a regular throughout his spell at Boundary Park. Strong, fearless and hard-tackling, he acquitted himself so well in the heart of the Latics defence that he soon took the eye of several larger clubs, and Norwich City paid a substantial fee for the former England Schoolboy international in mid-season 1935–36. A subsequent move to Luton Town came just three months before the outbreak of World War Two, during

which he served as a gunner in the Royal Artillery. Burke had just one outing with Southport in August 1946 before resuming his trade as a bricklayer.

BURNETT, George Gordon

Goalkeeper

Born: Birkenhead, 11 February 1920. Died: Birkenhead, 29 April 1985.
Career: Litherland Boys' Club. Everton amateur May, professional September 1938. Wartime guest with Millwall, Wrexham, Tranmere Rovers, and Manchester United. South Liverpool loan 1951. OLDHAM ATHLETIC October 1951, fee £2,000. Ellesmere Port 1955.

■ George Burnett was a hurried signing by the Latics when they lost the services of first-team goalkeeper Fred Ogden, who had broken a collarbone at Bradford City in October 1951. A cool and thoroughly capable goalkeeper, Burnett starred in the Third Division North Championship season of 1952–53, missing only four matches throughout the successful campaign. Earlier in his career, Burnett appeared for Everton in the FA Cup semi-final of 1950 and was ever present for three seasons leading to the resumption of normal League football in 1946–47.

BURNS, Leo Francis

Half-back

Born: Manchester, 3 August 1932. Career: Manchester City amateur season 1951–52. OLDHAM ATHLETIC September 1953 to June 1956.

■ A National Serviceman in the RAF for much of his spell with the Latics, blond-haired Leo Burns was demobilised during the early weeks of season 1955–56. As deputy for Wilf Hobson he appeared in four mid-season League outings that yielded but a single point. These came during a run of 12 matches without a win in what proved to be his and player-manager Hardwick's last season at Boundary Park.

BURNS, Oliver Houston

Inside-forward

Born: Larkhall, Lanarkshire, 16 May 1914. Died: Halifax, December 1989.
Career: Royal Albert. Queen of the South August 1935. Airdrieonians January 1938. Glenavon July 1938. Burnley March 1939. Wartime guest with Halifax Town and Hamilton Academical. St Johnstone loan August 1945. OLDHAM ATHLETIC October 1946, fee £1,000. Halifax Town September 1947. Nelson 1949.

■ A well-travelled inside-forward who had sampled football in Scotland, Ireland and England before the outbreak of World War Two, Oliver Burns was a brainy player, distinguished by his ability to place a cross-field pass with unerring accuracy.

BURRIDGE, Ben James Herbert

Half-back

Born: Beamish, Co. Durham, 11 March 1898.
Died: Oldham, 22 December 1977.
Career: Oxhill Villa. Houghton Rovers amateur, professional August 1920. Annfield Plain. Darlington November 1921. Sheffield Wednesday June 1926, fee £1,200. OLDHAM ATHLETIC June 1930, fee £460. Macclesfield Town August 1931. Hyde United June 1933. Hurst June 1934, player-manager June 1935 to July 1938. Wartime guest with Ashton National.

■ A seasoned campaigner by the time he arrived at Boundary Park, Ben Burridge had captained Sheffield Wednesday's reserves to the Central League Championship in 1929. He was expected to challenge for a first-team spot with Athletic, but the well-established middle

line of Adlam, Seth King and Goodier remained the favoured choice of manager Andrew Wilson.

BURROWS, George Baker

Inside-forward

Born: Hetton-le-Hole, Co. Durham, 2 March 1900.
Died: Houghton-le-Spring, 9 August 1979.
Career: Hetton Celtic. OLDHAM ATHLETIC December 1919, fee £10. West Ham United June 1921.

■ Nineteen-year-old inside-forward George Burrows' excellent start in Athletic's reserves saw him score four goals in his first four matches. A Division One debut followed, and in his second outing he struck a spectacular winner at Newcastle United. The explosive start was not maintained, however, and Athletic replaced youth with experience when they signed 34-year-old Bill Halligan, the Irish international inside-forward.

BUTCHER, Richard Tony

Midfield

Born: Peterborough, 22 January 1981.
Career: Northampton Town trainee. Rushden & Diamonds November 1999 to October 2001. Kettering Town August 2001. Lincoln City November 2002. OLDHAM ATHLETIC July 2005. Lincoln City loan October 2005. Peterborough United June 2006. Notts County July 2007.

■ After an unhappy start to his Athletic career, Richard Butcher returned after a loan spell with Lincoln City and established himself in central midfield, scoring four goals in 39 appearances. With a year left on his contract, Butcher opted to join Peterborough United in the summer of 2006, linking for a third time with the then Posh manager Keith Alexander.

BUTLER, Charles Reginald

Inside-forward

Born: Barry, Glamorgan, 20 March 1908.
Died: Hendon, 7 July 1983.
Career: Barry Town. Charlton Athletic amateur February 1928. Chatham loan. Cardiff City trial July 1930. Thames October 1930. Bath City August 1931. Blackburn Rovers November 1931. Bath

City loan 1932. New Brighton August 1933. OLDHAM ATHLETIC July 1935, fee £200. Tranmere Rovers July 1936. Tunbridge Wells Rangers March 1937. Cork City July 1937. South Liverpool December 1937.

■ Welsh-born of English parents, Charlie Butler first played regularly in League football during two seasons of Third Division North fare with New Brighton. He was one of three former Rakers who joined the Latics in the summer of 1935. Butler played 13 times during Athletic's first campaign in the Third Division North, but lacked pace to complement his sound knowledge of play and cool distribution.

BUTLER, Reuben

Centre-forward

Born: Stillington, Co. Durham, 10 October 1890.
Died: Heworth, Co. Durham, 15 July 1958.
Career: Stillington St John's. Stockton Amateurs 1910–11. Spennymoor United 1911–12. Middlesbrough amateur May 1912, professional October 1912 Hartlepools United loan May 1914. OLDHAM ATHLETIC May 1920, fee £1,850. Bury July 1923, fee £375. Bradford City October 1924. Crewe Alexandra March 1926. Rochdale May 1926. Accrington Stanley May 1927. Great Harwood August 1929. Northwich Victoria December 1929. Bacup Borough February 1930. Reverted to amateur status August 1932 and appointed player-coach

to Rossendale United's reserve team. Bacup Borough manager June 1933 to May 1937.

■ At the zenith of his powers, Reuben Butler's skill was unquestioned. He forged his reputation during a lengthy spell with Middlesbrough either side of World War One, during which he served with the Tank Corps in France. A dashing, fearless leader, he led Athletic's scoring lists in both of his two seasons at Boundary Park, despite being sidelined for three months in 1921–22 with a broken ankle. Joining Bury, he assisted them to promotion into the First Division, scoring 13 goals in 20 matches in 1923–24.

BUTLER, Thomas

Outside-right

Born: Atherton, 28 April 1918.
Career: Astley & Tyldesley Colliers. Bolton Wanderers September 1936. Macclesfield Town 1937. OLDHAM ATHLETIC February 1938. Middlesbrough March 1939, fee £1,500. Wartime guest with Bolton Wanderers, Ashton National, OLDHAM ATHLETIC and Chester. OLDHAM ATHLETIC August 1946, fee £500. Accrington Stanley July 1947. Wigan Athletic 1953.

■ A tricky customer on the right-wing, Tommy Butler joined Bolton Wanderers at 18 years of age, but suffered a broken left leg and when recovered was transferred to Macclesfield Town. He returned to League football with the Latics and his performances quickly earned him an upward move to

Middlesbrough. The outbreak of World War Two saw Butler back at Boundary Park as a guest player, and he rejoined on a permanent basis in August 1946. A year later he joined Accrington Stanley, where he clocked up in excess of 200 League appearances in a six-year stay. Two brothers were also players – William won three FA Cup medals with Bolton Wanderers and was capped by England, while Herbert Butler assisted Blackpool and Crystal Palace. A nephew, Dennis Butler, played for Bolton Wanderers and Rochdale.

BUTTERWORTH, Harry

Half-back

Born: Unsworth, Manchester, 1885.
Career: Unsworth Parish Church. Preston North End September 1904. Barrow October 1906. OLDHAM ATHLETIC May 1908. Queen's Park Rangers August 1910. Millwall Athletic 1912–1919. Subsequently coached in Holland.

■ Of moderate height and stocky build, reserve wing-half Harry Butterworth made 10 early-season League appearances in Athletic's Division Two promotion-winning side in 1909–10. In his second season with Queen's Park Rangers Butterworth made 15 appearances for the Southern League champions, but missed out when QPR contested the FA Charity Shield against Football League champions Blackburn Rovers at White Hart Lane in May 1912.

Proceeds of this match, incidentally, were being donated to the Titanic Disaster fund.

BUXTON, Stephen

Left-back

Born: South Bank, 3 February 1885.
Died: South Bank, 21 April 1953.
Career: South Bank. Brentford August 1908. OLDHAM ATHLETIC August 1911, fee £425. Darlington May 1913. Wartime guest with OLDHAM ATHLETIC, Chesterfield Municipal and Blyth Spartans. Ashington July 1920. Workington. South Bank Gasworks amateur May 1924. Appointed to Committee of South Bank June 1935.

■ Steve Buxton was a member of the South Bank side beaten 9–1 by Athletic in the FA Cup in December 1906. He arrived at Boundary Park after three seasons with Brentford, where he missed only three matches in three seasons. Although small for a defender he earned fulsome praise from the *Athletic News* correspondent reporting on a First Division match between Athletic and Manchester City in October 1911. 'I greatly admired the play of Buxton. For a man of his inches he is a truly remarkable player, speedy, a clever and judicious tackler, a fine kick with either foot, and, above all, scrupulously fair.' Sadly, Buxton's immense promise was cruelly cut short by a serious knee injury after just four matches in season 1912–13. He did, however, return to Boundary Park as a guest during World War One, when he was serving in the Royal Army Medical Corps.

BYROM, Thomas

Inside-forward

Born: Blackburn, 1889.
Died: Blackburn, 8 June 1958.
Career: Blackburn Victoria Cross. Blackburn Rovers June 1911. Wartime guest with Burnley. Rochdale June 1920. OLDHAM ATHLETIC December 1920, fee £1,150. Chorley September 1922.

■ Tom Byrom began with his local club, Blackburn Rovers, and was leading goalscorer in their Central League team in 1912–13. Some years later, his nine goals in 18 Central League matches for Rochdale induced the Latics to pay a hefty fee for his services but he failed to impress at Boundary Park, losing his place after just five First Division matches.

CALLAGHAN, Aaron Joseph

Defender

Born: Dublin, 8 October 1966.
Career: Stoke City apprentice February 1983, professional November 1984. Crewe Alexandra loan November 1985. OLDHAM ATHLETIC October 1986, fee £10,000. Crewe Alexandra May 1988, fee £16,000. Preston North End August 1992 to December 1993, fee £20,000. Crusaders. St Patrick's Athletic. Glenavon loan. Dundalk 2000–02.

■ Republic of Ireland Under-21 international Aaron Callaghan scored his first League goal in only his second full appearance for Athletic. His winner against Barnsley on 26 September 1987 earned him an extended run as central defensive partner to Andy Linighan, but he ended the season in reserve, having lost out to the outstanding local youngster Mike Flynn. In his first season with Crewe Alexandra, Callaghan helped them win promotion from Division Four.

CAMERON, Alexander Ramsey

Full-back

Born: Leith, 5 October 1943.

Career: St Bernard's Athletic. Hibernian September 1962. OLDHAM ATHLETIC May 1964 to March 1965.

■ After a dismal start to season 1964–65 – only two League wins in the first 17 engagements – Alex Cameron lost his place in mid-October and failed to regain it. The reintroduction of Ken Branagan at right full-back coincided with a mid-season revival that lifted the side from the foot of Division Three.

CAMPBELL, Alexander Ferguson 'Sandy'

Inside-forward

Born: Dalmuir, Clydebank, 24 January 1897.
Died: Blackpool, 25 April 1975.
Career: Old Kilpatrick. Glasgow Ashfield. Queen's Park 1919. OLDHAM ATHLETIC amateur June, professional August 1920. Swansea Town June 1922, fee £70. OLDHAM ATHLETIC May 1923, retired due to injury May 1924, but resumed with Mossley July 1927.

■ Sandy Campbell was twice a Scottish Juvenile Cup winner with Old Kilpatrick before signing a professional form with Glasgow Ashfield. After World War One he joined the famous amateurs, Queen's Park, and 12 months later the Latics signed him. In two spells at Boundary Park he was a warm favourite. A dapper little inside-forward with twinkling feet, he revealed clever touches and was a most attractive player to watch. Ankle and knee injuries curtailed his playing career, and he later joined the Oldham Rugby League Club committee.

CAMPBELL, Charles

Right-half

Born: Oban, 27 February 1928.
Career: Rutherglen Glencairn. OLDHAM ATHLETIC November 1949. Hyde United 1950.

■ Marine engineer Charles Campbell had previously refused offers to turn professional when approached by two Scottish League clubs but he accepted the offer of a one-month trial with the Latics, which was rewarded by a contract for the remainder of the season. He had a brief taste of first-team football following Billy Spurdle's transfer to Manchester City, but was not retained in the close season.

CAMPBELL, John

Forward

Born: Liverpool, 17 March 1922.
Died: Spain, 17 February 2007.
Career: Cammell Laird FC. Liverpool April 1943. Wartime guest with Chester and Blackburn Rovers. OLDHAM ATHLETIC July 1956. Blackburn Rovers youth coach March 1957.

■ Jackie Campbell was a player of ripe experience, with 245 League and Cup appearances to his credit when he joined Athletic. A skilful and versatile player, he was probably best as a forward but equally adept in the middle line. He began with Athletic at inside-left, with another ex-Blackburn Rover, Dave Pearson, as his inside partner. In a season remarkable only for the number of team changes

made by manager Ted Goodier, Campbell appeared in all forward positions except the centre before requesting his release in order to return to Blackburn Rovers to take up a coaching appointment.

CARLISLE, Richard Wright

Centre-half

Born: Preston, 9 September 1899.
Died: Preston, 1975.
Career: South Liverpool. Preston North End amateur October 1909. Padiham 1912. South Liverpool 1913. Wartime guest with Preston North End. OLDHAM ATHLETIC October 1919. Wigan Borough May 1921. Morecambe player-coach July 1922, retired 1929. Preston North End coach September 1930.

■ Richard Carlisle was a reserve central-defender 'adept at taking both man and ball', according to one contemporary correspondent! He followed former Athletic manager Herbert Bamlett to Springfield Park and made 32 appearances (3 goals) in Wigan Borough's first season in the Football League. Appointed player-coach to Morecambe, he was a Lancashire Combination Championship winner in 1925.

CARMICHAEL, Robert

Inside-forward

Born: Paisley, 1885.
Career: Shettleston FC. Sunderland January 1907. St Mirren 1908. OLDHAM ATHLETIC May 1909, fee £90. Third Lanark 1910. Bailleston Thistle. Clyde December 1911. Shelbourne, Ireland, 1915.

■ When the Latics won promotion to Division One in the 1909–10 season, the solidly-built Bob Carmichael lost his place after playing in the opening five fixtures of the season, which had yielded only two points. In July 1943, at the age of 59, he was appointed assistant-trainer to Arthur Dixon – a former Athletic player – at Glasgow Rangers.

CARNEY, David

Midfield

Born: Sydney, Australia, 30 November 1983.
Career: Everton trainee, professional January 2000. OLDHAM ATHLETIC non-contract August 2003. Halifax Town March 2004. Sydney FC Australia May 2004.

■ Following his release by Everton, Dave Carney accepted a one-month trial at Boundary Park. The Australian midfielder replaced Carlos Roca for the second half of the Carling Cup tie against Scunthorpe United and showed promise in a bruising encounter that saw Athletic's Darren Sheridan and Danny Boshell red-carded, along with Scunthorpe's Matt Sparrow. Carney was not offered an extension to his trial, though, with manager Dowie considering that he had sufficient options in midfield.

CARRICK, James

Half-back

Born: Boothstown, 17 February 1901.
Career: Plank Lane FC, Leigh, November 1919. Airdrieonians trial. Manchester City amateur season 1919–20. Exeter City June 1920. OLDHAM ATHLETIC June 1921, fee £650. Stockport County June 1923, fee £150. Barrow July 1924. Bradford Park Avenue July 1925. Accrington Stanley May 1927. Torquay United June 1928. Accrington Stanley May 1929. Burton Town July 1930. Stalybridge Celtic August 1930.

■ Jim Carrick enjoyed an excellent start to his career, recording 41 appearances and three goals for Exeter City in 1920–21. He nevertheless spent his two seasons at Boundary Park in reserve, failing to dislodge the evergreen Elliot Pilkington. He subsequently assisted a further five League clubs, but his appearances in first-team football were

infrequent. His best seasonal return came at Torquay United, with 30 appearances and two goals in 1928–29.

CARROLL, John Patrick

Inside-forward

Born: North Bierley, 1890.
Career: Fryston Colliery. Castleford Town June 1923. Selby Town later in the same season. OLDHAM ATHLETIC July 1924, released April 1925.

■ In the season before he joined the Latics, John Carroll scored 37 goals for Castleford Town, and twice represented the Yorkshire League against the Irish League. A tall and forceful forager, he scored in wins against Stoke and Blackpool within his seven senior outings, but the signing of Jack Keedwell in October 1924 effectively ended Carroll's involvement at senior level. He was still turning out as an amateur with Selby Town in his 41st year.

CARROLL, Joseph

Forward

Born: Radcliffe, 6 January 1957.
Career: Bury Grammar School. OLDHAM ATHLETIC July 1975. Halifax Town loan September 1976, permanent November 1976 to May 1979.

■ Curly-haired Joe Carroll made his League debut at 18 years of age. He deputised on the left wing for both Alan Groves and Ian Robins in his handful of

League appearances before being loaned to Halifax Town in the early stages of 1976–77. The move was made permanent after his impressive start, which included his first-ever League goal in a 6–0 win against Doncaster Rovers. Before leaving the Shay he totalled 76/6 League appearances and scored 16 goals.

CARSS, Anthony John

Midfield

Born: Alnwick, 31 March 1976.
Career: Alnwick Town. Bradford City associate schoolboy October 1990. Blackburn Rovers August 1994. Darlington August 1995. Cardiff City July 1997. Chesterfield September 1998. Carlisle United August 2000. OLDHAM ATHLETIC October 2000. Huddersfield Town August 2003. Retired due to injury November 2006. Preston North End Academy coach January 2007.

■ A clever and resourceful central or wide midfielder whose tireless displays immediately lifted the side, Tony Carss achieved a clean sweep of the Player of the Year awards in his first season. Injuries disrupted his second season and enforced a three-month lay-off. Out of contract in the summer and with the club on the brink of administration, he reluctantly departed to Huddersfield Town. Forced into early retirement at 30 years of age, Carss enrolled on a university degree course in sports writing and broadcasting.

CASHMORE, Arthur

Centre-forward

Born: Birmingham, 30 October 1893.
Died: West Bromwich, 1969.
Career: Stourbridge FC. Manchester United May 1913. OLDHAM ATHLETIC May 1914, fee £50. Darlaston FC September 1919. Cardiff City December 1919, fee £1,000. Notts County November 1921, fee £1,500. Darlaston FC July 1922. Nuneaton Town April 1923. Shrewsbury Town November 1923. Darlaston FC trial August–September 1925. Hereford United October 1927.

■ An attack leader with speed, dash and pluck, Arthur Cashmore proved a fine bargain. His eight goals in 16 matches helped Athletic finish runners-up in the Football League Championship in 1914–15. Cashmore enlisted in the army in 1915 and was wounded, but appearances in wartime football took his overall Athletic record to 38 goals in 67 appearances. Transferred to Cardiff City, he played in their first-ever Football League match, a 5–2 win against Stockport County on 28 August 1920.

CASSIDY, Laurence

Inside-forward

Born: Manchester, 10 March 1923.
Career: Manchester United amateur January 1947, professional February 1947. OLDHAM ATHLETIC July 1956 to June 1957.

■ A reserve centre-forward with Manchester United who combined football with his teaching duties in the Manchester district, Laurence Cassidy

became the Latics' fifth signing of the week when he joined in July 1956. He began in the first-team but after just three matches lost his inside-left spot to the former Blackburn Rovers inside forward, Jackie Campbell.

CAUNCE, Lewis

Goalkeeper

Born: Earlestown, 20 April 1911.
Died: Bury, 13 July 1978.
Career: Earlstown White Star. Burnley trial. Huddersfield Town August 1931. Rochdale July 1932. Wigan Athletic July 1933. OLDHAM ATHLETIC May 1935 to season 1940–41.

■ At 6ft 1in and 13st, Lewis Caunce was an ideally-built goalkeeper who shared the first-team spot with Harry Church in his first season at Boundary Park. Thereafter he dominated the position until the suspension of League football in 1939. War work in a tank manufacturing factory in Bury enabled Caunce to continue assisting Athletic during the first two seasons of regionalised football.

CECERE, Michael Joseph

Forward

Born: Chester, 4 January 1968.
Career: OLDHAM ATHLETIC trial October 1984, apprentice November 1984, professional January 1986. Huddersfield Town November 1988, fee £50,000 plus

£10,000 payable after 50 appearances. Stockport County loan March 1990. Walsall loan August 1990, permanent December 1990, fee £25,000. Exeter City January 1994. Rochdale July–December 1996.

■ Darkly handsome Mike Cecere developed in Athletic's Youth Team, partnering the emerging Wayne Harrison in attack. In his debut season, the powerfully-built and speedy striker had the unusual distinction of scoring a hat-trick against Blackburn Rovers, having been introduced as a second-half substitute. About six months earlier he had been on the verge of quitting to join the Police Force when the Latics had placed him on the free transfer list. Despite being troubled by injuries in his final two seasons of League football, Cecere's career figures amounted to 213/53 appearances and 60 goals.

CHADDERTON, Albert

Full-back

Born: Oldham, 22 November 1894.
Died: Oldham, 4 February 1963.
Career: Woodhouses FC. Army football. OLDHAM ATHLETIC November 1919 to June 1920.

■ Local product Albert Chadderton spent his season at Boundary Park in the reserves, playing in 34 matches and scoring once. His sole senior outing at Aston Villa – the season's FA Cup winners – proved a severe baptism. Directly opposed to the England international winger Charlie Wallace, it was a 'backs-to-the-wall' afternoon at Villa Park, resulting in a comfortable 3–0 victory for the home side.

CHADWICK, Clifton

Outside-right

Born: Bolton, 26 January 1914.
Career: Turton FC. Fleetwood. Bolton Wanderers trial. OLDHAM ATHLETIC October 1933. Middlesbrough February 1934, fee £1,000. Wartime guest with Rochdale, Bolton Wanderers, OLDHAM ATHLETIC, Nottingham Forest and Manchester United. Hull City September 1946, fee £650. Darlington July 1947. Stockton August 1948.

■ Once described as a 'pocket Hercules', the lightweight wingman was only 19 years old when he stepped straight into Athletic's first-team after just two outings in the Northern Midweek League. Fearless and terrier-like despite his lack of inches, he played in just 21 consecutive matches before First Division Middlesbrough snapped him up. He subsequently returned to the Latics as a wartime guest, and later still as Stockton's outside-left, when they visited Boundary Park in a first-round FA Cup tie on 26 November 1949.

CHALMERS, Aaron

Defender/Midfield

Born: Miles Platting, 2 February 1991.
Career: OLDHAM ATHLETIC Centre of Excellence Under-9s, apprentice May 2007.

■ Twelve months on from striving to hold down a place in Athletic's talented youth team, first-year apprentice Aaron Chalmers made his senior debut from the bench against Leyton Orient at Boundary Park on 12 April 2008. A glimpse of his undoubted potential was revealed when he volleyed at goal after setting up the chance with an audacious chip over his head in the 2–0 victory. The same match also featured the debut of another youth-team product, Ashley Kelly.

CHAMBERS, William Thomas

Centre or Inside-forward

Born: Wednesbury, 10 August 1906.
Died: Wednesbury, 1978.
Career: Wednesbury. Worcester City 1927. Shrewsbury Town 1928. West Bromwich Albion Reserves. Darlaston. Burnley May 1929, fee £250. Lovell's Athletic. Lancaster City August 1930. Shrewsbury Town August 1931. Darlaston later in the same

season. *Halifax Town June 1932. Bolton Wanderers July 1934, fee £500. OLDHAM ATHLETIC May 1934, in exchange for F.V. Swift. Chester June 1936, fee £175. Bath City July 1938. Darlaston September 1939.*

■ Centre-forward Bill Chambers was leading goalscorer in the Third Division North in 1933–34, his 30 goals for Halifax Town earning him an upward move to Bolton Wanderers. He arrived at Boundary Park in an exchange transfer that took goalkeeper Fred Swift to Bolton, but he failed to find his best form with Athletic. Said to be lacking pace, he had a disappointing season, losing his first-team place in October and failing to regain it thereafter.

CHAPMAN, Edwin

Forward

Born: Blackburn, 2 May 1919.
Died: Blackburn, 4 December 1977.
Career: Darwen Reserves. Blackburn Rovers amateur, professional May 1936. Accrington Stanley July 1938. OLDHAM ATHLETIC June 1939. Wartime guest with Aldershot. Blackburn Rovers September 1945. Stockport County August 1946 to June 1947.

■ Eddie Chapman's initial season at Boundary Park was curtailed by the outbreak of World War Two after he had appeared at outside-right in the first three matches of 1939–40. In regional matches during the war he scored 34 goals in 73 appearances, and when the retained list was published in June 1946 he was offered terms but declined, subsequently moving to Stockport County.

CHAPMAN, Leslie

Midfield

Born: Oldham, 27 September 1948.
Career: Chadderton Grammar School. High Barn FC. Huddersfield Town amateur September 1965. OLDHAM ATHLETIC trial September 1966, professional January 1967. Huddersfield Town September 1969, in exchange for David Shaw plus £35,000. OLDHAM ATHLETIC December 1974, in part exchange for Colin Garwood. San Jose Earthquakes. US, loan May–August 1978. Stockport County May 1979. Bradford City February 1980, fee £10,000. Rochdale June 1983, caretaker manager March 1984 then assistant player-manager June 1984.

Stockport County player-manager July 1985. Preston North End player-assistant manager August 1986 then manager January 1990 to September 1992. Manchester City reserve-team coach January 1993, subsequently kit manager. Huddersfield Town coaching staff until October 1997.

■ Les Chapman began as an outside-left, later moving to a midfield role. A tireless worker with boundless enthusiasm for the game, his long career spanned 22 seasons of League football. He gave excellent value to each of his six League clubs, and his two spells with the Latics accounted for a little over a third of his total of 725/22 appearances. Many felt that his final departure from Boundary Park was premature, as he had missed only five League games in the preceding four and a half seasons.

CHARLTON, Simon Thomas

Defender

Born: Huddersfield, 25 October 1971.
Career: Huddersfield Town trainee, professional July 1989. Southampton June 1993, fee £250,000. Birmingham City December 1997, fee £250,000. Bolton Wanderers July 2000. Norwich City July 2004, fee £250,000. OLDHAM ATHLETIC August 2006 to May 2007. Norwich City coach 2007.

■ Veteran defender Simon Charlton joined Athletic on a season-long deal following his summer 2006 release by Norwich City. In addition to his long experience at the very highest level of the game, Charlton could cover most berths

across the back-line or in midfield with equal faculty. Additionally, his reading of the game and organisational skills were a vital element in his 39 appearances. His League career began with Huddersfield Town, his debut coming against Crewe Alexandra in Division Three on 3 March 1990 in a team that included Mike Cecere, the former Athletic striker. Almost 17 years on, Charlton completed his 500th League appearance in Athletic's colours. He also memorably scored from well inside his own half with a massive clearance that deceived Gillingham's goalkeeper in the 4–1 victory at Boundary Park in September 2006.

CHARLTON, Stanley

Full-back

Born: Little Hulton, 16 November 1900.
Died: South Norwood, 1971.
Career: Little Hulton United. OLDHAM ATHLETIC August 1920. Rochdale May 1922. Exeter City August 1923. Crystal Palace May 1928, fee £750. Newport

County October 1932. Margate August 1933. Streatham Town amateur September 1934. Greenbroom Athletic amateur September 1935. Venner Sports, Surrey, amateur December 1936.

■ Stan Charlton kicked accurately and tackled well, and with youth on his side was expected to develop along the right lines. Unfortunately, a severe ankle injury, sustained in a reserve team match in 1921–22, led to his release. His undoubted potential was fully realised during five excellent seasons with Exeter City. Charlton's outstanding performances as the Grecians' skipper earned him a place in the FA Tour to Australia in 1925, and later in the same year he was at right-back for The Professionals versus The Amateurs in the Charity Shield Final at Tottenham. His son, Stanley junior, won England Amateur international honours before playing for Orient and Arsenal.

CHAYTOR, Kenneth

Inside-forward

Born: Trimdon, Co. Durham, 18 November 1937.
Career: Durham County Schoolboys. OLDHAM ATHLETIC amateur June 1954, professional November 1954. Witton Albion June 1960. Ashton United 1961–63.

■ Kenny Chaytor showed tremendous promise as a 16-year-old inside-forward, forcing his way into the League side while still not old enough to sign a professional form. Deceptively fast and elusive and with a strong shot in either foot, his introduction coincided with a remarkable revival that lifted the side from 18th to eighth within the space of a few weeks. Eight goals in 18 League appearances was an excellent start, and he was similarly effective in his second season with 11 goals in 30 matches. However, his bright star flickered and faded, and at the age of 22 he departed into non-League football.

CHURCH, Henry Boyce

Goalkeeper

Born: Castleford, 24 November 1904.
Died: Pontefract, 29 July 1984.
Career: Castleford Town. Bolton Wanderers October 1930. OLDHAM

ATHLETIC June 1935, fee £100. Exeter City loan October 1937, permanent November 1937 to May 1939.

■ Harry Church shared first-team duties with Lewis Caunce in 1935–36 and had returned to his native Castleford, working as a publican when Exeter City offered him a month's trial. He stayed with the Grecians until May 1939, when a proposed move to Bradford City was shelved at the outbreak of World War Two. Earlier in his career Church was Bolton's goalkeeper when the Burnden Park ground record was set, with 69,912 spectators attending the fifth-round FA Cup tie against Manchester City on 18 February 1933.

CLAMP, Edward

Goalkeeper

Born: Church Gresley, 13 November 1922.
Died: Swadlincote, 2 June 1990.

Career: Derbyshire Schoolboys. John Knowles FC. Moira United. Gresley Rovers. Derby County November 1947. OLDHAM ATHLETIC July 1949. Buxton August 1950.

■ Ted Clamp played in the Leicester Senior League at 14 years of age. Ideally built for his position, he nevertheless failed to establish himself in League football. He had made only one First Division appearance for Derby County, and in his three outings with Athletic he seemed short of confidence, conceding 11 goals.

CLARK, Ronald

Outside-left

Born: Clarkston, 21 May 1932.
Career: Forth Wanderers. Kilmarnock on provisional forms August 1949. Petershill Juniors. Kilmarnock professional April 1951. Gillingham July 1956. OLDHAM ATHLETIC June 1958. Bedford Town July 1959.

■ A Scottish Junior Cup winner with Petershill in 1951, outside-left Ronnie Clark made his senior debut with

Kilmarnock in the same year, but appeared in only 24 first-team matches during his five years at Rugby Park, scoring five goals. Two seasons with Gillingham provided more opportunities for the tall, well-built wingman, but on joining the Latics for their initial season in Division Four he lost his place to Peter Phoenix after just four early-season appearances.

CLARKE, Alfred

Inside-forward

Born: Hollinwood, 23 August 1926.
Career: Stalybridge Celtic. Crewe Alexandra February 1948. Burnley December 1948. OLDHAM ATHLETIC August 1952. Halifax Town March 1954. Nelson player-manager July 1956.

■ A vital part of Athletic's 1952–53 Third Division North Championship season, Alf Clarke controlled the ball well and was good at opening out the game. Sadly, the hard-won promotion was squandered, Athletic coming straight back down from Division Two the following season. Clarke departed the sinking ship in March of that term and wound up his League career with Halifax Town.

CLARKE, John Theodore Knight

Outside-right

Born: Lancaster, 19 January 1917.
Died: Lancaster, June 1989.
Career: New Mills FC. Lancaster Town. OLDHAM ATHLETIC amateur May 1935 to June 1937.

■ In two seasons as an amateur at Boundary Park John Clarke was called upon only once for first-team duty. The diminutive and lightweight wingman scored the opening goal against Barrow in a 4–3 win on his debut, prompting the local correspondent to label him 'the little big shot'.

CLARKE, Leon Marvin

Forward

Born: Birmingham, 10 February 1985.
Career: Wolverhampton Wanderers trainee, professional March 2004. Kidderminster Harriers loan March 2004. Queen's Park Rangers loan January 2006. Plymouth Argyle loan March 2006.

Sheffield Wednesday January 2007. OLDHAM ATHLETIC loan March 2007. Southend United loan August 2007.

■ In a season marked by the number of loan signings made by Athletic, the month spent at Boundary Park by Leon Clarke was a success all the way. Despite having played little for Sheffield Wednesday, the well-built striker revealed an excellent first touch and eye for goal. Athletic were undefeated during his loan spell, securing two wins and three draws, with Clarke scoring against Doncaster Rovers and twice against Brentford.

CLEGG, Michael Jaime

Defender

Born: Ashton-under-Lyne, 3 July 1977.

Career: Manchester United trainee July 1993, professional July 1995. Ipswich Town loan February 2000. Wigan Athletic loan March 2000. OLDHAM ATHLETIC February 2002, signing non-contract forms September 2004.

■ A winner of the FA Youth Cup with Manchester United in 1995, and with two Under-21 International caps, Michael Clegg nevertheless found it hard to fully establish himself with Athletic. The bulk of his first-team appearances came in season 2003–04, but he found himself out of favour under new manager Brian Talbot. In October 2006, Clegg was appointed strength and conditioning coach with Sunderland, having retired from professional football after leaving Athletic two years earlier.

CLEMENTS, Kenneth Henry

Defender

Born: Middleton, 9 April 1955.
Career: OLDHAM ATHLETIC B Team. Manchester City amateur July 1972, professional July 1975. OLDHAM ATHLETIC September 1979, fee £200,000. Manchester City loan March 1985. Bury March 1988, fee £20,000. Limerick, Ireland, 1990. Shrewsbury Town October 1990, retired due to knee injury July 1991. Hyde United commercial manager. Curzon Ashton, resuming as a player, September 1992.

■ Kenny Clements cost Athletic their then record fee of £200,000 when he was signed from Manchester City to succeed

Keith Hicks in central defence. During five and a half seasons at Boundary Park, he formed an excellent central defensive partnership with Paul Futcher. Both were perceptive users of the ball out of defence, and as a pair they formed a very effective barrier to opposing forwards. Quick to tackle and even quicker to recover, Clements was comfortable on the ball, despite being so obviously 'one-footed'. After 16 years as a professional footballer, Clements qualified as a driving instructor, but more recently has received commissions for his paintings, having launched a new career as an artist.

CLEMENTS, Paul Robert

Inside-forward

Born: Greenwich, 7 November 1946.
Career: West Ham United amateur. Hendon FC. Skelmersdale United. Toured Japan & Korea with Middlesex Wanderers May 1969. OLDHAM ATHLETIC amateur March, professional June 1971. Wigan Athletic November 1972, fee £1,500.

■ Paul Clements enjoyed much success with Skelmersdale United and was an FA Amateur Cup winner against Dagenham at Wembley in 1971. The holder of eight England Amateur international caps, he scored the only goal of the game on his debut for the Latics, but subsequently failed to find the net. He was, however, a classy forward with deft footwork, very adept at making openings for others.

CLITHEROE, Lee John

Winger

Born: Chorley, 18 November 1978.
Career: OLDHAM ATHLETIC trainee August 1995, professional July 1997. Lancaster City November 1999. Southport August–November 2003. Chorley 2004–05. Altrincham. Charnock Richard FC.

■ One of four young professionals released by Athletic in November 1999, Lee Clitheroe was the only one of the quartet with League experience. Considered a very promising youngster in his five senior outings, his progress was cruelly halted when he suffered a broken leg in a match against Walsall in December 1998.

COLLINS, James Patrick

Right full-back

Born: Urmston, 27 December 1966.
Career: Crystal Palace apprentice. OLDHAM ATHLETIC amateur June 1983, professional August 1984. Bury October 1986. Altrincham loan 1987. Fleetwood season 1987–88. Chorley August 1988. Accrington Stanley.

■ Jimmy Collins' sole League appearance came in the final fixture of season 1983–84. He was introduced at half-time, in place of the injured Bob Colville, in a match which produced the Latics' 16th away defeat of the season.

COLLINS, John William

Forward

Born: Chiswick, 10 August 1942.
Career: Brentford & Chiswick Schoolboys. Queen's Park Rangers ground staff, professional August 1959. OLDHAM ATHLETIC October 1966, fee £9,000. Reading August 1967, fee £6,360. Luton Town August 1969, fee £10,000. Cambridge United February 1971 to June 1973, fee £6,000. Queen's Park Rangers coach. Fulham reserve-team coach 1975. Watford coach 1975 to 1977. Brighton & Hove Albion assistant manager 1982.

■ A proven goalscorer with terrific stamina, John Collins made a sensational debut for the Latics in a floodlit friendly match, scoring six goals against Swiss team, FC Thun. His transfer deal included a provision for £75 to be paid to QPR for each goal scored, but this was dispensed with after a few weeks and a settlement made. Sadly, Collins and his family failed to settle in Oldham and in February 1967 he requested a transfer, Reading taking him homewards in the close season.

COLLINS, Robert Young

Forward/Midfield

Born: Govanhill, Glasgow, 16 February 1931.
Career: Polmadie Hawthorn Juveniles. Pollok Juniors August 1947. Celtic August 1948. Everton September 1958, fee £25,000. Leeds United March 1962, fee £25,000. Bury February 1967. Morton August 1969. Ringwood City, Melbourne, Australia player-coach August 1971. Hakoah, Sydney, Australia player-coach October 1971. Wilhelmina, Melbourne, Australia, player-coach. OLDHAM ATHLETIC player-coach October 1972. Shamrock Rovers loan. OLDHAM ATHLETIC assistant manager April 1973. Huddersfield Town manager July 1974 to December 1975. Leeds United youth coach July 1976. Hull City coach July 1977, manager October 1977 to February 1978. Blackpool coach March to May 1978. Barnsley youth coach October 1980, appointed manager February 1984 to June 1985. Guisley Celtic manager September 1987 to September 1988.

■ Bobby Collins's 10-year stint with Celtic (320 appearances and 116 goals) was followed by an equally impressive career in English football. He is perhaps best remembered as captain and midfield general of Don Revie's formidable Leeds United sides of the 1960s, and for his Footballer of the Year award in 1965.

Capped on 31 occasions by Scotland, he additionally represented the Scottish League in 15 matches. He was in his 43rd year when he made his final appearance in senior football with the Latics.

COLMAN, Edgar

Goalkeeper

Born: Oldham, 1 June 1905.
Died: Rochdale, 1979.
Career: Mossley. OLDHAM ATHLETIC amateur April 1926. Mossley November 1926. Eccles United 1927. Blackpool trial June 1927. Rochdale trial October 1927. Bacup Borough. Congleton Town February 1930.

■ Locally born goalkeeper Edgar Colman deputised twice for Athletic's Welsh international goalkeeper, Albert Gray in season 1926–27. Despite the fact that his experience at the time was limited, he could not be faulted in either match. He won particular praise for his debut display at Darlington, where he made several excellent saves in the 1–0 defeat.

COLQUHOUN, John

Inside-forward

Born: Stirling, 3 June 1940.
Died: Stirling, June 1996.
Career: Glasgow Celtic Boys' Club. Maryhill Harps. OLDHAM ATHLETIC August 1961, fee £6,000. Scunthorpe United June 1965. OLDHAM ATHLETIC November 1968. Ashton United 1970.

■ Hard working and adaptable, Johnny Colquhoun appeared in every forward position for the Latics. His early outings were at outside-left, and in an excellent first season he scored 12 League and Cup goals. In the 1962–63 promotion season he moved to inside-left to accommodate the newly signed wingman Colin Whitaker, and appeared in every League and Cup game, scoring 15 goals. Brought back to Boundary Park after a three-year spell with Scunthorpe United, he passed the career milestone of 400 League appearances. His son, John Mark, was capped by Scotland when a Heart of Midlothian player.

COLUSSO, Cristian

Midfield

Born: Buenos Aires, 7 February 1977.
Career: Rosario Central, Argentina 1994. Sevilla, Spain, for five months during 1998. Rosario Central 1998. OLDHAM ATHLETIC loan February to May 2002.

■ An Argentina International at both Under-20 and Under-23 levels, 'Inspector' Colusso (as he was quickly nicknamed by the fans) was certainly a class act. His introduction to life at Boundary Park must have been something of a culture shock as he made his debut against Brighton, from the bench, in monsoon conditions! Although his loan was undertaken with a view to a permanent engagement, no agreement was finalised and the player returned home at the end of the season.

COLVILLE, Robert John

Forward

Born: Nuneaton, 27 April 1963.
Career: Rhos United. OLDHAM ATHLETIC February 1984. Bury October 1986, fee £15,000. Stockport County loan September 1987, permanent December 1987, fee £5,000. York City May 1989, in exchange for Alan Dean. Kitchener Spirit, Canada, 1990. Darlington trial. Crewe Alexandra non-contract October-November 1990. Bangor City January 1991. Guisley 1991. Bangor City September 1992. Guisley 1993.

■ Blond-haired Bob Colville was an industrious forward, whole-hearted and full of unselfish running. Largely a reserve with Athletic, his best spell in the first-team came in the second half of season 1985–86, following the transfer of Mike Quinn to Portsmouth. After leaving Athletic, Colville's best season in League football came with Stockport County in Division Four in 1987–88, when he scored 17 League and Cup goals in 44 appearances.

CONSTANTINE, Leon

Forward

Born: Hackney, 24 February 1978.
Career: Edgware Town. Millwall August 2000. Leyton Orient loan August 2001. Partick Thistle loan January 2002. Brentford August 2002. Southend United August 2003. Peterborough United July 2004. Torquay United loan October, permanent December 2004, fee £75,000. Port Vale November 2005, fee £20,000. Leeds United August 2007. OLDHAM ATHLETIC loan March 2008.

■ A member of the Leeds United side who were humbled by Athletic at Elland Road on New Year's Day 2008, Leon Constantine scored Leeds's goal in the 3–1 defeat. He also suffered a broken arm in the same match, and was short of match action when he joined Athletic on loan, effectively replacing another loan signing, Jordan Robertson, who had returned to Sheffield United after an ankle injury. Constantine scored his first goal for Athletic against one of his former clubs, Millwall. He followed with another in the 4–1 defeat of Huddersfield Town. He was a late starter in League football and probably best remembered for his excellent scoring record during two seasons with Port Vale – 39 goals in 84/1 matches.

COOK, William

Full-back

Born: Preston, 16 January 1881.
Died: Burnley, 18 December 1947.
Career: St Stephen's, Preston. Preston North End January 1902. Ashton Town 1903. Rossendale United May 1904. OLDHAM ATHLETIC February 1908, fee £200. Wartime guest with Burnley 1916–17. Rossendale United August 1920.

■ Balding full-back Billy Cook's many attributes were vividly recorded in an *Athletic News* match report from season 1911–12: 'Cook was impassable. He was the monarch of all he surveyed, and a veritable Goliath, who kicked with tremendous power and certainty. And, for a man of his build, he showed excellent powers of recovery.' Certainly a great character in Athletic's early days, his robust approach on one occasion earned him a 12-month suspension, after he had been ordered off at Middlesbrough in April 1915. Convinced of his innocence, he refused to leave the field, causing the

game to be abandoned. Cook was a genuine all-rounder who played county cricket for Lancashire for two years from 1905, and he later enjoyed a lengthy career as a professional in both the Lancashire and Central Lancashire Leagues.

COOKSEY, Ernest George

Midfield

Born: Bishop's Stortford, 11 June 1980.
Career: Colchester United trainee. Heybridge Swifts. Bishop's Stortford. Bromley. Chesham United. Crawley Town July 2002. OLDHAM ATHLETIC August 2003. Rochdale September 2004. Boston United January 2007. Grays Athletic July 2007.

■ At either central or left midfield Ernie Cooksey was a fierce competitor who received his League baptism in Athletic's colours. As the Latics battled to stay in business and predators swooped to strip the club's best playing assets, Cooksey was among the desperately needed reinforcements recruited to boost the sadly depleted squad. In the traumatic season that followed, the hard-working midfielder was immediately impressive. His six goals from midfield included two in a 3–0 win against Carlisle United in the FA Cup first-round tie at Boundary Park. Athletic's supporters, former players and club have all combined to help raise finance for drugs, urgently needed by their former player who is battling cancer. Various events have included a benefit match at Boundary Park, which was attended by approximately 1,500 spectators.

COOPER, Arthur

Goalkeeper
Born: Sheffield, c.1895.

Career: Beighton FC. Wartime guest with Nottingham Forest. Grimsby Town. Sheffield Wednesday and Birmingham. Barnsley May 1919. OLDHAM ATHLETIC August 1922, released April 1923, fee £100.

■ Arthur Cooper guarded Barnsley's goal for three seasons after World War One and had the experience of 103 League and Cup matches. He proved a useful reserve with Athletic, but was unable to break Howard Matthew's monopoly of the position. A life-saver as well as a goal-saver, in November 1916 Cooper was complimented at Leeds Assizes for having rescued a child from drowning in the canal at Sheffield.

COOPER, Kenny

Striker

Born: Baltimore, US, 21 October 1984.
Career: Dallas Mustangs, US. Manchester United January 2004. OLDHAM ATHLETIC loan January–March 2005. Dallas Mustangs, US, January 2006.

■ A lively striker who lacked nothing in physique at 6ft 3in and 14st, Kenny Cooper controlled the ball quickly and was direct and forceful in the dribble. The highlight of his two-month sojourn at Boundary Park came on 5 March 2005, his double strike in the 3–0 win against Port Vale ending a depressing run of six consecutive defeats.

COPE, William Arthur

Full-back

Born: Stoke-on-Trent, 25 November 1884. Died: Hartshill, Stoke-on-Trent, 18 February 1937.
Career: Mount Pleasant. Burslem Port Vale August 1904. Stoke July 1907. OLDHAM ATHLETIC June 1908, fee £300. West Ham United May 1914, fee £150. Wrexham July 1922, retired 1923.

■ A capable full-back on either flank and noted for the length of his clearances despite his modest physique and size-four boots, Billy Cope was unfortunate to spend his early days with two clubs who both resigned from the Football League. Despite this, he went on to enjoy a lengthy career, and was still turning out with Wrexham at the age of 38. His Athletic appearances were limited due to

the talented array of full-backs on the club's books, but his best seasonal return was 19 matches and one goal in 1910–11, Athletic's first season in the top flight.

CORAZZIN, Giancarlo Michele 'Carlo'

Forward

Born: New Westminster, Canada, 25 December 1971.
Career: Vancouver 86ers, Canada. Cambridge United December 1993, fee £20,000. Plymouth Argyle March 1996, fee £150,000. Northampton Town July 1998. OLDHAM ATHLETIC July 2000. Vancouver Whitecaps June 2003.

■ At the time of his departure from Boundary Park, Canadian International striker Carlo Corazzin had scored 10 goals in 55 matches for his country. A not dissimilar ratio to his 24 in 129 matches for the Latics which, even allowing for

injury problems, was something of a disappointment. Overall, however, his career record in League football was somewhat better at 111 goals in 367 matches.

CORBETT, Peter

Goalkeeper

Born: Preston, 5 March 1934.
Died: Preston, 27 July 2007.
Career: Preston North End June 1956. Workington August 1957. OLDHAM ATHLETIC July 1959 to June 1960.

■ Peter Corbett conceded 10 goals in his first three matches, and two months later had another unhappy outing when Liverpool beat the Latics 8–0 in a first-round Lancashire Senior Cup tie at Anfield. Two excellent performances against Doncaster Rovers over the Christmas period helped restore his confidence but at the end of the season – the worst in Athletic's history, finishing 23rd in Division Four – he was one of seven players released on a free transfer.

CRAIG, Robert McAllister

Inside-forward

Born: Airdrie, 8 April 1935.
Career: Bicester. Blantyre Celtic. Third Lanark November 1955. Sheffield Wednesday November 1959, fee £6,500. Blackburn Rovers April 1962, fee £20,000. Celtic October 1962, fee £15,000. St Johnstone August 1963, in exchange for

Robert Young. OLDHAM ATHLETIC March 1964, fee £5,000. Toronto City, Canada, May 1965. Johannesburg Wanderers, South Africa, until November 1965. Third Lanark February 1967.

■ Bobby Craig returned to English football with the Latics after a two-season spell in his native Scotland. He was expected to take over the mantle of play-maker from Bobby Johnstone, who was nearing retirement and increasingly troubled by knee injuries. Craig did not lack skill on the ball, but his form was very inconsistent and he was unable to hold down a first-team place in a very poor Athletic side, which came close to relegation from Division Three.

CRANSTON, William

Wing-half

Born: Kilmarnock, 18 January 1942.
Career: Saxone Youth Club. Blackpool August 1960. Preston North End December 1964, fee £7,000. OLDHAM ATHLETIC July 1970 to July 1973, fee £6,000.

■ Bill Cranston enjoyed a memorable debut in League football. Two days after his 20th birthday he helped Blackpool beat Wolverhampton Wanderers 7–2 in a First Division fixture. With Preston North End, he was voted Player of the Year in his final season, a depressing term that ended in relegation from Division Two. Signed by Athletic and installed as captain, the hard-working and untiring defender led the side to promotion from Division Four in his first season.

CRAWFORD, John Campbell 'Ian'

Inside-forward

Born: Falkirk, 27 June 1922.
Died: 1966.
Career: East Stirlingshire. Morton. Raith Rovers. Ayr United. OLDHAM ATHLETIC July 1952, fee £750. Halifax Town July 1954. Macclesfield Town 1955. Montrose August 1956. East Stirlingshire manager, director and later chairman.

■ A short and stocky inside-forward, Ian Crawford lacked a yard of pace but his nifty footwork and eye for an opening made him a dangerous opponent. His handy knack of being in the right place at the right moment often resulted in a close-range strike at goal. Despite failing to win a regular place, his seven goals in just 14 matches was a very useful contribution as the Latics won the Third Division North Championship in season 1952–53.

CREANEY, Gerard Thomas 'Gerry'

Forward

Born: Coatbridge, 13 April 1970.
Career: Nottingham Forest Boys' Club. Celtic Boys' Club 1984. Celtic May 1987. Everton trial 16 January 1994. Portsmouth 26 Jan 1994, fee £600,000. Manchester City September 1995, fee £1.1million plus Paul Walsh. OLDHAM ATHLETIC loan March–May 1996. Ipswich Town loan October 1996. Burnley loan September 1997. Chesterfield loan January 1998. West Bromwich Albion trial July 1998. St Mirren October 1998. Notts County February–May 1999. Queen of the South trial November 2000.

■ After failing to impress with Manchester City following his £1.1 million transfer, the first of Gerry Creaney's loan spells took him to Boundary Park, and in the final stages of season 1995–96 he helped preserve Athletic's Division One status. Within his brief stay, the Scotland B and Under-21 international missed from the penalty spot for the first time in his career (against Wolverhampton Wanderers) but scored his 100th career goal (against Southend United).

CROMPTON, Norman

Half-back

Born: Farnworth, 7 April 1904.
Died: Bolton, February 1991.
Career: Little Hulton United. Denbigh United September 1925. OLDHAM ATHLETIC May 1926. Queen's Park Rangers May 1928. Horwich R.M.I. June 1930. Darwen June 1931. Prescot Cables. Lancaster Town July 1935. Rossendale United June 1936. Wigan Athletic January 1937. Burton Sports coach February 1939.

■ One of a pair of centre-halves signed on the same day in May 1926, Jack Armitage from Burnley was immediately installed at senior level, while Norman Crompton's role remained that of understudy throughout his two years at Boundary Park. After a season in reserve with Queen's Park Rangers, Crompton returned north to join Horwich RMI. He later helped Darwen win the Championship of the Lancashire Combination and reach the third round of the FA Cup, earning a money-spinning tie against Arsenal at Highbury in January 1932.

CROFT, Lee David

Midfield

Born: Billinge, near Wigan, 21 June 1985.
Career: Garswood United. Manchester City trainee, professional July 2002. OLDHAM ATHLETIC loan November 2004 to February 2005. Norwich City August 2006, fee £700,000.

■ In 2004–05, the season in which Ronnie Moore replaced Brian Talbot as Athletic's manager, England Schools and Youth international Lee Croft was just one of a welter of loan signings fielded during the campaign. Although League form was decidedly below par, Croft made an immediate impact, resulting in a mid-season burst of four consecutive League wins. The lively midfielder also starred in the FA Cup run to round four, earning warm praise for his outstanding display in the team's courageous performance against Bolton Wanderers.

CRONIN, Lance

Goalkeeper

Born: Brighton, 11 September 1985.
Career: Crystal Palace professional September 2002. Wycombe Wanderers loan March–May 2005. OLDHAM

ATHLETIC non-contract November 2005. Shrewsbury Town February 2006. MK Dons trial. Gravesend & Northfleet August 2006. Ebbsfleet United May 2007.

■ Briefly with Athletic as reserve goalkeeper to Chris Day, Lance Cronin was quickly called upon when summoned from the bench at Chasetown in an FA Cup first-round tie. He was released following the loan signing of Lee Grant from Derby County. He was an FA Trophy winner with Ebbsfleet, who beat Torquay United 1–0 at Wembley on 10 May 2008.

CROOK, George

Inside-forward

Born: Hutton Henry, County Durham, 30 January 1935.
Career: Durham junior football. OLDHAM ATHLETIC February 1953. Middlesbrough November 1958 to June 1960. Toronto Ukrainians, Canada, February 1961.

■ For two seasons, before a National Service posting to Germany intervened, George Crook made good progress as a tricky inside man, very adept at providing openings for his colleagues. He was demobilised from the Army in October 1958 and transferred to Middlesbrough the following month, but in two seasons he failed to reach senior level. At the age of 26 he emigrated to Canada.

CROSS, David

Centre-forward

Born: Heywood, 8 December 1950.
Career: Heywood Schoolboys. Rochdale August 1969. Norwich City October 1971, fee £40,000. Coventry City November 1973, fee £150,000. West Bromwich Albion November 1976, fee £120,000. West Ham United December 1977, fee £180,000. Manchester City August 1982, fee £135,000. Vancouver Whitecaps, Canada, April–September 1983. OLDHAM ATHLETIC October 1983. Vancouver Whitecaps, Canada, April 1984. West Bromwich Albion October 1984. Bolton Wanderers July 1985. Bury loan January–May 1986. Aris Salonika, Cyprus, player-coach 1987. Altrincham coach 1987–88. Watford scout. OLDHAM ATHLETIC assistant youth coach August 1997, reserve-team coach January 2002. Blackburn Rovers Academy coach May 2003.

■ A forceful striker with a good first-time shot and outstanding in the air, David Cross's physical presence made him a handful for defenders, and netted him a career total of over 250 goals. Athletic were one of a number of clubs chasing his signature following his return from a spell in the North American League, and he proved to be an excellent short-term acquisition. His goals helped the Latics to important victories against Portsmouth, Fulham and Leeds United, before he returned to Vancouver Whitecaps.

CROSSLEY, Mark Geoffrey

Goalkeeper

Born: Barnsley, 16 June 1969.

Career: *Nottingham Forest trainee June 1985, professional July 1987. Millwall loan February 1998. Middlesbrough July 2000. Stoke City loan November 2002 and again March 2003. Fulham August 2003, fee £500,000. Sheffield Wednesday loan November 2006. OLDHAM ATHLETIC June 2007.*

▪ Widely travelled Welsh international goalkeeper Mark Crossley began with Nottingham Forest and in 15 years at the City Ground made around 400 senior appearances. First capped by England at Under-21 level, he subsequently switched allegiance and represented Wales, winning one B and eight full caps. He was an FA Cup finalist in 1991 and in 1994 helped Forest win promotion into the Premier League. Shortly after joining Athletic he recorded his 500th senior appearance. At 6ft and 16 stones, Crossley presents a formidable barrier to opposing forwards and his calm and confident displays have served Athletic well in his first season, his wide experience helping to improve the entire defensive unit of the team.

CROSSLEY, Terence Gordon

Outside-left

Born: Rockferry, 24 February 1936.
Career: Bangor University. Portmadoc. OLDHAM ATHLETIC amateur August 1957, professional July 1958 to June 1959.

▪ A BSc on the staff of Chorlton Grammar School, Terry Crossley's debut came in the midst of a flu epidemic that decimated the Boundary Park ranks. The virus affected 10 players, trainer Jimmy Kelly and even the club groundsman. Six

months later, Crossley scored on his second and final League appearance, a 4–2 win against Bradford Park Avenue.

CROWE, Dean Anthony

Forward

Born: Stockport, 6 June 1979.
Career: Stoke City trainee, professional September 1996. Northampton Town loan February 2000. Bury loan March 2000, permanent August 2000. Plymouth Argyle loan August 2001. Luton Town loan September, permanent October 2001. York City loan September 2003. OLDHAM ATHLETIC March–May 2004. Leek Town September 2004. Stockport County non-contract August 2005. Witton Albion January 2006 released November 2007. Offerton Green FC permit player.

▪ Dean Crowe was one of five transfer deadline signings made by new manager Brian Talbot following his appointment in March 2004. In his first full appearance the diminutive striker scored against one of his former clubs, Luton Town, in a 1–1 draw at Kenilworth Road, his speculative cross from well out on the touchline drifting over the embarrassed Hatter's 'keeper. Overall, however, he failed to make a real impact and was not offered an extension to his short-term contract.

CRUMBLEHULME, Kevin

Wing-half

Born: Manchester, 17 June 1952.
Career: Cleworth Road Youth Club. OLDHAM ATHLETIC associate schoolboy, apprentice September 1967,

professional July 1970. Fleetwood 1972. Mossley December 1972. Stalybridge Celtic 1974.

▪ Kevin Crumblehulme was invited for trials at Boundary Park at 15 years of age. Despite a lengthy association with Athletic – he was approaching his 20th birthday when he made his League debut – the youthful wing-half failed to establish himself at senior level. In non-League circles he won a Cheshire County League Championship with Stalybridge Celtic in 1979–80 and also appeared in representative matches with the Cheshire County League XI.

CUMMING, Lawrence Stanley Slater

Inside-forward

Born: Londonderry, 10 April 1905.
Career: Alloa Athletic August 1926. Huddersfield Town March 1928. OLDHAM ATHLETIC October 1929, fee £900. Southampton June 1930, fee £500. Alloa Athletic 1931. Queen of the South August 1933, fee £100. Hamilton Academical July 1938.

▪ Within days of joining Athletic, Lawrie Cumming won his third Northern Ireland cap, and his form at Boundary Park was quite outstanding. Neat and clever in his footwork, he was a scorer of spectacular goals, often from long range. Sadly, injury sidelined him at a crucial point in the campaign and Athletic's promotion hopes evaporated. After returning to Scotland as a part-time professional, Cumming worked in the advertising department of a Scottish daily newspaper.

CUNLIFFE, Thomas

Outside-left

Born: Simms-lane-End, near Wigan, c.1886.
Career: Hooley Hill FC 1902. Earlestown FC March 1905. Blackburn Rovers March 1906. St Helens Recreation June 1907. Liverpool February 1916 to October 1917. Altrincham. OLDHAM ATHLETIC August 1919 to June 1920. Mossley.

■ Tom Cunliffe began in football at 12 years of age as an outside-left with Audenshaw in the Sunday School League. He made his League debut with Blackburn Rovers in April 1906, but his next taste of League action came some 13 years later with the Latics. Between times he had lengthy spells in Lancashire Combination football, and during World War One made 57 appearances for Liverpool. His season at Boundary Park was spent as understudy to George Wall but he proved a very useful man in the reserves, scoring six goals in 35 appearances.

CURRAN, James

Goalkeeper

Born: Macclesfield, 24 September 1947.
Career: Lancashire Schoolboys. Manchester United amateur May 1963. Newcastle United amateur 1965–66. OLDHAM ATHLETIC trial August 1966, professional December 1966. Crewe Alexandra April 1967. Witton Albion. Irlam Town.

■ Flame-haired Jimmy Curran won County Schools honours at both football and cricket, and had football trials for England Schoolboys. In a brief spell with

the Latics he deputised for David Best in four matches, receiving mixed reviews: 'Uncertain in the air' being one lukewarm verdict. During his spell with Crewe Alexandra he was fielded as a full-back in their reserve team. He later coached Manchester United's A Team.

CURRIE, David Norman

Forward

Born: Stockton-on-Tees, 27 November 1962.
Career: Stockton Schoolboys. Middlesbrough February 1982. Darlington July 1986. Barnsley February 1988, fee £150,000. Nottingham Forest January 1990, fee £750,000. OLDHAM ATHLETIC August 1990, fee £460,000. Barnsley September 1991, fee £250,000. Rotherham United loan October 1992. Huddersfield Town loan January 1994. Carlisle United July 1994. Scarborough January–April 1997.

■ Athletic's record transfer fee was almost doubled when David Currie was signed from Nottingham Forest for £460,000. Despite the heavy outlay, Currie failed to establish a regular first-team place, and might have joined Blackburn Rovers just prior to the transfer deadline in March of his first season but preferred to stay and fight for a first-team place. Flashes of excellent and at times flamboyant ball control marked his varied career in which he played exactly 500 games for nine League clubs and scored 132 goals.

CUTTING, Jack Andrew

Inside-forward

Born: Fleetwood, 15 April 1924.
Died: Fleetwood, 24 April 1985.
Career: RAF football. Manchester United amateur July to December 1945. OLDHAM ATHLETIC amateur June, professional November 1946. Fleetwood September 1947. Accrington Stanley June 1948 to January 1950. Fleetwood September 1950. Northwich Victoria 1952–53. Winsford United.

■ Blond-haired and forceful, former RAF Pilot Officer Jack Cutting was a whole-hearted forager, usefully able to occupy any forward position. He failed to establish himself with Athletic but had a productive season with Fleetwood (18 goals in 38 matches) after leaving

Boundary Park. In a second spell in League football with Accrington Stanley, he scored five goals in 25 matches.

CYWKA, Tomasz

Midfield

Born: Gliwice, Poland, 27 June 1988.
Career: Gwarek Zabrze, Poland. Wigan Athletic August 2006. OLDHAM ATHLETIC loan October–December 2006.

■ Polish Under-21 midfielder Tomasz Cywka, on loan from Wigan Athletic, made his Athletic debut in the Johnstone's Paint Trophy defeat by Chesterfield at Boundary Park on 1 November 2006. The match also marked the debut, from the bench, of teenage goalkeeper Adam Legzdins, and the team that day featured seven players aged 20 or less. Cywka subsequently featured as a late substitute in four League matches before being recalled to Wigan just prior to Christmas 2006.

D'ARCY, Michael Eamonn

Goalkeeper

Born: Crumlin, Ireland, 8 March 1933.
Career: Dundalk. Bury trial. OLDHAM ATHLETIC trial August, professional September 1954, fee £150. Shamrock Rovers 1956. Drumcondra 1962. Hollyhead later in the same year. Shamrock Rovers 1966.

■ Eamonn D'Arcy had trials with Bury and the Latics prior to season 1954–55, and a month after signing professional forms at Boundary Park took over the

first-team jersey. Competition from Burnett, Fred Ogden and Bollands restricted his opportunities and he returned to Ireland, initially as a part-time player with Shamrock Rovers. He played against Manchester United's pre-Munich side in the 1957–58 European Cup and also won representative honours, playing for the League of Ireland on 10 occasions.

DAVIES, Craig Martin

Forward

Born: Burton upon Trent, 9 January 1986.
Career: Manchester City juniors. Oxford United trainee, professional February 2005. Verona, Italy, January 2006. Wolverhampton Wanderers season-long loan August 2006. OLDHAM ATHLETIC June 2007, fee £65,000.

■ Athletic first encountered Craig Davies in January 2007 when the strong running striker scored Wolves' second goal in the third round FA Cup tie at Molineux which ended all square at 2–2. The Wales international spent a season on loan with the Wolves after an unhappy spell in Italy, where he had failed to acclimatise. Following his signing by Athletic, Davies enjoyed an excellent pre-season which continued with an opening day strike against Swansea City and another goal and two assists in the 4–1 defeat at Mansfield Town in the Carling Cup. Athletic's leading scorer with 14 goals, he is expected to add further international honours in the summer after adding to his Under-21 caps in the 2–0 defeat by England in May 2008.

DAVIES, David Walter

Centre-forward

Born: Treharris, Glamorgan, 1 October 1888.
Career: Merthyr Town. Treharris. OLDHAM ATHLETIC May 1912, fee £180. Stockport County March 1913. Sheffield United April 1913. Merthyr Town season 1919–20. Treharris Albion.

■ Centre-forward Walter Davies won his second Wales cap while on Athletic's books. Despite a scoring debut against the season's FA Cup winners, Aston Villa, the lightly-built, ball-playing attack leader was restricted by injury to just 10 appearances.

DAVIS, Eric William Charles

Centre-forward

Born: Stonehouse, Plymouth, 26 February 1932.
Died: Plymouth, 24 July 2007.
Career: Tavistock. Plymouth Argyle August 1952. Scunthorpe United July 1957, fee £2,000. Chester February 1959. OLDHAM ATHLETIC trial September-October 1960.

■ Signed by Athletic on a month's trial after two seasons with Chester, Eric Davis scored on his debut but declined to sign permanently due to business commitments. In season 1957–58 he scored 19 goals in 25 matches for Scunthorpe United, champions of the Third Division North.

DAVIS, Thomas Lawrence

Centre-forward

Born: Dublin, 3 February 1911.
Career: Cork City. Shelbourne. Exeter City trial. Boston Town August 1931. Torquay United June 1932. New Brighton August 1933. FC de Metz, France, May 1935. OLDHAM ATHLETIC June 1935, fee £250. Tranmere Rovers February 1938. Cork City June 1938. Dundalk April 1939. Workington July 1939. Wartime guest with Dundalk, Drumcondra, Shelbourne and Belfast Distillery. VVV (Venlo), Holland manager-coach August 1947.

■ Good ball control, a fierce shot, and outstanding headwork all combined to make Tommy Davis a very potent attacking force. He first came to prominence with New Brighton, scoring 50 League goals in just 76 matches. In 1936–37, Davis scored 35 League and FA Cup goals which remains Athletic's record for goals scored in a season. He made his international debut in the same season, and marked the occasion by scoring twice for Ireland against Germany. Davis was reported to have emigrated to Cannes, France, after leaving the game.

DAW, Edwin Charles

Goalkeeper

Born: Doncaster, 1876.
Died: Leicester, 1944.
Career: Hexthorpe Wanderers. Sheffield United trial. Grimsby Town November 1896. Barnsley October 1897. Rushden Town May 1898. Luton Town May 1899. Leicester Fosse May 1900. New Brompton June 1902. Doncaster Rovers November 1904. Bradford City November 1905.

OLDHAM ATHLETIC May 1906. Belmont Works amateur November 1907. Leicester Fosse April 1910.

■ Teddy Daw was Athletic's last line of defence for much of season 1906–07, when the Championship of the Lancashire Combination was secured. In the same term, they enjoyed a lengthy run in the FA Cup, progressing through five qualifying rounds and the first round proper before being drawn to play Liverpool at home. Sadly, the Latics' unfortunate custodian suffered acute embarrassment when he allowed an 87th minute shot from Liverpool's Billy McPherson to roll between his legs for the only goal of the game.

DAY, Christopher Nicholas

Goalkeeper

*Born: Walthamstow, 28 July 1975.
Career: Tottenham Hotspur trainee, signing professional April 1993. Crystal Palace August 1996, fee £225,000. Watford July 1997, fee £225,000. Lincoln City loan December 2000. Queen's Park Rangers July 2001. Aylesbury loan October 2002. Preston North End loan February 2005. OLDHAM ATHLETIC August 2005. Millwall July 2006.*

■ After starting his Athletic season as first-choice goalkeeper, England Under-21 international Chris Day appeared in 30 consecutive League matches. He was dropped following a 3–2 defeat at Huddersfield Town in late January and replaced by loan signing Lee Grant.

Although contracted to Athletic for a further 12 months, Day opted to leave in the summer. Despite interest from several clubs he elected to take a homeward move, switching to Millwall on a free transfer.

DEARDEN, William

Inside-forward/Winger

*Born: Oldham, 11 February 1944.
Career: Oldham Schoolboys. OLDHAM ATHLETIC from school (briefly on Wolverhampton Wanderers' books as an amateur). OLDHAM ATHLETIC professional September 1963. Crewe Alexandra December 1966. Chester June 1968. Sheffield United April 1970, fee £10,000. Chester loan February 1976, permanent July 1976. Chesterfield August 1977, retired from playing 1980, appointed youth coach then trainer October 1981. Mansfield Town trainer 1983, subsequently appointed assistant manager. Port Vale assistant manager July 1994. Mansfield Town manager July 1999. Notts County manager January 2002 to January 2004. Blackpool assistant manager. Mansfield Town manager December 2006 to March 2008.*

■ An apprentice plumber during his early days as a Latics part-timer, Billy Dearden revealed glimpses of real potential in Athletic's reserves, yet failed to reach the same effectiveness during infrequent first-team appearances. Released on a free transfer in 1966, he eventually fulfilled his potential during six seasons with Sheffield United, his overall League career totalling 101 goals in 405 appearances. A late entrant into

management, he commenced a second spell with Mansfield Town in 2006 at the age of 62, becoming the third-oldest manager in the Football League behind Sir Alex Ferguson and Dario Gradi MBE.

DEVLIN, Thomas

Inside-forward

*Born: Bellshill, Lanarkshire, 10 April 1903. Died: Fairfield, Connecticut, US, February 1979.
Career: Vale of Clyde. Shawfield Juniors. Kilsyth Rangers. Third Lanark A Team April 1922. King's Park FC. Birmingham September 1924. Preston North End January 1926, fee £362. Liverpool May 1927, fee £250. Swindon Town June 1928, fee £200. Brooklyn Wanderers, US, May 1929. Aberdeen June 1931. Walsall August 1932. Boston Fall River, US, c.1932–33. Zurich, Switzerland, September 1933. Fleetwood December 1933. OLDHAM ATHLETIC September 1934 to April 1935. Racing Club de Roubaix, France, player-coach 1935–36. Fleetwood August 1937.*

■ Tom Devlin's 'rolling stone' League career, which embraced 10 other senior clubs in four countries concluded at Boundary Park. Elder brother William had similar tendencies, clocking up 14 clubs in England, Scotland, Ireland and Wales.

DIAMOND, John James

Centre-forward

*Born: Middlesbrough, 30 October 1910. Died: Royton, Oldham, 8 July 1961.
Career: Beverley White Star. Hull City amateur July, professional September*

1931. Newark Town March 1932. Shelbourne, Ireland, August 1932. Southport June 1933. Barnsley November 1934, fee £1,500. Cardiff City May 1935. Bury June 1936. OLDHAM ATHLETIC March 1937. Hartlepools United January 1939. Hyde United June 1939.

■ Speedy, resolute and quick to seize an opportunity, Jack Diamond's greatest asset was his superb aerial ability. In August 1937, in Athletic's pre-season trial match, he scored a first half hat-trick. Switching sides at half-time, he scored another three, yet still finished on the losing side! Initially kept out of Athletic's side by Tommy Davis, his performances in the opening matches of 1937–38 – following on from his double hat-trick – ensured his retention. After Royal Navy service during World War Two, Diamond returned to live in the Oldham district and worked as an iron moulder in a local foundry.

DICKENSON, James

Half-back

Born: Pittington, County Durham, 1907.
Career: Easington Colliery Welfare. Hartlepools United May 1930. Blackpool June 1931. OLDHAM ATHLETIC June 1932. Torquay United May 1934. Scarborough July 1935. Hordon Colliery Welfare July 1936.

■ Jim Dickenson was a member of the Durham Constabulary during his Hartlepools United days. He did not reach

senior level with Blackpool, and in two seasons at Boundary Park was principally a Central League player. A move south to Torquay United afforded him more opportunities in a side that featured another three ex-Latics players – Tom Pickersgill, Ernie Steele and Fred Flavell.

DICKINSON, Leonard

Inside-forward

Born: South Elmsall, Yorkshire, 6 March 1942.
Career: Sheffield Wednesday February 1960. OLDHAM ATHLETIC June 1961, fee £100. Altrincham July 1962. Witton Albion June 1963. Buxton October 1964. Ashton United January 1966. Mossley August 1966. Altrincham 1972–73.

■ A lightly-built opportunist inside-forward, Len Dickinson found few opportunities in his season at Boundary Park, despite scoring five goals – including a seven-minute hat-trick – on his debut for Athletic's reserves against Lytham on 19 August 1961. His first-team chance was delayed until March 1962, when he scored vital goals against Exeter City and Wrexham within the space of a week. He subsequently enjoyed a lengthy and productive spell with Mossley, scoring 84 goals in 338 appearances.

DIVERS, John

Inside-forward

Born: Clydebank, 6 August 1911.
Died: Glasgow, 8 June 1984.
Career: Rothesay Royal Victoria 1930. Renfrew Juniors 1931. Celtic December

1932. Morton loan 1942, permanent October 1945. OLDHAM ATHLETIC August 1947. Morton October 1947. Portadown, Ireland, player-manager September to November 1950.

■ John Divers had the briefest of associations with the English game. His debut for the Latics was ended within minutes by injury and, within a few weeks of arriving at Boundary Park, he returned to Scotland to rejoin Morton. A nephew of the famous Irish international 'Patsy' Gallagher, Divers was capped by Scotland in October 1938 and was a member of Celtic's Championship-winning squad in the same year.

DIXON, Arthur

Half-back

Born: Chadderton, 1892.
Died: Shaw, 25 December 1965.
Career: Washbrook Primitive. Woodhouse. Tonge 1910. OLDHAM ATHLETIC amateur January 1912, professional Sept 1913. St Mirren loan February 1916. Rangers August 1918, fee £1,250. Cowdenbeath October 1927. Dolphin FC, Dublin, manager August 1930. Rangers trainer & physiotherapist July 1932. Partick Thistle trainer August 1947. Third Lanark trainer. Everton, chief scout in Scotland. OLDHAM ATHLETIC physiotherapist July 1962.

■ A ball-boy and programme seller at Boundary Park during his youth, on leaving school Arthur Dixon became an apprentice turner at Platt Brothers, the local textile machinery manufacturers. Munitions work took him to Scotland, where he eventually won a total of eight medals with Glasgow Rangers. He was invariably the only player in the side without international or inter-League representative honours, as well as being the sole Englishman among Scots and the occasional Irishman. Some 50 years after first signing for the Latics he returned to Oldham and worked as club physiotherapist until his death.

DODDS, John Thomas

Outside-left

Born: Hexham, 1885.
Career: Northern Star, Hexham. Newcastle United August 1905. OLDHAM ATHLETIC August 1908, fee £100. Heart of Midlothian June 1909, fee £50. Darlington 1910–11. Merthyr Town September 1911. Stalybridge Celtic until May 1915, when he enlisted into the Footballers' Battalion.

■ One of three Newcastle United players recruited by the Latics in the summer of 1908, Jack Dodds was unfortunate to be injured in only his second appearance at Blackpool, and more seriously hurt in a reserve team match in December. The arrival of Joe Donnachie from Everton further restricted his opportunities, leading to his transfer to Hearts in June 1909.

DODDS, William

Inside-forward

Born: Sunderland, 1885.
Career: Sunderland Royal Rovers. Southwick May 1904. Burslem Port Vale June 1906. OLDHAM ATHLETIC June 1907. Linfield, Ireland, 1908.

■ Billy Dodds joined Athletic after his club, Burslem Port Vale, resigned from the Football League. Originally an outside-left, he began with the Latics at inside-right, and it was from this position that he scored Athletic's first-ever goal in a Football League match. This came in the 3–1 opening day victory at Stoke on 7 September 1907. Some two years later, when Boundary Park hosted an Inter-League match against the Irish League, Dodds was travelling reserve for the Irish team. His son, James, won Irish Schools and junior international honours and assisted Linfield, Fulham and Gillingham in the 1930s.

DOLPHIN, Alfred

Outside-right

Born: Redditch, 1890.
Died: Bromsgrove, 1940.
Career: Nuneaton Town. OLDHAM ATHLETIC May 1919, fee £100. Notts County June 1920, fee £100. Darlington June 1921. Stockport County June 1922. Walsall July 1923. Weymouth 1924.

■ At 29 years of age Alf Dolphin was a late starter in League football, who assisted five League clubs in as many

seasons. A fast moving wingman with good ball control, his promising start with the Latics was abruptly halted by injury in mid-season. He assisted Darlington to the Third Division North runners-up position in 1921–22, scoring three goals in 33 appearances.

DONACHIE, William 'Willie'

Full-back

Born: Castlemilk, Glasgow, 5 October 1951.
Career: Glasgow United. Celtic ground staff. Manchester City amateur October 1968, professional February 1969. Portland Timbers, US, March 1980, fee

£200,000. Norwich City September 1981, fee £200,000. Burnley November 1982. OLDHAM ATHLETIC July 1984, appointed player-coach July 1985, retired as a player June 1994 and subsequently appointed assistant manager. Everton assistant manager November 1994. Manchester City coach February 1998. Sheffield Wednesday assistant manager November 2001. Ipswich Town assistant manager October 2002. Millwall assistant manager, caretaker manager September 2006, manager November 2006 to October 2007.

■ One of soccer's evergreen players, Willie Donachie was an influential figure in Athletic's defence, his vast experience enabling him to read the game well and react accordingly. Reluctantly, he retired from playing at the age of 42 having been named as substitute on a number of occasions in 1991–92 and 1992–93 without getting onto the pitch. Donachie's outstanding career was rewarded with 35 caps for Scotland, including appearances in the World Cup Finals of 1974 and 1978. He also completed a fraction short of 700 matches with his four League clubs.

DONNACHIE, Joseph

Outside-left

Born: Kilwinning, Ayrshire c.1885.
Career: Rutherglen Glencairn. Albion Rovers. Greenock Morton March 1905. Newcastle United June 1905. Everton February 1906. OLDHAM ATHLETIC October 1908, fee £250. Wartime guest

with Everton and Liverpool. Rangers March 1919, fee £800. Blackpool June 1920. Chester player-manager 1921.

■ Joe Donnachie first crossed the border in 1905, but his stay with Newcastle United was not prolonged, and his subsequent role with Everton, as understudy to Jack Sharp, afforded him few opportunities. His move to the Latics, however, was a success from the outset. Considered one of the best wingers ever to play for Athletic, his talents were neatly summed up by his former colleague Charlie Roberts in 1921: 'I never saw a player who could beat an opponent as simply as Joe Donnachie. He was a real artist, but it was really amusing to Donnachie and us all at Oldham when some Southern scribe described Joe as the speedy Donnachie. Joe was anything but speedy, but what he lacked in speed he had in brains, and that is what is wanted in present football more than ever.' In April 1913 he was rewarded with the first of his three Scotland caps against England, and in 1913–14 he scored Scotland's goal in their 1–1 draw against Ireland. Donnachie's career ended at Chester and he took over a local hostelry, The Mariner's Arms, in 1923. His son, Joe junior, at one time on Liverpool's books, was killed in a flying accident during World War Two.

DOUGHERTY, Joseph

Centre-forward

Born: Darlington, 1894.
Died: Darlington, 1959.
Career: Darlington Forge. Leeds City February 1914. OLDHAM ATHLETIC April 1919, fee £100. Hartlepools United March 1921 to January 1923. Lincoln City trial January–February 1924.

■ Joe Dougherty had played just once for Leeds City before World War One, and came to Boundary Park, initially on trial, over the Easter period of 1919. Two days after signing a professional form he celebrated by scoring a hat-trick against Rochdale. When normal peacetime football resumed in August 1919 he commenced as first-team centre-forward but lost his place by November and was transfer listed in December. Later with Hartlepools United, Dougherty made 33

appearances, mainly at wing-half, in their first season in the Football League.

DOUGLAS, George Harold

Outside-right

Born: Stepney, London, 18 August 1893.
Died: Southborough, Kent, 24 January 1979.
Career: Ilford FC. Leicester Fosse amateur May 1912, professional May 1913. Wartime guest with Arsenal and Norwich City. Burnley February 1921, fee £1,600. OLDHAM ATHLETIC May 1922, fee £750. Bristol Rovers August 1926, fee £100. Tunbridge Wells player-manager July 1928. Dover United, reinstated amateur November 1930.

■ An extremely promising schoolboy footballer, George Douglas captained West Ham to the English Schools Shield in 1907 and appeared for London

Schools against Glasgow. He won two England Amateur International caps in 1913, but his League career with Leicester Fosse was interrupted by the outbreak of World War One, during which he served with the Leicestershire Royal Horse Artillery. He arrived at Boundary Park from Burnley, and for four seasons dominated the outside-right position. Although slim and short in stature he was an elusive opponent with deft footwork and the ability to centre accurately. A provider rather than a goalscorer on his own account, his career aggregate figures were 309 League appearances and 24 goals.

DOUGLAS, William

Centre-forward

Born: Porth, 1892.
Career: Cwm FC. Cardiff City. OLDHAM ATHLETIC June 1913, fee £15. Wrexham 1914. Wartime guest with OLDHAM ATHLETIC.

■ Billy Douglas was a versatile footballer who appeared in several outfield positions and also as goalkeeper for Cardiff City. He assisted the Bluebirds to the Championship of the Southern League Second Division in 1912–13, but was unable to carry forward his success on moving to Boundary Park. Douglas enlisted in the Royal Flying Corps during World War One and made the odd guest appearance for the Latics in wartime football.

DOWD, Henry William

Goalkeeper

Born: Salford, 4 July 1938.
Career: Blackley ICI. Manchester City amateur January 1958, professional July 1960. Stoke City loan October 1969. Charlton Athletic loan August 1970. OLDHAM ATHLETIC December 1970 to June 1974. Northwich Victoria (five matches) 1977–78.

■ Harry Dowd followed the legendary Bert Trautmann in Manchester City's goal and enjoyed a successful career at Maine Road, appearing in 219 League and Cup matches. He won a Second Division Championship medal in 1966 and an FA Cup-winners' award in 1969. Signed by Athletic's manager Jimmy Frizzell during his first full season in

charge, seven wins in the next eight matches ensued, leading eventually to promotion from Division Four. He was later to feature in a second promotion campaign, although he lost his place to the emerging Chris Ogden in mid-season 1973–74. A goalkeeper with bags of confidence, Dowd at times induced heart-stopping moments by dribbling round onrushing forwards outside his own penalty area.

DOWKER, Thomas

Outside-left

Born: Speke, Liverpool, 7 November 1922.
Died: Wigan, December 2001.
Career: South Liverpool. OLDHAM ATHLETIC July 1947 to June 1948.

■ Tom Dowker was recruited from South Liverpool following a successful season in 1946–47 when they finished third in the Cheshire League, two points adrift of the champions, Wellington Town. Athletic fielded seven outside-lefts during the season, Dowker making only one senior appearance, in the 4–1 defeat at Rotherham United on 1 September 1947.

DOWN, David Frederick 'Dickie'

Centre-forward

Born: Bristol, 7 July 1948.
Career: Bristol City apprentice September 1963, professional September 1965. Bradford Park Avenue October 1967.

OLDHAM ATHLETIC October 1968 to March 1969. Bristol Rovers trial 1969. Swindon Town trial August 1969.

■ Centre-forward Dickie Down was manager Rowley's first signing after he had been appointed for a second spell in the Boundary Park hot seat. Down had scored six goals in 30 League matches for Bradford Park Avenue in 1967–68, but his spell at Boundary Park was blighted by a serious ankle ligament injury, sustained in his second outing. He was restricted to just nine League appearances as Athletic finished 24th in Division Three and were relegated.

DOWNES, Percy

Outside-left

Born: Langold, 19 September 1905.
Died: Gainsborough, November 1989.
Career: Dinnington Main Athletic. Huddersfield Town trial. Gainsborough Trinity March 1924. Blackpool November 1924, fee £500. Hull City February 1932. Stockport County August 1932. Burnley May 1934. OLDHAM ATHLETIC May 1936. Gainsborough Trinity May 1938.

■ Although nearing the end of his League career, Percy Downes successfully took over the left-wing berth vacated by Arthur Buckley's transfer to Leeds United. In earlier days the speedy and elusive wingman won a Second Division Championship medal with Blackpool in 1930. Later with Stockport County, he scored four goals in their record League win, 13–0 against Halifax Town in January 1934. Downes' lengthy League career spanned 377 matches and 73 goals.

DOWNIE, Alexander Leck Brown

Half-back

Born: St Rollox, Glasgow, 1876.
Died: Withington, Manchester, 9 December 1953.
Career: Glasgow Perthshire. Third Lanark October 1898. Bristol City May 1899. Swindon Town August 1900. Manchester United October 1902. OLDHAM ATHLETIC October 1909, fee £600. Crewe Alexandra player-coach 1911–12. Old Chorltonians (Manchester Amateur League) coach.

■ When Alex Downie made his first appearance for the Latics in October 1909 they were without a victory. His astute captaincy and influence on the side improved matters to such an extent that they won promotion to Division One. They went from New Year's Day 1910 until the end of the season and lost only one match, clinching promotion on goal average. Downie made his reputation with Manchester United, for whom he appeared in 191 League and Cup matches. A golfer of much more than average ability, Downie was a qualified engineer who held a responsible position on the Munitions Board during World War One.

DOYLE, John Alexander 'Ally'

Full-back

Born: Limavady, Northern Ireland, 25 October 1949.
Career: Limavady Technical School. Coleraine. OLDHAM ATHLETIC trial June 1965, professional October 1966 to June 1969.

■ Ally Doyle won schools and youth international honours as an inside-forward. After only 14 Lancashire Combination outings he suffered a broken leg in a training accident in January 1967 but recovered to make his League debut nine months later. A clever, quick-thinking player, Doyle lacked any physical advantage and rather surprisingly made his mark as a full-back after being tried in that position in an emergency. His cousin, goalkeeper Eric McManus, enjoyed a lengthy career in

English football, most notably with Notts County and Bradford City.

DRYBURGH, Thomas James Douglas

Outside-left

Born: Kirkcaldy, Fife, 23 April 1923.
Career: Lochgelly Albert. Aldershot June 1947. Rochdale July 1948. Leicester City August 1950, fee £6,500. Hull City May 1954. King's Lynn June 1955. OLDHAM ATHLETIC trial August 1957. Rochdale November 1957 to June 1958. Lancaster City.

■ Tommy Dryburgh's first sporting love was ice-hockey. He starred with the Kirkcaldy Fliers club, but after wartime Navy service turned his attentions to soccer. He was only briefly associated with Athletic, after spending a season in

non-League football. In four seasons with Leicester City, he made 99 League and Cup appearances and scored 30 goals. Dryburgh's League career totalled 220 appearances and 51 goals.

DUBOSE, Winston S.

Goalkeeper

Born: Florida, US, 28 July 1955.
Career: Tampa Bay Rowdies May 1977. Tulsa Roughnecks April 1983. Tampa Bay Rowdies 1984. OLDHAM ATHLETIC trial September, professional October 1988 to April 1989. Retired 1992.

■ United States international goalkeeper Winston Dubose played in only one first-team match, a second-round Football League Cup tie against Darlington which Athletic won 4–0. The signing of Jon Hallworth in February 1989 led to the release of the American international. Dubose retired from football in 1992 and is currently director of business development with Bayshore Technologies of Tampa Bay.

DUDLEY, Craig Bryan

Forward

Born: Ollerton, 12 September 1979.
Career: Notts County trainee August 1996, professional April 1997. Shrewsbury Town loan January 1998. Hull City loan November 1998. Telford United loan March 1999. OLDHAM ATHLETIC March 1999. Chesterfield loan August 1999. Scunthorpe United loan February 2002. Burton Albion, August 2002. Hyde United August 2005. Ashton United 2006. Gurnos Rangers 2007–08.

■ A combination of raw pace and whole-hearted commitment made Craig Dudley a potent attacking force, but injuries and an asthmatic condition blighted his three years at Boundary Park. A former England Youth international alongside Michael Owen, he failed to realise his early promise and stepped down into Conference football at the age of 23.

DUFFY, Gerald

Centre-forward

Born: Middlewich, Cheshire, 12 September 1934.

Career: Middlewich FC. OLDHAM ATHLETIC May 1956. Witton Albion July 1959. Nantwich 1961. Borough United 1963. Winsford United July 1966. Colwyn Bay January 1967.

■ At 5ft 9in and 11st, Gerry Duffy lacked physical advantage for his role of attack leader. He was, nevertheless, dashing, elusive and persistent and favoured the direct route to goal. His best season at Boundary Park was 1957–58, when he netted 17 League and Cup goals in 34 appearances. After leaving League football, Duffy sampled European competition with Borough United, and was a scorer in the 1963–64 European Cup-Winners' Cup first round against Sliema Wanderers (Malta).

DUNGWORTH, John Henry

Forward

Born: Rotherham, 30 March 1955.
Career: Huddersfield Town apprentice July 1970, professional April 1972. Barnsley loan October 1974. OLDHAM ATHLETIC May 1975. Rochdale loan March 1977. Aldershot

September 1977. Shrewsbury Town November 1979, fee £100,000. Hereford United loan October 1981. Mansfield Town August 1982. Rotherham United February 1984, player-coach 1986. Frickley Athletic 1988. Sheffield United youth development officer 1990. Huddersfield Town Academy coach 1999, first-team coach December 2006 to April 2008.

■ John Dungworth assisted nine League clubs in an outstanding career totalling 455/29 League appearances and 115 goals, figures that had seemed highly unlikely when he was released by Athletic on a free transfer in May 1977. After two seasons with Aldershot his value had soared to £100,000. In his second season (1978–79) he broke the Shots' scoring record with 26 goals in Division Four matches and an additional eight in FA Cup ties. Shrewsbury Town paid their record fee to take him to Gay Meadow in the following season. In later seasons he switched roles, usually appearing in midfield or defence for Rotherham United.

DUXBURY, Lee Edward

Midfield

Born: Skipton, 7 October 1969.
Career: Bradford City trainee, professional July 1988. Rochdale loan January 1990. Huddersfield Town December 1994, fee £250,000. Bradford City November 1995, fee £135,000. OLDHAM ATHLETIC March 1997, fee £350,000. Bury August 2003. Farsley Celtic September 2004. Glentoran. OLDHAM ATHLETIC reserve team manager June 2006.

■ Lee Duxbury was welcomed back to Boundary Park in June 2006 having been swiftly recruited to the backroom staff by new manager John Sheridan. Originally joining Athletic as a player in March 1997, Duxbury became a great crowd favourite, impressing with his unquenchable enthusiasm and immense capacity for work. He also had the priceless knack of breaking through opposing defences to register important goals. His 39 strikes for the Latics included 10 in season 2000–01, which made him leading goalscorer for the season.

DYSON, James

Inside-forward

Born: Middleton, 4 March 1907.
Died: Oldham, 4 January 2000.
Career: Northwich Victoria. OLDHAM ATHLETIC amateur February, professional March 1928, fee £20. Grimsby Town March 1932, fee £2,350. Nottingham Forest February 1938 to May 1939. Wartime guest with Accrington Stanley and OLDHAM ATHLETIC. Chadderton FC manager post-war.

■ The type of signing that most managers dream about, Jimmy Dyson cost just £20. Quickly established in the first team, he was leading goalscorer in 1930–31 with 16 in 36 League matches, but it was his constructive play and deft footwork that remained in the mind, along with his reputation as an expert

from the penalty spot. Reluctantly sold in the midst of a financial crisis in season 1931–32, he made 147 League and Cup appearances for Grimsby Town, scoring 39 goals, assisting the Mariners in their 1933–34 Second Division Championship side. A move to Nottingham Forest came on the eve of World War Two, during which he served with the Royal Marines in Egypt, Sicily and Ceylon.

EARDLEY, Neal James

Full-back

Born: Llandudno, 6 November 1988.
Career: Conway County Schools. North Wales Boys. Wrexham juniors 2000–02. OLDHAM ATHLETIC Centre of Excellence 2002, trainee July 2005, professional September 2006.

■ Wales international full-back Neal Eardley has continued to enhance his reputation with both club and country in

2007–08. A product of Athletic's excellent youth system, he has risen through the ranks from Under-14 level to become one of the outstanding prospects in League One. Latics' Young Player of the Year in 2006–07, he recovered from an unfortunate start when red-carded in the opening fixture at Tranmere Rovers and received a three-match ban. He was rarely absent thereafter, completing 41 appearances during the season. A late-season switch in April 2008 might well cause manager Sheridan a future selection problem. Moved from his usual role at right-back into central midfield, Eardley looked immediately at home and injected much needed energy and firepower in support of the front players.

EATON, Clifford

Inside-forward

Born: Oldham, 15 October 1910.
Died: Chelmsford, 1979.
Career: Lees Road Lads. Hurst 1931. Portsmouth amateur December 1933. Rochdale November 1934. OLDHAM ATHLETIC June 1936 to May 1938. Wartime guest with OLDHAM ATHLETIC.

■ Cliff Eaton made his debut in League football with Rochdale, appearing in 35 League and Cup matches and scoring four goals. He was initially offered a month's trial at Boundary Park, though this was subsequently extended and he remained on the books for two seasons. Despite being the cleverest forward in the reserves – he scored 16 goals in 1937–38 – Eaton was never given more than the odd game in the first team.

EAVES, Thomas Albert

Full-back

Born: Mawdesley, Leeds, 1 January 1914.
Died: Denton, Manchester, 16 December 2001.
Career: Leyland Motors 1934–35. OLDHAM ATHLETIC November 1936. Reading July to November 1946. Leyland Motors April 1947. Stalybridge Celtic July 1947. Hyde United September 1947.

■ A reliable auxiliary for either full-back position, Bert Eaves met opponents squarely and was a hard man to pass. His best season came in 1937–38 when he appeared in 19 League matches as deputy for Norman Price. A cartilage operation restricted him to just six matches in 1938–39, but he recovered to assist Athletic in 79 wartime games.

ECCLESTON, W.

Centre-forward

Career: Accrington Stanley January 1901. Barrow September 1901. Kettering Town November 1901. Barrow September 1904. OLDHAM ATHLETIC May 1905. Barrow February 1906, in exchange for T. Lawrenson.

■ Eccleston scored twice in five FA Cup ties in season 1905–06, both goals coming in the 3–1 win at Stalybridge Rovers which took Athletic to the fourth qualifying round. At this point they faced a Football League club and lost 2–1 at Hull City. In February of the same season an exchange deal took Eccleston back to Barrow for a third time. A local correspondent considered him 'Always a trier, but too slow.'

ECKERSLEY, Frank

Goalkeeper

Born: Chorlton, Manchester, 12 November 1912.
Died: Manchester, 25 January 1992.
Career: Pelaw CWS. Derby County January 1930. Linfield, Ireland, July 1933. Wigan Athletic June 1935. Manchester City May 1936, fee £400. OLDHAM ATHLETIC June 1937 to April 1939.

■ Frank Eckersley assisted Linfield to the Irish League and Cup double in 1934, but he did less well in League football. Despite his association with three League clubs, his solitary first-team appearance was his debut for Athletic, in a 3–1 win against Stockport County on 17 April 1939.

EDGE, Thomas

Outside-right

Born: Leigh, 28 April 1895.
Died: Stockport, 1966.
Career: Brook Valley. Stockport County

reserves during World War One. Manchester City October 1919. Treherbert June 1920. OLDHAM ATHLETIC January 1921. Exeter City May 1921. Blackpool May 1922. New Brighton June 1923. Winsford United 1924.

■ Rather ironically, Tom Edge's best season in League football was his last, as he made 26 appearances and scored two goals in New Brighton's first season in the Third Division North. An ankle injury blighted his sojourn at Boundary Park after he had briefly sampled First Division football. While on Exeter City's books he represented the Southern League against the Central League in March 1922.

EDMONDS, Neil Anthony

Defender/Midfield

Born: Accrington, 18 October 1968.
Career: Hyndburn and Lancashire Schoolboys. Arsenal associate schoolboy. OLDHAM ATHLETIC apprentice April 1985, professional June 1986. Rochdale loan September 1988, permanent November 1988 to February 1990. Chorley. Swedish football. Preston North End trial. East Bengal FC, Calcutta, India for 3 months. Bangor City January 1991. Stalybridge Celtic April 1991. Played in Finland 1991. Chadderton FC loan February 1992. Horwich RMI loan August 1993. Leigh RMI loan September 1995. Accrington Stanley July 1996.

■ Blond-haired and versatile, Neil Edmonds began at left-back and was introduced just prior to the Play-off matches in 1986–87. He was unable to dislodge seasoned campaigners Andy Barlow and Willie Donachie, and a loan

spell to Rochdale was made permanent. Edmonds found regular first-team football at Spotland and in 1988–89, operating in a midfield role, he scored eight goals in 34/5 matches.

EDWARDS, Paul Anthony

Left-winger.

Born: Manchester, 1 January 1980.
Career: Ashton United. Doncaster Rovers February 1998. Knutsford Town. Altrincham. Swindon Town August 2001. Wrexham July 2002. Blackpool July 2004. OLDHAM ATHLETIC August 2005. Port Vale June 2007.

■ After a bright start to his Athletic career, speedy and hard-working Paul Edwards was injured at Nottingham Forest in his second season and the knee ligament injury kept him out for almost three months. In the meantime, Simon Charlton and Chris Taylor became firmly established on Athletic's left side. Edwards made 69 appearances for Athletic but declined a new contract, opting to follow Craig Rocastle to Port Vale.

EDWARDS, Paul Francis

Defender

Born: Shaw, Lancashire, 7 October 1947.
Career: St Joseph's, Shaw. Chadderton Schoolboys. Manchester United amateur December 1963, professional February 1965. OLDHAM ATHLETIC loan September-October 1972, permanent March 1973, fee £15,000. Stockport County loan January 1977, permanent August 1978 to July 1980, fee £10,000. Ashton United.

■ The small cotton township of Shaw launched the career of Paul Edwards. While a pupil at St Joseph's RC School he was recommended for a trial with Manchester United and eventually made his first team bow at right-back on a close season tour of Australia. The tall, calm defender was capped by England Under-23s on three occasions and made 68 appearances for United before linking with Athletic, initially on loan. Four goals in his 11-match loan spell led to his permanent recruitment later that season. The skilful utility defender went on to complete in excess of 100 League appearances for Athletic, including 24 in the 1973–74 Third Division Championship season.

EDWARDS, Stephen Gerald

Full-back

Born: Birkenhead, 11 January 1958.

Career: Ellesmere Port Schoolboys. OLDHAM ATHLETIC associate schoolboy October 1973, apprentice June 1974, professional January 1976. Crewe Alexandra February 1983. Rochdale July 1984. Tranmere Rovers October 1984. Oswestry Town 1986. Fleetwood 1987. Northwich Victoria 1987. Mossley March 1990. Vauxhall GM, North West Counties League, 1990. Caernarfon Town 1991. Mold 1992–93.

■ In seven years as a professional with Athletic, Steve Edwards completed 89 senior matches. He captained both the youth and reserve teams before making his League debut aged 20. Originally a midfield player, he switched to full-back, but despite quite lengthy spells of first-team football in 1978–79 and 1981–82 he faced strong competition from the likes of Ronnie Blair, Nicky Sinclair and John Ryan.

ELLIS, Anthony Joseph

Forward

Born: Salford, 20 October 1964.
Career: Horwich RMI. Bolton Wanderers trial. Northwich Victoria 1986. OLDHAM ATHLETIC August 1986. Preston North End October 1987, fee £23,000. Stoke City December 1989, fee £250,000. Preston North End August 1992, fee £50,000 plus Graham Shaw. Blackpool July 1994, fee £165,000. Bury December 1997, fee £70,000. Stockport County February 1999,

fee £25,000. Rochdale November 1999. Burnley July 2001 to April 2002. Leigh RMI August 2002.

■ In the season that Athletic's new plastic pitch was unveiled, Tony Ellis was one of manager Joe Royle's early signings. A striker with good close control who could pass and shoot accurately, his potential was quite obvious although he had to leave Boundary Park to find regular first-team football. In a lengthy career he commanded some significant transfer fees, making 457/60 appearances for seven League clubs, and scoring 179 goals. In June 2007 he was recruited to the backroom staff at Rochdale, one of his former clubs.

EYRE, John Robert

Forward

Born: Hull, 9 October 1974.
Career: OLDHAM ATHLETIC associate schoolboy January 1989, trainee August 1991, professional July 1993. Scunthorpe United loan December 1994, permanent July 1995, fee £40,000. Hull City July 1999. OLDHAM ATHLETIC July 2001. North Ferriby United May 2005. Brigg Town.

■ In two separate spells with Athletic, eight years apart, John Eyre proved a versatile striker and midfielder, excellent in combination and with a good turn of pace. He made his Athletic debut from the bench at Chelsea in October 1993. A Darren Beckford goal was enough to secure the points, one of only nine Premier League victories during the

relegation season. A successful loan spell with Scunthorpe United was made permanent, and Eyre starred in their 1998–99 Third Division promotion season, scoring 15 goals in 41 League matches. Returning to Boundary Park after a two-year spell with Hull City, he added a further 98/20 League matches and 14 goals in a four-year stint that made full use of his extreme versatility.

EYRES, David

Winger

Born: Liverpool, 26 February 1964.
Career: Rhyl. Blackpool August 1989, fee £10,000. Burnley July 1993, fee £90,000. Preston North End October 1997, fee £80,000. OLDHAM ATHLETIC October 2000. Hyde United 2006. Mossley October 2006.

■ A late starter in League football, David Eyres was 25 years old when he signed for Blackpool. In what proved to be a highly successful career, the predominately left-footed wingman/striker assisted Blackpool to promotion from Division Four before former Blackpool manager Jimmy Mullen paid £90,000 to take him to Turf Moor. In a splendid first season Eyres scored 26 League and Cup goals and also scored in his third Play-off Final in four years as Burnley beat Stockport County 2–1 to win promotion to Division One. A third promotion followed with Preston North End, who won the Division Two Championship in 1999–2000. Joining Athletic on a free

transfer in October 2000, the 36-year-old flankman's arrival immediately lifted the side and, in his first full season, 16 goals in all competitions won him the sponsor's 'Player of the Season' award. Throughout his stay of almost six years at Boundary Park, Eyres' service from wide on the left was a feature of the team's attacking play. Finally released by manager Moore in May 2006 after 234 matches for Athletic, the 42-year-old winger signed off in typical fashion, rounding Scunthorpe United's goalkeeper to score in the 1–1 draw at Boundary Park that concluded season 2005–06.

FACEY, Delroy Michael

Forward

Born: Huddersfield, 22 April 1980.
Career: Huddersfield Town trainee, professional May 1997. Bolton Wanderers July 2002. Bradford City loan November 2002. Burnley loan February 2003. West Bromwich Albion January 2004, fee £100,000. Hull City July 2004. Huddersfield Town loan February 2005. OLDHAM ATHLETIC March 2005. Tranmere Rovers August 2005. Rotherham United August 2006. Gillingham June 2007. Wycombe Wanderers loan March 2008.

■ A transfer deadline day signing, powerful striker Delroy Facey found himself unable to dislodge the successful front partnership of Luke Beckett and Chris Killen and was released in late August of the following season.

FAIRCLOUGH, David

Forward

Born: Liverpool, 5 January 1957.
Career: Liverpool apprentice July 1973, professional January 1974. Toronto Blizzard, Canada, April–August 1982. Lucerne FC, Switzerland, July 1983. Manchester City trial February 1985. Norwich City March 1985. OLDHAM ATHLETIC August 1985. Rochdale July 1986. KSK Beveren, Belgium, August 1986. Tranmere Rovers June 1989. Wigan Athletic September 1990 to May 1991. Knowsley United.

■ England Under-21 International David Fairclough spent most of his season at Boundary Park in the reserves, his 16 goals helping them to

win the Championship of the Central League Division Two. In earlier days the flame-haired Liverpool 'Super-sub' scored 52 goals for the Reds and was a European and UEFA Cup winner. Since retiring, Fairclough has worked as a freelance journalist and in the insurance business.

FARMER, William Henry

Goalkeeper

Born: Guernsey, 24 November 1927.
Career: St Martin's, Guernsey. Nottingham Forest May 1951. Brush Sports, Loughborough, June 1957. OLDHAM ATHLETIC July 1957, fee £400. Worcester City July 1958. Coventry City trial August–September 1959. Corby Town 1959–60.

■ In six seasons with Nottingham Forest Bill Farmer appeared in 52 League matches. He joined the Latics, as a replacement for Derek Williams after appearing in eight matches during Forest's 1956–57 Second Division promotion campaign. Farmer endured a

torrid time in his five outings for Athletic, conceding 13 goals. He was replaced by David Teece, and did not reappear in the first team after September.

FAULKNER, Michael

Inside-forward

Born: Conisbrough, 3 January 1950.
Career: Sheffield United associate schoolboy December 1964, apprentice August 1965, professional December 1967. OLDHAM ATHLETIC July 1969. Morecambe March 1970. Gainsborough Trinity March 1971.

■ Mike Faulkner played in two of the three friendly matches in Athletic's pre-season Scottish tour of August 1969, scoring at Arbroath after coming off the bench. In 17/1 matches for the reserves, Faulkner scored 11 goals (including four in one match against Tranmere Rovers Reserves) but was released into non-League football without adding to his solitary first-team appearance in the 1–1 draw at Crewe Alexandra on 20 September 1969.

FAWLEY Ronald

Outside-left/Left-back

Born: Ashton-under-Lyne, 22 April 1927.
Died: Tameside, 1982.
Career: Ashton United. OLDHAM ATHLETIC amateur August 1950, professional June 1951. Northwich

Victoria 1958. Stalybridge Celtic 1960–62. Glossop 1962–63.

■ Local product Ronnie Fawley received a League baptism with the Latics while still on amateur forms. Lightweight and speedy, he revealed early promise on the left wing in 16 appearances before signing as a part-time professional in June 1951. An adaptable performer, Fawley proved equally at home after switching to left-back in his last two seasons.

FAY, James Albert

Half-back

Born: Southport, 29 March 1884.
Died: Southport, 4 March 1957.
Career: Chorley 1903. Oswaldtwistle Rovers May 1904. OLDHAM ATHLETIC May 1905. Bolton Wanderers September 1911, fee £750. Wartime guest and team manager of Southport Vulcan. Southport May 1921 to 1923. Hesketh Park FC as a reinstated amateur until 1925.

■ Jimmy Fay's first contract with Athletic, signed and witnessed on 13 May 1905, provided for wages of 30 shillings (£1.50) per week in the playing season plus travelling expenses. Three years later he was earning £4 per week in both the playing season and during the summer, reflecting the rapid advance of himself and the team in the intervening years. In six full seasons Fay was one of Athletic's most

valuable players, missing only one match, and this in Lancashire Combination days. A clever and consistent half-back, the greatest testimony to his versatility came in season 1909–10, when he was asked to play at inside-right and proved an instant success. By scoring 26 goals in 38 matches, he was largely instrumental in taking Athletic into the top flight as runners-up to Manchester City. During his lengthy stint as a Bolton Wanderer, he was appointed to the committee of the Players' Union. He was elected chairman in 1922 and secretary from 1929 until 1952.

FERGUSON, Charles

Defender

Born: Glasgow, 22 April 1930.
Career: Benburb Juniors. Heart of Midlothian August 1951. Hamilton Academical May 1953. Accrington Stanley May 1954. Rochdale September 1955, fee £500. OLDHAM ATHLETIC July 1959. Rossendale United player-coach August 1961.

■ A former Ayrshire miner, Charlie Ferguson began in England with Accrington Stanley. A move to Rochdale brought regular first-team football for the first time, and in four seasons at Spotland the fearless and robust defender appeared in 150 League matches, scoring three goals. He was Athletic's most consistent defender in his

first season, missing just one match, but in 1960–61, under new manager Jack Rowley, he lost his place after appearing in the first 12 League matches, 10 of which were lost.

FERGUSON, James Cameron Mars

Goalkeeper

Born: Glasgow, 20 February 1935.
Career: Dundee. Falkirk 1958. OLDHAM ATHLETIC May 1959. Crewe Alexandra August 1960. Darlington July 1962 to June 1963. Stenhousemuir.

■ Goalkeeper Jimmy Ferguson began with Dundee as understudy to Billy Brown, the Scottish international who later starred with Tottenham Hotspur. In one season at Boundary Park he placed himself in the firing line with great courage and no little skill, but his efforts alone were insufficient to prevent the side from a second successive re-election application to Division Four.

FERGUSON, John Theodore Hever

Outside-left

Born: Edinburgh, 14 June 1939.
Career: St Andrews United. OLDHAM ATHLETIC November 1956 to May 1958.

■ Recruited from Scottish junior ranks and given an early League debut at the age of 17, John Ferguson's fast-moving and direct wing play held much promise. Sadly, this was curtailed when he contracted meningitis just prior to Christmas 1958, and the illness brought about his premature retirement from the game.

FERGUSSON, William Alexander

Centre-forward

Born: Willenhall, 2 March 1897.
Died: Walsall, December 1986.
Career: Sunbeam Motor Works. OLDHAM ATHLETIC January 1923. Reading June 1924, fee £100. Rochdale June 1925. Rotherham United June 1926. Worcester City July 1927.

■ Billy Fergusson had netted 35 goals for Sunbeam Motor Works in the season that

Athletic signed him. He was given an early introduction into Division One and scored the only goal of the game against Blackburn Rovers in his second appearance, but made little further headway before joining Reading in June 1924. He later enjoyed a productive spell with Rochdale, scoring 19 goals in 21 matches in 1925–26.

FERRIER, Ronald Johnson

Inside-forward

Born: Cleethorpes, 26 April 1914.
Died: Cleethorpes, 11 October 1991.
Career: Grimsby Wanderers. Grimsby Town May 1933. Manchester United May 1935. OLDHAM ATHLETIC March 1938.

Wartime guest with Mossley, Wrexham, Grimsby Town, Southampton, Reading, Crystal Palace, West Ham United and Plymouth Argyle. Lincoln City August 1947. Grimsby Town Juniors player-coach November 1949. Lysaghts Sports, Scunthorpe, player-coach July 1950.

■ In the final peacetime season, 1938–39, Ron Ferrier was Athletic's leading scorer with 24 League and Cup goals in 34 matches. Taking into account his appearances for Athletic during wartime, he played in 116 matches and scored 66 goals. Sadly, when normal League football resumed in 1946–47 he made only intermittent appearances, his form seemingly lost. Ferrier scored seven goals for Manchester United reserves against Bury reserves in March 1936.

FIELDEN, Alwyn

Centre-forward

Born: Denshaw, near Oldham, 1920.
Career: Denshaw FC. Hurst January 1936. Manchester CWS. Droylsden. OLDHAM ATHLETIC amateur November 1938. Witton Albion August 1939.

■ Eighteen-year-old amateur centre-forward Alwyn Fielden made his bow as a late replacement for the injured Ron Ferrier in the New Year's Eve clash with local rivals Rochdale. Although finishing on the losing side in his solitary appearance, he had the satisfaction of scoring Athletic's goal in the 2–1 defeat.

FILLERY, Michael Christopher

Midfield

Born: Mitcham, 17 September 1960.
Career: Merton Schoolboys. Chelsea apprentice. Sutton United loan January 1976. Chelsea professional August 1978. Queen's Park Rangers August 1983, fee £200,000. Portsmouth July 1987. OLDHAM ATHLETIC October 1990, fee £30,000. Millwall loan March 1991. Torquay United loan September 1991. Crawley FC player-coach June 1992.

■ With a wealth of top-class experience when he joined Athletic, 30-year-old Mike Fillery was expected to give a touch of extra guile and variety in midfield. Sadly, however, he suffered a knee ligament injury 13 minutes into his debut for Athletic. He spent six weeks in plaster and was out of action until January 1991. In March 1991 he was loaned to Millwall and offered to them at £50,000, but a second loan spell at Torquay preceded his move into the Beazer Homes League, as player-coach of Crawley FC.

FINNEY, William Arthur

Centre-half

Born: Nottingham, 17 July 1901.
Died: Doncaster, 3 February 1976.
Career: Goldthorpe United. Wath Athletic 1921. Bury May 1923. OLDHAM ATHLETIC November 1929 to May 1932. Hereford United June 1933.

■ Former collier William Finney began with Bury but had to wait patiently for a place in the first team. He actually qualified for a benefit at Gigg Lane, despite figuring in only 36 matches. The total had risen to 70 before Athletic signed him, but again he was largely in reserve, making only two League appearances in his first season. An injury to club captain Seth King in 1931–32 eventually enabled Finney to establish a regular place. Although appearing slight and frail for his role as centre-half, he was a hard-fighting player who lasted the most strenuous game better than most.

FIRM, Neil John

Central-defender

Born: Bradford, 23 January 1958.
Career: Leeds United apprentice July 1974, professional January 1976. OLDHAM ATHLETIC loan March–May 1982. Peterborough United August 1982. Diss Town January 1986.

■ Neil Firm was signed on loan from Leeds United following Kenny Clements's cartilage injury in late season 1981–82. Less mobile than the unfortunate Clements, at 6ft 4in and 13st 7lb Firm nevertheless presented a formidable physical barrier. With Peterborough United he appeared in 71/1 League matches and scored three goals before an Achilles injury ended his senior career.

FITTON, Fred

Inside-forward

Born: Bury, 12 January 1905.
Died: Middleton, 1970.
Career: Adlington. Burnley May 1928. OLDHAM ATHLETIC amateur June, professional August 1930. Southend United November 1931, fee £150. Accrington Stanley July 1932. Rochdale November 1933. Nelson trial August 1934. Runcorn September 1938, manager November 1946.

■ A lithe inside-forward of some promise, Fred Fitton scored five goals in 10 senior appearances for Athletic and

was a regular marksman in the Central League side. After leaving Boundary Park, he proved to be a regular goalscorer throughout his career. With Accrington Stanley in 1932–33, he scored 24 goals in 42 matches. In non-League football he assisted Runcorn to the Championship of the Cheshire County League in 1939.

FITTON, John

Goalkeeper

Born: Royton, Oldham, 12 January 1951.
Career: Chadderton Juniors. OLDHAM ATHLETIC from school August 1966, professional October 1968. Skelmersdale United loan August 1972. Mossley October 1974. Chadderton loan 1976. Retired in

1981 but had a brief comeback with Chadderton that was ended by a back injury.

■ Fifteen-year-old goalkeeper John Fitton's first outing for Athletic was a painfully short one as he broke an arm within five minutes of the kick-off in a B Team fixture. He made his League debut at 18 years of age, but a three-match run as deputy for the injured Barry Gordine was the extent of his involvement at senior level. Fitton joined Mossley in 1974 and embarked on a seven-year, 350 plus appearances stint, which took in an FA Trophy Final appearance at Wembley in 1980.

FLAVELL, Frederick

Inside-forward

Born: Northwich, 5 September 1904.
Died: Cheshire, 10 December 1981.
Career: Northwich Victoria. Witton Albion. OLDHAM ATHLETIC amateur September, professional October 1930. Torquay United June 1932. Witton Albion November 1935.

■ The departure of Stewart Littlewood to Port Vale in March 1931 afforded Fred Flavell the opportunity to stake his claim for the centre-forward berth, but he failed to seize his opportunity. After two seasons of reserve team football, Flavell migrated South to Torquay United along with Matt Gray's brother, Alfred. At Plainmoor he scored 25 goals in 46 matches, and was a finalist in the Third Division South Cup in 1934.

FLEETWOOD, Thomas

Half-back

Born: Toxteth Park, 6 December 1888.
Died: Bolton, 1945.
Career: Hindley Central. Rochdale October 1908. Everton March 1911, fee £460. Wartime guest with Tranmere Rovers. OLDHAM ATHLETIC August 1923, fee £750. Chester September 1924.

■ Tom Fleetwood began as an inside-forward, but Everton lost little time in switching him to a half-back role. Tireless and enterprising, he gave splendid service in a 12-year stay at Goodison Park, appearing in 35 League matches in 1914–15 when Everton were Football League Champions. After 285 League and Cup appearances he joined the Latics and was immediately installed as captain. Sadly, he injured an ankle at Blackpool on his debut, was sidelined for six weeks, and thereafter failed to regain form and fitness.

FLEMING, Craig

Defender

Born: Calder, Halifax, 6 October 1971.
Career: Yorkshire Schoolboys. Halifax Town trainee, professional March 1990. OLDHAM ATHLETIC August 1991, fee £80,000 plus £70,000 after 40 appearances. Norwich City June 1997, fee £600,000. Wolverhampton Wanderers loan 19 January 2007. Rotherham United 31 January 2007. King's Lynn September 2007, retired March 2008.

■ A versatile defender, able to operate in a central role or at right full-back, Craig Fleming was Joe Royle's fourth close season capture in 1991, as Athletic prepared for their return to the top flight.

At 19 years of age he was probably considered one for the future, but in the event he quickly won a first-team place. At the end of the relegation season 1996–97, Norwich City paid £600,000 for his transfer, and in the 2006–07 season his outstanding service to the Canaries was rewarded with a richly deserved testimonial.

FLEMING, Craig Matthew

Forward

Born: Stockport, 1 December 1984.
Career: OLDHAM ATHLETIC School of Excellence 1997, trainee, released June 2004.

■ Two goals for the youth team in midweek earned Craig Fleming a place on the bench for Athletic's League trip to Blackpool on 26 January 2004. His 84th minute introduction as replacement for Scott Vernon made the 19-year-old forward the 15th player to make his League debut during the season. In his final year at trainee level he failed to win a professional contract and was released in the shake-up following the appointment of Brian Talbot as manager.

FLOYD, Peter

Goalkeeper

Born: Huncoat, near Accrington, 8 July 1899.
Died: Hyndburn, 1979.
Career: Huncoat Baptists FC. Accrington Stanley amateur, professional April 1921. Clitheroe 1925. Lancaster Town July 1926.

OLDHAM ATHLETIC May 1928. Lancaster Town 1929, retiring later the same year.

■ Ideally proportioned goalkeeper Peter Floyd played in 29 matches for Accrington Stanley in 1922–23. A spell in non-League football preceded his arrival at Boundary Park, Athletic signing him to replace Jack Prince as reserve goalkeeper. As deputy to Jack Hacking he was restricted to three senior appearances, all of them coming when Hacking was on international duty. A part-time professional throughout his career, Floyd was a miner who completed 50 years of service at Calder and Huncoat Collieries.

FLYNN, Michael Anthony

Defender

Born: Oldham, 23 February 1969.

Career: Oldham Schoolboys. OLDHAM ATHLETIC apprentice July 1985, professional February 1987. Norwich City December 1988, fee £100,000. Preston North End December 1989, fee £125,000. Stockport County March 1993, fee £125,000. Stoke City loan January 2002. Barnsley March 2002. Blackpool January 2003. Accrington Stanley September 2004. Hyde United November 2005. Stalybridge Celtic December 2006. Radcliffe Borough 2007–08.

■ A tall, uncompromising central defender, Mike Flynn made his Latics debut at 18 years of age. He was still only 19 when First Division Norwich City paid £100,000 for his services. Mike played in every League game for

Stockport County in their Division Two promotion season of 1996–97, and helped them reach the semi-finals of the Coca-Cola Cup. In a lengthy professional career Flynn clocked up 767 Football League appearances and scored 31 goals.

FORAN, Mark James

Defender

Born: Aldershot, 30 October 1973.
Career: Millwall trainee, professional November 1990. Sheffield United August 1993, fee £25,000. Rotherham United loan August 1994. Wycombe Wanderers loan August 1995. Peterborough United February 1996, fee £40,000. Lincoln City loan January 1997. OLDHAM ATHLETIC loan March 1997. Crewe Alexandra December 1997, fee £25,000. Bristol Rovers August 2000. Telford United August 2002. Northwich Victoria July 2003 to May 2006.

■ Towering central-defender Mark Foran's single substitute appearance for the Latics came in the relegation season 1996–97. He began with Millwall but made his first appearance at League level with Sheffield United. Despite association with nine League clubs, his total appearances, including substitutions, amounted to a modest 90.

FORBES, Terrell Dishan

Right full-back

Born: Southwark, 17 August 1981.
Career: West Ham United trainee, professional July 1999. AFC Bournemouth loan October 1999. Queen's Park Rangers

July 2001. Grimsby Town September 2004. OLDHAM ATHLETIC July 2005. Yeovil Town June 2006.

■ Versatile defender Terrell Forbes appeared at right full-back, wing-back and in central defence during his season at Boundary Park. Despite making 36 appearances during the campaign his form was patchy and with 12 months left on his contract he was released. Forbes was quickly fixed up when he reunited with his former Grimsby Town manager, Russell Slade, at Yeovil Town.

FORD, Kenneth

Outside-right

Born: Sheffield, 1 December 1940.
Career: Local junior football. Sheffield Wednesday professional March 1960. OLDHAM ATHLETIC June 1961 to June 1962, fee £100.

■ A cousin of David Ford, the England Under-23 international forward who also began with Sheffield Wednesday, Ken Ford was without League experience when signed by Athletic. The short, stocky wingman operated in the shadows of Bazley and Phoenix at Boundary Park and made only six first-team appearances. He was one of eight players released at the season's close.

FOSTER, Anthony Joseph

Midfield

Born: Dublin, 13 February 1949.
Career: Bolton Athletic, Dublin. Arsenal trial July 1965, professional February 1966. OLDHAM ATHLETIC trial August

1966, professional September 1966. St Patrick's Athletic October 1967.

■ The youngest son in a family of nine, Tony Foster worked in the sheet metal trade after leaving school. A Republic of Ireland Schoolboy international against England at Northampton in 1964, he was signed by Arsenal as a 16-year-old. He was released shortly after signing a professional form with the Gunners and was given trials by Athletic in their pre-season Irish tour. In the club's summer tour of Rhodesia and Malawi in 1967 he scored 11 goals in six matches, but failed to reproduce similar fireworks in Division Three and was released after an unhappy season in which his form fluctuated alarmingly.

FOSTER, Clifford Lake

Outside-left

Born: Rotherham, 1904.
Died: Rotherham, 8 January 1959.
Career: Scunthorpe & Lindsay United February 1923. Rotherham United March 1924. Bournemouth & Boscombe Athletic May 1925. Shirebrook March 1926. Morecambe September 1926. Manchester City April 1927. OLDHAM ATHLETIC May 1928. Halifax Town March 1929 to June 1930.

■ One of soccer's happy wanderers, reserve wingman Cliff Foster played only

once for Athletic, taking his career total to just 12 League matches, despite his association with four senior clubs. A move to Halifax Town afforded him more opportunities. Prior to his release in 1930 he totalled 31 League appearances and scored seven goals.

FOSTER, Robert

Goalkeeper

Born: Dean, near Bolton, 1911.
Career: Farnworth Standard. Burnley Reserves. Accrington Stanley amateur January 1932. Southampton May 1932. Wrexham June 1933. Bury August 1935. OLDHAM ATHLETIC September 1936. Mossley November 1937. Wartime guest

with Tranmere Rovers and Bolton Wanderers.

■ Bob Foster was running his newsagents business when Athletic offered him a month's trial as cover for injured reserve-team goalkeeper, Fred Collinge. Signed for the remainder of the season, Foster was given an early League debut and in his 11 outings proved a reliable second string to Lewis Caunce, exhibiting coolness under pressure and safe handling.

FOWEATHER, Vincent James

Inside-forward

Born: Hollinwood, Oldham, 1896.
Died: Oldham, 10 May 1966.
Career: Albert Mount FC. Crewe Alexandra 1919. OLDHAM ATHLETIC June 1920. Rochdale May 1922. Macclesfield Town April 1923. Eccles United trial October 1923. Stalybridge Celtic October 1923. Macclesfield Town August 1924. Lancaster Town August 1925.

■ Locally born Vincent Foweather's senior outings with Athletic all came in season 1920–21, and within a run of five consecutive First Division outings he scored in the 2–0 home win against Manchester City in February 1921. He left Athletic along with Richard Jones and Bill Bradbury, all taking the short journey to Rochdale. After retiring from the game he worked variously as a local

publican, managed the Savoy Billiard Hall for 20 years and latterly worked in the offices of Oldham Council.

FOX, Raymond

Outside-left

Born: Didsbury, Manchester, 13 December 1934.
Career: HM Forces football. OLDHAM ATHLETIC amateur August 1957 to April 1958.

■ For the opening fixture of 1957–58, the final season of Third Division North competition, Athletic manager Ted Goodier fielded five new players. Only one of them, centre-half Ian Muir, appeared regularly during the season, casting doubt on the manager's recruiting policies. Amateur wingman Ray Fox, who two months earlier had been demobilised after National Service, was discarded after a single outing in a season that saw no less than eight outside-lefts fielded.

FRANKS, Albert Edward S.

Outside-left

Born: Small Heath, Birmingham, 1892.
Career: Cradley Heath. OLDHAM ATHLETIC May 1912 to April 1913.

■ In 1911–12, his second season with Cradley Heath, Albert Franks scored 22 goals and was selected to represent Birmingham Juniors against Glasgow Juniors at Coventry. Shortly afterwards he arrived at Boundary Park. As deputy

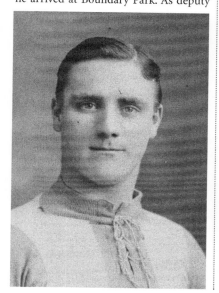

for Athletic's international wingman, Joe Donnachie, he made only one senior appearance but enjoyed a productive spell at reserve level, scoring nine goals in 44 matches.

FREEMAN, Reginald Fidelas Vincent

Full-back

Born: Birkenhead, 20 December 1897.
Died: Wickersley, near Rotherham, 4 August 1955.
Career: Wallasey Rovers. Harrowby 1918. Yorkshire Amateurs. Northern Nomads 1919. OLDHAM ATHLETIC January 1921. Middlesbrough April 1923, fee £4,000. Rotherham United August 1930, fee £150, player-manager January 1935, continuing as manager after retiring as a player. Sheffield United manager August 1952.

■ Reg Freeman made the transition from amateur ranks into Division One with surprising ease and was without a challenger for his position at Boundary Park, appearing in 93 consecutive

matches before injury broke the sequence. A gentlemanly full-back of style, grace, and outstanding ability, the club's ever-present financial problems brought about his transfer to Middlesbrough and Athletic dropped out of the top flight in the month following his departure. Freeman won a Second Division Championship medal with Middlesbrough in 1927 and in a lengthy association with Rotherham United was successful in guiding them to promotion from Division Three North after narrowly missing out three times running from 1947.

FRIZZELL, James Letson

Utility player

Born: Greenock, 16 February 1937.
Career: West of Scotland Schoolboys. Greenock Belaire 1952. Largs Thistle 1954. Greenock Morton 1955. OLDHAM ATHLETIC May 1960, fee £1,500, first-team coach September 1968, caretaker manager December 1969, manager March 1970 to June 1982. Manchester City assistant manager July 1983, manager October 1986, general manager May 1987, chief scout May 1994, stadium manager c. 2000 until May 2001.

■ Jimmy Frizzell's 22 years as player and then manager of the Latics began in 1960, and considering the modest transfer fee of £1,500 he can rightly be considered the club's all-time bargain buy. Initially a forceful, strong running inside-forward,

he was the club's leading scorer in 1961–62 with 24 goals. By the mid-1960s he had been successfully converted to wing-half, and later still to full-back. Appointed caretaker manager in late December 1969 following the departure of Jack Rowley, he appeared to be faced with a hopeless task as the team had won only four League matches. He nevertheless steered the team to nine wins and six draws and was given the job on a permanent basis in March 1970. Promotion from Division Four swiftly followed, plus the £70,000 prize for the Ford Sporting League trophy. Having lifted the Latics into Division Two in 1974 and consolidated their position at this level, he was sensationally dismissed. Over 6,000 spectators attended Frizzell's testimonial match – 2,000 more than the average League attendance for the season; proof, if any were needed, of his popularity with the Oldham sporting public.

FRYATT, James Edward

Centre-forward

Born: Swaythling, near Southampton, 2 September 1940.
Career: Moor End United Youth Club. Charlton Athletic October 1957. Southend United June 1960, fee £600. Bradford Park Avenue June 1963, fee £2,500. Southport March 1966, fee £4,000. Torquay United March 1967, fee £5,000. Stockport County October 1967, fee £7,000. Blackburn Rovers October 1968, fee £24,000. OLDHAM ATHLETIC February 1970, fee £8,000. Southport November 1971. Philadelphia Atoms, US, 1973 and again 1974. Stockport County September 1974. Torquay United December 1974. Chorley January–March 1975. Hartford Bi-Centennials, US, April–June 1975. Philadelphia Atoms, US, July–August 1975. Las Vegas Quicksilver, US, assistant manager 1977, later manager.

■ Centre-forward Jim Fryatt made a sensational start to his Athletic career. In the last two months of season 1969–70, the powerful and fearless marksman netted 11 goals in just 16 matches, including a four-goal blast against Chester on 28 March. Five goals in the opening four League matches of 1970–71 set the tone for a magical season in which

promotion from Division Four was secured, and the Ford Sporting League trophy won. Athletic probably never had a better pair of strikers in tandem than Jim Fryatt and David Shaw. Each played in 45 League matches in 1970–71, Fryatt scoring 24 goals and Shaw 23. Balding and with Dickensian sideboards, the strongly built Fryatt had a fierce shot with both feet, but his headwork was his strongest asset. Whether soaring at the far post or diving parallel to the ground to convert a low centre, his headed goals were the ones that remained in the memory.

FRYER, John Hilary

Centre-forward

Born: Manchester, 24 June 1924.
Died: Bury, March 2004.
Career: Goslings FC. Wartime guest with Dundee United. OLDHAM ATHLETIC May 1947. Wigan Athletic November 1948.

■ The Latics were Jack Fryer's first senior club, although he had guested for Dundee United while training at a naval establishment during World War Two. Noted for his opportunism near to goal, he nevertheless failed to retain his position as attack leader. His best individual performance came in the first away victory of the season, against Darlington on 27 September 1947, when he scored two goals in Athletic's emphatic 6–0 victory.

FUTCHER, Benjamin Paul

Central-defender

Born: Manchester, 20 February 1981.
Career: OLDHAM ATHLETIC amateur 1995, trainee July 1997, professional July 1999. Stalybridge Celtic loan August 2001, permanent January 2002. Doncaster Rovers March 2002. Lincoln City August 2002. Boston United July 2005. Grimsby Town January 2006. Peterborough United August 2006. Bury June 2007.

■ Ben Futcher was first associated with the Latics at 14 years of age, and even at that early stage he stood 6ft 2in tall and wore size 12 and a half boots. He first broke into the senior squad in season 1999–2000, but found it difficult to graduate beyond reserve team football. At the start of season 2000–01 he was loaned to Stalybridge Celtic (managed by his father, Paul), and when his Athletic contract was cancelled by mutual consent in January 2002 he signed for Stalybridge permanently. He has subsequently established himself in League football, proving skilful on the ball and totally dominant in the air. Ben's father, Paul, and uncle, Ron – the famous Futcher twins – starred for Athletic in the 1980s.

FUTCHER, Paul

Defender

Born: Chester, 25 September 1956.
Career: Chester apprentice July 1972, professional January 1974. Luton Town June 1974, fee £100,000. Manchester City June 1978, fee £350,000. OLDHAM ATHLETIC August 1980, fee £150,000. Derby County January 1983, fee £100,000. Barnsley March 1984, fee £30,000. Halifax Town July 1990. Grimsby Town loan January 1991. Darlington manager March–May 1995. Dundalk, Ireland, August 1995. Droylsden September 1995. Gresley Rovers joint manager (with Gary Birtles) November 1995. Southport player-manager June 1997. Stalybridge Celtic manager June 2001 to March 2002. Ashton United manager February to December 2005.

■ Seventeen-year-old Paul Futcher commanded a fee of £100,000 after just 20 League appearances with Chester, and his immense potential was fully realised in a career covering eight League clubs and a fraction short of 700 appearances. The winner of 11 England Under-21 caps, he narrowly failed to graduate to full international status. A cool and very competent defender with the ability to springboard counter-attacks with perceptive passing out of defence, his vision and assurance on the ball made him one of the best back four players to represent the Latics. He hails from a remarkable family of footballers, Paul's elder brother, Graham, played for Chester in the early 1970s, while twin brother, Ron, assisted Athletic between 1985–87. Paul's son, Ben, became the third family member to represent the Latics when he made his League debut in October 1999.

FUTCHER, Ronald

Forward

Born: Chester, 25 September 1956.
Career: Chester apprentice July 1972, professional January 1974. Luton Town July 1974. Minnesota Kicks, US, May–August 1976, May–August 1977 and May–August 1978. Manchester City August 1978, fee £75,000. Minnesota Kicks, US, April 1979. Portland Timbers, US, April–August 1982. Southampton trial January 1983. Tulsa Roughnecks, US, April–September 1983. NAC Breda, Holland. Tulsa Roughnecks May–September 1984. Barnsley December 1984. OLDHAM ATHLETIC July 1985, fee £15,000. Bradford City loan March 1987, permanent April 1987, fee £40,000. Port Vale August 1988. Burnley November 1989, fee £60,000. Crewe Alexandra August 1991 to May 1992. Droylsden October 1995.

■ Ron Futcher celebrated his Latics home debut with a goal after four minutes and added a second in a rousing 4–3 win against Shrewsbury Town. He proved a bargain signing and his ratio – close to a goal every other game – made him a highly effective, if not very elegant, attack leader. Ron Futcher's League career took in nine clubs and he scored 149 goals in 364/33 appearances.

GANNON, John Spencer

Midfield

Born: Wimbledon, 18 December 1966.
Career: Wimbledon apprentice, professional December 1984. Crewe Alexandra loan December 1986. Sheffield United February 1989. Middlesbrough loan November 1993. OLDHAM ATHLETIC March 1996 to April 1997.

■ John Gannon's Sheffield United career began with promotions in successive seasons to take the Blades from Division Three to Division One. He also enjoyed three seasons in the Premier League between 1991–94. He nevertheless spent an unrewarding year at Boundary Park. A knee operation in the summer of 1996 kept him out until October, and the following April he was released after making just one League appearance during the relegation season. Since retiring as a player, Gannon has worked as assistant manager at Mansfield Town, and joined Notts County in a similar capacity in June 2006. He was appointed first-team coach by Leeds United in November 2007, but a change of management in late January 2008 resulted in his dismissal.

GARDNER, Samuel Frederick

Centre-forward

Born: Pendleton, 1915.
Career: McMahon's FC (Manchester League). OLDHAM ATHLETIC amateur September 1937, professional November 1937 to May 1938.

■ Despite an outstanding goalscoring record at reserve level, 25 goals in 28 Lancashire Combination matches in 1937–38, Sam Gardner was restricted to two senior appearances in the Northern Section Cup ties against Southport. A 1–1 draw at Boundary Park on 15 March was followed on 29 March 1938 by the replay, which Athletic lost 3–0. Two months later, Gardner was one of seven professionals given free transfers.

GARDNER, Stephen David

Midfield

Born: Hemsworth, 7 October 1958.
Career: Barnsley Schoolboys. Ipswich Town apprentice July, professional October 1975. OLDHAM ATHLETIC December 1977, fee £10,000. Karlskrona, Sweden, April 1981.

■ Steve Gardner won England schoolboy honours but was without League experience when he joined Athletic at 19 years of age. He settled well into Athletic's midfield initially but faded from the scene after the signing of Ged Keegan from Manchester City. In the two seasons prior to his move to Sweden, Gardner appeared almost exclusively at reserve level.

GARLAND, Ronald

Centre-forward

Born: Middlesbrough, 28 July 1931.
Died: Oldham, 31 March 1989.
Career: South Bank St Peter's. OLDHAM ATHLETIC amateur September 1951,

professional December 1951. Mossley loan March 1956, permanent 1956. Stalybridge Celtic February 1957.

■ Flame-haired attack leader Ronnie Garland lost two years of his career to National Service, which was spent mainly in Korea. He played football after the war had ended and was a member of the army team that toured Japan. In season 1955–56 he was given a six-match run at centre-forward in a deeper lying role, and initial victories against Hartlepools United and Crewe Alexandra resulted. It was not, however, a position that suited him, as he was essentially a bustling leader who employed direct methods.

GARNETT, Shaun Maurice

Central-defender

Born: Wallasey, 22 November 1969.
Career: Tranmere Rovers associate schoolboy, trainee June 1986, professional June 1988. Chester City loan October 1992. Preston North End loan December 1992. Wigan Athletic loan February 1993. Swansea City March 1996, fee £200,000. OLDHAM ATHLETIC September 1996, fee £150,000. Halifax Town October 2002. Morecambe loan November 2003, permanent December 2003, released April 2004. Tranmere Rovers youth team manager.

■ A fierce tackling, uncompromising defender, Shaun Garnett lived only a stone's throw from Tranmere Rovers's ground and he joined them straight from school. His 12 years at Prenton Park included three Wembley appearances, two in successive Play-off Finals and one in the Final of the Leyland DAF Cup against Bristol Rovers in May 1990. Briefly associated with Swansea City, who

were relegated two months after he joined them, he moved up two divisions when recruited by the Latics. Sadly, a serious cruciate ligament injury curtailed Garnett's excellent period of service in the heart of Athletic's defence.

GARWOOD, Colin Arthur

Forward

Born: Heacham, Norfolk, 29 June 1949.
Career: Peterborough United amateur September 1966, professional July 1967. OLDHAM ATHLETIC July 1971, fee £12,000. Huddersfield Town December 1974, fee £15,000 plus Les Chapman. Colchester United February 1976, fee £5,000. Portsmouth March 1978, fee £25,000. Aldershot February 1980 to 1982 fee £54,000. King's Lynn. Boston United 1983.

■ England Youth international Colin Garwood maintained an excellent scoring ratio throughout 15 seasons of League football, amassing 159 goals in 425 League appearances. He began at the age of 18 and scored on his debut for Peterborough United. After a slow start at Boundary Park, his form and confidence improved greatly. In the 1973–74 Third Division Championship side, his 16 League goals came in just 28 matches and included seven in seven matches in April, as the title push gathered momentum.

GAYLE, Andrew Keith

Winger

Born: Manchester, 17 September 1970.
Career: OLDHAM ATHLETIC trainee July 1987, professional July 1989. Crewe Alexandra February 1990. Bury August 1990 to 1991. Horwich RMI. Naxxar Lions,

Malta, trial October 1991. Horwich RMI November 1991. Stalybridge Celtic. Accrington Stanley. Horwich RMI. Ashton United. Flixton. Witton Albion. Chorley. Oldham Town. Nantwich Town. Rossendale United. St Helens Town. Mossley 2000.

■ Andy Gayle's League career consisted of just two substitute appearances: one for the Latics and one for Crewe Alexandra. His Latics debut came in the final match of season 1988–89, a 2–2 draw against Swindon Town. He subsequently gathered no moss in non-League football!

GAYNOR, Leonard Alfred

Inside-forward

Born: Greasley, Notts, 22 September 1925. Career: Gilbrook Villa 1944. Ilkeston Town 1945. Brinsley 1946. Eastwood Colliery 1947. Hull City April 1948. Bournemouth & Boscombe Athletic June 1951. Southampton March 1954. Aldershot February 1955. OLDHAM ATHLETIC July 1957, in exchange for Trevor Lawless plus a fee. Yeovil Town January 1958. Cambridge City.

■ A constructive inside-forward with wide experience, Len Gaynor had captained Aldershot for two years prior to his move to Boundary Park. The veteran playmaker had an unhappy sojourn, and was dropped after playing in the first four matches. He was then one of 10 players sidelined by a severe 'flu virus.

GEE, Arthur

Inside-forward

Born: Earlestown near Warrington, 1892. Died: Werneth, Oldham, 6 August 1959. Career: Earlestown FC amateur 1908, professional June 1911. OLDHAM ATHLETIC June 1911, fee £30. Wartime guest with Liverpool and Everton. Stalybridge Celtic July 1921. Rochdale May 1922. Ashton National April 1923. Crewe Alexandra January 1924. Nuneaton Town. Ferranti's FC May 1924. Mossley September 1926. Witton Albion October 1927. Platt Brothers, Oldham, manager 1946–47.

■ Arthur Gee was one of Athletic's youngest professionals in their early days as a Football League club. An outstanding junior, he progressed through the ranks at Boundary Park,

establishing himself at senior level in 1912–13. Although small and lightly built, he was a continual source of anxiety to the opposition, quick in thought and action and with some remarkable goals to his credit. Either side of World War One he scored 42 League goals in 112 matches. During the war he worked as a riveter at Liverpool docks but was able to play fairly frequently for Athletic in wartime football, scoring a further 46 goals in 119 matches.

GEMMELL, Eric

Centre-forward

Born: Prestwich, Manchester, 7 April 1921.
Died: Cambridge, 20 February 2008.
Career: Manchester United amateur April 1941. Goslings FC 1945. Manchester City March 1946. Ashton United loan 1946–47. OLDHAM ATHLETIC June 1947. Crewe Alexandra February 1954. Rochdale September 1954. Buxton April 1956. Nantile Vale, Wales, player-manager July 1960.

■ Centre-forward Eric Gemmell signed an amateur form with Manchester United at 20 years of age, but crossed the city to sign his first professional form with Manchester City after leaving the navy. Tall and lithe and with a prematurely receding blond hairline, Gemmell was an excellent ball-player who held his line together in masterly fashion. In January 1952 in a League match against Chester on a snowbound Boundary Park he scored seven goals (six in succession) in a resounding 11–2 win. It was the best individual scoring performance in a League match since April 1936, when Joe Payne scored 10 for

Luton Town against Bristol Rovers. For many years Gemmell held Athletic's record of 109 goals in League matches, a total finally overtaken in April 1989 by Roger Palmer. Although approaching the veteran stage and increasingly troubled by injuries, Gemmell's 23 League goals in just 27 League matches was a key element in the Championship winning season of 1952–53. In addition to his talents as a footballer, Gemmell spent summer months as a professional with the Levenshulme Cricket Club.

GERRARD, Paul William

Goalkeeper

Born: Heywood, Lancashire, 22 January 1973.
Career: OLDHAM ATHLETIC associate schoolboy February 1987, trainee August 1989, professional November 1991. Everton July 1996, fee £1 million. Oxford United loan December 1998. Ipswich Town loan November 2002. Sheffield United loan August 2003. Nottingham Forest March 2004. Sheffield United September 2006. Blackpool loan January–May 2008.

■ Paul Gerrard graduated through Athletic's youth system to become an England Under-21 player with the outstanding record of 13 clean sheets in 18 matches. Tall, brave, excellent in the air and an accomplished shot stopper, his career was initially plagued by knee injuries and he underwent operations on both following dislocation problems. Linked with Everton long before his £1 million transfer became a reality, he spent long periods as deputy to Neville Southall and later Thomas Myhre. Towards the end of his Nottingham

Forest spell in February 2006, a return to Boundary Park ended painfully, a knee injury sustained in the match resulted in a lengthy lay-off.

GIDDINGS, Stuart James

Full-back

Born: Coventry, 27 March 1986.
Career: Coventry City trainee, professional June 2004. OLDHAM ATHLETIC loan August 2007.

■ England Youth international left-back Stuart Giddings had been restricted to just three games in two seasons at Coventry City, having had two knee operations and hamstring problems. Despite the setbacks, Giddings had recently been handed a new contract by the Sky Blues. Loaned to Athletic by their former manager Ian Dowie, Giddings was straight into action in the season's opening victory against eventual champions Swansea City. He gave further steady performances against Mansfield Town and Carlisle United before suffering an ankle injury which opened the way for 18-year-old Ryan Bertrand to take over the left-back position.

GILL, Wayne John

Midfield

Born: Chorley, 28 November 1975.
Career: Blackburn Rovers trainee, professional July 1994. Dundee United loan May 1998. Blackpool March 2000. Tranmere Rovers July 2000. OLDHAM ATHLETIC October 2001, fee £70,000. Grimsby Town trial February 2003. Rochdale trial July 2003. Scarborough August 2003. Droylsden 2004.

■ Wayne Gill's time with Athletic was cruelly curtailed by injuries. An ankle injury sustained in his third appearance kept him out until March 2002, and at this point he was injured again in a reserve team match and he did not reappear at senior level. The attacking midfielder scored seven goals in just 12 League matches for Blackpool, but his career figures were a modest 22/9 appearances and nine goals. After retiring, Gill studied physiotherapy at Salford University and went back into the game when he was appointed physiotherapist to Lancaster City.

GILLESPIE, Robert

Inside-forward

Born: Manchester, 20 October 1904.
Died: Manchester, 1971.
Career: Newton Heath Loco. OLDHAM ATHLETIC amateur August, professional October 1924. Luton Town July 1926. Port Vale May 1927. Wrexham September 1930. Northwich Victoria October 1930. Barrow August 1931 to June 1932. Boston Town September 1933. Nelson August 1934. Brierley Hill Alliance July 1935. Ashton National March 1936.

■ An impressive display for Newton Heath Loco in the Oldham Charity Cup Final at Boundary Park earned Bob Gillespie his chance in League football. A dapper, hard working little inside-forward with neat ball control, he made his League debut while still an amateur but was quickly rewarded with a professional contract. Quite lengthy spells of first-team football in his first season came to an abrupt end when he

was crowded out by new signings Pynegar, Ormston and Horace Barnes.

GLENNIE, James

Full-back

Born: Aberdeen 1905.
Career: Aberdeen Park Vale. Accrington Stanley trial 30 September to 4 October 1924. Burnley trial 7 October 1924. OLDHAM ATHLETIC professional 11 October 1924. Scunthorpe & Lindsay United August 1925.

■ James Glennie declined Accrington Stanley's terms following a week's trial, and then failed to impress in a trial with Burnley's Midweek League team. Arriving at Boundary Park later in the same week he was quickly fixed up, but the consistency of Athletic's full-backs, Sammy Wynne and Harry Grundy, restricted Glennie to a solitary League appearance.

GLOMBARD, Luigi

Forward

Born: Paris, France, 21 August 1984.
Career: Nantes, France. Cardiff City July 2006. Leicester City loan January 2007. OLDHAM ATHLETIC March 2007. Grenoble Foot 38, France, May 2007.

■ Athletic only just completed the paperwork to beat the season's transfer deadline when they recruited Luigi Glombard on loan from Cardiff City. In jocular mood, the Latics' website ran an April fool story that his signing had breached international regulations and an 18-point deduction had been enforced – a little heartless by website manager Stuart Vose, as if supporting the Latics was not stressful enough!

GOODFELLOW, Sydney

Half-back

Born: Wolstanton, Staffordshire, 6 June 1915.

Career: Silverdale FC. Hanley FC. Port Vale amateur, signing professional November 1936. Glentoran, Ireland, July 1937. Rochdale May 1938. Chesterfield April 1939, fee £595 plus Arthur Richardson. Doncaster Rovers May 1948. OLDHAM ATHLETIC September 1950, fee £750. Accrington Stanley June 1952. Wellington Town August 1953. Stafford Rangers trial December 1953. Oswestry Town March–May 1954.

■ A member of the Doncaster Rovers side that won the Championship of the Third Division North in 1950, Syd Goodfellow arrived at Boundary Park in the week following manager Billy Wootton's resignation. Athletic had sustained six defeats in the opening eight matches of 1950–51 but the craggy wing-half immediately stiffened the middle line, and remained a regular under new player-manager George Hardwick.

GOODIER, Edward

Half-back

Born: Little Hulton, 15 October 1902.
Died: Farnworth, 4 November 1967.
Career: Brookhouse United. Bolton Wanderers amateur May 1921. Huddersfield Town May 1922. Lancaster Town August 1924. OLDHAM ATHLETIC June 1925. Queen's Park Rangers November 1931, together with Leslie Adlam for a combined fee of £1,500. Watford June 1935, fee £1,000. Crewe Alexandra June 1936. Rochdale June 1937, appointed player-manager September 1938. Birmingham manager November 1944 to May 1945. Wigan Athletic manager June 1952. OLDHAM ATHLETIC manager May 1956 to June 1958.

■ A blond-haired six-footer who took only size five in football boots, Ted Goodier captained Lancaster Town for a season before joining Athletic. He had to wait patiently for a first-team place, eventually establishing himself after Jimmy Naylor was transferred to Huddersfield Town. Goodier missed only four matches in 1929–30, when Athletic finished third in Division Two and posted their record Boundary Park attendance of 46,471 for the FA Cup fourth-round tie against Sheffield Wednesday. The Latics had progressed to round four by beating Wolverhampton Wanderers, Goodier scoring the only goal of the game with virtually the last kick of the match.

GOODWIN, Leslie

Outside-left

Born: Ardwick, Manchester, 30 April 1924.
Died: Workington, 20 December 2002.
Career: Haughton Green. Blackpool amateur. OLDHAM ATHLETIC August 1944. Southport July 1947, retired due to injury July 1949.

■ A speedy and determined wingman despite his lightweight build, Leslie Goodwin began with Athletic during wartime and played in 57 regional matches and scored four goals. He was one of 10 forwards retained by Athletic in June 1946, but was restricted to just seven late-season appearances before joining Southport in the close season. After just 16 matches and two goals, a combination of ill health and a groin injury terminated his career.

GOODWIN, William

Full-back

Born: Mold, Wales, 16 January 1892.
Died: Middleton, 1972.
Career: Mold Town. Bangor College. Holywell FC. Wrexham. OLDHAM ATHLETIC amateur July 1913, professional July 1914. Wartime guest with Sheffield United August 1915. Crewe Alexandra May

1921. *OLDHAM ATHLETIC June 1925. Congleton Town April 1926. Mossley July 1928 to February 1930.*

■ Wales Amateur and Victory International Billy Goodwin was a powerfully built and speedy full-back. He was able to match most wingmen for speed, recording 11 seconds in the 100-yards sprint in 1919. During World War One he served in Italy with the Royal Welsh Fusiliers. A schoolteacher by profession, he returned to Boundary Park for a second spell in 1925 but made only a further three senior appearances.

GORAM, Andrew Lewis

Goalkeeper

Born: Bury, 13 April 1964.
Career: Bury and Manchester Schoolboys. West Bromwich Albion apprentice June 1980. OLDHAM ATHLETIC August 1981. Hibernian October 1987, fee £325,000. Rangers June 1991, fee £1 million. Notts County non-contract 3 September 1998. Sheffield United 7 September 1998. Motherwell January 1999. Manchester United March 2001, fee £100,000. Boreham Wood July 2001. Hamilton Academical trial August 2001. Blackpool trial. Coventry City September 2001 to February 2002. OLDHAM ATHLETIC March 2002. Motherwell goalkeeping coach July 2003. Queen of the South until July 2003.

■ Andy Goram was born in Lancashire but qualified for Scotland by parentage. His father, Lewis Goram, was Bury's goalkeeper from 1950 to 1956. An extremely agile and confident goalkeeper, Goram became the third Latics player to be capped by Scotland, and the first World Cup player when selected for the 1986 Finals in Mexico. In his second season at Boundary Park he became first choice and was named Player of the Year by the Latics' supporters' club. He helped Athletic to the brink of Division One in 1986–87, but despite the club's best defensive performance since season 1910–11, they lost out in the Play-off stage to Leeds United. Early in the following season he was transferred to Hibernian for a £325,000 fee. In the summer of 1989, the multi-talented Goram became a double international when he represented Scotland at cricket in a NatWest Trophy

match against Yorkshire. A £1 million fee took him to Rangers in June 1991, and the following year he won his 25th Scotland cap and was awarded a silver medal to mark the milestone. Seven seasons of outstanding success with Rangers included five Scottish League Championship medals, but his international career ended in controversial circumstances in 1998. He walked out of the Scotland camp in New Jersey, USA, during warm-up preparations for the World Cup Finals in France, blaming media intrusion into his private life. After an absence of 15 years he returned to assist Athletic during an injury crisis but perhaps wished that he had not – Cardiff City inflicting the Latics' worst ever defeat at Boundary Park by 7–1.

GORDINE, Barry

Goalkeeper

Born: Bethnal Green, London, 1 September 1948.
Career: Bexley United 1964. Gravesend & Northfleet January 1967. Sheffield United amateur November 1967, professional June 1968. OLDHAM ATHLETIC loan December 1968, permanent May 1969, fee £3,000. Southend United August 1971. Brentford October 1974.

■ Despite being short in stature for his position, Barry Gordine was an extremely agile last line of defence, while his coolness under pressure inspired confidence in his co-defenders. Following a lengthy loan spell, his signing was made permanent in May 1969, and in his final season at Boundary Park he appeared in 17 matches in the 1970–71 promotion season.

GORTON, Andrew William

Goalkeeper

Born: Salford, 23 September 1966.
Career: OLDHAM ATHLETIC amateur June 1983, professional July 1985. Stockport County loan December 1986 to February 1987. Tranmere Rovers loan May 1988. Stockport County August 1988, fee £15,000. Lincoln City August 1989, fee £15,000. Glossop August 1990, fee £10,000. OLDHAM ATHLETIC February to March 1991, fee £3,000. Crewe Alexandra non-contract April 1991. Witton Albion September 1991. Mossley loan October 1991. Bury non-contract July 1992, professional October 1992. Altrincham loan March to May 1993. Bury contract cancelled October 1993.

■ Opportunity knocked for Andy Gorton following Athletic's sale of their Scotland international goalkeeper Andy Goram to Hibernian in October 1987. The young stand-in looked a worthy successor, handling well and confidently while commanding his area. Sadly, his temperament did not match his talent, off-field indiscretions resulted in him being placed on the transfer list in April 1988. Gorton was offered a second opportunity in February 1991, but within a month his contract was cancelled, following allegations of drink driving and an arson charge.

GOUGH, Harold

Goalkeeper

Born: Newbold, near Chesterfield, 31 December 1890.
Died: Castleford, 1970.

Career: Castleford Town. Bradford Park Avenue March 1910. Castleford Town August 1911. Sheffield United April 1913, fee £40. Wartime guest with Leeds City and Hibernian. Castleford Town January 1925. Harrogate October 1926. OLDHAM ATHLETIC February 1927, fee £450. Bolton Wanderers December 1927, fee £25. Torquay United June 1928, retired due to injury in 1930.

■ England international goalkeeper Harold Gough had been out of League football for three years when Athletic signed him, and was well into the veteran stage, having made his League debut in season 1910–11. Signed to replace Welsh International Bert Gray, it was Jack Hacking who won the first-team jersey after Gough conceded 14 goals in four matches. Gough was a member of the Sheffield United team that won the FA Cup in 1915. After leaving Boundary Park he assisted Bolton Wanderers briefly before spending a further two seasons with Torquay United, in the course of which he recorded his 300th League outing.

GRABBAN, Lewis James

Forward

Born: Croydon, 12 January 1988.
Career: Crystal Palace trainee, professional July 2006. OLDHAM ATHLETIC loan August–October 2006. Motherwell loan August 2007. Millwall January 2008, fee £150,000.

■ Recruited on loan by Athletic in mid-August 2006, teenage striker Lewis Grabban injected some much-needed pace into Athletic's attack. Associated with Crystal Palace from the age of 13, his senior experience was limited to two Carling Cup outings but at youth and reserve team level he scored in excess of 50 goals. After two early season starts, Grabban spent much of his second month at Boundary Park on the substitutes' bench and was recalled by Palace due to his lack of first-team action.

GRAHAM, Richard Ean

Defender/Midfield

Born: Dewsbury, 28 November 1974.
Career: Tadcaster FC. Charwell Lions,

Leeds. OLDHAM ATHLETIC trainee August 1991, professional July 1993, retired due to knee injury June 2000.

■ Republic of Ireland Under-21 international Richard Graham made his Athletic debut in the Premier League at 19, and during a lengthy career at Boundary Park formed excellent central defensive pairings with Steve Redmond and Doug Hodgson. Injured shortly after making his debut and out for four months, he was subsequently to spend longer spells on the sidelines, and his cruel luck with injuries finally curtailed his career at the early age of 26. Graham nevertheless recorded commendable career totals of 174 senior appearances and 15 goals.

GRAINGER, Dennis

Outside-left

Born: Royston, Barnsley, 5 March 1920.
Died: Duckmanton, near Chesterfield, 6 May 1986.
Career: South Kirby. Southport amateur August 1937, professional October 1938. Wartime guest with Doncaster Rovers, Millwall, Walsall, Rotherham United, Lincoln City and Sheffield United. Leeds United September 1945, fee £1,000. Wrexham November 1947. OLDHAM ATHLETIC June 1951, in part-exchange for Bill Jessop. Bangor City August 1952. Flint Town August 1953.

■ Despite his previous and quite substantial experience, Dennis Grainger failed to establish himself at Boundary Park, with Bill Ormond dominating the left-wing position in a potent attack that recorded 90 League goals during the season. Dennis Grainger's brother Jack

played for Southport, and three footballing cousins included two England Internationals – Colin (Sheffield United, Sunderland and England), Jack (Rotherham United and Lincoln City) and Edwin Holliday (Middlesbrough and England).

GRANT, Anthony Paul Shaun Andrew Daure

Midfield

Born: Lambeth, 4 June 1987.
Career: Chelsea from the age of nine, trainee, professional February 2005. OLDHAM ATHLETIC loan January 2006. Wycombe Wanderers season-long loan July 2006. Luton Town loan November 2007 to January 2008.

■ Perhaps it was the climate change from London to Oldham, but on-loan midfielder Anthony Grant immediately succumbed to a bout of flu that reduced his opportunities during a one-month loan deal from Chelsea. In the briefest of stays at Boundary Park, Grant showed undoubted pedigree. A holding central midfielder with a cultured style, the England Under-19 international continued to enhance his reputation during a season-long loan with Wycombe Wanderers in 2006–07.

GRANT, Lee Anderson

Goalkeeper

Born: Hemel Hempstead, 27 January 1983.

Career: Derby County trainee 2000, signing professional February 2001. Burnley loan November 2005. OLDHAM ATHLETIC loan January to May 2006. Sheffield Wednesday July 2007.

■ Despite having lost his senior place at Derby County and fallen to third choice, England Under-21 goalkeeper Lee Grant was a key element in the Latics' late-season push towards the Play-offs in 2005–06. After replacing Chris Day in Athletic's goal he almost immediately recorded five clean sheets, a feat last achieved by Andy Goram in the early weeks of season 1986–87.

GRAY, Albert

Goalkeeper

Born: Tredegar, Wales, 23 September 1900. Died: Cleveleys, near Blackpool, 16 December 1969. Career: Ebbw Vale 1921. OLDHAM ATHLETIC May 1923. Manchester City January 1927, fee £2,250. Manchester Central loan August 1929. Coventry City August 1930. Tranmere Rovers June 1931. Chester June 1936. Waterford, Ireland, September 1938. Congleton Town 1938–39.

■ For many years Athletic's most capped player (nine of his 24 awards came while at Boundary Park), Bert Gray was first capped in 1924, when he was reserve to Howard Matthews in Athletic's goal and had only played in two League matches. Nevertheless, he helped Wales to win the Home International Championship, conceding only one goal in the three matches played. At 6ft 3in Gray combined reach, agility and courage. He

completed 101 appearances for Athletic before joining Manchester City, where he was a Second Division Championship winner in season 1927–28. Gray was also an excellent golfer and three times winner of the Merseyside Footballers' Golf Championship.

GRAY, Andrew David

Midfield

Born: Harrogate, 15 November 1977. Career: Leeds United trainee, professional July 1995. Bury loan December 1997. Nottingham Forest September 1998, fee £175,000. Preston North End loan February 1999. OLDHAM ATHLETIC loan March 1999. Bradford City August 2002. Sheffield United February 2004. Sunderland August 2005, fee £1.1 million. Burnley March 2006, fee £750,000. Charlton Athletic January 2008.

■ The son of Frank Gray, the Scottish international left-back, Andy followed in his father's footsteps by beginning with Leeds United and then being transferred to Nottingham Forest. He joined Athletic on a one-month loan around the Easter period of 1999 with the club in the midst of a crisis. His debut at Wycombe came in what was described as the season's worst performance, and in his four outings he struggled to make an impression in a side that narrowly avoided relegation to Division Three. Andy's uncle, Scottish international Eddie Gray, played for and managed Leeds United.

GRAY, Matthew

Inside-forward/Half-back

Born: Westhoughton, 18 April 1907. Died: Oldham, 18 September 1985. Career: Hindley Green Athletic. Tranmere Rovers amateur. Atherton FC September 1927. OLDHAM ATHLETIC May 1928 to 1945.

■ Matt Gray gave Athletic many years of yeoman service, initially in the forward line and later at centre-half. When any position in the side presented a problem, Matt Gray could be relied upon to provide the solution. He was awarded a well-deserved benefit match in April 1937. Seven of the Latics' 1929–30 side played for the 'Old Boys XI' who lost 3–1 to Matt Gray's XI, with 5,509 spectators attending

the match. Matt's brother, Alfred, was also on the Latics' books but did not appear in the first team, though he did sample League action with Torquay United and Lincoln City in the 1930s.

GREAVES, Ian Denzil

Full-back

Born: Shaw, near Oldham, 26 May 1932. Career: St Joseph's, Shaw. OLDHAM ATHLETIC trial. Buxton United amateur 1949. Manchester United May 1953. Lincoln City December 1960. OLDHAM ATHLETIC May 1961, fee £2,000. Altrincham June 1963. Northern Rhodesia national coach May 1964. Huddersfield Town coach August 1964, manager June 1968 to June 1974. Bolton Wanderers assistant manager August 1974, manager October 1974 to January 1980. Hereford United assistant manager July to December 1980. Oxford United manager December 1980 to February 1982. Wolverhampton Wanderers manager February to August 1982. Mansfield Town manager January 1983 to February 1989.

■ A tall, fair-haired full-back, Ian Greaves first came to prominence at Old Trafford in an extended spell of first-team duty during the closing stages of season 1955–56, when 10 wins and four draws helped Manchester United to clinch the League Championship. Shortly after the Munich disaster, he featured in the FA Cup Final against Bolton Wanderers, collecting a runners-up medal. After his playing career ended, Greaves had an outstanding career in management, winning the Second Division Championship with Huddersfield Town in 1969–70, and with Bolton Wanderers in 1977–78. He also

took Mansfield Town to promotion from Division Four in 1985–86 and to Wembley in May 1987, when they won the Freight Rover Trophy Final against Bristol Rovers.

GREEN, Harry

Outside-right

Born: Sheffield 5 August 1907.
Died: Sheffield, 1980.
Career: Sheffield junior football. OLDHAM ATHLETIC November 1928. Mexborough March 1929. Leeds United April 1930. Bristol City May 1934. York City June 1935. Frickley Colliery March 1937.

■ A former steel-foundry worker, Harry Green was a tricky wingman despite his light build and lack of inches. He played in only one first team match for Athletic and this coincided with the worst defeat of the season, a 6–0 defeat at Bristol City. Season 1935–36 with York City proved to

be the high point of his career, the diminutive wingman scoring eight goals in 43 League and Cup matches.

GREEN, Ian

Goalkeeper

Career: OLDHAM ATHLETIC trainee July 1977 to May 1979.

■ Ian Green's debut was of 10 minute's duration, when he replaced broken leg victim John Platt after 80 minutes of the Anglo-Scottish Cup tie against Sheffield United on 5 August 1978. Athletic won 1–0 and Green held the position for the visit of Sunderland three days later, although he had to take a day off from his full-time job as a brewery storekeeper to play in the game. The rookie goalkeeper performed with great credit in the 2–1 win but Peter McDonnell played in all the subsequent rounds including both legs of the Final, won by Burnley 2–1 on aggregate. In the Sir Fred Pontin Gold Cup six-a-side competition in the same month Athletic reached the Wembley Final and beat Southampton 3–0 to lift the trophy. The match took place prior to the Ipswich Town v Nottingham Forest Charity Shield Final. For the record the Latics' line up was Ian Green, Mark Hilton (captain), Paul Atkinson, Tim Jordan, Jim Steel and Paul Heaton. The substitutes were David Barnett and Nick Sinclair. As winners they each received a silver medal.

GREENHALL, George Edward

Centre-half

Born: Liverpool, 5 November 1937.
Career: Andover FC. Manchester City November 1958 to May 1960. OLDHAM ATHLETIC September 1960. Altrincham August 1961. Stafford Rangers August 1963 to February 1964. A knee injury kept him out of football until he resumed with Ashton United 1966. Congleton Town September 1966 to 1971.

■ A former police cadet and army paratrooper, George Greenhall shared the centre-half berth with veteran skipper Billy Spurdle in his single season at Boundary Park. A quick and forceful tackler and effective in the air, he appeared in half of the season's matches but was one of the 10 players released in the close season.

GREGAN, Sean Matthew

Central-defender

Born: Guisborough, 29 March 1974.
Career: Stockton West End. St Michael's (Billingham). Darlington trainee, professional January 1991. Preston North End November 1996, fee £350,000. West Bromwich Albion August 2002, fee £1.5 million. Leeds United September 2004. OLDHAM ATHLETIC loan November 2006, permanent January 2007.

■ Sean Gregan began as a midfield player but was switched to central defence during his time as a trainee with Darlington. He joined Athletic from Leeds United on an initial loan deal, having fallen out of favour with new manager Dennis Wise. With Stefan Stam ruled out by ankle ligament damage, the powerful 32-year-old was recruited until New Year's Day when the transfer window opened and a permanent deal was struck. The vastly experienced pivot scored on his debut in the pulsating 4–3 FA Cup first-round victory at Kettering Town, and helped Athletic reach the Play-off semi-finals at the end of his first season. Sadly, a torn Achilles sidelined Gregan for over five months of the 2007–08 season and despite his Man of the Match display at Swindon Town on his return in April, the 3–0 defeat effectively ended Athletic's hopes of a Play-off place.

GREW, Mark Stewart

Goalkeeper

Born: Bilston, Staffordshire, 15 February 1958.

Career: *Bilston and Moxley Schoolboys. West Bromwich Albion apprentice 1973, professional June 1976. Wigan Athletic loan December 1978. Notts County loan March 1979. Leicester City July 1983, fee £60,000. OLDHAM ATHLETIC loan October 1983. Ipswich Town March 1984, fee £60,000. Fulham loan September 1985. West Bromwich Albion loan January 1986. Derby County loan March 1986. Port Vale June 1986. Blackburn Rovers loan October to December 1991. Cardiff City August 1992. Stafford Rangers. Port Vale goalkeeping coach August 1994, youth coach December 1994, assistant manager June 1999 to December 2002.*

■ Mark Grew completed in excess of 200 League and Cup appearances for Port Vale and assisted them to promotion from Division Three in 1989. His career was also notable for the number of loan spells he undertook, leading to his sobriquet 'The Loan Ranger.' One such temporary move brought Grew to Boundary Park in October 1983. He was one of four goalkeepers fielded by the Latics in 1983–84. In addition to regular choice Andy Goram, 18-year-old Brian Parkin and loan signing Jeff Wealands also made their debuts during the campaign.

GRICE, Robert

Half-back

Born: *Sutton, St Helens, 12 April 1907.*
Died: *Oldham, 5 August 2004.*
Career: *Peasley Cross Athletic. St Helens Town. Runcorn 1924–25. Conway FC. Sutton Commercial February 1928. Colwyn Bay March 1929. Flint Town. Liverpool amateur. Skelmersdale United. Ashton National. Peasley Cross Athletic*

September 1930. New Brighton October to December 1932. Peasley Cross Athletic. OLDHAM ATHLETIC January 1933. Southport June 1935. Stalybridge Celtic August 1936. Clitheroe October 1936. Ashton National March 1937.*

■ A collier straight from school at the age of 14 years, Bob Grice's early football was played in Wales and the Merseyside district. Rugged, vigorous, and extremely capable, he played with no frills and he was equally at home at centre-half or full-back. His signing in late season 1932–33 enabled Matt Gray, who had acted as emergency centre-half for much of the season, to resume his more favoured inside-right role. Athletic had lost eight consecutive matches prior to Grice's signing, but they then won the next four and ended the season with a flourish. An unusual football connection surrounded his sister, who was a goalkeeper with Dick Kerr's famous Ladies Football team of the 1920s.

GRIFFIN, Adam

Left full-back

Born: *Salford, 26 August 1984.*
Career: *Salford Schoolboys. OLDHAM ATHLETIC associate schoolboy July 2000, professional August 2003. Oxford United loan November 2005. Stockport County loan January 2006, permanent August 2006.*

■ A product of Athletic's youth system, Adam Griffin made his first senior appearance, from the bench, in the final

League match of 2001–02. He was just 17 years of age at the time. A cool and plucky defender or wing-back, he progressed well until season 2005–06. Under new manager Ronnie Moore, however, Griffin fell totally out of favour and spent much of his final season out on loan.

GRIFFITHS, Arthur

Outside-right

Born: *Hartshill, Staffordshire, c.1885.*
Career: *Hartshill junior football. Stoke September 1905. OLDHAM ATHLETIC August 1908. Stoke 1909. Wrexham August 1912.*

■ Versatile utility forward Arthur Griffiths joined Athletic after his previous club, Stoke, had resigned from the Football League. A lively attacking force at either outside-right or in either inside-forward berth, he scored four League goals in 25 matches before returning to Stoke who, incidentally, did not gain re-election to the League until 1919–20. On 20 January 1917, just before Athletic's wartime game against Stoke, Arthur Griffiths was a welcome visitor to the Latics' dressing room. He had just returned from 20 months of active service in France and was unfit for football, suffering from trench foot.

GROBBELAAR, Bruce David

Goalkeeper

Born: *Durban, South Africa, 6 October 1957.*
Career: *Vancouver Whitecaps. Crewe Alexandra loan December 1979 to May 1980. Liverpool March 1981, fee £250,000. Stoke City loan March 1993. Southampton August 1994. Plymouth Argyle August 1996. Oxford United 17 September 1997. Sheffield Wednesday 23 September 1997. OLDHAM ATHLETIC professional December 1997, non-contract January 1998. Chesham United August 1998. Bury non-contract September 1998. Lincoln City non-contract December 1998. Northwich Victoria October 1999. Super Sport, South Africa, manager December 1999 to October 2001. St Hellenic, South Africa, coach December 2001.*

■ Towards the end of his distinguished career, 40-year-old Bruce Grobbelaar achieved three clean sheets in his four

£40,000. OLDHAM ATHLETIC February 1974, fee £10,000. Blackpool November 1977.

■ Alan Grove's spell with the Latics was the most productive of his tragically curtailed career. In an explosive start he scored in each of his first three matches and won a medal for his part in the run-in to the Third Division title in 1974. A powerful and aggressive wingman and a great crowd favourite, he remained an almost automatic choice throughout his stay at Boundary Park. Tragically, he died from a heart attack at the untimely age of 29, leaving a widow, Debbie, aged just 16. A crowd of 4,396 spectators attended a benefit match for his dependants, when Blackpool visited Boundary Park in July 1978.

GRUNDY, Harry

Full-back

Born: Little Hulton, 18 September 1893.
Died: Bolton, 15 April 1979.

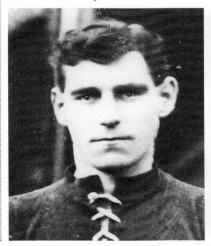

late-season outings for Athletic in 1997–98, the two wins and two draws lifting the team to the comparative respectability of 13th place in Division Two. Best remembered as Liverpool's flamboyantly entertaining last line of defence in their decade of success in the 1980s, the Zimbabwe international's honours included six League Championships, three FA Cups and three Football League Cups. He additionally was a European Cup winner in 1984 and a finalist in the following year. The bribe accusations levelled at Grobbelaar in November 1994, involving Malaysian betting syndicates, caused the biggest furore in the game since 1964, when the three Sheffield Wednesday players, Swann, Kay and Lane were similarly accused and subsequently banned from the game. The FA decided that there was a case to answer, but in the March 1997 corruption trial the jury failed to reach a verdict. At the age of 49 Grobbelaar came out of retirement to play for Glasshoughton Welfare in an emergency and assisted his team to a 2–1 win.

GROVES, Alan

Winger

Born: Ainsdale, Southport, 24 October 1948.
Died: Royton, Oldham, 15 June 1978.
Career: Blowick FC. Southport amateur August, professional December 1968. Chester July 1970. Shrewsbury Town February 1971, fee £5,000. Bournemouth & Boscombe Athletic October 1972, fee

Career: Rothwell's Athletic. Wharton Lads. Little Lever Colliery. OLDHAM ATHLETIC amateur August, professional September 1914, retired May 1930.

■ Harry Grundy first worked as a cotton mill hand, becoming a 'half-timer' at the age of 12. He enjoyed a 16-year career with the Latics as a totally reliable full-back, equally at home on either flank. The resolute, broad-shouldered defender completed 289 League and Cup matches, and a further 99 during World War One. He was awarded a richly deserved benefit in April 1924 with a guarantee of £500. Later, he was auditor to the Players' Union between 1931–32. A nephew, Arthur Grundy, signed an amateur form with Athletic in February 1939.

HACKING, John

Goalkeeper

Born: Blackburn, 22 December 1898.
Died: Accrington, 1 June 1955.
Career: Blackburn Schoolboys. Grimshaw Park Co-operative, Blackburn. Blackburn Rovers A Team. Blackpool January 1919. Wigan Borough trial 1925. Fleetwood October 1925. OLDHAM ATHLETIC May 1926. Manchester United March 1934. Accrington Stanley player-manager May 1935, retiring as a player December 1935. Barrow manager May 1949 to 1955.

■ Jack Hacking was signed from Lancashire Combination Cup winners Fleetwood after Blackpool had released him on a free transfer in 1925. The Latics were noted for their excellent goalkeepers in the inter-war period and the wonderfully consistent and reliable

Hacking proved a worthy successor to such notables as Howard Matthews, Ted Taylor and Bert Gray. In eight seasons at Boundary Park the former grocery store assistant served Athletic with distinction. He also gained international recognition despite playing his club football in the old Second Division. In the twilight of his career Hacking helped Manchester United avoid relegation to Division Three. In the late stages of season 1933–34 a succession of inspired performances by the veteran 'keeper ensured United's survival. Hacking's son, John junior, was also a goalkeeper with Accrington Stanley and Stockport County. He was also a guest player with Manchester United during World War Two at only 18 years of age.

HADDINGTON, William Raymond

Inside-forward

Born: Scarborough, 18 November 1923.
Died: Adelaide, Australia, 26 July 1994.
Career: Bradford Park Avenue amateur June 1942. Wartime guest with Bradford City, Halifax Town, York City, Plymouth Argyle, Portsmouth and Exeter City. OLDHAM ATHLETIC August 1947. Manchester City November 1950, fee £8,000. Stockport County December 1951, fee £2,500. Bournemouth & Boscombe Athletic August 1952. Rochdale October

1952. Halifax Town November 1953. Bedford Town 1953–54. Juventus FC, Australia 1958.

■ In Athletic's long history there have undoubtedly been many better all-round players than Ray Haddington, but none with his explosive shooting powers and willingness to take on the opposition goalkeeper from seemingly impossible distances and angles. Acknowledged in his day as the strongest hitter of a dead ball in the Northern Section of Division Three, he was fortunate at Boundary Park to have ball-playing inside partners of the quality of Eric Gemmell and Harry Stock, both perfect foils for Haddington's lethal finishing. Although his transfer to Manchester City was a matter of great regret to the Latics faithful, the transfer fee helped finance Athletic's move to bring in England international full-back George Hardwick as player-manager.

HAINING, William Wallace

Central-defender

Born: Glasgow, 2 October 1982.
Career: St Mungo's School, Glasgow. Falkirk FC Youth Team. Glasgow Rangers Juniors c.1996. OLDHAM ATHLETIC associate schoolboy July 1999, professional October 2001. St Mirren July 2007.

■ Will Haining was a member of Glasgow Rangers' highly successful youth set-up in the late 1990s, collecting a finalists' medal for his appearance in the World Youth Club Championship against Atletico Madrid. He made his first start for Athletic in the final fixture

of season 2001–02 and first appeared regularly from mid-season 2002–03, the campaign that ended in Play-off defeat by Queen's Park Rangers. Aerially dominant and totally fearless, he endured an injury-plagued season in 2005–06 but signed off in the following term having missed only one match. Appointed captain in succession to Chris Swailes in early season, he led by example, guiding the team to the Play-off semi-finals. Although offered a new contract, his eight-year Athletic career ended when he made a homeward move to Scottish Premier League side, St Mirren.

HALFORD, David

Outside-left

Born: Croxley Green, Hertfordshire, 19 October 1915.
Died: Tadcaster, July 2007.
Career: York Schoolboys. Rowntree's FC, York. Scarborough November 1932. Derby County December 1932. Bolton Wanderers June 1936, fee £1,650. OLDHAM ATHLETIC June 1938. Wartime guest with Queen's Park Rangers, Watford and Crystal Palace.

■ An England Schoolboy International against Scotland and Wales in 1930, David Halford left his job in a chocolate factory to join Derby County at 17 years of age. Bolton Wanderers paid a substantial fee for him but in two seasons at Burnden Park he played in only eight matches. A stylish and subtle dribbler, Halford was the provider of many scoring opportunities for his inside men and proved a good marksman himself, scoring 11 goals in 28 League and Cup appearances.

HALL, Allan Samuel

Half-back

Born: Urmston, Manchester, 26 May 1938. Career: Lancashire Schoolboys. Manchester United amateur May 1955. Wellington Boys. OLDHAM ATHLETIC November 1957. Winsford United August 1961 to February 1962. Ashton United. Winsford United August 1964. Buxton 1967–68.

■ Allan Hall won an England Youth cap, despite not being a regular in Manchester United's star-studded youth team. He

was employed as an apprentice engineer when signed as a professional by Athletic, and in four seasons at Boundary Park the lightly built, creative midfielder played under three managers. Just under half of his 79 senior appearances were made under new manager Norman Dodgin in 1958–59, his opportunity arising when Peter Neale was transferred to Scunthorpe United.

HALL, Christopher Michael

Forward

Born: Manchester, 27 November 1986.
Career: OLDHAM ATHLETIC trainee July 2003, professional October 2005. Stalybridge Celtic July 2007.

■ Chris Hall's best season, when he scored three vital goals in four FA Cup ties, ended when he suffered a broken leg in a training ground accident in February 2007. Tall, muscular and uncompromising, Hall developed through youth ranks and was progressing well in his usual role of impact substitute when his season ended prematurely. Four months later, the 20-year-old striker decided to quit professional football, foregoing the final year of his contract. Quoting only 'personal reasons' for his surprise decision, his interests in acting and modelling were thought to be the underlying reasons for his departure. Two months later Hall signed on part-time forms with Stalybridge Celtic, Athletic retaining his League registration and compensation rights.

HALL, Daniel Andrew

Central-defender

Born: Ashton-under-Lyne, 14 November 1983.
Career: Ashland University. Tameside Centre of Excellence. OLDHAM ATHLETIC trainee, Scarborough loan 2003, OLDHAM ATHLETIC professional August 2003. Shrewsbury Town July 2006. Gretna January to May 2008.

■ Danny Hall was among a welter of departures from Boundary Park as new manager John Sheridan made moves to reshape the squad inherited from Ronnie Moore. The powerfully built central defender graduated through Athletic's youth system to make 71 starts and eight substitute appearances, but a serious knee injury sustained in February 2004 cruelly halted his progress. Hall reached Wembley with Shrewsbury Town in season 2006–07 but his big day ended in disappointment as Bristol Rovers won the League Two Play-off Final by 3–1.

HALL, Fitz

Central-defender

Born: Walthamstow, 20 December 1980.
Career: West Ham United trainee. Barnet February 2000. Chesham United. OLDHAM ATHLETIC trial December 2001, professional March 2002, fee £20,000. Southampton July 2003, fee £250,000. Crystal Palace August 2004, fee £1.5 million. Wigan Athletic June 2006, fee £3 million. Queen's Park Rangers January 2008.

■ The escalating value of his transfer fees – even allowing for inflation – give a true reflection of the rapid progress made by Fitz Hall since his departure from

Boundary Park in July 2003. The former building site worker began with West Ham United at the tender age of nine but was recruited by the Latics from the Ryman League, courtesy of a recommendation by Chesham United's then manager Bob Dowie, brother of Athletic manager Ian. The lanky central defender made the step up into League football with apparent comfort and bags of confidence. His subsequent step up to the Premier League completed an amazing and meteoric rise for the 22-year-old defender.

HALL, James Franklin

Full-back

Born: Burnage, Manchester, 7 May 1945.
Career: Manchester Schoolboys. Manchester City amateur c. 1960. Mather & Platt FC. OLDHAM ATHLETIC amateur May 1963, professional July 1966. Port Elizabeth, South Africa, April 1967. Altrincham, briefly, in the mid-1970s.

■ Jimmy Hall was working as a maintenance engineer at Mather & Platt's Newton Heath works when he was invited for trials at Boundary Park. He made two League appearances before signing professional forms, but subsequently appeared in only one League Cup tie before emigrating. He played as a part-time professional in South Africa, combining football with work as a representative for a sportswear company. Returning to the UK, he had a short spell with Altrincham before opening a sports shop in Bramhall.

HALLAM, Jack

Half-back

Born: Hadfield, 23 May 1910.
Died: Hadfield, February 1995.
Career: Hadfield Star. Wigan Borough amateur February, professional April 1931. OLDHAM ATHLETIC December 1931. Stockport County trial August–September 1932. Fulham trial October-December 1932. Hyde United. Hadfield Star amateur December 1933. Hollingworth FC amateur September 1934.

■ Jack Hallam's signing came a few weeks after his previous club, Wigan Borough, resigned from the Football League. He had the dubious honour of being Borough's last goalscorer prior to their resignation, his winner coming in their penultimate fixture on 17 October 1931 in a 3–2 win against Carlisle United. Hallam's debut for Athletic, against Bury in a 2–1 defeat at Boundary Park in January 1932, was his only senior outing and was also his last at League level.

HALLE, Gunnar

Defender/Midfield

Born: Oslo, Norway, 11 August 1965.
Career: Nesjar Juniors 1980. Larvik Turn 1982. Lillestrom 1985, fee £9,000. OLDHAM ATHLETIC trial December 1990, professional February 1991, fee £280,000. Lillestrom loan May–July 1994. Leeds United December 1996, fee £400,000. Bradford City June 1999, fee £200,000. Wolverhampton Wanderers loan March 2002. Lillestrom 2002.

Aurskog/Finstadbru player-coach 2004. Lillestrom assistant coach 2005 to November 2006. Viking coach 2006–07.

■ Gunnar Halle was one of the earliest Norwegian imports into English football and the blond-haired Scandinavian gave Athletic six years of splendid service. Athletic's most capped player began in Norway as a forward, later switching to midfield and then to full-back. His best position was a matter of debate, but he was probably most effective at right full-back or on the right side of midfield. At international level Halle won 24 of his 63 caps while at Boundary Park, and in 1992 scored a hat-trick for his country in a 10–0 win against San Marino in a World Cup qualifier. He also took part in the World Cup Finals in America in 1994.

HALLIGAN, William

Inside-forward

Born: Bogginfirm, County Antrim, Ireland, 18 February 1886.
Career: Belfast Celtic. Belfast Distillery. Leeds City May 1909. Derby County February 1910, fee £400. Wolverhampton Wanderers June 1911, fee £450. Hull City May 1913, fee £600. Wartime guest with Manchester United, Rochdale, Stockport County and Chesterfield. Preston North End July 1919. OLDHAM ATHLETIC January 1920, fee £750. Nelson July 1921, fee £75, retired May 1922.

■ Irish international Bill Halligan scored five goals in his first five matches for the Latics, prompting one correspondent to report 'Halligan was the artist of the line, who passed and headed the ball with the skill of an accomplished inside-forward.'

On Christmas Day 1920 he had the misfortune to break his ankle, shortly after scoring the only goal of the match against Bradford Park Avenue, and did not appear for Athletic again before his close season transfer to Nelson. During the course of his final season at Seedhill, he scored his 100th goal in League football.

HALLWORTH, Jonathan Geoffrey

Goalkeeper

Born: Stockport, 26 October 1965.
Career: Stockport and Greater Manchester Schoolboys. Ipswich Town apprentice, professional May 1983. Bristol Rovers loan January 1985. OLDHAM ATHLETIC February 1989, fee £75,000. Cardiff City August 1997 to January 2001, when he retired due to a knee injury. OLDHAM ATHLETIC goalkeeping coach September 2001 to January 2002.

■ Jon Hallworth's career with Athletic began in outstanding fashion, resulting in an unbeaten run of 10 games. The tall, blond, shot-stopper gave loyal service during his lengthy stay at Boundary Park despite fierce competition from Andy Rhodes and later from Paul Gerrard. Hallworth was ever present in the 1990–91 Championship season, and missed only one League match in 1991–92 as Athletic returned to the top flight. He appeared in the FA Cup semi-finals of 1990 and 1994, but lost out to Andy Rhodes for a place in the Football League Cup Final against Nottingham Forest in 1990, having played in five of the earlier rounds. Following retirement, he briefly returned to Boundary Park as part-time goalkeeping coach while also running his own business in the Stockport area.

HALOM, Victor Lewis

Forward

Born: Coton Park, Burton upon Trent, 3 October 1948.
Career: Burton and South Derbyshire Schoolboys. Charlton Athletic apprentice April 1964, professional January 1966. Orient loan August 1967, permanent October 1967, fee £5,000. Fulham November 1968, fee £35,000. Luton Town September 1971, fee £35,000. Sunderland February 1973, fee £35,000. OLDHAM ATHLETIC July 1976, fee £25,000.

Rotherham United player-coach February 1980, fee £25,000. Northwich Victoria, briefly, during 1981–82. Frederikstad, Norway, coach 1982. Barrow manager July 1983. Rochdale manager May 1984 to December 1986. Burton Albion manager September-October 1987. North Shields.

■ Strong, aggressive striker Vic Halom arrived at Boundary Park after much success with Sunderland. He was an FA Cup winner in 1973, and also assisted his side to promotion from Division Two in 1976. He had an excellent first season at Boundary Park, scoring 23 League and Cup goals and passing the milestone of 100 career goals. His strike-rate diminished in subsequent seasons when he was deployed in a central-midfield role. Halom's career aggregate figures were 435 League matches and 131 goals. In November 2007 Bulgaria-based Halom was recruited by Newcastle United as a scout in Eastern Europe.

HALSALL, Alan

Goalkeeper

Born: Menai Bridge, Anglesey, 17 November 1940.
Career: Skelmersdale United. Manchester United amateur December 1961. Blackpool April 1962. OLDHAM ATHLETIC July 1963 to June 1964. Wigan Athletic June 1967 to 1968.

■ Alan Halsall appeared twice for First Division Blackpool in the final weeks of season 1961–62, and spent the following term in reserve. He fared little better in his season at Boundary Park, where he was again restricted to two senior appearances as Johnnie Bollands dominated the position.

HAMILTON, James 'Snowy'

Full-back

Born: Burslem, c.1884.
Career: Burslem Town September 1902. Burslem Port Vale March 1903. OLDHAM ATHLETIC June 1907 to April 1911.

■ 'Snowy' Hamilton (so named on account of his white-blond hair) was a typical full-back of his day, with 13 stones to throw usefully into the fray. As

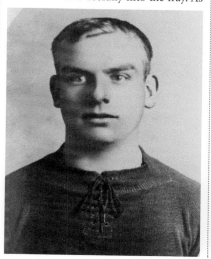

one correspondent noted 'He effectively discharged the first duty of a full-back: cleared his lines promptly, and never indulged in anything ornamental.' Hamilton joined Athletic along with Billy Dodds from Burslem Port Vale, whose resignation from the Football League led to Athletic's election in 1907–08.

HANCOCK, Henry Bentley

Inside-forward

Born: Tranmere, 1874.
Died: Birkenhead, 8 August 1924.
Career: Melrose FC September 1892. Tranmere Rovers trial October 1902. Melrose FC November 1902. Port Sunlight May 1903. Stockport County c. February/March 1905. Blackpool May 1905. OLDHAM ATHLETIC May 1906. Manchester City May 1908. West Bromwich Albion February 1909. Brierley Hill Alliance April 1910, retired due to injury in 1912.

■ Among the best of Athletic's early inside-forwards, Harry Hancock scored 23 of the team's 105 goals in Lancashire Combination matches and six in eight FA Cup ties. As the Latics began their adventure as a Football League club in 1907–08, Hancock remained a fixture at inside-left until a serious ankle injury sidelined him for some two months from February 1908. Athletic narrowly missed out on promotion at the first attempt, finishing third in Division Two.

HARDIE, John Clarke

Goalkeeper

Born: Edinburgh, 7 February 1938.
Career: Penicuik Thistle. Hibernian. Falkirk 1959–60. OLDHAM ATHLETIC July 1960. Chester July 1961. Bradford Park Avenue December 1963. Crystal Palace August 1970 to October 1971, fee £5,000.

■ During his period of National Service John Hardy was a regular member of the Scottish Command XI. Joining Falkirk, he was just one of nine goalkeepers fielded by the Bairns in season 1959–60, surely something of a record. In his season at Boundary Park he contested the first-team jersey with Jim Rollo, but with Chester and Bradford Park Avenue he was first choice. His Park Avenue career wound up in their last match as a Football League club, at Aldershot on 20 April 1970, the game marked his 265th League appearance for them. Outside of football, Hardie was a qualified cabinet-maker.

HARDMAN, John Andrew

Half-back

Born: Miles Platting, Manchester, 1889.
Died: Killed in action in France, February 1917.
Career: Longfield FC. OLDHAM ATHLETIC amateur December 1910, professional March 1911. Pontypridd August 1912. Derby County August 1913. Bristol Rovers October 1914.

■ Jack Hardman's game featured quick and forceful tackling and his defensive work was better than his ball distribution. He appeared only twice for the Latics, but after just one season with Pontypridd, Derby County signed him and he sampled relegation and promotion in two seasons at the Baseball Ground. He was serving in the army as a sergeant, when his death in action was reported in February 1917.

HARDWICK, George Francis Moutry

Full-back

Born: Saltburn, 2 February 1920.
Died: Middlesbrough, April 2004.
Career: South Bank East End 1934. Middlesbrough amateur October 1935, professional April 1937. Wartime guest with Nottingham Forest, Birmingham, Chelsea, West Bromwich Albion, Reading and Lovell's Athletic. OLDHAM ATHLETIC player-manager November 1950 to May 1956, fee £15,000. US 7th Army, Stuttgart, Germany, director of coaching August 1956. Holland national team manager-coach January to June 1957. PSV Eindhoven, Holland, coach August 1957 to May 1958. Middlesbrough coach August 1961 to November 1963. Sunderland manager November 1964 to May 1965. Gateshead manager May 1968 to February 1970.

■ A cool, polished full-back with great tactical awareness, George Hardwick

captained every team that he played for, from Southbank East End to England and Great Britain. He won 13 England caps and played in 17 wartime internationals. Athletic's youngest-ever manager, his influence and ability lifted the Latics from 21st position to mid-table in his first season. Fourth position in 1951–52 was followed by the Championship in 1952–53, but at this point lack of finances to strengthen the side proved fatal. Without a win in the first eight matches in Division Two, the side were just not good enough, and the hard-won promotion was squandered due to a lack of backing for the player-manager. In recent years George Hardwick has been named among the 100 leading players of the century, and a statue of him has been unveiled at the Riverside Stadium.

HARDY, John James

Centre-half

Born: Sunderland, 19 February 1899.
Died: Sunderland, 10 January 1932.
Career: Wearmouth Colliery. Sunderland Celtic. Manchester United amateur November 1920. South Shields April 1921. Derby County August 1924, fee £1,500. Grimsby Town July 1925, fee £750. OLDHAM ATHLETIC January 1927, fee £750. South Shields October 1927, fee £200. Boldon Colliery. Scarborough Town August 1930. West Stanley December 1930. Clapton Orient September to December 1931.

■ John Hardy made his debut for South Shields in Division Two in November 1921 and was rarely absent thereafter. He did not enhance his reputation in a season at the Baseball Ground, but in 1925–26 he helped Grimsby Town win the Third Division North title. Thereafter his fortunes declined, as he was unable to graduate beyond reserve-team football at Boundary Park, and his eventual homecoming to the South Shields club saw them relegated from Division Two in 1927–28. His untimely death, at 32 years of age, was as a result of pneumonia.

HARDY, Lee

Winger

Born: Blackpool, 26 November 1981.
Career: Blackburn Rovers trainee. OLDHAM ATHLETIC July 2001. Macclesfield Town June 2002. Hucknall Town trial September 2003. Leigh RMI trial September 2003. Ayr United December 2003. St Johnstone June 2004. Hamilton Academical January 2005.

■ A season as understudy to Athletic's Player of the Year, David Eyres, proved almost totally unrewarding for left-winger Lee Hardy, who was restricted to one substitute appearance. His career took an upturn when he moved to Ayr United, his form at Somerset Park quickly earning him an upward move to St Johnstone. At Hamilton Academical a serious ankle injury robbed him of a place in the Bell's League Challenge Cup Final against St Mirren in November 2005.

HARGREAVES, Frank

Inside-forward

Born: Ashton-under-Lyne, 16 November 1902.
Died: Tameside, September 1987.
Career: New Moss Colliery. Ashton National. Hurst FC. Stalybridge Celtic. Droylsden United. Manchester North End September 1923. OLDHAM ATHLETIC October 1923. Everton May 1924, fee £750. OLDHAM ATHLETIC May 1925, fee £250. Rochdale August 1930. Bournemouth & Boscombe Athletic July 1931. Watford October to December 1931. OLDHAM ATHLETIC March 1932, reserve team trainer August 1933, first team trainer July 1936 to September 1948.

■ Slightly-built and artistic, and an exponent of the defence-splitting pass, Frank Hargreaves possessed fine dribbling skills. He was not at his best, however, on heavy grounds and he generally disappointed as a marksman. His debut for the Latics came in a match that created a piece of soccer history. Athletic's full-back, Sammy Wynne, scored twice for the Latics and also netted two own-goals in the 3–2 win against Manchester United on 6 October 1923. Hargreaves was a fine servant as both player and trainer. During World War Two he served with the Eighth Army and was evacuated from Dunkirk.

HARRIS, James

Centre-forward

Born: Birkenhead, 18 August 1933.
Career: Birkenhead Schoolboys. Everton amateur 1948, professional September 1951. Birmingham City December 1960, fee £20,000. OLDHAM ATHLETIC July

1964. Tranmere Rovers August 1966. Rhyl Athletic October 1966. St Patrick's FC November 1966, retired May 1967.

■ Within three months of his League debut with Everton, Jimmy Harris played for England Under-23s versus Scotland at Hillsborough and scored once in England's 3–1 win. He scored 72 goals for Everton in 207 League and Cup matches, including a hat-trick at Tottenham in October 1958 when Everton lost 10–4. He had scored in excess of a century of goals in top-class soccer prior to his move to Boundary Park, but he found less success with the Latics, scoring seven in 31/1 matches. After retiring from the game Harris worked as a steward at the Prenton Golf Club, Merseyside.

HARRIS, Joseph

Centre-forward

Born: Belfast, 8 April 1929.
Career: Belfast Distillery. Larne FC. Blackburn Rovers January 1951, fee £3,300. OLDHAM ATHLETIC March 1953. Belfast Crusaders July 1954.

■ Joe Harris was a big-hearted player with useful versatility. Aside from his normal position of centre-forward, he made several appearances at outside-right, a position left vacant following the sale of Jimmy Munro to Lincoln City. Harris's best performance in Athletic's colours came in March 1954 when his

two well-taken goals against Leeds United helped secure a welcome 4–2 victory. Sadly, it was one of only eight wins recorded in the Latics' unhappy sojourn in Division Two. In July 1954 he returned to Ireland, where he had first come to prominence with Belfast Distillery.

HARRIS, Neil

Centre-forward

Born: Shettleston, 30 October 1894.
Died: Swindon, 3 December 1941.
Career: Vale of Clyde. Partick Thistle June 1913. Wartime guest with Belfast Distillery, Kilmarnock and Fulham. Newcastle United May 1920, fee £3,300. Notts County November 1925, fee £3,000. Dublin Shelbourne May 1927. OLDHAM ATHLETIC July 1927, fee £400. Third Lanark March 1929, fee £400. Burton Town player-manager July 1929. Belfast Distillery manager May 1932. Swansea Town manager July 1934. Swindon Town manager May 1939 to 1941.

■ Neil Harris won his Scotland cap against England at Wembley in 1924 and his FA Cup medal in the same year, scoring one of Newcastle United's goals in the 2–0 win against Aston Villa. A seasoned campaigner by the time he reached Boundary Park, Harris made an immediate impact, scoring seven goals in his first six appearances, but he lost out in 1928–29 when George Taylor and, later, Stewart Littlewood were introduced. Neil's son, John Harris, assisted Chelsea between 1945–56 and later managed Chester and Sheffield United.

HARRIS, William

Goalkeeper

Born: Oakham, Dudley, Staffordshire, 1 December 1918.
Died: Dudley, 20 February 1996.
Career: Oakham Juniors. Whiteheath Vics 1934. West Bromwich Albion amateur October 1936, professional February 1937. Wartime guest with Shrewsbury Town. OLDHAM ATHLETIC June 1946, fee £150. Accrington Stanley August 1947. Dudley Town player-coach July 1950. Bilston United player-manager 1953–55. Scouted for West Bromwich Albion on retirement.

■ Bill Harris made his League debut with West Bromwich Albion as a 19-year-old, but wartime army service intervened. He was wounded at Normandy but made a full recovery and joined the Latics for the resumption of normal League football in 1946–47. Ideally built for his position, he was a reliable and consistent goalkeeper, particularly good when fielding high shots and crosses. Transferred to Accrington Stanley after one season at Boundary Park, he made 99 appearances in three seasons at Peel Park.

HARRISON, Wayne

Inside-forward

Born: Stockport, 15 November 1967.
Career: Stockport Schoolboys. OLDHAM ATHLETIC associate schoolboy January 1983, apprentice April 1984, professional December 1984. Liverpool January 1985, fee £250,000. OLDHAM ATHLETIC loan January–March 1985. Crewe Alexandra loan December 1988. Career ended by knee injury April 1991.

■ Superb balance, speed, and deadly accuracy near goal marked Wayne Harrison as a unique talent in Athletic's youth and reserve teams, and the blond-haired 17-year-old starlet stepped into League football to instant acclaim from all quarters. His diamond-bright potential netted Athletic a record fee when Liverpool invested heavily in his undoubted promise. Sadly, in a Liverpool

Central League match in May 1990, his career was cruelly ended when the cruciate and medial ligaments of his right knee were irreparably damaged. After three operations he was advised by specialists to retire or face permanent disability. Athletic entertained Liverpool at Boundary Park in a benefit match for him in April 1992.

HARTFORD, Richard Asa

Midfield

Born: Clydebank, 24 October 1950.
Career: Drumchapel Amateurs. West Bromwich Albion amateur May 1966, professional November 1967. Manchester City August 1974, fee £250,000. Nottingham Forest June 1979, fee £500,000. Everton August 1979, fee £400,000. Manchester City October 1981, fee £350,000. Fort Lauderdale Strikers, US, May 1984. Norwich City November 1984. Norway coaching appointment 1985. Bolton Wanderers player-coach July 1985. Stockport County player-coach June 1987. OLDHAM ATHLETIC March 1989. Shrewsbury Town player-coach July 1989, caretaker manager January 1990, manager January 1990 to January 1991. Bury non-contract February 1991. Boston United February–May 1991. Blackburn Rovers coach 1991, reserve team trainer 1992. Stoke City assistant manager November 1993. Manchester City assistant manager July 1995, caretaker manager August 1996, reserve-team coach 1997 to May 2005.

■ Dismissed only a matter of days earlier from his post as manager of Stockport County, 38-year-old midfielder Asa Hartford was immediately offered a short-term playing contract by Athletic, whose midfield options were severely restricted by injuries. Hartford enjoyed a long and successful career, in terms of League matches alone, he made 725/19 appearances and scored 63 goals. His international career spanned 10 years and half a century of Scotland caps. He was named Asa after the celebrated American singer Asa Yoelson, whose stage name was Al Jolson.

HARTLE, Barry

Outside-left

Born: Salford, 8 August 1939.
Career: Salford Boys' Club. Watford

August 1956. Sheffield United June 1960, fee £3,000. Carlisle United July 1966, fee £14,000. Stockport County September 1967. OLDHAM ATHLETIC June 1970. Southport July 1971. Macclesfield Town 1972. Buxton 1974. Witton Albion 1975. Hyde United 1976–77.

■ Barry Hartle was a member of the Watford side who won promotion from Division Four in 1959–60, and in his first season with Sheffield United the Blades were promoted to Division One. After making a bright start with Athletic he was unfortunate to be injured in early season, and was unable to regain his place as promotion from Division Four was achieved. Hartle rounded off his League career with Southport, reaching the personal milestone of 300 League appearances in their colours. He subsequently worked as a postman in Stockport, and later as a taxi driver.

HARTLEY, Edmund

Role: Outside-right

Born: Burnley, 5 May 1932.
Career: Burnley amateur June, professional November 1950. Rossendale United. OLDHAM ATHLETIC July 1956. Chorley October 1956.

■ Eddie Hartley's brief stay at Boundary Park featured a single senior outing in a 2–1 defeat at Stockport County on 3 September 1956. At the end of the following month he returned to Lancashire Combination football with Chorley. At Victory Park he enjoyed considerable success, being a Combination Cup winner in 1958, and a member of successive Combination Championship sides in 1960 and 1961. The club awarded him a benefit in May 1961.

HASLAM, Harry

Left full-back

Born: Manchester, 30 July 1921.
Died: 10 September 1986.
Career: Manchester United amateur October 1938. Wartime guest with Stockport County. Rochdale amateur May 1945. OLDHAM ATHLETIC May 1946. Brighton & Hove Albion September 1947. Leyton Orient July 1948. Guildford City October 1949. Hastings United player & assistant manager. Eastbourne United manager. Gillingham coach. Barry Town manager August 1956–59. Tonbridge manager February 1960. Fulham chief scout July–November 1968. Luton Town coach and promotions manager 1969, manager May 1972 to January 1978. Sheffield United manager January 1978 to May 1981. England scout 1981.

■ A burly, strong-tackling full-back, Harry Haslam found little success in League football, seven matches for Leyton Orient in 1947–48 being his best seasonal return. His cheerful demeanour and sunny personality, allied with a sound knowledge of the game and great motivational skills were, however, successfully harnessed in managerial roles. After a lengthy apprenticeship in non-League circles, he was appointed coach and promotions manager of Luton Town. Taking over as manager following the departure of Alec Stock in May 1972, he guided the Hatters into the top flight in 1974.

HASSON, William Craig

Outside-left

Born: Glasgow, 12 June 1905.
Died: Kensington, 1976.
Career: Shettleston Juniors. Clyde September 1926. OLDHAM ATHLETIC October 1928, fee £150. Millwall May 1934. Chesterfield May to September 1935.

■ A Scotsman born of Irish parents, Bill Hasson spent two years with Clyde and had figured in 47 Scottish League matches when Athletic paid £150 for his transfer. The diminutive wingman established himself immediately on arrival at Boundary Park. Excellent ball control and skill in the dribble made him one of the outstanding outside-lefts in the Second Division. He enjoyed an outstanding season with Athletic in 1929–30 – the team finished third in Division Two – and he scored 10 goals in 40 League matches.

HATELEY, Anthony

Centre-forward

Born: Derby, 13 June 1941.
Career: Normanton Sports Club. Derby County associate schoolboy April 1955. Notts County amateur May 1956, professional June 1958. Aston Villa August 1963, fee £20,000. Chelsea October 1966, fee £100,000. Liverpool July 1967, fee £100,000. Coventry City September 1968, fee £80,000. Birmingham City August 1969, fee £72,000. Notts County November 1970, fee £20,000. OLDHAM ATHLETIC July 1972, fee £5,000. Bromsgrove Rovers May 1974. Prescot Town July 1975. Keyworth United December 1978.

■ Powerfully built and noted for his heading ability, Tony Hateley commanded some very sizeable fees in a career covering seven League clubs and an impressive return of 210 goals in 429 matches. At Boundary Park, his failure to make a full recovery from a cartilage operation was a great disappointment. Tony Hateley's son, Mark, inherited his father's heading ability and won 32 England caps between 1984 and 1992.

HAYES, William

Half-back

Born: Runcorn, Cheshire, 8 June 1919.
Died: South Cheshire, September 2002.
Career: Halton Juniors. OLDHAM ATHLETIC amateur December 1936, professional January 1937. Wartime guest with Runcorn 1945–46. Mossley 1951–52.

■ Two trial games in Athletic's Midweek XI were sufficient to impress and Bill Hayes went on to make his League debut at 19 years of age. Wartime service in the Cheshire Regiment interrupted his promising start, but he returned to give five seasons of splendid service in post-war football. Equally at home in any half-back position, Hayes was not a showy player, but he tackled with great determination and was a hard man to pass. He was awarded a benefit match in May 1949 and the game attracted 11,391 spectators. After leaving the Latics he took over the Brighton Hotel in Oldham.

HAZELL, Reuben Daniel

Central-defender

Born: Birmingham, 24 April 1979.
Career: Aston Villa trainee, professional March 1997. Tranmere Rovers August 1999. Torquay United January 2002. Kidderminster Harriers August 2004. Chesterfield August 2005. MK Dons trial 2007. OLDHAM ATHLETIC September 2007.

■ Impressive displays in the heart of Athletic's defence earned the stylish defender a long-term contract after he had completed two monthly engagements. Initially in partnership with Sean Gregan and later with Stefan Stam, when club skipper Gregan suffered an Achilles tendon injury at Doncaster Rovers on 23 October, Hazell's versatility was an added bonus. The experienced defender has looked comfortable in any position across the back four, a bonus in a season when manager Sheridan's selection options have been restricted by serious injuries to key personnel.

HEATH, Donald

Winger

Born: Stockton-on-Tees, 26 December 1944.
Career: Stockton-on-Tees Schoolboys. Middlesbrough amateur August 1960, professional December 1962. Norwich City July 1964, fee £15,000. Swindon Town September 1967, fee £7,000. OLDHAM ATHLETIC July 1970. Peterborough United July 1972. Hartlepool July 1973. Gateshead 1974–75. Crook Town July 1975.

■ A fleet-footed wingman who centred with nice judgement, Don Heath was an

integral part of Athletic's free-scoring attack in season 1970–71 when promotion from Division Four was secured. Earlier in his career he assisted Swindon Town to promotion from Division Three in 1968–69, and memorably was a member of the Swindon side that pulled off a famous giant-killing act at Wembley by beating Arsenal 3–1 in the Football League Cup Final.

HEATON, John Hagues

Outside-left

Born: Preston, 11 April 1916.
Died: Preston, 27 December 1979.
Career: Northern Nomads. OLDHAM ATHLETIC amateur August 1938 to May 1939.

■ A schoolteacher at Preston Grammar School, John Heaton's first match for Athletic was on Boxing Day 1938, but the match against Stockport County had to be abandoned due to fog after 63 minutes with Athletic losing 1–0. Heaton's official League debut was postponed for only one day, however, as he played and scored in the return match at Edgeley Park, won 3–1 by Stockport County.

HEATON, Paul John

Midfield

Born: Hyde, Cheshire, 24 January 1961.
Career: Manchester City trial. OLDHAM ATHLETIC associate schoolboy November 1976, apprentice June 1977, professional January 1979. Rochdale, initially on loan, permanent March 1984. Rovaniemi, Finland, 1986. Kajaani, Finland, 1988. Mikkeli, Finland.

■ Despite an almost fragile physique in his early days, Paul Heaton was always a clever and direct dribbler, who never lacked the confidence to take an opponent on. He made his League debut as a 17-year-old, but was particularly impressive during Joe Royle's first season as manager (1981–82), scoring 14 League and Cup goals in 44/2 appearances. Increasingly troubled by knee injuries, he nevertheless recorded 151 senior appearances before ending his League career with Rochdale. His first club in Finland was Rovaniemi, a club situated within the Arctic Circle and probably little different from Boundary Park in mid-winter!

HEATON, Thomas

Half-back

Born: Blackburn, 1 June 1897.
Career: Blackburn Rovers April 1915.

OLDHAM ATHLETIC June 1923, fee £150. Manchester North End August 1927. Toronto Transportation Commission, Canada, May 1929. Retired from playing in 1930 after breaking a leg.

■ Tommy Heaton appeared in 59 League and Cup matches for his home-town club Blackburn Rovers. He stepped straight into Athletic's first-team on arrival but failed to establish himself, losing his place after just four outings. He did much better the following season when his dour defensive qualities were exactly what the side needed in their desperate struggle to avoid relegation, happily averted by wins in the final two League matches.

HEMSLEY, Charles James

Centre-forward

Born: Brighton, 17 August 1888.
Died: Brighton, 29 March 1986.
Career: Ewbank FC. Accrington Stanley during World War One. OLDHAM ATHLETIC November 1919, fee £200, retired in 1922 after breaking a leg. Accrington Stanley trainer July 1925. Lytham St Annes coach.

■ Born by the sea, Charlie Hemsley served in the Royal Navy both before and during World War One. He began in football with Accrington Stanley and his record as a fine opportunist centre-forward quickly attracted several clubs. Hemsley had a very unfortunate start in Athletic's colours. Having scored one of three goals against Manchester United at Old Trafford, and with the Latics 3–0 ahead, fog descended and the game had

to be abandoned 15 minutes from time. A compound fracture of the leg ended his football career, but he played club cricket until the age of 70 and lived in Brighton to the grand old age of 97.

HENRY, Anthony

Midfield

Born: Houghton-le-Spring, 26 November 1957.
Career: Manchester City apprentice July, professional December 1974. Bolton

Wanderers September 1981, fee £125,000. OLDHAM ATHLETIC March 1983, fee £21,000. Stoke City December 1987, fee £30,000. Mazda, Japan, June 1989. Shrewsbury Town August 1991 to June 1992. Hyde United February 1993.

■ Tony Henry spent seven years with Manchester City and won an FA Cup medal for his substitute appearance in the Centenary Final in 1981. He did not appear in the replay, memorably won by Spurs thanks to a wonder goal by the Argentine international, Ricky Villa. With Bolton Wanderers, Tony was leading scorer in each of his two seasons at Burnden Park, and at £21,000 he proved to be an absolute bargain for the Latics, appearing in more than 200 matches and scoring 27 goals.

HENRY, Nicholas Ian

Midfield

Born: Liverpool, 21 February 1969.
Career: Liverpool Schoolboys. OLDHAM ATHLETIC associate schoolboy January

1985, trainee July 1986, professional July 1987. Halmstad, Sweden, loan March 1988. Sheffield United February 1997, fee £500,000 plus Doug Hodgson. Walsall March 1999. Tranmere Rovers June 1999. Scarborough player-coach August 2002, later manager until October 2005.

■ Midfield ball-winner Nick Henry began in Athletic's first team in season 1989–90, and was an integral part of Athletic's successes in the early 1990s. His very first goal at senior level in the fourth-round Littlewoods Cup tie against League champions and First Division leaders, Arsenal was one to savour. His 30–yard right foot volley literally flew into the bottom right-hand corner of John Lukic's goal to make the score 2–0 in an unforgettable night at Boundary Park that ended in a 3–1 victory, en route to the Wembley Final against Nottingham Forest.

HERBERT, Frank

Half-back

Born: Stocksbridge, Sheffield, 29 June 1916.
Died: Wortley, Yorkshire, 1972.
Career: Sheffield amateur football. Sheffield Wednesday May 1938. Bury October 1945. OLDHAM ATHLETIC June 1946 to May 1947.

■ An undisclosed but 'substantial' fee brought Frank Herbert to Boundary Park. Sadly, he failed to impress during a run of four early season outings and the right-half spot was eventually secured by local product, Jack Bowden.

HESELTINE, Wayne Alan

Full-back

Born: Bradford, 3 December 1969.
Career: Manchester United associate schoolboy November 1984, trainee July 1986, professional December 1987. OLDHAM ATHLETIC December 1989, fee £40,000. Bradford City August 1992 to May 1994. Guisley FC 1994.

■ In January 1990 utility defender Wayne Heseltine replaced the injured Andy Barlow for the last 14 minutes of

the FA Cup replay against Birmingham City and retained his place for the visit to Swindon Town three days later. Sadly, at the end of the same month, he suffered a broken leg and knee ligament damage in a reserve team match at Coventry City. He did not add to his two outings but enjoyed his first experience of regular first-team football after joining Bradford City, appearing in 51/3 Division Two matches.

HESHAM, Frank

Outside-right

Born: Manchester, c.1881.
Died: Killed in action, France, 17 November 1915.
Career: Gorton St Francis. Manchester City November 1896. Crewe Alexandra June 1901. Accrington Stanley 1903–04. Stoke May 1904. Leyton FC May 1905. OLDHAM ATHLETIC July 1907. Preston North End September 1909, fee £25. Croydon Common November 1909. Hyde United September 1910. Crewe Alexandra later in 1910. Newton Heath Alliance September 1913.

■ Frank Hesham was born within sight of Manchester City's Hyde Road ground and joined his local club as a youngster. A variety of moves preceded his arrival at Boundary Park for Athletic's first season as a Football League club. Although he did not start the season as first choice outside-right, he quickly won the position, and his speedy and direct flank play netted him nine League and Cup goals in 29 appearances. A disappointing

start to the new campaign brought about innumerable team changes, and Arthur Griffiths, the new recruit from Stoke, took over the outside-right position. Frank Hesham lost his life during World War One while serving as a gunner with the Royal Garrison Artillery on the western front, leaving a widow and one child.

HEWITSON, Robert

Goalkeeper

Born: Blyth, Northumberland.
Career: Morpeth Harriers November 1900. Barnsley May 1903. Crystal Palace May 1905. OLDHAM ATHLETIC May 1907. Tottenham Hotspur July 1908. Croydon Common 1909 to 1910.

■ Athletic's first goalkeeper in the Football League, Bob Hewitson retained the position until the final two months of the campaign. In February 1908, he was alleged to have hurled a lump of Boundary Park mud at referee Mr T.P. Campbell in an ill-tempered 3–3 draw against Fulham and was suspended by the FA. Shortly after returning to action he was in trouble again and was suspended sine die by Athletic's directors on a charge of insubordination. Hewitson departed to Tottenham Hotspur in the close season, and by coincidence his debut for Spurs came in their very first appearance in a Football League match.

HEY, Charles

Full-back

Born: Salford, 1899.
Died: Rochdale, 1942.
Career: Gorton FC. Hurst January 1922. OLDHAM ATHLETIC May 1925. Hurst June 1930. Stockport July 1931. Rossendale United May 1932.

■ An extremely versatile reserve able to occupy most outfield positions, Charlie Hey made all but one of his first-team appearances during season 1926–27, deputising at outside-right for Jack King, and at left full-back for Teddy Ivill. He was generally fielded at full-back in Athletic's reserve team, for whom he made 141 appearances. During summer months he played cricket for Reddish CC.

HEYWOOD, Frederick

Inside-left

Born: Turton, c.1881.
Career: Turton FC. Newcastle United September 1900. Blackpool June 1902. Reading 1903. Blackpool July 1904. OLDHAM ATHLETIC May 1905. Darwen August 1906. Turton FC November 1908. Chorley.

■ Fred Heywood made his debut in Division One with Newcastle United in February 1901 and scored three goals in 13 consecutive appearances up to the end of the season. His first spell with Blackpool saw him miss just one League match in 1902–03 as inside partner to the amateur international outside-left, Harold Hardman. After a season with Reading he returned to Bloomfield Road but appeared only once at senior level before joining the Latics in May 1905. In addition to his five FA Cup appearances, Heywood played in 31 Lancashire Combination fixtures and scored seven goals.

HIBBERT, William

Centre-forward

Born: Golborne, 21 September 1884.
Died: Blackpool, 6 March 1949.
Career: Plank Lane Juniors. Newton-le-Willows. Bryn Central May 1905. Bury May 1906. Newcastle United October 1911, fee £1,950. Wartime guest with Arsenal, Bury, Sheffield Wednesday, Rochdale. Hartlepools United and Leeds City. Bradford City May 1920, fee £700. OLDHAM ATHLETIC May 1922, fee £500. Bridgend Town manager May 1923. Fall River Marksmen, US, coach July 1923. Hamilton Steelworks, Canada, September 1923. Saskatchewan Swastikas, Canada, October 1923. J & P Coates, Rhode Island, US, November 1923, coach season 1925–26. Gymnastic Club Valencia, Spain, coach June 1927. Wigan Borough trainer May 1928. Burscough Rangers coach February–March 1930. Budapest FC, Hungary, coach August 1930. Buxton November 1930.

■ A nimble, slightly-built centre-forward, Billy Hibbert was Newton-le-Willows' attack leader in January 1905 when they opposed the Latics in a Lancashire Combination B Division fixture. In a remarkable match, the Latics won 11–0 with Plumpton scoring the first five goals and Shoreman the final six. Latics went on to win promotion and Billy Hibbert eventually played for England and enjoyed a career which spanned 387 First Division matches and 174 goals. He rounded off his League career with a season at Boundary Park, and retired at the age of 38, never having played outside of the top flight.

HICKS, Keith

Central-defender

Born: Oldham, 9 August 1954.
Career: OLDHAM ATHLETIC associate schoolboy January 1970, apprentice December 1970, professional August 1972. Hereford United September 1980. Rochdale July 1985 to February 1987. Hyde United March 1987. Mossley player-manager 1987. Hyde United. Radcliffe Borough 1990–91. Mossley October 1991. Bacup Borough September 1992. Rossendale United trial January 1993. Chadderton coach season 1993–94. Rochdale Centre of Excellence director of coaching.

■ Fair-haired and lantern-jawed, Keith Hicks was established in Athletic's back four while still a youngster, his League debut coming just 14 months after signing on schoolboy forms. After just three appearances in his debut season, he began 1972–73 as first choice in central defence and played in every match during the season. Hicks missed only two matches in the following term, when the Championship of the Third Division was won. His long association with Athletic ended when he moved to Hereford United, where he clocked up 201 League appearances in a five-year stay. A groin injury sustained during his second season with Rochdale brought an end to his League career.

HILL, Clinton Scott 'Clint'

Central-defender

Born: Huyton, 19 October 1978.
Career: Tranmere Rovers trainee, professional July 1997. OLDHAM ATHLETIC July 2002, fee £225,000. Stoke City July 2003, fee £120,000. Crystal Palace loan November–December 2007, permanent January 2008.

■ Clint Hill joined Tranmere Rovers as a 15-year-old and went on to complete 170 matches. He also made a Wembley League Cup Final appearance against Leicester City in February 2000. One of his early matches for the Latics was against Tranmere and the no-nonsense centre-half crowned an impressive display by opening the scoring with a powerful header in Athletic's 2–0 victory. Sadly, a broken leg restricted Hill to 25 appearances, and in the close season he joined the general exodus from Boundary Park as chairman Moore withdrew financial support and the club faced the biggest crisis of its long history.

HILTON, Mark Gerard

Midfield

Born: Middleton, 15 January 1960.
Career: Stoke City associate schoolboy March 1976. OLDHAM ATHLETIC apprentice July 1976, professional January 1978. Bury August 1981 to June 1983. Oldham Town. Ashton United player-assistant manager 1988–89. Mossley player-manager. Ashton United October 1990. Mossley. Accrington Stanley 1991. Ashton United 1992. Curzon Ashton 1993. Oldham Town player and joint manager October 1993.

■ Mark Hilton spent five years with Athletic as a sturdy, hard-tackling midfielder who appeared to be making

steady progress, culminating in 24 League appearances in 1979–80. The following term, however, he lost out to new signing Ryszard Kowenicki and departed to Bury in search of first-team football. A year later, he suffered a broken leg in a Lancashire County Cup match, ironically against the Latics at Boundary Park.

HILTON, William Ashton

Right-back

Born: Oldham, 14 April 1911.
Died: Royton, Oldham, 31 January 1989.
Career: Bedford Lads. New Mills FC. OLDHAM ATHLETIC amateur May 1933, professional July 1934, retired due to knee injury during wartime season 1944–45.

■ Full-back Billy Hilton was educated at Coldhurst School, Oldham, and served his time as a fitter at Platt Brothers engineering works. The departure of Billy Porter to Manchester United in January 1935 opened the way for Hilton, who appeared in the final nine Division Two matches of 1934–35 and remained as Athletic's right-back for the remainder of his career. In addition to his 138 senior appearances, Hilton played in a further 98 wartime matches. He started a taxi business in 1948 and was proprietor of the Windmill Garage at Royton from 1952 to 1973. He was also chairman of Royton Council in 1962–63 and a Liberal Councillor for 17 years until 1978.

HITCHEN, Trevor

Half-back

Born: Sowerby Bridge, 25 September 1926.
Career: Sowerby Bridge Boys' Brigade.
Halifax Town amateur August 1943. Notts
County May 1945. Wartime guest with
Arsenal 1945–46. Wellington Town.
Southport January 1949. OLDHAM
ATHLETIC August 1956. Wigan Athletic
player-manager 1957. Southport manager
June 1958. Formby FC player 1959, later
manager and then chairman.

■ Trevor Hitchen became a familiar figure
on Third Division North grounds,
completing 266 League and Cup
appearances (37 goals) for Southport in a
seven and a half-year stay. He was an early
signing by Athletic's new manager Ted
Goodier but remained a peripheral figure,
his three League starts being made in three
different positions. In November 1973,
Hitchen was chairman of Formby when
they reached the first round proper of the
FA Cup for the first time in the club's
history. Latics were the visitors and won
2–0, George Jones scoring both goals.

HOBSON, Wilfred

Half-back

Born: Delves Lane, Consett, 26 January
1932.
Career: Crookshall juniors. Durham
County youths. West Stanley FC 1949.
OLDHAM ATHLETIC January 1953.
Gateshead June 1959.

■ A fine defensive wing-half, Wilf
Hobson was a speedy and forceful tackler
with an immense capacity for work. In
1959, his five years of consistent service
were rewarded with a benefit that was
shared with Bill Naylor. Athletic opposed
an 'All Stars XI' and won 6–4, with one of
their goals scored by guest star Len
Shackleton. Wilf Hobson's cousins,
Bobby and Tommy Lumley were inside-
forwards who began their League careers
with Charlton Athletic. A carpenter by
trade, when married in 1956 he made
most of the furniture in his new home.

HODGE, Martin John

Goalkeeper

Born: Southport, 4 February 1959.
Career: Southport Trinity. Plymouth
Argyle apprentice September 1975,
professional February 1977. Everton July
1979, fee £135,000. Preston North End
loan December 1981. OLDHAM
ATHLETIC loan July–September 1982.
Gillingham loan January 1983. Preston
North End loan February 1983. Sheffield
Wednesday loan August 1983, permanent
September 1983, fee £50,000. Leicester City
August 1988, fee £250,000. Hartlepool
United August 1991. Rochdale July 1993.
Plymouth Argyle August 1994, fee £10,000.
Sheffield Wednesday goalkeeping coach
July 1996, later reserve-team coach, first-
team coach June 2001 to October 2002.
Rochdale goalkeeping coach January 2003.
Leeds United goalkeeping coach July 2004.

■ Martin Hodge was manager Joe
Royle's first signing. His three-month
loan deal, however, was cancelled due to
illness after he had appeared in the
opening four matches of the season. A
safe handling and consistent goalkeeper,
Hodge joined Sheffield Wednesday and
during season 1986–87 broke the club
record for consecutive appearances (214
in League and Cup).

HODGSON, Douglas John Houston

Central-defender

Born: Frankston, Australia, 27 February
1969.
Career: Heidelberg FC, Australia. Sheffield
United July 1994. Plymouth Argyle loan
August 1995. Burnley loan October 1996.

OLDHAM ATHLETIC February 1997.
Northampton Town loan 9 October,
permanent 12 October 1998 to January
2000, fee £20,000.

■ A hard-tackling, robust central-
defender, Doug Hodgson also appeared
as a striker for the Latics and did not
look out of place, as he had originally
played as a forward in Australia.
Involved in a very serious car crash at
the age of 15, he received multiple
injuries and had to wear a neck brace
for three years, and it was a neck injury
sustained during his spell with
Northampton Town that ended his
League career some 16 years later.

HODKINSON, Andrew James

Midfield

Born: Ashton-under-Lyne, 4 November
1965.
Career: Tameside Schoolboys. Bolton
Wanderers apprentice. OLDHAM

ATHLETIC August 1983. Stockport County amateur August 1985, professional November 1985. Scunthorpe United August 1988, fee £10,000. Hyde United 1990. Goole Town 1991.

■ England Schoolboy International Andy Hodkinson looked an extremely promising prospect at 18 years of age. In the final home match of his debut season his first League goal proved to be the winner in a 2–1 victory against Grimsby Town, a result that ensured Athletic's survival in Division Two. Stockport County signed him following his release from Boundary Park, and in three seasons at Edgeley Park he was rarely absent, playing in 126/4 League and Cup matches and scoring 19 goals.

HODKINSON, David

Outside-left

Born: Lancaster, 18 January 1945.
Career: Lancashire Youth. OLDHAM ATHLETIC apprentice October 1961, professional February 1963.

■ David Hodkinson made his League debut against Doncaster Rovers in a 3–1 win at Boundary Park on 11 November 1961. Still two months away from his 17th birthday, he was one of Athletic's youngest debutants. Much later in the season, he deputised for John Bazley in the Easter Monday match against Tranmere Rovers at Boundary Park and again finished on the winning side in a 2–0 victory. Hodkinson emigrated to Canada in 1969 and became a headmaster in Ontario.

HODSON, James

Full-back

Born: Horwich, 5 September 1880.
Died: Holland, February 1938.
Career: St Helens Recreation July 1900. Bury May 1902. OLDHAM ATHLETIC June 1905, fee £15. Wartime guest with Southport Vulcan. Belfast Celtic (very briefly) May 1919. Brentford May 1919. Guildford United coach-manager February 1922. Berehem Sports Club, Antwerp, June 1923.

■ Jimmy Hodson's Athletic career began at Hudson Fold in the Lancashire Combination and 10 years later it was terminated by World War One, with the Latics runners-up for the First Division Championship. He began in League football with Bury and was reserve full-back in the squad that won the FA Cup Final in 1903. Although built along hefty lines, he combined strength with surprising pace for a man of his build. He was also remarkably free from injury, as his overall appearance figures reflects. Taking into account his first two seasons of Lancashire Combination football, he averaged 36 matches per season for 10 years.

HOLDEN, Andrew Ian

Central-defender

Born: Flint, 14 September 1962.
Career: Shotton Westminster. Rhyl FC. Chester City August 1983. Wigan Athletic October 1986, fee £45,000. OLDHAM ATHLETIC January 1989, fee £130,000, reserve-team coach 1992 until May 1997. Everton youth-team coach July 1997,

subsequently reserve-team coach. Tranmere Rovers assistant manager May 2001.

■ Andy Holden was working as a machine operator in a North Wales paper mill and playing part-time for Rhyl when Chester City signed him a month prior to his 21st birthday. A rock-hard central defender, he assisted Chester to promotion from Division Four in 1985–86. He subsequently cost Athletic £130,000, and in the season that Roger Palmer broke Athletic's all-time record for League goals, Andy Holden weighed in with four from just 13 matches, his aerial strength from set-pieces providing a real threat to opposing defences. No fewer than 12 knee and ankle operations combined to restrict the desperately unfortunate Holden to a solitary Wales cap and eventually terminated his playing career.

HOLDEN, Dean Thomas John

Defender

Born: Salford, 15 September 1979.
Career: Bolton Wanderers trainee, professional December 1997. OLDHAM ATHLETIC loan October 2001, permanent May 2002. Peterborough United July 2005. Falkirk January 2007.

■ Tall, strong and two-footed, England Youth International Dean Holden performed equally well in defence or at right wing-back. Initially a loan signing by Andy Ritchie, he was secured on a free

transfer, with a sell-on clause, in May 2002. After completing 124 senior appearances and captaining the side from 2004, Holden was out of contract in the summer of 2005 and joined Peterborough United. In January 2008 the 28-year-old defender fractured his tibia and fibula in a tackle with Celtic's Stephen McManus but is targeting a return to full fitness prior to the 2008–09 season.

HOLDEN, James Stewart

Defender

Born: Grange Moor, Yorkshire, 21 April 1942.
Career: Skelmanthorpe FC. Huddersfield Town from school May 1957. OLDHAM ATHLETIC July 1965. Rochdale January 1967. Wigan Athletic 1967. Hyde United December 1967. Stalybridge Celtic August 1968.

■ Stewart Holden was asked to fill a variety of roles during his spell with Athletic, appearing at full-back, wing-half and inside-forward. In short, a very useful utility player, but he was not commanding a regular League berth at the time of his transfer to Rochdale. A talented amateur cricketer, he played for Heyside C.C. for many years and later served on their committee.

HOLDEN, Richard William 'Rick'

Outside-left

Born: Skipton, 9 September 1964.
Career: Skipton LMS. Carnegie College. Burnley March 1986. Halifax Town September 1986. Watford March 1988, fee £125,000. OLDHAM ATHLETIC August 1989, fee £165,000. Manchester City July 1992, in exchange for Steve Redmond and Neil Pointon plus £300,000. OLDHAM ATHLETIC October 1993, fee £450,000. Blackpool September 1995. Peel FC. Isle of Man July 1996. Barnsley assistant manager.

■ Part of a great succession of Oldham Athletic wingmen down the years, Rick Holden was among the finest. A real wonder worker on the flank, he was able to avoid the sternest challenges and deliver quality crosses, sometimes from seemingly impossible angles. A real handful for opposing defenders, he was one of the brightest stars in a virile Athletic attack, and many were disappointed when he left

to join Manchester City in a transfer valued at £900,000. His second spell at Boundary Park was less successful as it encompassed relegation from the Premier League and a faltering start in Division One. In September 1995, with 20 months of his contract still to run, Holden requested and was granted a free transfer, having passed exams to qualify as a chartered physiotherapist.

HOLLIS, Ellis

Half-back

Born: Darwen.
Career: Darwen May 1905. Nelson 1909. OLDHAM ATHLETIC June 1911 to May 1914.

■ Ellis Hollis spent three years with Athletic but made only two first-team appearances. His debut was not a happy one, resulting in a 7–1 defeat at Blackburn Rovers in season 1912–13. Throughout his spell at Boundary Park his prospects of advancement were slim in the extreme with Athletic invariably fielding a middle line of three internationals.

HOLT, Andrew

Defender

Born: Stockport, 21 May 1978.
Career: Stockport Schoolboys. Manchester City School of Excellence 1989–92. OLDHAM ATHLETIC associate schoolboy 1992, trainee July 1994, professional July 1996. Hull City loan

March 2001, permanent May 2001, fee £150,000. Barnsley loan August 2002. Shrewsbury Town loan March 2002. Wrexham August 2004. Northampton Town July 2006.

■ Strapping defender Andy Holt made his first League appearance at 19 years of age, but did not become a regular until season 1998–99. For two seasons his pace, power, and attacking instincts from left wing-back attracted the attention of bigger clubs, but in 2000–01 his form faltered and he lost his place to Mark Innes.

HOLT, David

Defender

Born: Padiham, 26 February 1952.
Died: New Zealand, October 2003.
Career: Padiham Spotlights. Bury from school, professional October 1969. OLDHAM ATHLETIC December 1974, fee £25,000 plus Tony Bailey. Burnley July 1980 to June 1983, fee £45,000.

■ After joining Bury straight from school David Holt appeared in 189/6 League and Cup matches and scored nine goals. He cost Athletic a record fee in December 1974, and in six seasons gave excellent value, initially at left-half and later at left-back, partnering Ian Wood. Holt won a Division Three Championship medal with Burnley in 1981–82 and retired to pursue business interests in 1983. He died after suffering a heart attack in New Zealand where he had established a postal courier service.

HOLT, Edward

Outside-right

Born: Newton Heath, Manchester, 1881.
Career: Newton Heath Athletic. Newton Heath FC March 1899 to 1900. Newton Heath Athletic. OLDHAM ATHLETIC June 1904 to March 1906.

■ On trial at Newton Heath (the forerunners of Manchester United) wingman Teddy Holt was given a run out in a Second Division match against Chesterfield. Despite scoring one goal in the Heathens' 2–1 win, he was not offered a permanent engagement. He signed for the Latics in June 1904 and played in 28 of the 34 Lancashire Combination B Division matches during the season when promotion was secured. He did not feature regularly during the following season, and was suspended sine die by Athletic's directors after arriving late for a match in March 1906.

HOLT, Raymond

Centre-half

Born: Thorne, Yorkshire, 29 October 1939.
Career: Moor End FC. Huddersfield Town May 1958. OLDHAM ATHLETIC July 1965. Halifax Town July 1966. Scunthorpe United July 1968 to 1970. Worksop Town.

■ Ray Holt had three years to wait for a first-team outing with Huddersfield Town, but he began immediately at senior level with Athletic. He was not alone in enduring a torrid time at

Boundary Park, collecting only two winning bonuses from his 14/1 League outings. He did not appear at senior level again following Jimmy McIlroy's appointment as manager in mid-term. With his two subsequent clubs, Holt was generally a first-team player, appearing in 86 League matches for Halifax Town, and 50 for Scunthorpe United.

HOOLICKIN, Garry John

Defender

Born: Middleton, 29 October 1957.
Career: Middleton Schoolboys. Lancashire Schoolboys. OLDHAM ATHLETIC apprentice April 1974, professional July 1975, retired 1989.

■ Versatile defender Garry Hoolickin could play equally well at right-back or in central defence, and was a conspicuous figure in the Latics' defence in the early 1980s. For years in the shadow of Ian Wood, the popular, flame-haired defender nevertheless completed in excess of 200 senior appearances before a cruciate knee injury ended his 15 years at Boundary Park. He subsequently worked as a licensee in Middleton, and more recently in the property business. His son, Anthony, was a trainee with the Latics but did not reach professional status.

HOOLICKIN, Stephen

Right-back

Born: Moston, Manchester, 13 December 1951.

Career: Middleton Schoolboys. OLDHAM ATHLETIC associate schoolboy August 1966, apprentice April 1967, professional December 1969. Bury August 1973. Carlisle United October 1976, fee £20,000. Hull City December 1980, retired March 1982.

■ Seven years on from joining the Latics on schoolboy forms, Steve Hoolickin, elder brother of Garry, joined Bury on a free transfer. He had played in only eight League matches for Athletic, but missed only two first-team matches in his first season at Gigg Lane as Bury won promotion from Division Four. He played in 140 League matches for Bury, 143 for Carlisle United and 31 for Hull City. He eventually settled in Carlisle, where he was employed in the building trade.

HOOPER, Daniel

Centre-half

Born: Darlington, 15 September 1893. Died: Mansfield, 1973. Career: Harrogate Hill United. Darlington Rise Carr. OLDHAM ATHLETIC March 1919. Shildon Athletic July 1920. Darlington Rise Carr, reinstated amateur, October 1922. Lincoln City trial September 1924.

■ Danny Hooper gained a reputation in Army football in France when serving with the Royal Garrison Artillery. After demobilisation, he helped Rise Carr win the Darlington Charity Cup, and joined Athletic in March 1919. He was unfortunate to sustain a serious ankle injury on his debut and was sidelined for two months, thereafter operating – along with brother Fred – almost exclusively at reserve team level.

HOOPER, Frederick William

Inside-forward

Born: Darlington, 14 November 1894. Died: Darlington, 1982. Career: Darlington Rise Carr. Wartime guest with Grimsby Town. OLDHAM ATHLETIC March 1919. Darlington 1920. Rochdale August 1926. Consett October 1927.

■ The younger brother of Daniel Hooper, Fred was an inside-forward with a neat first touch and an eye for goal. He was much the cleverest forward in Athletic's reserves, finishing as leading scorer with 10 goals in 39 appearances. In six seasons with his home-town club, Darlington, Hooper scored 64 goals in 164 League and Cup matches and won a Third Division North Championship medal in 1925. In addition to Fred and Danny, the Hooper family of footballers also included Mark (Sheffield Wednesday) and Carl (Lincoln City).

HOPE, James Richard

Outside-right

Born: Weston, near Runcorn, 1907. Died: Chorlton-cum-Hardy, 27 July 1967. Career: Northwich Victoria. Witton Albion January 1928. Winsford United August 1929. OLDHAM ATHLETIC May 1931 to April 1932. Runcorn August 1932. Winsford United. Stalybridge Celtic August 1933. Clayton Aniline, reinstated amateur, December 1935.

■ One of a number of Cheshire County League recruits to assist the Latics in the 1930s, Hope's debut coincided with one of the best victories in a disappointing season, a 5–2 win against Notts County on 14 September 1931. After appearing in four consecutive Second Division matches in the same

month he did not feature again, Leslie Smalley being the player most favoured at outside-right.

HOPKINSON, Edward

Goalkeeper

Born: Wheatley Hill, Durham, 29 October 1935. Died: April 2004. Career: Royton Secondary Modern School. Chadderton Schoolboys. Lancashire Schoolboys. Mill Brow, Chadderton. Haggate Lads. OLDHAM ATHLETIC amateur 1951–52. Bolton Wanderers amateur August, professional November 1952, retired due to injury November 1969 and appointed to the club's coaching staff. Stockport County assistant manager July 1974. Ashton United manager. Bolton Wanderers goalkeeping coach 1979.

■ Eddie Hopkinson was one of the youngest ever players to represent Athletic when he made his debut in January 1952 at the age of 16 years and 75 days. He played only three times but in his second match, on a snowbound Boundary Park, Athletic ran riot, beating Chester 11–2. He joined First Division Bolton Wanderers in 1952, and ended his first campaign with an ever-present record. Before injury forced his retirement in 1969 he had appeared in a club record 519 League games. He was a member of Bolton Wanderers's FA Cup-winning side in 1958 and won 14 England caps. A true all-rounder, he played cricket and water polo for Royton and was an accomplished golfer. His son Paul, also a goalkeeper, played in League football for Stockport County.

HORROCKS, Harry

Outside-right

Born: Chorlton, Manchester, 10 May 1897.
Died: Dewsbury, 1973.
Career: Norman Athletic. Cleckheaton. Manchester City amateur season 1920–21. Bolton Wanderers amateur June 1921, professional June 1922. OLDHAM ATHLETIC July 1922. Crewe Alexandra July 1924. OLDHAM ATHLETIC trial October 1926.

■ At just 5ft 5in and 10st 3lb Harry Horrocks lacked any physical advantage, but was nevertheless a keen and spirited forager with sufficient skill to compensate. Although signed as a winger, he appeared mainly at inside-right in 15 matches in his debut season and scored Athletic's last Division One

goal in the relegation campaign of 1922–23. Despite an end-of-season clear out that saw six forwards released Horrocks was retained, but appeared in only eight of the Second Division matches in 1923–24.

HORSBURGH, John James

Goalkeeper

Born: Edinburgh, 17 November 1936.
Career: Dundee. OLDHAM ATHLETIC trial May, professional August 1961 to March 1962.

■ Johnny Horsburgh was on Dundee's transfer list when he accepted Athletic's invitation for a trial in a benefit match in aid of the Players' Benevolent Fund, held at Boundary Park in May 1961. Duly signed, he became one of four goalkeepers on Athletic's books, and with only three teams to play them in, the seriously under-employed Horsburgh even played as a wingman in the reserves before his contract was cancelled in March 1962.

HORTON, Leslie

Defender

Born: Salford, 12 July 1921.
Career: Tyldesley United. Rochdale April 1941. Rossendale United. OLDHAM ATHLETIC January 1944. Wartime guest with Hartlepools United. Carlisle United August 1948. Rochdale April 1950. York City July 1950. Halifax Town March 1951. Ashton United player-manager October 1952. Chloride Recreation player-

manager 1955, rejoined as manager October 1962.

■ Versatile defender Les Horton began with Athletic in wartime football, and when normal League fare resumed in 1946, he began a sequence of 75 consecutive League matches which was only interrupted by injury. Principally a wing-half, he was also a very capable full-back and even played odd games as an emergency centre-forward. His final appearance for Halifax Town was his 200th in League football. Horton subsequently worked for Chloride in Manchester, retired in 1979 and settled in Carnforth.

HOTTE, Mark Stephen

Central-defender

Born: Bradford, 27 September 1978.
Career: Rugby League for Bradford Northern Juniors in 1987–88, before switching to football. North of England Schoolboys. OLDHAM ATHLETIC trainee August 1995, professional July 1997. Scarborough January 2002. York City June 2005. Scarborough June 2006. Droylsden June 2007. Farsley Celtic January 2008.

■ Although lacking height Mark Hotte competed well in the air and his speed off the mark and man-marking skills were decided assets. The signing of experienced central defender Stuart Balmer from Wigan Athletic effectively ended Hotte's involvement at senior

level, and after just two substitute appearances in 2001–02 he was transfer listed and joined Scarborough in January 2002.

HOULAHAN, Harold

Inside-forward

Born: Coundon, County Durham, 14 February 1930.
Career: Durham City. Newcastle United February 1951. OLDHAM ATHLETIC May 1952. Darlington January 1954. Spennymoor United 1955–56.

■ A final career aggregate of 11 League goals in just 29 matches was a healthy scoring ratio, but inside-forward Harold Houlahan failed to establish himself in senior football. He scored three goals in six matches for the Latics and eight in 23 matches for Darlington.

HOWARTH, Christopher

Goalkeeper

Born: Bolton, 23 May 1986.
Career: Bolton Wanderers trainee. Stockport County loan January–February 2006. OLDHAM ATHLETIC loan August 2006. Carlisle United loan March 2007, permanent May 2007.

■ Signed on loan as cover for Les Pogliacomi, Chris Howarth was handed an early opportunity when the Australian's knee injury opened the way for his first taste of senior football. Fourth-choice goalkeeper at Bolton Wanderers, Howarth had spent a spell on loan at Stockport County without first team involvement. After coming off the bench on his debut, a 1–0 defeat by Port Vale, Howarth's first start against Swansea City saw him save a penalty and keep a clean sheet in the season's first victory. Sadly, he became the second Athletic goalkeeper to be injured when he was forced to limp off the pitch with a thigh strain in the Carling Cup defeat at Rotherham United.

HOWE, Frederick

Centre-forward

Born: Bredbury, Cheshire, 24 September 1912.
Died: Stockport, October 1984.
Career: Wilmslow. Hyde United. Stockport County amateur November 1930, professional September 1931. Hyde United September 1933. Liverpool March 1935. Manchester City June 1938. Grimsby Town October 1938. Wartime guest with Stockport County and Watford. OLDHAM ATHLETIC July 1946 to 1947. Ashton United February 1948, continuing as coach from July 1948.

■ 'A strong, well-made and fast attack leader who liked the ball pushed through between the backs.' Fred Howe was so described in a Manchester City football programme in 1938. World War Two robbed Howe of a large portion of his career, but despite approaching the veteran stage when he joined Athletic in July 1946 he was leading scorer with 20 goals in just 31 matches.

HOWSON, William

Inside-forward

Born: Garforth, Yorkshire, 22 October 1892.
Died: Bradford, 1959.
Career: Castleford Town 1919. Bradford City March 1920. OLDHAM ATHLETIC May 1923, fee £200. Halifax Town August 1924 to 1926.

■ One of several new forwards signed by Athletic following their relegation from the top flight in 1923, Billy Howson was a small but sturdy inside-forward with useful top-flight experience. During the course of his season at Boundary Park, Howson appeared in all forward positions apart from outside-left before losing his place to the amateur international J.E. Blair. Two seasons with Halifax Town wound up Howson's League career with aggregate figures of 39 goals in 126 appearances.

HUDSON Christopher John

Midfield

Born: Middleton, 25 November 1964.
Career: Manchester City Juniors. OLDHAM ATHLETIC September 1982. Kronfors, Sweden, June 1986. Rochdale non-contract February–May 1987.

■ Young reserve midfielder John Hudson was drafted in at left-back during season 1983–84 when a suitable replacement for the departed John Ryan was sought. The 13 starts and two substitute appearances he made accounted for the bulk of Hudson's senior appearances, as he was cruelly plagued by a succession of knee injuries

during his last two seasons at Boundary Park. For the past three years John has worked for the PFA as a head of community liaison.

HUDSON, Mark Alexander

Midfield

Born: Guildford, 30 March 1982.
Career: Aldershot School of Excellence. Swindon Town School of Excellence. Fulham Juniors 1995, professional July 1999. OLDHAM ATHLETIC loan August 2003 and again November 2003. Crystal Palace January 2004, fee £550,000.

■ Towering centre-back Mark Hudson impressed on his debut at Brentford with his unruffled approach and ability on the ball. He was one of a number of loan signings made by manager Ian Dowie following the exodus of star players during Athletic's major financial crisis in 2003. After two months on loan Hudson declined a long-term deal but subsequently returned for a further month, having failed to break into Fulham's first team in the interim. When manager Ian Dowie departed Boundary Park for Crystal Palace in December 2003, one of his first signings was Mark Hudson.

HUGHES Andrew John

Midfield

Born: Longsight, Manchester, 2 January 1978.
Career: Stockport Schoolboys. OLDHAM ATHLETIC associate schoolboy February 1992, trainee July 1994, professional January 1996. Notts County January 1998, fee £150,000. Reading July 2001, fee £300,000. Norwich City July 2005, fee £500,000. Leeds United August 2007.

■ A hard-tackling right-sided midfielder with plenty of pace and confidence, Andy Hughes nevertheless departed Boundary Park having played very few matches in his final season. A move to Notts County in mid-term brought almost instant success as the Magpies swept to the Championship of Division Three with a massive 17–point margin over runners-up Macclesfield Town. Hughes has subsequently enhanced his reputation with Reading, Norwich City and Leeds United.

HUGHES, Lee

Forward

Born: Smethwick, 22 May 1976.
Career: Warley & West Midlands Schoolboys. Kidderminster Harriers. West Bromwich Albion May 1997, fee £250,000. Coventry City August 2001, fee £5 million. West Bromwich Albion August 2002 to May 2004, fee £2.5 million. OLDHAM ATHLETIC August 2007.

■ The former roofer lived the dream when he joined West Bromwich Albion, the team he had supported from boyhood, from non-League Kidderminster Harriers. At either side of a £5 million transfer to Coventry City he completed a century of goals for the Albion before his contract was cancelled following the well-documented off-the-field problems that brought his football career to an abrupt halt. After serving three years of a six-year sentence he joined Athletic, whose representatives had visited him in Featherstone prison to arrange the controversial move to Boundary Park. It could be said that the ex-Premier League striker's incarceration robbed him of the prime years of his career, but in an injury-plagued first season he nevertheless showed heartening glimpses of his predatory finishing skllls. Seven goals in as many matches in mid season included the campaign's only hat-trick, clinically completed, despite his predictably abusive 'welcome' to the New Den.

HUGHES, Mark Anthony

Midfield

Born: Dungannon, Northern Ireland, 16 September 1983.
Career: Tottenham Hotspur trainee, professional July 2001. Northampton Town loan August–September 2004. OLDHAM ATHLETIC loan November 2004, permanent February 2005. Thurrock FC September 2006. Chesterfield November 2006. Stevenage Borough January 2007. Chester City July 2007.

■ Defensive midfielder Mark Hughes has represented Northern Ireland at every level up to full international, his two caps coming in the summer of 2006 when he was still registered with Athletic. Hughes made an excellent start at Boundary Park but fell out of favour following the appointment of new manager John Sheridan and had the last nine months of his contract paid up.

HULME, Aaron

Full-back

Born: Manchester, 1883.
Died: Failsworth, near Manchester, November 1933.
Career: Newton Heath Athletic. Colne FC May 1904. OLDHAM ATHLETIC October 1904. Manchester United May 1906. Nelson 1909. Hyde FC March 1910. St Helens Recreation August 1912. Newton Heath Athletic August 1913.

■ In addition to four FA Cup tie appearances for Athletic, Aaron Hulme featured regularly in two seasons of Lancashire Combination football, totalling 50 appearances. He helped lift Athletic from the B Division of the Combination in 1904–05, but left to join Manchester United at the end of the following season. He played in only four League matches in two seasons for United before returning to Lancashire Combination football. Aaron Hulme lost his life as a result of a motoring accident and was buried at Failsworth Cemetery on 6 November 1933.

HUMPHRIES, John Stephen

Forward

Born: Farnworth, 18 July 1964.
Career: OLDHAM ATHLETIC apprentice June 1980, professional July 1982. Rochdale loan March 1984. Horwich RMI October 1984. Telford United.

■ In Joe Royle's first season in charge of Athletic, 18-year-old John Humphries

was just one of several strikers tried by the new manager. With Rodger Wylde first choice, several pairings were tried, Darron McDonough being the most successful. Humphries was loaned to Rochdale in March 1984, and six outings before the end of the season proved to be his last in League football.

HUNTER, Allan

Central-defender

Born: Sion Mills, County Tyrone, Northern Ireland, 30 June 1946.
Career: Coleraine amateur 1962, professional 1965. Leeds United trial 1965. OLDHAM ATHLETIC January 1967, fee £5,000. Blackburn Rovers June 1969, fee £30,000. Ipswich Town September 1971, fee £60,000 plus Robert Bell. Colchester United player-manager May 1982 to January 1983, later returning as assistant manager until November 1987.

■ Allan Hunter had all the attributes necessary for success in central defence, and within 13 months of joining Athletic he was very unfortunate to miss the chance of his first full cap when he damaged knee ligaments playing for the reserves in February 1968. Good in the air and with outstanding control on the ground, the long striding Hunter was obviously destined for bigger things. He netted Athletic a handsome profit when he moved at the close of the relegation

season 1968–69 to Second Division Blackburn Rovers. Ipswich Town took him into Division One, where he enjoyed great success, appearing in 280 League matches. Capped by Northern Ireland at Amateur, Youth, and Under-23 levels, he won 53 full caps and was an FA Cup winner with Ipswich Town in 1978.

HUNTER, George Charles

Centre-half

Born: Peshawar, India 1885.
Died: Lambeth, London, February 1934.
Career: Maidstone. Croydon Common August 1907. Aston Villa February 1908. OLDHAM ATHLETIC January 1912. Chelsea March 1913. Manchester United March 1914 to January 1915, fee £1,300. Wartime guest with Croydon Common, Brentford and Birmingham. Portsmouth August 1919, retired 1922.

■ Standing just 5ft 6in tall, 'Cocky' Hunter was whole-hearted, tough, and a vicious tackler who never knew when he was beaten. Sadly, his temperament regularly brought him into conflict with both referees and the game's authorities, and his hurried exit from Boundary Park was followed by a similar departure from Stamford Bridge a little over a year later. Manchester United made him club captain but he set the worst possible example – less than a year on he was suspended sine die for breaches of training regulations. In earlier days Hunter was twice a Football League representative and a member of the Aston Villa side that won the League Championship. Hailing from a military background and born within 10 miles of the Khyber Pass, he saw active service in both France and Gallipoli during World War One.

HURST, John 'Jack'

Centre-half

Born: Lever Bridge, near Bolton, 27 October 1914.
Died: Harrow, February 2002.
Career: Lever Bridge. Bolton Wanderers amateur October 1932, professional May 1933. Wartime guest with Swindon Town, York City, Reading and Norwich City. OLDHAM ATHLETIC February 1947, fee £1,510. Chelmsford City August 1951.

■ Jack Hurst served as a gunner in the Royal Artillery during World War Two. He was evacuated from Dunkirk in 1940 and served in El Alamein, Tobruk and Italy before being demobilised in October 1945. Rejoining Bolton Wanderers in season 1945–46 he played in eight rounds of the FA Cup including the semi-final against Charlton Athletic at Villa Park. He joined the Latics in the closing stages of the following season and, apart from his final season when he lost out to Archie Whyte, was a prominent figure in Athletic's rearguard for four seasons. On retirement, teetotaller Jack became a Heywood publican before moving to Middlesex where he worked in a pharmaceutical laboratory until retirement age.

HURST, John

Defender

Born: Blackpool, 6 February 1947.
Career: Blackpool Schoolboys. Everton apprentice September 1962, professional October 1964. OLDHAM ATHLETIC June 1976 to June 1981.

■ A polished wing-half with superb anticipation, John Hurst's First Division pedigree enabled him to see a move beyond the next and, as with all gifted players, he always appeared to have time to spare in achieving his ends. In a career spent entirely in the top two divisions Hurst amassed over 500 League appearances and scored 14 goals. During his lengthy spell with Everton he won nine England Under-23 caps, was an FA Cup finalist in 1968 and a League Championship winner in 1970.

HUTCHINSON, James Arthur

Inside-forward

Born: Sheffield, 28 December 1915.
Died: Sheffield, November 1997.
Career: Aqueduct FC, Sheffield. Sheffield United November 1937. Wartime guest with Bradford Park Avenue, Bradford City, Hull City, Lincoln City and Port Vale. Bournemouth & Boscombe Athletic June 1946. Lincoln City November 1946. OLDHAM ATHLETIC February 1949, retired due to injury August 1950.

■ Jimmy Hutchinson made his name with Lincoln City as a persistent, strong running forward with a good shot in either foot. He scored 32 goals in 41 matches in 1947–48 when the Imps won the Championship of the Third Division North. A bright start to his Latics career was sadly cut short by an injury sustained at Southport in October 1949. During World War Two he served in the Royal Navy on-board HMS *Rodney* on Malta convoys. His son, Barry, also an inside-forward with a fine scoring record, netted 116 League goals in a career spanning six League clubs in the 1950s and 1960s.

INNES, Mark

Defender/Midfield

Born: Bellshill, Glasgow, 27 September 1978.
Career: Lanarkshire Schoolboys. Mill United, Airdrie. Yett Farm Boys' Club. OLDHAM ATHLETIC trainee August 1994, professional October 1995.

Chesterfield loan December 2001, permanent January 2002. Port Vale March 2005. St Mirren trial July 2006. Hyde United September 2007.

■ A talented schools footballer and Scotland Youth international, Mark Innes broke into the League side with a regular run of matches on the left side of midfield in 1998–99 and scored a timely first goal against Reading in a 2–0 victory that ensured Division Two survival. Increasingly involved at senior level over the following two seasons, it was surprising that he featured only as a substitute in 2001–02, apart from two starts in the LDV Vans Trophy matches.

IRONSIDE, Ian

Goalkeeper

Born: Sheffield, 8 March 1964.
Career: Barnsley September 1982. Matlock Town. North Ferriby United. Scarborough March 1988. Middlesbrough August 1991, fee £40,000. Scarborough loan March 1992. Stockport County September 1993. Scarborough March 1995. OLDHAM ATHLETIC July 1997, retired due to injury 1998.

■ Ian Ironside can have few happy memories of Boundary Park, as he was Scarborough's goalkeeper on the receiving end of Frank Bunn's double hat-trick in the Latics' 7–0 Football League Cup victory in October 1990. During his season at Boundary Park the unfortunate Ironside suffered a thigh muscle injury and also had operations on both ankles that forced his retirement from the game. Ian is the son of Roy Ironside, a goalkeeper during the 1950s and 1960s, with 333 League appearances for Rotherham United and Barnsley.

IRVINE, David

Forward

Born: Cockermouth, 10 September 1951.
Career: Workington May 1970. Everton January 1973, fee £35,000. Sheffield United loan September 1975. OLDHAM ATHLETIC June 1976. Fort Lauderdale Strikers, US, April 1977. Tulsa Roughnecks, US, June 1980. Atlanta Chiefs, US, July 1980. San Jose Earthquakes, US, June 1981.

■ England Youth international Dave Irvine, a free transfer signing by Athletic, shared forward duties with David Shaw and Vic Halom. Eight goals in 23 starts and four appearances from the bench was a respectable return, but his true potential was realised during five seasons in the North American Soccer League, his best return coming in 1978 when he scored 21 goals for Fort Lauderdale Strikers.

IRWIN, Joseph Denis

Full-back

Born: Cork, Ireland, 31 October 1965.
Career: Turners Cross College, Cork. Leeds United apprentice March 1982, professional November 1983. OLDHAM ATHLETIC May 1986. Manchester United June 1990, fee £625,000. Wolverhampton Wanderers July 2002.

■ Full-back Denis Irwin is best

remembered at Boundary Park for his speedy breaks out of defence, followed by accurate, early balls into the opponents penalty area. He also packed a powerful right-foot shot and was particularly dangerous from free-kicks, even from long distance. The only player to be capped at six levels by Ireland, Irwin announced his retirement from international football in January 2000 after 56 caps, making his final appearance against Turkey in November 1999. With more than 500 senior outings with Manchester United and a collection of medals that included seven Championships, two European trophies, three FA Cups and one League Cup, Irwin rounded off his long and successful career with two seasons at Wolverhampton Wanderers.

IVILL, Edward

Full-back

Born: Little Hulton, 7 December 1898.
Died: Accrington, 24 November 1979.
Career: Bolton Wanderers amateur. Atherton FC. OLDHAM ATHLETIC July 1924. Wolverhampton Wanderers November 1932. Charlton Athletic January 1933, fee £1,700. Accrington Stanley July 1935, reserve-team coach August 1936. Clitheroe August 1937.

■ 'Consistency personified' would be a fair appraisal of Teddy Ivill's Athletic career. He captained Atherton for two seasons from centre half-back, but eventually settled at full-back after

moving to Boundary Park. During a spell of five seasons from 1927 to 1932 Ivill did not miss a single League or Cup match. He was awarded a benefit match in May 1932 and, six months later, was transferred to Wolverhampton Wanderers. Teddy's son, Jeffrey, was an amateur with the Latics in the 1940s, but did not reach senior level.

JACK, Rodney Alphonso

Forward

Born: Kingstown, St Vincent, 28 September 1972.
Career: Lambada, Barbados, August 1994. Torquay United October 1995. Crewe Alexandra August 1998, fee £650,000. Rushden & Diamonds July 2003. OLDHAM ATHLETIC July 2004. Waterford United April 2005. Crewe Alexandra August 2006 to May 2007. Southport July 2007.

■ Rodney Jack arrived at Boundary Park as a seasoned performer with almost 350 League and Cup games and 85 goals to his credit. He followed manager Brian Talbot to Athletic after Rushden & Diamonds were relegated from the Football League. With 75 full caps for St Vincent and the ability to fill any forward or wide midfield position, he started brightly but was seriously injured in October while on international duty with St Vincent. Although he recovered in late season, new manager Ronnie Moore opted to pay up the remainder of his one-year contract in April 2005.

JACKSON, Albert

Defender

Born: Manchester, 12 September 1943.
Career: Manchester United Juniors.
OLDHAM ATHLETIC amateur 1961,
professional December 1962. Mossley loan
September 1962. Bangor City May 1966.
Wigan Athletic. Mossley 1975–76.

■ Albert Jackson made his League debut at centre-half, but the bulk of his first team outings came as centre-forward. When new manager Gordon Hurst was installed for 1965–66, Jackson was his first choice as attack leader. He had scored four goals in 17 League and Cup matches at the time of the appointment of Jimmy McIlroy as player-manager in mid-season, but did not appear again at senior level following the Irish international's arrival.

JACKSON, Harry

Inside-forward

Born: Shaw, near Oldham, 12 May 1934.
Career: Chadderton Schoolboys.
OLDHAM ATHLETIC June 1951.
Rochdale October 1955. Northwich
Victoria 1956. Stalybridge Celtic June
1956. Mossley February 1957.

■ An outstanding all-round sportsman as a junior, Harry Jackson represented Lancashire Schoolboys in both swimming and cricket before becoming a professional footballer. As an opening batsman he reached Minor Counties level with Lancashire. In club cricket with Crompton he scored a 50 on every ground in the Central Lancashire League. He made only 10 senior appearances for Athletic, a total that included a single

outing at Chester in September 1952, the season in which Athletic went on to secure the Championship of the Third Division North. Further opportunities were denied him when he was called up for National Service in the same month.

JACKSON, Norman Edward

Full-back

Born: Bradford, 6 July 1925.
Died: Chesterfield, September 2003.
Career: Manningham Mills FC. Sheffield
Wednesday October 1948, fee £25. Bristol
City June 1954, fee £750. OLDHAM
ATHLETIC July 1956 to June 1957.

■ In a modest League career of just 41 matches Norman Jackson nevertheless featured in two Championship-winning sides. He made 10 appearances for Second Division champions Sheffield Wednesday in 1951–52 and played in seven matches for Bristol City in 1954–55 when they were Third Division South champions. His season with Athletic was plagued by injury, which resulted in a cartilage operation in January 1957. Aside from football, Jackson spent his summers playing cricket in the Bradford League.

JACKSON, Robert

Full-back

Born: Middleton, 5 June 1934.
Career: Lancashire Schoolboys. OLDHAM
ATHLETIC amateur June 1949, professional
August 1951. Lincoln City March 1955.
Wisbech Town 1964 to October 1966.

■ An outstanding schoolboy footballer, Bob Jackson made his League debut at 17 years of age in season 1951–52, shortly after signing part-time professional

forms. By season 1954–55 he had claimed the first-team spot at right-back from Les Smith, and his outstanding promise was rewarded with a place in the Third Division North representative side that season. Just prior to the transfer deadline in March 1955 he moved to Lincoln City, where he went on to complete 235 League appearances.

JARRETT, Jason Lee Mee

Midfield

Born: Bury, 14 September 1979.
Career: Blackpool trainee, professional July
1998. Wrexham October 1999. Bury July
2000. Wigan Athletic March 2002, fee
£75,000. Stoke City loan January 2005.
Norwich City July 2005. Plymouth Argyle
loan November 2005. Preston North End
March 2006. Hull City loan November
2006. Leicester City loan February 2007.
Queen's Park Rangers loan October 2007.
OLDHAM ATHLETIC loan January 2008.

■ The all-action central-midfielder was a key member of Wigan Athletic's 2002–03 Division Two Championship side but a broken leg restricted him to 4/10 appearances in 2004–05 when promotion to the Premier League was gained. Despite having played little first-team football for Preston North End all season, Jarrett was immediately impressive on his debut, assisting Athletic to their first home win for two months. His one-month loan deal was immediately extended to cover the remainder of the season, and the energetic midfielder showed increasing evidence of his higher-level experience as his match fitness improved. His three goals in two games in March were an added bonus.

JARVIS, John Brian

Half-back

Born: Bangor-on-Dee, 26 August 1933.
Died: Shrewsbury, January 2004.
Career: Wrexham amateur May 1951, professional July 1952. OLDHAM ATHLETIC July 1959. Bankstown, Sydney, Australia, March 1963. Altrincham September 1963. Australian football April 1964. Witton Albion. Colwyn Bay August 1966. Borough United September 1966 to May 1967.

■ Once described as 'a hunk of Welsh granite', wing-half Brian Jarvis joined Wrexham as an amateur straight from school and signed professional forms on completion of his RAF National Service. He had appeared in 64 League matches for the Robins when he joined the Latics and was one of four new signings included in the season's opening fixture, a 2–0 win against Bradford Park Avenue. Stocky, hard-working and fearless, Jarvis proved a great clubman whose final season saw the Latics promoted from Division Four.

JEAVONS, William Henry

Outside-right

Born: Woodhouse Mill, near Sheffield, 9 February 1912.
Died: Burnley, 2 April 1992.
Career: Woodhouse Brunswick. Trials with Huddersfield Town and Chesterfield October 1930. Scarborough trial April 1931. Chesterfield amateur August, professional December 1931. Burnley June

1932. Accrington Stanley June 1933. OLDHAM ATHLETIC February 1934. Southport July 1934. Wrexham July 1935. Shrewsbury Town December 1935. Burton Town August 1936. Worcester City January 1938. Wartime guest with Burnley.

■ Signed two days after Athletic's sale of Cliff Chadwick to Middlesbrough, Billy Jeavons scored in his second outing, a 2–0 win against Blackpool, but played in what proved to be his last match the following week, a 5–2 defeat at Bradford City. Sadly, he failed to reproduce the form that had seen him score seven goals in 17 matches for Accrington Stanley, a sequence that began with a stunning debut against New Brighton in November 1933 when he scored twice in a 3–0 victory. A Burnley native for 60 years, Jeavons worked as an engineer with Joseph Lucas until retirement in 1974.

JENNINGS, Alf

Outside-right

Born: Finsbury Park, 30 May 1904.
Died: Enfield, February 1994.
Career: Barnet FC. Tottenham Hotspur September 1922. Poole Town August 1925. OLDHAM ATHLETIC May 1926. Poole Town May 1927.

■ Athletic gave the tall, long-striding wingman Alf Jennings a second chance in senior football but he failed to capitalise after starting the season as first-choice outside-right, and returned to Poole Town after a season of reserve team football. In earlier days he spent three years with Tottenham Hotspur without reaching senior level.

JEPSON, Ronald Francis

Forward

Born: Stoke-on-Trent, 12 May 1963.
Career: Nantwich Town. Port Vale March 1989. Peterborough United loan January 1990. Preston North End February 1991, fee £80,000. Exeter City July 1992, fee £60,000. Huddersfield Town December 1993, fee £60,000. Bury July 1996, fee £40,000. OLDHAM ATHLETIC January 1998, fee £30,000. Burnley July 1998, reserve team manager 2002. Gillingham assistant manager, manager November 2005 to September 2007. Huddersfield Town assistant manager April 2008.

■ Despite a late start in League football Ronnie Jepson proved to be an extremely durable performer. Although operating mainly from the bench, the flame-haired striker was still playing for Burnley at 37 years of age. Prior to joining the Latics, Jepson assisted Bury to the Division Two Championship in 1996–97, but the goals had dried up in the following season when Athletic signed him in January 1998. In nine matches Jepson scored four goals and helped lift Athletic to 13th position in Division Two, but in May he departed Boundary Park, in company with the manager who had signed him, Neil Warnock.

JESSOP, William

Outside-left

Born: Preston, 22 April 1922.
Died: Stafford, May 1994.
Career: Preston Schoolboys. Preston North End September 1940. Wartime guest with Accrington Stanley, Notts County, Walsall & Fulham. Stockport County May 1947. OLDHAM ATHLETIC February 1948, fee £1,250. Wrexham June 1951, in part exchange for Dennis Grainger. Bloxwich Strollers July 1952. Nuneaton Borough July 1953. Rugby Town July 1958. Hinckley Athletic December 1958.

■ At 14 years of age Billy Jessop was a member of the Preston Schoolboys team that jointly held the English Schools' Challenge Shield. He was taken onto North End's ground staff straight from school, but departed Deepdale at the

close of the first peacetime season and scored his first League goal on his debut for Stockport County. Whether fielded at inside or outside-left, Jessop was a lively attacking force with admirable ball control. His best season at Boundary Park was 1949–50 when he missed only one match during the season, scoring nine goals in 46 League and Cup matches.

JOBSON, Richard Ian

Central-defender

Born: Cottingham, Yorkshire, 9 May 1963. Career: Nottingham and English Universities. Burton Albion August 1981. Watford November 1982, fee £22,000. Hull City February 1985, fee £40,000. OLDHAM ATHLETIC August 1990, fee £460,000. Leeds United October 1995, fee £1million. Southend United loan January 1998. Manchester City March 1998. Watford loan October 2000. Tranmere Rovers loan December 2000, permanent March 2001. Rochdale player-coach September 2001, retired May 2003.

■ England B international Richard Jobson, a versatile and polished defender, was originally plucked out of non-League football by Watford's manager Graham Taylor. In a lengthy subsequent spell with Hull City he made 219/2 League appearances, and the cultured central defender found immediate success at Boundary Park, making 43/1 appearances in the Division Two Championship campaign

of 1990–91. Apart from a spell on the sidelines due to injury in season 1994–95, his wonderful consistency ensured that he otherwise missed very little first-team action. An injury-plagued spell with Leeds United followed, but in season 1999–2000 he appeared in 43/1 matches for Manchester City who won promotion to the Premier League. Jobson's League career ended at Rochdale with the impressive overall record of 580/8 League matches and 40 goals.

JOHN, Raymond Charles

Inside-forward

Born: Swansea, 22 November 1932. Career: Swansea Schoolboys. Tottenham Hotspur amateur January 1950. Barnsley May 1953. Exeter City July 1954. OLDHAM ATHLETIC December 1958, in part-exchange for Jimmy Thompson. Margate July 1960.

■ Ray John signed his first professional form with Barnsley, but made his debut in League football with Exeter City. In four years with the Grecians he scored 18 goals in 143 matches and rejoined his former boss, Norman Dodgin, when he joined the Latics midway through season 1958–59. He scored five goals in 19 matches as Athletic finished the season in 21st position in Division Four, but his second season was curtailed by a serious knee injury as Athletic slumped to 23rd place in the table.

JOHNSON, Harry

Inside-forward

Born: Radcliffe, 4 December 1910. Died: Scunthorpe, 10 December 1981. Career: Great Harwood. Winsford United. Bury trial December 1929. West Bromwich Albion amateur April 1930. Stalybridge Celtic amateur 1931. OLDHAM ATHLETIC January 1931. Southend United May 1934. Exeter City June 1936. Scunthorpe United July 1937 to 1940.

■ Former cotton mill worker Harry Johnson was a bustling raider and a dangerous marksman anywhere near to goal. He marked his League debut by heading a fine goal against Southampton, and while his scoring ratio with Athletic was a respectable one he did even better in his first season with Southend United, scoring 15 in just 23 matches. When Scunthorpe United won the Midland League Championship in 1938–39 he

hardly knew failure, scoring the remarkable total of 51 goals. An all-round sportsman, Johnson spent summer months playing for Radcliffe Cricket Club in the Central Lancashire League.

JOHNSON, Jermaine

Forward

Born: Kingston, Jamaica, 25 June 1980.
Career: Tivoli Gardens, Jamaica. Bolton Wanderers September 2001, fee £750,000. OLDHAM ATHLETIC loan November 2003, permanent March 2004. Contract cancelled February 2005, then re-signed on non-contract forms March 2005. Tivoli Gardens, Jamaica May 2005. Bradford City June 2006. Sheffield Wednesday January 2007, fee £500,000.

■ 'JJ' Johnson began at Boundary Park on a lengthy loan spell from Bolton Wanderers. He initially scored four goals in 14 appearances and, when released by the Wanderers, became one of new manager Talbot's five transfer deadline signings. The pacy Jamaican international suffered from inconsistent form during a frustrating spell at Boundary Park when his finishing failed to match his occasionally brilliant approach play.

JOHNSTON, Thomas Bourhill

Centre-forward

Born: Loanhead, Midlothian, 18 August 1927.
Career: Loanhead Mayflower. Peebles Rovers May 1949. Third Lanark trial. Kilmarnock November 1949. Darlington April 1951. OLDHAM ATHLETIC March 1952. Norwich City June 1952, fee £500. Newport County October 1954, fee £3,000. Leyton Orient February 1956, fee £6,000 plus Mike Burgess. Blackburn Rovers March 1958, fee £15,000. Leyton Orient February 1959. Gillingham September 1961, fee £3,000. Folkestone Town player-coach July 1962. Lytham St Annes October 1965. Emigrated to Australia in February 1972 and coached Lysaghts FC.

■ A former miner who gave up pit work after having a leg broken and nearly losing an arm, centre-forward Tommy Johnston led Kilmarnock's goal-scoring

lists in his debut season with 15 in just 19 League and Cup matches. He went on to amass 238 League goals in 406 matches in an outstanding career but was at Boundary Park only a matter of weeks after failing to dislodge Eric Gemmell as attack leader. Subsequently, a total of 43 goals in 1957–58 made him the leading scorer in the Football League. Johnston holds the Leyton Orient club record for most League goals (121), and most goals in a season (35 in 1957–58).

JOHNSTON, William Cecil

Inside-forward

Born: Coalisland near Dungannon, Northern Ireland, 21 May 1942.
Career: Coalisland Rangers. Glenavon amateur 1960. OLDHAM ATHLETIC June 1966 to October 1968. Coleraine. Crusaders coach 1970, later manager. Glenavon manager 1985.

■ Despite having played Rugby Union at school, and later combining soccer with his profession as a schoolteacher, Billy Johnston won every available honour in Irish football. Capped at both amateur and full levels and with seven appearances for the Irish League, he seemed the ideal successor to Jimmy McIlroy in Athletic's attack. Sadly, in the first minute of his sixth League match at Middlesbrough, Johnston suffered a compound fracture of his right ankle, and was sidelined for the remainder of the season. A complete recovery eluded him and in October 1968 he reluctantly announced his retirement.

JOHNSTON, William Gifford

Forward

Born: St George's, Edinburgh, 16 January 1901.
Died: Newton Heath, Manchester, 23 November 1964.
Career: Edinburgh Schoolboys. Dalkeith Thistle. Selby Town December 1918. Huddersfield Town November 1920, fee £250. Stockport County December 1924, fee £1,500. Manchester United October 1927, fee £3,000. Macclesfield Town June 1929. Manchester United May 1931. OLDHAM ATHLETIC May 1932, fee £300. Frickley Colliery player-manager June 1935 to late 1936.

■ During three seasons at Boundary Park Billy Johnston was the schemer of the attack, his vision and ball control from the midfield area effectively keeping Athletic's attack on the move. In earlier days he captained Edinburgh

Schoolboys and played twice for Scotland Schools. He scored 65 career goals in 256 League appearances for his four senior clubs, enjoying two separate spells with Manchester United which might have totalled three, but Athletic refused to consider an approach from Old Trafford in February 1934. An excellent golfer, Johnston later became a licensee in Salford before moving to Abergele in a similar capacity.

JOHNSTONE, Robert 'Bobby'

Inside-forward

Born: Selkirk, 7 September 1929.
Died: Selkirk, 22 August 2001.
Career: Newtongrange Bluebell. Newtongrange Star. Hibernian 1946. Manchester City March 1955, fee £22,000. Hibernian September 1959, fee £12,000. OLDHAM ATHLETIC October 1960, fee £4,000. Witton Albion May 1965 but retired very shortly afterwards due to injury. Later coached Mount Pleasant of the Oldham Amateur League.

■ The home debut of Bobby Johnstone, against Exeter City on 15 October 1960 attracted a crowd of 17,116 spectators to Boundary Park. – the highest home attendance for six and a half years. Johnstone immediately brought flair and

excitement back to a club starved of hope and success. Although lacking mobility in later seasons due to a troublesome knee injury, he remained an essential element, always likely to lay on a goalscoring opportunity with his perceptive, defence-splitting passing ability. In earlier days he was a member of the 'Famous Five' Hibernian international forward line and won successive Scottish League titles in 1951 and 1952. At the time of his move to Athletic, Johnstone had scored exactly 100 Scottish League goals and was the holder of 17 international caps. With Manchester City he appeared and scored in the FA Cup Finals of 1955 and 1956. After retiring from the game he settled in the Hollinwood area and starred as a crown-green and flat bowler. His biography *Bobby Johnstone: The Passing Of An Age*, written by John Leigh and published by Breedon Books, is a fitting tribute to an outstanding footballer.

JOHNSTONE, William

Inside-forward

Born: Markinch, Fife, 18 May 1901.
Died: St Andrew's, Fife, 1976.
Career: Fife Juniors. Rosslyn Juniors. Dundee United. Kings' Park February 1922. Clyde during season 1922–23. Reading October 1926, fee £1,125. Arsenal March 1929, in exchange for J.C. Barley. OLDHAM ATHLETIC January 1931, fee £2,130. Clyde October 1933.

■ Billy Johnstone scored 36 goals for Clyde in season 1925–26, assisting them

to promotion from the Second Division of the Scottish League. Reading paid a four-figure fee for him and his goals helped take the Berkshire club to the semi-final of the FA Cup in 1927. A significant fee was required to bring him to Boundary Park, despite the fact that he had played little first-team football for Arsenal. The former miner made an immediate impact at Boundary Park, however, scoring 13 goals in his first 16 outings.

JONES, Alexander

Central-defender

Born: Blackburn, 27 November 1964.
Career: Bury Schoolboys. Blackburn Rovers associate schoolboy. OLDHAM ATHLETIC apprentice July 1981, professional December 1982. Stockport County loan October 1984. Preston North End July 1986. Carlisle United September 1989. Rochdale June 1991, fee £17,500. Motherwell January 1992, fee £40,000. Rochdale loan September 1992, permanent December 1992, fee £30,000. Halifax Town March 1994. Stalybridge Celtic 1995. Chorley loan April–May 1996. Southport July 1996. Lancaster City March 1997. Radcliffe Borough player-manager June 1998. Ramsbottom United player-coach January 1999.

■ The son of inside-forward George Jones, a member of Athletic's 1973–74 Third Division Championship-winning team, Alex made his Latics debut at 18 years of age but failed to establish

himself, and was released on a free transfer in May 1986. He joined Preston North End and was immediately successful, making maximum appearances in the Division Four promotion campaign of 1986–87, North End's first season on their new plastic pitch. Jones remained at Deepdale to complete 100/1 League appearances, the major part of his career aggregate of 215/5 games for five Football League clubs.

JONES, Arthur

Outside-right

Born: Gwersyllt, Denbighshire, 22 August 1912.
Died: Wrexham, March 2002.
Career: Cross Street FC. Holyhead. Wrexham amateur 1931, professional May 1932. Hyde United September 1932. OLDHAM ATHLETIC July 1935. Bradley Rangers January 1940. Wartime guest with Bath City and Tranmere Rovers.

■ Arthur Jones had scored 22 goals for Hyde United in the season prior to his move to Boundary Park. In addition to neat footwork and the ability to centre accurately, the popular Welshman was not afraid to cut inside for a shot, 30 goals in 98 League matches being an excellent ratio for a wide player. His finest individual performance came during his first season at Boundary Park when he scored four goals – including one penalty – against his previous club, Wrexham, in a 5–2 victory.

JONES, Charles

Outside-left

Born: Troedyrhiw, near Merthyr Tydfil, 12 December 1899.
Died: Brentwood, Essex, April 1966.
Career: Cardiff City 1919. Stockport County August 1921. OLDHAM ATHLETIC March 1923, fee £1,000. Nottingham Forest September 1925, fee £750. Arsenal May 1928, fee £4,800. Notts County manager May to December 1934. Crittalls Athletic secretary-manager March 1935 to 1939.

■ Stockport County were the first team to win the Championship of the new Third Division North in season 1921–22, with wingman Charlie Jones a major contributor with nine goals in 34 matches. He joined Athletic in the late stages of the following term, but was unable to halt the team's relegation from the top flight. It was not until his move to Nottingham Forest that his career took an upturn, resulting in the first three of his eight Wales international caps. His career peaked when he switched to left-half to make way for the youthful 'Boy' Bastin in the Arsenal team. A key element in the Gunners' domination of the English League, Jones won three League Championships in the early 1930s. Sadly, he did less well in management, only one win in 17 matches prompting Notts County to sack him after only seven months in charge at Meadow Lane.

JONES, Christopher Martin Nigel

Forward

Born: Altrincham, 19 November 1945.
Career: Cheshire Schoolboys. Manchester City professional May 1964. Swindon Town July 1968. OLDHAM ATHLETIC loan January 1972. Walsall February 1972, fee £8,000. York City June 1973, fee £7,000. Huddersfield Town August 1976. Doncaster Rovers July 1977. Darlington loan January 1978. Rochdale December 1978. Bridlington 1980. Frickley Colliery manager February 1981. Rowntree Mackintosh, York, reinstated amateur.

■ Chris Jones was signed on a month's loan from Swindon Town, but did not complete the spell, Walsall stepping in with the required fee of £8,000 for his transfer. A centre-forward who liked a change, his most settled spell – at York City – was also his most successful. His 33 League goals in 94/1 matches included 17 in 41 matches in 1973–74, when York won promotion into Division Two for the first time in the club's history.

JONES, Ellis

Inside-forward

Born: Spennymoor, 5 April 1900.
Died: Spennymoor, 1972.
Career: Crook Town. Willington Athletic. Stanley United. Spennymoor United. Hull City May 1925. Annfield Plain August 1926. OLDHAM ATHLETIC February

1928. *Workington October 1929. Spennymoor United September 1930. Crook Town. Brackhall Colliery Welfare March 1931.*

■ Stocky, fair-haired inside-left Ellis Jones was given a second opportunity at League level by Athletic, after an earlier and undistinguished season with Hull City in 1925–26 when he scored once in eight Second Division outings. He was credited with 36 goals for Annfield Plain in the season that Athletic signed him, but despite a scoring debut at Preston North End Jones spent much of his time in the reserves before returning to the North East in October 1929.

JONES, Evan

Centre-forward

Born: Trehafod near Pontypridd, 20 October 1888.
Died: Bedwellty area, 1972.
Career: Trehafod. Aberdare 1908–09. Chelsea September 1909. OLDHAM ATHLETIC February 1911. Bolton Wanderers May 1912, fee £750. Wartime guest with Cardiff City and Newport County. Swansea Town August 1919. Pontypridd July 1920. Porth August 1921 to 1923.

■ A short and stocky centre-forward noted for his fierce shooting, Evan Jones was the second player in Athletic's history to win international recognition. A month after George Woodger's England cap against Ireland in February 1911, Jones was capped by Wales against Scotland at Cardiff. Athletic's first season

in the top flight proved to be a very satisfactory one; their seventh place finish owing much to a late burst of eight goals in 15 matches by the Wales international.

JONES, George Alexander

Forward

Born: Chapelfield, Radcliffe, 21 April 1945.
Career: Bury Schoolboys. Bury amateur 1960, apprentice September 1961, professional June 1962. Blackburn Rovers March 1964, fee £30,000. Bury November 1966, fee £17,000. OLDHAM ATHLETIC March 1973, fee £10,000. Halifax Town February 1976, fee £3,000. Southport January 1977. Lancaster City 1978. Radcliffe Borough November 1978. Prestwich Heys. Hyde United. Prestwich Heys.

■ George Jones scored 133 League and Cup goals for Bury in two spells, and was a week short of his 30th birthday when he arrived at Boundary Park. Signed to replace David Shaw, who had been transferred to West Bromwich Albion, he was quickly dubbed 'road-runner' by the fans on account of his seemingly limitless capacity for action and willingness to chase apparent lost causes. He played a key role in Athletic's Division Three Championship of 1973–74, scoring 10 goals in 26/6 matches, and an additional three in six FA Cup ties. His son, Alex (q.v.), was a central-defender who began with Athletic in the early 1980s.

JONES, George Benjamin 'Benny'

Inside-forward

Born: Newtown, North Wales, 29 January 1907.
Died: Bolton, 1982.
CAREER: Newtown. Bolton Wanderers

June 1927. *Hamilton Academical February 1929. Swindon Town May 1930. Rochdale August 1931. OLDHAM ATHLETIC March–April 1932. Wigan Athletic September 1932. Nelson 1933. Southend United July 1934. (In November 1935 the FA refused him permission to play as an amateur with Astley Bridge FC, Bolton). Crusaders 14 April 1937. Portadown 23 April 1937. Bangor August 1937. Crusaders May 1938.*

■ Recruited by Athletic on the same day that popular inside-forward Jimmy Dyson departed to Grimsby Town, Benny Jones's six-week Athletic career spanned just two matches within the same number of days over the Easter period in 1932. Both ended in heavy defeats – 5–1 at Manchester United. followed by 5–0 at Plymouth Argyle. When playing in Ireland he was also employed as a teacher at the Methodist College, Belfast.

JONES, John Thomas

Goalkeeper

Born: Holywell, Flintshire, 25 November 1916.
Died: Holywell, Flintshire, 1978.
Career: Flint Town. Port Vale amateur July 1936, professional December 1936. Northampton Town May 1937. Wartime guest with Wrexham, Arsenal, Bradford Park Avenue, Notts County, Hull City, Rochdale and Manchester City. OLDHAM ATHLETIC August 1948 to July 1949, fee £250.

■ John Jones won Wales Schoolboy caps against England, Scotland and Ireland. He spent a mixed season at Boundary Park, equally sharing first-team duties with Fred Ogden. Certainly lacking

height for his position, he was not at his best in dealing with lofted crosses into his area, but he was extremely agile and brave and a good shot-stopper.

JONES, Paul Bernard

Central-defender

Born: Ellesmere Port, 13 May 1953.
Career: Wirral Youth. Shell FC. Bolton Wanderers apprentice July 1969, professional June 1970. Huddersfield Town July 1983. OLDHAM ATHLETIC December 1985, fee £10,000. Blackpool March 1987. South African football May 1988. Stalybridge Celtic. Wigan Athletic January 1989. Galway United, Ireland, February 1989. Rochdale March 1989. Stockport County June 1989. Hinckley Town October 1990. Bramhall FC. Droylsden January 1992. Cheadle Town manager May 1992. Mossley assistant manager November 1992. Mold FC 1993. Stockport Georgians manager. Cheadle Town manager. Wilmslow Albion manager July 1996.

■ In 14 years with Bolton Wanderers central defender Paul Jones won Second and Third Division Championship medals while amassing 441/4 League appearances and 38 goals. He joined the Latics after a two-year spell with Huddersfield Town, and gave excellent value for his very modest transfer fee of £10,000. Despite the signing of central defender Andy Linighan from Leeds United the following month, Paul Jones retained his place alongside the newcomer. Their combined efforts lifted Athletic from a mid-season slump to an eight-place finish in Division Two.

JONES, Paul Neil

Central-defender

Born: Liverpool, 3 June 1978.
Career: Tranmere Rovers apprentice, professional December 1995. Barrow 1997. Leigh RMI. OLDHAM ATHLETIC November 1999 to July 2002.

■ An aggressive, hard-tackling defender, Paul Jones made 16 League appearances in his debut season. He also scored his first senior goal, the winner in a 2–1 win against Wigan Athletic on 11 April 2000. After that promising start he was cruelly plagued by shin splints injuries, and in what proved to be his final senior appearance, the unfortunate central-defender signed off by scoring Athletic's winner against Oxford United in a 3–2 victory at Boundary Park on 2 December 2000.

JONES, Richard

Half-back

Born: Ashton-in-Makerfield, 6 June 1901.
Career: Skelmersdale United. OLDHAM ATHLETIC May 1920, fee £20. Rochdale May 1922. Stockport County June 1923. Exeter City August 1924. Bristol Rovers August 1925. Colwyn Bay United October 1925. Bath City 1926. Wigan Borough October 1926. Northwich Victoria July 1927. Ashton St Thomas, Wigan, reinstated amateur October 1931.

■ Dick Jones was first noted by Athletic in the ranks of Skelmersdale United, who won the double of the Liverpool County Combination Championship and the Liverpool Cup in season 1919–20. Hard-working and fearless, his League debut was made against Liverpool and he enjoyed lengthy spells of first-team action in his first season. Jones's progress was cruelly halted in his second term when a knee injury sustained in a second-round FA Cup tie at Barnsley effectively ended his involvement at senior level. He subsequently enjoyed a good season with Rochdale in 1922–23, missing only six matches during the term. A highlight in non-League football came when he captained the Northwich Victoria side that won the Cheshire Senior Cup in April 1929.

JONES, Sidney

Forward

Born: Langley Park, Co. Durham, 10 August 1915.
Died: Burnley, February 1984.
Career: Gretna FC. Carlisle United May 1934. Gateshead May 1935. Manchester United January 1936. Burnley May 1936. OLDHAM ATHLETIC November 1936 to January 1938.

■ Despite association with four League clubs before reaching his 21st birthday, Sid Jones's potential remained unrealised at senior level. At Boundary Park his qualities of dash and enthusiasm were insufficient to win him promotion to the

League side. His solitary appearance at Wrexham in January 1937 revealed a lack of steadiness when shooting, and failure to bring the ball under control quickly. Twelve months on, Jones requested to be released from his contract to enable him to join the Burnley Police Force.

JONES, Thomas

Forward

Born: Rhosymedre, Wrexham, c. 1896.
Career: Acretair. Rhosymedre. Army football. Manchester United amateur November 1918. OLDHAM ATHLETIC July 1919. Accrington Stanley September 1920.

■ Utility forward Tom Jones was spotted in army football by Manchester United when he was stationed at Heaton Park during World War One. He was operating in Athletic's reserve team when a telegram inviting him to represent Wales in the Victory International against England on 18 October 1919 arrived too late to enable him to travel. On what should have been his big day, he turned out for the Latics reserves at Rochdale. He was recalled to senior action for the match against Sheffield United at Boundary Park in November 1919, and scored two of Athletic's goals in the 4–0 victory. It was the best result of the season, but the result and Jones's performance were not sustained.

JONES, Thomas

Centre-half

Born: Little Hulton, c.1916.
Career: Little Hulton FC. Accrington Stanley amateur May, professional August 1937. OLDHAM ATHLETIC January 1939. Wartime guest with Accrington Stanley, Blackburn Rovers and Rochdale.

■ Tom Jones was signed by Athletic to understudy club captain Beaumont Ratcliffe but had made just one appearance before the outbreak of war in September 1939. He had several outings as a guest player with Rochdale, but in April 1945 he was seriously wounded in action and had to have both feet amputated. Accrington Stanley played Rochdale in two matches for his benefit, at Peel Park and at Spotland, with both matches well attended. Elder brother William W. Jones played League football for Accrington Stanley in 1931–32.

JORDAN, Timothy Edwin

Forward

Born: Littleborough, 12 April 1960.
Career: OLDHAM ATHLETIC amateur October 1976, professional June 1978. IFK Eskilistuna, Sweden, April 1981. Later played in Norwegian football.

■ Although Tim Jordan failed to establish himself in League football he did play for the Latics at Wembley. This was in the Pontins' Youth Challenge six-a-side final against Southampton, won 3–0 by the Latics youngsters, the match taking place before the 1978 Charity Shield game between Ipswich Town and Nottingham Forest.

JOYCE, Walter

Half-back

Born: Oldham, 10 September 1937.
Died: 29 September 1999.
Career: Lancashire Schoolboys. Burnley amateur July 1953, professional November 1954. Blackburn Rovers February 1964, fee £10,000. OLDHAM ATHLETIC September 1967, coaching staff 1969–70 season. Rochdale manager June 1973 to May 1976. Bolton Wanderers coach & assistant manager until December 1985. Preston North End coach 1986, youth development officer September 1992. Bury youth coach and scout 1994. Manchester

United scout and youth development officer 1997 to 1999.

■ Walter Joyce captained Oldham and Lancashire Schoolboys, and Burnley took him onto their ground staff straight from school. In almost 10 years at Turf Moor he twice captained Burnley's reserves to successive Central League titles and appeared in 89 League and Cup matches at senior level. A successful spell with Blackburn Rovers followed and he joined Athletic in the month of his 30th birthday. He gave two years of excellent service at wing-half before being promoted onto the coaching staff. Rochdale invited him to become their manager in 1973 but his time at Spotland began appallingly. Their record of just two wins in 46 League matches constituted an unwanted Football League record. Joyce nevertheless remained for a further two seasons before embarking on a highly successful coaching career.

JOYNSON, George Edward

Inside-forward

Born: Birkenhead, 1889.

Died: Liscard, Wirral, 20 July 1914.
Career: Wallasey Rovers. OLDHAM ATHLETIC July 1912, fee £30.

■ George Joynson scored 27 goals for Wallasey Rovers in season 1911–12 to earn his upward move. Despite playing only five times in Athletic's First Division side, he was leading scorer for Athletic Reserves in both of his seasons at Boundary Park. His death came in tragic circumstances and at the untimely age of 24 when he expired in the summer of 1914 as a direct result of sunstroke.

KALALA, Jean-Paul (Kamudimba)

Midfield

Born: Luburbashi, DR Congo, 16 March 1982.
Career: OGC Nice, France. Grimsby Town July 2005. Yeovil Town July 2006. OLDHAM ATHLETIC June 2007.

■ Although born in Congo, Kalala moved with his family at the age of one to France, where his football career began with his home-town team Nice. A full international, Kalala appeared in two Finals of the African Nations Cup, and commenced his third season in English football when he joined Athletic from Yeovil Town in June 2007. He was manager Sheridan's fifth summer signing, and he arrived at Boundary Park as long-serving defender Will Haining departed to St Mirren. In 2006–07 Kalala made 35/3 League appearances for Yeovil, assisting the Glovers to the League One Play-off Final against Blackpool at Wembley. A regular first-team player early in the season, Kalala lost his place in October. Recalled for the

third-round FA Cup tie at Everton, he played a full part in Athletic's stunning victory but failed to hold his place and was released on a free transfer with one year remaining on his original contract.

KANE, Paul James

Midfield

Born: Edinburgh, 8 September 1965.
Career: Salvesen Boys' Club. Hibernian July 1982. OLDHAM ATHLETIC January 1991, fee £350,000. Aberdeen November 1991, fee £350,000. Barnsley loan August 1995. Viking FK Stavanger, Norway 1996. St Johnstone July 1997, player and Under-18 coach.

■ Although Paul Kane made sufficient appearances to qualify for a Championship medal in his first season at Boundary Park, the close season return of Mike Milligan from Everton, and the September signing of Neil McDonald, combined to make Kane's opportunities very limited. Athletic made him available for transfer, and were able to recoup from Aberdeen the full £350,000 transfer fee, paid to Hibernian earlier in the year.

KEEDWELL, John Henry

Centre-forward

Born: Ellesmere Port, 12 January 1901.
Died: Ellesmere Port, 14 January 1958.
Career: Liverpool amateur November 1922, professional January 1923. Manchester City amateur August 1924. OLDHAM ATHLETIC October 1924. Llandudno loan December 1925. Chester March 1928. Colwyn Bay United August 1928. Runcorn September 1929. Mold October 1929.

■ Jack Keedwell found little success in a struggling Athletic side, whose lack of firepower led to a season spent in the lower reaches of Division Two. When the final fixture came around, Athletic were in dire straits. Their visit to Selhurst Park, the new ground of Crystal Palace, saw them needing a result to retain their Second Division status. Jack Keedwell, in what proved to be his final outing for the Latics, memorably scored the only goal of the game, a result which kept Athletic up and condemned Palace to accompany Coventry City into Division Three.

KEEGAN, Gerard Anthony

Midfield

Born: Little Horton, Bradford, 3 October 1955.
Career: Sale Schoolboys. Manchester City apprentice August 1971, professional March 1973. OLDHAM ATHLETIC February 1979, fee £25,000. Mansfield Town October 1983. Rochdale July 1984. Altrincham September 1984.

■ Flame-haired 'Ged' Keegan's influence in midfield, plus that of Simon Stainrod shortly afterwards, did much to steer Athletic away from the bottom of the table and into the respectability of a 14th-place finish. The England Under-21 international, who was a Football League Cup winner with Manchester City in 1976, served Athletic consistently well in a holding midfield role. A high work rate and the ability to keep things simple were features of his play, and he rarely wasted a pass out of defence.

KEELEY, Glen Matthew

Central-defender

Born: Barking, Essex, 1 September 1954.
Career: Ipswich Town apprentice July 1970, professional August 1972. Newcastle United July 1974, fee £70,000. Blackburn Rovers August 1976, fee £30,000. Birmingham City loan August 1982. Everton loan October-December 1982. OLDHAM ATHLETIC August 1987, fee £15,000. Colchester United loan February 1988. Bolton Wanderers September 1988 to April 1989. Chorley. Clitheroe to January 1991. Chester City loan August 1992.

■ Awarded the club captaincy on arrival at Boundary Park, the vastly experienced Glen Keeley failed to impress in an uncertain central-defensive partnership with Andy Linighan, which also featured Tony Henry in a new role as sweeper. The season ended with a new centre-back pairing of Mike Flynn and Ian Marshall, Keeley spending a brief loan spell in Division Four with Colchester United prior to a final move in League circles to Bolton Wanderers.

KEELEY, John Henry

Goalkeeper

Born: Plaistow, Essex, 27 July 1961.

Career: South East Essex Schoolboys. Southend United apprentice, professional July 1979 to December 1984. Maldon Town. Chelmsford City. Brighton & Hove Albion August 1986, fee £1,500. OLDHAM ATHLETIC August 1990, fee £240,000. Oxford United loan November 1991. Reading loan February 1992. Chester City loan August and November 1992. Colchester United July 1993. Chelmsford City early March 1994, Stockport County March 1994. Peterborough United January–February 1995. Chelmsford City 1995. Canvey Island 1995. Worthing 1997. Brighton & Hove Albion non-contract November 2001 while employed as goalkeeping coach. Portsmouth goalkeeping coach May 2007.

■ Prior to joining Athletic, goalkeeper John Keeley had spent four excellent seasons with Brighton, his record of 19 clean sheets helping the Seagulls to promotion from Division Three in season 1987–89. He cost Athletic a record fee of £250,000 in August 1990, but the outstanding form and remarkable consistency of Jon Hallworth restricted Keeley to just two senior outings in his three seasons at Boundary Park, at the conclusion of which he was released on a free transfer. Mishaps and injuries also contributed to his lack of success and made his stay such a harrowing and unrewarding one. All told, his varied and eventful career spanned 257 League matches.

KEIZERWEERD, Orpheo Henk

Forward

Born: Surinam, 21 November 1968.

Career: Lelystad. AZ 67. Sloterplas. Stormvogels. Stade Rodez, France, December 1993. OLDHAM ATHLETIC non-contract March–May 1993. FC Groningen trial 1993. Den Bosch October 1993.

■ Dutch trialist Keizerweerd was a free agent when he joined Athletic in the closing months of Premiership season 1992–93. His only senior involvement during his three-month sojourn at Boundary Park was an appearance from the bench at Liverpool on 10 April 1993.

KELLARD, Thomas

Inside-forward

Born: Oldham, 30 November 1904.
Died: Oldham, March 1986.
Career: Chamber Colliery. Hurst FC. Ashton National. OLDHAM ATHLETIC amateur. Glossop September 1926. Hurst FC October 1926. OLDHAM ATHLETIC professional November 1926. Queen's Park Rangers May 1928. Burton Town August 1929. Hurst FC September 1929. Mossley January 1931. Stalybridge Celtic August 1933. Ashton National August 1936. Ashton United 1937 to 1939. Post-war coach Bardsley FC and OLDHAM ATHLETIC A Team.

■ A keen sprinter in his younger days Tom Kellard first trained with Athletic when he was about 16 years old, but it was some years later when he became a professional at Boundary Park. He made his League debut in a 3–2 victory against Manchester City in February 1928 but was released on a free transfer just three months later. He joined Queen's Park Rangers but remained for just one season, returning homewards to play in local non-League football.

KELLY, Ashley Craig

Midfield

Born: Tameside, 22 December 1988.
Career: Manchester City juniors. Trafford Boys. OLDHAM ATHLETIC trainee June 2005, non-contract June 2006. Leigh RMI loan October 2007. Barrow loan December 2007. OLDHAM ATHLETIC professional July 2007, released May 2008.

■ Following loan spells with Leigh RMI and Barrow in 2007–08, Ashley Kelly was an unused substitute on seven occasions before making his League debut, as a 79th minute substitute, for Sean Gregan in the 2–0 home win against Leyton Orient on 12 April 2008. Without further senior appearances, and with his contract up, he was released along with another of Athletic's young midfielders, Michael Pearson.

KELLY, A.C.P.

Winger

Career: Oswaldtwistle Rovers. OLDHAM ATHLETIC May 1905. Oswaldtwistle Rovers September 1906. Brynn Central June 1907.

■ Kelly made his debut in the opening fixture of season 1905–06. An attendance of approximately 8,000 saw the former Oswaldtwistle Rovers wingman score Athletic's first goal of the Lancashire Combination campaign, a 1–1 home draw against Atherton Church House. During the season, in addition to his three FA Cup appearances and two goals, Kelly made a further 28 Combination appearances and scored three goals.

KELLY, Gary Alexander

Goalkeeper

Born: Fulwood, near Preston, 3 August 1966. Career: Newcastle United apprentice, signing professional June 1984. Blackpool loan October 1988. Bury October 1989, fee £60,000. OLDHAM ATHLETIC loan August 1966, permanent September 1996 to December 2002, fee £10,000. Northwich Victoria February 2003. Leigh RMI September 2003, resigned position of assistant manager November 2004.

■ Gary Kelly had the experience of 263 League and Cup matches in a seven-year spell with Bury and, prior to that, 60 with Newcastle United. Initially signed on loan

by Athletic as cover for Jon Hallworth, the Republic of Ireland Under-21 and B international was afforded an early chance when Hallworth was injured and Kelly finished his first season at Boundary Park with 46 League and Cup appearances and the Player of the Year Trophy. A safe-handling, confident goalkeeper who placed his clearances to advantage, Kelly completed 225 League appearances for Athletic and more than of 500 for his five League clubs. He retired at the age of 38 after suffering a hand injury in September 2004. Gary hailed from a remarkable family of goalkeepers: his father, Alan, won 47 Republic of Ireland caps, while Gary's brother, Alan junior, represented the Republic on 34 occasions.

KELLY, John

Midfield

Born: Bebington, Merseyside, 20 October 1960.
Career: Cammel Laird FC. Tranmere Rovers September 1979. Preston North End October 1981, fee £50,000. Chester City August 1985. Swindon Town June 1987. OLDHAM ATHLETIC November 1987, fee £35,000. Walsall August 1989. Huddersfield Town loan March-May 1990, permanent February 1991. Chester City July 1992 to June 1993.

■ A lively performer throughout a lengthy League career spanning eight clubs, in excess of 400 appearances and 63 goals, Republic of Ireland Under-21 international John Kelly became Athletic's second £35,000 signing in November 1987, closely following Earl Barrett's recruitment from Manchester City. The lively Merseysider endured a

seven-month lay-off following an ankle injury sustained on New Year's Day 1988, but recovered to appear in 41/1 Division Two matches the following term. Rather surprisingly, after netting six goals in support of a virile attack that registered 81 League and Cup goals, the club captain was placed on the transfer list just five days before the start of the new season and was quickly snapped up by Walsall.

KELLY, Norman

Midfield

Born: Belfast, 10 October 1970.
Career: Dundonald Boys High School. Dungoyne. Glentoran 1985. Trials with Chelsea and Manchester United. OLDHAM ATHLETIC amateur June, trainee July 1987, professional July 1989. Wigan Athletic loan October 1989. IFK Stromstad, Sweden, loan March 1990. Dunfermline Athletic March 1991. Bolton Wanderers trial May 1993. Raith Rovers January 1994. Glentoran loan February 1994.

■ Two weeks' training at Boundary Park during school holidays eventually resulted in Norman Kelly signing a YTS form. Considering the honours gained at Schoolboy and Under-21 levels, the Irish midfielder's subsequent League aggregate of six substitute appearances (four during his loan spell with Wigan Athletic) was an extremely disappointing outcome.

KEMP, Gilbert

Inside-forward
Born: Wallasey, 1888.

Died: Don Valley, 1951.
Career: Wallasey Rovers. OLDHAM ATHLETIC amateur December 1911, professional January 1912, fee £200. Wartime guest with Bradford Park Avenue. Bradford City July 1919. Coventry City October 1919. Grimsby Town January to May 1920, fee £300. Doncaster Rovers 1920.

■ Gilbert Kemp was a star in the West Cheshire League with Wallasey Rovers. At Boundary Park he won a regular berth in 1914–15 and his excellent return of 19 goals in 42 matches took Athletic to within a whisker of the First Division Championship, Everton taking the title by the slender margin of one point. In the first peacetime season after World War One, Kemp failed to settle, assisting three League clubs in 1919–20 before dropping into non-League circles with Doncaster Rovers.

KENNEDY, Fred

Inside-forward

Born: Black Lane, Bury, 23 October 1902.
Died: Failsworth, 14 November 1963.
Career: Rossendale United 1920. Manchester United May 1923. Everton March 1925, fee £2,000. Cowdenbeath loan July 1925. Middlesbrough May 1927, fee £600. Reading May 1929, fee £500. OLDHAM ATHLETIC October 1930, fee £200. Rossendale United September 1931. Northwich Victoria December 1931. Racing Club de Paris, France, September 1932. Blackburn Rovers August 1933. Racing Club de Paris, France, June 1934. Stockport County July 1937.

■ Fred Kennedy began in League football with Manchester United and made his debut against the Latics at Boundary Park on 6 October 1923. A piece of soccer history was made that day when Athletic's full-back, Sammy Wynne, scored twice for his own side and two own goals in the Latics' 3–2 win. Some seven years later Kennedy joined Athletic but disappointingly failed to hold a place in the first team. He subsequently enjoyed both League and Cup wins in French football with Racing Club de Paris.

KENNY, William Aidan

Midfield

Born: Liverpool, 19 September 1973.
Career: Everton associate schoolboy November 1989, trainee June 1990, professional June 1992 to February 1994. OLDHAM ATHLETIC August 1994, contract cancelled March 1995. Barrow October 1995 to 1996.

■ England Under-21 midfielder Billy Kenny was dismissed by Everton in February 1994 because of his addiction to cocaine. Athletic's manager Joe Royle, a former playing colleague of Billy's father at Everton, agreed to give the troubled midfielder a second chance. There was little doubt that Kenny had ability, but his efforts to gain match fitness were unsuccessful, and his final appearance for the reserves in January 1995 ended when he was substituted at half-time. Released by Athletic in March, he assisted Barrow in 1995–96, scoring two goals in 24 matches.

KERR, James

Outside-left

Born: Lemington-on-Tyne, Northumberland, 3 March 1932.
Died: 1994.
Career: Newcastle United Juniors. Blyth Spartans 1952. Lincoln City November 1952. OLDHAM ATHLETIC June 1954. North Shields August 1956.

■ Jimmy Kerr was a junior with Newcastle United before his period of National Service, but after demobilisation joined Blyth Spartans. Within a matter of months he was signed by Lincoln City and made 14 Second Division appearances in his first season. Adroit in footwork and with a fair turn of speed, Kerr was a tearaway wingman who at times was guilty of running the ball too far. He had strong competition from Harry McShane for the left-wing spot in his first season, but began 1955–56 as first-choice number 11. Sadly, his career was abruptly ended by a knee injury sustained in the Christmas Eve fixture against Scunthorpe United.

KEY, Lance William

Goalkeeper

Born: Kettering, 13 May 1968.
Career: Histon FC. Sheffield Wednesday April 1990. York City loan October 1991. OLDHAM ATHLETIC loan October 1993. Oxford United loan January 1995. Lincoln City loan August 1995. Hartlepool United

loan December 1995. Rochdale loan March 1996. Dundee United July 1996. Sheffield United March 1997. Rochdale August 1997. Northwich Victoria loan December 1998, permanent March 1999. Altrincham loan February 2000. Kingstonian June 2001. Histon September 2004.

■ A graduate from the Eastern Counties League, goalkeeper Lance Key was playing for Sheffield Wednesday's A Team when he received the call to help the Latics, who had both Paul Gerrard and Jon Hallworth out injured. It was a massive step up for the tall, blond-haired Key, but his outstanding displays against Chelsea and Newcastle United earned him the match sponsor's Man of the Match award on both occasions.

KILCLINE, Brian

Central-defender

Born: Nottingham, 7 May 1962.
Career: Nottingham Schoolboys. Notts County apprentice 1978, professional May 1980. Coventry City June 1984, fee £60,000. OLDHAM ATHLETIC August 1991, fee £400,000. Newcastle United loan February, permanent March 1992, fee £250,000. Swindon Town January 1994, fee £90,000. Mansfield Town December 1995. Halifax Town November 1997. Altrincham player-coach to October 1998.

■ Signed by Athletic on the eve of their debut in Division One, England Under-21 international Brian 'Killer' Kilcline proved a useful squad member, but the problem of where to fit him into the side was never adequately resolved. In earlier days, the Viking-like, flamboyant defender

famously captained Coventry City to their first-ever FA Cup Final success in 1987. After leaving Athletic he captained Newcastle United to promotion and a place in the FA Premier League in 1993.

KILKENNY, Neil Martin

Midfield

Born: Middlesex, 19 December 1985.
Career: Queensland Boys, Australia. Arsenal trainee 2002. Birmingham City January 2004. OLDHAM ATHLETIC loan November 2004 to May 2005 and again July 2007. Leeds United January 2008.

■ Born in London but raised in Australia, Neil Kilkenny was eligible to represent England, Ireland and Australia. Capped at Youth level by England he nevertheless opted to represent Australia and made his full international debut against Liechtenstein in a 3–1 win in June 2007. Busy and with great vision, the young midfielder was immediately at home when loaned to Athletic in November 2004, scoring twice on his full debut at Bradford City. His loan spell was quickly extended to cover the remainder of the season and his contribution did much to save Athletic from relegation to the League's bottom tier. Following a second, equally successful, loan spell at Boundary Park, moves to make the deal a permanent one were unfortunately unsuccessful. A six-figure transfer fee was agreed with Birmingham City, and a lucrative contract offered to the talented midfielder. All were disappointed, however, when he opted to join Leeds United. He was quickly into his stride at Elland Road, assisting his new club to the League One Play-off Final. The Wembley fixture ended in cruel disappointment, Yorkshire rivals Doncaster Rovers winning the trophy, and with it promotion to the Championship.

KILLEN, Christopher John

Forward

Born: Wellington, New Zealand, 8 October 1981.
Career: Mirimar Rangers, New Zealand. Manchester City March 1999. Wrexham loan September 2000. Port Vale loan September 2001. OLDHAM ATHLETIC July 2002, fee £250,000. Hibernian January 2006. Celtic May 2007.

■ Unfortunate with injuries throughout most of his spell at Boundary Park, New Zealand international striker Chris Killen was under-employed during 2003–04 (seven starts, six from the bench and two goals). Although not entirely free from injury in 2004–05 he enjoyed his best season, scoring 15 League and Cup goals. His exit from Boundary Park came in acrimonious circumstances, with Athletic's owners threatening to sue Killen for libel after he intimated that they had interfered with team selection, putting pressure on manager Moore to leave him out of the side.

KING, Dennis

Winger

Born: Bearpark, Co. Durham, 16 September 1932.
Died: Durham Central, September 1988.
Career: Durham County Youths. Bradford Park Avenue September 1950. Spennymoor United. OLDHAM ATHLETIC June 1954, fee £350. Chorley July 1956 to 1958.

■ Dennis King, a nippy and versatile forward, began with Bradford Park Avenue at 18 years of age but failed to reach senior level. A spell with Spennymoor United followed and despite interest from Luton Town and Mansfield the 21-year-old wingman accepted Athletic's terms. As understudy to Tommy Walker, the former Newcastle United wingman, King was restricted to just seven senior appearances in his first season. He found more opportunities in 1955–56, underlining his

versatility by appearing on both wings and at centre-forward, scoring seven goals in 15 League appearances.

KING, George Colin

Inside-forward

Born: Combs, Derbyshire, 8 December 1900.
Died: Preston, June 1991.
Career: Manchester Schoolboys. Old Chorltonians amateur. Manchester United trial 1922. OLDHAM ATHLETIC professional August 1922. Old Chorltonians reinstated amateur July 1923. Dick Kerr's FC amateur September 1928.

■ George King represented Manchester Schoolboys in the Final of the English Schools Shield and played in an England Schools trial match at York. After two trial games with Manchester United he joined the Latics and was offered terms for a second season but declined, preferring to rejoin amateur ranks. For many years employed as chief accountant at Dick Kerr's Preston works, he played both cricket and football for the works teams, the football team playing in the Lancashire Combination at that time.

KING, John

Outside-right

Born: Pendlebury, 8 December 1902.
Died: Salford, 4 March 1988.
Career: Newton United. Mossley 1924. OLDHAM ATHLETIC October 1926, fee £150. Rossendale United September 1931. Ashton United 1932. Mossley October 1932. Ashton National November 1932. Stalybridge Celtic February 1933. Ashton National September 1933. Pendlebury FC. Bacup Borough August 1936. South Liverpool March 1937.

■ Two days after signing, Jack King was pitched straight into Athletic's Division Two side, and made 27 League appearances in his first season. The following season was his best, eight goals in 42 League and Cup matches being an excellent return for a wide player. Increasingly troubled by knee injuries, King eventually accepted compensation and drifted into non-League circles. Two years after leaving Boundary Park his form with Ashton National attracted the attention of First Division Huddersfield

Town, but after two Central League games the FA blocked the move on account of his earlier compensation settlement. By 1939 King was starring in another sport, having taken up baseball with Swinton and Pendlebury.

KING, Seth

Centre-half

Born: Penistone, 14 February 1897.
Died: Leigh, 8 February 1958.
Career: Penistone Church FC. Huddersfield Town amateur 1919–20. Penistone FC. Sheffield United November 1920, fee £10. OLDHAM ATHLETIC May 1929 to February 1932, fee £400. Denaby United August 1932, retired July 1934.

■ Seth King spent eight and a half years with Sheffield United and was a member of the Blades' FA Cup-winning team in 1925. He was a seasoned campaigner by the time he joined Athletic and club captain, Jack Hacking, sportingly handed over the leadership to him. A whole-hearted pivot of the attacking type, for two seasons he did not miss a game in League or Cup, but in the second game of season 1931–32 he sustained a knee injury at Barnsley and thereafter appeared only occasionally. His contract was cancelled by mutual consent in February 1932 and he took over the tenancy of the Castle Inn, Hillsborough, Sheffield. At the time of his death, just days from his 61st birthday, Seth King was running a newsagents in Leigh.

KINNELL, George

Midfield/Forward

Born: Dunfermline, 22 December 1937.
Career: Crossgates Primrose. Trials with East Fife and Raith Rovers. Aberdeen February 1959. Stoke City November 1963, fee £27,000. OLDHAM ATHLETIC August 1966, along with Keith Bebbington, for a combined fee of £25,000. Sunderland October 1966, fee £20,000. Middlesbrough October 1968. Juventus FC, Melbourne, Australia, June 1969.

■ George Kinnell's departure from Boundary Park brought a quick and handsome profit after just two months, but he had quickly become a crowd favourite on account of his instant success as a goalscorer – eight in just 12 matches – and the Latics faithful were less than pleased to lose his services. George was a cousin of the late Jim Baxter, the celebrated Scottish international wing-half.

KIRKPATRICK, Ernest

Inside-forward

Born: Farnworth, 27 March 1898.
Died: Heywood, 20 March 1971.
Career: Fleetwood early in season 1923–24. OLDHAM ATHLETIC September 1925, fee £250. Fleetwood August 1927. Chorley February 1928. Bournemouth & Boscombe Athletic May 1929. Chorley June to November 1930. Fleetwood Windsor Villa coach and groundsman January 1931.

■ Ernest Kirkpatrick found opportunities difficult to come by but scored three goals in 13 League matches in his first season. After only two first-team outings in 1926–27 he rejoined Fleetwood and, aside from a season with Bournemouth, spent the remainder of his career in Lancashire Combination circles. His three Combination Championship wins – with Fleetwood in 1924 and twice with Chorley in 1928 and 1929 – constituted a record.

KNIGHT, David Sean

Goalkeeper

Born: Houghton-le-Spring, 15 January 1987.
Career: Middlesbrough trainee, professional February 2005. Darlington loan December 2005. OLDHAM ATHLETIC loan August–September 2006. Swansea City August 2007.

■ England Youth international goalkeeper David Knight was an FA Youth Cup winner with Middlesbrough in 2004 but his only League experience before his Athletic debut was with Darlington, for whom he made three appearances over the New Year period of 2006. The fourth goalkeeper used by Athletic with the season only six matches old, Knight spent a traumatic month at Boundary Park. Unluckily sent off on his debut – his red card was later overturned – he then missed games due to illness and hip and neck injuries.

KNIGHTON, Kenneth

Full-back/Midfield

Born: Mexborough, 20 February 1944.
Career: Mexborough Rovers. Wath Wanderers. Wolverhampton Wanderers apprentice July 1960, professional February 1961. OLDHAM ATHLETIC November 1966, fee £12,000. Preston North End December 1967, fee £35,000. Blackburn Rovers July 1969, fee £45,000. Hull City March 1971, fee £60,000. Sheffield Wednesday August 1973, fee £50,000, coaching staff April 1976. Sunderland coach 1978, manager June 1979 to April 1981. Orient manager October 1981 to May 1983. Dagenham manager 1984–85. Trowbridge Town manager 1985 to January 1988. Portishead manager 1991 to 1993.

■ With only 13/3 League appearances for Wolverhampton Wanderers in six years at Molineux, blond-haired Ken Knighton sampled regular first-team football for the first time with Athletic. It was quickly apparent that he was destined for a bigger stage, and the escalating value of his subsequent transfer fees confirmed the early prognosis. In a career spanning six League clubs, he played in 340/9 League games and scored 25 goals.

KOFFMAN, Sidney John 'Jack'

Outside-left

Born: Prestwich, Manchester, 3 August 1920.
Died: Camberwell, Surrey, 24 May 1977.
Career: Audenshaw United. Bolton Wanderers December 1944. Manchester

United May 1945. Stalybridge Celtic November 1945. Hull City June 1946. Northwich Victoria October 1946. Congleton Town later in season 1946–47. OLDHAM ATHLETIC June 1947. Ashton United August 1948.

■ Jack Koffman began in wartime football with Bolton Wanderers, making his first-team debut against Everton in January 1945. Later in the same year he joined Manchester United but was released after six months and joined Stalybridge Celtic. In June 1946 he joined Hull City, appearing in four matches before returning to Cheshire League football. He failed to capitalise at Boundary Park after starting 1947–48 as first choice outside-left, with manager Wootton trying seven players in the number-11 jersey during the season.

KOWENICKI, Ryszard Stefan

Midfield

Born: Lodz, Poland, 22 December 1948.
Career: Widzew Lodz, Poland. OLDHAM ATHLETIC December 1979, fee £12,000. Bradford City trial August–September 1981.

■ Lengthy transfer negotiations and much red tape preceded Ryszard Kowenicki's eventual arrival at Boundary Park, Latics manager Jimmy Frizzell succeeding in clinching all aspects of the deal after five previously unsuccessful attempts. With only 48 hours in which to prepare for his debut, the Polish

midfielder was immediately impressive in his winning start against a strong Chelsea side. Known as 'Ricky' to his teammates, he was a colourful character with a luxuriant droopy moustache, his appearance putting one in mind of a Wild West 'Wanted' poster! His game featured non-stop running, explosive shooting and a remarkable long-throw technique. His goals were generally of the long-range, spectacular variety.

KYRATZOGLOU, Alexandros Bassilios

Forward

Born: Armidale, Australia, 27 August 1974.
Career: IEK Athens, Greece. OLDHAM ATHLETIC non-contract October-November 1997.

■ Alex Kyratzoglou spent two months at Boundary Park on non-contract forms. Although arriving with good credentials, the powerfully-built Australian striker made only one senior outing from the bench at Millwall during his trial period and was not offered a permanent engagement.

LARGE, Frank

Centre-forward

Born: Leeds, 26 January 1940.
Died: Westport, Ireland, 9 August 2003.
Career: Holbeck Loco. British Railways, Halifax. Halifax Town June 1959. Queen's Park Rangers June 1962, fee £7,500. Northampton Town March 1963, fee £8,500. Swindon Town March 1964, fee £10,000. Carlisle United September 1964,

fee £6,500. OLDHAM ATHLETIC December 1965, fee £7,500. Northampton Town December 1966, fee £14,000. Leicester City November 1967, fee £20,000. Fulham June 1968. Northampton Town August 1969. Chesterfield November 1972. Baltimore Comets, US, April 1974. Kettering Town September 1974.

■ One of soccer's happy wanderers, Frank Large was a tremendous worker who spared no effort to get at any half-chance in the penalty area. He proved an excellent short-term signing for Athletic, helping to pull the side away from the threat of relegation with seven goals in 18 League outings in 1965–66. Despite suffering a broken jaw that sidelined him for six matches in the following term, he had scored 12 League and Cup goals in 17 matches when his transfer to Northampton Town netted almost double the fee that Athletic had paid for him a year earlier. Large won Third Division Championship medals with Northampton Town in 1963 and with Carlisle in 1965.

LAWLESS, Arthur Trevor

Centre-half

Born: Retford, 28 March 1932.
Career: King Edward VI School, Retford. Blackpool A Team. Billingham Synthonia Recreation. Worcester City amateur 1953. Plymouth Argyle July 1955. OLDHAM ATHLETIC July 1956, fee £100. Aldershot July 1957. Southport July 1958. Ton Pentre 1959. Loughborough United player-manager May 1960. Stamford Town player-manager June 1963. Sutton Town manager May 1966.

■ Despite association with four League clubs, Trevor Lawless totalled only 34 appearances in his career. Joining Athletic in June 1956 he was not called upon until 1 December, when he deputised at right-back for Lewis Brook. Later in the same month, an injury to Eddie Murphy gave Lawless a five-match run at centre-half but he played in only three more matches before moving to Aldershot. A season with Southport wound up his League career, and he subsequently qualified as a senior FA coach and moved into management in the Midland League. An all-round sportsman, Lawless appeared in Minor Counties cricket for Nottinghamshire Second XI in the 1950s.

LAWRENCE, Valentine

Half-back

Born: Arbroath, 5 May 1889.
Died: Camberwell, 1961.
Career: Dundee Violet. Forfar Athletic.

Newcastle United trial April 1911. Manchester City July 1911. Arbroath. OLDHAM ATHLETIC May 1913, fee £50. Leeds City May 1914. Dundee Hibs September 1915. Morton February 1918. Dumbarton November 1918. Hartlepools United February–March 1919. Darlington. Southend United August 1921. Abertillery July 1922. Tunbridge Wells Rangers August 1923.

■ The outstanding form shown by Athletic's all-international half-back line of Moffat, Roberts and Wilson restricted Val Lawrence to a solitary League outing during his season at Boundary Park – a 2–1 win at Derby County on 22 November 1913. For the reserve team he made 23 appearances and scored one goal.

LAWSON Alan

Defender

Born: Lennoxtown, 13 September 1941.
Career: Campsie Black Watch. Lennoxtown. Ashfield Juniors. Celtic 1960. OLDHAM ATHLETIC June 1964. Ashton United 1970.

Craggy and uncompromising defender Alan Lawson spent six years with the Latics, serving under five different managers – a fair indication of the turbulent times at Boundary Park in the 1960s. He was the first substitute used by the Latics in League football when he replaced the injured Albert Jackson against Peterborough United on 28 August 1965. He marked the occasion by scoring his solitary League goal.

LAWTON William

Half-back

Born: Ashton-under-Lyne, 4 June 1920.
Career: Ferranti FC. OLDHAM ATHLETIC February 1945. Chester October 1949. Bacup Borough 1950–51. Colwyn Bay July 1951.

A tall, dark-haired wing half-back, Bill Lawton had a neat touch on the ball and was an accomplished initiator. He was recruited by Athletic during wartime and was rarely absent in season 1945–46, playing in 32 Third Division (North West) matches and four FA Cup ties. He found fewer opportunities when normal League football resumed in 1946–47 and had been absent from the first team for nine months when he was transferred to Chester. Lawton was better known as a cricketer, who began locally with the Werneth club. He played in County cricket with Lancashire and Cumberland, and was a professional with several League clubs in the post-war period. Lawton is the husband of Dora Bryan, the popular stage, screen and TV actress.

LEDGER, Robert Hardy

Utility player

Born: Craghead, Co. Durham, 5 October 1937.
Career: Doncaster Schoolboys. Yorkshire Schoolboys. Huddersfield Town amateur 1952, professional October 1954. OLDHAM ATHLETIC May 1962, fee 'about £6,000'. Mansfield Town December 1967. Barrow October 1969 to June 1970. Lancaster City.

Bob Ledger began with Athletic as an orthodox right-winger. In his first season his accurate crossing of the ball did much to help the side to a total of 95 goals and he scored eight himself as Athletic won

promotion from Division Four. In later seasons his utility value proved a tremendous asset. It was during Les McDowall's spell as manager that Ledger was switched to full-back. He was well settled in this role when asked to take the centre-forward position by Jimmy McIlroy in season 1967–68. Typically, he responded to the call and scored a hat-trick against Scunthorpe United in his first match. One of the best utility players to represent the Latics, Bob Ledger was a worthy winner of the club's very first Player of the Year award in 1967.

LEE Alfred

Half-back

Born: Farnworth, 11 June 1927.
Died: Bolton, March 1991.
Career: Bolton Wanderers October 1948. OLDHAM ATHLETIC July 1950, fee £250. Colwyn Bay August 1951.

Alf Lee was without League experience when he joined Athletic, but was given an early opportunity by manager Billy Wooton. In his second outing he scored the only goal of the game against Chester,

but following the appointment of new player-manager, George Hardwick, Lee remained in reserve. At this level he prospered, leading the reserves scoring list with 14 goals in 32 matches.

LEE, David John Francis

Midfield

Born: Basildon, 28 March 1980.
Career: Tottenham Hotspur trainee, signing professional July 1998. Southend United August 2000. Hull City June 2001. Brighton & Hove Albion January 2002. Bristol Rovers loan October 2002. Thurrock FC. OLDHAM ATHLETIC non-contract September 2004, professional October 2004. Thurrock FC November 2004. Stevenage Borough trial February 2005. Aldershot Town February 2005.

Tenacious midfielder David Lee's activities were almost entirely confined to reserve team football after he left Southend United. Initially signed on non-contract forms following his summer release by Brighton, David Lee failed to arrest Athletic's shaky start to season 2004–05, and became surplus to requirements in November when a trio of loan signings – Hughes, Croft and Kilkenny – immediately brought about an improvement in results.

LEE, Robert Martin 'Rob'

Midfield

Born: Plaistow, 1 February 1966.
Career: Hornchurch FC. Charlton Athletic July 1983. Newcastle United September 1992, fee £700,000. Derby County February 2002, fee £250,000. West Ham United August 2003. OLDHAM ATHLETIC non-contract November 2004. Wycombe Wanderers March 2005, retired May 2006.

Veteran England international Rob Lee left West Ham United in the summer of 2004 and the following November was a surprise signing by Athletic on non-contract forms. In the briefest of stays, he appeared in just one match at Boundary Park, the LDV Vans Trophy Northern quarter-final Cup tie against Hartlepool United, won 3–1 by Athletic. Later in the same season he joined Wycombe Wanderers and made 40 League appearances for the Chairboys prior to retiring at the age of 40. In addition to his

21 full caps, Lee appeared twice for England at Under-21 level and once for England B. In the 1992–93 season he scored 10 goals in 36 League matches for Division One champions Newcastle United and his overall career figures amounted to an impressive 662/41 League matches and 104 goals.

LEEDHAM, Frederick

Inside-forward

Born: Lye, Worcestershire, 21 February 1909. Died: Lye, Worcestershire, 21 December 1996.
Career: Worcestershire Amateurs. West Bromwich Albion amateur April 1926. Kidderminster Harriers amateur May 1926. West Bromwich Albion professional February 1928, fee £300. Kidderminster Harriers July 1929. Bradford Park Avenue August 1931, fee £160. Accrington Stanley June 1933. OLDHAM ATHLETIC February 1935, in exchange for Frank Britton plus £225. Cheltenham Town August 1937. Revo Electric FC reinstated amateur August 1939.

■ A neat and stylish ball worker, Fred Leedham was an outstanding junior who, in teenage years, toured the US with Worcestershire Amateurs. He made his League debut with West Bromwich Albion but first sampled regular League football with Bradford Park Avenue. A spell with Accrington Stanley preceded his move to Boundary Park. A shrewd and often unorthodox inside-forward, his clever manoeuvring was seen to best effect during season 1935–36, when he scored nine goals in 30 League appearances.

LEGZDINS, Adam Richard

Goalkeeper

Born: Penkridge, 28 November 1986. Career: Birmingham City trainee. Halifax Town loan November 2005 to January 2006. Birmingham City professional July 2006. OLDHAM ATHLETIC loan October–November 2006. Macclesfield Town loan January–February 2007. Halifax Town loan August 2007 to 2008.

■ Athletic moved to take 19-year-old Adam Legzdins on loan from Birmingham City when their two reserve goalkeepers, Terry and Ryan Smith, were both sidelined by injury. Legzdins's sole appearance came when he was introduced as a second-half substitute for Les Pogliacomi in a side containing seven teenagers for their Johnstone's Paint Trophy, northern section, second-round tie at Boundary Park on 1 November 2006, won 1–0 by Chesterfield.

LEIGH, Thomas 'Ginger'

Left full-back

Born: Hollins, 1888. Died: Manchester, 25 May 1914. Career: Earlestown July 1902. Ashton Town May 1904. OLDHAM ATHLETIC May 1906. Fulham May 1907. Queen's Park Rangers 1910. Croydon Common 1911. Rochdale June 1912. South Liverpool February 1913.

■ A dashing type of full-back who favoured a robust approach, Leigh joined Athletic prior to their final season as a non-League club. He failed to establish himself, appearing in only three Lancashire Combination matches and two FA Cup ties. Seven years after leaving Athletic he took his own life in tragic circumstances. Having entered a Manchester hospital for an operation on a football injury, surgeons discovered that he was suffering from cancer. Tragically, the 26-year-old Leigh jumped out of the hospital window to his death.

LESTER, Hugh

Outside-left

Born: St Helens. Career: St Helens Recreation. Earlestown November–December 1910. Liverpool December 1911. OLDHAM ATHLETIC May 1913. Wartime guest with Liverpool and Prescot FC. Reading 1919–20. Hurst FC.

■ A noted amateur sprinter with a best time of 10 and a half seconds for the 100 yards, Hugh Lester was expected to provide competition for Joe Donnachie's outside-left position. In the event, the Scottish international continued to monopolise the position and Lester was switched to left-back in the Central League side. It was in this berth that he made his solitary League outing at Notts County in season 1914–15.

LESTER, Michael John Anthony

Midfield

Born: Gorton, Manchester, 4 August 1954. Career: Middleton Juniors. OLDHAM ATHLETIC from school, apprentice September 1969, professional December 1972. Manchester City November 1973, fee £50,000. Stockport County loan August 1975. Washington Diplomats, US, March 1977. Grimsby Town November 1977. Barnsley October 1979. Exeter City August 1981. Bradford City February 1982. Scunthorpe United March 1983, fee £7,000. Hartlepool United loan January 1986. Stockport County September 1986. Scarborough March 1987. Ludvika, Sweden 1987. Blackpool non-contract December 1987. Chorley. Mossley February 1990. Manchester City School of Excellence coach. American coaching appointment. Runcorn coach January–March 1996.

■ Blond-haired Micky Lester joined Athletic from school, shortly after returning from an American tour with Manchester Schoolboys. He was just 18 when he made his Boxing Day debut and would have probably appeared even earlier had he not been laid up with cartilage trouble for much of season 1970–71. Manchester City paid £50,000 for his potential, after he had played in 11 matches of Athletic's Division Three Championship season, 1973–74. Subsequent moves in a nomadic career resulted in his association with a further eight League clubs, plus two spells abroad in the US and Sweden. In terms of League matches alone, his career figures totalled 347/10 appearances and 42 goals.

LEWIN, Derek James

Inside-forward

Born: Manchester, 18 May 1930. Career: St Anne's Athletic. OLDHAM ATHLETIC amateur August 1953. Bishop

Auckland. Accrington Stanley amateur October 1957. Manchester United amateur February 1958.

■ Derek Lewin's League career comprised just 10 games for the Latics and one against them. He was a greatly admired player in the unpaid ranks, despite finding little time for training due to the pressures of his family food importing business. He joined Manchester United in the wake of the Munich air disaster and helped them recruit players for their reserve team. Associated with the Bishop Auckland club during a period of great success, Lewin scored in each of their three FA Amateur Cup appearances at Wembley. He won five England Amateur international caps and was a Great Britain representative in the 1956 Melbourne Olympics.

LEWIS, Jonathan

Inside-forward

Career: Wrexham. OLDHAM ATHLETIC May 1905. Broughton United February 1906.

■ Lewis remained a peripheral figure during his spell at Hudson Fold. He appeared in only one Lancashire Combination fixture, a 1–0 defeat at Stalybridge Rovers. In the FA Cup competition he – and the Latics – faced Football League opponents for the very first time, losing 2–1 at Hull City. Incidentally, Lewis's remuneration during his Athletic days was seven shillings and sixpence per week (equivalent to 37½p in today's money).

LIDDELL, Andrew Mark

Forward/Winger

Born: Leeds, 28 June 1973.
Career: Barnsley trainee, professional July 1991. Wigan Athletic October 1998, fee £350,000. Sheffield United July 2004. OLDHAM ATHLETIC June 2005.

■ Despite missing four months of the season due to an Achilles injury, Athletic's popular wingman was welcomed back to action in April and in the same month was offered a new contract, reflecting his continuing value to the side. In a career spanning 17 years and over 600 appearances, the former Scottish Under-21 international continues to hold the ball up well, centres accurately and is a reliable

man from the penalty spot. His experience was sadly missed during his enforced injury lay-off. Earlier in his career, Liddell spent seven years with Barnsley and six with Wigan Athletic, with whom he won a Second Division Championship medal in 2002–03.

LIDDELL, John Cairney

Centre-forward

Born: Stirling, 13 December 1933.
Died: Grangemouth, 16 March 1999.
Career: Kilsyth Rangers. Cambuslang Rangers. St Johnstone April 1959. OLDHAM ATHLETIC September 1960. Worcester City April 1962. Mossley October 1962 to February 1963.

■ Centre-forward John Liddell cost Athletic an undisclosed 'four-figure fee' when he moved to Boundary Park after helping St Johnstone into the Scottish First Division, scoring 36 goals in their 1959–60 promotion campaign. The former lorry driver largely failed to realise expectations, although his preference for taking the shortest route to goal resulted in a respectable scoring

ratio – 11 in 24 matches – before his move into non-League football with Worcester City.

LIGHTFOOT, Christopher Ian

Defender

Born: Warrington, 1 April 1970.
Career: Chester City trainee, signing professional July 1988. Wigan Athletic July 1995, fee £87,500. Crewe Alexandra March 1996. OLDHAM ATHLETIC loan September 2000. Kidderminster Harriers trial, late season 2000–01. Queen's Park Rangers trial July 2001. Morecambe July 2001. Runcorn player-manager October 2003. Marine FC December 2004, appointed coach January 2005.

■ Athletic's manager Andy Ritchie took strapping defender Chris Lightfoot on loan from Crewe in an effort to shore up a leaky rearguard and escape the relegation zone. Lacking match fitness the tall central-defender was substituted after 59 minutes on his debut, but the goalless draw helped stem the tide of defeats. Although Athletic's defence had looked less vulnerable during his brief stay, his month's loan was not extended when Shaun Garnett regained fitness.

LINIGHAN, Andrew

Central-defender

Born: Hartlepool, 18 June 1962.
Career: Henry Smith's Boys' Club. Hartlepool United September 1980. Leeds United May 1984, fee £20,000. OLDHAM ATHLETIC January 1986, fee £55,000. Norwich City March 1988, fee £350,000. Arsenal June 1990, fee £1.25 million. Crystal

Palace January 1997, fee £150,000. Queen's Park Rangers loan March 1999. Oxford United December 2000. St Albans City 2001.

■ A tall and commanding central defender, England B international Andy Linighan was effective in both penalty areas, his height and aerial ability making him an ideal target man at corners and free-kicks. He was one of a number of ex-Leeds United players who found success with the Latics; Denis Irwin, Tommy Wright and Andy Ritchie all come to mind. Subsequently, his most successful period came with Arsenal, a personal highlight being his extra-time winner in the FA Cup Final against Sheffield Wednesday in 1993. Andy's father, Brian, played for Lincoln City and Darlington in the 1950s, of his five sons, four played professional football, odd man out, Mark, played as a semi-professional.

LISTER, Herbert Francis 'Bert'

Centre-forward

Born: Miles Platting, Manchester, 4 October 1939
Died: Manchester, 16 July 2007.
Career: Manchester Schoolboys. Bogart Hole Clough FC. Manchester City amateur December 1954, professional November 1957. OLDHAM ATHLETIC October 1960, along with Ken Branagan for a combined fee of £10,000. Rochdale January 1965, fee £2,250. Stockport County January 1967. Altrincham December 1967 to February 1969. Stalybridge Celtic September 1969.

■ Bert Lister captained Manchester Schoolboys and was taken onto Manchester City's books while serving an electrical apprenticeship. After three years as a professional at Maine Road he was transferred to the Latics, along with full-back Ken Branagan. Although lacking any physical advantage for his position as attack leader Lister was, nevertheless, tenacious, hard-working and a superb opportunist. He memorably scored six goals – all right-foot shots – on a snowbound Boundary Park on Boxing Day 1963 in the Latics' all-time record 11–0 victory.

LITCHFIELD, Peter

Goalkeeper

Born: Manchester, 27 July 1956.
Career: Droylsden. Preston North End January 1979. Bradford City July 1985. OLDHAM ATHLETIC loan October 1988. Scunthorpe United July 1989 to 1991.

■ Peter Litchfield spent three weeks on loan with Athletic when first-choice goalkeeper Andy Rhodes was out of action with a knee ligament injury. Only one point was gathered from the three matches in which he played, leaving the side eighth from bottom of Division Two. Athletic recovered, however, losing only twice in their final 20 matches, but it had been a difficult season in which they used four goalkeepers in League and Cup matches, and fielded five of their trainee professionals at senior level.

LITTLEJOHN, Adrian Sylvester

Forward

Born: Wolverhampton, 26 September 1970.
Career: West Bromwich Albion trainee.

Walsall May 1989. Sheffield United August 1991. Plymouth Argyle September 1995, fee £100,000. OLDHAM ATHLETIC March 1998, in exchange for Phil Starbuck. Bury November 1998, fee £75,000. Sheffield United non-contract October-December 2001. Played in China and the US. Barnsley trial January 2003. Port Vale February 2003. Lincoln City August 2004. Rushden & Diamonds January 2005. Mansfield Town September 2005. Leek Town December 2005. Kettering Town March 2006. Retford United June 2007. Sheffield United Under-14 coach, football development officer April 2008.

■ Adrian Littlejohn's transfer was completed on deadline day in March 1998, and the speedy striker made a promising start, scoring against League leaders Watford in a rousing 2–2 draw. In his fourth appearance, the former England Youth international scored twice against his previous club, Plymouth Argyle. In the new season, under new manager Andy Ritchie, the goals dried up and he departed to Bury, again linking up with manager Neil Warnock.

LITTLEWOOD, Christopher Stewart

Centre-forward

Born: Treeton, Rotherham, 7 January 1905.
Died: Rotherham, 2 January 1977.
Career: Hardwick Colliery. Chesterfield amateur January 1924. Matlock Town. Sheffield Wednesday January 1925. Luton Town July 1925. Williamthorpe Colliery. Alfreton Town trial October 1926. Port Vale November 1926. OLDHAM ATHLETIC January 1929, fee £1,300 plus Albert Pynegar. Port Vale March 1931, fee £1,550. Bournemouth & Boscombe

Athletic July 1933. Altrincham July 1934 to 1936. Northwich Victoria 1937–38.

■ Stewart Littlewood's effective centre-forward play brought him 27 goals in 38 League matches in season 1929–30, one short of Frank Newton's record of 28 in 1907–08. The well-travelled attack leader scored 48 goals in just 81 appearances for Athletic before returning to Port Vale in March 1931. On 24 September 1932 he scored six goals against Chesterfield in a 9–1 victory, and his double hat-trick remains to this day the most goals scored by a Port Vale player in one match.

LIVERMORE, David

Midfield

Born: Edmonton, 20 May 1980.
Career: Arsenal trainee, professional July 1998. Millwall July 1999, fee £30,000. Leeds United July 2006. Hull City August 2006, fee £400,000. OLDHAM ATHLETIC loan January 2008.

■ Born at Edmonton and a Spurs supporter as a youngster, David Livermore was associated with his home-town club from the age of seven. He switched to Arsenal at the age of 10 but made his League debut with Millwall, for whom he completed 312 senior appearances in a seven-year stay. Highlights included the League One title in 2000–01, the FA Cup Final of 2004 against Manchester United at the Millennium Stadium, and matches against Ferencvaros in the UEFA Cup in the following season. A 10-day sojourn with Leeds United was followed by a move to Hull City, from whom he joined Athletic on loan in a trasnfer-deadline swoop in January 2008. The left-sided midfielder settled well at Boundary Park and Athletic were prepared to extend his loan for a third month, but the former Millwall captain decided to return to Hull, not wishing to risk injury before seeking a new club in the close season.

LOCHHEAD, Andrew Lorimar

Centre-forward

Born: Milngavie, Glasgow, 9 March 1941.
Career: Renfrew Juniors. Sunderland trial. Burnley December 1958. Leicester City October 1968, fee £80,000. Aston Villa February 1970, fee £30,000. OLDHAM

ATHLETIC August 1973, fee £15,000, appointed player-coach July 1974. Denver Dynamos, US, loan April–June 1974. Padiham FC manager 1975–76.

■ Latics manager Jimmy Frizzell finally solved a long running centre-forward problem when he recruited the craggy, vastly experienced Andy Lochhead. The Latics attack had lacked a focal point ever since the departure of Jim Fryatt to Southport in November 1971. Although Lochhead was not a regular scorer for Athletic, his all-round ability to win the ball in the air and his physical presence made him an ideal target man who created numerous chances for his colleagues. In his one full season at Boundary Park Athletic won the Third Division title. It was a fitting finale to a long and successful playing career that spanned 436/10 League matches and 158 goals.

LOMAX, Kelvin

Right-back

Born: Bury, 12 November 1986.
Career: Woodhey High School (Bury). OLDHAM ATHLETIC Centre of Excellence 1996, trainee July 2003, professional July 2005. Rochdale loan September 2007.

■ Kelvin Lomax made his senior debut under manager Brian Talbot in the final fixture of 2003–04 at Notts County. As a second-half substitute for Darren Sheridan, he made an impressive start despite being in his first year as a trainee. Further progress of 7/2 League appearances in 2004–05 ended following the appointment of new manager Ronnie Moore in 2005. Released in April 2006 in a season blighted by injury, Lomax was handed a second channe by

new manager John Sheridan, who re-signed the 19-year-old defender in July 2006. Two months on loan to Rochdale provided the opportunity for a run of 10 first-team matches, and his first start of the season for the Latics came in the shock 1–0 FA Cup victory against Premier League opponents Everton at Goodison Park. In addition to setting up Gary McDonald for the winning wonder strike, Lomax's goalline clearance from McFadden's shot capped a wonderful defensive performance. In the following month his reward was a new, three-and-a-half-year contract.

LONERGAN, Darren

Defender

Born: Cork, Ireland, 28 January 1974.
Career: Waterford. Liverpool trial April 1994. OLDHAM ATHLETIC September 1994 to 1997. Bury trial October-November 1997. Rochdale, trial. Walsall, trial. Stalybridge Celtic November 1997. Hyde United. Macclesfield Town August 1998 to April 1999. Southport trial.

■ Impressive displays in Athletic's A Team and reserves ensured that Darren Lonergan remained for a lengthy spell at Boundary Park, but he ultimately failed to make the grade at senior level. In earlier days Lonergan appeared in three Gaelic football All-Ireland Finals with Waterford Schoolboys before switching to soccer.

LONGMUIR, Archibald MacDonald

Inside-forward

Born: Saltcoats, Ayr, 17 April 1897.
Career: Ardrossan Winton Rovers. Wartime guest with Aberdeen. Celtic May 1920. Blackburn Rovers November 1921, fee £1,000. OLDHAM ATHLETIC August 1923, fee £500. Wrexham June 1924 to May 1930, fee £400. Cowdenbeath loan July 1925.

■ Although he scored on his debut for Athletic, a 2–2 draw at Blackpool on the opening day of season 1923–24, Archie Longmuir enjoyed little further success, and it was left to Wrexham to bring out the best in him. In a six-year stay at the Racecourse he completed a total of 254 League and Cup matches, scoring 39 goals, mainly from outside-right. After retiring from the game he was in business in the Wrexham area, and in December 1935 scooped the football pools, winning just short of £17,000.

LOURENCO DA SILVA, Louis Carlos

Midfield

Born: Luanda, Angola, 5 June 1983.
Career: Sporting Lisbon, Portugal. Bristol City loan March 2001. OLDHAM ATHLETIC loan July–December 2002.

■ Capped by Portugal at every level from Under-16 to Under-20, Lourenco made his debut for Sporting Lisbon at 16 but had played mostly in their B team, for whom he scored 33 goals in 2001–02. Described by Ian Dowie as 'quick, bright and sharp', the Angolan youngster, nicknamed 'Jimmy' by his teammates, failed to secure a regular berth during his loan spell and returned to Portugal after five months of his one-year loan. He nevertheless left behind an abiding memory when scoring against Huddersfield Town at Boundary Park in September 2002. Introduced after 66 minutes to replace Wayne Andrews, Lourenco scored Athletic's fourth goal with a stunning overhead kick, giving a glimpse of the quality that earned him national honours.

LOW, Joshua David 'Josh'

Winger

Born: Bristol, 15 February 1979.
Career: Bristol Rovers School of Excellence, trainee, professional August 1996. Farnborough Town loan November 1998. Leyton Orient May 1999. Cardiff City November 1999. OLDHAM ATHLETIC August 2002. Northampton Town August 2003, fee £165,000. Leicester City June 2006. Peterborough United January 2007.

■ Capable of outstanding performances, whether at wing-back or on the right-side of midfield, Josh Low enhanced his reputation in a season at Boundary Park, despite a troublesome hamstring injury that restricted his appearances. The former Wales Under-21 international created many opportunities, mainly in the counter-attack, his searing pace making him a truly potent attacking force.

LOWE, John

Outside-right

Born: Ripley, Derbyshire 1895.
Career: Ripley Colliery. Sheffield Wednesday trial. Hartshay Colliery. Chesterfield Municipal May 1920. Bolton Wanderers October 1921, in exchange for Tom Broome. Port Vale May 1923. OLDHAM ATHLETIC May 1928. Rotherham United August 1929. Ripley Town October 1929, committee member from March 1933.

■ A clever, ball playing wingman, John Lowe was said to lack pace, but his centres were invariably accurate. He did not miss a match with Port Vale in the 1924–25 and 1925–26 seasons, and went on to record 128 consecutive appearances between April 1925 and March 1927. Sadly, he failed to find his best form after joining Athletic, losing his first-team spot to Jack King after just seven appearances.

LOWRIE, Thomas

Half-back

Born: Glasgow, 14 January 1928.
Career: Clydesdale Juniors. Troon Athletic. St Mirren. Manchester United August 1947. Aberdeen March 1951. OLDHAM ATHLETIC August 1952 to June 1955, fee £3,000. Droylsden August 1958.

■ Tommy Lowrie was an excellent wing-half in typical Scottish style – constructive, comfortable on the ball, and an arch exponent of the defence-splitting pass. He learned his football with minor teams in Glasgow after spending time as a wartime evacuee in Perth. He made his Manchester United debut in April 1948 against Manchester City, before a crowd in excess of 71,000 at Maine Road. He joined Athletic after 18 months with Aberdeen, and won a Third Division North Championship medal in his first season.

LYONS, George

Forward

Career: Black Lane Temperance. Manchester United April 1904. OLDHAM ATHLETIC July 1906. Rossendale United November 1906. Salford United October 1907.

■ George Lyons spent two seasons with Manchester United without managing to graduate, appearing in just four League matches and one FA Cup tie before being released. He joined the Latics for what proved to be their final season as a non-League club but made an early season departure to Rossendale United after just one first-team outing.

McALLISTER, Alexander 'Sandy'

Centre-half

Born: Kilmarnock c.1878.
Died: Italy, 31 January 1918.
Career: Dean Park, Kilmarnock. Carrington Vale. Kilmarnock FC 1896. Sunderland December 1896. Derby County June 1904. OLDHAM ATHLETIC 1905 to 1906. Spennymoor United July 1909.

■ Former coal-miner Sandy McAllister appeared in 225 League and Cup matches and scored five goals for Sunderland, winning a Championship medal in 1902. He then spent just one season with Derby County before joining Athletic. The small but strongly-built pivot gave good value during his season at Hudson Fold being ever-present in Lancashire Combination and FA Cup matches. His total of 10 goals for the season included nine from the penalty spot, reflecting the robust nature of the game at that time. McAllister died of food poisoning while serving as a private with the Northumberland Fusiliers in Italy during World War One.

McBRIDE, Joseph

Winger/Midfield

Born: Glasgow, 17 August 1960.
Career: St Mungo's Academy, Glasgow. Everton apprentice September 1976, professional August 1978. Rotherham United August 1982. OLDHAM ATHLETIC September 1983, fee £45,000. Hibernian January 1985, fee £20,000. Dundee December 1988, fee £50,000. East Fife July 1991. Albion Rovers player-coach March 1994 to mid-season 1995–96.

■ Joe McBride was transfer listed at the end of his first season with Athletic in which injuries hampered his progress. In mid-season 1984–85 he was transferred to Hibernian for less than half the fee Athletic had paid for him. Despite McBride's fine footballing pedigree – his father, also Joe, was a Scottish international centre-forward – he failed to win a regular place in Athletic's starting line up, despite his ability to occupy midfield or wing positions. Considered an outstanding prospect in his early days, McBride had represented Scotland Schools and went on to win Youth and Under-21 international honours.

McCALL, Peter

Half-back

Born: West Ham, 11 September 1936.
Career: King's Lynn. Bristol City amateur October 1952, professional April 1955. OLDHAM ATHLETIC May 1962, fee £1,000. Hereford United July 1965 to June 1967.

■ Peter McCall was evacuated to Norfolk as a youngster and began his football career with King's Lynn. Upon joining Bristol City, National Service with the 10th Hussars effectively delayed

his senior debut until April 1958. He had made 78 League appearances for the Robins at the time of his transfer to Athletic and he was immediately successful, his fine attacking play from right-half being a major element in Athletic's promotion season of 1962–63.

McCARTHY, Philip Paul

Wing-half

Born: Liverpool, 19 February 1943.
Died: Liverpool, December 1996.
Career: Marine FC. Skelmersdale United amateur 1962. OLDHAM ATHLETIC trial February, professional July 1965. Halifax Town January 1966 to 1971.

■ Phil McCarthy failed to make the grade with Athletic but his career took an upturn following his transfer to Halifax Town. In a lengthy spell at the Shay he made 180/1 League appearances and scored 14 goals. Highlights included promotion from Division Four in 1969, and a third-place finish in Division Three in 1971.

McCARTHY, Sean Casey

Forward

Born: Bridgend, 12 September 1967.
Career: Bridgend Town. Swansea City October 1985. Plymouth Argyle August 1988, fee £50,000. Bradford City July 1990, fee £250,000. OLDHAM ATHLETIC December 1993, fee £500,000. Bristol City loan March 1998. Plymouth Argyle August 1998. Exeter City July 2001, retired June 2003.

■ A burly, powerful forward, Sean McCarthy had 104 League goals to his credit when Athletic signed him from Bradford City. Despite his previous scoring record, McCarthy failed to deliver the goals necessary for Premier League survival, four in 19/1 matches reflecting his difficulty in adjusting to life at the highest level. In Graeme Sharp's first season as manager McCarthy scored 18 of the team's 60 League goals but his scoring ratio dipped in his final two seasons, and he was transfer listed in January 1998. In a second spell with Plymouth Argyle he passed the milestone of 500 League appearances, and his final career figures totalled 172 goals in 478/69 League matches.

McCORMACK, Francis Adamson 'Frank'

Centre-half

Born: Glasgow, 25 September 1920.
Career: Parkhead Juniors. Clyde c.1943. OLDHAM ATHLETIC November 1949, fee £7,000. Morton August 1953.

■ Despite costing Athletic a considerable fee, Frank McCormack failed to impress at Boundary Park. Matters were not helped by his dispute with the club regarding his desire to continue in his trade as a house-plasterer. McCormack claimed it had been agreed he could work as well as play football, but the club's directors insisted that he should be a full-time player. The impasse was never resolved, and although he remained on Athletic's retained list until 1953, McCormack left Boundary Park for good in the 1950 close season.

McCORMICK, Patrick

Inside-forward

Born: Cleator Moor, 7 January 1914.
Died: Cleator Moor, 25 August 1991.
Career: Cleator Moor. Preston North End amateur October 1933. Morecambe July 1935. OLDHAM ATHLETIC May 1936. Workington August 1939.

■ Patrick McCormick was playing regularly for Preston North End reserves at 19 years of age, but he was allowed to leave Deepdale and made his mark with Morecambe, scoring 33 goals in season 1935–36. Combining good ball control with speed, he made a promising start with Athletic, scoring 11 League and Cup goals in 31 matches in his first season. Sadly, he failed to maintain the form that had marked him as such a fine prospect, and the majority of his final two seasons at Boundary Park was spent at Lancashire Combination level.

McCREADY, Bernard Thomas

Goalkeeper

Born: Dumbarton, 23 April 1937.
Career: Dumbarton St Patrick's. Renfrew Juniors. St Mirren trial February 1955. Hibernian trial April 1955. Celtic May 1955. Rochdale May 1957. OLDHAM ATHLETIC March to June 1959. Clyde trial. Buxton August 1959.

■ Goalkeeper and chartered accountant Benny McCready spent two years as a reserve goalkeeper with Glasgow Celtic, and a similar period with Rochdale for whom he completed 31 League and Cup appearances. He was signed by Athletic at Easter 1959 and provided some competition for David Teece during the closing weeks of Athletic's first season in the newly formed Division Four. Despite a number of impressive displays during his brief stay, McCready was not retained as Athletic made a clean sweep of their goalkeeping staff following a disappointing 21st-place finish.

McCUE, John William

Centre-half

Born: Longton, Staffordshire, 1899.
Career: Sandbach Ramblers. Stoke City amateur 1924. Stafford Rangers. OLDHAM ATHLETIC October 1925, fee £200. Sandbach Ramblers June 1926. Oswestry Town November 1926. Denbigh August 1927.

■ John McCue spent a season in reserve with Athletic and, in what seemed like an afterthought, he was introduced for the final fixture of the season. His solitary League appearance proved a memorable one as goals by Albert Pynegar (4), Frank Hargreaves (3) and a penalty by full-back Sammy Wynne rounded off Athletic's season with a thumping 8–3 home victory against Nottingham Forest.

McCUE, John William

Full-back

Born: Stoke-on-Trent, 22 August 1922.
Died: Barlaston, Stoke-on-Trent, 19 November 1999.
Career: Longton & North Staffordshire Schoolboys. Stoke City amateur November 1939, professional April 1940. Wartime guest with Darlington 1945–46. OLDHAM ATHLETIC September 1960. Macclesfield Town July 1962.

■ For many years Stoke City's record for League appearances was held by full-back John McCue, until his total of 502 was eventually overtaken by the current record-holder, Eric Skeels with 506. Initially joining Athletic on a month's trial at the age of 38, the veteran defender spent two years at Boundary Park and is best remembered in partnership with

Ken Branagan. The two vastly experienced backs effectively tightened the defensive lines as the Bobby Johnstone-inspired attack lifted Athletic from the doldrums.

McCURLEY, Kevin

Centre-forward

Born: Consett, Co. Durham, 2 April 1926.
Died: Broadstairs, Kent 5 May 2000.
Career: Worthing. Brighton & Hove Albion September 1948. Liverpool June 1951. Colchester United March 1952. OLDHAM ATHLETIC June 1960. Tonbridge March 1961. Ramsgate Athletic June 1962. Canterbury City July 1963. Snowdown Colliery.

■ The scorer of exactly 100 League goals at the time of his signing, the unfortunate Kevin McCurley was carried off the field, two minutes before half-time on his debut, suffering from a dislocated kneecap. During the period of his incapacity a trio of new signings, Bert Lister, John Liddell and Bobby Johnstone, kept McCurley out of the first team picture, despite his having scored twice in his come-back game in the reserves in late October.

McDONALD, Gary Matthew

Midfield

Born: Irvine, 10 April 1982.
Career: Abbey Boys' Club (Ayreshire). Kilmarnock Youths. Kilmarnock June 1999. OLDHAM ATHLETIC June 2006. Aberdeen May 2008.

■ Gary McDonald won a Scottish Cup medal at Under-15 level with Abbey BC and represented Scotland from Under-16s to Under-20s level. Subsequently

capped by Scotland B, he completed 116 appearances and scored 14 goals before leaving Rugby Park. He became manager Sheridan's first signing in June 2006 and he enjoyed a productive first season with seven goals from 44/5 League and Cup appearances. Despite starting 2007–08 from a position on the bench, the industrious midfielder eventually regained a starting spot. His first goal of the season was the match winner in the FA Cup victory at Doncaster Rovers, and he repeated the feat with a strike that shook the football world when his stunning 25-yard volley knocked Everton out of the third round of the FA Cup. Not surprisingly, at the end of season awards ceremony at Boundary Park, McDonald's strike was voted Goal of the Season. Out of contract at the end of the campaign, McDonald declined Athletic's offer and signed a pre-contract agreement with Scottish Premier League Club Aberdeen.

McDONALD, Hugh Lachlan

Goalkeeper

Born: Kilwinning, Ayrshire, 20 December 1881.
Died: Plumstead, London, 27 August 1920.
Career: Ayr Westerlea. Ayr FC. Maybole FC. Ayr Academical. Beith FC July 1905. Woolwich Arsenal January 1906. Brighton & Hove Albion May 1906. Woolwich Arsenal May 1908. OLDHAM ATHLETIC July 1910. Bradford Park Avenue December 1911. Woolwich Arsenal December 1912. Fulham November 1913. Bristol Rovers February 1914.

■ In August 1908 the *Athletic News* considered McDonald 'A formidable opponent for a nervous forward.' He was certainly an imposing figure and, considering his bulk, amazingly agile. He joined Athletic for their first season in Division One and the seventh-place finish achieved owed much to McDonald and his co-defenders, who conceded only 41 League goals in the 38–match programme. Three matches into the new season he was deposed by Howard Matthews and refused to travel to Everton with the reserves. He was fined, suspended for one month, and transfer listed. On retirement from the game McDonald became a publican in Plumstead.

McDONALD, Neil Raymond

Midfield

Born: Willington Quay, near North Shields, 2 November 1965.
Career: Wallsend Boys' Club. Newcastle United apprentice, signing professional February 1983. Everton August 1988, fee £525,000. OLDHAM ATHLETIC October 1991, fee £500,000. Bolton Wanderers July 1994. Preston North End November 1995, fee £40,000, youth-team coach March 1997 to 1998. Bolton Wanderers coach

2000. Crystal Palace assistant manager 2005–06. Carlisle United manager June 2006 to August 2007. Lincoln City assistant manager November 2007. Leeds United first-team coach February 2008.

■ Neil McDonald began with the Newcastle United first team at 16 years of age. At either midfield or right-back, he completed 185/18 League and Cup matches, scoring 28 goals. Transferred to Everton in August 1988, a highlight was his appearance in the all-Merseyside FA Cup Final of 1989. After 100/14 matches and seven goals he became the fifth former Everton player signed by Latics manager Joe Royle. McDonald was expected to give greater variety to Athletic's midfield with his experience, range of passing, and ability to strike from deep positions. Sadly, the England Under-21 international failed to impress at Boundary Park. Transfer listed in July 1993 after just 24/5 first-team appearances, he eventually joined Bolton Wanderers on a free transfer but tragically suffered a broken leg in his second match.

McDONNELL, Peter Anthony

Goalkeeper

Born: Kendal, 11 June 1953.
Career: Netherfield. Bury March 1974. Liverpool May 1974, fee £25,000. Dallas Tornado, US, April 1978. OLDHAM ATHLETIC August 1978, fee £18,000. Barrow 1983, manager July–November 1984. Morecambe. Barrow 1988 to 1993.

■ In four years with Liverpool, Peter McDonnell was totally overshadowed by England goalkeeper Ray Clemence. McDonnell's debut for Athletic actually doubled his number of League

appearances, and it was a traumatic start for the bearded goalkeeper. On a sunny opening day of the season at Luton Town the home side won 6–1, all their goals coming in the second half after Athletic had led at half-time. Generally first choice throughout his Athletic career, McDonnell was a courageous goalkeeper, quick to take responsibility in his own penalty area.

McDONOUGH, Darren Karl

Midfield

Born: Antwerp, Belgium, 7 November 1962.
Career: OLDHAM ATHLETIC associate schoolboy December 1977, apprentice July 1979, professional January 1980. Luton Town September 1986, fee £87,000. Newcastle United March 1992, fee £90,000, retired due to Achilles injury April 1994.

■ Darren McDonough announced his arrival in League football as an 18-year-old apprentice by scoring with a spectacular long-range volley at Notts County on his debut. In the course of exactly 200 senior matches for the Latics, the aggressive, committed displays of the wonderfully versatile McDonough made him a firm favourite at Boundary Park. Probably best as a central defender but also capable in midfield or as a striker – he scored 10 goals in 1982–83 – he was one of the most whole-hearted players ever to pull on an Athletic shirt.

McGARVEY, Scott Thomas

Forward

Born: Glasgow, 22 April 1963.
Career: Celtic Boys' Club. Manchester United associate schoolboy November 1978, apprentice June 1979, professional April 1980. Wolverhampton Wanderers loan March–May 1984. Portsmouth July 1984, fee £85,000. Carlisle United loan January 1986, permanent August 1986. Grimsby Town March 1987. Bristol City September 1988. OLDHAM ATHLETIC May 1989 to September 1990, fee £22,000. Wigan Athletic loan September-October 1989. Mazda, Hiroshima, Japan, June 1990, fee £20,000. Aris, Limassol, Cyprus, September 1992. Derry City, Ireland, player-coach 1993. Witton Albion February 1994. Barrow March 1994.

■ A fair-haired Glaswegian, Scott McGarvey made his full debut for Manchester United as a 19-year-old, and this was swiftly followed by his first appearance for Scotland Under-21s in April 1982. Despite being a prolific scorer in United's junior sides, his career at senior level did not progress as expected. Associated during a nomadic career with eight League clubs, McGarvey totalled 152/27 League appearances and scored 39 goals. Despite a scoring debut at Swindon Town in January 1990, his spell at Boundary Park was disappointing as he failed to establish a regular place in Athletic's potent attack that totalled 110 goals in 65 League and Cup matches in 1989–90.

McGILL, James Hopkins

Full-back

Born: Bellshill, Lanarkshire, 2 October 1939.
Died: Chester, October 2006.
Career: Larkhall Thistle. Partick Thistle January 1957. OLDHAM ATHLETIC May 1959. Crewe Alexandra August 1960. Chester October 1962. Wrexham October 1963. Macclesfield Town May 1964. Bournemouth & Boscombe Athletic trial October 1964. Bangor City July 1965. Porthmadog.

■ Jimmy McGill began in football as a forward, but in three seasons with Partick Thistle was converted to a defender. Athletic fielded the apprentice joiner in both full-back berths, at centre-

forward, and finally at right-half. The latter seemed to be his best position, as his speed, stamina and frequent up-field bursts helped forge a link between defence and attack that had been sadly lacking all season. McGill's career in English football totalled 168 League appearances and four goals.

McGINLAY, John

Forward

Born: Inverness, 8 April 1964.
Career: Nairn County. Sunderland trial 1985. Elgin City. Shrewsbury Town February 1989. Bury July 1990, fee £175,000. Millwall January 1991, fee £80,000. Bolton Wanderers September 1992, fee £125,000. Bradford City November 1997, fee £625,000. OLDHAM ATHLETIC October 1998, retired due to Achilles injury January 1999. Gresley Rovers manager 2001.

■ John McGinlay's League career ended with Athletic when he took the decision to retire after less than five months at Boundary Park. Bradford City had released him in September 1998, and it was hoped that the experienced Scotland international would add some much-needed presence to Athletic's shot-shy attack. Sadly, the injury problems that had prompted his early release from Bradford City continued to hamper his performances, leading to his decision to retire. In his five years at Burnden Park, McGinley enjoyed a memorable season in 1994–95. In addition to registering his

100th League goal, he collected a Coca-Cola Cup finalists' medal and assisted Bolton Wanderers to promotion into the Premier League via a Wembley Play-off victory against Reading. McGinley was capped twice by Scotland at B level and won 13 full caps between 1994–97.

McGINN, William Bell

Full-back

Born: Kilwinning, Ayrshire, 2 February 1943.

Career: Ardrossan Winton Rovers. OLDHAM ATHLETIC November 1963. Rossendale United 1966.

■ Throughout his stay at Boundary Park Billy McGinn faced stiff competition from more experienced defenders. In his first season he made only three senior appearances as deputy for the former Sheffield United back, Barry Taylor. Although Taylor departed in the close season, he was replaced by the stylish ex-Blackpool full-back Barrie Martin. McGinn's first opportunity of regular senior action came following a mid-term reshuffle in which Martin was moved to left-half. The young Scot took his chance well during 23 League and Cup outings, and commenced 1965–66 as first-choice left-back but lost out in mid-season following the appointment of Jimmy McIlroy as manager.

McGLEN, William

Defender

Born: Bedlington, 27 April 1921.
Died: Burgh-le-Marsh, Skegness, 23 December 1999.

Career: Blyth Spartans. Manchester United amateur January, professional May 1946. Lincoln City July 1952. OLDHAM ATHLETIC February 1953, in exchange for Jimmy Munro. Lincoln City trainer 1956. Skegness Town coach-manager June 1967 to August 1968.

■ At the outset of his career Billy McGlen was recommended to Manchester United after playing services football in Italy during World War Two. Principally a steady left-back, he was versatile enough to successfully occupy the left-wing berth in early 1950–51 following Charlie Mitten's defection to Bogota. He joined Athletic from Lincoln City to fill a gap caused by injury to player-manager George Hardwick and proved to be an inspired signing. Playing in the final 11 matches of the season, of which only two were lost, McGlen did much to help Athletic clinch the Championship of the Third Division North.

McGOWAN, Gerard James

Outside-left

Born: Kilwinning, Ayrshire, 4 August 1944.
Career: Ardeer Recreation. OLDHAM ATHLETIC November 1963. Hyde United August 1966. Bangor City 1967.

■ Gerry McGowan waited patiently for the best part of two years before sampling first-team football, and although he scored against Peterborough United in his second League outing it

was seven months before he earned a recall. That match at Southend United also marked the debut of Athletic's player-manager, Jimmy McIlroy.

McGUIRE, Michael James

Midfield

Born: Blackpool, 4 September 1952.
Career: Lancashire Schoolboys. Coventry City apprentice November 1969, professional July 1970. Norwich City January 1975, fee £60,000. Tampa Bay Rowdies, US, April–August 1978. Barnsley March 1983, fee £30,000. OLDHAM ATHLETIC January 1985. Blackpool August 1987. Grantham Town March

1988. Joined the PFA in June 1987, initially as YTS co-ordinator. Retired from playing in 1991. Appointed deputy chief executive of the PFA July 2002.

■ Former England Youth international Mick McGuire joined Athletic as a vastly experienced midfielder with over 200 League and Cup appearances with Norwich City and an overall career record in excess of 300 League matches. He joined an Athletic side deep in relegation trouble, but his influence and ability to control events from midfield immediately improved performances and guided the side well clear of the drop. He had an excellent season in 1985–86, appearing in 40 League matches, but in the season that followed he featured little.

McILROY, James

Inside-forward

Born: Lambeg near Lisburn, Northern Ireland, 25 October 1931.
Career: Craigavad. Glentoran August 1949. Burnley March 1950, fee £8,000. Stoke City March 1963, fee £30,000. OLDHAM ATHLETIC manager January 1966, player-manager March 1966. Stoke City coach August 1968. Bolton Wanderers coach and assistant manager August 1970, briefly team manager, resigned November 1970.

■ Jimmy McIlroy's career began at 17 years of age when Glentoran added the apprentice bricklayer to their payroll.

Less than a year later he embarked for Burnley and a glittering career was highlighted by the Division One Championship in 1960, European Cup entry the following season, and a Wembley appearance in the FA Cup Final against Tottenham Hotspur in 1962. After 13 years at Turf Moor he was transferred to Stoke City and two months later picked up a Division Two Championship medal. In international football he won 55 Northern Ireland caps which included an appearance in the 1958 World Cup quarter-finals. The wonderfully gifted inside-forward had not intended to play again after joining Athletic as manager, but with his team floundering in the relegation zone he resumed as a player. McIlroy made his final appearance for the Latics against Peterborough United at Boundary Park on 26 August 1967. He finished his career with 568/6 League appearances and 131 goals. After leaving the game he worked as a journalist for a Burnley newspaper.

McILVENNY, Robert

Inside-forward

Born: Belfast, 7 July 1926.
Career: Balmoral United. Glentoran 1942. Distillery. Merthyr Tydfil 1947. OLDHAM ATHLETIC March 1950, fee £3,000. Bury August 1954. Southport August 1955. Barrow July 1957. Yeovil Town 1959. Colwyn Bay player-manager 1960–62. Southport A Team trainer 1966 to February 1968.

■ The son of an Irish international, Bobby McIlvenny was one of the smallest players ever to represent Athletic. Just

under 5ft 4in in height and weighing a little over 10st, he was quick, elusive and direct in style. He was also extremely hard working and appeared to cover every blade of grass during a game. He scored eight goals in 37 matches in Athletic's 1952–53 Championship-winning side, and memorably scored twice at Luton in the Latics' first Division Two fixture since 1935. Subsequent spells in League football with Barrow and Southport took his career aggregate figures to 271 League matches and 64 goals. Bobby's elder brother, Pat McIlvenny, played for Brighton & Hove Albion and Aldershot in the 1950s.

McKENNAN, Peter Stewart

Inside-forward

Born: Airdrie, 16 July 1918.
Died: Dundonald, Ayrshire, October 1991.
Career: Whitburn Juniors. Edinburgh Juniors. Partick Thistle July 1935. Wartime guest with Linfield and Glentoran. West Bromwich Albion October 1947, fee £10,650. Leicester City March 1948, in exchange for Jack Haines plus £6,000. Brentford September 1948. Middlesbrough May 1949, fee £7,500. OLDHAM ATHLETIC July 1951, fee £3,000. Coleraine player-coach July 1954.

■ Peter McKennan made his senior debut with Partick Thistle at 17 years of age, and was on the brink of full

international honours when World War Two interrupted his promising career. Following demobilisation, a series of fairly rapid moves ensued, and his longest spell in the League came with Athletic, where he teamed up with his former Middlesbrough colleague, player-manager George Hardwick. Strong and forceful in possession and with wonderful ball control, McKennan favoured the direct route to goal, and his never-say-die-spirit was always a source of inspiration to his teammates. Despite being increasingly troubled by knee injuries, he was a key member of the 1952–53 Championship side, scoring 10 goals in 32 matches.

McLEAN, Ian James

Left-back

Born: Leeds, 13 September 1978.
Career: Bradford City associate schoolboy April 1994, trainee July 1995, professional January 1997. OLDHAM ATHLETIC October 1998. Gainsborough Trinity June 2000.

■ Full-back Ian McLean was released by Bradford City after a three-year association in which he reached professional level but failed to graduate beyond reserve team football. Offered a trial by the Latics, he was quickly drafted into senior action. After making five League appearances in his first season, McLean appeared only once in 1999–2000 as Andy Holt continued to dominate the left wing-back position.

McMAHON, Ian

Defender

Born: Wells, 7 October 1964.
Career: Thornham Schoolboys. Manchester City juniors 1977. OLDHAM ATHLETIC associate schoolboy October 1980, apprentice July 1981, professional October 1982. Rochdale loan January, permanent February 1984 to March 1986. Subsequently worked in the commercial departments of Rochdale Hornets, Oldham and Halifax Rugby League clubs. Hull City and Doncaster Rovers Football League clubs. In January 2001 emigrated to US to take up the post of general manager with a professional football team located in Des Moines, Iowa.

■ Ian McMahon was a talented all-

rounder who played rugby league as a schoolboy before becoming a professional footballer. He subsequently played cricket for Werneth and rugby union for Oldham Vets. He had appeared only twice for Athletic when a loan move to Rochdale, which quickly became permanent, offered him the opportunity of regular first-team football. In a little over two years he appeared in 104 League and Cup matches and scored eight goals. Sadly, in the season that he was voted Rochdale's Young Player of the Year a cartilage operation developed complications that ended his career at just 21 years of age.

McMANUS, Brendan

Goalkeeper

Born: Kilkeel, Northern Ireland, 2 December 1923.
Career: Newry Town. Huddersfield Town October 1945. OLDHAM ATHLETIC July 1947, fee £200. Bradford City October 1948, fee £675. Frickley Colliery 1953. Scarborough July 1955 to 1956.

■ Brendan McManus, a tall and extremely agile goalkeeper, handled the ball well, his judgement and fielding of high crosses being a particular strong point. His transfer to Bradford City, after just one season at Boundary Park was a disappointment to his many admirers,

but the move enabled him to team up once again with David Steele, the manager who had first brought him into League football with Huddersfield Town. Ironically, in his first season at Valley Parade McManus starred in home and away victories against the Latics over the Christmas period in 1948. A personal memory of the genial Irishman surrounded his mode of transport as I, when an autograph-hunting schoolboy, often accompanied him as he pushed his bicycle up Sheepfoot Lane after the match!

McNEILL, Alexander 'Alan'

Midfield

Born: Belfast, 16 August 1945.
Career: Crusaders. Glentoran loan 1967. Middlesbrough August 1967, fee £10,000. Huddersfield Town November 1968. OLDHAM ATHLETIC October 1969. Stockport County July 1975. Witton Albion 1977–81.

■ A strongly-built, attacking midfielder, Alan McNeill made an immediate impact at Boundary Park. Prior to his arrival the team had gone nine matches without a League victory, but their fortunes took a much-needed upturn which eventually led to promotion in season 1970–71. Despite being dogged by injuries in season 1973–74 he won a Division Three Championship medal for his 13/5 League appearances. McNeill's League

career wound up with two seasons at Stockport County, but in non-League circles he played in the Huddersfield League until the age of 46.

McNIVEN, David Jonathan

Forward

Born: Leeds, 27 May 1978.
Career: Lytham St Annes YMCA. OLDHAM ATHLETIC trainee July 1994, professional October 1995. Linfield loan March 1997. Vasalund, Sweden, loan June–October 1997. Chesterfield trial January 1998. Scarborough loan February 2000. Southport March 2000. York City August 2000 to May 2001. Chester City September-October 2001. Hamilton Academical November 2001. Northwich Victoria July 2002. Leigh RMI July 2003. Queen of the South July 2004. Scarborough January 2006. Morecambe July 2006.

Stafford Rangers loan January 2007, permanent August 2007. Farsley Celtic February 2008.

■ David McNiven is the twin brother of Scott (below) and son of David senior, the Scottish Under-21 international forward who scored 85 goals in a career spanning four League clubs in the 1970s and 1980s. In the final home match of his debut season, David's appearance from the bench created a record, as it was the first time that twins had been fielded in a match by Athletic. (Twins Paul and Ron Futcher both played for Athletic in the 1980s, but not at the same time.) David failed to graduate at Boundary Park, his appearances from the bench far outweighing his starting appearances. In more recent times, he appeared as a substitute in Morecambe's victorious Wembley Play-off Final in 2007 that won The Shrimps promotion to the Football League.

McNIVEN, Scott Andrew

Full-back

Born: Leeds, 27 May 1978.
Career: Lytham St Annes YMCA. OLDHAM ATHLETIC trainee July 1994, professional October 1995. Oxford United June 2002. Mansfield Town July 2004. Chester City July 2005. Macclesfield Town trial July 2006. Morecambe non-contract 18–30 August 2006. Fleetwood Town trial November 2006. Farsley Celtic July 2007.

■ The twin brother of David McNiven (above), Scott's League career commenced when he made his Athletic

debut at Barnsley a few weeks short of his 17th birthday. Called into Scotland's Under-21 squad at 17 years of age, his debut against the Faroe Islands sadly lasted for only 40 minutes as he was sent off for two bookable offences. At either right-back or in central midfield Scott served Athletic with distinction in over 250 senior appearances and it was a matter of some surprise when he was released as a free agent at the close of season 2002–03. Diagnosed with testicular cancer during his season with Mansfield Town, he happily made a full recovery. In August 2007 the McNiven twins were in direct opposition for the very first time in a competitive match, the Farsley Celtic versus Stafford Rangers Blue Square Premier fixture, won 1–0 by Farsley.

McSHANE, Henry 'Harry'

Outside-left

Born: Holytown, Lanarkshire, 8 April 1920.
Career: Bellshill Athletic. Blackburn Rovers amateur January 1937, professional February 1937. Wartime guest with Manchester City, Blackpool, Reading and Port Vale. Huddersfield Town September 1946. Bolton Wanderers July 1947. Manchester United September 1950, in exchange for John Ball. OLDHAM ATHLETIC February 1954, fee £750. Chorley player-coach 1955–56. Wellington Town 1956–57. Droylsden August 1958. Stalybridge Celtic coach October 1961.

■ Harry McShane was two months short of his 34th birthday when he was signed by the Latics. Still a speedy and dangerous wingman, he was never over-elaborate, preferring to make ground by the shortest route. He was immediately plunged into Athletic's ultimately unsuccessful battle against relegation from Division Two, making his debut at Blackburn Rovers, where his career had commenced some 17 years earlier. A member of the Manchester United squad when they won the Championship of Division One in 1951–52, McShane retained his links with Old Trafford through United's Old Players' Association. Harry's son, Ian, is the film and television actor, perhaps best known for his role as the antiques dealer in the TV series *Lovejoy*.

McTAVISH, John Kay

Inside-forward

Born: Govan, Glasgow, 7 June 1885.
Died: Glasgow, 1926.
Career: Petershill. Falkirk 1905. OLDHAM ATHLETIC June 1910. Tottenham Hotspur January 1911. Newcastle United April 1912, fee £650. Partick Thistle June 1913, fee £500. York City 1914. Goole Town February 1915. Wartime guest with Falkirk. East Fife 1919. East Stirlingshire 1921. Dumbarton until 1924.

■ Scottish international John McTavish joined Athletic for their first season in Division One, but in his home League debut against Newcastle United he was injured and did not re-appear for the second half. It was an unfortunate start for the ball-playing Scotsman who, just three months earlier, had been capped against Ireland. He remained for only six months at Boundary Park, and moved rapidly thereafter, playing in 40 matches for Spurs and 39 for Newcastle United before returning to Scotland to join Partick Thistle.

McVITIE, George James

Winger

Born: Carlisle, 7 September 1948.
Career: Carlisle Schoolboys. Carlisle United apprentice May 1964, professional December 1965. West Bromwich Albion August 1970, fee £30,000. OLDHAM

ATHLETIC August 1972, fee £20,000. Carlisle United December 1975, fee £12,000. Queen of the South 1981–82.

■ A real touchline artist with an exciting turn of pace, former England Schoolboy international George McVitie appeared in every League and Cup match during the Championship-winning campaign of 1973–74, scoring 10 goals in 54 matches. His transfer fee was the highest ever paid by Athletic at the time, and although McVitie's appearances were restricted by illness in his first season, he was undoubtedly good value thereafter. Athletic supporters of a certain age will no doubt recall with relish the wing pairing of McVitie with Alan Groves during the run-in to the Division Three-Championship title in 1974.

MADDISON, John Arden Brown

Wing-half

Born: Usworth near Chester-le-Street, 12 February 1900.

Died: Rugeley, 19 August 1987.
Career: Usworth Colliery. Stoke November 1923. Port Vale October 1924. OLDHAM ATHLETIC May 1927. Burton Town August 1929. Mansfield Town August 1933. S.C. Nimes, France, December 1934. Gresley Rovers February 1935. Sutton Town September 1935. Gresley Rovers, reinstated amateur November 1936.

■ A curly-haired and combative wing-half, Arden Maddison was given few senior opportunities as understudy to the consistent Leslie Adlam. He also made the wrong kind of headlines in the first of his infrequent appearances when he was ordered off the field during an ill-tempered derby game against Manchester City.

MAGEE, Eric

Inside-forward

Born: Lurgan, Northern Ireland, 24 August 1947.
Career: Glenavon 1962. Bolton Wanderers trial. OLDHAM ATHLETIC May 1967, fee £4,200. Port Vale July 1969 to May 1970. Linfield 1970–77.

■ Eric Magee first encountered the Latics when he scored against them for Glenavon in a match on the pre-season tour of Ireland in the summer of 1966. About a year later he followed Billy Johnston to Boundary Park and made a scoring debut on the summer tour to

Rhodesia and Malawi. Enthusiastic and dashing, the blond-haired inside-forward, who won Northern Ireland Youth and Amateur international caps, enjoyed his best season in 1967–68 with seven goals in 28 matches. In the relegation season that followed injuries kept him sidelined for lengthy spells. After a season with Port Vale Magee returned to Ireland where he appeared in four Irish Cup Finals with Linfield, but was unfortunate to finish on the losing side on each occasion.

MAKIN, Christopher Gregory

Full-back

Born: Manchester, 8 May 1973.
Career: Boundary Park Juniors. FA National School Lilleshall while an OLDHAM ATHLETIC associate schoolboy June 1987, trainee August 1989, professional November 1991. Wigan Athletic loan August–November 1992. Preston North End loan September 1993. Marseille, France, July 1996. Sunderland August 1997, fee £500,000. Ipswich Town March 2001, fee £1.25 million. Leicester City August 2004. Derby County loan February–May 2005. Stoke City trial July 2005. Reading August 2005. Southampton August 2006, retired due to hip injury April 2008.

■ Excellent pace and distribution, crisp tackling and the ability to occupy both full-back and midfield positions

combined to make Chris Makin an impressive prospect who represented England at Schools, Youth and Under-21 levels. He actually made his League debut in Division Three with Wigan Athletic during a successful loan spell in which he scored twice for the other Latics. He made his Oldham debut in the Premiership versus Arsenal in October 1993 and was a losing FA Cup semi-finalist in the same season. During the summer of 1996 he joined one of Europe's top clubs, Marseille, on a free transfer. He cost Sunderland £500,000 just a year later and was a Division One Championship winner in 1999.

MAKIN, Joseph

Full-back

Born: Ancoats, Manchester, 21 September 1950.
Career: St Anne's, Newton Heath. Manchester Schoolboys. OLDHAM ATHLETIC apprentice April 1966, professional October 1967 to June 1968. St George's Cross FC, Australia.

■ At 16 years and 7 months Joe Makin was one of Athletic's youngest debutants, but lost his first-team place in the opening weeks of season 1967–68 with the team anchored at the foot of Division Three. Originally fielded at outside-left in Athletic's reserve team, he lacked the necessary pace for a wingman and was later switched to full-back.

MALLON, James Gillan

Centre-forward

Born: Glasgow, 28 August 1938.
Career: Partick Thistle from school, professional March 1956. OLDHAM ATHLETIC March 1959. Stranraer 1960. Morton 1962. Barrow October 1965. Altrincham 1969.

■ Centre-forward Jimmy Mallon scored four goals in 12 League matches in the final two months of Athletic's first season in Division Four, but it was insufficient to turn the tide in a depressing season that ended in a re-election application. Twelve months after joining the Latics he received his call-up papers and joined the Cameronians (Scottish Rifles). Mallon subsequently re-appeared in English football with Barrow and in a stay of almost four years at Holker Street appeared in 167 League and Cup matches and in 1966–67 assisted Barrow to promotion from Division Four.

MALPAS, Edward

Centre-half

Born: Wolverhampton, 6 September 1904.
Died: Guernsey, 11 November 1968.
Career: Chertington. Shrewsbury Town 1923. Cannock Town. Aston Villa November 1924, fee £50. Blackpool June 1927. OLDHAM ATHLETIC March 1928. Kidderminster Harriers September 1928.

■ Darkly handsome Ted Malpas was deposed after appearing in three consecutive matches in March 1928, the last of which took place at Wolverhampton Wanderers, a club with strong family connections. Ted's father,

Billy Malpas, was Wolves' centre-half in the FA Cup Finals of 1893 and 1896. Ted joined the Wolverhampton Police Force in 1928, and in 1946 he moved to the Channel Islands where he worked as a physiotherapist and scouted for Nottingham Forest.

MARDON, Paul Jonathon

Defender/Midfield

Career: Boco Juniors. Bristol City trainee June 1985, professional January 1988. Doncaster Rovers loan September 1990. Birmingham City August 1991, fee £115,000. West Bromwich Albion November 1993, fee £400,000. OLDHAM ATHLETIC loan January–April 1999. Plymouth Argyle loan September 2000. Wrexham loan October 2000, retired due to injury May 2001.

■ Paul Mardon scored Athletic's winner at Notts County on his debut and his outstanding aerial ability brought him further headed goals against Lincoln City and Preston North End during the course of his highly successful loan spell. The tall and powerful central-defender won Wales B and full international honours but injuries blighted his final two seasons, during which he did not appear at senior level for West Bromwich Albion.

MARLOR, Alan

Right-back

Born: Oldham, 20 January 1924.
Died: Oldham, January 1996.
Career: OLDHAM ATHLETIC September 1945. Ashton United June 1946.

■ Locally-born full-back Alan Marlor appeared in 30 League North West matches and four FA Cup ties in season 1945–46, usually in tandem with Tommy Shipman. When the retained list was published in June 1946, Marlar, Boothman and Clough were the trio of full-backs offered terms, but Marlor declined, opting to join Ashton United.

MARRISON, Thomas

Inside-forward

Born: Rotherham, 1881.
Died: Sheffield, 21 August 1926.
Career: Walkley School. Sheffield Wednesday February 1902. Rotherham Town September 1906. Nottingham Forest November 1906. OLDHAM ATHLETIC June 1911, fee £200. Bristol City May 1912 to May 1913.

■ Tommy Marrison began with Sheffield Wednesday and scored the only goal of the match on his debut, but his first prolonged spell of regular League action came with Nottingham Forest. He again scored on his first appearance in November 1906 and Forest went on to clinch the Championship of Division Two, Marrison scoring six goals in 25 matches. Departing Forest in the wake of their relegation from Division One in 1910–11, he joined Athletic for their second season in the top flight. Marrison lost his place in mid-term, following a 6–1 defeat at Aston Villa on Boxing Day 1911 and spent a final season in Division Two with Bristol City.

MARSH, John Stanley

Inside-forward

Born: Failsworth, 31 August 1940.
Career: Little Hulton United. OLDHAM ATHLETIC October 1957. Witton Albion June 1960. Ashton United August 1962. Mossley 1962–63. Llandudno. Hyde United. Northwich Victoria August 1965 to May 1966. Stalybridge Celtic 1967–68.

■ Johnny Marsh began in Athletic's reserve team at 17 years of age and was a regular scorer throughout the season in which the team scored 135 goals in 38 matches and clinched the Championship of the Lancashire Combination Second Division. Despite the promising start he had a very lengthy wait for a first-team

opportunity, and played only twice at senior level after spending the best part of three seasons in the reserves.

MARSHALL, Alfred Willis

Wing-half

Born: Darlington, 1888.
Died: Darlington, 30 June 1923.

Career: Darlington St John's. Darlington St Augustine's. Fulham September 1909. OLDHAM ATHLETIC June 1920, fee £2,500.

■ Characterised by a peculiar knock-kneed running style, Alf Marshall was capable of sending an opponent the wrong way when running straight ahead. Recruited by Fulham from Northern League football, the lightly-built wing-half recorded exactly 100 League appearances for the Cottagers, although his career was interrupted by military service during World War One. He was slow to settle with Athletic but improved to the extent that he was appointed club captain in succession to Reg Freeman. In his final season at Boundary Park Marshall suffered a serious breakdown in health. An operation in the summer failed to save him and he died at his home in Darlington at the untimely age of 35.

MARSHALL, Ian Paul

Central-defender/Forward

Born: Liverpool, 20 March 1966.
Career: Everton from school, apprentice July 1982, professional March 1984. OLDHAM ATHLETIC (after two weeks

on loan) March 1988, fee £100,000. Ipswich Town August 1993, fee £750,000. Leicester City August 1996, fee £875,000. San Jose Earthquakes, US, trial June 2000. Stoke City trial July 2000. Queen's Park Rangers trial August 2000. Bolton Wanderers non-contract August, professional October 2000. Blackpool loan November 2001, permanent January 2002, retired due to injury March 2002.

■ Although initially recruited to replace the departed Andy Linighan in central defence, Ian Marshall subsequently proved to be a very potent force in attack. Deceptive pace and a sound technique reaped a rich harvest of goals in seasons 1990–91 and 1991–92, with the eccentric Scouser heading Athletic's goalscoring charts with 17 from only 25/1 League appearances when the Second Division Championship was clinched. In the following campaign, which marked Athletic's return to the top flight, he scored 10 League goals in 41 matches. He was desperately unlucky when injury caused him to miss out on Athletic's appearance in the Littlewoods Cup Final at Wembley in 1990. Later in his career Marshall made substitute appearances for Leicester City in the Worthington Cup Finals of 1999 and 2000, collecting a winners' medal in the latter, a 2–1 victory against Tranmere Rovers. In April 2007 it was reported that Marshall was living in the Canadian province of Newfoundland, where he had set up a football training camp.

MARSHALL, James Hynd

Inside-forward

Born: Glenguie, Peterhead, 9 June 1890.
Died: Cathcart, Glasgow, 8 July 1958.
Career: Vale of Grange. Bo'ness. Partick Thistle November 1911. Bradford City June 1914, fee £1,500. OLDHAM ATHLETIC September 1920, fee £2,250. Bangor FC. Southport January 1924. Rotherham County June 1924. Lincoln City December 1924. Queen of the South June 1925. Stranraer. Coached in Holland 1929–39. Newport County trainer July 1946 to May 1948. Bolton Wanderers scout.

■ Jimmy Marshall's transfer fee of £2,250 constituted a very heavy investment by Athletic's directors, as the team struggled to retain their top-flight status after World War One. They finally succumbed to relegation in 1922–23, and the season proved to be Marshall's last at Boundary Park. The tall and willowy forward had a deceptive body swerve and was a constructive player but disappointed as a marksman, and was transfer listed at £1,000 in April 1923. Nine months later, following a spell in non-League football, he joined Southport on a free transfer. He subsequently spent 10 years coaching in Holland, and was fortunate to escape on the last boat out of Amsterdam following the German occupation. He subsequently worked on munitions at De Havilland's Bolton factory, and in February 1945 was an unsuccessful applicant for the post of Athletic manager.

MARSHALL, William

Full-back

Born: Belfast, 11 July 1936.
Died: Hartlepool, 20 April 2007.
Career: Lomond Star. Distillery. Burnley amateur September, professional October 1953. OLDHAM ATHLETIC August 1962. Hartlepools United August 1964. Horden Colliery Welfare 1966.

■ Despite being capped twice by Northern Ireland B while on Burnley's books, Billy Marshall appeared in only nine League and Cup matches in as many years at Turf Moor. With the Clarets' reserves he won a Central League Championship medal in 1960 and was

twice a Lancashire Senior Cup winner. He was installed as club captain on joining Athletic and held the left-back spot for much of the promotion season that followed. He found less favour under new manager Les McDowall in 1963–64 and departed in the close season.

MARSLAND, Gordon

Half-back

Born: Blackpool, 20 March 1945.
Career: Blackpool apprentice September 1961, professional May 1962. Carlisle United June 1965. Bristol Rovers June 1969. Crewe Alexandra loan September-October 1970. OLDHAM ATHLETIC loan March–April 1971.

■ Athletic's promotion winning side of 1970–71 enjoyed a fairly settled look, although they fielded three goalkeepers, with Short and Gordine finally giving way to Harry Dowd. Wing-half Gordon Marsland's loan to Athletic was intended to provide defensive cover for Brian Turner, who had been sidelined with knee ligament damage. In the event, Marsland's debut and only starting appearance, was as deputy for Ian Wood, whose absence robbed him of an ever-present record for the season.

MARTIN, Barrie

Full-back

Born: Birmingham, 29 September 1935.

Career: Highfield Youth Club. Blackpool December 1953. OLDHAM ATHLETIC August 1964, fee £10,000. Tranmere Rovers June 1965 to 1968, fee £4,000.

■ Full-back Barrie Martin spent almost 11 years with Blackpool as a stylish, sharp-tackling defender. He made his first-team debut in April 1958 and had completed 209 League and Cup matches when Athletic paid the second-highest fee in their history to recruit him. In a season when relegation from Division Three was only narrowly averted, Martin was one of the few successes in a disappointing campaign. He left Boundary Park after one season for a bargain fee of £4,000 and in season 1966–67 helped Tranmere Rovers to promotion from Division Four.

MARTIN, John Charles

Centre-half

Born: Leeds, 25 July 1903.
Died: Padiham, 31 December 1976.
Career: Burnley A Team January 1922. Accrington Stanley amateur July, professional November 1924. Blackpool February 1926, fee £1,300. Southport June 1927. Macclesfield Town July 1929. Southport May 1930. Nelson November 1930. Wigan Borough July 1931. OLDHAM ATHLETIC November 1931 to May 1932, fee £50.

■ A hefty centre-half who gave the ball plenty of boot out of defence, Jack Martin joined Athletic following Wigan Borough's withdrawal from the Northern Section of Division Three, but a knee injury sustained at Valley Parade in February 1932 brought a premature

end to his career. He subsequently became a coal merchant in Padiham and then worked as a tackler in the local weaving industry.

MARTIN, William Thomas John

Centre-forward

Born: Millwall, London, 27 April 1883.
Died: Stepney, London, 11 December 1954.
Career: Millwall St John's. Millwall Athletic October 1901. Hull City August 1904. Clapton Orient May 1906. Stockport County May 1908. OLDHAM ATHLETIC February 1909, in exchange for William Andrews. Millwall Athletic July 1910.

■ A wing-half in his early days, Bill Martin was with Hull City when they gained admission to Division Two of the Football League. Later, with Clapton Orient, the blond-haired half-back was moved up to centre-forward. Despite lacking finesse in ball control he proved a dangerous marksman, finishing as leading goalscorer in both of his seasons at Millfields Road. An exchange deal brought him to Athletic in the late stages of season 1908–09 but he failed to establish himself beyond reserve team football, appearing in only three matches in 1909–10 as Athletic won promotion from the Second Division.

MATTHEWS, William Howard

Goalkeeper

Born: Roadend, Worcestershire, 29 November 1885.
Died: Oldham, 9 February 1963.
Career: Oldbury St John's. Langley St Michael's. Burslem Port Vale amateur May 1906. Burton United July 1907. OLDHAM ATHLETIC April 1908. Port Vale October 1926. Halifax Town August 1928. Chester November 1930. Oswestry Town.

■ Howard Matthews played in 14 seasons of League football for the Latics and made a further 122 appearances during World War One. Although slightly built he was amazingly agile with an uncanny positional sense that made goalkeeping look easy. Consistently brilliant for years, he was unfortunate to

be playing at the same time as the great Sam Hardy, otherwise he would surely have been capped by England. A teetotaller and non-smoker, he was a model professional and a wonderful ambassador for the club. A civil servant by profession, Matthews was a devoutly religious man who for 30 years was secretary of the Tudor Lodge of Freemasons. He was awarded two benefits by Athletic, with guarantees of £250 in November 1913 and £500 in May 1922. His career was an extremely lengthy one, as he was still in League football with Halifax Town in his 45th year.

MAWSON, Craig John

Goalkeeper

Born: Skipton, 16 May 1979.
Career: Burnley trainee July 1995, professional July 1997. Halifax Town February 2001. Morecambe August 2001. OLDHAM ATHLETIC August 2004. Hereford United October 2004. Halifax Town June 2006.

■ Craig Mawson began with Burnley but made his League debut during a brief spell with Halifax Town. Three successful seasons with Morecambe followed and he returned to League football when he joined Athletic. Mawson was beaten six times on his home debut in the second-round Carling Cup tie against Tottenham Hotspur on 21 September 2004 and he was released the following month. In May 2006 he was Hereford United's goalkeeper in the Conference Play-off Final against Halifax Town at the Walkers Stadium, Leicester. Twice coming from behind in a gripping encounter, Hereford won 3–2 after extra-time to regain Football League status.

MAYOR, Jack

Wing-half

Born: Morecambe, October 1916.
Career: Morecambe amateur. OLDHAM ATHLETIC professional May 1936 to May 1938.

■ Two seasons spent exclusively at reserve-team level concluded in May 1938 when Jack Mayor was granted a free transfer. Of the 25 professionals on the books, 17 were offered terms and the only released player for whom a fee was asked was Paddy Robbins. Mayor's single senior outing came in the Northern Section Cup tie against Southport on 29 March 1938, which Athletic lost 3–0.

MELVILLE, Leslie

Half-back

Born: Ormskirk, 29 November 1930.
Career: Liverpool County FA. Everton professional April 1950. Bournemouth & Boscombe Athletic July 1956. OLDHAM ATHLETIC March 1958. Worcester City August 1958 to 1960.

An England Youth international against Scotland in season 1948–49, Les Melville became a professional with Everton at the age of 19, but in six years at Goodison Park failed to reach senior level, his League debut coming with Bournemouth & Boscombe Athletic in 1956–57. After the briefest of stays at Boundary Park he moved into non-League football with Worcester City, and hit the headlines during their FA Cup adventure in 1958–59. After winning four qualifying rounds, Worcester then beat Chelmsford City, Millwall and Liverpool before losing 2–0 to Sheffield United in round four.

MIDDLETON, Harry

Outside-right

Born: Northwich c.1902.
Career: Ashton Heys FC. Witton Albion December 1922. OLDHAM ATHLETIC October 1923. Witton Albion 1927. Northwich Victoria 1929. Hurst FC. North Western Road Car Co, Northwich, reinstated amateur August 1930.

■ Recruited from Cheshire League football, Harry Middleton sampled modest amounts of Second Division football during his four years at Boundary Park without managing to dislodge George Douglas, who dominated the outside-right berth. Dark-haired and dashing, Middleton gave good service in Athletic's reserves, but when released on a free transfer in April 1927 he returned to non-League football with Witton Albion.

MILDENHALL, Stephen James

Goalkeeper

Born: Swindon, 13 May 1978.
Career: Swindon Town Trainee, professional July 1996. Gloucester City loan November 1996. Salisbury City loan August 1997. Notts County July 2001, fee £150,000. OLDHAM ATHLETIC December 2004. Grimsby Town June 2005. Yeovil Town July 2006.

■ A tall and commanding goalkeeper, Steve Mildenhall did not appear on the losing side during his brief spell at Boundary Park. Injury curtailed his season, however, and he was released in the close season. He has subsequently failed narrowly to win promotion with both Grimsby Town and Yeovil Town, both unsuccessful in Play-off encounters. In earlier days, Mildenhall scored a winning goal for Notts County against local rivals Mansfield Town in a first-round League Cup tie at Field Mill. A free-kick, from within his own half of the field, was misjudged by the Stags goalkeeper and proved to be the winner in a thrilling 4–3 victory.

MILLER, Stanley

Outside-left

Born: Prestwich, 1883.
Career: Eccles FC 1902. Sale Holmefield 1905–06. Springfield FC 1906–07. Broughton FC 1907. OLDHAM ATHLETIC amateur May 1909 to May 1913. Stalybridge Celtic September 1914 to May 1915. Middlesex Footballer's Battalion.

■ A slim and speedy amateur outside-left, Stanley Miller displayed such fine form in Athletic's reserves that he deposed Scottish international Joe Donnachie in the first team and made 27 appearances in the 1909–10 promotion winning side. In the close season he was rewarded with a place in the FA amateur party that toured Denmark. He found less success in Division One, where his methods were said to lack the necessary variety to trouble the best defenders. During his Athletic days Miller combined football with his work as a yarn salesman with a Preston agency.

MILLIGAN, George Harry

Half-back

Born: Failsworth, 31 August 1917.
Died: Rhyl, 26 November 1983.
Career: Manchester North End. OLDHAM ATHLETIC amateur March, professional May 1935. Everton May 1938, fee £3,150. Wartime guest with Droylsden, OLDHAM ATHLETIC, Crystal Palace, Chelsea, Reading and York City. Everton scout. Rhyl Athletic manager, and later director.

■ George Milligan made the transition from Latics supporter to professional with his favourite club at 17 years of age. Rarely absent in the two seasons prior to World War Two, his vision and control from wing-half made him a magnet for bigger clubs and Everton paid a very substantial fee for him in May 1938. He was with Everton when war broke out and joined the Grenadier Guards Armoured Division in February 1941, serving with Bryan Johnston, the cricket commentator. He made guest appearances for a number of clubs during wartime, but did not return to Everton after demobilisation. After moving to live in Rhuddlan, North Wales, he built up a successful holiday caravan site with his brother.

MILLIGAN, Michael Joseph John

Midfield

Born: Moss Side, Manchester, 20 February 1967.
Career: Manchester County Schoolboys. Manchester City associate schoolboy. Flixton

FC. OLDHAM ATHLETIC apprentice December 1984, professional March 1985. Everton August 1990, fee £1 million. OLDHAM ATHLETIC July 1991, fee £600,000. Norwich City June 1994, fee £850,000. Blackpool July 2000 to March 2002.

■ Mike Milligan appeared in eight seasons of football for the Latics as a gritty ball-winner and provider from midfield. Athletic's captain in the Littlewoods Cup Final of 1990, he was capped at four levels by the Republic of Ireland and was unfortunate not to add to his single full cap as he was surprisingly omitted from Jack Charlton's squad for the US World Cup Finals in 1994. He left Boundary Park to join Everton for a club record £1 million, but was back after one season having been in and out of the team following a knee injury that sidelined him for two months. He returned to rejoin the newly-promoted Latics in another record deal and gave a further three years of 100 per cent endeavour before being transferred to Norwich City following Athletic's relegation from the Premier League in 1994.

MILLWARD, Alan Ernest

Goalkeeper

Born: Oldham, 18 October 1910.
Died: Southport, 29 June 1998.
Career: An amateur throughout, he assisted Northern Nomads and Middlesex Wanderers. OLDHAM ATHLETIC September 1931 and September 1936.

■ Locally-born amateur goalkeeper Alan Millward played only once for Athletic and was beaten five times at Plymouth Argyle on Easter Monday 1932. A solicitor

by profession, he served in RAF Coastal command during World War Two as a Sunderland flying boat navigator, reaching the rank of Flight Lieutenant before his demobilisation in April 1946.

MILNE, John Buchan

Full-back

Born: Rosehearty, Aberdeen 27 April 1911. Died: Cheadle, Cheshire 6 September 1994.
Career: Fraserburgh. Plymouth Argyle May 1933. Southend United June 1937, fee £250. Barrow August 1946. OLDHAM ATHLETIC August 1947 to July 1948.

■ Recruited by the Latics within a month of his 37th birthday, John Milne lost his place after appearing in the two opening fixtures of 1947–48. Thereafter mainly appearing at reserve team level, the solid and workmanlike full-back nevertheless performed well in late season when recalled following Ben Bunting's absence due to a cartilage injury.

MISKELLY, David Thomas

Goalkeeper

Born: Newtonards, Northern Ireland, 3 September 1979.
Career: Dungoyne Boys' Club. Glentoran. OLDHAM ATHLETIC trainee September 1996, professional July 1997. Portadown June 2003. Macclesfield Town January 2004. Portadown.

■ Northern Ireland Youth and Under-21 international David Miskelly came close to winning a full cap but was still recovering from a shoulder injury and therefore unable to respond to a call-up

into the senior squad in February 2002. Despite his lengthy stay at Boundary Park Miskelly was short of first-team opportunities, being mainly in the shadow of the ever-consistent Gary Kelly. After returning to Ireland following his release in the summer of 2003 Miskelly joined Macclesfield Town in January 2004, but did not appear at senior level.

MITCHELL, John

Inside-forward

Career: Glengowan Rangers. Airdrieonians 1902. Glentoran 1907. OLDHAM ATHLETIC May 1909. Glentoran June 1910.

■ Lightly-built and prematurely balding inside-right John Mitchell was one of three new forwards fielded on the opening day of season 1909–10, and he scored one of Athletic's goals in the 2–2 draw at Birmingham. Without a win in the opening five matches, Mitchell was deposed and spent the remainder of the season at reserve level. Despite the poor start, Athletic went on to win promotion to the top flight with an attack dominated by Fay (26 goals), Montgomery (16) and Toward (13).

MITCHELL, Peter

Full-back

Born: Oldham, 5 August 1946.
Career: St Patrick's FC. Oldham Community Centre FC. OLDHAM ATHLETIC amateur November 1965, professional July 1966 to January 1967.

■ Peter Mitchell began as a wing half-back in youth soccer, converting to full-back during his stay at Boundary Park. His League debut was made – as an amateur – as a second-half substitute for Alan Lawson at Southend United in March 1966. The welcome 2–1 victory also marked the debut of Athletic's player-manager Jimmy McIlroy. Peter Mitchell's father, Billy, was a forward with Oldham Rugby League Club.

MOFFAT, Hugh

Half-back

Born: Congleton, January 1885.
Died: Macclesfield, 14 November 1952.
Career: Congleton Town. Burnley amateur January 1904, professional 1905.
OLDHAM ATHLETIC December 1910, fee £490. Chesterfield Municipal 1919. Congleton Town 1920.

■ Hugh Moffat made his League debut in the Second Division with Burnley in April 1904. The left-sided defender appeared in eight seasons of League football at Turf Moor, recording 214 matches and 13 goals. He joined Athletic at the mid-point of their first season in Division One, and remained a regular throughout his five seasons at Boundary Park. In the season that he won his England cap, the versatile Moffat appeared for Athletic in both full-back berths, at centre-forward, and in his usual right-half position. Hugh's son, Stanley, assisted several League clubs in the inter-war period, including Birmingham and Millwall.

MOLANGO, Maheta

Forward

Born: St Imier, Switzerland, 24 July 1982.
Career: Atletico Madrid. SV Wacker Burghaused, Austria. Brighton & Hove Albion August 2004. Lincoln City loan August 2005 to January 2006. UB Conquense, Spain, loan. Wrexham loan November 2006. OLDHAM ATHLETIC loan August 2006.

■ As the team made a faltering start to the 2006–07 campaign, Maheta Molango was Athletic's first scorer, breaking the team's duck in their third fixture. The 1–0 victory against Swansea City gave manager John Sheridan his first win in full-time management courtesy of Molango's close-range header and the goalkeeping heroics of rookie Chris Howarth. After six appearances, three as substitute, Molango returned to the Withdean Stadium at the end of his largely unimpressive one-month loan spell.

MOLYNEUX, William Stanley

Goalkeeper

Born: Ormskirk, 10 January 1944.
Career: English Electric FC. Earle FC. Liverpool amateur 1961, professional November 1963. OLDHAM ATHLETIC June 1967. Buxton loan March 1969. Wigan Athletic August 1969.

■ A small but spring-heeled goalkeeper,

Bill Molyneux signed amateur forms with Liverpool at 17 years of age. An apprentice toolmaker at English Electric, he spent a lengthy period in reserve at Anfield, appearing only once in the First Division. He first played for Athletic against Rio Tinto, Rhodesia, in the 1967 pre-season tour, but then had 16 months to wait before making his League debut following the departure of David Best to Ipswich Town. He was then replaced by loan signing Barry Gordine after a six-match run that brought only one win.

MONTGOMERY, William

Inside-forward

Born: Gourock, Renfrewshire, 1885.
Died: Oakland, California, US, 21 November 1953.
Career: Kilwinning Rangers. Rutherglen Glencairn. Bradford City November 1905. Sunderland July 1907. OLDHAM ATHLETIC October 1909, fee £350. Rangers June 1912, fee £200. Dundee February 1913.

■ A short but solidly built inside-forward, Montgomery arrived at Boundary Park via Sunderland, where in two seasons he had been restricted to just 10 League outings. He very quickly made his mark with Athletic, however, scoring 16 goals in 28 matches in the Division Two runners-up team of 1909–10. Although he was the scorer of Athletic's first ever goal in Division One, at Aston Villa on 3 September 1910, by mid-season he had lost his place to George Woodger, whose outstanding form

during the campaign earned him an England cap.

MOONEY, Simon G.

Midfield

Born: Rochdale, 23 September 1970.
Career: OLDHAM ATHLETIC trainee July 1987, professional August 1989 to May 1990.

■ Fair-haired central-defender Simon Mooney's single senior appearance came when he was introduced as a substitute after 59 minutes of the Simod Cup tie at Middlesbrough on 14 December 1988. He replaced Paul Warhurst in a match that ended with Athletic down to nine men when Ian Marshall and Roger Palmer were both injured late in the game. Middlesbrough won by a single penalty scored by Dean Glover.

MOORE, Kevin Thomas

Central-defender

Born: Grimsby, 29 April 1958.
Career: Humberside schoolboys. Grimsby Town June 1976. OLDHAM ATHLETIC February 1987, fee £100,000. Southampton August 1987, fee £125,000. Bristol Rovers loan January 1992 and again October 1992. Fulham July 1994, retired June 1996.

■ Former England Schoolboy international Kevin Moore was Joe Royle's most expensive signing in February 1987, but his stay was brief. When Athletic failed to win promotion after losing in the Play-off tournament,

Kevin Moore departed to Southampton, managed at that time by his former Grimsby Town colleague and defensive partner, Chris Nicholl. Kevin Moore won a Division Three Championship with Grimsby Town in 1980. He was one of five members of the Moore family to assist the Mariners – Norman (debut 1946) and brother Roy (1948). Roy's three sons continued the link – Kevin (1976), Dave (1978) and Andy (1984).

MOORE, Neil

Central-defender

Born: Liverpool, 21 September 1972.
Career: Everton associate schoolboy February 1988, trainee June 1989, professional June 1991. Blackpool loan September 1994. OLDHAM ATHLETIC loan February 1995. Carlisle United loan August 1995. Rotherham United loan March 1996. Norwich City January 1997. Burnley August 1997. Macclesfield Town non-contract December 1999. Telford United March 2000.

■ Neil Moore was briefly associated with Athletic on loan at a time when both Richard Jobson and Craig Fleming were long-term casualties, and Richard Graham was struggling to shake off a knee injury. Latics manager Graeme Sharp had attempted to sign Moore earlier, but at the conclusion of his loan period no firm bid was made. Prior to moving into non-League football with Telford United, Moore assisted eight League clubs, his best spell at Burnley covering 53/4 matches and four goals.

MORGAN, Stephen James

Forward

Born: Wrexham, 28 December 1970.

Career: OLDHAM ATHLETIC trainee July 1987. Wrexham loan March 1990. Rochdale March 1991, released 1992. Two-week trial with a club in Belgium. Stalybridge Celtic August 1992. Colwyn Bay loan November 1992, permanent 1993.

■ Wales Schoolboy and Youth international Steve Morgan starred in Athletic's B and reserve teams, winning a Lancashire League Division Two Championship in season 1987–88. Despite being among the youngest players to make a League debut the Welshman ultimately failed to live up to expectations, scoring his first League goal in Wrexham's colours during a loan spell at the Racecourse.

MORRISEY, John Joseph

Winger/Midfield

Born: Liverpool, 18 April 1940.
Career: Liverpool from school, signing professional May 1957. Everton September 1962, fee £12,000. OLDHAM ATHLETIC May 1972 to February 1973.

■ Johnny Morrisey began with Liverpool but made his name during 10 seasons with Everton, scoring 50 goals in 314 appearances and winning two League Championships. Sadly, despite the odd flash of skill, he failed to do himself justice during a brief spell at Boundary Park. Son Johnny Morrisey junior was a flying wingman with Tranmere Rovers who made 586 appearances and scored 63 goals in all competitions between 1985–99.

MORROW, John James

Winger

Born: Belfast, 20 November 1971.
Career: Linfield. Rangers July 1988.

Grimsby Town and Preston North End trials July 1996. OLDHAM ATHLETIC trial July, professional August 1996 to April 1997. Greenock Morton August 1997.

■ Wingman John Morrow joined Athletic after eight years at Ibrox and immediately had ankle trouble in the pre-season tour of Ireland. Things did not improve for the unfortunate Irishman who appeared short of match fitness in two League outings and then suffered torn lateral knee ligaments in a training accident.

MOSS, Frank

Goalkeeper

Born: Leyland, 5 November 1909.
Died: Heswall, 7 February 1970.
Career: Leyland Motors. Preston North End amateur October 1927, professional February 1928. OLDHAM ATHLETIC amateur 8 May, professional 20 May 1929. Arsenal November 1931, fee £2,225. Heart of Midlothian manager March 1937 to August 1940.

■ Initially in reserve to Jack Hacking at Boundary Park, Frank Moss eventually replaced the England international in mid-season 1930–31. Arsenal's manager Herbert Chapman moved in with a substantial bid for his services, and in the month of his transfer Moss took over from Charlie Preedy in Arsenal's goal. At the end of his first season he played in the FA Cup Final against Newcastle United. Considered one of the best goalkeepers

of the 1930s, it was success all the way with three League Championships, two Football League XI appearances and four England caps. Misfortune occurred in the last of his Championship-winning seasons when Moss sustained a severe dislocated shoulder injury in March 1935 at Everton. Despite a lengthy battle to regain full fitness he was unable to continue as a goalkeeper, although Arsenal attempted to convert him to an outfield role in their reserve team before he announced his retirement.

MOULDEN, Paul Anthony Joseph

Forward

Born: Farnworth, 6 September 1967.
Career: Bolton Borough Schoolboys. Bolton Lads' Club. Trials with Manchester United, Everton, Bolton Wanderers and Leeds United. Manchester City apprentice June 1984, professional September 1984. AFC Bournemouth August 1989, fee £160,000. OLDHAM ATHLETIC March 1990, for a then record fee of £225,000. Molde, Norway, loan 1992. Brighton & Hove Albion loan August–October 1992. Birmingham City March 1993, fee £150,000. Huddersfield Town March–May 1995. Stockport County trial. Rochdale August 1995. Accrington Stanley July–October 1996. Leigh RMI November 1996. Bacup Borough January 1998. Castleton Gabriels October 1999.

■ Athletic's most expensive signing since they paid £200,000 for Kenny Clements,

England Schools and Youth international Paul Moulden was destined to make more substitute appearances than starts in a disappointing spell at Boundary Park. A prodigious goalscorer as a junior, his feat of scoring 289 goals for Bolton Lads' Club in 40 matches in 1981–82, won him an entry in the *Guinness Book of Records*. He began with Manchester City and scored 17 League and Cup goals in their promotion-winning side of 1988–89. He had scored 13 League goals in 32 matches for Bournemouth in the season that Athletic signed him, but he was initially restricted due to being Cup tied, thus missing out as Athletic reached the Littlewoods Cup Final and the FA Cup semi-final. In the promotion season that followed he scored three goals in 11/13 appearances, but an ankle operation restricted his appearances to just two from the bench in 1991–92 and he was transfer listed at the end of the season.

MUIR, Ian Baker

Centre-half

Born: Motherwell, 16 June 1929.
Career: Thorniewood United. Motherwell 1950. Bristol Rovers June 1953. OLDHAM ATHLETIC June 1957, fee £200. Rhyl July 1958. Dolgellau August 1960. Colwyn Bay August 1962.

■ A tall, willowy centre-half, Ian Muir followed in his father's footsteps when he joined Bristol Rovers in June 1953. His father, John Muir had also assisted

Rovers and Luton Town in the inter-war period. Ian had made only 26 League appearances in four seasons at Eastville, but he successfully held off the challenge of Eddie Murphy for the first-team centre-half berth during his single season at Boundary Park.

MULVANEY, Richard

Defender

Born: Sunderland, 5 August 1942.
Career: Silksworth Colliery. Billingham Synthonia. Merton Colliery. Blackburn Rovers February 1964. OLDHAM ATHLETIC August 1971. Rochdale October 1974 to October 1976. Gateshead 1977. Chester-le-Street player-coach.

■ A solid, uncompromising centre-half, Dick Mulvaney appeared in 44 consecutive League matches in his first season at Boundary Park but thereafter was restricted by injuries, managing 44 starts in the following two seasons. During a six-year spell with Blackburn Rovers he appeared in 145/6 League matches and won two Central League Championship medals. His three years at Boundary Park saw the club progress rapidly towards promotion in season 1973–74, during which campaign Mulvaney appeared in just over half of the League matches. Brother Jimmy was an inside-forward with Hartlepools United, Barrow and Stockport County in the 1960s and early 1970s.

MUNDY, Harold James 'Jimmy'

Midfield/Forward

Born: Wythenshawe, 2 September 1948.
Career: Ashland Rovers. Manchester City amateur August 1966, professional

January 1968. OLDHAM ATHLETIC loan September-December 1970. Bangor City 1971. Stafford Rangers March–November 1972.

■ Jimmy Mundy left his job as an insurance agent to sign professional forms with Manchester City. An extremely versatile player, Mundy had played at the back, in midfield, and in the forward line during his stay with Manchester City. He joined Athletic on a three month loan spell, but requested his release after two months due to a lack of first-team opportunities.

MUNRO, James Ferguson

Outside-right

Born: Elgin, 25 March 1926.
Died: Elgin, 22 June 1997.
Career: West End FC, Elgin. Wartime guest with Aberdeen. Dunfermline Athletic May 1946. Waterford, Ireland, July 1947. Manchester City November 1947. OLDHAM ATHLETIC March 1950, fee approx. £6,000. Lincoln City February 1953, in exchange for Billy McGlen. Bury January 1958, fee £2,000, released June 1959. Weymouth FC. Poole Town 1960–61. Ely City player-coach 1961–62.

■ Scotsman Jimmy Munro's game featured tricky dribbling and a go-ahead, enthusiastic style. He quickly became a great crowd favourite at Boundary Park, where he was mainly employed as a dashing right-winger, with a liking to cut inside for a shot on goal. He had played in 33 matches in the 1952–53 Third Division North Championship season, and 128 overall, when he was involved in the exchange deal that brought Billy McGlen to Boundary Park. Munro gave good value to each of his four League clubs, totalling 346 appearances and 56 goals.

MURPHY, Edward Cullinane

Centre-half

Born: Glasgow, 1 June 1934.
Career: Clyde. OLDHAM ATHLETIC June 1956. Bangor City 1959. A broken leg ended his playing career in 1965. Bacup Borough manager August 1967.

■ Eddie Murphy left Clyde following their relegation from Division A of the Scottish League. Although he gained

little senior experience during his spell at Shawfield Park, the tall and lithe centre-half settled well at Boundary Park, playing in 41 League and Cup matches in his first season. Murphy faced increasing competition from Ian Muir in 1957–58 and Wally Taylor in his final season. Outside of football he was employed as a painter and decorator.

MURPHY, John

Centre-forward

Born: Blantyre, Ayrshire, 29 August 1912.
Career: Auchinleck Talbot. OLDHAM ATHLETIC October 1934. Workington August 1935. Ards, Ireland, August 1936.

■ Despite an excellent debut when he scored twice against Norwich City in a 4–2 victory at Boundary Park in December 1934, John Murphy scored only once in the next six matches, all of which ended in defeat. At the end of the season, and with the club facing the prospect of Third Division North football for the first time, 11 players, including John Murphy, were granted free transfers.

MURPHY, William

Outside-left

Born: St Helens, 23 May 1894.
Died: St Helens, 1975.
Career: Peasley Cross Juniors. Alexandra Victoria. Wartime guest with Liverpool. Manchester City amateur February 1918, professional May 1919. Southampton August 1926, fee £350. OLDHAM

ATHLETIC June 1929, in exchange for Bert Watson. Tranmere Rovers July 1930. Ellesmere Port Town September 1932. U.B.G., St Helens September 1934.

■ Brought to Boundary Park from Southampton in a deal that saw long-serving wingman Bert Watson move in the opposite direction, 'Spud' Murphy scored on his mid-season debut at Bristol City, but failed to dislodge Bill Hasson and was restricted to just two senior appearances. Earlier in his career Murphy assisted Manchester City to the runners-up position for the League Championship in season 1920–21, scoring eight goals in 40 matches.

MURRAY, Kenneth

Inside-forward

Born: Darlington, 2 April 1928.
Died: Newcastle upon Tyne, 8 January 1993.
Career: Bishop Auckland. Darlington July 1950. Mansfield Town July 1953. OLDHAM ATHLETIC March 1957, fee £1,500. Wrexham February 1958. Yeovil & Petters United July 1959. Gateshead August 1959 to May 1960.

■ Inside-forward Ken Murray was a proven goalscorer who totalled 110 League goals in 293 matches for his five senior clubs. He was part of a double swoop into the transfer market by Athletic's manager Ted Goodier when signed along with Tommy Wright, whose son, Tommy, also played for Latics and was appointed assistant manager in 2006. In a little under a year at Boundary Park

his 'shoot on sight' policy made him a dangerous forward when anywhere near to goal. Athletic's decision to transfer him in the late stages of 1957–58 proved an unwise one, as their ultimate placing of 15th in Division Three North condemned them to become founder members of Division Four.

MURRAY, Paul

Midfield

Born: Carlisle, 31 August 1976.
Career: Carlisle United trainee July 1993, professional June 1994. Queen's Park Rangers March 1996, fee £300,000. Southampton August 2001. OLDHAM ATHLETIC December 2001. Beira Mar, Portugal, May 2004. Carlisle United May 2006. Gretna June 2007 to May 2008.

■ In his final season at Boundary Park club captain Paul Murray led a successful battle against relegation, leading from the front by scoring nine goals in 41 League matches. Sadly, with his contract up at the close of the season, Athletic lost the battle to keep their inspirational midfielder. In accepting a two-year contract with Beira Mar of Portugal he linked for a fourth time with coach Mick Wadsworth, after working with him at Carlisle United, Southampton and the Latics. During his spell with Queen's Park Rangers Murray won England caps at B and Under-21 levels.

NAYLOR, Harold Francis

Centre-forward

Born: Leeds, 6 June 1928.
Died: North Yorkshire, April 2005.
Career: Mossley. OLDHAM ATHLETIC amateur 1950–51. Stalybridge Celtic 1951–52.

■ The younger brother of Athletic's long-serving defender Bill Naylor, Harold was a last-minute selection to lead the Latics' attack at Bradford City in April 1951. In addition to his solitary League outing Naylor played in seven reserve team matches and scored 8 goals. He also played in the Festival of Britain friendly against Bohemians on 12 May 1950.

NAYLOR, James

Wing-half

Born: High Crompton, 2 March 1901.
Died: Shaw, 31 August 1983.
Career: Shaw Parish Church FC. Shawside FC. OLDHAM ATHLETIC amateur May 1920, professional October 1922. Huddersfield Town December 1928, fee £3,750. Newcastle United July 1930, fee £4,000. Manchester City October 1932. OLDHAM ATHLETIC loan February–May 1933. Macclesfield Town February 1934. Nelson August 1935. Wigan Athletic August 1937 to 1938.

■ England trialist Jimmy Naylor first caught the attention of Athletic officials when playing for Shawside against Corpus Christi in a junior Cup Final staged at Boundary Park. The sequel was his signature on amateur forms, and the

start of an association with the Latics covering seven seasons of League football. His first season at senior level was not an auspicious one for the club, as they were relegated into the Second Division. Playing in 19 out of a possible 26 matches in his debut season, he then missed just six matches in the following five seasons. Naylor was a brilliant attacking half-back, whose deft footwork and precision passing was capable of prising open the tightest of defences. Huddersfield Town paid a substantial fee to take him to Leeds Road, and he was immediately at home in the top flight. Polished displays quickly attracted the attention of England selectors, leading to an appearance for 'The Rest' against England in an international trial match at Hillsborough in February 1929. A Wembley appearance in the 1930 FA Cup Final was the undoubted highlight of Naylor's career, despite the fact that Arsenal, for the first time in their history, won the trophy by 2–0. A final call from his first love, the Latics, saw him return to Boundary Park, on loan from Manchester City until the end of the 1932–33 season, and he had the satisfaction of helping his old club to avoid relegation. Spells in non-League soccer followed before retirement at the end of the 1937–38 season.

NAYLOR, Thomas William 'Bill'

Defender

Born: Leeds, 7 December 1924.
Career: Outwood Stormcocks. Huddersfield Town February 1943. OLDHAM ATHLETIC March 1948 to June 1959, fee £600.

■ At either full-back or centre-half Bill Naylor's commanding height gave him an advantage when the ball was in the air. On the ground, he tackled strongly with 'safety first' his prime concern. His long spell of service was rewarded with two benefits before he retired in June 1959. Brother Harold made one appearance for the Latics in 1950–51. Bill's son, Stuart, won England B honours as a goalkeeper and gained wide League experience, most notably with West Bromwich Albion between 1986–96.

NDIWA-LORD, Kangana

Defender

Born: Maquela do Zombo, Angola, 28 February 1984.
Career: Djurgaarden, Sweden. Bolton Wanderers July 2003. OLDHAM ATHLETIC loan August 2003. Rochdale loan February 2004. Stalybridge Celtic June 2004.

■ Towering teenage central-defender Ndiwa arrived at Boundary Park via an extremely circuitous route. Raised in Congo, he won Sweden Youth international honours in his adopted country and had been with Bolton Wanderers for only a matter of weeks when he was loaned to Latics to gain first-team experience. The DR Congo

international made three starts and one substitute appearance in a patched-up Athletic side in the throes of serious financial difficulties which led to the club being put into administration.

NEALE, Peter

Half-back/Forward

Born: Chesterfield, 9 April 1934.
Career: Mansfield Town amateur. Markham Sports Club. OLDHAM ATHLETIC January 1953. Scunthorpe United October 1958, fee £2,500. Chesterfield October 1966, fee £2,000. Scarborough July 1968. Alfreton Town January 1969.

■ Recruited by Athletic from a Chesterfield junior side, blond-haired Peter Neale worked at Bardsley Colliery during his early days at Boundary Park. His career was interrupted by call-up for National Service, and he spent two years in Germany with the RAF. Released from the Forces in 1955, he signed full-time professional forms and missed only one match during his debut season. At either inside-forward or wing-half his all-action style and consistently spirited performances served Athletic well, his best season, 1957–58, ending with figures of 16 League goals in 38 matches. Mainly at centre-half in later years, Neale gave excellent service to both Scunthorpe

United and Chesterfield, altogether appearing in more than 400 League appearances in a career spanning three League clubs.

NEWTON, Leonard Francis 'Frank'

Centre-forward

Born: Denaby, 1882.
Died: Warsop, 27 February 1959.

Career: Grassmoor Red Rose. Chesterfield Town May 1902. Leyton FC May 1905. Bradford City May 1906. OLDHAM ATHLETIC September 1907, fee £25. Bradford Park Avenue November 1909. Burnley January 1911 to May 1912.

■ 'Certain mannerisms on the field of play' (according to one contemporary scribe) resulted in Frank Newton being nicknamed 'Mary Ann'. At some 100 years' remove it is difficult to imagine why, as he was also described as a well-built centre-forward, well suited to heavy conditions. He was also a potent attacking force – in Athletic's first season as a Football League club he scored 30 goals in 39 League and Cup matches. Newton dominated Athletic's attack for two seasons, scoring 47 goals in just 86 appearances.

NOLAN, Michael William

Full-back

Born: Dublin, 8 July 1950.
Career: Larksview FC, Dublin. OLDHAM ATHLETIC apprentice July

1966, *professional August 1967 to June 1968.*

■ Despite his promise as a schoolboy international, which saw him offered trials by Blackburn Rovers and Wolverhampton Wanderers, Nolan's form and confidence dipped alarmingly during his final season at Boundary Park. Sadly he proved to be yet another Irish import who failed to fulfil the promise shown at junior levels. Mike's uncle, Ronnie Nolan, played for Shamrock Rovers for 15 years.

NORD, John Gaiger

Outside-left

Born: Sunderland, 16 May 1895.
Died: Sunderland, 16 February 1978.
Career: Shotton Colliery Welfare. OLDHAM ATHLETIC amateur July, professional August 1919, released May 1922.

■ As understudy to two of Athletic's finest outside-lefts, George Wall and Bert Watson, John Nord was seriously short of first-team action. Recommended to Athletic by their full-back, Billy Cook, who had played alongside the diminutive outside-left in army football during World War One, Nord's opportunities were further restricted by a serious knee injury sustained in his first season.

NUTTALL, Martin

Forward

Born: Oldham, 12 September 1961.
Career: Grange School. OLDHAM ATHLETIC apprentice August 1978, professional September 1979. Halifax Town August 1982 to June 1984.

■ Martin Nuttall starred in schools football and scored 40 goals for Athletic's youth and reserve teams in season 1979–80. His introduction to the League side came in 1980–81, a term in which Athletic scored only 39 goals in 42 Division Two matches, and it was probably unrealistic to expect the youthful striker to succeed where more experienced forwards had failed to deliver. A willing worker with a neat first touch, his introduction nevertheless sparked a run of three victories, and his first League goal, scored after 86 minutes, ensured both points at Cardiff City in

Athletic's 2–0 victory. In what proved to be manager Jimmy Frizzell's last season in charge, Nuttall lacked senior opportunities and departed to Halifax Town within a month of his 21st birthday. In two seasons of Division Four football at the Shay he scored 10 League goals in 39/11 appearances. Subsequently employed as a financial advisor, Nuttall was still enjoying football in the Rochdale Alliance League well beyond his 40th birthday.

O'CALLAGHAN, Brendan Richard

Forward/Central-defender

Born: Bradford, 23 July 1955.
Career: Doncaster Rovers professional July 1973. Stoke City March 1978, fee £40,000. OLDHAM ATHLETIC February 1985, fee £35,000, retired due to injury January 1986.

■ Brendan O'Callaghan won six full caps for the Republic of Ireland and was equally at home in either attacking or central defensive roles. He was pitched straight into Athletic's relegation battle and proved a valuable squad member, providing height and strength in both attack and defence. Injured after playing in nine matches, he was to appear only once more before a persistent groin injury ended a fine career that spanned 450 League matches and 110 goals.

O'DONNELL, James

Inside-forward

Born: Methil, Fifeshire, 18 April 1934.
Career: Wellesley Juniors. Blackburn Rovers professional May 1952. OLDHAM ATHLETIC October 1953. Stalybridge Celtic October 1956. Leeds United January 1957, fee £1,400. Peterborough United 1957. Northwich Victoria. Accrington Stanley trial September-October 1960. Prescot Cables July 1962. Caernarvon Town player-manager August 1962.

■ Despite a famous footballing pedigree, ginger-haired Jimmy O'Donnell failed to make the grade in senior football. A nephew of the famous O'Donnell brothers of Celtic and Preston North End fame, Jimmy joined Athletic on a free transfer from Blackburn Rovers while serving in the RAF. He made little impact in his infrequent appearances and was similarly unsuccessful when given a second opportunity by Leeds United, failing to reach senior level at Elland Road.

O'DONNELL, Richard Mark

Goalkeeper

Born: Sheffield, 12 September 1988.
Career: Wisewood Juniors. Sheffield Schoolboys. Sheffield United Academy. Sheffield Wednesday July 2005. York City loan March–May 2007. Rotherham United loan January–April 2008. OLDHAM ATHLETIC loan March–May 2008.

■ Initially signed on a seven-day emergency loan from Sheffield Wednesday to cover for the injured Mark Crossley, Richard O'Donnell's debut – and his first Football League appearance – saw him on the receiving end of a first-half bombardment at Luton Town. Athletic lost 3–0 with all of Luton's goals coming in the space of 15 first-half minutes. With his loan extended, O'Donnell featured in successive 1–1 draws against Millwall and Doncaster Rovers and appeared from the bench for the final 30 minutes of the season's last match, the stunning 4–1 victory at Crewe Alexandra.

OGDEN, Christopher John

Goalkeeper

Born: Oldham, 3 February 1953.
Career: Lancashire Schoolboys. OLDHAM

ATHLETIC associate schoolboy 1967, amateur August 1969, professional July 1971. Swindon Town August 1978. Rotherham United November 1979. Bath City. Cheltenham Town. Chamber FC reinstated amateur 1988–89.

■ The son of Fred Ogden, Chris continued the family tradition as Athletic's goalkeeper. Of similar height to his father but of heavier build, Chris endured a shaky start, conceding 16 goals in his first six League matches when deputising for the injured Harry Dowd in 1971–72. Some two years later he won the first-team jersey during the Division Three Championship season of 1973–74, and did so well that a club record sequence of 10 consecutive League victories ensued.

OGDEN, Frederick

Goalkeeper

Born: Oldham, 3 April 1925.
Died: Oldham, 2 February 2008.
Career: Edge Lane Boys' Club. OLDHAM ATHLETIC amateur during season 1941–42, professional December 1947. Chesterfield June 1955. OLDHAM ATHLETIC March 1956. Nelson July 1956. Buckley & Taylor, Oldham, reinstated amateur October 1957. OLDHAM ATHLETIC A Team trainer August 1959, reserve team trainer, and in February 1967 given control of the club's juniors.

■ A popular figure beneath the crossbar, Fred Ogden was considered rather lightweight for his position but his cat-like agility, anticipation and a safe pair of hands effectively compensated for any lack of physical advantage. First choice goalkeeper until a fractured collar bone led to his replacement by George Burnett, Fred was unlucky to miss out in the 1952–53 Championship campaign, being restricted to just four appearances. Fred's son Chris followed the family tradition as Latics' last line of defence.

O'HALLORAN, Matthew Vincent

Midfield

Born: Nottingham, 18 November 1982.
Career: Derby County trainee, professional July 2002. OLDHAM ATHLETIC August 2003. Chesterfield December 2003. Boston

United August 2004. King's Lynn February 2005. Boston United September 2007.

■ Matt O'Halloran joined Athletic during the club's financial crisis and appeared in a variety of positions in the course of his 17 appearances, 14 coming from the bench. His single goal was a timely one – a last-minute winner against Rushden & Diamonds at Boundary Park on 30 August 2003. In December 2006 he was a member of the King's Lynn side that hosted Athletic in the FA Cup second-round tie. The Linnetts had won five earlier matches but their dream ended in front of Sky cameras, Athletic winning 2–0.

OLNEY, Ian Douglas

Forward

Born: Luton, 17 December 1969.
Career: Ebley FC. Aston Villa apprentice, professional July 1988. OLDHAM ATHLETIC May 1992, fee £700,000. Kidderminster Harriers August 1996. Halesowen Town January–May 2000.

■ Record signing Ian Olney joined Athletic for their debut in the newly-formed FA Premier League, and the tall England Under-21 international striker led the scoring charts with 12 League goals and one in the FA Cup. It was the season best remembered for Athletic's 'great escape' from relegation, thanks to unlikely but timely victories in the final three matches against Aston Villa, Liverpool and Southampton. In November of the following season Olney suffered a medial ligament injury at West Ham and was sidelined for 18 months. In February 1996 he reluctantly decided to retire, and worked as a partner in a fitted kitchen company in the Midlands.

O'LOUGHLIN, William James

Winger

Born: Bolton, 18 January 1937.
Career: Bury amateur. Rossendale United. OLDHAM ATHLETIC February 1960. Wigan Athletic August 1961. Prescot Cables August 1963. Stalybridge Celtic August 1964.

■ Billy O'Loughlin began with Athletic as a part-time professional while working as a butcher in Bolton. Recruited from Lancashire Combination football, he was drafted straight into League action at outside-right, and he added some much-needed dash and enthusiasm to proceedings. Under new manager Jack Rowley in season 1960–61, O'Loughlin signed full-time forms and appeared on both wings in the opening months before losing his place to Bob Rackley.

ORLYGSSON, Thorvaldur 'Toddy'

Midfield

Born: Odense, Denmark, 2 August 1966.

Career: K.A. Akureyri, Iceland. Nottingham Forest December 1989, fee £175,000. Stoke City August 1993. OLDHAM ATHLETIC December 1995, fee £180,000. Heart of Midlothian trial May 1997. Retired June 1999 and returned to Iceland as coach to K.A. Akureyri.

■ Although born in Denmark, Toddy Orlygsson was qualified to play for Iceland and won 41 caps for his adopted country. A tribunal was needed to resolve his transfer fee to Boundary Park, his signing was intended to cover the enforced lay-off of skipper Nick Henry due to a back injury. Ironically, Orlygsson himself was plagued by injuries throughout much of his time at Boundary Park. He was particularly missed in the latter stages of season 1996–97 when a calf strain sidelined him as Athletic fought an unsuccessful relegation battle and descended into the Second Division.

ORMANDY, Jack

Outside-left

Born: Liverpool, 25 January 1912.
Died: Dewsbury, January 1997, age 85.
Career: Prescot Cables. Bradford City June 1932. Bury June 1936. Southend United June 1939. OLDHAM ATHLETIC July 1946. Halifax Town July 1947 to June 1948.

■ A tricky and nimble little wingman, Jack Ormandy joined Athletic at 34 years of age but was still a lively performer. His deft footwork and inviting centres provided much of the ammunition for Athletic's other veteran forward of the immediate post-war era, Fred Howe, who scored 20 League goals in 1946–47.

ORMOND, William

Outside-left

Born: Greenock, 26 August 1926.
Died: October 1992.
Career: Arthurlie. Partick Thistle November 1945. Blackpool October 1947. OLDHAM ATHLETIC December 1949. Barrow February 1954. Scunthorpe United August 1958. Weymouth 1959. Barnstaple Town July 1962.

■ A strong and forceful wingman, Bill Ormond was equally at home on either wing and enjoyed an excellent season in 1952–53, scoring 11 goals in 43 League matches in the Championship-winning side. He left during the course of the Division Two campaign that followed and gave four seasons of excellent service to Barrow, often shining against his former Boundary Park colleagues in Third Division North encounters.

ORMONDROYD, Ian

Forward

Born: Bradford, 22 September 1964.
Career: Thackley FC. Bradford City September 1985. OLDHAM ATHLETIC loan March 1987. Aston Villa February 1989, fee £600,000. Derby County September 1991, fee £350,000. Leicester City March 1992. Hull City loan January 1995. Bradford City July 1995, fee £75,000. OLDHAM ATHLETIC September 1996. Scunthorpe United September 1997, fee £25,000, retired 1998. Subsequently appointed Bradford City Community Officer.

■ Nicknamed 'Sticks', the towering striker bridged a nine and a half year gap when he joined Athletic from Bradford City in September 1996. He had made the identical move, although on a temporary basis, almost a decade earlier. Although approaching the veteran stage in September 1996, his versatility and high work-rate served Athletic well until his surprise transfer to Scunthorpe United, just four months after he had signed a new one-year deal in May 1997.

ORMSTON, Arthur

Centre-forward

Born: Amble, 3 June 1900.
Died: Oldham, 13 October 1947.
Career: Radcliffe United, Ashington. South Shields October 1920, fee £75. Chesterfield May 1921. Durham City September 1922. Coventry City March 1923. Barrow August 1923. Wigan Borough March 1924, fee £30. OLDHAM ATHLETIC June 1925, fee £25. Bradford City October 1926, fee £650. Bristol Rovers June 1927, fee £300. OLDHAM ATHLETIC November 1928, fee £425. Blyth Spartans September 1930. Stalybridge Celtic October 1930. Macclesfield Town July 1931 to January 1932.

■ Making his debut in Second Division football with the Latics, fearless and bustling centre-forward Arthur Ormston began with a hat-trick against Fulham, and followed up with five goals against Stoke City just two days later. Eight goals in two matches from a player costing just £25 constituted an almost unbelievable

start. A second spell at Boundary Park was not a success, despite the fact that he cost £400 more than he had done some three years earlier.

OUTHWAITE, George

Goalkeeper

Born: Ferryhill, 19 May 1928.
Died: Spennymoor, 27 July 2006.
Career: Chilton Colliery. OLDHAM ATHLETIC amateur March 1956.

■ One of two amateur goalkeepers fielded by Athletic in the late stages of season 1955–56, George Outhwaite's debut at Gateshead resulted in Latics' second away win of an unhappy season that ended with the resignation of player-manager George Hardwick.

OVER, Eric

Outside-left

Born: Sheffield, 5 July 1933.
Career: Sheffield United November 1954. Barrow January 1956. OLDHAM ATHLETIC December 1957, fee £450, retired June 1958.

■ After two seasons at Bramall Lane, locally-born wingman Eric Over joined Barrow. One week after scoring Barrow's winning goal at Boundary Park on 1 December 1956 he suffered a broken leg in a second-round FA Cup tie at Chesterfield. He was fully recovered by the time he joined Athletic, but despite having held a first-team place during his brief stay Over announced his retirement in the close season and joined Grimsby Borough Police. He did, however, continue to play for the Police team, a side that featured eight ex-professionals. Not surprisingly they won the Police Trophy for the fifth time in 1958–59.

OWEN, Gareth David

Central-defender

Born: Pontypridd, 21 September 1982.
Career: Stoke City trainee, professional July 2001. Tiverton Town loan. OLDHAM ATHLETIC loan January–April 2004. Torquay United loan July–August 2004. OLDHAM ATHLETIC loan March–May 2005, permanent March 2005, fee £50,000. Stockport County loan August 2006, permanent June 2007.

■ Following two separate loan spells from Stoke City, Gareth Owen signed a three-year contract with Athletic in March 2005. Considered 'one for the future' when signed, the Wales Youth defender never fully established himself, his best run in the team being halted by injury. Loaned to Stockport County for the full season 2006–07, he was given the captain's armband and led County to a club record nine consecutive wins, all achieved without conceding a goal. Despite his Athletic contract having a year to run, his wish to join County on a full-time basis was agreed by manager John Sheridan in June 2007.

PALMER, Roger Neil

Midfield

Born: Manchester, 30 January 1959.
Career: Manchester City apprentice May 1975, professional March 1977. OLDHAM ATHLETIC November 1980 to May 1994, fee £70,000.

■ Signed following the sale of Simon Stainrod to Queen's Park Rangers, Roger Palmer proved to be one of Athletic's best-ever buys. The holder of the club's record for total goals (156), his tally was almost entirely scored from midfield, a testament to his lung-bursting work-rate and priceless knack of arriving at just the right moment in the opponent's penalty area.

Wonderfully consistent throughout his 13 and a half year career with Athletic, Palmer was rewarded with a highly successful testimonial at the close of the Division Two Championship campaign. Manchester City, Palmer's former club, were the visitors and 15,000 spectators turned out to give their record goalscorer a memorable night. In a rare interview 10 years later with Athletic's popular programme editor, Gordon Lawton, Athletic's reclusive hit-man recalled his special memories. These included a Wembley appearance in the Littlewoods Cup Final, a hat-trick against Manchester City at Maine Road and his record-breaking goal against Ipswich Town, which took him beyond Eric Gemmell's previous record total. Players he considered the best during his spell at the club were: Earl Barrett (the best ever). Frank Bunn (who had a deft touch and could bring the ball down and lay it off in the same movement) and Rick Holden (a magic left foot, and knew just when to deliver the ball).

PARKER, Derrick

Forward

Born: Wallsend, 7 February 1957.
Career: Northumberland Schoolboys. Burnley apprentice, professional February 1974. Southend United February 1977, fee £10,000. Barnsley February 1980, fee £60,000. OLDHAM ATHLETIC August 1983, fee £40,000. Doncaster Rovers loan

December 1984. Burnley October 1985, fee £10,000, released May 1987. Finland football. Rochdale October 1987. North Ferriby United. Altrincham. Northwich Victoria January 1988. Frickley Athletic October 1990. Hyde United November 1991. Bishop Auckland January 1992. Irlam FC February 1992.

■ Despite netting over a century of goals in his career, Derrick Parker's strike rate at Boundary Park was disappointing. A hard-working forward with sufficient skill to retain possession while awaiting support, Parker had a traumatic start with Athletic, being dropped, injured and transfer listed, all within three months of signing.

PARKIN, Brian

Goalkeeper

Born: Birkenhead, 12 October 1965.
Career: OLDHAM ATHLETIC amateur December 1982, professional March 1983. Crewe Alexandra November 1984. Crystal Palace June 1988. Bristol Rovers November 1989. Wycombe Wanderers July 1996. Shrewsbury Town September 1998. Notts County October 1998. Wimbledon March 1999. Yeovil Town 1999. Bristol Rovers professional October 1999, non-contract August 2000.

■ A former oil refinery worker, Brian Parkin lacked opportunities as Andy Goram dominated the goalkeeping position during his spell with Athletic. The ideally-built goalkeeper blossomed on leaving Boundary Park, eventually

totalling 396 League appearances which included 241 for Bristol Rovers with whom he won a Division Three Championship medal in 1990.

PARKIN, Sam

Forward

Born: Roehampton, 14 March 1981.
Career: Chelsea from school, professional August 1998. Millwall loan September 2000. Wycombe Wanderers loan November 2000. OLDHAM ATHLETIC loan March–May 2001. Northampton Town loan July 2001–May 2002. Swindon Town August 2002. Ipswich Town July 2005, fee £450,000. Luton Town August 2006, fee £340,000.

■ Three starting appearances and four from the bench netted Sam Parkin three goals during his brief but successful loan spell with Athletic. An attack leader with an excellent physique and a strong shot in either foot, his full potential was first realised during a three-year spell with Swindon Town for whom he scored 73 goals in 135/7 matches.

PARKINSON, Henry

Inside-forward

Born: Little Hulton, 1899.
Died: Oldham, 22 January 1994.
Career: Raphael Street Wesleyans. Breightmet United. Altrincham 1920. OLDHAM ATHLETIC November 1921. Macclesfield Town. Hazel Grove August 1922. Brentford July 1923. Lytham 1924. Morecambe. Lostock Hall October 1927. Lytham November 1929. Ribble Motors 1931.

■ Parkinson was an outstanding amateur who represented Cheshire County in the same month that he made his debut for Athletic reserves in October 1921. Reported to show a 'nice ball playing style', he nevertheless found difficulty in adapting to the pace of First Division football.

PARNABY, Thomas William

Outside-left

Born: South Shields, 6 January 1922.
Died: South Hams, Devon, 4 December 2004.
Career: Durham County Schoolboys.

Plymouth Argyle amateur June 1939, professional July 1939. OLDHAM ATHLETIC June 1947. Winsford United July 1948.

■ Former Royal Marine Commando Tommy Parnaby became a Latics player in a wholesale recruiting campaign by manager Billy Wootton – the former Plymouth Argyle wingman was his sixth capture in the space of one week in June 1947. Although he scored in his second appearance for the Latics, a 5–1 defeat by Rotherham United, the dreadful start to the season brought sweeping changes and Parnaby did not re-appear after playing in seven of the opening 10 fixtures of the season.

PATEMAN, George Edward

Centre-forward

Born: Chatham, 18 May 1910.
Died: Rochester, 23 March 1973.
Career: Canterbury Waverley. Gillingham June 1929. Portsmouth July 1931. OLDHAM ATHLETIC May 1933. Bradford City June 1934. Clapton Orient July 1935. Reading October 1935, fee £350. Accrington Stanley August 1936, fee £100. Southport February 1937, in exchange for Frank Curran. Barrow June 1937 to May 1939. Shorts Sports player-manager 1946–47.

■ A lively leader with a good eye for goal, George Pateman spent a season at Boundary Park as understudy to Tommy Reid. The tall and lithe centre-forward certainly made the most of his limited opportunities, scoring four goals in just

seven appearances. Throughout his career Pateman experienced much of the variety of football, assisting nine League clubs. In retirement he worked as personnel manager at Shorts, the aircraft manufacturers.

PATERSON, Alexander Adam

Inside-forward

Born: Kirkfieldbank, near Lanark, 18 May 1897.
Career: Lanark United. OLDHAM ATHLETIC April 1921 to May 1922.

■ Scotland Junior international Alex Paterson was given a run out in the final fixture of season 1920–21, a 2–1 home defeat by Huddersfield Town. Lightweight to the point of frailty – standing 5ft 6in and weighing less than 10st – he did not add to his one senior appearance.

PATERSON, Andrew

Half-back

Born: Leeholme, 19 January 1909.
Died: Chadderton, 11 December 1989.
Career: Grays United. Middle Docks. Hebburn Colliery. Stockport County amateur August 1930. Gateshead October 1931. Wigan Athletic July 1934. OLDHAM ATHLETIC May 1937. South Shields 1939. Wartime guest with OLDHAM ATHLETIC.

■ Prior to joining Athletic, Andy Paterson was a member of the Gateshead team who finished runners-up for the Third Division North Championship in

season 1931–32. He next captained Wigan Athletic to two consecutive Cheshire League Championships. Athletic were rich in half-back talent in the late 1930s, and Paterson did not appear regularly. As a wartime player with Athletic he had a lucky escape when a German bomb fell in the backyard of the house in which he was living. This was just prior to Christmas 1941 and in the same air raid Boundary Park suffered £671-worth of damage to the ground, every window in the offices and the main stand being shattered.

PEARS, John

Outside-left

Born: Ormskirk, 23 February 1907.
Career: Westhead St James. Skelmersdale United June 1926. Burscough Rangers December 1926. Liverpool amateur August 1927, professional March 1928. Rotherham United August 1928. Accrington Stanley May 1929. OLDHAM ATHLETIC July 1930. Preston North End March 1934. Sheffield United November 1934, fee £1,500. Swansea Town August 1935, fee £350. Hull City June 1937, fee £100. Rochdale June 1938. Mossley September 1938.

■ A match-winning left-winger and a great favourite with the Athletic crowd, John Pears' attributes lay in his great speed and a tremendous shot in his left foot. With an inclination to meet right-wing centres with a first-time volley, his goals were often of a spectacular nature. His 34 goals in 97 appearances earned him an upward move and he

helped Preston North End win promotion to the First Division, having joined them just prior to the transfer deadline in 1934.

PEARSON, David Thomson

Inside-forward

Born: Dunfermline, 9 November 1932.
Career: Kelty Burnside. Comrie Colliery 1949. Blackburn Rovers November 1949. Ipswich Town May 1954, fee £2,000. Darwen 1955–56. OLDHAM ATHLETIC August 1956. Rochdale March 1957. Crewe Alexandra May 1958. Chorley 1959–60. Third Lanark trial February 1961.

■ One of the few players to mark his League debut with a hat-trick, Dave Pearson was manager Goodier's 13th close season signing in 1956. Despite his

wonderful start in the 4–3 win against Halifax Town, Pearson's goals had dried up by mid-December and the team's form plummeted, with only two League wins recorded in the second half of the season. Despite a very creditable career average of a League goal in every other game, Pearson's career figures amounted to a relatively modest 61 matches and 31 goals.

PEARSON, Horace

Goalkeeper

Born: Tamworth, 6 April 1907.
Died: Bristol, November 1989.
Career: Tamworth Castle. Nuneaton Town 1928. Luton Town January 1929. Blackpool May 1929. OLDHAM ATHLETIC November 1931. Coventry City May 1933. Newport County May 1937. Barry Town 1938. Bristol City September 1938. Scarborough July 1946.

■ Horace Pearson joined Athletic as back-up to England international Jack Hacking following the transfer of Frank Moss to Arsenal. Within four months he had taken over the first-team jersey, but Hacking responded to the challenge and was back as first choice midway through the following season. Pearson played in two Championship-winning sides during his career. In 1930 he assisted Blackpool to win the Second Division title, and with Coventry City he won a Third Division South Championship medal in 1936.

PEARSON, Michael Thomas

Defender/Midfield

Born: Bangor, North Wales, 19 January 1988.
Career: OLDHAM ATHLETIC trainee, professional July 2006. Farsley Celtic loan October–December 2007.

■ Youth-team product Michael Pearson appeared to have made the breakthrough in February 2007 when he made his first senior appearance from the bench against Millwall. The 19-year-old Welshman was a late replacement for Will Haining in the 2–1 defeat that knocked Athletic off the top of the table, marking a triumphant return to Boundary Park for Millwall manager Willie Donachie. In the following May, Pearson captained the Athletic youth squad in their groundbreaking tour to Bangladesh. Without further involvement at senior level in 2007–08 and with just seven reserve team outings Pearson was released in May 2008.

PEDERSEN, Tore Andre

Defender

Born: Fredrikstad, Norway 29 September 1969.
Career: Selbak 1975–87. Lillestrom 1988. Fredrekstat 1989. IFK Gothenberg 1990. SK Brann, Bergen, Norway 1993.

OLDHAM ATHLETIC December 1993, fee £500,000. SK Brann, Bergan, May 1994. Safrecce, Hiroshima, Japan, August 1994. FC St Pauli, Germany, 1995. Blackburn Rovers September 1997, fee £500,000. Eintracht Frankfurt October 1998, fee £225,000. Wimbledon July 1999. Trosvik, Norway March 2001.

■ Cultured central-defender Tore Pedersen was the second Norwegian international to join Athletic when he followed Gunnar Halle to Boundary Park in December 1993. Despite a highly successful career at international level – he won 46 caps for his country – Pederson's brief flirtation with English football proved disappointing. His Athletic career was terminated by a knee injury in March 1994, sustained in the sixth-round FA Cup win at Bolton Wanderers.

PEMBERTON, Martin Calvin

Forward

Born: Bradford, 1 February 1976.
Career: OLDHAM ATHLETIC associate schoolboy May 1990, professional July 1994. Ards, Ireland, loan January–February 1997. Doncaster Rovers March 1997. Scunthorpe United non-contract March 1998. Hartlepool United July 1998. Harrogate Town September 1998. Bradford Park Avenue. Mansfield Town August 2000, fee £10,000. Stockport County May 2002. Rochdale loan January–May 2004. Farsley Celtic November 2004.

■ A serious back injury restricted Martin Pemberton's opportunities with Athletic, and despite making a full recovery the youthful striker appeared in only six matches, all of these from the substitute's bench. Subsequently converting to full-back, Pemberton completed a career total of 106/27 League appearances, his final outing, with Rochdale, coming on 10 January 2004 in a 1–0 defeat at Yeovil Town. In non-League circles, his club Farsley Celtic won promotion to the Blue Star Premier League (formerly the Conference) in 2007. Outside of football, it was reported in February 2003 that Martin had a girlfriend recognisable to millions – Kimberley Walsh from the pop group Girls Aloud.

PENNINGTON, James

Outside-right

Born: Golborne, 26 April 1939.
Career: Manchester City amateur December 1955, professional August 1956. Crewe Alexandra March 1961. Grimsby Town April 1963, fee £2,000. OLDHAM ATHLETIC July 1965. Rochdale July 1966. Northwich Victoria 1967 to 1969.

■ Jim Pennington was a lightweight and tricky wingman who joined Athletic after two years with Grimsby Town, for whom he totalled 89 League matches and scored eight goals. In a season at Boundary Park he eventually lost out in mid-term, following Jimmy McIlroy's appointment as manager. His only goal for Athletic was made before the season's largest attendance of 35,330 spectators, in the FA Cup third-round replay at West Ham United on 24 January 1966. The Hammers won 2–1 after drawing 2–2 at Boundary Park two days earlier.

PENNINGTON, Thomas E.

Goalkeeper

Born: c.1887.
Career: Newton FC. Whitchurch February 1907. Reading May 1907. Saltney FC September 1908. OLDHAM ATHLETIC September 1909 to May 1910. Fulham trial October 1912.

■ Reserve goalkeeper Tom Pennington made only one senior appearance for

Athletic and contemporary reports suggested that he performed with great credit in the season's first victory, a 2–1 away win at Burnley.

PHILLISKIRK, Anthony

Forward

Born: Sunderland, 10 February 1965.
Career: Sunderland Schoolboys. Durham County Schoolboys. Sheffield United August 1983. Rotherham United loan October 1986. OLDHAM ATHLETIC July 1988, fee £25,000. Preston North End February 1989. Bolton Wanderers June 1989, fee £50,000. Peterborough United October 1992, fee £85,000. Burnley January 1994, fee £80,000. Carlisle United loan October 1995. Cardiff City December 1995, fee £60,000. Halifax Town loan December 1997. Macclesfield Town loan December 1997. OLDHAM ATHLETIC coaching staff June 1998, initially as youth-team coach then first-team coach and assistant manager, reverting to youth-team coach January 2004.

■ Tony Philliskirk was capped twice by England Under-18 Schoolboys and scored on both occasions, against Scotland at Falkirk and, one week later, against Wales at Shrewsbury. Although short of opportunities with Athletic due to the excellent form of Andy Ritchie and Frank Bunn, the tall fair-haired striker went on to score a total of 110 League goals in a career spanning 10 League clubs and 352/56 appearances. Son Danny, despite having made only fleeting appearances in the Athletic youth team, was snapped up by Chelsea in June 2007 on a contract set to run until 2011.

PHILPOTT, Alan

Utility player

Born: Stoke-on-Trent, 8 November 1942.
Career: Stoke Schoolboys. Stoke City apprentice, signing professional November 1959. OLDHAM ATHLETIC November 1967, fee £7,500. Stafford Rangers January 1969. Eastwood FC, Hanley. Port Vale youth coach.

■ In a lengthy spell with Stoke City, Alan Philpott had gained a thorough grounding as a utility man, having occupied nine outfield positions during his eight years at the Victoria Ground. Assured in link-up play and with a good range of passing, he looked most comfortable in a midfield role with Athletic, but he was off-loaded by new manager Jack Rowley within two months of his appointment.

PHOENIX, Peter Patrick

Outside-left
Born: Salford, 31 December 1936.

Career: Stretford Schoolboys. Lostock Gralam. Manchester City amateur May 1955. Stoke City amateur. Tamworth FC. OLDHAM ATHLETIC amateur, professional 24 February 1958. Rochdale October 1962, in exchange for Colin Whitaker. Exeter City October 1963. Southport January 1964. Stockport County July 1964. Wigan Athletic August 1965. Witton Albion 1965. Bangor City 1966–68. Massey Ferguson FC.

■ Peter Phoenix was an enterprising wingman who took over the number-11 jersey from Eric Over in 1957–58, the final season of regional Third Division football. His quick, go-ahead methods were best seen in 1958–59 when he was leading scorer with 14 League and Cup goals. Later adapting to the role of an attacking wing-half, Phoenix completed 178 appearances and scored 31 goals before leaving Boundary Park early in the 1962–63 promotion season. His career thereafter was undistinguished, spanning five clubs in less than three years. Nevertheless, he continued to play as an amateur beyond his 50th birthday, retiring only after suffering a broken leg in a Manchester Amateur League match.

PICKERING, William Henry

Full-back

Born: Sheffield, 10 December 1919.
Died: Selby, 16 November 1983.
Career: Sheffield Schoolboys. Sheffield Wednesday amateur May, professional October 1937. Wartime guest with Leeds United. OLDHAM ATHLETIC July 1948, fee £1,000. Gainsborough Trinity September 1951. Worksop Town coach

1962–63, manager September 1964. Goole Town manager until April 1972.

■ Able to occupy either flank, former England Amateur international Bill Pickering began at right-back but after seven matches switched to the left, where he remained a fixture. His partnership with Tommy Bell in 1948–49 was particularly effective in a season when sixth place in the Third Division North was achieved. The quick-moving and stylish defender gave excellent service in two years at Boundary Park, 87 appearances in two seasons being an accurate reflection of his consistency.

PICKERSGILL, Thomas

Half-back

Born: St Helens, 19 February 1908.
Died: Knowsley, July 1991.

Career: Runcorn. OLDHAM ATHLETIC May 1930. Rhyl 1932. Torquay United May 1933. Accrington Stanley June to October 1935. Fleetwood December 1935. Rhyl January 1936.

■ Tom Pickersgill graduated to League football after a season spent in Athletic's reserve side. He made a shaky start as visitors Manchester United won 5–1 on his debut, and one week later a trip to Bradford Park Avenue resulted in a 5–0 defeat. A second opportunity presented itself later in the same season and this coincided with a much better run of results, Pickersgill's consistent displays earning him a lengthy run of first-team football.

PILKINGTON, Elliot

Half-back

Born: Radcliffe, 2 April 1890.
Died: Bury, 23 November 1945.
Career: Salford United. OLDHAM ATHLETIC May 1910. Llandudno August 1926. Macclesfield Town August 1927.

■ Elliot Pilkington began as an inside-forward and headed the scoring charts for Athletic Reserves in his first two seasons, finally breaking into the first team in season 1914–15, when Athletic finished runners-up for the Football League Championship. Later settling at centre-half, he successfully marshalled Athletic's defence in the first seven seasons of post-war football. His benefit match at Boundary Park in March 1921 accurately reflected his popularity with the Oldham sporting public, attracting a crowd of 19,440. On retiring from the game he worked as a coal merchant in Radcliffe.

PILKINGTON, Samuel Turnell

Outside-right

Born: Accrington, 1890.
Career: Accrington Stanley October 1906. Colne FC August 1907. Haslingden. OLDHAM ATHLETIC February 1911. Haslingden June 1912. Accrington Stanley July to October 1913.

■ Sam Pilkington first played for Accrington Stanley as a 16-year-old, and in summer months he was a talented batsman with Accrington CC of the Lancashire League. After World War One, as secretary-manager of Accrington Stanley he was largely instrumental in the revival of the club, leading to their election to the new Third Division North in 1921. In business as a cotton merchant, he was elected Mayor of Accrington in November 1942 and was President of the Lancashire Combination from 1946 to 1968.

PLATT, John Roger

Goalkeeper

Born: Ashton-under-Lyne, 22 August 1954.
Career: Ashton United. OLDHAM ATHLETIC amateur October 1971, professional March 1974. Bury August 1981. Bolton Wanderers July 1983. Tranmere Rovers loan November 1984. Preston North End February 1985. OLDHAM ATHLETIC amateur December 1986. Stalybridge Celtic August 1987. Hyde United 1990. Stalybridge Celtic until January 1993.

■ A courageous goalkeeper with a keen positional sense, John Platt's fearlessness at times proved to be his undoing as he

missed large parts of two seasons due to serious injuries. Throughout his spell he was challenged for the first-team spot, initially by Chris Ogden and later by Peter McDonnell. Platt made 109 League appearances for the Latics and 185 in his career overall. He was appointed stadium manager at Boundary Park in August 1986 and currently works as Football in the Community officer.

PLAYER, Percival Roy Ivan

Centre-half

Born: Portsmouth, 10 May 1928.
Died: Rutland, 15 April 1992.
Career: Portsmouth amateur. Grimsby Town amateur, professional December 1953. OLDHAM ATHLETIC June 1959, fee £300. Gainsborough Trinity August 1960. Spalding United 1961 to May 1964.

■ Roy Player first came to the attention of Grimsby Town while serving in the district with the RAF. He made 57 appearances in his five years with the Mariners before being transferred to Athletic in the summer of 1959. As deputy for centre-half Wally Taylor he made only two first-team appearances. In

the second of these he was unfortunately credited with an own-goal in the 4–2 defeat against Crewe Alexandra on Good Friday 1960.

POGLIACOMI, Leslie Amado

Goalkeeper

Born: Perth, Australia, 3 May 1976.
Career: Marconi Stallions Under-11s 1987. New South Wales Schoolboys. Adelaide City 1997. Wollongong Wolves 1998. Parramatta Power 2000. Wolverhampton Wanderers trial February

2002. OLDHAM ATHLETIC July 2002. Blackpool August 2005. OLDHAM ATHLETIC June 2006 to February 2008.

■ In April 2008 Athletic sadly parted company with their popular 31-year-old Australian goalkeeper when he returned to Australia for major reconstruction surgery to his knee. Chronic injury problems having sidelined him for almost all of the 2007–08 season. Of Argentinean descent, Pogliacomi moved to Australia with his family in 1983, and first became a professional footballer at the age of 18. He joined Athletic following an unsuccessful trial with Wolverhampton Wanderers and achieved a record of 19 clean sheets in his first season, assisting the team to reach the end-of-season Play-offs. In December 2004 he recorded his 100th Athletic appearance, and after a season spent with Lancashire neighbours Blackpool the 6ft 5in shot-stopper returned to Athletic as new manager John Sheridan took over. A sixth-place finish took Athletic to the Play-offs, but Pogliacomi was injured in the semi-final first leg. His 46 appearances during the season triggered a one-year extension to his contract, but continuing injury problems in his final season restricted him to just three appearances for the reserves.

POINTON, Neil Geoffrey

Left-back

Born: Church Warsop, 28 November 1964.
Career: Scunthorpe United apprentice, professional August 1982. Everton November 1985, fee £75,000. Manchester City July 1990, in exchange for Andy Hinchcliffe plus £200,000. OLDHAM ATHLETIC July 1992, fee £60,000. Heart of Midlothian October 1995. Walsall July 1998. Chesterfield January 2000. Hednesford Town player-coach June 2000, player-manager December 2000. Retford United manager. Mossley February 2003.

■ A member of Everton's 1987 Championship-winning side, uncompromising left-back Neil Pointon had the benefit of over 300 League appearances when he joined Athletic along with Steve Redmond in the summer of 1992. A worthy successor to Andy Barlow, Pointon proved to be an

accomplished defender who weighed in with vital goals as the Latics accomplished a last-gasp escape from Premier League relegation. The following season Pointon scored against Manchester United in the FA Cup semi-final and the replay, but United went on to claim the trophy with a 4–0 win against Chelsea in the Final. With Heart of Midlothian, Pointon appeared in the Scottish Cup Final in 1996 and the League Cup Final in 1997, and he later captained Walsall to promotion from Division Two in 1999.

POLLITT, Michael Francis

Goalkeeper

Born: Farnworth, 29 February 1972.
Career: Manchester United associate schoolboy October 1987, trainee July 1988, professional July 1990. OLDHAM ATHLETIC loan October–November 1990. Bury July 1991. Lincoln City December 1992. Darlington August 1994. Notts County November 1995, fee £75,000. OLDHAM ATHLETIC loan August–November 1997. Gillingham loan December 1997. Brentford loan January 1998. Sunderland February 1998, fee £75,000. Rotherham United July 1998. Chesterfield August 2000. Rotherham United May 2001. Wigan Athletic June 2005, fee £200,000. Ipswich Town loan November 2006. Burnley loan January 2007.

■ Mike Pollitt did not progress beyond the bench in his first loan spell with Athletic, but seven years later proved to be an extremely capable goalkeeper in his 16 appearances as deputy for injury victim Gary Kelly. In the same season he undertook four separate loan spells from Notts County, but when his career reached a settled phase he won promotions with Rotherham United in 2000 and Chesterfield in 2001. In 2006 he was Wigan's goalkeeper in the Carling Cup Final against Manchester United at the Millennium Stadium. Sadly, his big day was ruined when he sustained a hamstring injury and was substituted after just 14 minutes.

POLLOCK, William

Half-back

Born: Barrhead, Renfrewshire, 7 June 1920.
Career: Manchester United amateur May 1946. OLDHAM ATHLETIC July 1947 to 1948. Fleetwood 1949–50.

■ Bill Pollock was very much a fringe player in 1947–48 when Athletic fielded no fewer than 30 players in League matches. One of eight new players paraded on the opening day at Chester, he was deposed after appearing in the first four matches and failed to regain his place.

PORTER, Christopher John

Forward

Born: Wigan, 12 December 1983.
Career: Queen Elizabeth Grammar School Old Boys, Blackburn. Bury March 2003. OLDHAM ATHLETIC July 2005. Motherwell July 2007.

■ Chris Porter began with Bury appearing alongside Dave Nugent when he made his debut against Macclesfield Town in March 2003. How the Shakers must have regretted being unable to hang on to the two youngsters who developed into such outstanding forwards. Despite being troubled by a persistent knee problem throughout much of his time at Boundary Park, Porter's 23 goals in 2006–07 took Athletic to the brink of promotion. Sadly, Athletic's leading scorer refused terms and signed a two-year contract

with Motherwell, becoming the second Athletic player to cross the border after Will Haining had signed with St Mirren. Neither player commanded a transfer fee, and particularly in Porter's case, Athletic must in hindsight have wished that they had accepted a six-figure bid made by Plymouth Argyle in the January 2007 transfer window.

PORTER, William

Full-back

Born: Fleetwood, July 1905.
Died: Ashton-under-Lyne, 28 April 1946.
Career: Fleetwood Windsor Villa. Fleetwood FC November 1925. OLDHAM ATHLETIC May 1926. Manchester United January 1935. Wartime guest with OLDHAM ATHLETIC, Manchester City, Blackburn Rovers, Accrington Stanley and Newcastle United. Hyde United player-manager from early 1944–45 to 1946.

■ A tall, polished, and industrious full-back, Billy Porter recovered well from a broken leg sustained in his first season at Boundary Park. His long-standing partnership with Teddy Ivill was a particularly successful and long-lasting one. In nine years with Athletic Porter clocked up 284 appearances, while his co-defender Ivill played in 285 matches. At Manchester United Porter was ever present in 1935–36 when the Second Division Championship was won. War work at Metropolitan Vickers enabled him to play regularly throughout World

War Two as United's captain, he also guested regularly for other clubs, Athletic included.

PRENDERVILLE, Barry

Defender

Born: Dublin, 16 October 1976.
Career: Cherry Orchard FC. Coventry City August 1994. Hibernian loan September 1998. Ayr United June to October 1999. St Patrick's Athletic, Dublin. OLDHAM ATHLETIC September 2000. Shelbourne January 2002.

■ Strapping defender Barry Prenderville arrived at Boundary Park via a wandering path, having sampled Irish, English and Scottish football beforehand. Knee and hamstring injuries blighted his

first season at Boundary Park, but he was at his best during Athletic's bright start to season 2001–02. After the departure of manager Andy Ritchie, however, Prenderville was one of six players swiftly off-loaded.

PRICE, Norman Malcolm

Full-back

Born: Dumfries, 2 March 1904.
Died: Dumfries, 15 April 1977.
Career: Glasgow Ashfield. Ayr United March 1928. Bristol Rovers July 1930. Nithsdale Wanderers loan May 1931. Accrington Stanley June 1931. Coleraine, Ireland July 1934. Stalybridge Celtic August 1935. OLDHAM ATHLETIC May 1936. Gainsborough Trinity June 1938.

■ A Scottish full-back of formidable physical proportions who arrived at

Boundary Park with a wide variety of experience. Norman Price was generally first choice with Athletic alongside Billy Hilton when the team finished fourth in consecutive Division Three North seasons between 1936–38.

PRINCE, Jack

Goalkeeper

Born: Crewe, 6 June 1906.
Died: Crewe, 13 October 1971.
Career: Nantwich Town. OLDHAM ATHLETIC November 1927. Port Vale May 1928. Rochdale August 1930. Wrexham November 1931. Shrewsbury Town December 1931. Northwich Victoria

August 1933. Nantwich Town. Crewe Alexandra July 1937.

■ A useful reserve goalkeeper Prince was unable to break the Jack Hacking monopoly in 1927–28, apart from one outing when Hacking was playing for the Football League. Prince subsequently sampled relegation and promotion with Port Vale, making 12 appearances in 1929–30 when the Third Division North Championship was secured.

PURCELL, Llewellyn

Inside-forward

Born: Boothstown, 30 April 1909.
Died: Barton Irwell, 1980.
Career: Pendlebury FC. Bolton Wanderers amateur December 1926. Winsford United December 1930. OLDHAM ATHLETIC November 1931, fee £50. Stockport County trial August–September 1932. Witton Albion January 1933. Rossendale United July 1933. Mossley Common United, Manchester, amateur November 1933. Glossop coach after World War Two. Atherton Collieries coach June 1949.

■ Athletic retained Llewellyn Purcell for the remainder of the 1931–32 campaign following an initial one-month trial. He appeared only once at senior level, in the 2–1 defeat by Bury at Boundary Park on 16 January 1932.

PYNEGAR, Albert

Inside-forward

Born: Basford, 24 September 1895.
Died: Basford, 26 March 1978.
Career: Eastwood Rangers. Sutton Town 1913. Leicester City May 1920. Coventry City January 1924. OLDHAM ATHLETIC July 1925, fee £1,200. Port Vale January 1929, in exchange for Stewart Littlewood plus £200. Chesterfield October 1930, fee £250. Rotherham United August 1932, fee £25. Sutton Town April 1934.

■ Albert Pynegar started with a bang at Leicester City, scoring 61 goals in all competitions in his first season, including six on his debut against Derby County reserves on 28 August 1920. He was a regular scorer for Athletic, ending his first season by scoring four goals in an 8–3 hammering of Nottingham Forest. After leaving Athletic Pynegar won

consecutive Third Division North Championships with Port Vale in 1930 and with Chesterfield in 1931. His career aggregate figures were impressive – 174 League goals in 366 matches.

QUINN, Michael

Forward

Born: Liverpool, 2 May 1962.
Career: Derby County apprentice July 1978. Wigan Athletic September 1979. Stockport County July 1982. OLDHAM ATHLETIC January 1984, fee £52,000. Portsmouth March 1986, fee £150,000. Newcastle United August 1989, fee £680,000. Coventry City November 1992,

fee £250,000. Plymouth Argyle loan November 1994. Watford loan March 1995. Hong Kong football May 1995. PAOK, Greece, July 1995–1996.

■ An ideally-built attack leader, Mike Quinn's game featured powerful and aggressive running and an in-built radar for goals. He moved up two divisions when he joined Athletic, and after a modest start of five goals in 14 matches, the burly Scouser scored freely in the two seasons preceding his big-money transfer to Portsmouth. In season 1989–90 he scored 34 goals for Newcastle United, a total that made him the Football League's leading goalscorer. Quinn was also credited with the Premier League's 2000th goal when he scored for Coventry City against Manchester City on 19 February 1994.

QUINN, Noel Peter Anthony

Outside-right

Born: Dublin, 2 November 1949.
Career: Caffery's College, Dublin. Manchester United amateur October 1966. Blackburn Rovers amateur December 1966. OLDHAM ATHLETIC trial December 1966, professional January 1967. Drumcondra, December 1967.

■ At the time of his signing, Noel Quinn became the ninth Irishman on the playing staff at Boundary Park. The Republic of Ireland Schoolboy international failed to make the grade with Athletic, lacking stamina and tenacity to complement his natural ability on the ball.

QUIXALL, Albert

Inside-forward

Born: Sheffield, 9 August 1933.
Career: Sheffield Schoolboys. Meynell Youth Club. Sheffield Wednesday amateur May 1948, professional August 1950. Manchester United September 1958, fee £45,000. OLDHAM ATHLETIC September 1964, fee £8,500. Stockport County July 1966. Altrincham November 1967. Radcliffe Borough.

■ Flaxen-haired Albert Quixall was a ball-juggling inside-forward who sported short shorts at a time when the vogue was for long ones. He was the

subject of a British record transfer fee when he moved to Manchester United in the aftermath of the Munich tragedy. Capped by England at Schools, Under-23 and B levels he went on to win five full caps and was four times a Football League representative. The winner of two Second Division Championships with Sheffield Wednesday, Quixall was an FA Cup winner with Manchester United in 1963. In the following season he was troubled by injuries and lost his first-team place, leading to his £8,500 transfer to Athletic. Restricted by continuing injury problems throughout his time at Boundary Park, Athletic fans saw only too briefly a glimpse of Quixall's unique body swerve and scheming abilities.

RACHUBKA, Paul Stephen

Goalkeeper

Born: San Luis Obispo, California, US, 21 May 1981.
Career: Manchester United trainee June 1997, professional July 1999. Royal Antwerp, Belgium, loan 2001. OLDHAM ATHLETIC loan November 2001– February 2002. Charlton Athletic May 2002, fee £200,000. Burnley loan January 2004. Huddersfield Town loan March 2004. MK Dons loan August 2004. Huddersfield Town loan November 2004, permanent December 2004. Peterborough United loan December 2006. Blackpool loan January 2007, permanent June 2007.

■ All three of Athletic's goalkeepers were injured when Paul Rachubka arrived at

Boundary Park, initially on a one-month loan. This was subsequently extended and, in view of his outstanding displays, efforts were made to make his move permanent. Sadly for Athletic, the young goalkeeper opted to remain on United's books, although he has had a variety of clubs since leaving Old Trafford. He was Blackpool's goalkeeper in the League One Play-off semi-finals against Athletic, and in the Seasiders' Wembley victory against Yeovil Town in 2007.

RACKLEY, Robert William

Outside-left

Born: Teignmouth, 15 March 1940.
Career: Newton Abbot Spurs. Exeter City April 1958. Bristol Rovers July 1960. OLDHAM ATHLETIC October 1960 to June 1961. Folkestone Town. Halifax Town trial October-November 1962. Bridgwater Town 1963–64. Taunton Town 1965–66.

■ A fair-haired wingman with a direct approach, Bob Rackley scored twice in five matches during a one-month trial period and was rewarded with a contract for the remainder of the season. He had the satisfaction of opening his scoring account against one of his previous clubs, Exeter City, at Boundary Park on 15 October 1960. The same match was also notable for the debut of Scottish international inside-forward Bobby Johnstone, an event that attracted a bumper crowd of 17,116 spectators.

RADCLIFFE, Mark

Goalkeeper

Born: Hyde, Cheshire, 26 October 1919.
Career: Hyde Schoolboys. OLDHAM ATHLETIC December 1942. Wartime guest with Manchester United and Chelmsford City. Fulham August 1946. Witton Albion 1948. Rochdale November 1952. Knutsford manager. Witton Albion manager.

■ Mark Radcliffe was Athletic's regular goalkeeper for three wartime seasons, playing in exactly 100 matches. Later as reserve to Irish international Ted Hinton at Fulham, he found opportunities limited, but played in 10 Division Two matches and one FA Cup tie in season 1946–47.

RAMSAY, Allan Andrew

Outside-left

Born: Liverpool, 1882.
Career: Barrow April 1905. OLDHAM ATHLETIC May 1906. Liverpool May 1907. Camell Laird September 1908.

■ In addition to three goals in eight FA Cup matches, Allan Ramsey netted 10 goals in 36 Lancashire Combination fixtures in season 1906–07 when Athletic lifted the Championship trophy. Life as a Football League club began for Athletic the following season, but Ramsey had departed in an upward move to Liverpool in the close season.

RAMSEY, Donald

Outside-right

Born: Manchester, 27 September 1928.
Career: OLDHAM ATHLETIC amateur June 1946, professional November 1946 to June 1950.

■ National Service commitments interrupted Don Ramsey's fledgling career and after demobilisation he made two early season appearances as deputy to Frank Tomlinson in 1949–50. He finished on the winning side on both occasions but without further senior opportunities he was released at the end of the season.

RATCLIFFE, Beaumont

Defender

Born: Bolton-on-Dearne, 24 April 1909.
Died: Overpool, 30 March 2003.
Career: Bradford Park Avenue amateur December 1930. Charlton Athletic trial September 1931. New Brighton October 1931. Le Havre, France, 1935. OLDHAM ATHLETIC June 1935, fee £500. Wartime guest New Brighton, Reading, Southport,

Manchester United, Tranmere Rovers and Arsenal. Reading May 1946. Watford May 1948, fee £750. Runcorn player-manager June 1949. Earlestown player-coach August 1951.

■ A popular and inspiring captain during his Athletic days, playing initially at full-back but subsequently at centre-half, Beau Ratcliffe led many spirited promotion attempts. None were successful unfortunately, but successive finishes of seventh, fourth (twice) and fifth ranked Athletic as serious contenders on each occasion. During wartime RAF service he was wounded and held as a prisoner-of-war in Italy but was able to resume with Reading in 1946, and made a final move in League circles to Watford at the age of 39. Outside of football, Ratcliffe was a family butcher in Birkenhead.

REDFEARN, Neil David

Midfield

Born: Dewsbury, 20 June 1965.
Career: Yorkshire Schoolboys. Nottingham Forest apprentice July 1981 to February 1982. Bolton Wanderers June 1982. Lincoln City March 1984, fee £8,250. Doncaster Rovers August 1986, fee £17,500. Crystal Palace July 1987, fee £100,000. Watford November 1988, fee £150,000. OLDHAM ATHLETIC January 1990, fee £150,000. Barnsley September 1991, fee £150,000. Charlton Athletic July 1998, fee £1 million. Bradford City August

1999, fee £250,000. Wigan Athletic March 2000, fee £112,500. Halifax Town player-coach March 2001, caretaker manager September–October 2001. Boston United player and assistant manager August 2002. Rochdale March 2004. Scarborough May 2004, caretaker manager October 2005, manager until July 2006. Bradford Park Avenue (as a player) July 2006. Northwich Victoria manager June 2007. Frickley Athletic September 2007.

■ Neil Redfearn had a long and distinguished professional career, but unfortunately only a relatively small part of it was spent with Athletic. A compactly built driving force from central midfield, he was a highly consistent performer and earned himself a place in Athletic folklore by scoring the injury time penalty-kick against Sheffield Wednesday that clinched the Second Division Championship in May 1991.

REDMOND, Stephen

Defender

Born: Liverpool, 2 November 1967.
Career: Liverpool and Merseyside Schoolboys. Manchester City associate schoolboy October 1982, professional December 1984. OLDHAM ATHLETIC July 1992, fee £300,000. Bury July 1998. Leigh RMI August 2003.

■ Steve Redmond was Manchester City's youngest-ever captain and played in every match when promotion to Division One was secured in 1989. After completing

272/4 matches and scoring seven goals for City, Steve joined the Latics, and proved a shrewd capture. Consistently reliable in central defence, he read the game well and his experience helped Athletic survive their first season in the newly-formed Premier League. The former England Under-21 international completed six years at Boundary Park before joining Bury on a free transfer in July 1998.

REEVES, David Edward

Forward

Born: Birkenhead, 19 November 1967.
Career: Wirral and Cheshire Schoolboys. Heswall. Sheffield Wednesday August 1986. Scunthorpe United loan December 1986 and October 1987. Burnley loan November 1987. Bolton Wanderers August 1989, fee £80,000. Notts County March 1993, fee £80,000. Carlisle United October 1993, fee £121,000. Preston North End October 1996. Chesterfield November 1997, player exchange plus £100,000. OLDHAM ATHLETIC loan December 2001, permanent January 2002. Chesterfield loan August 2002, permanent December 2002. Ards, Ireland, July 2004. Mansfield Town trial September 2004. Swindon Town trial October 2004. Scarborough January 2005. Alfreton Town assistant manager January 2007. Sutton Town 2007.

■ Initially on loan to Athletic from Chesterfield in a complicated deal that took Mark Allott and Mark Innes to Saltergate on loan, David Reeves made an immediate impact, scoring three goals in his first two outings, and his move was quickly made permanent. Rated as one of the best strikers in the lower divisions, he captained Carlisle to promotion in 1994–95, scoring 21 of their 67 League goals that season. David is the twin brother of Alan, for eight years a Swindon Town central-defender.

REID, James

Wing-half

Born: Kilmarnock, 1886.
Career: Belfast Celtic. Glentoran 1906. OLDHAM ATHLETIC August 1908 to April 1910. Glentoran.

■ Despite scoring twice on his debut at Bradford Park Avenue, Jamie Reid made little further headway with Athletic. His father played for Kilmarnock in the 1890s, and four of his brothers also played professional football – Max and John for New Brighton, Davie for Everton and Willie for Heart of Midlothian and Hibernian.

REID, Paul Robert

Midfield

Born: Warley, Worcestershire, 19 January 1968.

Career: Leicester City apprentice July 1984, professional January 1986. Bradford City loan March 1992, permanent July 1992, fee £25,000. Huddersfield Town May 1994, fee £70,000. OLDHAM ATHLETIC March 1997, fee £100,000. Bury July 1999. Swansea City July 2002. Carmarthen Town March 2003.

■ Paul Reid took the short trip over the Pennines to join Athletic on transfer deadline day in March 1997, joining on the same day as Matthew Rush. Paul gave excellent value for his £150,000 transfer fee, despite operating in a side that lost its Division One status and then found life little easier in Division Two. Consistent and totally committed throughout the full 90 minutes of every match, he continued in the same vein following his move to Bury, where he passed the personal milestone of 500 senior appearances in season 2000–01.

REID, Thomas Joseph

Centre-forward

Born: Motherwell, 15 August 1905. Died: Prescot, Liverpool, 1972. Career: Blantyre Victoria. Clydebank

1925. Liverpool April 1926, fee £1,000. Manchester United February 1929. OLDHAM ATHLETIC loan March 1933, permanent June 1933, fee £400. Barrow September 1935. Prescot Cables September 1936. Rhyl Athletic January 1938.

■ Ten goals in 13 matches during the course of his loan spell led to Tommy Reid's permanent move to Boundary Park, with the Latics' Supporters' Club donating the £400 fee for his transfer. He headed the scoring charts in 1933–34 with 17 League and Cup goals, but in the relegation season that followed he was in and out of the side, scoring nine goals in 24 outings. A season with Barrow brought his League career to a close, his career figures in the Football League amounting to 147 goals in 246 matches.

RHODES, Andrew Charles

Goalkeeper

Born: Askern, 23 August 1964.
Career: Barnsley apprentice, professional August 1982. Doncaster Rovers loan October 1985, permanent November 1985, fee £25,000. OLDHAM ATHLETIC March 1988, fee £55,000. Dunfermline Athletic July 1990, fee £100,000. St Johnstone July 1992. Bolton Wanderers loan February 1995. Preston North End loan October 1995. Airdrieonians December 1995, fee £50,000. Scarborough loan November 1997. Halifax Town late season 1997–98. Emley FC 1988. Barnsley non-contract June 2001. OLDHAM ATHLETIC goalkeeping coach. Barnsley goalkeeping coach September 2001. Ipswich Town goalkeeping coach until May 2008.

■ Throughout his time at Boundary Park Andy Rhodes was strongly challenged by Jon Hallworth, both being excellent shot-stoppers with Hallworth holding a slight edge on the kicking side. It was Rhodes who received the nod when Athletic contested the Littlewoods Cup Final at Wembley in 1990, but a few months later he was transferred to Dunfermline.

RICHARDS, Marc John

Forward

Born: Wolverhampton, 8 July 1982.
Career: Blackburn Rovers trainee, professional July 1999. Crewe Alexandra loan August 2001. OLDHAM ATHLETIC loan October-November 2001. Halifax Town loan February 2002. Swansea Town November 2002. Northampton Town July 2003. Rochdale loan March 2005. Barnsley August 2005. Port Vale July 2007.

■ Marc Richards established something of a record when he made his Athletic debut as a 67th-minute substitute for John Eyre. Before making contact with the ball he was booked for a late challenge on a Bristol City defender. The unhappy debut aside, the young striker showed some nice touches on the ball and, in Andy Ritchie's final match as manager, scored a brilliant individual goal to seal Athletic's 2–0 win against Tranmere Rovers in the LDV Vans Cup tie.

RICHARDSON, John Pattison

Outside-right

Born: Bedlington, 9 July 1909.
Died: Ashington, 20 November 1979.
Career: Ashington Colliery Welfare September 1929. Newbiggin FC. OLDHAM ATHLETIC November 1935. Newbiggin West End 1936. Ashington June 1937.

■ John Richardson was working as an electrical engineer and playing in amateur football when he was spotted by Athletic and invited for trials. His debut in League football resulted in the best win of the season, 6–0 against New Brighton on 9 November 1935. Nevertheless, Richardson was deposed after just three consecutive League outings. His brother, James Robert, played in Newcastle United's FA Cup-winning side of 1932 and was capped twice by England in 1933.

RICHARDSON, Lee James

Midfield

Born: Halifax, 12 March 1969.
Career: Halifax Town associate schoolboy April 1985, trainee August 1986, professional July 1987. Watford February 1989, fee £175,000. Blackburn Rovers July 1990, fee £250,000 including part-exchange for A.J. Kennedy. Aberdeen September 1992, fee £152,000. OLDHAM ATHLETIC August 1994, fee £300,000. Stockport County loan August 1997. Huddersfield Town October 1997, fee £65,000. Bury loan August 1999. Livingston February–March 2001. Chesterfield August 2000, assistant manager 2002, caretaker manager March 2007, manager April 2007.

■ Recruited by Athletic following their relegation from the Premier League, Lee Richardson made a dream start, scoring two spectacular goals as Athletic kicked-off in Division One with a 5–2 home win against Charlton Athletic. Despite having gained a reputation as a hard man during his Aberdeen days, the long-haired and bearded midfielder proved more constructive than destructive at Boundary Park, doing his best work when in possession of the ball, rather than when trying to win it back. Prior to joining

Athletic Richardson played in the Scottish Cup Final against Rangers in May 1993. Although he scored past former Athletic goalkeeper Andy Goram, Rangers won 2–1.

RICHARDSON, Lloyd Matthew

Midfield/Winger

Born: Dewsbury, 7 October 1977.
Career: FA National School of Excellence, Lilleshall. OLDHAM ATHLETIC associate schoolboy November 1991, trainee July 1994, professional October 1994. Vasalund, Sweden loan August–September 1997. Hyde United August 1998. Droylsden August 2001.

■ Lloyd Richardson completed a two-year residential scholarship at the FA National School at Lilleshall and represented England at Under-15 and Under-16 levels. He quickly reached professional status with Athletic but failed to graduate to senior level, his second-half substitute appearance at Oxford United on 15 February 1997 being his only taste of League action.

RICHARDSON, Stuart

Wing-half

Born: Leeds, 12 June 1938.
Career: Bethel United. Methley United. Queen's Park Rangers November 1956. OLDHAM ATHLETIC July 1959 to June 1960.

■ Recruited on a free transfer from Queen's Park Rangers, Stuart Richardson vied with Brian Jarvis and Billy Spurdle for a first-team berth during a single season at Boundary Park, appearing in approximately half of the season's fixtures. His brother, Geoffrey, played several games for Athletic reserves in the same season.

RICKERS, Paul Steven

Midfield

Born: Leeds, 9 May 1975.
Career: Leeds City Schoolboys. Tadcaster FC. OLDHAM ATHLETIC associate schoolboy July 1990, trainee August 1991, professional July 1993. Northampton Town July 2002. Leigh RMI loan January 2004. Trials with Macclesfield Town and Dundalk, Ireland. Bury non-contract. Farsley Celtic February 2004. Frickley Athletic October 2006. Goole AFC. Guisley AFC August 2007.

■ First associated with the Latics at the age of 14, Paul Rickers attended the School of Excellence and accepted schoolboy forms despite interest from three other League clubs. In a lengthy spell of service at Boundary Park Rickers impressed as a tireless midfielder, and was also able to occupy the right wing-back position when required. First established at senior level in season 1995–96, he missed very few matches

until 2001–02 when he fell out of favour following the November appointment of Mick Wadsworth as chief coach. He nevertheless graced Athletic's colours in a fraction less than 300 appearances.

RICKETTS, Michael Barrington

Forward

Born: Birmingham, 4 December 1978.
Career: Walsall trainee, professional September 1996. Bolton Wanderers July 2000, fee £500,000. Middlesbrough January 2003, fee £2.2 million. Leeds United July 2004. Stoke City loan February 2005. Cardiff City loan August 2005. Burnley loan January 2006. Southend United July 2006. Preston North End January 2007. OLDHAM ATHLETIC July 2007. Walsall loan November 2007 to January 2008. Southampton trial March 2008. San Jose Earthquakes, US, trial April 2008.

■ Hailed as a key element in Athletic's new-look strikeforce for the 2007–08 season, former England international striker Michael Ricketts scored from the penalty spot within two minutes on his debut against Swansea City. His second goal, in the 3–0 win at Walsall, lifted Athletic from the foot of the table. Some five weeks later, however, he was dropped and swiftly shipped out on an initial three-month loan to Walsall. Ironically, the on-loan striker scored against Athletic when the Saddlers visited Boundary Park and won 2–0 in late December. His Athletic contract was cancelled at the conclusion of his loan with Walsall and in April Rickett's attempts to revive his flagging career spanned unsuccessful trials at Southampton and in America with San Jose Earthquakes.

RIDDING, William

Forward

Born: Heswall, Cheshire, 4 April 1911.
Died: Heaton, Bolton, 20 September 1981.
Career: Tranmere Rovers amateur April 1927, professional May 1928. Manchester City March 1930, fee £3,000. Manchester United December 1931, fee £2,500 plus Billy Dale & Harry Rowley. Northampton Town August 1934. OLDHAM ATHLETIC October 1935. Crewe Alexandra trial October 1936. Tranmere Rovers A Team coach September 1938, manager July 1945. Bolton Wanderers trainer August 1946, temporary manager October 1950 to February 1951, appointed secretary-manager January 1957, resigned August 1968.

■ Tranmere Rovers' reputation for fine centre-forwards appeared to be continuing when the youthful Bill Ridding netted 12 in 13 League matches in 1929–30. Hailed as a worthy successor to earlier notables, 'Dixie' Dean and 'Pongo' Waring, his true potential was never fully realised as cartilage problems blighted his career and caused his early retirement at just 24 years of age. He nevertheless enjoyed a very long and successful career in management with Bolton Wanderers. He was also a qualified physiotherapist and chiropodist, and in 1950 was trainer to England's World Cup party.

RIDINGS Frank

Inside-forward

Born: Radcliffe, 30 April 1910.
Died: Whitefield, 12 April 1969.
Career: Bury A Team 1927. Stalybridge Celtic amateur 1931. Great Harwood. Blackburn Rovers A Team. Glossop FC. Burscough Rangers. OLDHAM ATHLETIC January 1933. Nelson October 1934.

■ Athletic's similarly named inside-forward trio of Johnson, Johnstone and Johnston was briefly dismantled by the introduction of Frank Riding, but the new recruit failed to improve matters, a further two defeats bringing the total of consecutive losses to seven. Three loan signings eventually proved to be Athletic's salvation. Tommy Reid and Harry Rowley from Manchester United and Jimmy Naylor from Manchester City all contributed to a marked improvement in results that led to a comfortable escape from relegation.

RITCHIE, Andrew Timothy

Forward

Born: Bradford, Manchester, 28 November 1960.
Career: Manchester United associate schoolboy October 1975, apprentice September 1977, professional December 1977. Brighton & Hove Albion October 1980, fee £500,000. Leeds United March 1983, in exchange for Terry Connor. OLDHAM ATHLETIC August 1987, fee £50,000. Scarborough August 1995. OLDHAM ATHLETIC player and assistant manager February 1997, player-manager May 1998, manager May 2001,

resigned October 2001. Leeds United Youth Academy director January 2002. Barnsley Academy director January 2004, caretaker manager March 2005, manager May 2005 to November 2006. Huddersfield Town manager April 2007 to April 2008.

■ A dashing and dextrous striker with an assured touch on the ball and a great shot in either foot, Andy Ritchie was an immediate success with Athletic, scoring 20 League and Cup goals in his first season. In 1989–90 he netted 28 (his best ever return), including 10 goals in the Football League Cup run that memorably took the Latics to Wembley for the first time, only to be narrowly beaten by Nottingham Forest. The following season saw Athletic champions of Division Two, Ritchie scoring 15 League goals during the campaign. Increasingly troubled by injuries in subsequent seasons, he nevertheless celebrated his 100th goal for the club during season 1994–95 before joining Scarborough on a free transfer in the summer. Rejoining Athletic as player and assistant manager on the day that Graeme Sharp was replaced by Neil Warnock, Ritchie's days as a player were drawing to a close, his last goal coming in the 3–0 victory against Wrexham at Boundary Park on 27 January 1998. At the time of his sensational dismissal from the managerial role in October 2001, Athletic had slipped from the top of the League to eighth in Division Two after taking just one point from their previous five matches.

ROACH, Neville

Forward

Born: Reading, 29 September 1978.
Career: Reading trainee August 1996, professional May 1997. Kingstonian loan January 1998. Slough Town loan September 1998. Bury trial February 1999. Wycombe Wanderers trial February 1999. Southend United February 1999 to May 2000, fee £30,000. Kingstonian trial. Eastern Pride, Australia, 2000. St Albans City February 2001. OLDHAM ATHLETIC March to May 2001. Torquay United non-contract August 2001. Stevenage Borough November 2001. Slough Town December 2001. Basingstoke Town August 2002. Eastleigh FC July 2004. Oxford United loan November 2005 to February 2006. Basingstoke Town May 2006. Maidenhead United. Farnborough Town October 2007.

■ Recruited on a short-term contract on transfer deadline day 2001, Neville Roach failed to make a senior breakthrough until the very last match of the 2000–01 campaign. Athletic were comprehensively beaten by a Millwall side celebrating the Second Division Championship, and Roach's 28 minutes of action, as a replacement for Carlo Corazzin, proved insufficient to earn him a further contract.

ROBBINS, Patrick

Outside-left

Born: Birr, Ireland, 18 November 1913.
Died: County Cleveland March 1986.
Career: Stockton-on-Tees. Middlesbrough September 1933. Blackburn Rovers February 1934. OLDHAM ATHLETIC May 1935. Hartlepools United June 1938. Accrington Stanley July 1939. Wartime guest with York City.

■ Although Paddy Robbins began on the left wing, the inside berth proved to be his best and he was a key member of the team that twice finished in fourth position in the League table. He was placed on the transfer list at £350 after three years with Athletic and spent a season with Hartlepools United. His promising start with Accrington Stanley – he scored twice in three appearances – was abruptly terminated when the outbreak of World War Two ended League football for the duration.

ROBERTS, Charles

Centre-half

Born: Darlington, 6 April 1883.
Died: Manchester, 7 August 1939.
Career: Bishop Auckland. Grimsby Town April 1903. Manchester United April 1904, fee £600. OLDHAM ATHLETIC August 1913, fee £1,750, retired during World War One due to injury. OLDHAM ATHLETIC manager June 1921, resigned December 1922.

■ An outstanding attacking centre-half with all the attributes of speed, skill on the ball and constructive passing, England international Charlie Roberts enjoyed great success with Manchester United in a lengthy association that covered 299 League and Cup appearances and 23 goals. He captained United to their first FA Cup win against Bristol City at Crystal Palace in March 1909, and to two League Championships. He cost Athletic a record fee in August 1913 and proved an inspirational captain who led the team with outstanding success in the two seasons leading up to the suspension of

League football due to World War One. Fourth place in Division One in 1913–14 was followed by the runners-up position in 1914–15, when failure to win either of their last two home matches cost Athletic the title. His later, 18-month spell as manager of Athletic was, in contrast, a totally unrewarding one.

ROBERTSON, Jordan

Forward

Born: Sheffield, 12 February 1988.
Career: Sheffield United trainee, professional July 2006. Torquay United loan November 2006. Northampton Town January 2007. Dundee United loan August 2007. OLDHAM ATHLETIC loan March 2008.

■ Signed from Sheffield United on an emergency loan deal for one month, the 20-year-old striker came as a replacement for leading scorer Craig Davies, who was out with a hamstring injury. In an earlier loan spell with Northampton Town, Robertson marked his debut with a goal against the Latics in January 2007. He repeated the feat in his first start for Athletic, ending a goal drought in away matches with the opening goal in the 3–0 win at Port Vale. Earlier in the season Robertson had scored four Scottish Premier League goals during his loan spell with Dundee United. Sadly, his Athletic sojourn ended painfully, an ankle ligament injury sustained in the 1–0 home defeat by Hartlepool United bringing his loan period to a premature end.

ROBINS, Ian

Midfield

Born: Bury, 22 February 1952.
Career: OLDHAM ATHLETIC apprentice September 1967, professional February 1970. Bury July 1977, fee £25,000. Huddersfield Town September 1978 to July 1982, fee £15,000.

■ Ian Robins began as an orthodox left-winger and when he made his League debut, at 17 years of age, he already had nice balance, plenty of confidence, and a sweet left foot. Switched to an attacking midfield role in 1971–72 he was immediately at home, and subsequently played an important part in the Third Division Championship campaign of 1973–74. After a season with Bury he moved to

Huddersfield Town for a bargain £15,000. In what was probably the best spell of his career, Robins was leading Town scorer in each of his first two seasons at Leeds Road, his 25 goals in 45 appearances being a major contribution to the Terriers' 1979–80 Division Four Championship success.

ROBINSON, John

Outside-right

Born: Chorley, 18 April 1936.
Career: Leyland Red Rose. Leyland Motors. Bury October 1954. OLDHAM ATHLETIC July 1961. Stalybridge Celtic September 1961. Fleetwood 1965–66.

■ Johnny Robinson began in League football with Bury and made his debut in Division Two at the age of 18 in December 1954. Three years later he fractured his right leg at Bradford Park Avenue and was out for almost two years. Joining Athletic on trial, he played in three matches but did not win a permanent contract, joining Stalybridge Celtic at the end of his trial period.

ROBINSON, Keith

Inside-forward

Born: Bolton, 30 December 1937.
Died: 25 December 2007.
Career: OLDHAM ATHLETIC October 1958. Horwich RMI August 1961.

■ Keith Robinson made rapid progress after joining Athletic from junior football in Bolton, appearing in 25 League matches in his debut season. In October 1959 he completed an apprenticeship and two years of National Service immediately followed. After demobilisation his earlier

form was never recaptured and Robinson's final season was spent almost entirely in the reserve team.

ROBSON, John Cecil

Outside-left

Born: Birtley, Co. Durham, 24 March 1906.
Died: Ashbourne, 20 October 1966.
Career: Berwick Main. Durham County Amateurs. Birtley. Burnley trial January 1923. Hull City March 1923. Reading August 1925, fee £50. Derby County June 1928, fee £1,500. Southend United June 1932, fee £750. Chester August 1933, fee £500. Rochdale November 1933. OLDHAM ATHLETIC June 1934. Hull Brewery reinstated amateur September 1936.

■ A winger built more on the lines of a full-back, Jack Robson was a forceful raider from the flanks, his acceleration and eye for an opening being particularly effective in his first season, when he scored eight League goals in 36 matches. A player with experience in all four divisions of the League, he missed only one match in Reading's Third Division South Championship side of 1925–26. Later with Derby County he scored five goals in the same number of matches in 1929–30 when the Rams were runners-up for the First Division Championship.

ROCA, Carlos Jose

Midfield

Born: Manchester, 4 September 1984.
Career: OLDHAM ATHLETIC trainee. Carlisle United June 2004. Northwich Victoria loan February 2005, permanent July 2005. Stalybridge Celtic August 2007. Altrincham February 2008.

■ Diminutive teenage midfielder 'Rocky'

Roca was given an early opportunity at senior level, and it was something of a sink-or-swim opportunity for the tricky youngster. He was one of two teenagers who made their debuts against Brighton in August 2003, Athletic's ranks being depleted by the wholesale exodus of senior players in the wake of the financial crisis that threatened the very existence of the club.

ROCASTLE, Craig Aaron

Midfield

Born: Lewisham, 17 August 1981.
Career: Gravesend & Northfleet. Ashford Town loan November 2001. Kingstonian December 2001. Ford United loan October 2002. Slough Town February 2003. Chelsea September 2003. Barnsley loan February 2004. Lincoln City loan March 2004. Hibernian loan August 2004. Sheffield Wednesday February 2005. Yeovil Town loan March 2006. OLDHAM ATHLETIC July 2006. Port Vale June 2007. Gillingham loan January 2008.

■ A cousin of the late David Rocastle of Arsenal and England fame, Craig made a relatively late start in League football. He first appeared regularly with Sheffield Wednesday and although he was involved in the first-team squad at Boundary Park throughout 2006–07, he was not fully established at any point. Wellens and McDonald providing stiff competition throughout the course of the season. Although contracted for a further year Rocastle was allowed to join Port Vale on a free transfer, and was followed to Vale Park within a matter of days by Paul Edwards.

ROLLO, James Shepherd

Goalkeeper

Born: Kildonan, Arran, Scotland, 16 November 1937.
Career: Blairgowrie Juniors. Jeanfield Swifts. Hibernian c.1954. Poole Town 1958. OLDHAM ATHLETIC May 1960. Southport July 1963. Bradford City July 1964. Scarborough July 1966 to 1968.

■ Born one of twins, Jim Rollo assisted Poole Town when stationed locally during his National Service. He joined the Latics at the close of season 1959–60, and was first-choice goalkeeper as the

new season opened. A cool and alert goalkeeper, Rollo starred in an eight-match run of League victories in mid-season, but in the 1962–63 promotion season he was restricted to 10 senior appearances when Johnny Bollands dominated the position. In 1989 he was involved in a horrific accident when a forklift truck that he was learning to drive fell onto him. He had to have his right leg amputated but, some three years later, he had recovered sufficiently to be able to take up scouting duties for Liverpool, mainly in the Highland League.

ROOKE, William

Left-half

Career: Stockport County 1903–04. Bristol East August 1904. OLDHAM ATHLETIC May 1905 to 1906.

■ In addition to his four appearances in the FA Cup, Billy Rooke played in 21 of the season's 38 Lancashire Combination A Division fixtures. His season ended prematurely on 27 January 1905 when he suffered a serious leg injury in the second half of the match against Blackburn Rovers reserves.

ROQUE, Miguel Farrero 'Miki'

Defender

Born: Tremp, Catalonia, 8 August 1988.
Career: Lleida, Spain. Liverpool August 2006. OLDHAM ATHLETIC loan March 2007. Xerezcd, Spain, loan 2007.

■ Teenage central defender Miki Roque sampled League football for the first time in Athletic's colours. A late replacement for Gary McDonald from the bench, Roque began on a winning note in the 1–0 home victory against promotion rivals Yeovil

Town. His Liverpool debut, again from the bench, was rather more prestigious as it came in a European Cup group match against Galatasaray in Turkey.

ROSCOE, Jack Houghton

Centre-forward

Born: Oldham, 28 January 1906.
Died: Oldham, 1969.
Career: Werneth Athletic. Witton Albion February 1927. OLDHAM ATHLETIC amateur. Mossley July 1928. OLDHAM ATHLETIC professional May 1931. Chester May 1932. Macclesfield Town October 1932. Hyde United 1934. Mossley August 1938.

■ 'A centre-forward showing a happy disposition to take the short route to goal and to shoot promptly.' So ran one correspondent's view of Jack Roscoe in 1931. Certainly his eight goals in 21 matches was a creditable effort, but his zestful approach and wholehearted efforts lacked ball control and subtlety. He prospered in non-League circles, most notably with Macclesfield Town in 1932–33, his 32 goals for them being a major contribution to their winning the

Championship of the Cheshire League. Lunchtimes at the Dee Mill at Shaw, where the author worked as a clerk in the late 1950s, usually included a scratch football match in the mill yard. A regular and enthusiastic participant was Jack Roscoe, despite his 50-plus years.

ROSS, Alan

Goalkeeper

Born: Ellesmere Port, 17 February 1933.
Career: An amateur throughout, with: Bishop Auckland. OLDHAM ATHLETIC September 1956. West Bromwich Albion February 1957. Formby. Southport May 1957. Blackburn Rovers August 1957. Accrington Stanley March 1958. Rochdale February 1959. OLDHAM ATHLETIC February 1959. Wigan Rovers 1959.

■ Alan Ross remained in the unpaid ranks throughout his playing career. He was working as a Civil Servant in Liverpool during his first spell at Boundary Park, but he later spent 21 years in Canada, lecturing at Newfoundland University. During that time he coached the national Youth team and became assistant coach to the Canadian national team.

ROUND, Elijah

Goalkeeper

Born: Stoke-on-Trent, 1882.
Career: Mexborough West End July 1902. Barnsley May 1904. OLDHAM ATHLETIC March 1908. Manchester United May 1909. Worksop Town December 1910. Mexborough 1911–12. Castleford Town May 1913. Wartime guest with Barnsley.

■ Signed following the sine die

suspension of goalkeeper Bob Hewitson, Elijah Round arrived at Boundary Park with the experience of 46 League and Cup appearances for Barnsley. He was also a total abstainer and non-smoker, and an altogether more circumspect character than his disgraced predecessor. Round stepped straight into Athletic's promotion challenge, and despite winning four and drawing three of their last eight matches the team failed narrowly, finishing third in Division Two. At the outset of the following season a hand injury, sustained during training, let in Howard Matthews whose outstanding displays ensured that he retained the position.

ROWLEY, Henry Bowater

Forward

Born: Bilston, Staffordshire, 23 January 1904.
Career: Bilston United. Walsall Wood. Burton Town 1926. Bilston United September 1926. Southend United trial November 1926. Bilston United December 1926. Shrewsbury Town February 1927. Manchester United May 1928, fee £100. Manchester City December 1931, in part exchange for Bill Ridding. OLDHAM ATHLETIC loan February 1933, permanent August 1933. Manchester United December 1934, fee £1,375. Burton Town player-manager July 1937, manager February 1938. Gillingham May 1938.

■ Inside-forward Harry Rowley originally arrived at Boundary Park on loan from Manchester City along with Jimmy Naylor, and the subsequent improvement in the side led to a successful fight against relegation. A

dire financial situation led to his transfer to Manchester United in December 1934, and Rowley's 19 goals in 37 matches helped United to win the Championship of Division Two in 1935–36.

RUSH, Matthew James

Winger

Born: Dalston, East London, 6 August 1971.
Career: Vista FC. West Ham United associate schoolboy 1984, trainee July 1988, professional March 1990. Cambridge United loan March 1993. Swansea City loan January 1994. Norwich City August 1995, fee £330,000. Northampton Town loan October 1996 and again in December 1996. OLDHAM ATHLETIC March 1997, fee £165,000, retired due to injury September 1998.

■ At the outset of his career, Matthew Rush impressed as a speedy wingman or wide midfield player with two good feet, the ability to go past defenders and useful aerial ability. All of which earned him four Under-21 international caps with the Republic of Ireland. Sadly, his time with Athletic was one long struggle for form and fitness, his problems dating back to a cruciate knee ligament operation some two years earlier. Following enforced retirement, Rush graduated with a degree in sports development from the University of East London.

RYAN, John Bernard

Left-back/Midfield

Born: Ashton-under-Lyne, 18 February 1962. Career: Mancunian Boys. OLDHAM ATHLETIC apprentice June 1978, Seattle Sounders, US, loan March–August 1979. OLDHAM ATHLETIC professional February 1980. Seattle Sounders, US, loan March–August 1980. Newcastle United August 1983, fee £235,000. Sheffield Wednesday September 1984, fee £40,000 plus Pat Heard. OLDHAM ATHLETIC August 1985, fee £25,000. Mansfield Town October 1987, fee £25,000. Chesterfield June 1989, fee £12,500 plus Steve Prindiville. Rochdale July 1991. Bury December 1993. Stalybridge Celtic July 1994. Radcliffe Borough August 1996, subsequently a director of the club from 1998.

■ Towards the end of his second season

of first-team football with the Latics, curly-haired left-back John Ryan was capped by England Under-21 against Hungary at St James' Park, Newcastle. Some four months later Newcastle United paid £235,000 to take the skilful, ball-playing defender to Tyneside, and in 1984 he appeared in 22 League matches as the Kevin Keegan-inspired Magpies won promotion to the First Division. A brief stay with Sheffield Wednesday preceded his return to Boundary Park, still at only 23 years of age. Sadly, his second spell with Athletic proved totally unrewarding. A double fracture of his left leg in a pre-season friendly at Tranmere Rovers restricted him to just one appearance in 1986–87 in which he was substituted at half-time having sustained a knee injury. John's brother David was a goalkeeper who appeared in League football with Port Vale and Southport.

SALLEY, George

Centre-half

Born: Newcastle upon Tyne, 1886.
Career: Wallsend Park Villa. OLDHAM ATHLETIC December 1910. Southport Central April 1912. Hurst November 1913 to 1914.

■ Strapping Northumbrian George Salley made a useful debut in a 1–0 win at Preston North End in September 1911. Although his robust approach was criticised, he was praised for his headwork and tackling. As understudy to club captain David Walders he was given few senior opportunities.

SALT, Phillip Thomas

Midfield

Born: Oldham, 2 March 1979.
Career: Chadderton Strikers. Ashton United Boys. OLDHAM ATHLETIC trainee August 1995, professional July 1997. Leigh RMI loan August–October 2001. Scarborough February 2002. Leigh RMI August 2002. Hyde United.

■ A member of Athletic's School of Excellence from the age of 11, midfielder Phil Salt was given his League debut at 18 years of age, but the ultimate goal of regular League football proved elusive. In August 2001 he requested a transfer and the following February joined Scarborough, along with Ryan Sugden, bringing the Conference club's quota of ex-Latics players at that time to four, following the earlier transfers of Mark Hotte and Paul Shepherd.

SANOKHO, Amadou

Midfield

Born: France, 1 September 1975.
Career: Nantes, France. Modena, Italy. Rondinella, Italy. Sanguistese, Italy. Burnley September 2004. OLDHAM ATHLETIC March–May 2005.

■ An imposing figure at 6ft 3in and built to match, Sanokho nevertheless failed to make the grade in English football. One start and three substitute appearances for Burnley preceded his free transfer to Athletic where he was restricted to one appearance from the bench against Sheffield Wednesday in the 1–1 draw at Boundary Park in April 2005.

SAWBRIDGE, John 'Jack'

Goalkeeper

Born: Wigan, 20 September 1920.
Died: Southport, 29 January 1984.
Career: King George V School. Crossens FC. OLDHAM ATHLETIC amateur June, professional September 1945 to December 1947. Chorley. Crossens FC. Skelmersdale United December 1948. Crossans FC.

■ In the days when goalkeepers were still occasionally referred to as 'custodians', Jack Sawbridge was a typical example, clad in the obligatory green woollen polo-necked sweater and with his corn-coloured hair hidden under a flat cap. Sawbridge turned professional at Boundary Park while serving in the RAF. In the final season of regional football, 1945–46, he had a lengthy run of first-team football, invariably showing sound judgement, an ability to field the ball smartly and clear his lines effectively. When normal peacetime football resumed, however, his role became that of a reliable second string to Bill Harris and later to Brendan McManus.

SCHOFIELD, Fred

Half-back

Born: Greenfield, Oldham, 15 September 1912.
Died: Greenfield, Oldham, 29 August 1975.
Career: Crompton Albion. New Mills FC. OLDHAM ATHLETIC amateur May, professional August 1933. Retired in May 1936 to join Oldham Police Force.

■ A strong-tackling, big-hearted left-half with an immense capacity for work.

Fred Schofield was attracting attention from more prominent clubs in 1935–36 when he took the surprising decision to retire from the game and join Oldham Police. He gained promotion during his time in the force, but after the war turned to industry and was secretary to a local firm. A man of many talents, Schofield was an accomplished pianist who gave radio recitals.

SCHOFIELD, Graham

Centre-half

Born: Manchester, 18 December 1950.
Career: Brookdale FC. OLDHAM ATHLETIC December 1968. Mossley 1972, retired due to injury in 1975.

■ A reserve centre-half during three seasons with Athletic, Graham Schofield suffered a broken leg in his last season at Boundary Park. He suffered even worse luck after joining Mossley, and by August 1974 he had been sidelined twice with fractured legs. He was widely rated as the

best centre-half in the Northern Premier League but he broke his leg yet again in 1975. Athletic visited Mossley in May 1975 to play in a benefit match for their injury-prone former player.

SCHOFIELD, Malcolm

Goalkeeper

Born: Failsworth, 8 October 1918.
Died: Truro, Cornwall, March 1985.
Career: Failsworth United Dairies FC. Newton Heath Loco. Newton Heath Athletic. OLDHAM ATHLETIC November 1937 to May 1947.

■ Malcolm Schofield's League debut came almost 10 years after he had first joined Athletic as a 19-year-old. World War Two was responsible for much of the delay, of course, his service as a sergeant gunnery instructor in the RAF taking him as far afield as Cairo. In a reserve team match against Rochdale reserves on 30 May 1947 Schofield had the misfortune to sustain a broken leg. It was very much a case of adding injury to insult as, in the previous month, the unfortunate goalkeeper had been advised that he could leave Athletic on a free transfer.

SCHOLES, Robert

Forward

Born: Higginshaw, Oldham, 9 June 1903.
Died: Oldham, 7 September 1987.
Career: OLDHAM ATHLETIC amateur trial August 1923. Glossop FC. OLDHAM ATHLETIC professional October 1924. Walsall June 1926. Mid Rhondda September 1927. Hollingworth FC. Hurst

FC September 1929. Stalybridge Celtic October 1930. Mossley 1935. Accrington Stanley trial August 1935. Ashton National October 1935. Crompton Albion reinstated amateur September 1936.

■ Bob Scholes possessed a fine turn of speed and was an extremely adaptable player. His five first-team appearances all came in 1924–25 when he occupied three different positions in the forward line. Walsall fielded him at outside-left in the opening matches of season 1926–27, but he spent much of the season on the other wing in their reserves. In May 1986, 82-year-old Bob admitted that he was not a great fan of today's football, commenting 'If they had to head the leather ball that we had, they would end up in hospital.'

SCHOLFIELD, Jack

Centre-forward

Born: Todmorden, 8 September 1902.
Died: Todmorden, 1979.
Career: Portsmouth Rovers (Lancashire). Aberdare Athletic August 1922. Atherton 1923–24. Lancaster Town July 1924. Barrow August 1925. OLDHAM ATHLETIC December 1925. Lancaster Town March 1927. Middlewich August 1927. Chester November 1928. Llandudno. Oakhill United, Todmorden amateur October 1932. Bourillion, Todmorden amateur September 1933.

■ Centre-forward Jack Scholfield starred in Lancashire Combination football with Atherton (27 goals in 1923–24) and Lancaster Town (27 again in 1924–25).

Stepping up to League level, he scored in each of his initial two outings with Barrow in the Third Division North. On joining Athletic in mid-season, however, he found the step up to Division Two a difficult transition, remaining for the most part a reserve-team player throughout his spell at Boundary Park.

SCOTT, James

Left-half

Born: Hetton-le-Hole, 7 September 1934. Career: Durham County Schoolboys. Burnley September 1951. OLDHAM ATHLETIC June 1961, retired June 1964.

■ A star in schoolboy football, Jim Scott scored a hat-trick for England Schoolboys against Scotland in the first Schools International played at Wembley

Stadium. In professional football, however, he was unable to establish himself beyond reserve team football with Burnley, although he did captain the Clarets' reserves to the Central League title in 1961. In three seasons at Boundary Park he was a cool, commanding defender who rarely made a mistake. He appeared in 29 League matches in the 1962–63 promotion season, but in the following term he appeared only four times and announced his retirement at the end of the season.

SCOTT, Robert

Inside-forward

Born: Bellshill, Lanarkshire 20 May 1930. Career: Stonehouse Violet. Burnbank Athletic. Dunfermline Athletic 1951. Alloa Athletic 1953–54. Accrington Stanley September 1954. Wrexham July 1959. OLDHAM ATHLETIC October 1959. Nelson June 1960. Bacup Borough.

■ One of many Scottish players recruited by Accrington Stanley's manager Walter Galbraith in the 1950s, Bert Scott spent just under five years with Stanley, scoring 43 goals in 162 League and Cup matches. In spells with Wrexham and Athletic in season 1959–60 he made little impact. Scott played only twice for Wrexham and failed to establish a regular place in a very poor Athletic side that finished 23rd in Division Four.

SCOTT, Robert 'Rob'

Defender

Born: Epsom, 15 August 1973. Career: Sutton United. Sheffield United August 1993, fee £20,000. Scarborough loan March 1995. Northampton Town loan November 1995. Fulham January 1996, fee £30,000. Carlisle United loan August 1998. Rotherham United November 1998, fee £50,000. OLDHAM ATHLETIC July 2005. Macclesfield Town September 2006. Halifax Town August 2007.

■ After just short of 200 appearances for Rotherham United, Rob Scott joined forces with his former Rotherham manager Ronnie Moore at Boundary Park. He made a bright start, scoring against Swindon Town in August, but a shoulder injury that required surgery ended his season prematurely in February. Out of favour under new manager John Sheridan, terms were agreed to cancel the remainder of his contract and the experienced utility player moved on to Macclesfield Town.

SCRINE, Francis Henry 'Frank'

Inside-forward

Born: Swansea, 9 January 1925. Died: Swansea, 5 October 2001. Career: Swansea Schoolboys. Swansea Town amateur May 1943, professional March 1944. OLDHAM ATHLETIC October 1953, fee £3,750. Llanelly 1956. Milford United January 1957. Ammanford. Pembroke Dock.

■ Frank Scrine represented Swansea Schoolboys and later the Royal Navy at rugby union, but made his name as a footballer. He spent 10 years with Swansea Town, winning a Third Division South Championship medal in 1949 and two Wales caps in season 1949–50. A strong running inside-forward with deceptive footwork and a good first-time shot, his best season at Boundary Park was 1954–54 when he appeared in 43 matches and scored 10 goals.

SEDDON, Roger Cowburn

Outside-left

Born: Bradley Fold, Bolton, 19 November 1903. Died: Blackburn, 14 May 1955.

Career: Black Lane Temperance 1923. Manchester United trial. Leyland January 1925. Congleton Town 1925. Chorley trial September-October 1925. OLDHAM ATHLETIC October 1925. Southport May 1926. Winsford United March 1927. Breightmet United September 1929. Winsford United November 1930. Rossendale United Sept 1932.

■ Roger Seddon made only one League appearance for Athletic, in a 2–1 defeat at Fulham on 23 January 1926. Transferred to Southport in the close season, Seddon made six League appearances and scored one goal but was released before the end of the season and returned to non-League football.

SERRANT, Carl

Left-back

Born: Bradford, 12 September 1975.
Career: OLDHAM ATHLETIC trainee, professional July 1994. Newcastle United July 1998, fee £500,000. Bury loan February 1999. Retired, due to injury, in January 2001. Bradford Park Avenue 2003. Droylsden. Farsley Celtic 2004. Crystal Palace coach November 2007.

■ A speedy and versatile defender with plenty of confidence and talent, Carl Serrant quickly attracted the attention of bigger clubs after a string of impressive displays at both club and representative levels. Sadly, his fledgling career was beset by injuries and his premature retirement was announced in January 2001. After studying for a sports science degree he returned to the game at non-League level and in May 2007 was a member of the Farsley Celtic side that won promotion to the Blue Star Premier League.

SEYMOUR, Thomas Gilbert

Full-back

Born: Yarm-on-Tees, 2 May 1906.
Died: Shrewsbury, 1983.
Career: Langley Park. Crook Town. Seaversham United. Bury April 1924. Swansea Town May 1927, fee £250. Connah's Quay December 1928. OLDHAM ATHLETIC May 1929. Shrewsbury Town June 1936, trainer 1939, chief scout and physiotherapist 1967.

■ Tommy Seymour's patience was finally

rewarded with a regular run in the first team in 1932–33. Finally finding his best position at right-back, he played in 101 out of a possible 102 matches up to the close of 1934–35. In his final season Billy Hilton and Beau Ratcliffe were the usual backs and Seymour left in the close season to join Shrewsbury Town. After three years as a player he was appointed trainer. After completing 30 years of service he was appointed chief scout and club physiotherapist.

SHACKLETON, Alan

Centre-forward

Born: Padiham, 3 February 1934.
Career: Burnley amateur. Bolton Wanderers amateur 1953–54. Burnley professional May 1954. Leeds United

October 1958, fee £8,000. Everton September 1959. Nelson 1960. OLDHAM ATHLETIC August 1961, fee £1,200. Tonbridge August 1962.

■ Six goals in his first seven matches was Alan Shackleton's dream start with Athletic. Despite his scoring burst (which included a hat-trick against Workington in his second match), Athletic made a very poor start to season 1961–62 and he lost his place to Bert Lister. Shackleton's career appearance record was modest, totalling only 97 League matches for four clubs. His return of 51 goals, however, illustrated that he was far from deficient as a goalscorer.

SHADBOLT, Joseph Arthur

Inside-forward

Born: Warrington, 1 August 1874.
Died: Southport, 1967.
Career: Birkdale South End. Southport Central April 1893. OLDHAM ATHLETIC May 1905. Hyde United 1909.

■ The scorer of Athletic's first-ever goal in an FA Cup tie, against Ashton Town on 7 October 1905, Joe Shadbolt was one of the team's most effective forwards in two seasons of Lancashire Combination football, scoring 39 goals in 63 matches. He was approaching veteran stage when he made his League debut for Athletic in December 1907 and scored in a 4–1 home win against Gainsborough Trinity. Throughout his Athletic career, Shadbolt trained at Southport. When the club insisted that he should live and train in Oldham he refused and left Boundary Park. He was for many years a painter and decorator in Southport.

SHARP, Arthur Alan

Inside-forward

Born: Nottingham, 9 July 1905.
Died: Carlisle, June 1991.
Career: Loughborough Corinthians. Mansfield Town February 1926. Blackpool July 1927. Reading May 1928. West Ham United March 1929. Newark Town September 1929. Carlisle United May 1930. Bristol City June 1932. Aldershot May 1933. OLDHAM ATHLETIC August 1934. Shrewsbury Town July 1935. Darlington August 1936. Shrewsbury Town February 1937. Scarborough August 1937.

■ Arthur Sharp was a Midland Combination Cup winner with Mansfield Town in 1927. He began in senior football with Blackpool in 1927 but it was not until 1930 that he made his first League appearance for Carlisle United in the Third Division North. Two seasons in the Southern section preceded his transfer to Athletic where he was unable to break into a side that finished 21st in Division Two and were relegated. Sharp's nomadic League career totalled 138 League matches and 29 goals.

SHARP, George Henry

Outside-left

Born: Bedlington, 20 July 1935.
Career: Darlington amateur May 1957. OLDHAM ATHLETIC amateur November 1957 to May 1958.

■ Amateur outside-left George Sharp lived up to his name by scoring within 10 seconds of the kick-off in his reserve team debut, he also added a second in a 7–1 win against Clitheroe. Despite the bright start he played only once in the League, Eric Over dominating the outside-left berth following his mid-season signing from Barrow.

SHARP, Graeme Marshall

Forward

Born: Glasgow, 16 October 1960.
Career: Eastercraigs FC. Dumbarton November 1978, fee £750. Everton April 1980, fee £120,000. OLDHAM ATHLETIC July 1991, fee £500,000, player-manager November 1994, resigned February 1997. Bangor City manager May 1997.

■ Graeme Sharp had all the necessary qualities for his position as attack leader. He held the ball up well, was excellent in the air and was an all-round centre-forward, rather than an out-and-out marksman. In an 11-year stay with Everton he formed impressive striking partnerships with Andy Gray and later with Gary Lineker. Sharp won 12 full caps for Scotland and his domestic honours included two Football League Championships, the 1984 FA Cup Final victory against Watford and the European Cup-Winners' Cup success in 1985. In April 1989 he scored his 100th goal in English League football at Charlton Athletic, his final Everton figures being 158 goals in 425/21 League and Cup matches. Sharp completed his first season at Boundary Park with 15 goals in 48 League and Cup matches, his total including four goals against Luton Town in the 4–1 home win in April 1992. In January 1993 after an

unbroken run of 74 games he was relegated to the substitutes's bench and later in the same month underwent an operation to cure a disc problem. In the season that Sharp took over as player-manager from Joe Royle he played in only 11/3 matches and scored three goals, thereafter continuing solely as manager, assisted by a former Everton colleague, Colin Harvey.

SHARRATT, Harold

Goalkeeper

Born: Wigan, 16 December 1929.
Career: An amateur throughout with: Wigan Athletic. Blackpool March 1952. Bishop Auckland. OLDHAM ATHLETIC March 1956. Bishop Auckland. Nottingham Forest February 1957. Bishop Auckland.

■ One of the outstanding amateur goalkeepers of the 1950s, Harry Sharratt appeared for Bishop Auckland in three consecutive FA Amateur Cup winning sides and won four England Amateur caps. He helped Athletic out of a goalkeeping crisis following the transfer of Johnny Bollands to Sunderland and his debut at Derby County was also the first time that Athletic contested a League match under floodlights.

SHAW, George

Outside-right

Born: Hyde, Cheshire c.1887.
Career: Hyde 1906–07. Denton October 1907. Hyde August 1908. OLDHAM ATHLETIC December 1908, fee £100. Hyde September 1910. Denton November 1913.

■ Signed by Athletic at the mid-point of their second season as a Football League club, George Shaw replaced Frank Hesham at outside-right and an initial nine-match run included his only senior goal, the winner against Fulham at Boundary Park in March 1909. He was exclusively a reserve in 1909–10, a term in which new signing Tommy Broad made one short of maximum appearances for the season.

SHAW, George David

Forward

Born: Huddersfield, 11 October 1948.
Career: Huddersfield Town from school, professional January 1967. OLDHAM

ATHLETIC September 1969, in part exchange for Les Chapman. West Bromwich Albion March 1973, fee £77,000. OLDHAM ATHLETIC October 1975, retiring January 1978 due to a knee injury.

■ In two separate spells at Boundary Park David Shaw's electrifying pace, stamina and flair for goals made him a firm favourite. His excellent record with the Latics eventually brought a big money transfer to West Bromwich Albion, but he failed to find his best form at the Hawthorns and was welcomed back to Boundary Park after scoring just 17 League goals in 65/17 matches. Increasingly troubled by a knee injury in his second spell, he was forced to retire or risk more serious and permanent damage. Shaw played in contact lenses and was colour-blind, but it would be difficult to name a more popular and effective striker, particularly in season 1970–71 when his lethal partnership with Jim Fryatt won Athletic promotion from Division Four and scooped the Ford Sporting League's £70,000 first prize. As a child, Shaw's family home at Dalton was adjacent to the old Leeds Road ground of Huddersfield Town. His grandfather, David Steele, was a member of Town's famous triple-title winning side of the 1920s and later managed the club. David Shaw achieved his life's ambition when he pulled on the Town shirt for his debut in the old Second Division in April 1967, and he has remained a big Town fan to this day. His son, Graeme, starred in another sport, playing rugby league with Bradford and Oldham.

SHAW, John

Centre-half

Born: Oldham, 2 October 1916.
Died: Middleton, 22 October 1973.
Career: South Shore Wesleyans. Lytham December 1933. OLDHAM ATHLETIC March 1934. Mossley July 1936. Grimsby Town May 1937. Birmingham March 1939. Wartime guest with Nottingham Forest, Watford and Crewe Alexandra. Mossley July 1946 to May 1951.

■ Locally-born centre-half John Shaw spent two seasons in reserve at Boundary Park before refusing terms for season 1936–37. He spent a season with Mossley before resuming in League football with Grimsby Town. The outbreak of World War Two halted his progress with Birmingham after 11 League appearances in 1938–39 and he did not figure in post-war League football.

SHEFFIELD, Laurence Joseph

Centre-forward

Born: Swansea, 27 April 1939.
Career: Swansea Schoolboys. Bristol Rovers July 1956. Barry Town loan January 1959. Newport County April 1962. Doncaster Rovers August 1965, fee £8,000 plus Alfred Hale. Norwich City November 1966, fee £15,000. Rotherham United August 1967, fee £17,000. OLDHAM ATHLETIC December 1967, fee £10,000. Luton Town July 1968. Doncaster Rovers October 1969. Peterborough United August 1970, fee £10,000. Doncaster Rovers youth coach.

■ A widely-travelled, sharp-shooting centre-forward. Laurie Sheffield had already scored over 100 League goals when he joined Athletic to take over as attack leader following Bob Ledger's transfer to Mansfield Town. Ironically, just 24 hours after being placed on the transfer list in early April 1968, he eased Athletic's relegation worries by scoring twice in a 4–1 win against Stockport County. In the close season he was on the move again, and his career finally spanned nine League clubs and 132 goals in 274/4 matches.

SHERIDAN, Darren Stephen

Midfield

Born: Manchester, 8 December 1967.
Career: Leeds United apprentice 1984. Winsford United. Barnsley August 1993, fee £10,000. Wigan Athletic July 1999. OLDHAM ATHLETIC July 2001. Clyde June 2004. St Johnstone July 2005. Barrow January 2007, joint manager 2007.

■ Darren Sheridan, brother of John, was a relative latecomer to League football with Barnsley, but in six years at Oakwell he was a regular first team man, appearing in 167/28 League and Cup matches and scoring seven goals. In two seasons with Wigan Athletic he figured in consecutive Play-off semi-finals but finished on the losing side on both occasions. Released after 56/10 League and Cup appearances and three goals he was reunited with his elder brother when Andy Ritchie brought him to Boundary Park. At either left-back or left-midfield Darren was a combative, all-action performer whose enthusiasm and will to

win made him a great crowd favourite, but his vigorous approach earned the displeasure of match referees on numerous occasions during his three years at Boundary Park.

SHERIDAN, John Joseph

Midfield

Born: Stretford, Manchester, 1 October 1964.

Career: Manchester City associate schoolboy. Leeds United March 1982. Nottingham Forest August 1989, fee £650,000. Sheffield Wednesday November 1989, fee £500,000. Birmingham City loan February 1996. Bolton Wanderers November 1996, fee £180,000. Huddersfield Town trial August 1998. Doncaster Rovers August 1998. OLDHAM ATHLETIC October 1998, player-coach September 2001, joint caretaker manager December 2003, assistant manager March 2004, youth coach November 2004, reserve-team coach, manager June 2006.

■ A star of two World Cups and three domestic Finals, John Sheridan began as a schoolboy with Manchester City but made his debut in League football with Leeds United in November 1982. Qualifying through his parents to represent the Republic of Ireland, he was capped 34 times, with his full international debut coming in March 1988. A very brief and unrewarding spell with Nottingham Forest preceded his move to Sheffield Wednesday where he was a Football League Cup winner in 1991, scoring the only goal goal after 38

minutes to beat the red-hot favourites, Manchester United. In season 1996–97 he added a Division One Championship medal to his collection as Bolton Wanderers took the title by the extraordinary margin of 18 points over runners-up Barnsley. Freed the following summer, he was operating in the Conference with Doncaster Rovers when Andy Ritchie brought him to Boundary Park. A play-maker of the highest calibre who rarely wasted a ball, Sheridan was a leader on the pitch and has continued to successfully guide Athletic in the managerial role.

SHIMWELL, Edmond

Full-back

Born: Birchover, Derbyshire, 27 February 1920.
Died: Blackpool, 3 October 1988.
Career: Wirksworth. Sheffield United amateur May 1938, professional January 1939. Blackpool December 1946, fee £7,000. OLDHAM ATHLETIC May 1957. Burton Albion July 1958, retired December 1958.

■ A strong and challenging full-back with a powerful and prompt clearance, England international Eddie Shimwell became the first full-back to score in a Wembley FA Cup Final when his powerfully-struck 14th minute spot-kick gave Blackpool the lead in 1948, although Manchester United ran out winners by 4–2. Shimwell appeared in each of Blackpool's three FA Cup Finals, finally picking up a winner's medal in the

'Matthews Final' of 1953. He had appeared in 324 League and Cup matches at the time of his free transfer to the Latics, but by this time in his 37th year he lost his place after appearing in the first five matches of 1957–58 and reappeared only twice. He demonstrated, however, that his prowess from the penalty spot remained undimmed when he scored a hat-trick of penalties for Athletic reserves at Nelson in a 7–0 win on 12 April 1958.

SHIPMAN, Thomas Eric Rollerson

Left-back

Born: Langwith, 4 August 1910.
Died: Langwith, 5 July 1972.
Career: Ripley Town amateur June 1927. Shirebrook December 1929. Birmingham May 1931. Blackpool May 1933. Reading June 1937. OLDHAM ATHLETIC June 1938. Mossley January 1946.

■ A strong-tackling, dour full-back whose hefty build was thrown unstintingly into the fray, Tommy Shipman was a mainstay of Athletic's team for several seasons, although the majority of his appearances were made in wartime football. He suffered a broken leg at Huddersfield Town in February 1945 and did not reappear when normal League football resumed in 1946–47. He played only twice for Mossley before retiring to become licensee of the Willow Bank Hotel in Oldham.

SHORT, Maurice

Goalkeeper

Born: Middlesbrough, 29 December 1949.
Career: Park End FC. Middlesbrough apprentice August 1966, professional February 1967. OLDHAM ATHLETIC June 1970. Grimsby Town loan January–March 1971. Whitby Town.

■ Maurice Short spent an unhappy season at Boundary Park, losing his first-team spot after just seven outings to Barry Gordine, who was in turn deposed by new signing Harry Dowd. Short conceded four goals at Grimsby Town on his debut, but in mid-season was loaned to the Mariners and played in 10 Division Four matches in a two-month loan spell before being released by Athletic.

SHUFFLEBOTHAM, John

Centre-half

Born: Macclesfield c.1888.
Died: Crewe, 1954.
Career: Old Mill FC. Small Heath March 1905. OLDHAM ATHLETIC June 1907. Portsmouth May 1909. Southport Central 1911, fee £15.

■ A reserve defender with Athletic in their first two seasons in the Football League, Jack Shufflebotham deputised in six matches for club skipper David Walders in 1908–09, after appearing just once the previous season. He found more opportunities with Portsmouth, playing in 21 Southern League matches and four

Cup ties. By October 1914 he had retired from the game and was working as a timber merchant's agent in the Birmingham district.

SIEVWRIGHT, George Edgar Smollett

Wing-half

Born: Broughty Ferry, Dundee, 10 September 1937.

Career: Broughty Athletic. Dundee United 1961. OLDHAM ATHLETIC June 1963, fee £500. Tranmere Rovers June 1964. Fee £1,000. Rochdale July 1965. Macclesfield Town August 1966. Mossley player-manager December 1972, manager 1973–74 season. Later managed Stalybridge Celtic.

■ Craggy Scot George Sievwright gave up his job as a baker to become a full-time professional with Dundee United, making his senior debut in October 1961. A hard-working, tenacious ball-winner from left-half, he was a commanding figure in Athletic's middle line during 1963–64, but was somewhat surprisingly transferred to Tranmere Rovers after just one season. The highlight of his subsequent spell in non-League football was a Wembley appearance in May 1970 when Macclesfield Town beat Telford United 2–0 in the FA Challenge Trophy Final, to become the first winners of the trophy.

SINCLAIR, Nicholas John Thomas

Right-back

Born: Manchester, 3 January 1960.
Career: Manchester Schoolboys. OLDHAM ATHLETIC June 1978. Wolverhampton Wanderers loan September 1984. Tranmere

Rovers October 1984 to May 1986. Chorlton Town 1989–90.

■ Curly-haired and sporting a moustache, Nicky Sinclair was a smoothly accelerating defender, at his best in a role that would be described as a wing-back in today's parlance. Sadly, his time at Boundary Park was cruelly hit by injuries, restricting him to just 79/2 appearances during his six years as an Athletic player.

SINKINSON, Frederick

Outside-right

Born: Middleton, c.1916.
Career: Buxton. Manchester North End. OLDHAM ATHLETIC amateur June 1937 to April 1938.

■ A fast-moving amateur outside-right, Freddie Sinkinson employed direct methods with some success for Athletic reserves during season 1937–38. His

return of 11 goals in 33 Lancashire Combination matches was a very creditable return for a wingman, but in terms of senior action he remained third choice behind Arthur Jones and Tommy Butler.

SINNOTT, Lee

Central-defender

Born: Pelsall, Staffordshire, 12 July 1965. Career: Rushall Olympic. Walsall apprentice September 1981, professional November 1982. Watford September 1983, fee £100,000. Bradford City July 1987, fee £130,000. Crystal Palace August 1991, fee £300,000. Bradford City loan December 1993, permanent January 1994, fee £50,000. Huddersfield Town December 1994, fee £105,000. OLDHAM ATHLETIC July 1997, fee £30,000. Bradford City loan March 1998. Scarborough June 1999. Leeds United Academy coach. Farsley Celtic manager June 2003. Port Vale manager November 2007.

■ Lee Sinnott captained the England Youth Team, played in League football at 16 years of age and was an FA Cup finalist with Watford at just 18 years of age. A tall, fair-haired central-defender, and long throw exponent, he joined Athletic to replace Craig Fleming and was the fifth Athletic player to join forces with manager Neil Warnock for a second time. A calf injury sidelined Sinnott for three and a half months in his first season and he was unable to regain a first-team place when recovered. It appeared that he would be leaving at the end of his first season, but a change of manager – Andy Ritchie replacing Neil Warnock – gave him an unexpected opportunity to continue his career, which eventually totalled 475/12 League appearances and 12 goals. In 2007 Sinnott guided Farsley Celtic to promotion to the Blue Star Premier League, assisted by a number of former Athletic favourites including Paul Rickers, Carl Serrant and Martin Pemberton.

SKIPPER, Peter Dennis

Central-defender

Born: Hull, 11 April 1958. Career: Hull Schoolboys. Carlisle United trial 1978. Hull City apprentice September 1978, professional February 1979. Scunthorpe United loan February 1980. Darlington May 1980. Hull City August 1982, fee £10,000. OLDHAM ATHLETIC October 1988, fee £40,000. Walsall July 1989. Wrexham non-contract September 1991. Wigan Athletic non-contract October 1991. Stafford Rangers August 1992. Wigan Athletic November 1992 to 1994.

■ A large proportion of Peter Skipper's career was spent in two separate spells with Hull City, and during his second spell the Tigers rose from Division Four to Division Two and were finalists in the Associate Members Cup. His total of 264/1 League appearances in this spell included a run of 149 consecutive matches. Athletic paid £40,000 for his transfer, which was rushed through one minute before the 5pm deadline, enabling him to make his debut the following day against Chelsea. While not the quickest of defenders, he provided a welcome touch of solidarity and was unfortunate to lose out when Athletic captured Welsh international Andy Holden from Wigan Athletic in January 1989. Skipper's senior career concluded at the age of 36, with career aggregate figures of 575/6 League appearances and 30 goals.

SLATER, Percival

Left-back

Born: Adlington, 1879. Career: Blackburn Rovers May 1899. Chorley August 1899. Manchester City May 1900. Bury June 1904. OLDHAM ATHLETIC May 1906, retired May 1907, but later noted to be assisting Chorley on amateur forms in season 1909–10.

■ One of five new players signed during manager David Ashworth's first week in office, Percy Slater appeared in 20 Lancashire Combination matches as Athletic took the League title on goal average from Liverpool reserves. Slater also played in all the season's FA Cup matches, the run ending with a 1–0 defeat by Liverpool at Boundary Park, a game watched by 21,538 spectators who paid a little over £619 at the gate. In the close season Slater retired from professional football to concentrate on business interests.

SLEEUWENHOEK, John Cornelius

Centre-half

Born: Wednesfield, 26 February 1944. Died: Birmingham, June 1989. Career: Aston Villa amateur June 1959, apprentice May 1960, professional March 1961. Birmingham City November 1967, fee £45,000. Torquay United loan March 1971. OLDHAM ATHLETIC July 1971 to May 1972.

■ Capped by England at Schools, Youth and Under-21 levels, John Sleeuwenhoek made his League debut with Aston Villa in April 1961 at the age of 17. He completed 260 League and Cup matches and was a Football League Cup finalist in

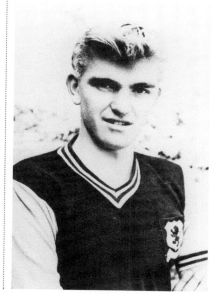

1963 before taking the short trip to Birmingham City. His move to Boundary Park proved unrewarding as he lost his place after just three early appearances, Dick Mulvaney retaining the centre-half berth for the rest of the season. The son of a Dutch parachute instructor, John Sleeuwenhoek died of a heart attack at the early age of 45. His son Kris was on the books of Wolverhampton Wanderers and Derby County without reaching senior level.

SMALLEY, Deane Alfie

Forward

Born: Chadderton, 5 September 1988.
Career: Our Lady's School (Royton). Middleton Colts. Oldham Schoolboys. North Side FC. OLDHAM ATHLETIC trainee July 2005, professional June 2007.

■ Following two substitute appearances in 2006–07, Deane Smalley has been involved in the majority of first-team matches in 2007–08. It has been a steep learning curve for the teenage striker, who scored 23 goals in 26 matches for Athletic's treble-winning youth team in 2006–07. Mainly appearing from the bench, he was unfortunate to damage ankle ligaments within 20 minutes when he made his first senior start in the Carling Cup tie at Burnley on 28 August. Quick and clever in possession with the ability to occupy central or wide right striking roles, Smalley has great enthusiasm and requires only a final polish to his finishing skills, so clinically exhibited in youth and reserve-team football.

SMALLEY, Leslie Wilfred

Outside-right

Born: Blackburn, 10 September 1911.
Died: Southampton, March 1983.
Career: Audley Range. Clitheroe 1931. OLDHAM ATHLETIC December 1931. Southport trial August 1933. Accrington Stanley trial September 1933. Hereford United October 1933. Clitheroe 1934. Morecambe. Moffatt's Works amateur February 1937.

■ Despite standing only 5ft 5in tall and weighing 9½st, Leslie Smalley appeared to have solved Athletic's problem outside-right position during the course of 14 matches and three goals in the latter stages of season 1931–32. The transfer of Freddie Worrall to Portsmouth in October of the same season had materially weakened Athletic's attack, but Smalley's inventive wing play helped steer the side clear of relegation. He was less successful in 1932–33 when a fractured leg sustained in a reserve match at Bradford Park Avenue eventually led to his release in the close season.

SMART, Allan Andrew Colin

Forward

Born: Perth, 8 July 1974.
Career: St Johnstone January 1991. Brechin City December 1991. Inverness Caledonian Thistle July 1993. Preston North End November 1994, fee £15,000. Carlisle United loan November 1995.

Northampton Town loan September 1996. Carlisle United October 1996. Watford July 1998, fee £75,000. Hibernian loan August 2001. Stoke City loan 6 November 1998. OLDHAM ATHLETIC 30 November 2001, fee £225,000, contract cancelled May 2002. Dundee United June 2002. Crewe Alexandra August 2003. MK Dons July 2004. Bury July 2005. Portadown, Ireland, June 2006. Burscough, season-long loan July 2007.

■ Athletic invested their largest fee for four years when they signed Allan Smart from Watford. Despite getting off the mark with the only goal of the LDV Vans Trophy tie at Notts County on 4 December 2001, the speedy and combative striker took some time to settle at Boundary Park. He did, however, score four goals in three matches, against Peterborough United, Brentford and Colchester United in late February and early March. Sadly, two serious off-the-field incidents in December and April led to his dismissal by the club after just five months of a contract that was originally scheduled to run until the summer of 2005.

SMELT, Tom

Centre-forward

Born: Rotherham, 25 November 1900.
Died: Rotherham, 1980.
Career: Mexborough Town. Chesterfield Municipal August 1920. Rotherham Town December 1920. Burnley amateur January 1921. Wombwell June 1921. Accrington Stanley October 1922. Exeter City September 1924. Chesterfield June 1925. Morecambe August 1926. Manchester City

April 1927. OLDHAM ATHLETIC May 1928. Crewe Alexandra June 1930. Scunthorpe United August 1931. Rotherham United September 1932 to 1933.

■ Centre-forward Tom Smelt made his League debut with Accrington Stanley and in his first season of senior football scored 13 goals in 25 matches. Thereafter he did little of note until arriving at Crewe Alexandra where he scored 11 goals in 39 League matches. The younger brother of Burnley full-back Len Smelt, Tom was a talented cricketer and professional for Crompton CC in the Central Lancashire League in 1930.

SMITH, Gordon Duffield

Midfield

Born: Kilwinning, Ayrshire, 29 December 1954.
Career: Kilmarnock Star. Kilmarnock June 1971. Rangers August 1977, fee £65,000. Brighton & Hove Albion June 1980, fee £400,000. Rangers loan December 1982 to January 1983. Manchester City March 1984, fee £35,000. OLDHAM ATHLETIC loan January 1986, permanent February 1986, fee £5,000. Admira Wacker, Vienna, June 1986. FC Basle, Switzerland, August 1987. Stirling Albion August 1988. St Mirren assistant manager May 1991 to 1993.

■ Any neutral observer who saw Gordon Smith miss the proverbial 'sitter' in the last minute of extra-time in the 1983 FA Cup Final must have felt some sympathy for the luckless midfielder who looked odds-on to score the winner. In the event the match was drawn and Manchester United won the replay by four clear goals. Smith was on Manchester City's books when he joined Athletic, initially on loan,

in mid-season 1985–86. Despite not having played a full first-team game all season the 31-year-old had an excellent debut against Wimbledon; calm and confident in possession, he helped the Latics to their first victory in 12 matches. At the conclusion of his month's loan, Athletic paid a nominal £5,000 for his transfer and their improvement in results continued through to the end of the season. Capped by Scotland at Under-21 and Under-23 levels, Smith was a treble winner with Rangers in 1978, and won both the Scottish Cup and the League Cup the following year. He is currently chief executive of the Scottish Football Association.

SMITH, Ian Paul

Midfield

Born: Easington, 22 January 1976.
Career: Peterlee Schoolboys. Sheffield Wednesday associate schoolboy. Burnley trainee, signing professional July 1994. OLDHAM ATHLETIC loan September-October 2000. Torquay United trial. Hartlepool United November 2001. Sheffield Wednesday July 2003. Kidderminster Harriers July 2005. Alfreton Town January 2006.

■ Paul Smith spent a month on loan at Boundary Park after losing his first-team place with Burnley. Unfortunately, his loan spell was abruptly terminated when he fell down an open manhole and needed 12 stitches in his shin. Returning to Turf Moor he passed the milestone of 100 League appearances for the Clarets before being released on a free transfer in the close season.

SMITH, Joseph Barry

Centre-forward

Born: South Kirkby, 15 March 1934.
Died: New Zealand, February 2007.
Career: Bradford Park Avenue ground staff. Farsley Celtic. Leeds United October 1951. Bradford Park Avenue May 1955. Wrexham June 1957. Stockport County July 1958. Headington United 1959. OLDHAM ATHLETIC August 1960. Bangor City December 1960. Southport August 1961. Accrington Stanley October 1961.

■ Sharp shooting centre-forward Barry Smith scored 28 goals – including four hat-tricks – for Bradford Park Avenue in season 1955–56. Despite the excellent start and a career scoring record of 55 goals in 102 League appearances, Smith was only 26 years old when he played his last League match. This was his solitary appearance for Athletic against Gillingham in September 1960.

SMITH, Leslie

Right-half, later right-back

Born: Manchester, 2 October 1920.
Died: Hazel Grove, 6 December 2001.
Career: Stockport County amateur. Huddersfield Town March 1946. OLDHAM ATHLETIC July 1949 to June 1956.

■ A pre-war amateur with Stockport County, Les Smith was called up and saw army service as a sergeant in Egypt. He joined Huddersfield Town after demobilisation and had made 37 First Division appearances when Athletic signed him as a part-time professional. Mainly a right-half, Smith was a solid and consistent performer who made 41 appearances in the 1952–53 Third Division North Championship side. In the middle of season 1953–54 he was switched to right-back, where he remained until his retirement in June 1956.

SMITH, Norman Henry

Inside-forward

Born: Burton upon Trent, 27 January 1924.
Died: Burton upon Trent,, 10 January 2000.
Career: Accrington Stanley amateur October 1945, professional February 1946. OLDHAM ATHLETIC June 1948, fee £400. Congleton Town July 1949.

■ Inside-forward Norman Smith joined Accrington Stanley from services football. He was offered full-time terms but declined, preferring to complete his apprenticeship as a printer. A tall, hard-working forward with deft footwork, he had scored six goals in 39 League appearances when Athletic signed him in June 1948. He made his debut in an early season 6–0 defeat at Hull City and then spent the remainder of the season in the reserves.

SMITH, Raymond

Forward

Born: Portadown, Northern Ireland, 20 November 1950.
Career: Glenavon amateur. OLDHAM ATHLETIC from school, apprentice June 1966, professional January 1968 to May 1969.

■ Ray Smith captained Northern Ireland Schoolboys in matches against England and Scotland but he eventually became yet another Irish youngster who failed to make the grade after a fine start in junior football. In 1967–68 he scored 10 goals in 33 matches to help Athletic Reserves win the Lancashire Combination Division Two Championship, but he was never a serious contender for a place in the League side.

SMITH, Stanley James

Centre-forward

Born: Kidsgrove, 24 February 1931.
Career: Stoke City amateur. Port Vale May 1950. Crewe Alexandra July 1957. OLDHAM ATHLETIC March–June 1958,

fee £250. Witton Albion 1959. Macclesfield Town 1960–63. Stafford Rangers August 1963. Runcorn 1965. New Brighton 1965–66. Winsford United player-manager to October 1966. Eastwood, Hanley. Northwich Victoria. Sandbach Ramblers player-manager 1968. Kidsgrove Athletic player-manager 1970. Barnton manager 1976. Alsager Town manager 1977–82.

■ Stan Smith left Crewe Alexandra just prior to the transfer deadline in March of his first season at Gresty Road, joining an Athletic team scrapping to avoid the possibility of becoming founder members of Division Four. It was the final season of Third Division football played on a regional basis and Athletic narrowly failed to finish in the top half of the table. Stan Smith was one of six players released in the close season, along with manager Ted Goodier, as Athletic prepared for life in football's basement.

SMITH, Terence

Goalkeeper

Born: Runcorn, 16 September 1987.
Career: Norton Juniors. OLDHAM ATHLETIC trainee, professional July 2006. Southport loan March 2007, permanent July 2007.

■ An early-season goalkeeping crisis led to a debut for 18-year-old youth-team product Terry Smith. In the Carling Cup tie at Rotherham United, Smith replaced the injured Chris Howarth after 34 minutes and conceded three second-half goals in the 3–1 defeat. Five days later, Smith was again called from the bench to replace loan signing David Knight who was red-carded after 39 minutes. In a

much more confident display, the rookie goalkeeper made several vital saves in the goalless encounter with Carlisle United. Knee and hand injuries disrupted his progress, and with no further involvement at senior level, Smith was released by manager Sheridan in April 2007.

SMITHURST, Edgar

Outside-right

Born: Eastwood, 5 November 1895.
Died: Rotherham, 1978.
Career: Doncaster West End. Doncaster Main Colliery. Wartime guest with Southampton and OLDHAM ATHLETIC. OLDHAM ATHLETIC professional May 1919. West Ham United March 1920. Chesterfield May 1921, fee £100. Doncaster Rovers February 1922. Brodsworth Colliery January 1924.

■ Following a spell as a guest player with Southampton, Edgar Smithurst was offered a trial by Athletic and was secured on League forms in time for the restart of normal League fare in 1919–20. He appeared only twice at senior level before moving south to join West Ham United. On the field of play he had to wear a glove to protect a bullet wound to his hand, sustained during service with the King's Own Yorkshire Light Infantry in France during World War One.

SNODIN, Glynn

Midfield

Born: Rotherham, 14 February 1960.
Career: Rotherham Schoolboys. Doncaster Rovers apprentice 1976, professional October 1977. Sheffield Wednesday June 1985, fee £135,000. Leeds United July

1987, fee £150,000. OLDHAM ATHLETIC loan August–September 1991. Rotherham United loan February 1992. Heart of Midlothian March 1992. Barnsley July 1993. Carlisle United player-coach July–September 1995. Gainsborough Trinity 1995. Scarborough youth coach July 1996. Doncaster Rovers assistant manager September 1998 to April 2000. Charlton Athletic reserve-team coach June 2000. Southampton coach March 2006. West Ham United coach June 2007.

■ At the time of his arrival at Boundary Park Glynn Snodin had played all of his football in Yorkshire. Commencing with Doncaster Rovers at the age of 17, he had completed 288/21 League matches and scored 61 goals at the time of his transfer to Sheffield Wednesday. After two years at Hillsborough he teamed up again with Billy Bremner, his former manager at Doncaster Rovers, who paid £150,000 to take him to Leeds United. Snodin was on a weekly contract when loaned to the Latics and he played little further League football, his final outing being for Barnsley in April 1995, taking his League career totals, including substitute appearances, to 498 and 73 goals. Glynn subsequently assisted Northern Ireland manager Nigel Worthington and is the elder brother of Ian Snodin.

SNODIN, Ian

Midfield/Full-back

Born: Rotherham, 15 August 1963.
Career: Doncaster Rovers apprentice, professional August 1980. Leeds United May 1985, fee £200,000. Everton January 1987, fee £840,000. Sunderland loan October 1994. OLDHAM ATHLETIC January 1995. Scarborough August 1997. Doncaster Rovers player-manager July 1998 to April 2000.

■ Ian Snodin won a Championship medal in his first season with Everton, playing alongside Graeme Sharp and Neil Adams. When Sharp took over as Athletic's manager his first signing was his former teammate Ian Snodin. The England B and Under-21 international made his debut for the Latics in place of suspended club skipper, Nick Henry, and was promptly suspended himself after being sent off on his debut for two

bookable offences. That unfortunate beginning aside, Ian Snodin served Athletic well as a hard-tackling defender or midfielder with excellent distribution, although in his final season at Boundary Park he was restricted to just 14 matches due to back and hamstring injuries.

SPEEDIE, Finlay Ballantyne

Inside-forward

Born: Dumbarton, 18 August 1880.
Died: Dumbarton, 5 February 1953.
Career: Arniston Thistle. Clydebank Juniors. Rangers October 1900. Newcastle United September 1906, fee £600. OLDHAM ATHLETIC May 1908, together with Willie Appleyard for a combined fee of £400. Bradford Park Avenue April 1909. Dumbarton September 1909, reserve-team coach September 1919.

■ One of a trio of Newcastle United players signed by Athletic for their second season in the Football League, Scotland international Finlay Speedie possessed great natural ability. Winner of League Championships in both Scotland and England (with Rangers in 1901 and 1902 and with Newcastle United in 1907), he played with equal faculty at inside-forward and centre-half during his 11-month stay with Athletic. During his glittering career with Glasgow Rangers he appeared in eight different positions, including goalkeeper, and was similarly versatile in his two seasons with Newcastle United, giving outstanding

performances in all areas of the field. During World War One he served with the Argyll & Sutherland Highlanders and was awarded the Military Medal.

SPENCE, Alan Nicholson

Inside-forward

Born: Seaham, 7 February 1940.
Career: Murton Colliery. Sunderland amateur March, professional September 1958. Darlington June 1960. Southport July 1963. OLDHAM ATHLETIC December 1968. Chester December 1969. Southport reserve-team coach 1970, trainer 1971. Skelmersdale United manager July 1972. Chorley manager October 1974, general manager May 1979. Saudi Arabia coaching appointment May 1982.

■ Seldom can a player have had such a down-to-earth introduction to senior football as that experienced by Alan Spence. He began with Sunderland in the 1957–58 season when they were relegated for the first time. Of the 97 goals conceded, seven of them (without reply) came in Spence's debut at Blackpool. He fared much better elsewhere, of course, setting a club record with Darlington by scoring in seven consecutive matches, but his best days were spent at Southport, where he netted a career total of 98 goals. Despite appearing in only half of the season's fixtures, he was Athletic's leading scorer

with 12 League goals in 1968–69. In his early days Spence won England Youth caps alongside Bobby Moore, Willie Carlin and Barry Bridges, playing in the Mini World Cup in 1958.

SPENCE, David McLachlan

Outside-left

Born: Paisley, 9 March 1896.
Died: Reading, 1961.
Career: St Mirren. Reading August 1920. Walsall August 1921. OLDHAM ATHLETIC November 1922, fee £440. Pontypridd June 1923. Aberdare October 1923. Coventry City 1924. Taunton United July 1926. Reading Serpills (Green Waves) reinstated amateur March 1929.

■ David Spence's career in League football commenced with Reading after wartime service with the Black Watch. He played in Reading's first fixture in the Football League, at Newport County, joining Walsall a year later. His move to the Saddlers coincided with their election to the new Third Division North, and in 15 months at Fellows Park Spence completed 49 League and Cup matches and scored four goals. The Latics were a struggling First Division side at the time of his signing, and the stocky wingman failed to make an impression in four first-team matches, lacking pace to complement his skill on the ball. An outstanding golfer, Spence was Scottish Amateur Champion in 1920.

SPENCE, Derek William

Forward

Born: Belfast, 18 January 1952.
Career: Belfast Crusaders. OLDHAM ATHLETIC September 1970. Bury February 1973, fee £2,250. Blackpool October 1976, fee £40,000. Olympiakos, Greece, 1977. Blackpool August 1978. Southend United December 1979, in exchange for Colin Morris. See Bee, Hong Kong, July 1982. Bury August 1983 to May 1984.

■ A lively, blond-haired forward, Derek Spence was leading scorer for Northern Ireland's Youth team in 1970. He began at Boundary Park by quickly netting six goals for the reserves but sadly his full potential was realised after he left Athletic. Spence won 29 caps with Northern Ireland while on the books of Bury, Blackpool and Southend United. In a record-breaking season at Roots Hall in 1980–81 he assisted The Shrimpers to the Championship of Division Four, the club's first Championship since a Southern League success 73 years previously. In League matches alone Spence scored a career total of 97 goals in 336/12 matches.

SPINK, Harry

Outside-left

Born: Blackburn, 21 September 1912.
Died: Blackpool, 1979.
Career: Blackburn Grammar School Old Boys. Darwen. Lancaster Town.

OLDHAM ATHLETIC November 1933. Rossendale United May 1935. Lancaster Town August 1936. Accrington Stanley trial November 1936. Bacup Borough March 1937.

■ The son of a former professional footballer with Nelson and Blackburn Rovers, Harry Spink was a lightly-built and speedy wingman who enjoyed an extended spell of senior action in his second season before losing his place in mid-term to the more experienced Jack Robson. Spink was one of 10 players released at the season's close as Athletic faced the uninviting prospect of Third Division football for the first time in their history.

SPOONER, Nicholas Michael

Central-defender

Born: Manchester, 5 June 1971.
Career: Bolton Wanderers trainee, professional July 1989. Charleston Battery, US, loan March 1999. OLDHAM ATHLETIC loan October 1998. Chester City November 1999. Charleston Battery, US, March 2000.

■ Nicky Spooner was still recovering from a long injury lay-off when he joined Athletic on loan from Bolton Wanderers. His debut at Millwall ended when two badly mistimed tackles resulted in his 48th-minute dismissal. His second appearance against local rivals Manchester City lasted for 71 minutes before he was replaced by substitute Mark Allott.

SPURDLE, William

Wing-half

Born: St Peter Port, Guernsey, Channel Islands, 28 January 1926.
Career: OLDHAM ATHLETIC amateur, professional March 1948. Manchester City January 1950, fee £10,000. Port Vale November 1956, fee £4,000. OLDHAM ATHLETIC June 1957, retired May 1963, subsequently appointed part-time trainer-coach to OLDHAM ATHLETIC reserves July 1965.

■ Billy Spurdle was evacuated from the Channel Islands during World War Two and was signed by Athletic as a part-time professional following his

demobilisation from the forces. Mainly operating from right-half he made an impressive start, appearing in 38 League and Cup matches in his first season of senior football. While never appearing to be in a hurry, his long, loping stride and sharp shooting made him a great favourite. During his lengthy spell with Manchester City he completed 172 League and Cup matches and scored 33 goals, and he became the first Channel Islander to appear in a Wembley Cup Final. Athletic paid a small fee to bring him back to Boundary Park from Port Vale in June 1957 and he played for a further six seasons before announcing his retirement at the age of 37, having completed exactly 200 League appearances in his two spells at Boundary Park.

STAFFORD, Harry Elijah

Full-back

Born: Heywood, 6 February 1907.
Died: Rochdale, December 1989.
Career: Heywood St James. OLDHAM ATHLETIC May 1927, retired due to injury May 1934. Reserve team trainer July 1936. Was re-engaged after the war as assistant trainer from January 1947. Rochdale trainer November 1950 to October 1951.

■ Popularly known as 'Tiny' Stafford, at a time when six-footers were much less common than they are today, the reserve full-back spent seven years on Athletic's books during the period when Teddy Ivill and Billy Porter were the automatic

selections at full-back. Sadly, he was seriously injured during one of his infrequent first-team outings, against Southampton in September 1933. Although he was operated on twice, Stafford was never fit enough to play again. In July 1936 he returned to Athletic as assistant to trainer Frank Hargreaves.

STAFFORD, Joseph

Full-back

Born: New Mills, Derbyshire, 14 August 1879.
Died: Oldham, 13 July 1957.
Career: Pine Villa 1895. Newton Heath Athletic. OLDHAM ATHLETIC 1899, retired 1913.

■ Joe Stafford moved to Oldham with his family around 1895 and took up employment in the local cotton-spinning industry. At about the same time he became associated with Pine Villa, and afterwards was a member of the Newton Heath Athletic team, winning both the Manchester League and the Manchester Junior Cup. He rejoined the Latics after their name had been changed from Pine Villa, and was elected captain of the club. He initially assisted in the winning of the Manchester Junior Cup and the Ashton Charity Cup and later guided the side to promotion from the B Division of the Lancashire Combination. He played in 13 matches in 1906–07, helping to secure the Lancashire Combination First Division title. When Athletic reached

their goal of Football League status in 1907, Joe Stafford was appointed captain of the reserve team. Although on the small side, Stafford was solidly built and remained a powerful back for the reserve team until his retirement in 1913. His brother, Jack, also played for Pine Villa and the Latics, but Joe Stafford was the only player in the history of the club to have played for Pine Villa and represented Oldham Athletic in a Football League fixture.

STAINROD, Simon Allan

Forward

Born: Sheffield, 1 February 1959.
Career: Hillsborough Celtic. Sheffield United apprentice July 1975, professional July 1976. OLDHAM ATHLETIC March 1979, fee £60,000. Queen's Park Rangers November 1980, fee £250,000. Sheffield Wednesday February 1985, fee £250,000. Aston Villa September 1985, fee £250,000. Stoke City December 1987, fee £90,000. Racing Club Strasbourg, France, loan. Rouen, France, June 1989, fee £70,000. Falkirk August 1990, fee £100,000. Dundee player and assistant manager February 1992, player-manager May 1992, director of football operations May 1993. Ayr United player-manager December 1993 to September 1995.

■ Although Athletic paid a then record fee for Simon Stainrod, they netted a handsome profit when they sold him to Queen's Park Rangers some 20 months

later. A great individualist and crowd favourite, at times he baffled his own teammates, nevertheless he shone as a provider of openings while scoring a fair quota of goals on his own account. Signed from Sheffield United, where he began in League football at the age of 17, he played his final game for the Latics at Queen's Park Rangers in November 1980, joining the Loftus Road club in the same week. Stainrod fitted in well at QPR, where he was an FA Cup finalist in 1982 and a Second Division Championship winner a year later. He later won Scottish League Division One Championships with Falkirk in 1991 and Dundee in 1992. In English League football he totalled 364/23 appearances and 107 goals, and in Scottish League matches added a further 30 goals in 94 matches.

STAM, Stefan

Defender

Born: Amersfoort, Holland, 14 September 1979.
Career: Grasshoppers. AFC 34. AZ67 Alkmaar. PSV Eindhoven. ADO Den Haag. Huizenn. OLDHAM ATHLETIC non-contract February, professional July 2005.

■ A Dutch gymnastic champion between the ages of 11 and 12, Stefan Stam also represented North Holland at football between the ages of 12 and 14. An Ajax supporter as a youngster, he was first spotted by AZ Alkmaar but made his senior debut with FC Eindhoven.

Capped by Holland at Under-18 and Under-20 levels, the cultured, left-sided defender endured two injury-plagued seasons at the start of his Athletic career but 2007–08 has seen the popular Dutchman enjoy an extended and injury-free run. This has followed extended and radical treatment in Holland to cure his acute hamstring problems.

STANDRING, Norman

Centre-forward
Born: Heywood.
Career: OLDHAM ATHLETIC amateur April 1944, professional April 1945. Northwich Victoria July 1946. Wellington Town October 1947.

■ Norman Standring joined Athletic during wartime and made a great impression in his debut season. The dashing centre-forward celebrated his first senior outing by scoring against Bury at Boundary Park in a 2–2 draw on Boxing Day 1944. He subsequently scored in each of six consecutive appearances and ended his first season with 14 goals in 16 matches. He had less success in 1945–46, scoring three goals in 11 regional matches, and two in FA Cup ties. Although offered terms by Athletic in June 1946 he declined and signed for Northwich Victoria, for whom he scored 29 goals in season 1946–47. Norman Standring's birth and death details have proved elusive, but an unconfirmed report intimated that he had died at the age of 45 in a road accident.

STANIFORTH, Archer Christopher 'Chris'

Centre-forward
Born: Carrington, Nottingham, 26 September 1895.
Died: Chesterfield, 24 December 1954.
Career: Nottingham Schoolboys. Notts County amateur 1913, Cresswell Athletic 1913. Chesterfield Municipal 1919. Cresswell Colliery. Mansfield Town March 1921. OLDHAM ATHLETIC May 1922, fee £400. Mansfield Town May 1924. Notts County December 1924, fee £800. Mansfield Town May 1926. Notts County May 1927, fee £800. Mansfield Town May 1928. Shirebrook player-coach June 1930. Grantham March 1931. Mansfield Town

player-coach September 1931. Sutton Town August 1932. Worksop Town August 1933. Cresswell Colliery player-manager 1934.

■ Chris Staniforth spent two seasons at Boundary Park, one in the First Division and one in the Second, following relegation in 1922–23. Weakness in attack cost Athletic their First Division status and, while Staniforth led the reserves scoring lists with 13 goals, he managed only three in 18 First Division matches. He fared little better in Division Two, but one goal famously knocked Sunderland out of the FA Cup in January 1924, Athletic beating their illustrious visitors 2–1 before a crowd of 24,726 at Boundary Park. Bought from and transferred back to Mansfield Town, Chris Staniforth was without doubt one of the best players in the 'Stags' long history, despite the fact that the bulk of his playing career was spent in Midland League and Combination soccer. Signing for the club on no less than five separate occasions, his overall record was 152 goals in just 160 matches.

STANTON, Clifford

Centre-forward

Born: Stockport, 12 August 1908.
Died: Holywell, 7 October 1970.
Career: Greek Street Baptists, Stockport. Altrincham July 1926. OLDHAM ATHLETIC May 1927. Macclesfield Town May 1929. OLDHAM ATHLETIC May 1930 to April 1931.

■ Neil Harris, the veteran Scottish international, was first-choice centre-forward with Athletic in 1927–28 but

during a spell when he was out with injury Cliff Stanton performed with credit, scoring four goals in eight matches. Stanton was released in the close season and joined Macclesfield Town where he scored 32 goals in 1929–30 and was selected to represent the Cheshire League. He rejoined Athletic in May 1930 but again failed to establish himself at League level, appearing in just five matches prior to his release in April 1931.

STARBUCK, Philip Michael

Forward/Midfield

Born: Nottingham, 24 November 1968.
Career: Nottingham Forest associate

schoolboy January 1983, apprentice July 1985, professional August 1986. Birmingham City loan March 1988. Hereford United loan February 1990. Blackburn Rovers loan September 1990. Huddersfield Town August 1991. Sheffield United October 1994, fee £150,000. Bristol City loan September 1995. RKC Waalwijk, Holland, loan. OLDHAM ATHLETIC August 1997. Plymouth Argyle March–May 1998, in exchange for Adrian Littlejohn. Cambridge City. Burton Town 2000–01. Leicester City reserve-team coach. Hucknall Town player-manager December 2001 to June 2003. Leigh RMI manager 2003 to November 2004. Arnold Town manager December 2004 to May 2006. Hednesford Town manager June 2006.

■ Phil Starbuck had the cruel misfortune to sustain a serious injury in pre-season training with Athletic and it was not until the following January that he was able to make his debut. Introduced into a struggling side with half of the season gone, he failed to halt the team's slide, collecting only one win bonus from his nine appearances. He had earlier enjoyed the best spell of his career with Huddersfield Town, appearing at Wembley in the 1994 Autoglass Final won by Swansea Town after extra-time and penalties.

STEEL, William James 'Jim'

Centre-forward

Born: Dumfries, 4 December 1959.
Career: Greystone Rovers, Dumfries. OLDHAM ATHLETIC apprentice December 1975, professional June 1978. Wigan Athletic loan November 1982. Wrexham loan January 1983. Port Vale March 1983, fee £10,000. Wrexham January 1984, fee £10,000. Deportivo La Coruna, Spain, loan 1987. Tranmere Rovers November 1987, fee £60,000. Retired 1992.

■ Jim Steel was only 18 years old when he made his League debut for Athletic and he marked the occasion by scoring twice in Athletic's first away victory of season 1978–79, a 3–1 victory at Cardiff City. Extremely well-built and brave, Steel controlled and distributed the ball well and his height gave him the advantage in aerial situations. Never a

prolific goalscorer, he was an excellent target man with a hardworking, unselfish approach. He retired from football in May 1992 to join Merseyside Police.

STEELE, Ernest

Outside-right

Born: Leigh, 28 October 1911.
Died: Tiverton, Devon, 16 April 1997.
Career: Rochdale amateur March 1931. Mossley amateur 1931. Rochdale professional August 1931. OLDHAM ATHLETIC August 1932. Torquay United May 1933. Notts County October 1934, fee £750. Bath City July 1936. Millwall December 1936. Crystal Palace September 1938. Wartime guest with Stockport County, Rochdale, Carlisle United, Sheffield United, Chesterfield, Leicester City and Swansea Town. Barry Town 1946. Hurst December 1946. Northwich Victoria 1947–48. Ossett Town.

■ Ernest Steele was a fine all-round sportsman, winning the East Lancashire Cross-Country Championship when a member of Middleton Harriers. He also played cricket for Middleton in the Central Lancashire League and represented Lancashire C.C.C. in Minor Counties matches. He was also a noted footballer, although success came late in his career with Millwall, Division Three South champions in 1937–38, and Crystal Palace, runners-up in Division Three South in 1938–39. During World War Two he served with the Royal Army

Service Corps, making guest appearances with a number of clubs. After a decade of service as Barnsley's groundsman he took up a similar position at Blundell public school at Tiverton. Steele collapsed and died at the age of 85 while watching a game of football between Tiverton Town and Taunton Town.

STENNER, Arthur William John

Outside-left

Born: Yeovil, 7 January 1934.
Career: Yeovil Town. St Austell while on National Service. Bristol City August 1954. Plymouth Argyle July 1955. Norwich City August 1956. Exeter City trial December 1956. OLDHAM ATHLETIC trial April 1957. Yeovil Town August 1957. Chard Town player-coach July 1959. Trowbridge Town September 1960. Poole Town November 1960. Weymouth. Bridport Town. Retired 1969.

■ Arthur Stenner was introduced into a very poor Athletic side and unsurprisingly struggled to make any impact. Because he was signed after the transfer deadline he was not eligible to play in matches involving promotion or relegation issues. This restricted him to just three appearances, one draw and two defeats. In the close season he followed Don Travis to Yeovil Town, later assisting several other Southern non-League clubs before retiring to devote his full attention to his furniture removals business.

STEPHENSON, Robert Leonard

Centre-forward

Born: Blackpool, 14 July 1930.
Career: Highfield Youth Club. Blackpool November 1948. Port Vale March 1955, fee £6,000. OLDHAM ATHLETIC June 1957, fee £1,025. Witton Albion December 1957.

■ Len Stephenson scored on his debut for Blackpool in season 1950–51, but with the wealth of forward talent available at Bloomfield Road in the 1950s he was restricted to just 24 League appearances in seven years. A transfer to Port Vale provided more opportunities with 61 League outings and 16 goals before Athletic signed him, along with Billy Spurdle, who was returning for a second spell at Boundary Park. While Spurdle prospered in his second spell, Stephenson unfortunately did not, remaining for less than half a season, having lost his starting role as centre-forward to Gerry Duffy.

STEVENS, Dennis

Half-back

Born: Dudley, 30 November 1933.
Career: Worcestershire Schoolboys. Bolton Wanderers amateur 1948, professional December 1950. Everton March 1962, fee £35,000. OLDHAM ATHLETIC December 1965. Tranmere Rovers March 1967, retired 1968.

■ Associated with Bolton Wanderers from the age of 15, Dennis Stevens made his League debut in Division One at 19. An inside-forward, Stevens came very

close to full international level – he was a squad member of the England party in April 1957 – and won Under-23 and Football League representative honours during his lengthy spell at Burnden Park. He was also an FA Cup winner against Manchester United in 1958. Everton paid a record fee for his transfer and he was ever present in their Championship-winning side of 1962–63. Along with several other signings – Blore, Large and Towers – Stevens helped steady Athletic's ship in the season when Jimmy McIlroy took over from Gordon Hurst in the managerial seat. His second season at Boundary Park got off to the worst possible start when he tore ligaments in the opening fixture against Leyton Orient and was restricted to only nine first-team matches.

STEWART, Robert

Left-back

Born: Loanhead, Midlothian, 13 March 1894.

Career: Broxburn United. Everton October 1915. Wartime guest with Tranmere Rovers. OLDHAM ATHLETIC May 1919. Exeter City June 1921, fee £350. Wigan Borough February 1923.

■ Bob Stewart played his first match for Athletic during the period of war football,

having been introduced to the club by Arthur Gee, when both players were working on Liverpool docks during World War One. Although possessing all the qualities necessary for a player occupying a rear position, his form was inconsistent. He also incurred a two-month suspension after being sent off against Arsenal in February 1920. In his second season at Boundary Park Stewart appeared infrequently and was made available for transfer in October 1920. It was not until the close season that he joined Exeter City, and his League career ended with three appearances for Wigan Borough.

STOCK, Harry

Inside-forward

Born: Stockport, 31 July 1918.
Died: Stockport, 1977.
Career: Cheadle FC. Stockport County July 1938. Wartime guest with Manchester United. OLDHAM ATHLETIC July 1948 to May 1951.

■ Harry Stock's influence and ability as a prompter of subtle attacks did much to redress Athletic's dreadful start to the 1948–49 season, which kicked-off with seven defeats in the opening eight matches. Partnering Haddington and Gemmell in the inside berths, a succession of brilliant performances attracted the interest of Aston Villa but Athletic refused their offer for his services. Sadly, his next two seasons at Boundary Park were dogged by the bugbear of injuries, a cartilage problem in 1950–51 restricting him to just one senior outing in his final season. Harry Stock departed Boundary Park in May 1951 to be followed, some 37 years later, by his grandson Paul Warhurst.

STOKES, Patrick

Outside-right

Born: Stockton-on-Tees, 1883.
Died: Durham, November 1959.
Career: Shildon Athletic. Denaby United. Grimsby Town May 1907. OLDHAM ATHLETIC November 1908, in exchange for Willie Appleyard. Released May 1909 but re-registered December 1910 to May 1911. Shildon Athletic December 1911.

■ Paddy Stokes made his League debut with Grimsby Town in Division Two in season 1907–08 and scored his first League goal against the Latics in March 1908. In November of the same year he joined Athletic in the exchange deal that took centre-forward Willie Appleyard back to Grimsby Town. Appleyard had failed to impress at Boundary Park and Stokes fared little better in two spells spent almost exclusively at reserve-team level.

STRINGER, Edmund

Inside-forward

Born: Sheffield, 6 February 1925.
Career: Norton Woodseats. OLDHAM ATHLETIC July 1949 to May 1950.

■ Eddie Stringer was a regular marksman in Lancashire Combination matches, forming a dangerous partnership with Albert Wadsworth. In a season when Athletic scored only 58 goals in 42 League matches, it was somewhat surprising that Stringer did not add to his solitary, early season outing at Crewe Alexandra.

STRINGFELLOW, Peter

Inside-forward

Born: Walkden, 21 February 1939.
Career: Walkden Town. Portsmouth trial. OLDHAM ATHLETIC December 1958. Sankey's FC December 1960. Gillingham December 1962. OLDHAM ATHLETIC loan January–February 1964. Chesterfield August 1964 to June 1965, in part exchange for Charlie Rackshaw.

■ Curly-haired and dashing, inside-forward Peter Stringfellow was Athletic's leading scorer with 11 in 31 appearances in 1959–60. Posted to Malaya on RAF National Service the following season, his registration was allowed to lapse and Gillingham stepped in for his signature. He won a Fourth Division Championship medal with the Gills in 1963–64, making 25 appearances during the season. Briefly on loan to Athletic in 1964, he did not appear in the first team and spent his final season of League football with Chesterfield.

SUGDEN, Ryan Stephen

Forward

Born: Bradford, 26 December 1980.
Career: Queensbury Celtic. OLDHAM ATHLETIC trainee July 1997, professional November 1998. Burton Albion loan April 2001. Scarborough February 2002. Chester City, June 2002. Burton Albion June 2003. Morecambe August 2003. Halifax Town July 2004.

■ A total of 38 goals in Athletic's youth and reserve teams in 1998–99 earned Ryan Sugden a League debut at the age of 18. His only senior goal, scored after coming on as a 90th-minute substitute

against Blackpool in April 2000, condemned The Seasiders to relegation from Division Two. Increasingly troubled by illness, he faded from the first-team scene. Out of contract in the summer of 2002, Sugden dropped to Conference level with Scarborough in February 2002.

SWAILES, Christopher William

Central-defender

Born: Gateshead, 19 October 1970.
Career: Ipswich Town trainee, professional May 1989. Peterborough United March 1991, fee £10,000. Boston United August 1991. Bridlington Town. Doncaster Rovers October 1993. Ipswich Town March 1995, fee £225,000. Bury November 1997, fee £200,000. Rotherham United July 2001. OLDHAM ATHLETIC July 2005 to December 2006. Hamilton Academical March 2007.

■ A recurring heel injury marred Chris Swailes's 18 months with Athletic, following his transfer from Rotherham United. Athletic's club captain was able to add little to his League career record of more than 400 League and Cup matches at the time of his arrival at Boundary Park. At his best, Swailes was a formidable and commanding central-defender with excellent leadership qualities. In December 2006 he reluctantly but amicably agreed a pay-off for the last few months of his contract. Three months on, he sampled Scottish football for the first time, signing a short-term contract with Hamilton Academical. In July 2007 he signed a new one-year deal and assisted the Accies to the Division One Championship in 2007–08.

SWALLOW, Ernest

Full-back

Born: Wheatley Hill, 9 July 1919.
Died: Doncaster, 18 January 1962.
Career: Bentley Colliery. Doncaster Rovers November 1941. Barnsley January 1948. OLDHAM ATHLETIC August 1950 to May 1951, fee £3,000. Doncaster Rovers trainer.

■ A full-back built on generous lines, Ernie Swallow was by no means a graceful defender, his game being more notable for the length and promptness of his clearances rather than for any attempt to employ scientific methods. He had been at Boundary Park for only three months when he was placed on the transfer list at his own request, the move coming within days of the appointment of new player-manager George Hardwick. Swallow was a member of the Doncaster Rovers side that took the Championship of Division Three North in 1946–47 with a record 72 points (a win was worth two points at that time). Ernie Swallow's son Barry made in excess of 500 League appearances as a centre-half with five different League clubs, most notably with York City.

SWAN, Iain

Central-defender

Born: Glasgow, 4 July 1980.
Career: Highbury Juniors. Glasgow Rangers School of Excellence. OLDHAM ATHLETIC trainee March 1996, professional November 1996. Leigh RMI loan February 2000. Partick Thistle loan March 2000. Leigh RMI August 2000. Morecambe May 2002. Lancaster City June 2005. Colwyn Bay August 2007.

■ Iain Swan was a regular in Athletic's reserves at 16 years of age. The youthful central-defender won most of the balls in the air but lacked in the art of distribution. He made his senior debut at 18 years of age as a 63rd-minute substitute in the third-round FA Cup tie against Premier League Chelsea, when two late goals from player-manager Gianluca Vialli ensured victory for the London team. Swan made his League debut against Wycombe Wanderers in March of the same season but added only one further senior outing to his tally.

SWAN, Ronald McDonald

Goalkeeper

Born: Plean, Stirlingshire, 8 January 1941. Career: Denny Rovers. Camelon Juniors. East Stirlingshire 1960. OLDHAM ATHLETIC May 1964. Luton Town January 1967. Altrincham August 1967. Buxton October 1967. Hyde United May 1968.

■ Goalkeeper Ron Swan began as a centre-half with Denny Rovers but switched roles and helped East Stirlingshire win promotion into Scottish League Division One in 1962–63. In two and a half seasons at Boundary Park, Swan shared first-team goalkeeping duties with Johnny Bollands before finally losing out to new signing David Best, following a shaky opening to season 1966–67. In 1971 Swan joined Oldham Police, and senior supporters will remember him as a popular and familiar figure, patrolling the perimeter of the Boundary Park pitch on match days.

SWARBRICK, James

Outside-left

Born: Lytham St Annes c.1881.
Career: Blackpool Etrurians. Chorley June 1900. Blackburn Rovers December 1901. Accrington Stanley loan April 1903. Brentford 1903. Grimsby Town July 1905. OLDHAM ATHLETIC May 1907. Southport Central November 1909. Stoke May 1910. Burslem Port Vale August 1911. Swansea Town December 1912 to 1913.

■ In a brilliant start to his Athletic career, outside-left Jimmy Swarbrick scored in each of the club's first two fixtures in the Football League. Sadly, in his third outing he suffered a compound fracture of his ankle after 55 minutes of the game against Bradford City. He was in hospital at Bradford for several weeks, and it was a little over a year before he reappeared in the League side. Shortly afterwards he was transferred to Southport Central. He did, however, return to League football and wound up in Southern League circles with Swansea Town, where he was a Welsh Cup winner in 1913.

SWEENEY, Andrew

Winger

Born: Oldham, 15 October 1951.
Career: Chadderton Schoolboys. OLDHAM ATHLETIC amateur November 1970, professional February 1971. Bury loan March 1973. Rochdale July 1975 to 1976. Mossley 1976. Stalybridge Celtic March 1977. Witton Albion 1977. Uppermill. Droylsden. Glossop.

■ Introduced to League action in the late stages of the 1970–71 promotion campaign, Andy Sweeney was part of the squad that lifted the Ford Sporting Trophy. The £70,000 prize money helped finance the building of a new stand on the Broadway side of Boundary Park. A lightweight and elusive wingman with more than one way of beating a full-back, Sweeney enjoyed some increasingly lengthy spells of senior action up until 1973–74, when the more experienced George McVitie dominated the right wing position.

SWIFT, Fred

Goalkeeper

Born: Royton, 13 February 1908.
Died: Blackpool, 1971.
Career: Lytham FC. Blackpool amateur July 1927, professional May 1929. Dick Kerr's FC August 1930. Chorley May 1931. OLDHAM ATHLETIC May 1933. Bolton Wanderers May 1935, in exchange for William Chambers. Shrewsbury Town June 1938. Swansea Town May 1939. Fleetwood 1946.

■ Tall, broad-shouldered and courageous, Fred Swift proved himself a worthy successor to Jack Hacking following the England international's transfer to Manchester United in March 1934. Athletic suffered relegation the following season but Swift was spared Third Division football, being snapped up by First Division Bolton Wanderers. A former lifeboatman, Swift served in the Royal Navy during World War Two and assisted Fleetwood in the first peacetime season. Fred's younger brother, Frank, was the famous Manchester City and England international goalkeeper who perished in the Munich air disaster when travelling as a journalist with the Manchester United party.

SWINBURNE, Alan Thomas Anderson

Goalkeeper

Born: Houghton-le-Spring, 18 May 1946.
Career: OLDHAM ATHLETIC apprentice August 1961, professional September 1963. Newcastle United June 1964.

■ Introduced to League football as a deputy for the injured Johnny Bollands, Alan Swinburne was beaten nine times in four mid-season matches in 1963–64 and did not get another opportunity. He also failed to reach first-team level with Newcastle United. By contrast, Alan's father Tom Swinburne was Newcastle United's goalkeeper on either side of World War Two and an England wartime international against Scotland in December 1939. Alan's younger brother, Trevor, the third goalkeeper in the family, served six League clubs in the 1970s and 1980s, totalling 343 League appearances.

TAIT, Jordan Alexander

Full-back

Born: Berwick, 27 September 1979.
Career: Newcastle United associate schoolboy 1994, trainee 1996, professional July 1998. Norwich City trial April 1999. OLDHAM ATHLETIC August 1999. Darlington October 2000. Arbroath July 2001. Ross County January 2003. Ayr United January 2004. St Johnstone July 2004. Berwick Rangers June 2005. Stenhousemuir December 2005.

■ Despite a lengthy association with Newcastle United, Jordan Tait failed to graduate to senior level and he fared little better elsewhere. Two substitute appearances for the Latics and two starts and a substitute appearance for Darlington were the sum total of his Football League career, though he has subsequently found more opportunities in the course of a wandering path through Scottish football.

TALBOT, George Robson

Goalkeeper

Born: Willington Quay, Wallsend, 15 July 1910.
Died: North Shields, 10 September 1990.
Career: Willington Athletic. Wallsend Town. Liverpool April 1933. OLDHAM ATHLETIC June 1934. Gateshead August 1935. Southport December 1935 to May 1937.

■ George Talbot spent a little over a season with Liverpool when Elisha Scott and Arthur Riley were the first-team goalkeepers. Moving to Boundary Park he was again cast in a reserve role, playing only twice at senior level. Talbot found more opportunities with Gateshead (12 appearances) and Southport (32 matches). Returning to the North East he was a river policeman and worked in the local shipyards until his retirement in 1975.

TALBOT, Robert Curry

Full-back

Born: North Hylton, Co. Durham, 20 September 1908.
Died: Wigan, 1971.
Career: Hetton United amateur October 1929. West Ham United May 1930. Burnley trial September 1931. West Stanley October 1931. Newport County August 1932. Wigan Athletic November 1933. OLDHAM ATHLETIC May 1935 to April 1936.

■ Talbot's first-team debut came on Christmas Day 1935 when a Billy Walsh hat-trick and a goal from Fred Leedham accounted for Tranmere Rovers in a 4–1 win. The return match at Prenton Park on Boxing Day was a different story, however, the Latics suffering their worst-ever League defeat by 13–4. Despite the crushing defeat, Talbot retained his place in the team and enjoyed a run in the side throughout January and February, his final total of 13 appearances being his best seasonal return in League football.

TANNAHILL, Robert

Forward

Born: Kilmarnock, c.1870.
Career: Kilmarnock August 1889. Blackburn Rovers trial January 1893. Bolton Wanderers February 1893. Tottenham Hotspur May 1897. Millwall Athletic October 1898. Chesterfield Town August 1899. Fulham May 1901. Grays United September 1904. OLDHAM ATHLETIC August 1905 to 1906.

■ Dubbed the 'Kilmarnock featherweight' during four seasons with Bolton Wanderers, Robert Tannahill's speed off the mark made him a dangerous raider from the wing. He appeared in the 1894 FA Cup Final when Notts County became the first side from Division Two to lift the trophy winning 4–1. The wingman was one of football's first 'rolling stones', his varied experience including spells in the Southern League and concluding with the Latics in Hudson Fold days.

TATTON, John Henry

Outside-right

Born: Dunston-on-Tyne, 23 November 1894.
Died: Dunston-on-Tyne, 1973.
Career: Dunston Atlas Villa. Newcastle United amateur June 1911. Gillingham July 1913. Preston North End July 1919. OLDHAM ATHLETIC February 1920, fee £400. Nantwich 1922–23.

■ A flyer on the right wing, Jack Tatton was able to show his heels to most backs. He was a most effective attacker when chasing a long ball; one contemporary player recalling that a ball played to his feet was not likely to produce anything in the way of fancy footwork. In May 1921 Athletic paid Aston Villa a significant fee for 36-year-old England international outside-right Charlie Wallace, a move that restricted Tatton to 13 League appearances in his final season.

TAYLOR, Alan

Goalkeeper

Born: Thornton, near Blackpool, 17 May 1943.
Career: Blackpool Rangers. Blackpool amateur 1962, professional October 1963. OLDHAM ATHLETIC loan December 1969. Stockport County loan August 1970. Southport July 1971. Blackpool Rangers 1974–76. Wren Rovers 1979. Blackpool Mechanics 1980–81.

■ Alan Taylor arrived on loan at Boundary Park in the month that Jack Rowley vacated the managerial seat and Jimmy Frizzell took over, initially as caretaker. Taylor played in successive 2–1 defeats before returning to Bloomfield

Road, then spending a second loan spell with Stockport County before joining Southport, where he won a Division Four Championship medal in season 1972–73.

TAYLOR, Christopher David 'Chris'

Winger

Born: Oldham, 20 December 1986.
Career: Saddleworth School. Springhead Juniors. OLDHAM ATHLETIC non-contract July 2004, professional February 2006. Barrow loan November 2005.

■ Locally born Chris Taylor is one of Athletic's brightest prospects. His tremendous pace and willingness to run at defenders has caused problems for opposition rearguards throughout another successful campaign in which he recorded 47/3 appearances in the 55-match campaign. Winner of the Young Player of the Year trophy in 2006–07, his game lacked only goals, but once off the mark, in his 52nd appearance at Carlisle United, he

promptly netted another two against Doncaster Rovers and one at Leyton Orient – four goals within the space of a fortnight. Able to occupy positions as diverse as left-back, central midfield, right or left-wing, a personal highlight for the flame-haired, Springhead-based Taylor came in November 2007 when he captained Athletic – the team he had supported since childhood – for the first time against Port Vale. The captain's armband was proudly retained as a memento of the occasion.

TAYLOR, Edward Hallows

Goalkeeper

Born: Liverpool, 7 March 1891.
Died: Golcar, Huddersfield, 5 July 1956.
Career: Marlborough Old Boys. Liverpool Balmoral. Lancashire County Amateurs. OLDHAM ATHLETIC February 1912, for a donation of £30. Wartime guest with Tranmere Rovers, Fulham and Liverpool. Huddersfield Town June 1922, fee £1,950. Everton February 1927, fee £1,650. Ashton National September 1928. Wrexham November 1928 to 1929.

■ Ted Taylor began with Liverpool Balmoral, his two brothers playing for the same team. He won several honours as an amateur, assisting Lancashire against London in a county match and also playing in the North versus South Amateur International trial match of 1912. After turning professional with the Latics he appeared in only 12 matches in three seasons while acting as understudy to Howard Matthews and at the outbreak of World War One he joined the Motor Transport Corps. Returning to Oldham after the hostilities, he eventually ousted

Matthews with a string of brilliant displays. Just prior to the opening of the 1922–23 season, Huddersfield Town manager Herbert Chapman paid just short of £2,000 for Taylor and within four months he won the first of his eight England caps. League Championship medals followed in 1924 and 1926, and he was unfortunate to miss out on a third after suffering a broken leg at Maine Road in October 1924. A third Championship medal eventually came his way at the age of 41, with Everton in season 1927–28. After retiring from the game, Taylor worked as a cotton broker in Liverpool.

TAYLOR, George

Centre-forward

Born: Failsworth, 23 January 1901.
Career: Ferranti FC. Hurst FC. OLDHAM ATHLETIC amateur December 1923, professional January 1925. Macclesfield Town 1929. Sandbach Ramblers November 1929. Hurst FC 1930. Newport County September 1933. Hurst FC August 1934.

■ At either centre or inside-forward George Taylor was a dangerous attacker, clever and strong on the ball and particularly effective in his headwork. Introduced during season 1924–25, he scored the only goal of the game at Stoke in his second appearance and, one week later, scored one of Athletic's goals in the 5–0 win against Coventry City. Tragedy struck when he broke his leg in his fourth match at South Shields on 21 February 1925, keeping him out of the first-team picture for 18 months. It was particularly noticeable that Athletic's

directors spent most of their transfer funds on forwards during the middle to late 1920s, the backs and halves remaining pretty constant throughout. George Taylor rarely started a new season as first choice, but once introduced he proved difficult to dislodge.

TAYLOR, George Barry

Full-back

Born: Sheffield, 3 December 1939.
Died: Chesterfield, March 1996.
Career: Sheffield United amateur August 1958, professional April 1959. OLDHAM ATHLETIC June 1963, fee £1,250. Chesterfield August 1964. Worksop Town July 1967.

■ Barry Taylor began as an outside-left in schoolboy and junior football, and continued as a winger in Sheffield United's Youth Team. After signing professional forms he was converted to full-back by manager Joe Mercer. Able to occupy either flank, Taylor was a cool, polished defender, usually sharing full-back duties alongside Ken Branagan or Billy Marshall. In a profession befitting a former 'Blade' and Sheffield native, Barry Taylor was a metallurgist.

TAYLOR, Joseph

Inside-forward

Born: Nottingham, 13 April 1905.
Career: Lenton United. Nottingham Forest October 1925. Ilkeston United July 1927. Blackpool May 1928. OLDHAM ATHLETIC May 1929. Notts County trial January 1932. Hurst FC March 1932. Yeovil & Petters United June 1934.

Nuneaton Town July 1935. Nottingham LMS reinstated amateur September 1936.

■ Joe Taylor had appeared only twice for Nottingham Forest at senior level when he was released and spent a season with Ilkeston United. Blackpool brought him back into League football but released him on a free transfer after just four League outings. Snapped up by the Latics, he enjoyed the best run of his career in late 1929–30 season. His six goals in 10 Division Two outings included a hat-trick in a 6–1 win against Bradford City in March 1930. Taylor additionally scored 22 goals for Athletic reserves before his season was ended by an injury sustained against Burnley on Easter Monday 1931.

TAYLOR, Joseph Thomas

Inside-forward

Born: Wednesbury, 11 April 1910.
Died: Oldham, 11 January 1977.
Career: Wednesbury FC. Leamington Town December 1930. West Bromwich Albion amateur March 1931. Shrewsbury Town July 1932. Luton Town May 1934. Carlisle United September 1935. Stockport County February 1937, fee £400. OLDHAM ATHLETIC July 1938, fee £200. Wartime guest with Halifax Town. Retired 1946.

■ Joe Taylor joined Athletic from Stockport County and by coincidence had played his first game for Stockport at Boundary Park in February 1937. Athletic were lying fourth in the League and Stockport third, and an attendance of over 23,000 saw the visitors win by 2–0, with Taylor scoring one of County's

goals. Although Stockport won promotion, they were relegated the following season and Taylor moved to Boundary Park, where he finished his playing days, making the bulk of his appearances in wartime football. He was licensee of the Nelson Inn, Union Street, Oldham after retiring from playing.

TAYLOR, Peter John

Winger

Born: Southend-on-Sea, 3 January 1953.
Career: Southend United apprentice January 1970, professional January 1971. Crystal Palace October 1973, fee £120,000. Tottenham Hotspur September 1976, fee £400,000. Orient November 1980, fee £150,000. OLDHAM ATHLETIC loan January 1983. Maidstone United March 1983. Exeter City non-contract October 1983. Maidstone United player-manager to October 1984. Chelmsford City coach 1984. Heybridge Swifts. Dartford manager

1989. Enfield manager June 1990. Watford assistant manager August 1991. Harlow Town player November 1991. Hendon manager August 1993. Southend United manager and School of Excellence Director December 1993. Dover Athletic manager November 1995. England Under-21 manager June 1996 to June 1999. Gillingham manger July 1999. Leicester City manager June 2000. Brighton & Hove Albion manager October 2001 to April 2002. Hull City manager October 2002. Crystal Palace manager June 2006 to October 2007. Stevenage Borough manager November 2007. Wycombe Wanderers manager May 2008.

■ Peter Taylor joined Athletic for a month's loan near to the end of a distinguished playing career. His debut at Rotherham United marked Athletic's first win in eight matches and ended the worst spell of Joe Royle's first season in charge. Taylor was first capped by England at semi-professional level and went on to win four Under-23 caps and four full caps. At the time of his full international debut he was the first Third Division player to be capped by England for 15 years. Taylor was in charge of a Sunday League team at the age of 17 while a fledgling professional at Southend United. Some 25 years later Glenn Hoddle appointed him England Under-21 manager and he additionally took charge of England on a caretaker basis in October 2000 following Kevin Keegan's resignation.

TAYLOR, Steven Jeffrey

Forward

Born: Royton, near Oldham, 18 October 1955.
Career: Bolton Wanderers apprentice July 1971, professional July 1974. Port Vale loan October 1975. OLDHAM ATHLETIC October 1977, fee £38,000. Luton Town January 1979, fee £50,000. Mansfield Town July 1979, fee £75,000. Burnley July 1980, fee £35,000. Wigan Athletic August 1983. Stockport County March 1984. Rochdale November 1984. Preston North End October 1986. Burnley August 1987. Rochdale March 1989 to March 1990. Mossley manager May to October 1993. OLDHAM ATHLETIC Under-16 manager September 1994.

Steve Taylor enjoyed a quite remarkable start with the Latics, being the team's only marksman in his first seven matches. He rounded off a highly successful first season with a hat-trick against Bristol Rovers, finishing with 21 League and Cup goals in 34 matches. Taylor's career eventually spanned 10 different League clubs, and in terms of League goals alone his career figures were 157 in 406/35 matches. His best seasonal return was with Rochdale in 1985–86, when his 31 goals in 51 League and Cup matches made him top overall scorer in Division Four.

TAYLOR, Walter Bingley 'Wally'

Centre-half

Born: Kirton-in-Lindsey, Lincolnshire, 30 October 1926.
Died: Scunthorpe, 18 August 2005.
Career: Grimsby Town amateur May, professional August 1944. Wartime guest with Nottingham Forest and Notts County. Southport July 1951, in part-exchange for Bill Bellas. OLDHAM ATHLETIC July 1958. Fee £500. Brigg Town 1960.

Former 'Bevan Boy' Wally Taylor had appeared in 21 League matches for Grimsby Town at the time of his transfer to Southport. In a stay of seven years at Haig Avenue he clocked up 269 League appearances, captaining the side from 1955 to 1958. He also captained the Third Division North XI against their Southern counterparts. At either centre-half or full-back he was a commanding presence in

Athletic's defence during his first season. In 1959–60, however, he was sidelined following a cartilage operation and then suffered a second knee injury, all of which restricted him to just eight matches.

TAYLOR, William

Half-back

Born: Southwell, c.1886.
Died: Nottingham, 7 May 1966.
Career: Southwell FC. Mansfield Mechanics. Notts County May 1908. Mansfield Mechanics 1912–14. Wartime guest with Shirebrook and Port Vale. Burnley October 1917. OLDHAM ATHLETIC November 1920, fee £2,000. Newark Town August 1925. Algerian coaching appointment 1926 to January 1927.

Although in the shadow of Burnley's celebrated middle line of Halley, Boyle and Watson at Turf Moor, Billy Taylor was the man who stepped in when any one of the trio were unable to turn out. He had original joined Burnley when serving in The Royal Garrison Artillery at Ripon. Transferred to the Latics in November 1920 he was a member of the first-team squad for five seasons, although the bulk of his 109 League appearances were made in First Division football. He appeared infrequently following relegation in 1923, by which time he was well into the veteran stage. After retiring from the game he was a nurseryman in Southwell for many years.

TEECE, David Alfred

Goalkeeper

Born: Rhodes, near Middleton, 1 September 1927.
Died: Rochdale, 3 March 2007.
Career: Hyde United. Hull City February 1952. OLDHAM ATHLETIC June 1956, fee £200. Buxton July 1959. A.V.Roe, Manchester, coach August 1960. Chadderton FC manager April 1965.

David Teece commenced in Cheshire League football and spent four years at Hull City, largely in the shadow of the Tigers' legendary goalkeeper, Billy Bly. A faltering start with the Latics saw him deposed by Derek Williams after nine goals were conceded in the first three

matches of the season. Williams received his National Service call-up papers in late season, resulting in a recall for Teece, who seized his opportunity and remained first-choice goalkeeper thereafter. His professional career ended at Boundary Park and he subsequently worked at British Aerospace as a draughtsman and fitter.

THOM, Stuart Paul

Central-defender

Born: Dewsbury, 27 December 1976.
Career: Nottingham Forest associate schoolboy April 1993, trainee September 1993, professional January 1994. Mansfield Town loan December 1997. OLDHAM ATHLETIC loan October 1998, permanent November 1998, fee £45,000. Scunthorpe United loan August 2000, permanent September 2000 to April 2002, fee £20,000. Barrow December 2002.

After five years spent at Nottingham Forest without reaching senior level, Stuart Thom arrived at Boundary Park on a month's loan that was quickly made permanent. He scored the first League goal of his career in a 2–0 win against Lincoln City in February 1999 and, in a season when relegation was narrowly avoided, his steady and reliable displays in central defence did much to improve the side's performances. Sadly, his second season at Boundary Park was plagued by injuries, restricting him to just 10 appearances. His two seasons with Scunthorpe United almost mirrored his time with the Latics, with a succession of injury problems restricting his appearances after a promising start.

THOMAS, William Edward

Half-back

Born: Chorlton, 16 March 1906.
Died: Oldham, 25 August 1956.
Career: Sutton Rovers. St Helens Town. Runcorn. Liverpool amateur February 1928. OLDHAM ATHLETIC January 1929. Rhyl. Tranmere Rovers May 1933. Rochdale June 1934. Ashton National July 1935. Runcorn 1938–39. OLDHAM ATHLETIC assistant trainer 1944–45, trainer 1948 to 1956.

■ Billy Thomas had a lengthy association with Athletic, but his playing days were spent mainly at reserve level, a knee injury proving troublesome throughout. He subsequently made just six appearances for both Tranmere Rovers and Rochdale before moving into non-League football. Returning to Boundary Park in the war years he appeared in a handful of Regional League matches, two as emergency goalkeeper, before joining the backroom staff. Senior Athletic supporters will doubtless remember Billy Thomas as Athletic's loyal and conscientious trainer, a position that he held for 12 years until his untimely death at 50 years of age.

THOMPSON, James (Senior)

Outside-right

Born: Chadderton, 24 January 1899.
Career: Bradbury's Works, Oldham. OLDHAM ATHLETIC amateur January 1917. Wartime guest with Burnley and Manchester City. OLDHAM ATHLETIC professional January 1920. Manchester City August 1920. Stalybridge Celtic June 1921. Ashton National September 1922. Port Vale January 1923. Blackpool June 1923. Accrington Stanley June 1924. Swindon Town June 1925. Crewe Alexandra July 1926. Hurst FC August 1928. Wilson's Brewery, Oldham, reinstated amateur November 1933.

■ Jimmy Thompson first played for the Latics during World War One when he was an apprentice engineer at Bradbury's, a local manufacturer of sewing machines and motor bikes. He served with the Oldham Comrades Battalion (Tenth Manchesters), and made guest appearances for Burnley and Manchester City during the war. He joined Athletic midway through the first peacetime season but played only twice for the Latics. His first taste of regular first-team football came with Stalybridge Celtic, whose first match, against Chesterfield, proved to be a record-breaking affair. Celtic won 6–0 to record their best-ever victory in a League match and Thompson's hat-trick was the first to be scored in the Third Division North. Jimmy Thompson's father, Joe, joined the Latics from Chadderton Athletic in season 1905–06 and played in five Lancashire Combination matches. James junior was the third generation of the family to play for the Latics.

THOMPSON, James (Junior)

Left-half

Born: Chadderton, Lancashire, 26 November 1935.
Died: Blackpool, 19 April 2002.
Career: Mill Brow FC. OLDHAM ATHLETIC amateur September 1952, professional January 1954. Exeter City December 1958, fee £3,000 plus Ray John. Rochdale March 1961, fee £2,000. Bradford City December 1965. Hyde United player-coach. Buxton player-manager May 1968.

■ An immensely promising schoolboy footballer, Jimmy Thompson was a member of the Oldham and District Schools party that toured France in April 1951. He joined Athletic on amateur forms in the following year and was a regular reserve-team player at 17 years of age. He developed into one of the best attacking wing-halves in the Northern Section and had scored 11 goals in 20 matches in 1958–59 at the time of his much-criticised transfer to Exeter City. The ensuing uproar prompted manager Dodgin to state publicly the reasons behind the move, which were, in a nutshell, 'Sell to survive' – it was ever thus! Jimmy Thompson completed a career aggregate of 436/1 League matches and scored 44 goals. His son Steve, in style and appearance on the field so reminiscent of his father, was on Latics' books as a youngster but began in League football with Bolton Wanderers. He assisted five League clubs as an attacking midfield player, recording career figures of 531/24 League matches and 71 goals.

THOMPSON, John

Defender

Born: Dublin, 12 October 1981.
Career: River Valley Rangers. Home Farm. Nottingham Forest July 1999. Tranmere Rovers loan October 2006 and again January 2007. OLDHAM ATHLETIC June 2007.

■ The fabled 'Luck of the Irish' certainly deserted Athletic's unfortunate defender, who suffered a broken nose on three separate occasions in his first month at Boundary Park. The tall and speedy Irish international started the season's opening eight matches before losing his first-team spot. A knee injury then

sidelined him from late October to March, aside from a brief involvement in the FA Cup win at Everton. A long-awaited 'come back' against Millwall lasted for just nine minutes when a reoccurrence of his medial ligament injury eventually required surgery. Certainly Athletic have yet to see the best of the likeable Irishman, and all will wish him an injury-free season in 2008–09.

THOMPSON, Neil

Full-back

Born: Beverley, 2 October 1963.
Career: Nottingham Forest apprentice, professional November 1981. Hull City August 1981. Scarborough August 1983. Ipswich Town June 1989, fee £100,000. Barnsley June 1996. OLDHAM ATHLETIC loan December 1997. York City player-coach March 1998, caretaker manager March 1999, player-manager May 1990 to February 2000. Scarborough manager October 2000 to September 2001. Boston United assistant manager, manager July 2002 to February 2004.

■ A player with all-round experience, Neil Thompson at various times appeared in the Premier League, all three divisions of the Football League and the Conference. He won four England semi-professional caps in the season that Scarborough won the Conference under manager Neil Warnock, who was Athletic's manager at the time of his temporary move to Boundary Park. In addition to his Conference title win, Thompson was involved with three other promotion sides: Hull City from Division Four in 1982–83, Ipswich Town from Division Two in 1991–92 and Barnsley from Division One into the Premier League in 1996–97.

THOMSON, Arthur Campbell

Centre-half

Born: Edinburgh, 2 September 1948.
Died: Edinburgh, 7 March 2002.
Career: Chelsea associate schoolboy 1963. Heart of Midlothian apprentice April 1964. OLDHAM ATHLETIC January 1970, fee £8,000. Raith Rovers December 1970, fee £2,000. Dalkeith Thistle 1972.

■ Arthur Thomson was released by Chelsea after a year on schoolboy forms and returned to Scotland to join Heart of Midlothian as an apprentice. He made his first-team debut in season 1966–67, appearing in the Scottish Cup Final in the following season when Hearts lost to Dunfermline by 3–1. The rugged Scot, who was one of Jimmy Frizzell's earliest signings, began as centre-half, later operating on the left side of a flat back four system. He made 18/1 first-team appearances and played a full part in Athletic's improvement that saw them steer clear of relegation. The following season, however, he started as first-choice centre-half but lost his place in mid-September and reappeared only twice before his cut-price sale to Raith Rovers. On retiring from the game he joined the Edinburgh City Police Force.

TIERNEY, Marc Peter

Left-back

Born: Prestwich, 23 August 1985.
Career: OLDHAM ATHLETIC non-contract July 2002, professional August 2003. Carlisle United loan December 2004. Shrewsbury Town January 2007.

■ Marc Tierney captained Athletic reserves at the age of 18 after being picked up in Manchester League amateur football. The strong, hard-tackling defender displayed useful versatility from the outset, able to occupy left-back or central-defensive positions. At the time of his transfer to Shrewsbury Town Tierney had faded from the first-team picture, with Simon Charlton and Paul Edwards dominating the left-back position. Tierney reached Wembley in the League Two Play-off Final against Bristol Rovers in May 2007, but his big day proved a disappointment as he was sent off and Shrewsbury lost 3–1.

TILLING, Harold Kynaston

Outside-left

Born: Warrington, 6 January 1918.
Died: Warrington, November 1998.
Career: Whitecross FC. OLDHAM ATHLETIC September 1942 to 1948. Wartime guest with Manchester United.

■ Liverpool had offered Harold Tilling professional terms before the war, but he was reluctant to leave his employment at that time. Five weeks on from his scoring debut for Athletic at Bury, he turned professional. In his first two seasons at Boundary Park Tilling appeared regularly, but in August 1944 he joined the army and was posted to Northern Ireland. In addition to five League and Cup appearances, Tilling scored 15 goals in 71 wartime matches.

TIPTON, Matthew John

Forward

Born: Conway, 29 June 1980.
Career: Maes-y-Bryn FC. Bangor City Juniors. OLDHAM ATHLETIC associate schoolboy October 1994, trainee July 1996, professional July 1997. Macclesfield Town February 2002. Mansfield Town trial August 2005. Bury August 2005. Macclesfield Town loan August 2006 to May 2007. Hyde United August 2007.

■ Matthew Tipton created a number of scoring records as a junior, at one stage netting 10 consecutive hat-tricks for his school in Welsh Schools Cup ties. He won Wales caps at Under-18 and Under-21 levels, first appearing for the Under-21s at the age of 17. At the same age he broke into Athletic's first team but failed to establish a regular place, at one stage spending a lengthy spell in the reserve side as a midfield player. At his best, Tipton's aggressive, all-action style and speed off the mark proved a handful for any defence, but his form lacked consistency. In January 2000 he was

transfer listed, but his response was positive and he went on to make his 100th League appearance during the course of season 2001–02 before his transfer to Macclesfield Town.

TOLSON, Neil

Forward

Born: Stourbridge, 25 October 1973.
Career: Walsall trainee, professional December 1991. OLDHAM ATHLETIC March 1992, fee £150,000. Bradford City December 1993, fee £50,000. Chester City loan January 1995. York City July 1996, fee £50,000. Southend United July 1999. Leigh RMI October 2002. Kettering Town trial January 2003. Halifax Town February 2003. Hyde United July 2003. Radcliffe Borough February 2006.

■ Eighteen-year-old Neil Tolson's spell with Athletic spanned First Division and Premier League days, but the inexperienced youngster was never selected in the starting line up during his 20 months at Boundary Park. He left to join Bradford City as part of the Sean McCarthy transfer package and later scored the 50th League goal of his career for Southend United. Neil Tolson is the grandson of the late Ray Westwood, the former Bolton Wanderers and England inside-forward.

TOMAN, Wilfred

Forward

Born: Bishop Auckland, 1874.
Career: Aberdeen Strollers. Aberdeen FC September 1892. Dundee. Victoria United July 1896. Burnley December 1896. Everton April 1899. Southampton May 1900. Austria national team coach May 1901. Everton June 1901. Stockport County January 1904. OLDHAM ATHLETIC trial October 1905. Newcastle United amateur August 1906.

■ Wilf Toman began in League football with Burnley and scored 19 goals in 33 matches in 1897–98 when the Clarets won promotion to Division One. Three years later he scored seven goals in 19 matches to assist Southampton to the Championship of the Southern League. A month's trial with Athletic was not extended after he had played in two Lancashire Combination matches and one FA Cup tie.

TOMLINSON, Francis Anthony 'Frank'

Outside-right

Born: Manchester, 23 October 1925.
Died: Oldham, 20 April 1999.
Career: Bolton Wanderers amateur. Goslings FC. Manchester United amateur October 1942. Goslings FC 1945–46. OLDHAM ATHLETIC November 1946. Rochdale November 1951. Chester August 1952. Ashton National 1953. Droylsden 1958–59. Bradford Park Avenue manager February to December 1970.

■ An enterprising wingman with all the necessary attributes of pace and footwork for his position, Frank Tomlinson scored in each of his first three appearances in the Latics' colours. His best season was 1948–49 when he scored 14 goals in 43 League and Cup matches. In September 1950 he suffered a broken leg when playing against York City and was sidelined for the remainder of the season. Many years after his playing career had ended Tomlinson was appointed manager of Bradford Park Avenue. With less than three months of the season remaining he had little opportunity to improve matters, and when the season closed with Bradford in bottom place they failed to gain re-election. In December he was dismissed for economic reasons.

TOMS, William Leon

Inside-forward

Born: The Curragh, Ireland, 19 May 1895.
Career: Bury Schoolboys. Altrincham.

Eccles Borough 1914. Wartime guest with Southport Vulcan. Manchester United amateur September 1919, professional October 1919. Plymouth Argyle September 1920, fee £500. OLDHAM ATHLETIC July 1921, fee £250. Coventry City July 1922, fee £150. Stockport County June 1923. Wrexham October 1923. Crewe Alexandra December 1924. Great Harwood October 1925 to January 1926. Winsford United August 1926. Eccles United November 1926. CWS Margarine Works, Manchester, reinstated amateur August 1929.

■ Prematurely balding inside-forward Billy Toms was still serving as an army lieutenant when he began with Manchester United. Short, and of stocky build, he possessed plenty of grit and he arrived at Boundary Park with a reputation as a sharp-shooter. His form dipped in mid-season, however, and he lost his place after appearing in the first 19 matches of the campaign, reappearing just once thereafter. He enjoyed a successful season with Coventry City after leaving Boundary Park, scoring 19 goals in 30 League matches. Crewe Alexandra was the last of his seven League clubs in a career that totalled 49 goals in 159 League matches.

TORRANCE, George Syme

Goalkeeper

Born: Glasgow, 27 November 1935.
Career: Thorniewood Athletic. Leicester City July 1954. OLDHAM ATHLETIC

August 1956. Rochdale September 1957. Albion Rovers.

■ Blond-haired and handsome, George Torrance spent two seasons with Leicester City but failed to reach League level, Johnny Anderson being first choice with Adam Dickson his deputy. A move to Athletic proved only marginally more rewarding in a season when Dave Teece and Derek Williams shared first-team duties. Rochdale found themselves with goalkeeping problems in September 1957 with all three of their goalkeepers sidelined. Torrance filled the breach in matches against Stockport County and Scunthorpe United before returning homewards to join Albion Rovers.

TOWARD, Alfred Vickers

Centre-forward

Born: Castleside, Consett, 1882.
Died: 19 May 1962.
Career: Leadgate Park. Hull City December 1908. OLDHAM ATHLETIC December 1909, fee £350. Preston North End October 1913, fee £450. Darlington September 1919 to December 1920. Leadgate Park.

■ Alf Toward scored 13 goals in 21 matches in his first season with Athletic. From his debut against Glossop on New Year's Day 1910 until the end of the season the team lost only one match. Toward was one of Athletic's scorers in the vital concluding match of the season against Hull City, Athletic winning 3–0 to edge the Tigers into third place, the Latics taking the runners-up spot behind Manchester City. He was the club's leading scorer in 1910–11 but lost his centre-forward spot in the same season to Evan Jones, the newly-signed Welsh international.

TOWERS, Ian Joseph

Forward

Born: Blackhill, 11 October 1940.
Career: Durham County Schoolboys. Burnley amateur July 1956, professional October 1957. OLDHAM ATHLETIC January 1966, fee £20,000. Bury July 1968 to March 1971, fee £10,000. Cape Town City, South Africa 1971. Hellenic, South Africa manager 1981.

■ A lively, blond-haired striker, Ian Towers spent almost 10 years with Burnley, but played mainly in the Central League side apart from season 1964–65 when he appeared in 21 First Division matches. One of four new signings fielded by Athletic on New Year's Day 1966, his nine goals in 20 appearances helped steer the side clear of relegation from Division Three. Ever present in League matches the following term, he enjoyed the best season of his career, notching 27 goals, four of which were scored in one match against Colchester United.

TRAVIS, Donald

Centre-forward

Born: Moston, Manchester, 21 January 1924.
Died: Yeovil, February 2002.
Career: Moston Fields. Manchester Schoolboys January 1937. Ferranti FC. Blackpool amateur July 1939. Goslings FC 1941. Wartime guest with Southend United, Plymouth Argyle, St Mirren and Cowdenbeath. West Ham United September 1945. Southend United May 1948, fee £4,000. Accrington Stanley December 1948. Crewe Alexandra November 1950. OLDHAM ATHLETIC October 1951. Chester February 1952. OLDHAM ATHLETIC August 1954, fee £570. Yeovil Town July 1957.

■ A familiar figure on Northern Section grounds, at 6ft 3in and with a physique to match, Don Travis possessed forceful qualities and a strong left foot and he scored many of his goals by sheer dash and perseverance. He was very successful in his second spell at Boundary Park, heading the club's scoring lists in three consecutive seasons between 1954–57. Travis served six League clubs and scored a total of 154 goals in 325 matches. His elder brother, Harry, played for Athletic during World War Two and was Bradford City's leading goalscorer in season 1935–36.

TREACY, Raymond Christopher Patrick

Forward

Born: Dublin, 18 June 1946.
Career: Home Farm FC. West Bromwich Albion apprentice August 1961,

professional June 1964. Charlton Athletic February 1968, fee £17,500. Swindon Town June 1972, fee £20,000 plus Arthur Horsfield. Preston North End December 1973, fee £30,000. OLDHAM ATHLETIC loan March 1975. West Bromwich Albion August 1976. Shamrock Rovers May 1977. Toronto Metros-Croatia, US May 1978. Shamrock Rovers assistant manager 1979. Drogheda United player-manager 1981. Home Farm FC manager 1986.

■ Ray Treacy made his full international debut for the Republic of Ireland before making his Football League debut for West Bromwich Albion. He went on to represent his country on 43 occasions and was awarded a testimonial by the FA of Ireland in 1989. His League career spanned 278/13 matches and 79 goals. One of his goals was scored for Athletic during his month's loan from Preston North End and it was a spectacular diving header that earned a share of the points against Oxford United. After retiring from the game he was an executive member of the PFA Committee and when he returned to Ireland Treacy ran a travel agency.

TRIPPIER, Austin Wilkinson

Forward

Born: Ramsbottom, 30 August 1909.
Died: Bury, 29 August 1993.
Career: Rochdale St Clement's. Rochdale amateur May 1928. Bury amateur July 1929. Rochdale professional October 1929. OLDHAM ATHLETIC May 1931. Southport July 1932. Chorley July 1933. Macclesfield Town August 1935. Bacup Borough June 1936 to 1937.

■ An injury sustained at Tottenham Hotspur just seven weeks after his debut effectively ended Austin Trippier's season with Athletic. Commissioned into the Royal Artillery in 1939, he rose to the rank of major and in 1941 was awarded the Military Cross for outstanding bravery under fire during the evacuation from Crete. He subsequently served in Egypt, France and Germany. After the war he returned to his profession as a stockbroker in Rochdale. His son, Sir David Trippier, was the former Conservative MP for Rossendale and a junior minister in the Department of the Environment.

TROTMAN, Neal Anthony

Defender

Born: Manchester, 26 April 1987.
Career: Reddish Boys. Fletcher Moss. Burnley trainee. OLDHAM ATHLETIC trainee 2005, July 2006. Halifax Town loan January–May 2007. Preston North End January 2008, fee £500,000.

■ First spotted in Burnley's youth team by manager John Sheridan when he was in charge of Athletic's youths, defender Neal Trotman was a trainee at Turf Moor but was released from his scholarship and snapped up by Athletic in 2005. His first professional contract was only of three-month's duration, but his battling displays in the heart of the reserve's defence earned him a contract extension in September 2006. At the time, manager Sheridan described Trotman as 'big, strong and aggresive, and with a good chance of progressing in the game'. The manager's prognosis proved to be well founded as the highly rated defender quickly attracted the attention of both Derby County and Preston North End, despite having appeared in just 22 League and Cup matches for Athletic. His move to Deepdale earned Athletic their highest incoming transfer fee since 1998.

TROTTER, Walter

Outside-left

Born: Oldham, 4 July 1905.
Died: Oldham, 1975.
Career: Chamber Colliery. OLDHAM ATHLETIC January 1927. Manchester North End September 1928. Manchester Central August 1931. Altrincham June 1932. Buxton October 1934.

■ For eight seasons in the 1920s Bert Watson totally dominated the first-team

outside-left berth. Local product Walter Trotter was just one of a long line of understudies who waited in vain for an extended run in the side. After his debut at Preston North End on 5 March 1927, Trotter reappeared in the final match of the season, a 3–2 home win against South Shields. Highlight of his trio of matches in 1927–28 was his first appearance of the season when he scored Athletic's opening goal in a 3–1 victory against Stoke at Boundary Park on 10 September 1927.

TUMMON, Oliver

Outside-right

Born: Sheffield, 3 March 1884.
Died: Sheffield, October 1955.
Career: South Street New Connexion, Sheffield. Sheffield Wednesday amateur March 1902, professional February 1903. Gainsborough Trinity June 1910, fee £40. OLDHAM ATHLETIC July 1912, fee £300. Sheffield United August 1919, following wartime guest appearances. Barnsley June 1920. Sir Albert Hawkes FC reinstated amateur May 1924. Nether Edge, Sheffield, amateur August 1924.

■ Oliver Tummon favoured a direct approach on the right wing. Short and powerfully built, he was not afraid to cut in on goal and possessed a strong shot in either foot. Athletic reached the semi-final of the FA Cup in 1913 and were runners-up for the League Championship in 1915, Tummon's spell at Boundary Park coinciding with the most successful period in the club's history. During World War One he returned to Sheffield to work in a munitions factory, and after retiring from senior football he continued to turn out in local amateur circles beyond his 40th birthday.

TURNER, Ben Howard

Central-defender

Born: Birmingham, 21 January 1988.
Career: Coventry City trainee, professional July 2006. Peterborough United loan September 2006 and November 2006. OLDHAM ATHLETIC loan February–March 2007.

■ Signed on a one-month loan from Coventry City in the midst of an injury crisis, strapping centre-half Ben Turner was unable to arrest the team's slide on his debut as Bournemouth inflicted a third consecutive defeat. Turner's inexperience was apparent when he was red-carded deep into injury time, for retaliation after he had been on the receiving end of a late tackle. A three-match ban effectively concluded his Athletic sojourn.

TURNER, Brian

Wing-half

Born: Salford, 23 July 1936.
Died: Sefton North, January 1999.
Career: Bury Amateurs. Bury FC amateur 1955, professional February 1957. OLDHAM ATHLETIC August 1970 to 1971. Mossley. Droylsden.

■ Brian Turner was released by Bury on a free transfer after 16 years, 454 League appearances and ever-present records in the promotion seasons 1961 and 1968. Initially offered a two-month trial by Athletic, this was subsequently extended to cover the remainder of the season. Most of his first team appearances were made as deputy for injury victim Billy Cranston in September and October during the successful 1970–71 campaign that ended in promotion from Division Four.

VALENTINE, Albert Finch

Centre-forward

Born: Higher Ince, near Wigan, 3 June 1907.
Died: Billinge, 12 March 1990.
Career: Horwich RMI. Southport amateur November 1928, professional January 1929. Cardiff City July 1929. Wigan Borough July 1931. Chester November 1931. Prescot Cables May 1932. Crewe Alexandra August 1932. Macclesfield Town August 1933. Halifax Town July

1934, fee £500. Stockport County June 1937. Accrington Stanley October 1937, fee £225. OLDHAM ATHLETIC August 1938 to 1941.

■ A widely-travelled opportunist centre-forward whose best days in League football were spent with Halifax Town. Albert Valentine netted 88 goals in three seasons at The Shay and also holds the club record for most League goals in a season, 34 in 1934–35. His Athletic career was spent almost entirely at reserve-team level despite scoring 28 goals in 29 Lancashire Combination matches in 1938–39. His commendable total included all five goals in the reserves 5–0 win against New Brighton reserves on 21 January 1939.

VALENTINE, Carl Howard

Winger

Born: Clayton, Manchester, 4 July 1958.
Career: Trafford Park Boys. OLDHAM ATHLETIC January 1976. Vancouver Whitecaps, Canada, February 1979, fee £86,000. OLDHAM ATHLETIC loan September-March 1980. West Bromwich Albion October 1984, fee £60,000. Witchita Wings January 1986. Cleveland Force August 1986. Calgary Kickers August 1897. Vancouver Whitecaps assistant coach 1994, player-coach March 1995.

■ Despite a lack of inches Carl Valentine was very solidly built and seemed able to ride the sternest challenge. With a good turn of speed and excellent ball control, he was an exciting wingman and an extremely elusive opponent along the touchline. His best season was 1977–78

when he featured in a nicely balanced attack that had Steve Taylor and Vic Halom as the main marksmen. During his association with Vancouver Whitecaps Valentine took out Canadian citizenship and played for his adopted country in the 1986 World Cup appearing against France, Hungary and the USSR in Group C of the final tournament.

VALENTINE, Frederick Edward

Outside-right

Born: Birkenhead, 1909.
Died: Claughton, Birkenhead, 22 October 1981.
Career: Tranmere Rovers amateur February 1928. Whitchurch. Oswestry January 1933. Runcorn July 1933. Hyde United August 1935. OLDHAM ATHLETIC May 1936 to April 1937.

■ Fred Valentine came to Boundary Park highly recommended, having scored 25 goals in 50 appearances for Hyde United in season 1935–36. He failed to establish himself beyond reserve team football, however, as Athletic's other Hyde United recruit, Arthur Jones, continued to dominate the first-team berth.

VALLANCE, William

Inside-forward

*Born: Bridgeton, Glasgow, 2 October 1916.
Died: Kirkintilloch, 13 August 1982.
Career: Congleton Town amateur.
OLDHAM ATHLETIC May 1938 to April
1939.*

■ In the season prior to joining Athletic Bill Vallance had scored 14 goals in 36 matches with Congleton Town, and picked up a Cheshire League Cup-winners' medal. His family had strong football connections, Bill's father James Vallance, was a player with Queen's Park and Bradford Park Avenue, and trainer to Stoke City for many years; younger brother, Tom, played for Torquay United and Arsenal; and his sister, Betty, married Stanley Matthews.

VERNON, Scott Malcolm

Forward

*Born: Manchester, 13 December 1983.
Career: OLDHAM ATHLETIC trainee,
professional July 2002. Blackpool loan
September 2004, permanent June 2005, in
exchange for Richie Wellens. Colchester
United loan March 2006, permanent
January 2008.*

■ The son of John Vernon, a winger on Stockport County's books in the mid-1970s, Scott made his Football League debut against his father's old team on 2 November 2002 and scored Athletic's second goal in a 2–0 victory. The

previous month he had scored twice in his first senior outing against Carlisle United in the LDV Vans Trophy. Season 2003–04 saw his breakthrough into regular first-team action and he responded with 14 goals in 32/17 matches. He did less well in 2004–05 but a highly successful loan spell with Blackpool in early season doubtless influenced his permanent move to Bloomfield Road in the summer of 2005.

VONK, Michel Christian

Central-defender

*Born: Alkmaar, Netherlands, 28 October
1968.
Career: AK 67 Alkmaar. SVV Dordrecht.
Manchester City March 1992, fee
£300,000. OLDHAM ATHLETIC loan
November-December 1995. Sheffield
United December 1995 to July 1998, fee
£350,000.*

■ Powerful central-defender Michel Vonk was loaned to the Latics from Manchester City in November 1995, and in the following month scored in his final appearance, a 2–2 draw at Crystal Palace. The clubs had agreed a fee of £350,000 for a permanent transfer, but Athletic failed to agree personal terms with the player and on the following day he was signed by Sheffield United.

WADDELL, George Boyd

Half-back

*Born: Lesmahagow, Lanarkshire, 29
November 1888.
Career: Dalziel Rovers. Burnbank Athletic.
Larkhill United. Rangers January 1909.
Kilmarnock loan September 1913. Bradford
City June 1914, fee £1,000. Royal Albert*

*August 1915. Stevenson United October
1915. Ayr United August 1916. Abercorn
May 1917. Preston North End September
1920, fee £1,750. OLDHAM ATHLETIC
July 1922, fee £250. Birmingham October
1922, fee £325. Hamilton Academical July
1923. New Brighton trial 1 November 1923.
Wolverhampton Wanderers 30 November
1923. Aberaman player-coach June 1924.*

■ Fair-haired Scottish half-back George Waddell joined the Latics for what was described as a 'bargain fee', but moved on after only four months at Boundary Park, continuing his travels in a varied career. His final three League appearances were made for New Brighton in their initial season as members of the Football League. In 1931 he was working for Ribble Motors at Preston and still turning out for the works team at 43 years of age.

WADSWORTH, Albert William

Inside-forward

*Born: Heywood, 22 March 1925.
Died: Bury, 26 March 1982.
Career: Manchester United amateur May
1946. Mossley 1947–48. Stalybridge Celtic
1948–49. OLDHAM ATHLETIC August
1949 to June 1953.*

■ Ray Haddington's transfer to Manchester City in November 1950 opened the way for Albert Wadsworth, and the dapper little inside-forward enjoyed his best run of first-team football in George Hardwick's first season in charge with 28 appearances. While lacking the explosive shooting of his predecessor, Wadsworth had a neat touch on the ball and his subtle support play effectively kept the attack on the move.

WAITE, William John

Centre-forward

Born: Newport, 29 November 1917.
Died: Weston-Super-Mare, 23 June 1980.
Career: Newport County amateur.
OLDHAM ATHLETIC amateur
September 1942. Manchester United
amateur November 1942. OLDHAM
ATHLETIC professional March 1946.
Worcester City 1947.

■ Centre-forward Bill Waite first played for Athletic in September 1942 when serving as a lance corporal in the Pioneer Corps, and stationed in the North West. He later played twice for Athletic in April and May 1946, following his demobilisation from army service in Germany. On the eve of the new season he suffered a broken collarbone in a pre-season trial. On his return to action he scored against Southport and later in the season scored twice against the same opponents. Despite his goal-a-game aggregate, Waite remained in reserve with Fred Howe the favoured selection as attack leader.

WALDERS, David

Centre-half

Born: Barrow-in-Furness c.1880.
Died: Burnley, April 1929.
Career: Barrow September 1901. Burnley July 1903. OLDHAM ATHLETIC May 1906, fee £125. Sparta Rotterdam, Holland, trainer-coach October 1912. Southport Central May 1913. Wartime guest with Burnley 1916.

■ One of an excellent nucleus of players who guided Athletic from the Lancashire

Combination to the heady heights of the First Division within the space of four seasons, David Walders was Athletic's first captain in the Football League. He stayed long enough to earn a benefit match, with a guarantee of £250, in March 1912, the home game against Sheffield Wednesday being set aside for him. In October of the same year he sailed from Hull to take up the post of trainer-coach to Sparta Rotterdam. In May 1913 he joined Southport Central and scored twice in their record FA Cup win, 9–0 against Portsmouth Rangers on 11 October 1913.

WALDERS, John 'Jack'

Outside-right

Born: Barrow-in-Furness, 1881.
Died: Burnley, 17 January 1924.
Career: Barrow. Burnley May 1904. OLDHAM ATHLETIC May 1906. Luton Town May 1907. Chorley October 1908.

■ Unlike brother David, Jack Walders spent only one season with Athletic, assisting them to the Championship of the Lancashire Combination before leaving to join Luton Town. Jack scored three goals in seven FA Cup appearances, and three in 25 Lancashire Combination matches. His death at the early age of 42 years was said to have been as a result of the 'severe privations' that he had experienced during wartime military service.

WALKER, George Samuel

Centre-half

Born: Oldham, 1905.
Career: Chadderton Amateurs. Hyde

United. OLDHAM ATHLETIC November 1925, fee £125. Buxton 1926. Manchester North End. Buxton.

■ George Walker played just twice for Athletic's first team before refusing the terms offered for 1926–27. He moved into non-League football with Buxton and was still captaining the Cheshire League side 10 years later.

WALKER, Robert Stephen

Left-back

Born: Bolton, 20 September 1985.
Career: OLDHAM ATHLETIC trainee September 2002.

■ A mixture of scholars, trialists and eight fit professionals comprised Athletic's first-team squad in early August 2003. Second-year scholar Rob Walker showed promise in pre-season friendly matches on the left side of midfield and was rewarded with a place in the season's opener against Brighton & Hove Albion at Boundary Park. Athletic's patched-up team lost 3–1 in what proved to be the 17-year-old's only senior appearance.

WALKER, Samuel

Centre-half

Born: Eccles, 22 April 1922.
Died: Stockport, March 1990.
Career: Darwen. OLDHAM ATHLETIC August 1947. Winsford United July 1948 to May 1953.

■ Sam Walker was a nicely-proportioned centre-half who was given his first-team opportunity in place of Ken Armitage in a midweek fixture at Rotherham United on 1 September 1947. Athletic lost 4–1 and Walker returned to Lancashire Combination football, not adding to his single senior outing.

WALKER, Thomas Jackson

Outside-right

Born: Cramlington, 14 November 1923.
Died: Middleton, 14 June 2005.
Career: Netherton. Newcastle United October 1941. Wartime guest with West Ham United. OLDHAM ATHLETIC February 1954, fee £2,500. Chesterfield February 1957, fee £1,250. OLDHAM ATHLETIC July 1957, retired April 1959.

■ A usefully two-footed player, at home on either wing, Tommy Walker was fast enough to have competed in the famous Powderhall athletics meetings and was the winner of many sprint handicaps. The tall and rangy winger won two FA Cup medals with Newcastle United during a career in Tyneside that totalled 204 League and Cup appearances and 38 goals. In two spells with Athletic he made 164 appearances before announcing his retirement in April 1959. Outside of football Walker was a Methodist lay preacher and ran a newsagents in Middleton for almost 30 years.

WALL, George

Outside-left

Born: Boldon Colliery, near Sunderland, 20 February 1885.
Died: Manchester, 1962.
Career: Boldon Royal Rovers. Whitburn 1901. Jarrow September 1903. Barnsley November 1903. Manchester United April 1906, fee £175. Wartime guest with Cowdenbeath. OLDHAM ATHLETIC March 1919, fee £200. Hamilton Academical June 1921. Rochdale June 1922. Ashton National September 1923. Manchester Ship Canal FC reinstated amateur 1924.

■ George Wall was one of the best outside-lefts in the game in the period before World War One, starring in a potent Manchester United attack that also featured the great Billy Meredith on the opposite wing. Season 1908–09 was the undoubted high point in his career, as he won three of his seven England caps and scored twice against Scotland to give England the Home Championship. He was also an FA Cup winner as United lifted the trophy for the first time. Following wartime service as a sergeant in the Black Watch, he joined Athletic and missed very few games in his two-year stay, exhibiting fine ball control and the ability to cut inside and shoot. After leaving Athletic he passed the milestone of 500 League appearances in Rochdale's colours.

WALLACE, Charles William

Outside-right

Born: Southwick, Durham, 20 January 1885.
Died: Sutton Coldfield, 7 January 1970.
Career: Southwick FC. Crystal Palace July 1905. Aston Villa May 1907. Wartime guest with Fulham and Arsenal. OLDHAM ATHLETIC May 1921, fee £1,000, retired April 1923.

■ England international wingman Charlie Wallace appeared in 10 seasons of League football with Aston Villa, scoring 57 League and Cup goals in 349 matches. He won FA Cup-winners' medals either side of World War One and was a key member of the Villa side that won the League Championship in 1910. Although very much at the veteran stage when he joined Athletic, Wallace commanded a sizeable fee and had an excellent first season at Boundary Park.

Frequently sidelined with injuries in his second term, he announced his retirement as Athletic dropped out of the top flight. He returned to Birmingham and worked as a painter and decorator in addition to working at Villa Park as a member of the backroom staff in various capacities until 1960.

WALSH, Daniel Gareth

Midfield

Born: Pontefract, Yorkshire, 16 September 1978.
Career: Kippax Juniors, Leeds. OLDHAM ATHLETIC trainee July 1996, professional July 1998. Lincoln City July 2001. Chesterfield December 2001 to April 2002. Kettering Town July 2002. Bradford Park Avenue November 2002.

■ A central midfielder with plenty of drive and a good range of passing, Danny Walsh was released at the end of his contract having failed to graduate at Boundary Park, with injuries and illness hampering his progress. His senior debut was probably the shortest on record as he replaced Mark Innes in the 86th minute against Burnley in April 1999.

WALSH, Gary

Goalkeeper

Born: Wigan, 21 March 1968.
Career: Wigan Schoolboys. Manchester United apprentice June 1983, professional April 1985. Airdrieonians loan August 1988. OLDHAM ATHLETIC loan November-December 1993. Middlesbrough August 1995, fee £500,000. Bradford City loan September 1997, permanent October 1997, fee £500,000. Middlesbrough loan September 2000. Wigan Athletic July 2003. Retired July 2005.

■ In what proved to be Athletic's final season in the Premier League, England Under-21 goalkeeper Gary Walsh played in six matches on loan from Manchester United when regular goalkeepers Hallworth and Gerrard were sidelined by injury. Despite his lack of opportunities at Old Trafford, Walsh proved an excellent stand in, the tall and commanding 'keeper assisting a struggling Latics side to two wins and a draw within his six-match spell in the firing line.

WALSH, Kevin William

Left-half

Born: Rochdale, 11 February 1928.
Career: St Patrick's Old Boys. OLDHAM ATHLETIC October 1949. Southport July 1952. Bradford City June 1954, in exchange for Bill Holmes. Southport July 1956. Mossley November 1956. Stalybridge Celtic 1957–58.

■ Local product Kevin Walsh was given his League debut in the final fixture of his first season at Boundary Park. He then made two early-season appearances in 1950–51 but was exclusively in reserve thereafter. Walsh found more opportunities with Southport, appearing in 67 matches in his first spell at Haig Avenue before his transfer to Bradford City. In 1955–56, having moved up from wing-half to inside-forward, he scored within eight minutes of the kick-off as the Bantams beat Athletic 3–1 in the first-round FA Cup tie at Valley Parade in November 1955.

WALSH, William

Inside-forward

Born: Blackpool, 1909.
Died: Blackpool, 3 November 1965.
Career: South Shore Wednesday. Fleetwood. Bolton Wanderers amateur August 1931, professional October 1931. Fleetwood July 1932. OLDHAM ATHLETIC November 1933, fee £125. Heart of Midlothian May 1936. Millwall October 1937, fee £2,500. Wartime guest with OLDHAM ATHLETIC, Southampton, York City, Rochdale, Blackpool and Blackburn Rovers.

■ Within three minutes of the kick-off in his debut at Brentford, Billy Walsh was on the score sheet. A regular goalscorer throughout, his best season at Boundary Park was 1935–36, when he headed the Third Division North scoring lists with 32 goals from 41 matches and a further two in three FA Cup matches. During his spell in Scotland with Heart of Midlothian he scored eight out of 15 goals in a second-round Scottish Cup tie against Kings Park. Walsh rounded off his League career in typical fashion, scoring 11 goals in 21 matches for Millwall in 1937–38, when the Lions won the Championship of the Third Division South.

WALTERS, George Archibald

Outside-left

Born: Glasgow, 30 March 1939.
Career: Clyde. OLDHAM ATHLETIC August 1959 to June 1960.

■ George Walters was able to occupy either wing position but appeared more at home on the left. Peter Pheonix was the main occupant of the outside-left berth during the 1959–50 season, Walters being just one of four others to wear the number-11 shirt. The campaign marked the lowest point in Athletic's history when they finished 23rd in Division Four. In late season Walters suffered a badly wrenched knee against Barrow at Boundary Park on April 2 and was sidelined for the remainder of the season.

WALTERS, Joseph

Inside-forward

Born: Stourbridge, April 1886.
Died: New Moston, Manchester, 24 December 1923.
Career: Wordsley Athletic 1900. Stourbridge August 1902. Aston Villa June 1905. OLDHAM ATHLETIC June 1912, fee £900. Wartime guest with West Ham United and Queen's Park Rangers. Accrington Stanley September 1920. Southend United September 1920, fee £200. Millwall Athletic May 1921. Rochdale October 1922. Manchester North End 1923. Crewe Alexandra November 1923.

■ A member of Aston Villa's League Championship-winning side in 1910, Joe Walters enjoyed three good seasons at Boundary Park before the outbreak of World War One. After service with the Royal Flying Corps he returned unscathed to recommence with the Latics in 1919–20. In what was virtually a new team from the side that had finished runners-up for the League Championship, a season of struggle ended with Athletic 17th in Division One. Despite being at the veteran stage when leaving Boundary Park, Walters saw plenty of first-team football subsequently. At the untimely age of 37, he died from pneumonia at his home in New Moston on Christmas Eve 1923.

WANN, Alexander Halley 'Sandy'

Right-half

Born: Stanley, Perthshire, 20 December 1940.
Career: Lincarty Juniors. Manchester City July 1958. St Mirren October 1960. OLDHAM ATHLETIC December 1960. Forfar Athletic August 1961. Northwich Victoria August 1963 to July 1965.

■ Sandy Wann began with Manchester City and spent two years on the Maine Road staff before returning to Scotland to sign for St Mirren. Two months on, he was spotted by a Latics scout and returned to Lancashire, initially on trial. An exuberant, bustling wing-half with 13-plus stones to throw usefully into the fray, he quickly won a first-team place. He was, nevertheless, on the move again in the close season. He briefly served in the Scottish Police Force but migrated south yet again when he joined Northwich Victoria.

WARD, Mark William

Winger/Midfield

Born: Huyton, 10 October 1962.
Career: Everton apprentice June 1979, professional September 1980. Northwich Victoria May 1981. OLDHAM ATHLETIC July 1983, fee £10,000. West Ham United August 1985, fee £250,000. Manchester City December 1989, fee £1 million. Everton August 1991, fee £1.1 million. Birmingham City loan March–May 1994, permanent August 1994, fee

£500,000. Huddersfield Town March–June 1996. Motherwell trial September 1996. Wigan Athletic non-contract September-October 1996.

■ One of six players who made their Athletic debuts during 1983–84, diminutive midfielder Mark Ward was the one outright success with a 100 per cent playing record in the season's 46 League and Cup matches. He was similarly consistent in the following term, completing a second ever-present season. On the eve of the 1985–86 term, however, First Division West Ham United swooped for his transfer. Assisting the Hammers to third place in the First Division set the tone for a successful spell that concluded when Manchester City agreed a £1 million-rated exchange deal to secure his services. His next port of call was at a club that had once rejected him – Everton, who had to pay £1.1 million to bring him back to Goodison Park. A loan spell with Birmingham City became permanent and Ward played in 43 matches in the Blues' Division Two Championship side of 1994–95. Brief spells with Huddersfield Town and Wigan Athletic wound up his League career, after which he sampled a variety of football including spells in the Channel Islands, Iceland, Australia, Hong Kong and New York. In May 2005 Ward was arrested on drug-trafficking charges and in October of the same year was sentenced to eight years in jail. Those who knew him at his peak and admired his skill as a footballer found it difficult to comprehend his quite spectacular fall from grace.

WARD, Wilkin

Outside-right

Born: Oldham, 1884.
Career: Whitworth FC. OLDHAM ATHLETIC September 1906. Bradford Park Avenue June 1908, fee £300. Rossendale United September 1910. Rochdale Hornets (Rugby League Club) September 1911.

■ A professional runner as well as a footballer, 'Wilkie' Ward scored on his debut in a 3–0 win at Stalybridge Rovers in March 1907. Six months on, he was at outside-right in Athletic's first Football League fixture, a 3–1 victory at Stoke. In the initial League season he contested the outside-right berth with Frank Hesham before leaving to join Bradford Park Avenue in what was their first season as a Football League club. A year with Rossendale United followed before he switched codes to assist Rochdale Hornets Rugby League Club as a wing-threequarter.

WARHURST, Paul

Defender

Born: Stockport, 26 September 1969.
Career: Manchester Schoolboys. Manchester City associate schoolboy 1984, trainee July 1986, professional July 1988. OLDHAM ATHLETIC October 1988, fee £10,000. Sheffield Wednesday July 1991, fee £750,000. Blackburn Rovers September 1993, fee £2.7 million. Crystal Palace July 1997, fee £1.25 million. Bolton Wanderers loan November 1998,

permanent January 1999, fee £800,000. Stoke City loan March 2003. Bolton Wanderers September 2003. Chesterfield October 2003. Barnsley December 2003. Carlisle United non-contract February 2004. Grimsby Town March 2004. Preston North End non-contract August 2004. Blackpool November 2004. Forest Green Rovers March 2005. Wrexham August 2005. Barnet March 2006. Northwich Victoria, very briefly caretaker manager September 2007.

■ First taken on by Manchester City at the age of 15, Paul Warhurst was 19 and relatively unknown when Athletic manager Joe Royle paid a modest £10,000 for his transfer. Initially lacking stamina to go with his great technique and electrifying pace, he did not play regularly until his second season. Warhurst's appearance at Wembley in the Littlewoods Cup Final against Nottingham Forest was the pinnacle of a season that had seen a remarkable rise in his fortunes. Mainly played in a lightning-quick central-defensive partnership with Earl Barrett, he was asked to fill in at right-back the following season after Denis Irwin moved to Manchester United. After being dropped in favour of Gunnar Halle he requested a transfer in February 1991 and joined Sheffield Wednesday for the first of his many subsequent moves. Along with eight England Under-21 caps, his club honours included appearances in the FA Cup and Football League Cup Finals with Sheffield Wednesday and a Premier League Championship with Blackburn Rovers in 1995. Paul's grandfather Harry Stock played for the Latics between 1948–51.

WARHURST, Roy

Wing-half

Born: Handsworth, Sheffield, 18 September 1926.
Career: Atlas & Norfolk Works FC. Huddersfield Town amateur 1943. Sheffield United amateur May 1944, professional September 1944. Birmingham City March 1950, fee £8,000. Manchester City June 1957, fee £10,000. Crewe Alexandra March 1959. OLDHAM ATHLETIC August 1960. Banbury Spencer August 1961.

■ Roy Warhurst was a Second Division Championship winner with Birmingham City in season 1954–55 and was desperately unlucky in the following season to miss the FA Cup Final against Manchester City due to injury. After two seasons with Manchester City and 17 months with Crewe Alexandra he arrived at Boundary Park with over 300 League appearances to his credit. Appointed club captain by new manager Jack Rowley, Warhurst played in eight of the first nine Division Four matches of season 1960–61 before being dropped with the side at the foot of the table. Retiring from the game in 1964 he become a scrap-metal dealer in Birmingham.

WARNE, Paul

Forward

Born: Norwich, 8 May 1973.
Career: Wroxham. Wigan Athletic July 1997, fee £25,000. Rotherham United January 1999. Mansfield Town loan November 2004. OLDHAM ATHLETIC July 2005. Yeovil Town June 2007.

■ Although the goals dried up for Paul Warne during Athletic's run to the Play-offs in 2006–07, the popular and hard working front man scored 11 goals in 50/4 matches and won the fans' vote as Player of the Year. Less than a week later he was released, his experience being a brusque reminder of football's roller-coaster fortunes. The veteran forward found no shortage of offers and was quickly fixed up with a two-year contract by Yeovil Town, promotion rivals in 2006–07.

WARNER, John

Wing-half

Born: Trelaw, Tonypandy, 21 September 1911.
Died: Tonypandy, 4 October 1980.
Career: Treorchy Juniors. Aberaman 1932. Swansea Town January 1934. Manchester United June 1938. OLDHAM ATHLETIC player-coach June 1951. Rochdale player-manager July 1952 to May 1953.

■ Recruited by Athletic as player-coach, Wales international Jack Warner was within a month of his 40th birthday when he made his debut at Southport. At the time he was the club's oldest debutant, but his ability to control the ball and deliver telling passes from midfield made him an influential member of the side, despite his age and greying locks. A season with Rochdale proved to be his last in League football and he retired, aged 42.

WATSON, Albert

Wing-half

Born: Bolton-on-Dearne, 1 June 1918.
Career: Huddersfield Town amateur September 1936, professional October 1936. OLDHAM ATHLETIC July 1948 to July 1950.

■ Albert Watson was captain of Huddersfield Town reserves in 1945 and made infrequent First Division appearances before his transfer to the Latics. Although lacking pace, he was a constructive wing-half whose game featured a quite remarkable long throw-in that was often used to advantage in the final third of the field. In 1949 he opened a sports outfitting shop in Sunderland with his brother Willie, the Sunderland and England wing-half and Yorkshire and England batsman.

WATSON, Mark Stewart

Central-defender

Born: Vancouver, Canada, 8 September 1970.
Career: Vancouver 86ers, Canada. Ipswich Town September 1993. Watford November 1993. Vancouver 86ers August 1995. Osters IFV, Sweden 1997. Oxford United December 1998 to May 2000. Wolverhampton Wanderers trial. DC United, US, trial. OLDHAM ATHLETIC non-contract September 2000, professional October 2000. St Johnstone trial. DC United, US, January 2001.

■ A widely travelled Canadian international central-defender who was offered a one-month deal and the opportunity to link up with international colleague, Carlo Corazzin. The fact that Athletic suffered heavy defeats in all three of Mark Watson's appearances suggested that he was not the man to halt the early season gloom and he was released at the end of his trial period.

WATSON, Reginald Herbert 'Bert'

Outside-left

Born: Latchford, near Warrington, 26 August 1900.
Died: Thelwell, Cheshire, 1971.
Career: Witton Albion. Manchester United trial. OLDHAM ATHLETIC December 1921, fee £300. Southampton June 1929, in exchange for William Murphy. Rochdale September 1931, retired February 1932.

■ Rejected by Manchester United after two trial games, Bert Watson was quickly spotted by Athletic and stepped straight into the first team. In eight seasons the speedy, sharp-shooting wingman's aggregate of 72 goals was the highest for any player in the pre-war period. He had three really outstanding seasons between 1925 and 1928, missing only eight first-team matches and scoring successive seasonal totals of 19, 15 and 17 goals. He was awarded a benefit with a guarantee of £500 in May 1928 and in the match against Hull City scored twice in the first five minutes to set up a 5–0 victory.

WATTS, Henry P.

Inside-forward

Career: Failsworth FC. OLDHAM ATHLETIC November 1907. Haslingden February 1911, in exchange for Sam Pilkington. Hurst FC February 1912.

■ Harry Watts scored a hat-trick against Blackpool reserves in his third appearance for Athletic reserves on 23 November 1907, and he was on the mark in his League debut against Fulham in February of the same year. He did well

as deputy for the injured Harry Hancock, scoring four goals in nine matches, but lacked opportunities thereafter.

WEALANDS, Jeffrey Andrew

Goalkeeper

Born: Darlington, 26 August 1951.
Career: Darlington Cleveland Bridge FC. Wolverhampton Wanderers apprentice June 1968, professional October 1968. Northampton Town loan February 1970. Darlington July 1970. Hull City March 1972, fee £10,000. Birmingham City July 1979, fee £30,000. Manchester United February 1983. OLDHAM ATHLETIC loan March 1984. Preston North End loan December 1984. Altrincham May 1985. Barrow August 1987. Altrincham 1988 to March 1992.

■ Efficient and unspectacular, Jeff Wealands began with Darlington before spending seven years with Hull City. In his first season with Birmingham City he helped them to win promotion from Division Two and picked up the Player of the Year award. He joined Athletic on loan from Manchester United where he was restricted to eight League and Cup appearances due to a troublesome back injury. Wealands was, nevertheless, still guarding Altrincham's goal at 40 years of age and during his spell at Moss Rose helped the Robins to beat First Division Birmingham City in the FA Cup third round at St Andrews in January 1986.

WEBSTER, Simon Paul

Central-defender

Born: Earl Shilton, Leicestershire, 20 January 1964.

Career: Mid Hertfordshire and Hertfordshire Schoolboys. Tottenham Hotspur apprentice May 1980, professional December 1981. Barnet loan December 1982. Exeter City loan November 1983. Norwich City loan January 1985. Huddersfield Town February 1985, fee £15,000. Sheffield United March 1988, fee £35,000. Charlton Athletic August 1990, fee £50,000. West Ham United June 1993, fee £525,000. OLDHAM ATHLETIC loan March 1995. Derby County loan August 1995. Retired November 1996.

■ A tall, commanding central-defender who was also able to occupy a full-back role when required, Simon Webster began as a Tottenham Hotspur apprentice but made the bulk of his senior appearances with Huddersfield Town (118 appearances and four goals) and Charlton Athletic (127 appearances and seven goals). The second broken leg of his career cruelly deprived him of the chance to establish himself in Premier League football, as he made only five substitute appearances for West Ham United in just over three years on their books. During his loan spell with Athletic he helped steer the team clear of relegation with four wins in his first five matches.

WELLENS, Richard Paul 'Richie'

Midfield

Born: Manchester, 26 March 1980.
Career: Manchester United trainee, professional May 1997. Blackpool March 2000. OLDHAM ATHLETIC July 2005. Doncaster Rovers July 2007.

■ Elegant midfielder Richie Wellens joined Athletic from Blackpool in the deal that took striker Scott Vernon to Bloomfield Road. Mature reading of the game plus a rousing enthusiasm were features of Wellen's two years at Boundary Park; he was also happily free from injury and completed 101 appearances, scoring eight goals. Rejecting Athletic's offer of a new contract, Wellens was quickly snapped up by League One rivals Doncaster Rovers and assisted them to promotion via the Wembley Play-off Final against Leeds United.

WELLOCK, Maurice

Inside-forward

Born: Bradford, 15 June 1902.
Died: Manningham, Bradford, 9 July 1967.
Career: Drummond Road School. Bradford Schoolboys. Bradford City July 1919. Halifax Town 1920. Blackpool July 1923, fee £250. OLDHAM ATHLETIC February 1927. Torquay United June 1927. Peterborough & Fletton United June 1928. Darlington June 1929. Halifax Town June 1932, club trainer October 1933 to May 1937.

■ A schoolboy international centre-forward with his native Bradford, Maurice Wellock's spell with Athletic was brief but eventful, beginning with a stunning four-goal debut at Grimsby Town. Despite the sensational start he lost his place after four consecutive appearances, reappearing only once before being released after just four months at Boundary Park. His most productive spell was with Darlington for whom he scored 74 League and Cup goals in 109 matches.

WEST, Edward

Left-back

Born: Parbold, 4 November 1930.
Died: Mansfield, April 2002.
Career: Sussex County Amateurs. Eastbourne United. Doncaster Rovers February 1953. Aldershot trial. Gillingham July 1954. OLDHAM ATHLETIC July 1957 to June 1961. Bankstown FC, Australia.

■ A fixture in Athletic's rearguard for three seasons, Ted West's game featured a well-timed and effective sliding tackle

and he was quick enough to surprise wingmen with his excellent powers of recovery. He finally lost out following the appointment of Jack Rowley as manager, who settled on a pairing of Ken Branagan and John McCue at full-back. West emigrated to Australia after leaving Boundary Park and continued in football with Bankstown FC, a club managed by Frank Broome, the former Aston Villa and England forward.

WEST, John

Inside-forward

Born: Oldham.
Career: Oldham Grammar School. Northern Nomads. OLDHAM ATHLETIC amateur April 1909. Aston Villa amateur November 1910.

■ A prominent local amateur, John West was recruited by Athletic in the midst of an injury crisis in late-season 1908–09. West's League debut at Leeds City was not distinguished and Athletic were beaten 3–0, not helped by a first-half injury to full-back Jimmy Hodson that left him a limping passenger on the wing. Shortly after his solitary League appearance West was called up as travelling reserve for the England Amateur International party's Easter tour to the Netherlands.

WEST, Thomas Norton

Forward

Born: Salford, 8 December 1916.
Died: Salford, May 1987.
Career: McMahon's FC. Stockport County March 1938. OLDHAM ATHLETIC July 1939. Rochdale June 1946. Nelson. Morecambe.

■ In the final season of regional football Ted West scored 13 goals in 20 matches and two in four FA Cup ties. Despite his excellent scoring record he was not retained and made the short journey to Rochdale along with Charlie Hurst, father of Geoff, England's World Cup hat-trick hero of 1966.

WHAITES, Alexander

Outside-left

Born: Most probably in Ireland c.1884.
Career: Linfield. Bradford City May 1904. OLDHAM ATHLETIC September 1907 to April 1909.

■ In one of his earliest senior outings with Bradford City, Alex Whaites scored two goals in a 9–0 FA Cup sixth qualifying round demolition of Sunderland West End. He joined Athletic as an emergency signing following the

early-season injury to Jimmy Swarbrick. Whaites had found little opportunity for first-team football at Valley Parade, but scored 10 goals in 39 matches for Athletic in his first season. Early honours in Irish football with Linfield included a League Championship in 1902 and an Irish Cup win in 1904.

WHELAN, Robert

Right-half

Born: Salford, 9 November 1930.
Career: Salford Youth Club. Manchester City April 1950. OLDHAM ATHLETIC July 1952. Accrington Stanley July 1953. Stalybridge Celtic June 1956.

■ Bob Whelan was unfortunate to sustain a quite serious injury within weeks of his promising League debut. In the 3–0 home win against Barrow his enthusiasm and studied use of the ball had impressed onlookers. In the season that the Latics won the Third Division North Championship, his role as understudy to Tommy Lowrie proved an unrewarding one.

WHITAKER, Colin

Outside-left

Born: Leeds, 14 June 1932.
Career: Farsley Celtic. Sheffield Wednesday November 1951. Bradford Park Avenue June 1953. Shrewsbury Town July 1956. Queen's Park Rangers February 1961. Rochdale May 1961. OLDHAM ATHLETIC October 1962, in exchange for Peter Phoenix. Barrow August 1964. Ashton United November 1964. Buxton 1965. Droylsden manager. Stalybridge Celtic player-manager 1967. Buxton manager 1970. Droylsden manager 1974. Buxton manager 1977 to 1980.

■ A speedy and confident winger who believed in taking the shortest route to goal, Colin Whitaker scored 109 League goals in 348 matches overall, his tally including nine hat-tricks and, in December 1958, four goals for Shrewsbury Town against Southport. He scored three of Athletic's 11 goals against Southport on Boxing Day 1962 and three against Peterborough United in September 1963. A fully qualified FA coach, he also played cricket for Castleton Moor in the Central Lancashire League and was an excellent golfer.

WHITE, Cornelius

Inside-forward

Born: Leicester, 10 March 1905.
Died: Leicester, 1975.
Career: Whitwick Imperial. Birmingham trial 1925. OLDHAM ATHLETIC February 1925, fee £25. Llandudno loan December 1925, permanent April 1926. Bacup Borough. Bangor City November 1926. Bradford City June 1928. Loughborough Corinthians July 1929. Hereford United. Nuneaton Town August 1933.

■ Cornelius White failed to graduate with Athletic and a loan spell with Llandudno became permanent and ultimately very successful. Bradford City gave him a second opportunity at League level and his debut at Valley Parade against Rotherham United on 25 August 1928 remains to this day Bradford City's record victory in League football. They opened the season by beating Rotherham 11–1, White being one of two forwards who registered hat-tricks. Despite the exceptional start, White played only four times during the season as Bradford City took the Third Division North title.

WHITE, Gwilym David 'George'

Right-back

Born: Doncaster, 25 February 1936.
Career: Plymouth Argyle amateur. OLDHAM ATHLETIC amateur August 1960 to May 1961.

■ White was serving in the RAF at the time of his isolated outing, a 5–1 defeat at Bradford Park Avenue on 27 August 1960. Athletic's problems at the back remained unresolved until manager Rowley recruited the vastly experienced Ken Branagan and John McCue.

WHITEHALL, Steven Christopher

Forward

Born: Bromborough, Wirral, 8 December 1966.
Career: Heswall. Stork FC. Southport 1989. Rochdale July 1991, fee £25,000. Mansfield Town August 1997. OLDHAM ATHLETIC July 1998, fee £50,000. Chester City loan September 2000, permanent

October 2000. Nuneaton Borough August 2001. Southport November 2001. Marine FC. Southport physiotherapist, joint caretaker manager January 2007.

■ Despite arriving at Boundary Park with excellent credentials as a goalscorer, Steve Whitehall failed to do himself justice, a succession of injuries doing nothing for his form or confidence, his first season yielding just four goals from 32/10 matches. Despite a better return in 1999–2000 (11 goals in 29/12 matches) he was loaned to Chester City in the early stages of 2000–01, and in October the move was made permanent, Athletic releasing him on a free transfer.

WHITTLE, Maurice

Left-back

Born: Wigan, 5 July 1948.
Career: Blackburn Rovers apprentice June 1963, professional October 1966. OLDHAM ATHLETIC May 1969. Fort Lauderdale Strikers, US, April to August 1977. Wigan Athletic. Fort Lauderdale Strikers, US, April 1978. Southport September 1978. Fort Lauderdale Strikers,

US, March–August 1979. Wigan Athletic. Bangor City. Stafford Rangers September 1979. Barrow October 1979–February 1982. Macclesfield Town. Lytham player-coach. Atherton player-manager. Barrow manager May–October 1985. OBS, Finland, manager.

■ Maurice Whittle was a distinctive figure on the field, characterised by his long curly hair, loping stride, and socks worn around his ankles. His long-running full-back partnership with Ian Wood was an extremely successful one and spanned promotion from Division Four in 1971 to the Third Division Championship in 1974. Whittle was a fierce striker of a dead ball, with free-kicks anywhere near to goal a speciality. He was also a very successful converter of penalty-kicks and his total of 41 goals from full-back was a handsome return.

WHYTE, Charles

Outside-right

Born: Bridgemill, Kincardineshire, 20 September 1911.
Career: Arbroath Ardenlea Juniors. Dundee United June 1932–April 1933. Arbroath. Rochdale trial August 1934. OLDHAM ATHLETIC trial November–December 1934. Nelson December 1934. Montrose January 1935.

■ Charlie Whyte failed in his attempts to establish himself in English League football. After leaving Arbroath he undertook a two-month trial with Rochdale. He appeared in nine consecutive League matches and scored one goal but was not offered a permanent engagement. Athletic similarly declined to extend his trial after he had played in two Second Division matches. Lancashire Combination club Nelson was his final port of call in English football, but after two months at Seedhill he returned to Scottish Second Division football with Montrose.

WHYTE, John Archibald 'Archie'

Centre-half

Born: Redding, Stirlingshire, 17 July 1919.
Died: Middleton, 1 October 1973.
Career: Armadale Thistle. Barnsley May 1938. OLDHAM ATHLETIC August 1950

to June 1956. Coaching staff until December 1960.

■ Archie Whyte began with Barnsley as an inside-forward but was successfully converted into a powerful and dominating centre-half. Moving to Boundary Park, he became a key figure in the Latics' improvement that culminated in the Third Division North Championship success in 1952–53. Whyte appeared in every League and Cup match during that campaign – just part of a run of exactly 100 consecutive outings that was only curtailed by injury in January 1954. Rarely absent throughout his six-year playing career, Whyte was rewarded with a benefit match on 5 May 1955. Many old favourites appeared in the Athletic XI including Ray Haddington, Jimmy Munro and Bobby McIlvenny. Their opponents, a 'Manager's XI' included internationals Peter Doherty, Johnny Carey and Frank Broome. For the record, a 3–3 draw resulted.

WIGGINS, Joseph Albert

Centre-forward

Born: Wembley, 1 April 1909.
Died: Wembley, 27 April 1982.
Career: Hanwell Town. Grays Thurrock 1926. Brentford August 1927. Leicester City May 1928, fee £1,400. Gillingham July 1934. Rochdale July 1935. OLDHAM

ATHLETIC May 1936. Stalybridge Celtic February 1937. Hurst FC April 1937. Rhyl until February 1946.

■ Joe Wiggins was signed by Athletic two days after the departure of centre-forward Billy Walsh to Heart of Midlothian. Walsh had broken Athletic's scoring record with 32 League goals in the previous season, so Wiggins had a hard act to follow. In the event, it was Tommy Davis who proved to be the worthy replacement, scoring 33 League goals during the season. Wiggins meanwhile shuttled between centre-forward and right-back in the reserves and was released before the end of the season.

WIJNHARD, Clyde

Forward

Born: Paramaribo, Surinam, 9 November 1973.
Career: Ajax. Groningen loan 1993–94. Ajax. RKC Waelwijk August 1995. Willem II Tilburg August 1997. Leeds United July 1998, fee £1.5 million. Huddersfield Town July 1999, fee £750,000. Preston North End, March 2002. Trials with Barnsley and Galatasaray. OLDHAM ATHLETIC non-contract August 2002, professional 30 August 2002. Vitoria Guimaraes, Portugal June 2003. Beira Mar, Portugal. Darlington October 2004. Macclesfield Town loan October 2005, professional January 2006. Brentford September–December 2006.

■ A centre-forward with experience at the highest level of the game and a former teammate of Dennis Bergkamp at Ajax, Clive Wijnhard was a free agent when offered a trial by Latics manager Ian Dowie. After scoring on his debut against Tranmere Rovers he was rewarded with a 12-month contract. Ten goals in his first 12 games was a dream start for the stylish and direct attack leader, but cartilage problems halted his progress and an 18-month lay-off was envisaged. A second opinion and a period of recuperation saw him back in late season, but he was unable to replicate his earlier scoring feats as Athletic's promotion push foundered in Play-off defeat by Queen's Park Rangers.

WILBRAHAM, Aaron Thomas

Forward

Born: Knutsford, 21 October 1979.
Career: Stockport County trainee, professional August 1997. Hull City July 2004, fee £100,000. OLDHAM ATHLETIC loan October-November 2004. MK Dons July 2005. Bradford City loan March 2006.

■ Loaned to Athletic from Hull City in October 2004, powerfully-built Aaron Wilbraham made an immediate impact, scoring both goals in Athletic's 2–1 victory at Stockport County, the scene of his former triumphs. A further four appearances for Athletic were less productive but on his return to Hull City Wilbraham assisted the Tigers to their second successive promotion. In 2007–08 Wilbraham was a Football League Two Championship winner with MK Dons.

WILDMAN, Arthur

Outside-right

Born: Bury, c.1885.
Career: Bury St Thomas. Freetown FC, Bury. OLDHAM ATHLETIC April 1904. Bury August 1904. OLDHAM ATHLETIC July 1905 to 1906.

■ Arthur Wildman first appeared for Athletic in their Manchester League days as a trialist outside-right from Freetown FC. He made his debut against Macclesfield on 1 April 1904 in a match won 4–0 by Athletic. Six months later, he was transferred to Bury, but spent a season in the reserve side at Gigg Lane. When re-signed by Athletic in July 1905 he became one of eight different players to occupy the outside-right berth during the course of the season.

WILKINSON, Harry

Centre-half

Born: Derker, Oldham, 2 May 1903.
Died: Glodwick, Oldham, 16 July 1997.
Career: Albert Mount. Wellington Albion. Werneth Amateurs. OLDHAM ATHLETIC amateur March 1921, professional May 1922. Bolton Wanderers July 1926. Mossley May 1927. Southport July 1928. Ashton National October 1928, retired 1929.

■ Local product Harry Wilkinson was an excellent club player, but in the role of understudy to Elliott Pilkington found opportunities limited, his cause was hampered by a series of injuries and illnesses which finally curtailed his career at the age of 26. In his infrequent appearances he impressed as a quietly effective defender and a good distributor with excellent aerial ability. In summer months he played in Central Lancashire League cricket with Oldham and Werneth. His father, Joe Wilkinson, was a hooker with Oldham Rugby League club for 14 years.

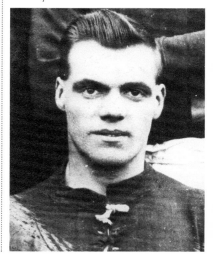

WILKINSON, Paul

Forward

Born: Grimoldby, near Louth, Lincolnshire, 30 October 1964.
Career: Clee Juniors. Grimsby Town associate schoolboy February 1980, apprentice July 1981, professional November 1982. Everton March 1985, fee £250,000. Nottingham Forest March 1987, fee £275,000. Watford August 1988, fee £300,000. Middlesbrough August 1991, fee £550,000. OLDHAM ATHLETIC loan October 1995. Watford loan November 1995. Luton Town loan March 1996. Barnsley July 1996. Millwall September 1997, fee £150,000. Northampton Town July 1998 to June 2000.

■ Paul Wilkinson spent a month on loan with Athletic in season 1995–96 but was sidelined for two matches after suffering a broken nose at Luton Town in his third outing in November 1995. His career began with great promise at Grimsby Town, where he began as a midfielder and was only tried in attack in an emergency. His powerful displays as a striker subsequently earned him England Under-21 recognition and a big-money move to Everton where he was a Football League Championship winner in 1987. Briefly with Nottingham Forest, he blossomed at Watford, being their leading goalscorer for three seasons before joining Middlesbrough. In 1994–95 he helped take Middlesbrough from Division One to the Premier League, but was then displaced by new signings Uwe Fuchs and Jan-Aage Fjortoft. In terms of League matches alone, Wilkinson's impressive career totalled 507/34 appearances and 154 goals.

WILKINSON, Wesley Michael

Forward

Born: Wythenshawe, 1 May 1984.
Career: Nantwich Town. OLDHAM ATHLETIC March 2004. Woodley Sports July 2005.

■ Nineteen-year-old striker or left-winger Wes Wilkinson was signed up at Boundary Park in the same week that new manager Brian Talbot took over from caretaker John Sheridan. In less than two seasons of North West Counties football with Nantwich Town Wilkinson had scored 41 goals. He made a most promising debut from the bench against Barnsley, replacing the injured Chris Killen after 45 minutes. Wilkinson was re-signed in the close season but injuries hampered his progress in 2004–05 and he was released in the summer.

WILLIAMS, Alan

Centre-half

Born: Bristol, 3 June 1938.
Career: Bristol and Gloucestershire Schoolboys. Bristol City amateur June 1955, professional September 1955. OLDHAM ATHLETIC June 1961, fee £1,000. Watford July 1965, fee £5,000. Newport County November 1966, fee £3,000. Swansea Town October 1968. Gloucester City June 1972.

■ Alan Williams averaged 43 League matches per season during his four years with Athletic, a true reflection of his consistent form and fitness. He appeared in every match in the Division Four promotion season of 1962–63, captaining the side from March until the end of the campaign. A rugged, no-nonsense pivot who used the ball well out of defence, his headwork was also a great asset in both defence and attack. Williams's career aggregate spanned 554/4 League matches and 25 goals, and on retirement he took over licensed premises near to Bristol City's Ashton Gate ground. His son Gary spent six years with the Latics.

WILLIAMS, Derek

Goalkeeper

Born: Mold, Flintshire, 15 June 1934.
Career: Bangor University. Mold Alexandra. Manchester City amateur May 1951. Mold Alexandra. Connah's Quay Nomads 1952–53. Bangor City 1953. Middlesex Wanderers 1954. Wrexham

amateur August 1954. Pwllheli 1955. Mold Alexandra 1955. OLDHAM ATHLETIC September 1956 to June 1959.

■ Welsh amateur international goalkeeper Derek Williams played once for Manchester City in the First Division as a 17-year-old, starring in a scoreless draw against Blackpool at Maine Road. He appeared for Wrexham in a dozen League matches in 1954–55, and was Athletic's first choice in 1956–57 until his call-up papers arrived in February 1957. Released by Athletic in June 1959, he took up rugby union and was good enough to represent Denbighshire and North Wales. Williams achieved a degree in mathematics and later qualified as a chartered accountant.

WILLIAMS, Gary Alan

Midfield

Born: Bristol, 8 June 1963.
Career: Bristol City apprentice June 1979, professional August 1980. Portsmouth non-contract December 1984. Swansea City January 1985. Bristol Rovers non-contract March 1985. OLDHAM ATHLETIC August 1985. Heart of Midlothian July 1991 to 1993. Bath City season 1993–94.

■ Gary Williams followed in his father Alan's footsteps by assisting both Bristol City and Athletic. Recommended to Latics manager Joe Royle by former playing colleagues at Bristol City, Gary was invited for trials. He scored in his

first Central League appearance at Scunthorpe and made his first-team debut at Huddersfield Town, as an emergency right-back in place of the injured Willie Donachie. In his best season at Boundary Park Williams scored nine League goals from midfield, plus one in the heartbreaking Play-off semi-final against Leeds United in May 1987, won by Leeds on the away goals rule with a goal scored in the last minute of normal time.

WILLIAMS, Jeffrey Bell

Inside-forward

Born: Salford, 11 January 1933.
Career: Salford and Lancashire Schoolboys. North Salford Youth Club. OLDHAM ATHLETIC June 1951 to April 1954.

■ Jeffrey Williams was serving in the Royal Corps of Signals at Catterick Camp when he made his debut in a goalless draw at Southport. It proved to be a solitary League appearance, as National Service took him to Germany where he did not kick a ball for a year. After demobilisation he returned to the Latics but failed to graduate beyond Lancashire Combination football. In season 1953–54 a back injury enforced his retirement from the professional game.

WILLIAMSON, Thomas

Half-back

Born: Salford, 16 March 1913.
Died: South Lowestoft, 28 June 1992.
Career: Pendleton Wednesday. Leeds United amateur July 1932, professional
September 1932. Northwich Victoria August 1933. OLDHAM ATHLETIC May 1935. Wartime guest with Rochdale April 1944. Fleetwood player-manager June 1947, retired 1957.

■ Tommy Williamson's Christmas Day 1935 debut with the Latics was a merry one, as a Billy Walsh hat-trick helped give Athletic the points in a 4–1 victory. One day later, however, in the return fixture at Tranmere, the Rovers ran riot, winning by the record scoreline of 13–4! Some weeks later, Williamson was injured, had a cartilage operation, and sat out the remainder of the season. Employed locally in aircraft engineering, he was able to play football throughout the war years and his total appearances for the club, in all competitions, was in excess of 400. He was the Latics' popular skipper on the resumption of normal League fare in 1946, and to mark his long service he was awarded a benefit match in April 1947. Over 22,000 spectators packed into Boundary Park for the match against an International XI, which included such famous names as Stanley Matthews, Stanley Mortenson, Frank Swift and George Hardwick. Williamson left Athletic to take over a business in Fleetwood, but at the same time applied for the manager's job at Boundary Park. He didn't get it, but subsequently proved that he had the ability, making his mark in Lancashire Combination circles with Fleetwood. After moving to Lowestoft, he managed Richards Ironworks and Brooke Marine, winning a string of trophies with both clubs.

WILSON, Clare

Half-back

Born: Boroughbridge, Yorkshire, 1886.
Career: Gateshead Town. Wallsend Park Villa. Bradford City February 1907. Glossop North End December 1908. OLDHAM ATHLETIC December 1911, fee £50. Gateshead September 1913.

■ Said to be lacking a little in pace but nothing in effort, Clare Wilson was a valued member of Athletic's staff during two seasons of First Division football. With internationals available for all three half-back positions, his appearances were limited but he was a first-class utility player, able to occupy all three half-back positions and the inside-forward berth with equal faculty.

WILSON, David

Left-half

Born: Irvine, Ayrshire, 14 January 1884.
Career: St Mirren 1901. Hamilton Academical August 1904. Bradford City November 1904. OLDHAM ATHLETIC May 1906, fee £90, player-coach September 1920. Nelson player-manager May 1921 to 1925. Exeter City manager March 1928 to February 1929.

■ David Wilson joined Athletic from Bradford City in Lancashire Combination days. In his first season he made maximum appearances, including Lancashire and Manchester Cup ties. He was eventually – but mistakenly – credited with 264 consecutive League appearances. He did in fact appear in 263 consecutive matches for

the club but this in all competitions, including minor Cup matches and friendly fixtures. In League and FA Cup matches alone he totalled 180 consecutive outings, not missing a game for almost four and a half seasons. Always the most consistent player, he was a glutton for work, playing the game from the first to the final whistle. One press comment from 1921 aptly summed up his many attributes: 'Always a player of remarkable stamina, he probably never had an equal as a defender. His energy was tireless, and the wonderful enthusiasm he introduced into his game was ever a great incentive to his colleagues.' He departed Oldham after a 15-year association to become player-manager of Nelson, at that time a Football League club operating in the Third Division North and in his second season at Seedhill he guided his team to the Championship. David Wilson was capped by Scotland in 1913, while his elder brother, Andrew, won six Scotland caps, two League Championships and one FA Cup medal with Sheffield Wednesday and was Athletic's manager from July 1927 to July 1932.

WILSON, John

Inside-forward

Born: Airdrie, 29 October 1916.
Career: Lochgelly Albert. Glasgow Celtic. Chesterfield May 1939. Wartime guest with Ballantyre Juniors, Hamilton Academical and Cowdenbeath. OLDHAM ATHLETIC July 1947, fee £500.

Accrington Stanley October 1948 to July 1950, fee £650.

■ Raised in the soccer-minded village of Blairhill, John Wilson was taken on to Glasgow Celtic's staff but did not reach senior level. A pre-war signing by Chesterfield, he returned to Scotland during World War Two and assisted Ballantyre Juniors to victory in the Hampden Park Cup. Never noted as a prolific goalscorer, he was an elusive dribbler and prompter-in-chief of Athletic's attack, his adroit passing skills being capable of unlocking the tightest defences. He left Boundary Park in the month of his 32nd birthday to join Accrington Stanley, but his spell at Peel Park was hampered by injuries, restricting him to 28 League appearances in two seasons.

WILSON, Ramon 'Ray'

Left-back

Born: Shirebrook, Derbyshire, 17 December 1934.
Career: Langwith Junction Imps. Huddersfield Town amateur May, professional August 1952. Everton July 1964, fee £25,000 plus Mick Meagan. OLDHAM ATHLETIC July 1969. Bradford City youth-team player-coach July 1970.

■ A one-time railway fireman in his native Derbyshire, Ray Wilson was a quick, decisive defender with exceptional creative skills. He developed with Huddersfield Town into one of the best

left-backs in the game, despite operating in an average Second Division side. After 12 years and the first 30 of his 63 England caps he was transferred to Everton and two years on was a member of England's successful World Cup-winning team. He was also an FA Cup winner in the same year. A knee injury sustained in training required surgery and he played in only 6/3 matches in 1968–69 and was released on a free transfer in the close season. Appointed captain on his arrival at Boundary Park, his time was blighted by injury and in mid-season he was replaced at left-back by Maurice Whittle. On leaving the game he joined his brother-in-law in the family undertaking business at Outlane, near Huddersfield.

WINN, Ashley

Midfield

Born: Stockton, 1 December 1985.
Career: OLDHAM ATHLETIC trainee July 2002. York City June 2005. Stalybridge Celtic July 2006.

■ Two brief substitute appearances against Swindon Town and AFC Bournemouth in October 2004 was the extent of Ashley Winn's Athletic career at senior level and he was one of several players released by Ronnie Moore in the close season.

WITHAM, Richard

Left-back

Born: Bowburn, Co. Durham, 4 May 1913.
Died: Blackpool, 29 October 1999.
Career: Bowburn Council School. Durham City. Huddersfield Town amateur April 1930, professional May 1930. Blackpool February 1934, fee £2,000. Wartime guest with Nottingham Forest. OLDHAM ATHLETIC June 1946 to May 1947.

■ Dick Witham began with Huddersfield Town at the age of 17, and despite his lack of senior experience commanded a useful fee from Blackpool some four years later. Before the outbreak of World War Two he completed 156 League and Cup matches and was a member of Blackpool's Second Division promotion-winning side in season 1936–37. Recruited by the Latics

for the resumption of League football after the war, he was first-choice left-back for the opening fixture against Carlisle United but lost his place immediately and played in only five first-team matches during the season.

WOLFENDEN, Matthew

Forward

Born: Oldham, 23 July 1987.
Career: OLDHAM ATHLETIC trainee July 2003, professional July 2006.

■ Locally born striker Wolfenden became one of Athletic's youngest Football League players when he made his debut, aged 16 years and 115 days, against Swindon Town in November 2003. Raised in a family of Latics supporters and associated with the Centre of Excellence from the of age of 10, Matty's early sporting prowess saw him represent Oldham and the North

West Counties League as a rugby league player. Football claimed him, however, and 2007–08 has seen him enjoy his most productive season in terms of appearances made and goals scored. Highlights included his first League goal at Boundary Park in the 3–2 win against Crewe Alexandra in October and a stylish lobbed third goal in the 3–0 victory at Port Vale in March.

WOLSTENHOLME, Arthur

Inside-forward

Born: Middleton, 14 May 1889.
Died: Manchester, 1958.
Career: Tonge FC. OLDHAM ATHLETIC March 1908. Blackpool December 1909. Gillingham August 1912. Norwich City July 1913. Lincoln City July 1914. OLDHAM ATHLETIC May 1919, fee £75. Newport County June 1920. Darlington June 1921. Nelson May 1922, appointed to training staff season 1923–24.

■ Fair-haired youngster Arthur Wolstenholme first became a regular during 1908–09, appearing in 26 League matches and scoring 10 goals. Three new signings featured in Athletic's opening fixture of 1909–10, and the former Sunderland forward, Montgomery, took over the inside-left berth. Wolstenholme departed in mid-season, the first of his many subsequent moves taking him to Blackpool where he scored 16 League and Cup goals in 81 matches. Thereafter it was a case of all-change at yearly intervals until the outbreak of World War One. When normal League football recommenced in 1919–20 he was cast in the role of Athletic's utility player, appearing in seven outfield positions in 22 First Division

appearances. Subsequent post-war highlights included his becoming the first player to score four goals in a Third Division North match – for Darlington against Chesterfield on 10 September 1921. Also, in his final season, he assisted Nelson to the Championship of the Third Division North, playing alongside former Athletic teammate David Wilson, the Seedhill club's player-manager.

WOOD, Ian Thomas

Full-back

Born: Radcliffe, 15 January 1948.
Career: Park Lane Olympic. OLDHAM ATHLETIC amateur November 1965, professional July 1966. Denver Dynamo, US, loan May 1974. San Jose Earthquakes, US, loan April–August 1978 and again May–August 1979. Burnley May 1980 to November 1981. Wichita Wings, US. Radcliffe Borough, subsequently becoming chairman until April 1996.

■ The holder of Athletic's all-time appearance record, blond-haired Ian Wood was first noted playing in Sunday League football in his native Radcliffe. Initially signed on amateur forms by manager Gordon Hurst as a budding centre-forward, he subsequently moved to wing-half, but finally found his best position at right-back, a role he adopted under the management of Jimmy McIlroy. A model professional, 'Woody' combined speed and strength with an excellent positional sense and an ability

to prompt attacks by skilful distribution out of defence. His long-running defensive partnership with Maurice Whittle was a key element in the 1973–74 Third Division Championship campaign. After 14 years at Boundary Park he left to join newly-relegated Burnley, but was released in November 1981 having failed to hold down a first-team place. Ian's son, Clark, signed trainee forms with Athletic in July 1987 but did not reach senior level.

WOOD, Neil Anthony

Midfield

Born: Manchester, 4 January 1983.
Career: Manchester United trainee July 1999, professional January 2000. Peterborough United loan September 2003. Burnley loan January 2004. Coventry City July 2004. Blackpool January 2006. OLDHAM ATHLETIC July 2006 to September 2007.

■ Ex-Manchester United midfielder Neil Wood turned down a new contract offer from Blackpool to join Athletic on trial in July 2006. One of six trialists on view at Haig Avenue, Wood was praised by manager Sheridan for his tidy use of the ball in the 5–0 hammering of Conference side Southport. Despite starting in the opening two fixtures of the season, Wood lost his place during the team's faltering start to the campaign. A cruciate knee injury sustained in training in January 2007 was followed by a lengthy spell of rehabilitation and in September 2007 his contract was cancelled by mutual consent, after he had started just five games and made two appearances from the bench.

WOOD, Norman

Outside-right

Born: Chadderton, 20 October 1921.
Died: Bridgnorth, May 2005.
Career: Chadderton Grammar School Old Boys. Grimsby Town trial. OLDHAM ATHLETIC amateur August 1937. Royton Amateurs. OLDHAM ATHLETIC amateur September 1946.

■ As a 16-year-old centre-forward Norman Wood scored 75 of Chadderton Grammar School Old Boys' 128 goals in season 1937–38 and represented Lancashire Grammar Schools. He also played for Royton Amateurs in the Lancashire & Cheshire Amateur League, scoring 20 goals. A trial with Grimsby Town followed, but he was studying for a position in the Civil Service and did not intend to take up football as a career. Norman Wood played only once for Athletic, as a late replacement at outside-right for Bill Blackshaw. A goalless encounter with Stockport County had few highlights, Athletic hanging on grimly for a draw after both full-backs, Boothman and Witham, had to retire due to injury.

WOOD, William

Inside-forward

Born: Parkgate, Rotherham, c.1900.
Career: Parkgate Christ Church. Retford. Wombwell c.1920. OLDHAM ATHLETIC March 1922, fee £500. Northampton June 1923. Swansea Town July 1924. Wellingborough. Rugby Town August 1929.

■ Willie Wood joined an Athletic side that had recorded just one win in their previous 11 matches, and were in grave danger of relegation from Division One. Wood's introduction at inside-right halted the slide, five wins and three

draws were accrued from the final 11 matches. After a bright start to 1922–23 when he scored in wins against Nottingham Forest and Bolton Wanderers, the team's form slumped. Numerous team changes, and a late season change of manager, failed to stop the rot and Athletic crashed out of the top flight. Willie Wood's son Barrie, also an inside-forward, played for Grantham against the Latics in a second-round FA Cup tie on 7 January 1967, having previously played in League football with Doncaster Rovers, Scunthorpe United and Barnsley.

WOODHALL, Brian Harold

Outside-left

Born: Chester, 6 June 1948.
Died: Chester, 4 May 2007.
Career: Overleigh Sunday School. Sheffield Wednesday apprentice August 1963, professional June 1965. OLDHAM ATHLETIC loan February–March 1970. Chester June 1970. Crewe Alexandra loan March–May 1971. Oswestry Town 1971. Colwyn Bay 1977.

■ Loaned to Athletic in February 1970, Brian Woodhall helped spark a revival with a goal in the 5–0 victory against Notts County on a snowbound Boundary Park, the Latics impressing in their best performance of the season. Although available for transfer, no deal was struck and Woodhall returned to Hillsborough. He commenced 1970–71 with his home-town club Chester but, despite a scoring debut at Brentford in the season's opener, he failed to maintain his place in the side and spent the final three months of the season on loan at Crewe Alexandra.

WOODCOCK, Ernest

Outside-left

Born: Salford, 14 May 1925.
Career: Salford Juniors. Blackburn Rovers amateur. Bury amateur May 1946, professional January 1947. OLDHAM ATHLETIC June 1948, fee £650. Stockport County September-October 1950.

■ A small and slightly-built wingman but one with plenty of skill and confidence, Ernie Woodcock scored the first goal of the 1948–49 season in a team featuring three other newly signed players. Five team changes immediately followed a disappointing display in the opening game, a 3–1 home defeat by Rotherham United, and despite his scoring debut Woodcock was one of the casualties. Reintroduced after a spell in reserve, he scored the only goal of the game against New Brighton at the Tower Grounds in early October, clinching the first away win of the season. Throughout his first season, when Athletic fielded four different left-wingers, Woodcock's main challenge was from Bill Jessop and it was the former Preston North End wingman who dominated the position in 1949–50.

WOODGER, George

Inside-forward

Born: Croydon, 3 September 1884.
Died: Croydon, 6 March 1961.
Career: Thornton Heath Wednesday. Croydon Wanderers. Crystal Palace October 1905. OLDHAM ATHLETIC September 1910, fee £750. Tottenham Hotspur May 1914, fee £325.

■ Rejoicing in the unusual nickname of 'Lady', George Woodger was an unlikely-looking footballer, prematurely balding and with an almost frail physique. Nevertheless, he was a player with splendid footwork, a polished style and great tactical awareness, and he was a key member of Athletic's First Division side for four seasons before returning south to join Tottenham Hotspur. The first Athletic player to win an international cap – for England against Ireland on 11 February 1911 – he retired during World War One and was subsequently employed as a fitter by Croydon Common Works Department.

WORRALL, Fred

Outside-right

Born: Warrington, 8 September 1910.
Died: Warrington, 13 April 1979.
Career: Witton Albion. Nantwich Town. Bolton Wanderers November 1928, registration cancelled by the Football League. OLDHAM ATHLETIC December 1928. Portsmouth October 1931, fee £3,000. Wartime guest with OLDHAM ATHLETIC, Droylsden, Blackpool and Manchester United. Crewe Alexandra April 1946. Stockport County September 1947. Chester coach July 1948. Warrington Rugby League FC trainer. Stockton Heath manager 1953.

■ A breach of signing-on regulations led to Bolton Wanderers being fined £50 and banned from signing Fred Worrall. Bolton's loss proved to be the Latics' gain as the sprightly and stockily-built wingman proved an instant success at Boundary Park. After three years in

which he missed just a handful of matches, Worrall was transferred to First Division Portsmouth. His speedy and direct wing play in the top flight eventually led to him being selected to represent the Football League, and he was subsequently awarded two England Caps. He also starred in Portsmouth's 1939 FA Cup Final triumph over Wolves, a match in which he played with a lucky sixpence in his boot and a miniature horseshoe in his pocket.

WORTHINGTON, Fred

Inside-forward

Born: Manchester, 6 January 1924.
Died: Warrington, 13 April 1979.
Career: Bradford FC (of Manchester). Bury amateur 1945, professional July 1947. Leicester City March 1951, fee £7,000. Exeter City July 1955. OLDHAM ATHLETIC July 1956. Chorley player-coach 1957. Mossley June 1958 to 1959. Ashton United until March 1961.

■ Fred Worthington made his League debut with Bury in September 1947, and appeared in 69 League matches before following his manager Norman Bullock to Leicester City. After 55 League matches and nine goals he was on the move again, a season in the south with Exeter City preceding his arrival at Boundary Park. Rather surprisingly he was given few opportunities, spending the first three months of the season in the reserve team. His talents as a subtle provider of

openings from midfield seemed deserving of a more regular place in the side that seemed to change on a weekly basis, the same 11 never playing together for more than three matches in a row. An early and unsuccessful 'rotation policy' by manager Goodier!

WRIGHT, Dennis

Outside-left

Born: Royton, Oldham, 9 January 1930.
Died: Rochdale, 7 April 2003.
Career: OLDHAM ATHLETIC amateur May 1946. Glasgow Rangers June 1947. OLDHAM ATHLETIC August 1951. Ashton United July 1952. Stalybridge Celtic 1956–57.

■ Speedy local wingman Dennis Wright played in three consecutive matches for Athletic in the first peacetime season, and at just 17 years of age he was deputising for a man

twice his age, 35-year-old Jack Ormandy. During National Service with Royal Scots Infantry he linked up with Glasgow Rangers but returned to Lancashire to take a three-year physiotherapy course at Salford University. He then spent a season with Athletic but was restricted to six League appearances due to the consistent displays of outside-left Billy Ormond. In November 1994, when in semi-retirement, Wright returned to Boundary Park as physiotherapist following the departure of Ian Liversedge.

WRIGHT, Ernest

Inside-forward

Born: Middleton, c.1912.
Career: Sedgeley Park. Queen's Park Rangers amateur August 1934, professional October 1934. Crewe Alexandra June 1935. Chesterfield May 1937, fee £125. OLDHAM ATHLETIC June 1938 to May 1939. Wigan Athletic August 1947.

■ During his spell with Chesterfield, the *Notts. Post Football Annual* for 1937–38 described Ernie Wright as 'a dextrous dribbler and a splendid shot'. This was only partly the case, as evidenced by his performances for Athletic, where he proved a fine schemer with neat ball skills. Shooting was not a strong point, however, his value being that of a provider of openings, rather than a scorer on his own account.

WRIGHT, John William 'Bill'

Goalkeeper

Born: Banks, Southport, c.1889.
Career: St Cuthbert's, Churchtown. Lytham FC September 1904. OLDHAM ATHLETIC May 1905. Southport Central 1908. Accrington Stanley September 1913. Manchester United September 1914.

■ A cool goalkeeper with a safe pair of hands, Bill Wright appeared in 35 Lancashire Combination matches in his first season and 14 in the following term when Athletic topped the League. Election to the Football League in the close season resulted in an all-round strengthening of the side, new signing Bob Hewitson from Crystal Palace appearing in most of the Division Two matches.

WRIGHT, Thomas

Outside-right

Born: Bland Hill, Clackmannanshire, 20 January 1928.
Career: Blairhall Colliery. Partick Thistle March 1945. Sunderland March 1949, fee £8,000. East Fife January 1955, in part exchange for Charlie Fleming. OLDHAM ATHLETIC March 1957, fee £500. North Shields 1957.

■ Direct in style and unstinting in effort, versatile forward Tommy Wright was capped by Scotland against the three home countries while on Sunderland's books. Signed by Athletic along with Ken Murray, the pair formed a new right-wing pairing on their joint debut, the resulting 3–2 win against Darlington on 9 March 1957 was the side's first League victory since 29 December 1956. Tommy

Wright scored in successive matches against Gateshead and Wrexham in the month of his signing, but the season concluded with a run of 12 matches without a win, and he left Boundary Park in the close season after the briefest of stays. His son, Thomas Elliot Wright, arrived at Boundary Park some 29 years later. Tommy senior is the uncle of Jackie Sinclair (Leicester City and Scotland) and Willie Sinclair (Huddersfield Town and Falkirk).

WRIGHT, Thomas Elliot

Forward

Born: Dunfermline, 10 January 1966.
Career: Hutchinsonvale. Leeds United apprentice April 1982, professional January 1983. OLDHAM ATHLETIC October 1986, fee £80,000. Leicester City August 1989, fee £650,000. Middlesbrough July 1992, fee £650,000. Bradford City July 1995 to June 1977. Kilmarnock trial July 1997. OLDHAM ATHLETIC August 1997. St Johnstone November 1997. Livingston March 1998. Doncaster Rovers August 1998. King's Lynn 2000, subsequently appointed assistant manager. OLDHAM ATHLETIC Under-16 coach, assistant manager June 2006.

■ Scotland Youth and Under-21 international Tommy Wright became the third ex-Leeds United player on the books of Athletic in October 1986, joining Denis Irwin and Andy Linighan. All three were to make significant contributions to Athletic

reaching the Play-offs in May 1987. Tommy Wright won the Junior Latics Player of the Year award at the end of his first season and he remained a popular player throughout, his scampering runs down the left flank being a feature of the Latics' attacking play and providing the springboard for many successful attacks. He was also a useful marksman on his own account, having a particularly good season in 1987–88 with 12 goals in 44/2 matches. Wright later returned to the Latics, somewhat unexpectedly, after being injured in France while playing in a pre-season trial with Kilmarnock. Requesting permission to train at Boundary Park, he was signed up after one day's training and scored the only goal of the game against Preston North End in his first full appearance. In June 2006 he was appointed assistant to manager John Sheridan. His father Tommy (senior) was a Scottish international winger who also assisted the Latics.

WYLDE, Rodger James

Inside-forward

Born: Stockport, 8 March 1954.
Career: Sheffield Schoolboys. Sheffield Wednesday apprentice July 1970, professional July 1971. Burnley loan November 1975. OLDHAM ATHLETIC February 1980, fee £75,000. Sporting Lisbon, Portugal, July 1983. Sunderland July 1984. Barnsley December 1984, fee £15,000. Rotherham United loan March 1988. Stockport County July 1988 to May 1989, appointed club physiotherapist June 1989.

■ Rodger Wylde began with his home-town club, Sheffield Wednesday, scoring 66 goals in 182 matches. He joined the Latics as a replacement for Vic Halom, who had left to join Rotherham United. Wylde proved a worthy successor, averaging just short of a goal every other game and leading Athletic's scoring lists in each of his three full seasons at Boundary Park. Clever and strong on the ball with a good first time shot, his best seasonal return was in 1982–83 (19 goals in 37/2 League matches), figures that earned him a move to Sporting Lisbon. At 34 years of age and, in his final season of League football, Wylde headed Stockport County's scoring list with 12 goals in 24/2 Division Four matches. He

subsequently became club physiotherapist at Edgeley Park. His overall figures in League football were 140 goals in 354/22 appearances.

WYNNE, Samuel

Full-back

Born: Neston, 26 April 1897. Died: Sheffield, 30 April 1927.
Career: Neston Comrades. Connah's Quay. Neston Colliery. OLDHAM ATHLETIC September 1921, fee £10. Bury December 1926, fee £2,250.

■ An article in the *Topical Times* magazine of 1930, penned by Athletic's former manager Herbert Bamlett, revealed that his signing of Sammy Wynne came about quite by chance. Having been recommended to view a number of players in a game to be played at Ellesmere Port, at about 2pm he was told that the game was not scheduled to start until the evening. Faced with a

wasted afternoon, Bamlett was advised that the Final of the Wirral Cup was being played at Port Sunlight so he went along to watch the game. He was particularly impressed by a full-back playing for Neston Colliery, and immediately after the game Mr Bamlett went into the dressing room, located Sammy Wynne in the bath and produced a signing-on form. With dripping hands, and still seated in the bath, Wynne rested the form on the back of Bamlett's wallet and signed. A back built on hefty lines, Wynne was noted for the length of his clearances and was a reliable man from the penalty spot. On 6 October 1923 he created a piece of soccer history when he scored two goals and two own-goals in Athletic's 3–2 win against Manchester United at Boundary Park. An upward move to First Division Bury in December 1926 ended in utter tragedy in the following April. When placing the ball for a free-kick after 38 minutes in the match against Sheffield United at Bramall Lane, Sammy Wynne collapsed on the pitch and died in the dressing room. The match was abandoned at half-time and receipts from the re-arranged game on 5 May were donated by Sheffield United to the player's widow.

YARWOOD, Jonathon

Full-back

Born: Huyton Quarry, near Liverpool, 9 January 1899.
Died: Liverpool, 1939.
Career: Blackmore Wanderers November 1919. Bury amateur August 1920. Atherton FC 1921. Everton May 1921, fee £500. OLDHAM ATHLETIC June 1922 to April 1925, fee £150. Liverpool Warehousing FC reinstated amateur October 1928.

■ Athletic opened negotiations for Yarwood's transfer shortly after his representative appearance for the Lancashire Combination against the Central League at Tranmere Rovers in April 1921. Everton were also interested, but after he opted to remain on Merseyside Yarwood spent a season in reserve at Goodison Park. A year later, Athletic finally succeeded in signing the powerfully-built full-back. Grundy and Freeman were Athletic's regular backs and Yarwood played in just five First Division

matches in his first season. He began 1923–24 as first-team left-back but his six consecutive appearances sadly proved to be his last. A broken leg and a subsequent cartilage operation combined to keep him out of the first-team picture until his release in April 1925.

YOUNG, Alexander Forbes 'Alan'

Forward

Born: Kirkcaldy, Fife, 26 October 1955.
Career: Kirkcaldy YMCA. OLDHAM ATHLETIC July 1974. Leicester City July 1979, fee £250,000. Sheffield United August

1982, fee £160,000. Brighton & Hove Albion August 1983, fee £140,000. Notts County September 1984, fee £55,000. Rochdale August 1986, fee £10,000 plus D. Thompson. Shepshed Charterhouse player-coach March 1988. Ilkeston Town 1989–90. Notts County coach and subsequently community officer. Chesterfield youth development officer 1998.

■ Alan Young made a rapid advance from Scottish junior football to the Second Division of the Football League, appearing in 21/6 matches and scoring seven goals in his first season at Boundary Park. The classy and confident attack leader saw less first-team action in the following two seasons but was on an upward curve at the time of his £250,000 transfer to Leicester City. In his first season at Filbert Street he spearheaded the Foxes charge into Division One, scoring 14 goals in 42 matches. Leicester lasted only one season in the top flight, but with the emerging Gary Lineker on the books, Young was transferred to Sheffield United. This proved to be just the first of a series of rapid moves, a knee injury finally curtailing his League career during which he scored 89 goals in 315/34 matches.

ZOLA-MAKONGO, Calvin

Forward

Born: Kinshasa, DR Congo, 31 December 1984.
Career: Northumberland County. Newcastle United trainee, professional January 2002. OLDHAM ATHLETIC loan August 2003. Everton trial. Tranmere Rovers July 2004.

■ Calvin Zola spent the first 15 years of his life in Congo before moving to England to study business management. A game for his college team and an appearance for Northumberland County was swiftly followed by a game for Newcastle United Under-19s – although he was only 16 – against Manchester United. Initially joining Athletic on a one-month loan, his stay was extended to cover the remainder of the season. Under manager Ian Dowie the tall but lightweight striker made an impressive start, but he failed to impress Brian Talbot whose five transfer deadline signings effectively ended Zola's season at senior level.

Oldham Athletic Managers

David Ashworth

April 1906 to April 1914 and January 1923 to July 1924

The appointment of David Ashworth virtually coincided with Athletic's return to Boundary Park from Hudson Fold in 1906. Born at Waterfoot in the Rossendale Valley in 1868, 'Little Dave', as he was affectionately known, was said to stand no more than 5ft tall and must have been one of the shortest managers ever. He began as a full-back with Newchurch Rovers, subsequently becoming their secretary-manager before turning to refereeing, later graduating to the Football League list. Then, as now, Athletic were not a club blessed with wealth, but Ashworth took the Latics from the mists of obscurity to the bright sunshine of the top flight within the space of four years. Leaving in April 1914 to manage Stockport County, he moved on to Liverpool in December 1919 and led them to the Division One championship in 1921–22. He was well on course for what was to become a

second League championship when he was induced by Athletic's directors to return, but he arrived too late to save the side from their first-ever relegation. After one season in Division Two, when Athletic finished seventh, he departed to Manchester City in July 1924. Among subsequent appointments were spells as Walsall's manager from February 1926 to February 1927, Caernarvon manager from June 1927 to May 1930 and Llanelly manager from July 1930. He died at Blackpool on 23 March 1947, aged 79.

Herbert Bamlett

June 1914 to May 1921

Athletic's second manager was also a former referee who officiated in the Latics' first-ever Football League match at Boundary Park against West Bromwich Albion on 14 September 1907. He officiated in nine international matches and was also referee when the Latics reached the FA Cup semi-final at Blackburn, against Aston Villa, in March 1913. Retiring at the very top, he was the youngest referee to take charge of an FA Cup Final, the all-Lancashire clash between Burnley and Liverpool in 1914. Born at Gateshead on 1 March 1882, Herbert Bamlett inherited a fine side at Boundary Park in the season that kicked-off with World War One already a month old. Sales of season tickets were drastically reduced as it seemed unlikely that football would be able to continue through the season. The club ran at a loss, with gate receipts as low as £77 for the February visit of Sunderland and a disappointing £88 for the visit of Manchester United two months later. Despite all the setbacks, Athletic enjoyed their best-ever season, finishing second in Division One, one point adrift of champions Everton. Bamlett joined the Royal Flying Corps in June 1916 and subsequently faced the unenviable task of reconstructing the team following his demobilisation in February 1919. Two seasons of indifferent performances led to his resignation in May 1921 to take charge of Wigan Borough's first season in

the new Third Division North. He subsequently managed Middlesborough from August 1923, and was Manchester United's manager from the summer of 1927 to April 1931. He died at his home, just a short distance from Manchester United's Old Trafford ground, in October 1941 after being in poor health for some time.

Charlie Roberts

July 1921 to December 1922

Despite his outstanding success as a fine, inspirational captain during his playing career, Charlie Roberts was unable to make his mark in management. Having led Athletic to successive finishes of fourth and second in the top flight, he was unable to lift the post-World War One side when he assumed control in July 1921. Relegation in his first season was only narrowly avoided thanks to an improved run of results from March onwards, after the team had failed to score a single goal in six matches prior to a surprise 1–0 win at Burnley that sparked a mini revival. Three wins and a draw in the opening five matches of 1922–23 proved to be a false dawn and a terrific slump followed. From 16 September to 27 January only two wins were recorded in 22 League games, and in the midst of the crisis Roberts resigned in December to be replaced by David Ashworth.

Bob Mellor

July 1924 to July 1927, July 1932 to May 1933 and May 1934 to February 1945

Associated with Athletic since 1906 and secretary since 1910, Bob Mellor retired in July 1953 and was succeeded by Frank Buckley, Mellor's assistant since 1947. Throughout his lengthy spell of service, Bob Mellor was called upon to fill the dual role of secretary-manager on three separate occasions, amounting to 15 years in all. He became full-time secretary on New Year's Day 1910 and proved to be something of a lucky mascot, as the team did not lose another match until Good Friday, and went on to win promotion to Division One. Always fulsome in his praise for long-serving club trainer Jimmy Hanson, Mellor readily acknowledged that it was Hanson who played a key role in the care and development of the playing staff, irrespective of who was manager at the time. Mellor was awarded the Football League's Long Service Medal in 1936, the presentation being fittingly made by Mr Charles E. Sutcliffe, who had acted as Athletic's solicitor when the company was floated in 1906. A life-long bachelor, Bob Mellor was born in a public house, the quaintly-named 'Waste Dealer's Arms', Bottom o'th'Moor, on 16 December 1877. He served in the Royal Army Medical Corps during World War One and died at the age of 89 in May 1967.

Andrew Wilson

July 1927 to July 1932

In a 20-year association with Sheffield Wednesday, Andrew Wilson scored 216 goals in 546 appearances, won League championship medals in 1903 and 1904, and was an FA Cup winner in 1907. The elder brother of Athletic's long-serving wing-half, David, Andrew won six Scotland caps, making his international debut versus England in 1907. He served in the 6th Highland Light Infantry in France and was seriously wounded, his left hand shattered by a piece of flying shrapnel. He joined Athletic as manager after a five-year stint with Bristol Rovers, and although his second season began disastrously, the mid-term introduction of Jimmy Dyson, Matt Gray, Freddie Worrall and Stewart Littlewood hauled the side from the foot of the table. In the following term (1929–30) promotion to Division One was missed by a single point, injuries weakening the side over the Easter period and resulting in a run-in of five matches that produced just two points. At the time of Andrew Wilson's move to Stockport County in July 1932, many of his better players had been sold without adequate replacement, and only four of his successful 1929-30 side remained on the books – Ivill, Gray, Porter and Hasson.

Jimmy McMullan

May 1933 to May 1934

During his playing days Jimmy McMullan was a fine skipper for both club and country, and famously captained the 'Wembley Wizards' who defeated England 5–1 in 1928. A lengthy stint with Partick Thistle began in 1913 and eventually totalled 352 appearances and 16 goals. He helped take the Jags to the Scottish Cup Final in 1921, appearing in nine earlier ties but missing the Final due to injury. He cost Manchester City £4,700 in February 1926 and won a Second Division Championship medal in 1928 and made two FA Cup Final appearances, finishing as runners-up, in 1926 and 1933. He was capped by Scotland on 16 occasions, was awarded four 'Victory International' caps and was a Scottish League representative. In a single season in charge at Boundary Park, McMullan guided Athletic to a commendable ninth place in Division Two. His best signings were goalkeeper Fred Swift, Cliff Chadwick and Peter Burke, but he lost Jack Hacking to Manchester United, John Pears to Preston North End, and Cliff Chadwick was snapped up by Middlesbrough after just 18 League matches and six goals. He left Athletic to become Aston Villa's first-ever manager in May 1934, moving to Notts County in November 1936 and finally to Sheffield Wednesday as secretary-manager in December 1937. Jimmy McMullan was born in Denny, Stirlingshire, on 26 March 1895 and died in Sheffield on 28 November 1964.

Frank Womack

February 1945 to April 1947

On 20 February 1945, Athletic's board of directors announced that they had arrived at a shortlist of six candidates – from an application list of 60 – for the position of manager. These included two former Athletic players: Jack Hacking who was manager of Accrington Stanley and James H. Marshall, who was coaching in Holland at the outbreak of war. The successful candidate, however, was Frank Womack, the former captain of Birmingham and manager of Torquay United, Grimsby Town, Leicester City and Notts County. A married man with three children, one daughter serving in the Wrens, he was appointed in late February and took over on Monday 5 March. Womack's 20-year playing career with Birmingham spanned 491 League appearances, a total which remains a club record to this day. He was a Second Division Championship winner with the Blues in 1920–21 and appeared twice for the Football League. His successes in management included Grimsby Town's Division Two championship in 1934, and a repeat performance with Leicester City in 1937. Although VE Day was celebrated in May 1945, football continued along wartime lines in 1945–46, but the FA Cup was contested, on a two-legged basis, for the first time since 1938–39. Athletic had an inconsistent season and went out of the FA Cup in round two,

beaten 4–3 on aggregate by Accrington Stanley. Many new signings were made prior to the resumption of normal League football, but despite 20 League goals from veteran centre-forward Fred Howe the team, sporting unfamiliar hooped jerseys, came close to a re-election application. Frank Womack resigned in April, a month that brought one draw and five defeats, the side finishing 19th and on an extremely low note, losing by 8–0 in the season's final fixture at Rotherham United. Frank Womack was born at Wortley, near Sheffield, on 16 September 1888 and died at Caistor, Lincolnshire, on 8 October 1968.

Billy Wootton

June 1947 to September 1950

Born in Longton, Staffordshire, on 27 August 1904, Billy Wootton's playing career as a full-back commenced with Stoke in 1924, followed by a seven-year spell at Port Vale. In 1930 he was reported to be combining football with his employment as a mould maker in a local pottery works. He joined Southend United in August 1932 but a serious knee injury cut short his League career. He was able to resume with Northwich Victoria in 1933–34 and was appointed player-manager in December 1934. His successes at the Drill Field included winning the Cheshire League Challenge Cup and the Cheshire Senior Cup. His Athletic appointment started very badly,

with only one win recorded in the opening 12 League matches of 1947–48. The side rallied to finish in 11th place, and they improved to sixth in 1948–49 after the customary indifferent start – two draws and six defeats in the first eight matches. The 1949–50 season ended with another 11th-place finish, and the highlight of the season – despite a 7–2 reverse – was the third-round FA Cup visit of star-studded Newcastle United, which drew 31,706 spectators to Boundary Park. Six defeats within the first eight matches of 1950-51 led to Wooton's resignation, although his three-year tenure had, on balance, left the club in a healthier state both financially and in terms of playing strength. He was quickly back into management with Halifax Town and later scouted for Sunderland.

George Hardwick

November 1950 to May 1956

A new and exciting era for the Latics was marked by the debut of player-manager George Hardwick, his initial appearance attracting 21,742 spectators to Boundary Park on 11 November 1950. The former captain of Middlesbrough and England cost Athletic a hefty £15,000 fee and he proved a sound investment. In his first full season the side challenged for promotion but finally finished in fourth place, 12 points adrift of champions Lincoln City. Eric Gemmell's 28 League goals for the season included seven against Chester and three hat-tricks, but it was an improved defensive performance in 1952-53 that clinched the Third Division North championship, one point ahead of Port Vale. Sadly, the long-awaited return to Division Two lasted for only one season. Athletic failed to win in their first eight matches, and a lack of backing for Hardwick in the transfer market squandered the hard-won promotion. Any hopes of a quick return were swiftly dashed, the only bright spot in season 1954-55 being Don Travis's 32 goals from centre-forward. Hardwick's final season in charge ended in a disappointing 20th-place finish, ironically little different from when he assumed control. The team had been in 21st place when he made his eagerly awaited debut against Lincoln City.

Ted Goodier

May 1956 to June 1958

Selected from 26 applicants for the task of succeeding George Hardwick, former Athletic wing-half Ted Goodier took over immediately following the Whitsuntide holidays in 1956. His previous managerial experience included a 14-year spell with Rochdale, a brief spell as caretaker at Birmingham, and a successful period with Wigan Athletic from July 1952. A non-League club at that time, the other Latics earned national recognition when holding mighty opponents Newcastle United to a 2–2 draw at St James' Park in the FA Cup third round in season 1953–54. Ted Goodier fielded 31 players in League matches in his first season, of which no fewer than 19 were new signings. Constant team changes were the order of the day and the side finished in a disappointing 19th place, having won only once in their last 22 fixtures. Unsurprisingly, attendance figures fell alarmingly: 13,306 for the season's opener, a 4–3 win against Halifax Town, and 3,068 for the final home match, a 2–1 defeat by Wrexham. The 1957–58 season ended with Athletic at their lowest-ever ebb, as founder members of Division Four. After a quarter of the season only six points had been won, it was not helped by a 'flu virus that decimated the playing staff. Although a long-awaited improvement occurred in late season it was a case of too-little, too-late and manager Goodier departed, having failed to halt Athletic's slide into soccer's basement.

Norman Dodgin

July 1958 to May 1960

Born at Sherrif Hill, Gateshead, on 1 November 1921, wing-half Norman Dodgin made 26 appearances in Newcastle United's Division Two promotion side in 1947–48. He was transferred to Reading in June 1950 and to Northampton Town in September 1951. He took his first step into management with Exeter City in August 1953, becoming one of the youngest managers in the game at just 31 years of age. He subsequently managed Yeovil Town and Barrow before arriving at

Boundary Park in July 1958. A great believer in youth, he had a reputation for spotting emerging youngsters and moulding them himself. No doubt it was this reputation that attracted cash-strapped Athletic, but successive re-election applications ensued and Norman Dodgin left Athletic, and football, after two seasons to take over a large newsagents business in Exeter. Norman's brother, Bill, managed Fulham from 1949 to 1953, as did Bill junior from 1968 to 1972, and later Northampton Town and Brentford. An amusing story – perhaps apocryphal – was told of Norman Dodgin's arrival at a new club. When introducing himself to one player with the words 'I'm Dodgin, the new manager,' he received a somewhat furtive reply 'So am I mate, you haven't seen him anywhere have you?'

Jack Rowley

July 1960 to May 1963 and October 1968 to December 1969

Jack Rowley became a professional with Wolverhampton Wanderers at 17 but was allowed to move to Bournemouth & Boscombe Athletic. By scoring 10 goals in his first 11 matches he soon attracted the attention of bigger clubs, Manchester United paying £3,000 for him in October 1937. At the outbreak of war he joined the South Staffordshire Regiment, and his performances as a guest player for Wolves, for whom he once scored eight goals in one match, eventually resulted in

his selection to represent England in a wartime international against Wales. Anti-tank gunner Rowley took part in the D-Day landings at Normandy but returned from active service to score 20 goals in 25 matches for Manchester United in season 1945–46. He scored twice in the 1948 FA Cup Final against Blackpool, and when United won their first post-war championship in 1951–52 his 30 League goals was a record until Dennis Violet scored 32 in 1959–60. He also won six England caps, the highlight being his four goals against Northern Ireland in 1949. In two spells as manager of Athletic, the promotion season of 1962–63 was his finest achievement, memorable for Bert Lister's 32 League goals, which included six against Southport on Boxing Day. Amazingly, Jack Rowley's 'reward' came three days after Athletic wound up their season with a 6–1 promotion celebration against Hartlepools United. So-called 'internal dissension' led Athletic's board to demand Rowley's resignation. He was later induced to return to Boundary Park for a second spell in charge but proved unable to lift a struggling side and was dismissed following five consecutive defeats spanning November and December 1969. In addition to his two spells in charge of Athletic, Jack Rowley also held managerial posts with Plymouth Argyle, Ajax, Bradford Park Avenue and Wrexham. He later ran a newsagents business in Shaw and died aged 79 at Ashton-under-Lyne. Jack's brother, Arthur Rowley, scored 433 League goals in 619 matches, most notably with Leicester City and Shrewsbury Town.

Les McDowall

June 1963 to March 1965

The son of a Scottish missionary, Les McDowall was born at Gunga Pur, India, on 25 October 1912. He originally worked as a shipyard draughtsman and during World War Two reverted to his profession but this time in an aircraft factory. His professional football career began with Sunderland in December 1932. Manchester City, teetering on the edge of relegation, paid £8,000 for him in March 1938 and he was still at Maine Road when City regained their top-flight

status after the war. After retiring and cutting his managerial teeth with Wrexham, he returned to Manchester City and in a 13-year spell guided them to two FA Cup Finals in successive years, winning the trophy on the latter occasion. A quiet but influential man, he was the architect of the famous 'Revie plan', which involved a deep-lying centre-forward (namely Don Revie). McDowall arrived at Boundary Park to take charge of a newly-promoted Athletic side who led the Third Division for a spell until injuries and loss of form resulted in a ninth-place finish. In the following season (1964–65) only two

wins were recorded in the first 17 matches, a mini-revival brought seven wins in nine matches but another slump saw the side on the edge of the relegation zone by Easter. At this point Athletic parted company with McDowall, who had failed to achieve a solitary away victory in 1965. He died in Northwich on 18 August 1991.

Gordon Hurst

May 1965 to January 1966

Gordon Hurst was born in Oldham on 9 October 1924 and commenced in football with Ferranti's Works in the Manchester Amateur League. He was on Athletic's books as an amateur during wartime, and it was during a services match in Kent that he was first noted by Charlton Athletic, who signed him as a professional in May 1946. In a distinguished career at the Valley, Hurst completed 378 First Division games, 24 FA Cup ties, and scored 81 goals from outside-right. He was an FA Cup winner in 1947, represented the Football League in 1951 and toured Australia with the FA Party in the same year. He joined Tunbridge Wells as player-manager in March 1958, coached Llandudno from June 1961 and in 1963 returned to Oldham to work in local government. In the following year he was appointed, on a part-time basis, to take charge of Athletic reserves in succession to Henry Cockburn. He was surprise choice as manager in May 1965, and his tenure was short-lived: after winning only three of 22 League matches he was replaced by

Jimmy McIlroy, initially continuing as assistant until July 1967 when he joined Rochdale as trainer-coach. He was appointed secretary to Bury in 1970, leaving in 1976. He died in Margate on 11 June 1980.

Jimmy McIlroy

January 1966 to August 1968

The Irish international inside-forward was a high-profile appointment in mid-season 1966–67 and he inherited a side at the foot of Division Three with only 13 points from 22 matches. He swiftly dismantled Gordon Hurst's team and rebuilt around a welter of new signings including Stevens, Blore, Large, Asprey and Towers. Narrowly avoiding relegation with a 20th-place finish, further recruitment continued apace with Kinnell, Bebbington and Billy Johnston joining in the summer, quickly followed by Best, Collins and Knighton. Despite leading the table for a spell in September, the promotion push was not sustained and the side finished 10th. The introduction of several young players including Ian Wood, Ronnie Blair and Les Chapman, who all showed rich promise, gave hope for the future, but a disastrous start to 1967–68 – only one win in the opening 12 League matches – quickly killed off any thoughts of promotion. Athletic finished in 16th place, and the new season had hardly kicked-off when McIlroy resigned to take over as head coach at Stoke City. After a spell out of the game he was briefly coach and then, for 18 days, assistant manager at Bolton Wanderers.

Jimmy Frizzell

March 1970 to June 1982

As a player, and later manager, Jimmy Frizzell spent a total of 22 years at Boundary Park and there can have been few more popular club servants. After a lengthy and distinguished playing career he was first given coaching duties in season 1968–69, following the departure of manager Jack Rowley. He initially took over as caretaker manager on 30 December 1969 in what appeared a hopeless position with only four League wins recorded. With 22 matches left in which to arrest the slide, his record of

nine wins and six draws was a truly remarkable performance and it earned him the position on a permanent basis in March 1970. In his first full season in charge Frizzell led the side to promotion from Division Four in an attacking extravaganza spearheaded by David Shaw and Jim Fryatt who scored 50 goals between them. Steady and continued progress eventually led to the side winning the championship of Division Three in 1973–74. Although life in Division Two proved more exacting, at the time of his sensational sacking in June 1982, Frizzell had laid firm foundations for the future of the club and was the second-longest serving manager in the Football League. After a year out of work he was appointed assistant to manager Billy McNeill at Manchester City, remaining at Maine Road in various capacities until May 2001.

Joe Royle

June 1982 to November 1994

Born in Norris Green, Liverpool, on 8 April 1949, Joe Royle joined Everton at 15 years of age, made his Football League debut a year later and was the spearhead of Everton's Championship-winning side of 1969–70. He registered over a century of goals before moving on to Manchester City in December 1974, Bristol City in November 1977 and finally to Norwich City in August 1980. Despite being described in his early days as a 'strapping

lad', his approach was never over-physical. He liked to play football, and this was reflected in the way his teams performed, winning with style and going for goals. He was a surprise appointment, following the sensational sacking of Jimmy Frizzell, as Athletic's directors had advertised for a player-manager and Royle's playing career had ended at the age of 32 due to a persistent knee injury. Seventh in Division Two in 1983–84 was a promising start for the new manager but the side flirted with relegation during the next campaign. Season 1986–87, the first in which the Play-offs were introduced, ended in heartbreak. A third-place finish would previously have earned promotion, but defeat by Leeds United ended hopes of a return to top-flight football. In December 1989, Royle was offered the post of manager by First Division Manchester City, but he put aside personal ambitions, feeling that he had unfinished business at Boundary Park. Nineteen Cup ties in 1989–90 included a Wembley appearance in the Littlewoods Cup Final against Nottingham Forest and two equally memorable semi-final clashes with Manchester United in the FA Cup. Sadly, the main objective, which was promotion from Division Two, ended in disappointment, four points short of the Play-offs. Never out of the top two places in 1990–91, Athletic famously clinched the Second Division Championship in the season's final fixture, a 3–2 victory against Sheffield Wednesday. In May 1991 Royle was named Second Division Manager of the Year. Athletic recorded their first victory in Division One for 68 years, beating

Chelsea 3–0 at Boundary Park, the cavalier spirit initially surviving in the top flight. Athletic scored 46 home League goals, a total only surpassed by Arsenal who netted 51. In the first Premier League season, relegation was only narrowly avoided thanks to unlikely victories in the season's final three matches, away at Aston Villa and at home to Liverpool and Southampton. Relegation followed in 1993-94 when the team's best form seemed to be reserved for Cup ties. Athletic were held to a draw in the FA Cup semi-final by Manchester United, for whom Mark Hughes scored a dramatic equaliser in the last minute of extra-time, but the Maine Road replay was a different story, United winning quite deservedly by 4–1. In November 1994 Joe Royle was appointed manager of Everton, succeeding sacked manager Mike Walker. By successfully avoiding relegation and lifting the FA Cup in his first season, his tenure as Everton's manager was off to a dream start. His subsequent appointments were with Manchester City, from February 1998 to May 2001, and Ipswich Town, from October 2002 to May 2006.

Graeme Sharp

November 1994 to February 1997

A £500,000 signing by manager Joe Royle in July 1991, Scotland international striker Graeme Sharp was appointed Athletic's manager in November 1997 following Royle's departure to Everton. Although initially appointed player-manager, Sharp played little following his appointment, bowing out with a final appearance against Sunderland at Boundary Park in January 1994. Some three years later he resigned, along with his assistant Colin Harvey, citing a lack of financial backing to strengthen a side bound for relegation from Division One. Succeeding the hugely popular Joe Royle was never going to be an easy task and the exit of many of the previous manager's high-profile signings in attempts to balance the books, effectively curtailed any hopes of promotion. Given that management at times requires difficult and controversial decisions, Sharp's release of Andy Ritchie on a free transfer in August 1995 was widely unpopular with the club's fans, many of

whom believed that local hero Ritchie would have been a better choice to take the club forward. After a spell in management with Bangor, Graeme Sharp returned to Everton as Fans Liaison Officer, combining his duties with media work.

Neil Warnock

February 1997 to May 1998

Born at Sheffield on 1 December 1948, wingman Neil Warnock assisted eight lower Division League clubs in 10 seasons, ending with over 300 career appearances and 36 goals to his credit. He stepped down to non-League football with Burton Albion in 1979 while practising as a chiropodist in Sheffield. Having moved around quite rapidly as a player, his colourful and at times controversial managerial career has run on similar lines, commencing with Gainsborough Trinity in 1980. Warnock first hit the headlines when he guided Scarborough into the Football League by winning the championship of the GM Vauxhall Conference in 1986–87. He subsequently took Notts County to successive promotions in 1990 and 1991, but they were relegated after just one season in the top flight. He arrived at Boundary Park following appointments with Torquay United, Huddersfield Town (Play-off winners Division Two 1995) and Plymouth Argyle (Play-off winners Division Three 1996). Succeeding Graeme Sharp, he inherited a poor side that suffered relegation to Division Two. In his single full season in charge at Boundary Park, Athletic entered the New Year in third place, but the promotion push faded to a disappointing 13th-place finish and he departed, by mutual consent, in May 1998. Quickly back in charge at Bury in June 1998, Warnock took over at Sheffield United in December 1999 and succeeded in taking them out of the Football League Championship in season 2005–06 as runners-up to Reading. Sadly, they lasted just one season in the Premier League, with defeat by Wigan Athletic on the final day of the season sealing their fate. Warnock resigned in May 2007, and after five months out of the game, he was appointed manager of Crystal Palace in succession to Peter Taylor.

Andy Ritchie

May 1998 to October 2001

Having returned to Boundary Park from Scarborough as player-coach in February 1997, Andy Ritchie took over as manager in May of the same year when Neil Warnock's contract was not renewed. Athletic flirted with relegation throughout his first season in charge, losing exactly half of their 46 League fixtures. Wins against Stoke City and Reading in the final two fixtures ensured safety, one point ahead of York City, who accompanied Northampton Town, Lincoln City and Macclesfield Town into Football League Division Three. Season 1999–2000 opened with five straight defeats and only one goal scored, but things could only improve, and the eventual placing of 14th was better than could have been forecast. A similar mid-table finish followed in 2000–01, 15th place resulting after the almost customary bad start, one win in the first 11 League matches. New millionaire owner Chris Moore terminated Ritchie's contract in October 2001 after the side had slumped from top position to eighth in Division Two. He was offered a place on Athletic's board as technical director but declined, leaving with a record of 51 wins, 39 draws and 64 defeats in League matches and 10 wins, three draws and 11 defeats in Cup ties. After a spell as Academy of Youth director at Leeds United, Ritchie took a similar position with Barnsley that eventually led to him taking over as manager in May 2005. Twelve months on, he led his team to promotion from Division One, but in November 2006 he was dismissed with Barnsley second bottom of the table. He was appointed manager of Huddersfield Town in April 2007 but departed, by mutual consent, on 1 April 2008 with the club in 14th place in League One.

Mick Wadsworth

November 2001 to May 2002

Athletic's fifth manager in seven years (with the title of head coach) arrived with an impressive CV, having worked for seven League clubs and also held coaching appointments for the FA which included work with England's 1990 World Cup squad. Selected from an initial list of 35 applicants, the former Southampton assistant manager was swiftly followed into Boundary Park by Ian Dowie as first-team coach. Following restructuring of Athletic's board in May 2002, Wadsworth was appointed a director of the club while continuing as head coach, having guided the team to ninth position in Division Two, their first top-half finish for 10 years. His sensational exit followed almost immediately, when he clashed with chairman Chris Moore over proposed cutbacks in youth development. He was out of work for only a matter of weeks, being appointed manager of Huddersfield Town in July 2002, but in less than a year he was replaced by Peter Jackson after suffering relegation from League Two. He was sacked as Congo coach in February 2004, following their defeat in all three matches in the African Cup of Nations. A spell in Portugal with Beira Mar was followed by 14 months as assistant to Shrewsbury Town manager Gary Peters until March 2006. More recently, as director of club development at Gretna, he has assisted them to a remarkable ascent into the Scottish Premier League. At the time of writing, however, relegation and administration threatens the very existence of the club.

Ian Dowie

May 2002 to December 2003

Born in Hatfield, Hertfordshire, on 9 January 1965, Northern Ireland international striker Ian Dowie began on schoolboy forms with Southampton but spells in non-League football followed before he joined Luton Town in December 1988. Although not the most

mobile or subtle forward, he was an excellent target man with outstanding headwork that made him a real threat to opposing defenders. In a career spanning six League clubs, Dowie scored 66 League goals in 278/45 appearances. A regular in the Northern Ireland side, which he captained on several occasions, he won 59 caps and scored 12 goals. First involved in coaching with Queen's Park Rangers, Dowie was briefly their caretaker manager from September 1998 and was appointed reserve-team manager in the summer of 1999. Initially joining Athletic as first-team coach, he worked well in tandem with head coach Mick Wadsworth and took over as manager following Wadsworth's resignation in May 2002. Six straight League wins took Athletic to the top of the table in early October and promotion looked a strong possibility throughout. However, a final placing of fifth and defeat by Queen's Park Rangers in the Play-offs brought the first speculation that Ian Dowie would be moving on, his first year in charge having been highly impressive. As the club teetered on the brink of liquidation in the summer of 2003, the vultures began to circle. Among the players to exit Boundary Park were Fitz Hall, Chris Armstrong, Clint Hill, Carlo Corazzin, Wayne Andrews, Tony Carss, Lee Duxbury and Josh Lowe. With the heart ripped out of Dowie's Play-off team, it was unsurprising that the disillusioned manager accepted an 18-month contract as Crystal Palace boss, just prior to Christmas 2003. In the best possible start, he guided Palace into the Premier League, via the Play-offs, in May 2004. Two years later he left to join Charlton Athletic, a move which so incensed Palace chairman Simon Jordan that he issued a writ to Dowie during the press conference announcing his arrival at the Valley. Dowie's departure from Charlton was equally dramatic as he was sacked in November 2006 after just 15 games in charge, following his spending of £11.2 million on six players who failed to halt the club's decline. His credibility was restored in February 2007 when Coventry City handed him a three-and-a-half-year deal. Taking over a side with one win in the previous 11 League matches and lying six points above the relegation zone, Dowie immediately lifted the side taking

14 points from his first six matches at the helm. As the Sky Blues passed into new ownership in 2008, the unfortunate Dowie was an early casualty. The new chairman, former Manchester City defender Ray Ranson, dismissed him in February 2008, just one year into a three-and-a-half-year contract. In May 2008 he was appointed first-team coach to one of his former clubs, Queen's Park Rangers.

Brian Talbot

March 2004 to March 2005

Born in Ipswich on 21 July 1953, Brian Talbot began with his home-town club as an apprentice in July 1970, turning professional in August 1972. He cost Arsenal a then club record fee of £450,000 in January 1979, later assisting Watford, Stoke City, West Bromwich Albion, Fulham and Aldershot. From the right side of midfield his game featured driving enthusiasm and 100 per cent commitment, and he amassed a career total of 600/22 League appearances and 84 goals. He won six England caps and his domestic honours included winning the FA Cup in successive seasons with Ipswich Town in 1978 and Arsenal in 1979. He had a spell as chairman of the PFA, resigning when he commenced in management with West Bromwich Albion in November 1988. Subsequent appointments included a four-year spell with Hibernians of Malta before he returned to the UK to take over at Rushden & Diamonds in March 1997. In a seven-year stay at Nene Park he won the Conference title in 2000–01 and the Championship of Division Three in 2002–03. Joining Athletic with the team involved in a relegation dogfight, he successfully steered the side to 15th position and safety, taking 19 points from the 12 remaining fixtures of the season. Despite a staff containing current internationals such as Killen, Johnson, Jack and Arber, League form in 2004–05 proved disappointing, the side reserving their best performances for extended runs in both the FA Cup and the LDV Vans Trophy. Six consecutive League defeats in February led to Talbot's resignation the following month. He subsequently joined Oxford United as manager in May 2005 but was dismissed in March 2006 with his side 22nd in

Division Three. At the end of the season they were relegated into the Conference. In May 2007 Talbot guided Marsaxlokk of Malta to the island title, and with it a place in the first qualifying round of the Champions League.

Ronnie Moore

March 2005-June 2006

Born at Liverpool on 29 January 1953, Ronnie Moore enjoyed a lengthy playing career that began and ended with Tranmere Rovers. Between times, he assisted Cardiff City, Rotherham United, Charlton Athletic and Rochdale. A versatile and hard-working performer, he totalled 610 League appearances and scored 157 goals. He was a key element in Rotherham's 1980–81 Third Division Championship side, scoring 23 League goals in 45 matches. His first, and very brief, experience of management came when he was appointed player-manager of Tranmere Rovers in February 1987, but unable to reach agreement on terms for a new contract he left in April of the same year. In a lengthy and largely successful spell in charge of Rotherham United, Moore led the Millers to successive promotions, from Division Three in 1999–2000 and from Division Two in 2000–01. Successfully steering Athletic from the lower reaches to preserve Division One status, he was indebted to Luke Beckett – an inspired loan signing – who netted six vital goals in just nine matches. Moore's single full season in charge was something of a roller-coaster campaign. In touch with the Play-off places throughout the greater part of the season, a disastrous

run-in – when only three points were taken from the final seven matches – was a massive disappointment. Despite a season of some progress, early season ticket sales were hugely disappointing and a combination of finances and fan-power influenced the board to part company with Ronnie Moore and his backroom staff, and appoint John Sheridan as new boss. Friends were reunited when Athletic visited Tranmere for the season's opener, with Ronnie Moore, Rover's new manager, getting the better of his former colleague John Sheridan with a 1–0 victory.

John Sheridan

June 2006

One of Athletic's best players since the heady days of Premier League football, John Sheridan was initially called upon to take over as caretaker manager before finally achieving his ambition of taking on the job on a full-time basis in June 2006. When Ian Dowie moved to Crystal Palace in December 2003, former youth coach Sheridan, assisted by David Eyres and Tony Philliskirk, took over. Twenty-four hours later Athletic beat League leaders Queen's Park Rangers, having taken just three points from the previous eight matches. After almost three months as caretaker Sheridan signed off with a 1–1 draw at Queen's Park Rangers and accepted the post of assistant to new manager Brian Talbot. Again passed over when Athletic turned to the more experienced Ronnie Moore in March 2005, Sheridan finally moved up from reserve team manager in June 2006 and exceeded all expectations by guiding his team into the Play-offs in his first season in charge. Although Athletic failed to reach the Play-offs in 2007–08, there were reasons to feel that progess had been made, particularly in the case of several of the club's home-grown players, who benefited from extended runs in the first team. In a season blighted by injuries to key personnel, the door opened for the younger element to stake their claim, and several of them enhanced their reputations. Given an injury-free run for the club's more experienced players, manager Sheridan must have an excelllent chance of mounting a serious promotion challenge in 2008–09.

Oldham Statistics

Leading scorers 1907–08 to 2007–08

	League		All Matches	
1907–08	F. Newton	28	F. Newton	30
1908–09	F. Newton	14	F. Newton	14
1909–10	J. Fay	26	J. Fay	26
1910–11	A. Toward	12	A. Toward	13
1911–12	E. Jones	17	E. Jones	17
1912–13	J. Walters	12	J. Walters	13
1913–14	A. Gee	12	A. Gee	12
1914–15	G. Kemp	16	G. Kemp	19
1919–20	A. Gee	13	A. Gee	13
1920–21	R. Butler	18	R. Butler	18
1921–22	R. Butler	13	R. Butler	13
1922–23	J. Marshall	6	J. Marshall	6
1923–24	J. Blair	14	J. Blair	15
1924–25	E. Pilkington	5	E. Pilkington	5
	R. Gillespie	5	R. Gillespie	5
	C. Jones	5	C. Jones	5
1925–26	A. Ormston	21	A. Ormston	23
1926–27	A. Pynegar	18	A. Pynegar	19
1927–28	A. Pynegar	18	A. Pynegar	19
1928–29	S. Littlewood	12	S. Littlewood	12
1929–30	S. Littlewood	27	S. Littlewood	29
1930–31	J. Dyson	16	J. Dyson	16
1931–32	W. Johnstone	11	W. Johnstone	11
	J. Pears	11	J. Pears	11
1932–33	J. Pears	13	J. Pears	13
1933–34	T. Reid	16	T. Reid	17
1934–35	W. Walsh	11	W. Walsh	12
1935–36	W. Walsh	32	W. Walsh	37
1936–37	T. Davis	33	T. Davis	38
1937–38	J. Diamond	17	J. Diamond	17
1938–39	R. Ferrier	23	R. Ferrier	24
1946–47	F. Howe	20	F. Howe	20
1947–48	W. Blackshaw	17	W. Blackshaw	17
			R. Haddington	17
1948–49	E. Gemmell	19	E. Gemmell	23
	R. Haddington	19		
1949–50	R. Haddington	19	R. Haddington	24
1950–51	E. Gemmell	20	E. Gemmell	22
1951–52	E. Gemmell	28	E. Gemmell	29
1952–53	E. Gemmell	23	E. Gemmell	25
1953–54	R McIvenny	6	R. McIlvenny	8
1954–55	D. Travis	32	D. Travis	32
1955–56	D. Travis	15	D. Travis	15
1956–57	D. Travis	14	D. Travis	14
1957–58	G. Duffy	16	G. Duffy	17
	P. Neale	16		
1958–59	P. Phoenix	13	P. Phoenix	14
1959–60	P. Stringfellow	11	P. Stringfellow	11
1960–61	H. Lister	16	H. Lister	21
1961–62	J. Frizzell	24	J. Frizzell	25
1962–63	H. Lister	32	H. Lister	35
1963–64	H. Lister	14	H. Lister	17
1964–65	J. Frizzell	10	J. Frizzell	10
			A. Bartley	10
1965–66	I. Towers	9	I. Towers	9
1966–67	I. Towers	27	I. Towers	27
1967–68	R. Ledger	11	R. Ledger	11
1968–69	K. Bebbington	12	K. Bebbington	13
	A. Spence	12		
1969–70	D. Shaw	12	D. Shaw	12
1970–71	J. Fryatt	24	J. Fryatt	26
1971–72	D. Shaw	18	D. Shaw	19
1972–73	D. Shaw	17	D. Shaw	18
1973–74	C. Garwood	16	C. Garwood	17
1974–75	I. Robins	9	I. Robins	9
1975–76	D. Shaw	13	D. Shaw	13
1976–77	V. Halom	19	V. Halom	23
1977–78	S. Taylor	20	S. Taylor	21
1978–79	A. Young	10	A. Young	14
1979–80	S. Stainrod	11	S. Stainrod	11
1980–81	R. Wylde	12	R. Wylde	12
1981–82	R. Wylde	16	R. Wylde	17
1982–83	R. Wylde	19	R. Wylde	19
1983–84	R. Palmer	13	R. Palmer	14
1984–85	M. Quinn	18	M. Quinn	21
1985–86	R. Futcher	17	R. Futcher	17
1986–87	R. Palmer	16	R. Palmer	17
1987–88	A. Ritchie	19	A. Ritchie	20
			R. Palmer	20
1988–89	R. Palmer	15	A. Ritchie	16
1989–90	R. Palmer	16	A. Ritchie	28
1990–91	I. Marshall	17	I. Marshall	17
			N. Redfearn	17
1991–92	G. Sharp	12	G. Sharp	13
1992–93	I. Olney	11	I. Olney	12
1993–94	G. Sharp	9	G. Sharp	11
1994–95	S. McCarthy	18	S. McCarthy	18
1995–96	L. Richardson	11	L. Richardson	11
1996–97	S. Barlow	12	S. Barlow	12
1997–98	S. Barlow	12	S. Barlow	13
1998–99	M. Allott	7	M. Allott	8
1999–2000	M. Allott	10	M. Allott	11
			S. Whitehall	11
2000–01	L. Duxbury	8	L. Duxbury	10
2001–02	D. Eyres	9	D. Eyres	12
	C. Corazzin	9		
2002–03	D. Eyres	13	D. Eyres	16
2003–04	S. Vernon	12	S. Vernon	14
2004–05	C. Killen	10	C. Killen	15
2005–06	L. Beckett	18	L. Beckett	18
2006–07	C. Porter	20	C. Porter	23
2007–08	C. Davies	11	C. Davies	14

Ever presents in a Football League season

	Games	
1907–08	38	J. Fay, D. Wilson
1908–09	38	J. Fay, D. Wilson
1909–10	38	J. Fay, D. Wilson
1910–11	38	J. Fay, D. Wilson, H. McDonald
1913–14	38	C. Roberts, D. Wilson, O. Tummon
1914–15	38	D. Wilson
1919–20	42	D. Wilson
1921–22	42	R. Freeman
1923–24	42	J. Naylor
1925–26	42	J. Naylor
1927–28	42	J. Naylor, E. Ivill
1928–29	42	E. Ivill
1929–30	42	E. Ivill, L. Adlam, S. King
1930–31	42	E. Ivill, S. King
1931–32	42	E. Ivill, W. Porter
1932–33	42	M. Gray
1933–34	42	W. Porter
1934–35	42	T. Seymour
1935–36	42	F. Schofield
1937–38	42	L. Caunce
1946–47	42	L. Horton
1948–49	42	W. Pickering
1950–51	46	T. Bell
1952–53	46	A. Whyte
1955–56	46	T. Walker
1962–63	46	K. Branagan, A. Williams, P. McCall, R. Ledger, J. Colquhoun
1966–67	46	I. Towers
1967–68	46	D. Best
1969–70	46	I. Wood
1970–71	46	M. Whittle, J. Bowie
1971–72	46	I. Wood
1972–73	46	I. Wood, M. Whittle, K. Hicks
1973–74	46	M. Whittle, G. McVitie
1974–75	42	C. Ogden
1976–77	42	L. Chapman
1978–79	42	L. Chapman, P. McDonnell
1980–81	42	R. Blair
1982–83	42	P. Atkinson
1983–84	42	M. Ward, R. Palmer
1984–85	42	M. Ward
1986–87	42	R. Palmer
1988–89	46	R. Palmer
1989–90	46	E. Barrett
1990–91	46	E. Barrett, J. Hallworth, A. Barlow
1991–92	42	A. Henry, G. Sharp
1992–93	42	M. Milligan
1996–97	46	P. Rickers
1999–2000	46	A. Holt
2003–04	46	L. Pogliacomi

Other appearances by competition

Texaco Cup (1974–75) and Anglo-Scottish Cup (1977–78 to 1980–81)
K. Hicks 17, J. Hurst 17, R. Blair 16, I. Wood 15/1, G. Bell 13, V. Halom 13, P. McDonnell 13, A. Young 12/3, C. Ogden 10, A. Groves 9/1, L. Chapman 9, P. Heaton 8/3, S. Taylor 8, S. Gardner 7/1, J. Steel 7/1, P. Edwards 7, S.

Edwards 7, C. Garwood 7, D. Holt 7, M. Whittle 7, G. Keegan 6, S. Stainrod 6, C. Valentine 6, A. Bailey 5, M. Hilton 5, G. Jones 5, P. Atkinson 4/1, I. Robins 4, G. Hoolickin 3/2, K. Clements 3, A. McNeill 3, G. McVitie 3, R. Mulvaney 3, R. Wylde 3, R. Kowenicki 2, P. Futcher 2, J. Platt 1/7, I. Green 1/1, D. Shaw 1, I. Buckley 0/1, A. Lochhead 0/1.

Goalscorers: Young 4, Stainrod 4, Garwood 3, Whittle 2, Blair 2, Halom 2, Taylor 2, Heaton 2, Steel 2, Atkinson 2, Wylde 2, Kowenicki 2, Groves 1, Hicks 1, McVitie 1, Jones 1,McNeill 1, Valentine 1, Hayes (Morton) og 1.

Third Division North Cup (1935–36 to 1938–39)

L. Caunce 7, A. Jones 7, B. Ratcliffe 7, W. Hilton 6, P. McCormick 5, P. Downes 4, N. Price 4, P. Robbins 4, G. Milligan 4, T. Williamson 4, A. Buckley 3, M. Gray 3, F. Schofield 3, T. Seymour 3, W. Walsh 3, J. Aspinall 2, H. Blackshaw 2, N. Brunskill 2, C. Butler 2, H. Church 2, T. Davis 2, J. Diamond 2, T. Eaves 2, S. Gardner 2, A. Paterson 2, A. Bailey 1, P. Burke 1, W. Chambers 1, C. Eaton 1, W. Hayes 1, S. Jones 1, F. Leedham 1, J. Mayor 1, T. Shipman 1, A. Valentine 1, W. Vallance 1, E. Wright 1.

Goalscorers: Walsh 3, A. Jones 2. McCormick 2, Robbins 2, Davis 2, Buckley 1, Schofield 1, Blackshaw 1, Butler 1, Chambers 1, Vallance 1, Wright 1.

Full Members' Cup (1986–87 to 1991–92)

A. Barlow 4, N. Henry 4, E. Barrett 4, R. Palmer 3/2, D. Irwin 3, M. Milligan 3, A. Ritchie 3, R. Holden 3, I. Marshall 2/1, W. Donachie 2, A. Linighan 2, M. Flynn 2, G. Williams 2, A. Rhodes 2, P. Warhurst 2, R. Jobson 2, N. Adams 1/1, T. Henry 1/1, A. Goram 1, P. Jones 1, T. Ellis 1, R. Futcher 1, M. Maguire 1, A. Gorton 1, A. Callaghan 1, N. Edmonds 1, J. Kelly 1, M. Cecere 1, T. Wright 1, T. Philliskirk 1, C. Blundell 1, S. McGarvey 1, J. Hallworth 1, D. Brazil 1, N. Redfearn 1, J. Keeley 1, C. Fleming 1, P. Kane 1, G. Sharp 1, R. Colville 0/1, G. Keeley 0/1, S. Mooney 0/1, N. Kelly 0/1, D. Currie 0/1, P. Bernard 0/1.

Goalscorers: Palmer 1, Marshall 1, Holden 1, Milligan 1.

Play-offs (1986–87 Divisions One & Two) (2002–03 Division Two) (2006–07 Football League Division One)

W. Haining 4, A. Goram 2, D. Irwin 2, A. Barlow 2, T. Henry 2, A. Linighan 2, K. Moore 2, R. Palmer 2, T. Wright 2, M. Milligan 2, G. Williams 2, J. Low 2, C. Armstrong 2, D. Sheridan 2, F. Hall 2, J. Eyre 2, P. Murray 2, W. Andrews 2, D. Eyres 2, L. Pogliacomi 2, R. Wellens 2, C. Taylor 2, S. Gregan 2, C. Porter 2, P. Warne 2, A. Liddell

2, M. Cecere 1/1, A. Blaney 1/1, P. Edwards 1/1, G. McDonald 1/1, I. Ormondroyd 1, D. Miskelly 1, C. Wijnhard 1, C. Hill 1, N. Eardley 1, S. Charlton 1, K. Lomax 1, C. Rocastle 1, C. Corazzin 0/2, T. Carss 0/2, L. Glombard 0/2, L. Duxbury 0/1, M. Wolfenden 0/1.

Goalscorers: Williams 1, Cecere 1, Eyres 1, Liddell 1, Wolfenden 1

Associate Members' Cup (1997–98 to 2007–08)

D. Holden 8/1, L. Pogliacomi 8, D. Eyres 7/1, G. Kelly 6, D. Sheridan 6, W. Haining 6, D. Hall 6, S. Vernon 5/2, M. McNiven 5/2, L. Duxbury 5, K. Betsy 5, N. Kilkenny 5, M. Allott 4/3, J. Eyre 4/3, D. Beharall 4/1, P. Rickers 4/1, A. Griffin 4/1, S. Garnett 4, C. Armstrong 4, M. Tipton 3/3, M. Innes 3/1, P. Salt 3, A. Holt 3, D. Boshell 3, A. Liddell 3, C. Taylor 3, A. Hughes 2/3, K. Lomax 2/2, P. Murray 2/1, J. Clegg 2/1, M. Tierney 2/1, A. Smart 2, S. Whitehall 2, J. Baudet 2, M. Hotte 2, S. Balmer 2, C. Killen 2, C. Zola 2, M. Appleby 2, L. Croft 2, A. Bruce 2, M. Bonner 2, G. Branston 2, P. Warne 2, S. Gregan 2, R. Bertrand 2, J.P. Kalala 2, C. Davies 2, C. Hall 1/3, M. O'Halloran 1/1, E. Cooksey 1/1, S. Stam 1/1, R. Wellens 1/1, J. Thomson 1/1, R. Graham 1, M. Richards 1, D. Boxall 1, S. McCarthy 1, J. McGinlay 1, C. Corazzin 1, S. Thom 1, P. Reid 1, P. Rachubka 1, N. Adams 1, J. Sheridan 1, R. Sugden 1, D. Miskelly 1, T. Carss 1, C. Hill 1, W. Andrews 1, Lourenco 1, M. Hudson 1, M. Arber 1, D. Lee 1, J. Johnson 1, A. Wilbraham 1, K. Cooper 1, R. Lee 1, C. Day 1, R. Scott 1, T. Forbes 1, M. Hughes 1, L. Beckett 1, N. Wood 1, T. Cywka 1, M. Crossley 1, N. Trotman 1, G. McDonald 1, M. Beresford 1, R. Hazell 1, M. Ricketts 1, N. Eardley 1, C. Dudley 0/2, C. Roca 0/2, Wolfenden 0/2, M. Rush 0/1, L. Richardson 0/1, P. Jones 0/1, P. Beavers 0/1, A. Ritchie 0/1, F. Hall 0/1, W. Wilkinson 0/1, C. Porter 0/1, A. Legzdins 0/1 M. Barlow 0/1, D. Smalley 0/1.

Goalscorers: Vernon 6, Eyres 3, Liddell 2, Richards 1, Eyre 1, Tipton 1, Duxbury 1, Salt 1, Smart 1, Kilkenny 1, Croft 1, Killen 1, Andrews 1, Holden 1, Boshell 1, Zola 1, Griffin 1, Appleby 1, Davies 1, Wolfenden 1.

Individual scoring feats

Seven goals in a game
E. Gemmell v Chester (h)
Division Three North   19 January 1952

Six goals in a game
B. Lister v Southport (h)
Division Four   26 December 1962
F. Bunn v Scarborough (h)
FL Cup third round   25 October 1989

Five goals in a game
A. Ormston v Stoke (h)
Division Two   14 September 1925

Four goals in a game
R. H. Watson v Stockton (a)
FA Cup fourth round   12 December 1925
A. Pynegar v Nottingham Forest (h)
Division Two   1 May 1926
M. Wellock v Grimsby Town (a)
Division Two   12 February 1927
A. Jones v Wrexham (h)
Division Three North   18 January 1936
W. Blackshaw v Halifax Town (a)
Division Three North   1 May 1948
D. Travis v Bradford Park Avenue (h)
Division Three North   18 April 1955
I. Towers v Colchester United (h)
Division Three   4 February 1967
J. Fryatt v Chester (h)
Division Four   28 March 1970
D. Shaw v Brentford (h)
Division Four   5 September 1970
G. Sharp v Luton Town (h)
Division One   11 April 1992
A. Ritchie v Torquay United (h)
FL Cup second round   24 September 1991
C. Corazzin v Wrexham (h)
Division Two   10 February 2001
C. Wijnhard v Mansfield Town (h)
Division Two   14 September 2002

Three goals in a game

8 times	E. Gemmell
5 times	T. Davis, B. Lister
4 times	R. Palmer
3 times	D. Shaw, W. Walsh
Twice	H. Hancock, F. Newton, G. Taylor, J. Pears, R. Ferrier, F. Howe, J. Frizzell, C. Whitaker, R. Ledger, C. Garwood, V. Halom, A. Young, R. Wylde, A. Ritchie, S. Barlow.
Once	J. Fay, A. Toward, G. Kemp, J. H. Marshall, A. Ormston, H. Barnes, A. Pynegar, L. Cumming, S. Littlewood, T. Reid, M. Gray, R. Haddington, P. McKennan, A. Clarke, K. Chaytor, T. Walker, D. Pearson, G. Duffy, J. Mallon, A. Shackleton, S. Taylor, M. Quinn, M. Cecere, R. Holden, I. Marshall, S. McCarthy, S. Vernon, C. Killen, C. Porter, L. Beckett. L. Hughes.

Top 20 appearances

		All Matches	League Matches
1.	Ian Wood	577/8	517/7
2.	Roger Palmer	477/59	419/47
3.	Ronnie Blair	406/15	359/13
4.	David Wilson	405	368
5.	Howard Matthews	368	344
6.	Jim Bowie	361/4	331/3
7 =	Jimmy Frizzell	341/9	308/9
7 =	Maurice Whittle	345/5	307/5
9.	Mike Milligan	334/2	278/1
10.	Nick Henry	319/13	264/9
11.	Matt Gray	303	289
12 =	Les Chapman	296/2	261/2
12 =	Paul Rickers	276/22	242/19
14 =	Harry Grundy	289	279
14 =	Jimmy Hodson	289	252
16.	Keith Hicks	284/2	240/2
17.	Teddy Ivill	285	276
18.	Billy Porter	284	274
19.	Andy Ritchie	233/49	201/42
20.	Elliot Pilkington	280	269

Most ever-present seasons

7	D. Wilson.
5	E. Ivill.
4	J. Fay, R. Palmer.
3	J. Naylor, I. Wood, M. Whittle.
2	W. Porter, S. King, L. Chapman, M. Ward, E. Barrett.

100 consecutive appearances

League

224	E. Ivill	April 1926 to October 1932
170	D. Wilson	September 1907 to December 1911
152	J. Fay	September 1907 to April 1911
147	I. Wood	March 1971 to April 1974
144	M. Whittle	October 1971 to December 1974
135	E. Barrett	March 1989 to February 1992
122	D. Wilson	April 1913 to May 1920
112	R. Palmer	December 1981 to September 1984

All matches

232	E. Ivill	April 1926 to October 1932
180	D. Wilson	September 1907 to December 1911
164	E. Barrett	March 1989 to February 1992
162	J. Fay	September 1907 to April 1911
159	M. Whittle	October 1971 to December 1974
158	I. Wood	March 1971 to April 1974
130	D. Wilson	April 1913 to May 1920
122	R. Palmer	December 1981 to September 1984
104	L. Caunce	February 1937 to April 1939
101	J. Naylor	December 1924 to February 1927
100	L. Chapman	February 1976 to March 1978

Progressive scoring records

Frank Newton set the first target in Oldham Athletic's opening League season scoring 28 League goals and adding another two in the FA Cup. The chart shows how individual scoring records have been beaten since then.

	League		All Matches	
1907–08	Frank Newton	28	Frank Newton	30
1935–36	Billy Walsh	32	Billy Walsh	37
1936–37	Tommy Davis	33	Tommy Davis	38

Top 20 scorers

		All Matches	League Matches
1.	Roger Palmer	157	141
2.	Eric Gemmell	120	109
3.	Andy Ritchie	107	84
4.	Bert Lister	97	81
5.	David Shaw	95	91
6.	Ray Haddington	73	63
7.	Bert Watson	72	64
8.	Don Travis	62	62
9 =	Matt Gray	58	58
9 =	Jimmy Frizzell	58	56
11.	Tommy Davis	57	51
12 =	Albert Pynegar	55	51
12 =	Billy Walsh	55	49
14.	Rodger Wylde	54	51
15 =	Vic Halom	51	43
15 =	Johnny Colquhoun	51	39
17.	Stewart Littlewood	48	46
18.	Frank Newton	47	45
19 =	Ian Robins	46	40
19 =	Keith Bebbington	46	39
19 =	Arthur Gee	46	43

Athletic Career Records

Below are the career records (League, FA Cup, League Cup and other matches) of every Athletic player to have played for the club commencing from 1905–06 when FA Cup matches were first contested. Football League appearances commence from season 1907–08. The years given are the first years of the seasons: for example 1946 means 1946–47. The 'others' list includes all competitions not accounted for in the rest of the table: Associate Members Cup, Full Members' Cup, Third Division North Cup, Texaco Cup, Anglo-Scottish Cup and League Play-offs. Substitute appearances are given to the right of full appearances, e.g. 14/4

Player	Played	LEAGUE A	LEAGUE G	FA CUP A	FA CUP G	FL CUP A	FL CUP G	OTHERS A	OTHERS G	TOTAL A	TOTAL G
Ackerley, S.	1961	2	0	0	0	0	0	0	0	2	0
Adams, N.J.	1988–93 & 1999–2000	149/36	27	21/1	3	17/2	1	2/1	0	180/40	31
Adams, R.M.	1953	23	1	2	0	0	0	0	0	25	1
Adebola, B.	2001	5	0	0	0	0	0	0	0	5	0
Adlam, L.W.	1922–30	279	9	11	1	0	0	0	0	290	10
Agar, A.	1932–35	96	28	5	1	0	0	0	0	101	29
Agogo, M.	1999	2	0	0	0	0	0	0	0	2	0
Aitken, W.C.	1968	1	0	0	0	0/1	0	0	0	1/1	0
Alden, N.E.	1935	1	0	0	0	0	0	0	0	1	0
Alessandra, L.	2007–	12/3	2	0/1	0	0	0	0	0	12/4	2
Aljofree, H.	2006	5	0	0	0	0	0	0	0	5	0
Allott.M.S.	1996–2001 & 2007	139/57	34	13/7	0	9/1	2	7/3	1	168/68	37
Anderson, D.E.	1981–83	4/5	0	0/1	0	0	0	0	0	4/6	0
Anderson, S.	1955–56	6	0	0	0	0	0	0	0	6	0
Andrews, W.M.H.	2002	28/9	11	2/1	0	1/2	0	3	1	34/12	12
Andrews, W.	1908	9	3	0	0	0	0	0	0	9	3
Antoine–Curier, M.	2003	5/3	2	0	0	1	1	0	0	6/3	3
Appleby, M.W.	2001–04	36/10	2	1	0	1	0	2	1	40/10	3
Appleyard, W.	1908	4	0	0	0	0	0	0	0	4	0
Arber, M.A.	2004	13/1	1	0	0	2	0	1	0	16/1	1
Armitage, J.H.	1926–28	90	3	4	0	0	0	0	0	94	3
Armitage, K.J.	1947	5	0	0	0	0	0	0	0	5	0
Armstrong, C.	2001–02	64/1	1	6	0	2	0	6	0	78/1	1
Aspden, T.E.	1905	0	0	1	0	0	0	0	0	1	0
Aspinall, J.	1936–38	11	0	0	0	0	0	2	0	13	0
Asprey, W.	1965–67	80	4	6	1	4	0	0	0	90	5
Aston, V.W.	1948–51	30	1	0	0	0	0	0	0	31	1
Atkinson, P.G.	1979–82 & 1985–87	168/8	12	5	0	14/2	1	4/1	2	191/11	15
Bailey, A.D.	1973–74	26	1	0	0	1	0	5	0	32	1
Bailey, A.	1933–36	53	12	4	2	0	0	1	0	58	14
Baker, B.H.	1928	1	0	0	0	0	0	0	0	1	0
Baldwin, W.	1932	1	0	0	0	0	0	0	0	1	0
Ball, J.A.	1950	7	1	0	0	0	0	0	0	7	1
Balmer, S.M.	2001	35/1	6	4	0	2	0	2	0	43/1	6
Banger, N.L.	1994–96	44/20	10	2/1	0	6	1	0	0	52/21	11
Barlow, A.J.	1984–94	245/16	5	19	0	22	0	6	0	292/16	5
Barlow, C.J.	1963	6	1	0	0	0	0	0	0	6	1
Barlow, M.J.	2003–06	1/9	0	0	0	0/2	0	0/1	0	1/12	0
Barlow, S.	1995–97	78/15	31	6/1	1	5/1	0	0	0	89/17	32
Barlow, T.H.	1906	0	0	3	3	0	0	0	0	3	0
Barnes, H.	1925–26	41	16	5	4	0	0	0	0	46	20
Barrett, E.D.	1987–91	181/2	7	14	1	20	1	4	0	219/2	9
Bartley, A.	1964–65	48/2	13	4	1	2	1	0	0	54/2	15
Bassindale, I.B.	1920–25	50	0	0	0	0	0	0	0	50	0
Baudet, J.	2001–02	34/10	3	2/2	0	2	0	2	0	40/12	3
Bazley, J.A.	1956–61	130	19	6	1	0	0	0	0	136	20
Beardall, J.T.	1969	21/1	10	3	0	1	0	0	0	25/1	10
Beavers, P.M.	1999	10/1	2	0	0	0/1	0	0/1	0	10/3	2
Bebbington, R.K.	1966–71	237	39	10	6	8	1	0	0	255	46
Beckett, L.	2004–05	36/7	24	1/2	0	0	0	1	0	38/9	24
Beckford, D.R.L.	1992–95	31/21	11	6/3	5	2	1	0	0	39/24	17
Beharall, D.	2001–04	58/2	3	8	0	4/1	0	4/1	0	74/4	3
Bell, G.T.	1974–78	166/4	9	7/1	0	9	0	13	0	195/5	9
Bell, P.	1919–21	18	2	0	0	0	0	0	0	18	2
Bell, T.A.	1946–51	170	0	11	0	0	0	0	0	181	0

Player	Played	LEAGUE A	G	FA CUP A	G	FL CUP A	G	OTHERS A	G	TOTAL A	G
Beresford, D.	1993–96	32/32	2	0/1	0	3/3	0	0	0	35/36	2
Beresford, M.	2007–	5	0	0	0	0	0	1	0	6	0
Bernard, M.P.	1977–78	6	0	0	0	1	0	0	0	7	0
Bernard, P.R.J.	1990–94	105/7	17	10	1	11/1	2	0/1	0	126/9	20
Bertrand, R.D.	2007–	21	0	0	0	1	0	2	0	24	0
Best, D.	1966–67	98	0	4	0	5	0	0	0	107	0
Beswick, I.	1958–60	47	0	2	0	0	0	0	0	49	0
Betsy, K.E.L.	2004	34/2	5	3	0	0	0	5	0	42/2	5
Betts, E.	1955–56	26	5	1	0	0	0	0	0	27	5
Bingham, J.G.	1969	16/1	3	1/1	1	0	0	0	0	17/2	4
Birch, B.	1959–60	35	11	2	0	2	1	0	0	39	12
Birkett, R.	1948	4	0	0	0	0	0	0	0	4	0
Black, P.M.	2007–	0/1	0	0	0	0	0	0	0	0/1	0
Blackshaw, H.K.	1936–38	62	15	3	1	0	0	2	1	67	17
Blackshaw, W.	1946–48	67	22	2	0	0	0	0	0	69	22
Blair, J.E.	1921–22	26	16	2	1	0	0	0	0	28	17
Blair, R.V.	1966–69 & 1972–80	359/13	22	15	0	16/2	1	16	2	406/15	25
Blaney, A.	2006	2/1	0	0	0	0	0	1/1	0	3/2	0
Blore, R.	1965–69	182/5	20	9	2	6	0	0	0	197/5	22
Blundell, C.K.	1987–89	2/1	0	0	0	1	0	1	0	4/1	0
Bollands, J.F.	1952–65	154	0	10	0	5	0	0	0	169	0
Bonner, M.	2003–05	26/7	1	0	0	1/1	0	2	0	29/8	1
Boothman, J.	1946–48	44	0	3	0	0	0	0	0	47	0
Boshell, D.K.	1999–2004	45/25	2	3/3	0	6	1	3	1	57/28	4
Boswell, W.	1931	2	1	0	0	0	0	0	0	2	1
Bottomley, W.	1907	13	0	0	0	0	0	0	0	13	0
Bourne, A.	1958–59	35	9	3	1	0	0	0	0	38	10
Bowden, J.	1945–48	72	1	5	1	0	0	0	0	77	2
Bowden, J.L.	1981–84	73/9	5	4	1	5	0	0	0	82/9	6
Bowie, J.M.	1962–71	331/3	37	18/1	2	12	3	0	0	361/4	42
Boxall, D.J.	1997–98	18	0	0	0	0	0	0	0	18	0
Bradbury, W.H.	1911–12 & 1919–20	74	5	3	0	0	0	0	0	77	5
Bradshaw, G.F.	1950	1	0	0	0	0	0	0	0	1	0
Braidwood, E.	1920–21	10	1	0	0	0	0	0	0	10	0
Bramwell, S.	1988	0/1	0	0	0	0	0	0	0	0/1	0
Branagan, J.P.S.	1973–76	24/3	0	0	0	2	0	0	0	26/3	0
Branagan, K.	1960–65	177	5	14	0	4	0	0	0	195	5
Branston, G.P.B.	2004–05	44/1	2	2	0	1	0	2	0	49/1	2
Brazil, D.M.	1990	1	0	0	0	0	0	1	0	2	0
Brelsford, B.	1926–27	9	0	1	0	0	0	0	0	10	0
Brennan, M.R.	1992–95	82/8	7	6	0	7	0	0	0	95/8	7
Brierley, K.	1945–54	125	10	9	1	0	0	0	0	134	11
Bright, D.	1968–69	19	0	0	0	0	0	0	0	19	0
Britton, F.	1934	1	0	0	0	0	0	0	0	1	0
Broad, J.	1913–14	15	5	0	0	0	0	0	0	15	5
Broad, T.H.	1909–11	96	9	8	0	0	0	0	0	104	9
Broadbent, F.	1921–22	12	4	2	3	0	0	0	0	14	7
Broadbent, W.H.	1920–23	12	1	0	0	0	0	0	0	12	1
Broadley, P.J.	1951	4	0	0	0	0	0	0	0	4	0
Bromage, R.	1983	2	0	0	0	0	0	0	0	2	0
Brook, L.	1947–56	189	14	7	0	0	0	0	0	196	14
Broome, A.H.	1924	4	0	0	0	0	0	0	0	4	0
Brown, A.	1928–32	44	0	3	0	0	0	0	0	47	0
Brown, H.	1931	1	1	0	0	0	0	0	0	1	1
Bruce, A.S.	2004	8/4	0	2	0	0	0	2	0	12/4	0
Brunskill, J.	1954	12	2	0	0	0	0	0	0	12	2
Brunskill, N.	1932–35	143	10	6	1	0	0	2	0	151	11
Brunton, M.	1906–07	1	0	9	8	0	0	0	0	10	8
Bryan, P.A.	1965	5/1	0	1	0	1	0	0	0	7/1	0
Bryceland, T.	1970–71	66	10	2	0	4	1	0	0	72	11
Buchan, M.M.	1983	28	0	0	0	2	0	0	0	30	0
Buckley, A.	1934–35	47	10	3	1	0	0	3	1	53	12
Buckley, I.	1971–74	5	0	0	0	0	0	0/1	0	5/1	0
Bullock, S.	1983–85	10/8	0	0	0	1	0	0	0	11/8	0
Bunn, F.S.	1987–91	75/3	26	2	1	8	8	0	0	85/3	35
Bunting, B.	1946–48	32	0	2	0	0	0	0	0	34	0
Burdess, J.	1963–65	3	0	0	0	0	0	0	0	3	0
Burgess, B.K.	2002	6/1	0	0	0	0	0	0	0	6/1	0
Burke, P.J.	1933–34	93	6	5	0	0	0	1	0	99	6

Player	Played	LEAGUE		FA CUP		FL CUP		OTHERS		TOTAL	
		A	G	A	G	A	G	A	G	A	G
Burnett, G.G.	1951–54	100	0	5	0	0	0	0	0	105	0
Burns, L.F.	1955	4	0	0	0	0	0	0	0	4	0
Burns, O.H.	1946	25	5	2	0	0	0	0	0	27	5
Burridge, B.J.H.	1930	6	0	0	0	0	0	0	0	6	0
Burrows, G.B.	1919	7	1	1	0	0	0	0	0	8	1
Butcher, R.T.	2005	32/4	4	3	0	0	0	0	0	35/4	3
Butler, C.R.	1935	13	0	0	0	0	0	2	1	15	1
Butler, R.	1920–22	77	34	1	0	0	0	0	0	78	34
Butler, T.	1937–38 & 1946	75	12	4	0	0	0	0	0	79	12
Butterworth, H.	1908–09	12	0	0	0	0	0	0	0	12	0
Buxton, S.	1911–12	27	0	1	0	0	0	0	0	28	0
Byrom, T.	1920	5	0	0	0	0	0	0	0	5	0
Callaghan, A.J.	1986–87	11/5	2	0	0	4	0	1	0	16/5	2
Cameron, A.R.	1964	15	0	0	0	1	0	0	0	16	0
Campbell, A.F.	1920–21 & 1923	41	8	0	0	0	0	0	0	41	8
Campbell, C.	1949	2	0	0	0	0	0	0	0	2	0
Campbell, J.	1956	26	5	2	0	0	0	0	0	28	5
Carlisle, R.W.	1919–20	5	0	0	0	0	0	0	0	5	0
Carmichael, R.	1909	6	1	0	0	0	0	0	0	6	1
Carney, D.	2003	0/1	0	0	0	0	0	0	0	0/1	0
Carrick, J.	1921–22	6	0	0	0	0	0	0	0	6	0
Carroll, J.P.	1924	7	2	0	0	0	0	0	0	7	2
Carroll, J.	1975	3/1	0	0	0	0	0	0	0	3/1	0
Carss, A.J.	2000–02	58/17	5	3	0	3/1	0	1/2	0	65/20	5
Cashmore, A.	1914	16	8	5	1	0	0	0	0	21	9
Cassidy, L.	1956	4	1	0	0	0	0	0	0	4	1
Caunce, L.	1935–38	134	0	6	0	0	0	7	0	147	0
Cecere, M.J.	1986–88	35/17	8	1/2	1	4/1	0	2/1	1	42/21	10
Chadderton, A.	1919	1	0	0	0	0	0	0	0	1	0
Chadwick, C.	1933	18	6	3	0	0	0	0	0	21	6
Chalmers, A.	2007–	0/2	0	0	0	0	0	0	0	0/2	0
Chambers, W.T.	1934	10	2	0	0	0	0	1	1	11	3
Chapman, E.	1945	0	0	4	2	0	0	0	0	4	2
Chapman, L.	1966–69 & 1974–78	261/2	20	10	1	16	2	9	0	296/2	23
Charlton, S.T.	2006	34	1	4	0	0	0	1	0	39	1
Charlton, S.	1920–21	6	0	0	0	0	0	0	0	6	0
Chaytor, K.	1954–59	77	20	3	0	0	0	0	0	80	20
Church, H.B.	1935	23	0	2	0	0	0	2	0	27	0
Clamp, E.	1949	3	0	0	0	0	0	0	0	3	0
Clark, R.	1958	4	0	0	0	0	0	0	0	4	0
Clarke, A.	1952–53	43	12	5	2	0	0	0	0	48	14
Clarke, J.T.K.	1936	1	1	0	0	0	0	0	0	1	1
Clarke, L.M.	2006	5	3	0	0	0	0	0	0	5	3
Clegg, M.J.	2001–03	40/6	0	2	0	1	0	2/1	0	45/7	0
Clements, K.H.	1979–84	204/2	2	8	0	12	0	3	0	227/2	2
Clements, P.R.	1971	32/2	0	1	0	0/1	1	0	0	33/4	1
Clitheroe, L.J.	1997–98	2/3	0	0	0	0	0	0	0	2/3	0
Collins, J.P.	1983	0/1	0	0	0	0	0	0	0	0/1	0
Collins, J.W.	1966	20/1	8	4	3	0	0	0	0	24/1	11
Collins, R.Y.	1972–73	6/1	0	2	1	0	0	0	0	8/1	1
Colman, E.	1925	2	0	0	0	0	0	0	0	2	0
Colusso, C.	2001	6/7	2	0	0	0	0	0	0	6/7	2
Colquhoun, J.	1961–64 & 1968–69	231/2	39	16	11	6	1	0	0	253/2	51
Colville, R.J.	1983–86	22/10	4	0/1	0	1	0	0/1	0	23/12	4
Constantine, L.	2007–	7/1	2	0	0	0	0	0	0	7/1	2
Cook, W.	1907–19	157	16	14	0	0	0	0	0	171	16
Cooksey, E.G.	2003	23/14	4	2	2	0	0	1/1	0	26/15	6
Cooper, A.	1922	9	0	0	0	0	0	0	0	9	0
Cooper, K.	2004	5/2	3	0/1	0	0	0	1	0	6/3	3
Cope, W.A.	1908–13	62	1	3	0	0	0	0	0	65	1
Corazzin, G.M.	2000–02	82/28	20	6/2	1	5/3	2	1/2	0	94/35	23
Corbett, P.	1959	10	0	0	0	0	0	0	0	10	0
Craig, R.M.	1963–64	18	4	0	0	1	1	0	0	19	5
Cranston, W.	1970–72	98/2	2	4	0	5	0	0	0	107/2	2
Crawford, J.C.	1952–53	24	8	0	0	0	0	0	0	24	8
Creaney, G.T.	1995	8/1	2	0	0	0	0	0	0	8/1	2
Crompton, N.	1926–27	9	0	0	0	0	0	0	0	9	0

Player	Played	LEAGUE A	LEAGUE G	FA CUP A	FA CUP G	FL CUP A	FL CUP G	OTHERS A	OTHERS G	TOTAL A	TOTAL G
Croft, L.D.	2004	11/1	0	3	1	0	0	2	1	16/1	2
Cronin, L.	2005	0	0	0/1	0	0	0	0	0	0/1	0
Crook, G.	1953–57	57	13	0	0	0	0	0	0	57	13
Cross, D.	1983	18/4	6	1	0	2	1	0	0	21/4	7
Crossley, M.G.	2007–	38	0	5	0	2	0	1	0	46	0
Crossley, T.G.	1957	2	1	0	0	0	0	0	0	2	1
Crowe, D.A.	2003	2/3	1	0	0	0	0	0	0	2/3	1
Crumblehulme, K.	1971	2	0	0	0	0	0	0	0	2	0
Cumming, L.S.S.	1929	25	11	1	0	0	0	0	0	26	11
Cunliffe, T.	1919	2	0	0	0	0	0	0	0	2	0
Curran, J.	1966	3	0	1	0	0	0	0	0	4	0
Currie, D.N.	1990	17/14	3	1	0	2/1	2	0/1	0	20/16	5
Cutting, J.A.	1946	4	1	1	0	0	0	0	0	5	1
Cywka, T.	2006	0/4	0	0	0	0	0	1	0	1/4	0
D'Arcy, M.A.	1954–55	45	0	2	0	0	0	0	0	47	0
Davies, C.M.	2007–	30/1	11	5	1	2	1	2	1	39/1	14
Davies, D.W.	1912	10	3	0	0	0	0	0	0	10	3
Davis, E.W.C.	1960	2	1	0	0	0	0	0	0	2	1
Davis, T.L.	1935–37	72	51	7	4	0	0	2	2	81	57
Daw, E.C.	1906	0	0	8	0	0	0	0	0	8	0
Day, C.N.	2005	30	0	4	0	1	0	1	0	36	0
Dearden, W.	1964–66	32/3	2	4	1	1	1	0	0	37/3	4
Devlin, T.	1934	2	0	0	0	0	0	0	0	2	0
Diamond, J.J.	1936–38	50	22	1	0	0	0	2	0	53	22
Dickenson, J.	1932–33	6	0	2	0	0	0	0	0	8	0
Dickinson, L.	1961	5	2	0	0	0	0	0	0	5	2
Divers, J.	1947	1	0	0	0	0	0	0	0	1	0
Dixon, A.	1913–14	30	0	1	0	0	0	0	0	31	0
Dodds, J.T.	1908	8	0	0	0	0	0	0	0	8	0
Dodds, W.	1907	13	3	0	0	0	0	0	0	13	3
Dolphin, A.	1919	16	0	0	0	0	0	0	0	16	0
Donachie, W.	1984–92	158/11	3	5/1	0	13/2	0	2	0	178/14	3
Donnachie, J.	1908–14	216	19	22	2	0	0	0	0	238	21
Dougherty, J.	1919–20	15	5	1	0	0	0	0	0	16	5
Douglas, G.H.	1922–25	134	8	7	1	0	0	0	0	141	9
Douglas, W.	1913	2	1	0	0	0	0	0	0	2	1
Dowd, H.W.	1970–73	121	0	5	0	5	0	0	0	131	0
Dowker, T.	1947	1	0	0	0	0	0	0	0	1	0
Down, D.F.	1968	9	1	1	0	0	0	0	0	10	1
Downes, P.	1936–37	51	4	3	0	0	0	4	0	58	4
Downie, A.L.B.	1909–10	48	0	1	0	0	0	0	0	49	0
Doyle, J.A.	1967–68	31/2	0	1	0	1	0	0	0	33/2	0
Dryburgh, T.J.D.	1957	1	0	0	0	0	0	0	0	1	0
Dubose, W.S.	1988	0	0	0	0	1	0	0	0	1	0
Dudley, C.B.	1999–2001	34/26	10	5/3	3	2/1	0	0/2	0	41/32	13
Duffy, G.	1956–58	58	21	4	2	0	0	0	0	62	23
Dungworth, J.H.	1975–76	2/2	0	0	0	0	0	0	0	2/2	0
Duxbury, L.E.	1996–2002	222/26	32	16/2	5	12	1	5/1	1	255/29	39
Dyson, J.	1927–31	122	40	4	0	0	0	0	0	126	40
Eardley, N.J.	2005–07	77/4	6	8	0	3	0	2	0	90/4	6
Eaton, C.	1936–37	2	0	0	0	0	0	1	0	3	0
Eaves, T.A.	1936–38	28	0	0	0	0	0	2	0	30	0
Eccleston, W.	1905	0	0	5	2	0	0	0	0	5	2
Eckersley, F.	1938	1	0	0	0	0	0	0	0	1	0
Edge, T.	1920	3	0	0	0	0	0	0	0	3	0
Edmonds, N.A.	1986–87	3/2	0	0	0	0/1	0	1	0	4/3	0
Edwards, P.A.	2005–06	39/21	0	2/2	0	1/1	0	1/1	0	43/25	0
Edwards, P.F.	1972–77	108/4	7	7	0	7	1	7	0	129/4	8
Edwards, S.G.	1977–82	77/3	0	3	0	5/1	0	7	0	92/4	0
Ellis, A.J.	1986	5/3	0	0	0	1	0	1	0	7/3	0
Eyre, J.R.	1993–94 & 2001–04	102/26	15	8/1	1	7/1	1	6/3	1	123/31	18
Eyres, D.	2000–05	187/20	33	15/2	5	8	2	9/1	4	219/23	44
Facey, D.M.	2004–05	1/8	0	0	0	1	0	0	0	2/8	0
Fairclough, D.	1985	6/11	1	1	0	1/1	2	0	0	8/12	3
Farmer, W.H.	1957	5	0	0	0	0	0	0	0	5	0
Faulkner, M.	1969	1	0	0	0	0	0	0	0	1	0
Fawley, R.	1950–57	94	9	4	1	0	0	0	0	98	10
Fay, J.A.	1905–11	154	37	21	3	0	0	0	0	175	40
Ferguson, C.	1959–60	57	0	3	0	1	0	0	0	61	0
Ferguson, J.C.M.	1959	36	0	3	0	0	0	0	0	39	0

Player	Played	LEAGUE		FA CUP		FL CUP		OTHERS		TOTAL	
		A	G	A	G	A	G	A	G	A	G
Ferguson, J.T.H.	1956	1	0	0	0	0	0	0	0	1	0
Fergusson, W.A.	1922–23	5	1	0	0	0	0	0	0	5	1
Ferrier, R.J.	1937–38	45	25	4	2	0	0	0	0	49	27
Fielden, A.	1938	1	1	0	0	0	0	0	0	1	0
Fillery, M.C.	1990	1/1	0	0	0	0	0	0	0	1/1	0
Finney, W.A.	1930	30	0	0	0	0	0	0	0	30	0
Firm, N.J.	1981	9	0	0	0	0	0	0	0	9	0
Fitton, F.	1930	9	4	1	1	0	0	0	0	10	5
Fitton, J.	1969	3	0	0	0	0	0	0	0	3	0
Flavell, F.	1930–31	4	0	0	0	0	0	0	0	4	0
Fleetwood, T.	1923	5	0	0	0	0	0	0	0	5	0
Fleming, C.	1991–96	158/6	1	11	0	12/1	0	1	0	182/7	1
Fleming, C.M.	2003	0/1	0	0	0	0	0	0	0	0/1	0
Floyd, P.	1928	3	0	0	0	0	0	0	0	3	0
Flynn, M.A.	1987–88	37/3	1	1	0	1/1	0	2	0	41/4	1
Foran, M.J.	1996	0/1	0	0	0	0	0	0	0	0/1	0
Forbes, T.D.	2005	33/6	0	3	0	1	0	1	0	38/6	0
Ford, K.	1961	5	1	1	0	0	0	0	0	6	1
Foster, A.J.	1965–66	8/1	0	0	0	1/1	1	0	0	9/2	1
Foster, C.L.	1928	1	0	0	0	0	0	0	0	1	0
Foster, R.	1936	10	0	1	0	0	0	0	0	11	0
Foweather, V.J.	1920	5	1	1	0	0	0	0	0	6	1
Fox, R.	1957	1	0	0	0	0	0	0	0	1	0
Franks, A.E.S.	1912	1	0	0	0	0	0	0	0	1	0
Freeman, R.F.V.	1920–22	101	0	3	0	0	0	0	0	104	0
Frizzell, J.L.	1960–69	308/9	56	22	1	11	1	0	0	341/9	58
Fryatt, J.E.	1969–70	76	40	1	0	4	2	0	0	81	42
Fryer, J.H.	1947	9	3	0	0	0	0	0	0	9	3
Futcher, B.P.	1999–2000	2/8	0	0/1	0	0	0	0	0	2/9	0
Futcher, P.	1980–82	98	1	3	0	10	0	2	0	113	1
Futcher, R.	1985–86	65	30	3	0	4	2	1	0	73	32
Gannon, J.S.	1995–96	6	0	0	0	0	0	0	0	6	0
Gardner, S.F.	1937	0	0	0	0	0	0	2	0	2	0
Gardner, S.D.	1977–80	41/12	1	3	0	2/1	0	7/1	0	53/14	1
Garland, R.	1954–55	9	3	1	0	0	0	0	0	10	3
Garnett, S.M.	1996–2001	165/8	9	12	0	7	0	4	0	188/8	9
Garwood, C.A.	1971–73	84/9	35	2/4	1	3	0	7	3	96/13	39
Gayle, A.K.	1988	0/1	0	0	0	0	0	0	0	0/1	0
Gaynor, L.A.	1957	5	0	0	0	0	0	0	0	5	0
Gee, A.	1911–20	112	43	7	3	0	0	0	0	119	46
Gemmell, E.	1947–53	195	109	23	11	0	0	0	0	218	120
Gerrard, P.W.	1992–96	118/1	0	7	0	7	0	0	0	132/1	0
Giddings, S.J.	2007–	2	0	0	0	1	0	0	0	3	0
Gill, W.J.	2001	3	0	0	0	0	0	0	0	3	0
Gillespie, R.	1924–25	27	5	1	0	0	0	0	0	28	5
Glennie, J.	1924	1	0	0	0	0	0	0	0	1	0
Glombard, L.	2006	3/5	1	0	0	0	0	0/2	0	3/7	1
Goodfellow, S.	1950–51	72	2	6	1	0	0	0	0	78	3
Goodier, E.	1925–31	113	2	3	1	0	0	0	0	116	3
Goodwin, L.	1946	7	0	0	0	0	0	0	0	7	0
Goodwin, W.	1914 & 1925	42	0	1	0	0	0	0	0	43	0
Goram, A.L.	1982–87	195	0	7	0	10	0	3	0	215	0
Gordine, B.	1968–70	83	0	4	0	1	0	0	0	88	0
Gorton, A.W.	1985–86	26	0	1	0	4	0	1	0	32	0
Gough, H.	1926	4	0	0	0	0	0	0	0	4	0
Grabban, L.J.	2006	1/8	0	0	0	1	0	0	0	2/8	0
Graham, R.E.	1993–99	139/11	14	13	1	11	0	0	0	163/11	15
Grainger, D.	1951	3	0	1	0	0	0	0	0	4	0
Grant, A.D.	2005	2	0	0	0	0	0	0	0	2	0
Grant, L.A.	2005	16	0	0	0	0	0	0	0	16	0
Gray, A.	1923–26	97	0	4	0	0	0	0	0	101	0
Gray, A.D.	1998	4	0	0	0	0	0	0	0	4	0
Gray, M.	1928–38	289	58	11	0	0	0	3	0	303	58
Greaves, I.D.	1961–62	22	0	0	0	0	0	0	0	22	0
Green, H.	1928	1	0	0	0	0	0	0	0	1	0
Green, I.	1978	0	0	0	0	0	0	1/1	0	1/1	0
Greenhall, G.E.	1960	25	0	3	0	2	0	0	0	30	0
Gregan, S.M.	2006–07	42	0	2/1	0	2	0	4	0	50/1	0
Grew, M.S.	1983	5	0	1	0	0	0	0	0	6	0
Grice, R.	1932–34	26	0	1	0	0	0	0	0	27	0
Griffin, A.	2001–04	58/4	3	4/1	0	2	0	4/1	1	68/6	4

Player	Played	LEAGUE		FA CUP		FL CUP		OTHERS		TOTAL	
		A	G	A	G	A	G	A	G	A	G
Griffiths, A.	1908	25	4	1	0	0	0	0	0	26	4
Grobbelaar, B.D.	1997	4	0	0	0	0	0	0	0	4	0
Groves, A.	1973–77	136/4	12	3/1	0	9	1	9/1	1	157/6	14
Grundy, H.	1914–28	279	0	10	0	0	0	0	0	289	0
Hacking, J.	1926–33	223	0	11	0	0	0	0	0	234	0
Haddington, R.W.	1947–50	117	63	9	10	0	0	0	0	126	73
Haining, W.W.	2001–06	147/8	11	9/1	1	4/1	0	10	0	170/10	12
Halford, D.	1938	26	11	2	0	0	0	0	0	28	11
Hall, A.S.	1957–60	74	5	3	0	2	0	0	0	79	5
Hall, C.M.	2003–06	7/36	1	0/7	4	0	0	1/3	0	12/46	5
Hall, D.A.	2002–05	57/7	1	7/1	0	1	0	6	0	71/8	1
Hall, F.	2001–02	44	5	3	1	4	0	2/1	0	53/1	6
Hall, J.F.	1965	2	0	0	0	1	0	0	0	3	0
Hallam, J.	1931	1	0	0	0	0	0	0	0	1	0
Halle, G.	1990–96	185/3	17	8	2	16	2	0	0	209/3	21
Halligan, W.	1919–20	28	9	0	0	0	0	0	0	28	9
Hallworth, J.G.	1988–96	171/3	0	20	0	20	0	1	0	212/3	0
Halom, V.L.	1976–79	121/2	43	9	3	9	3	13	2	152/2	51
Halsall, A.	1963	2	0	0	0	0	0	0	0	2	0
Hamilton, J.	1907–10	105	5	10	1	0	0	0	0	115	6
Hancock, H.B.	1906–07	27	7	12	9	0	0	0	0	39	16
Hardie, J.C.	1960	17	0	3	0	2	0	0	0	22	0
Hardman, J.A.	1911	2	0	0	0	0	0	0	0	2	0
Hardwick, G.F.M.	1950–55	190	14	13	0	0	0	0	0	203	14
Hardy, J.J.	1926	2	0	0	0	0	0	0	0	2	0
Hardy, L.	2001	0/1	0	0	0	0	0	0	0	0/1	0
Hargreaves, F.	1923, 1925–29 & 1932	103	17	1	0	0	0	0	0	104	17
Harris, J.	1964–65	28/1	7	1	0	2	0	0	0	31/1	7
Harris, J.	1952–53	27	4	0	0	0	0	0	0	27	4
Harris, N.	1927–28	39	16	1	0	0	0	0	0	40	16
Harris, W.	1946	32	0	2	0	0	0	0	0	34	0
Harrison, W.	1984	5/1	1	1/1	1	0	0	0	0	6/2	2
Hartford, R.A.	1988	3/4	0	0	0	0	0	0	0	3/4	0
Hartle, B.	1970	8/1	2	1	0	0	0	0	0	9/1	2
Hartley, E.	1956	1	0	0	0	0	0	0	0	1	0
Haslam, H	1946	2	0	0	0	0	0	0	0	2	0
Hasson, W.C.	1928–33	134	22	4	0	0	0	0	0	138	22
Hateley, A.	1973	1/4	1	0	0	0	0	0	0	1/4	1
Hayes, W.	1938–50	126	3	6	0	0	0	1	0	133	3
Hazell, R.D.	2007–	32/2	1	3/1	0	0	0	1	0	36/3	1
Heath, D.	1970–71	43/2	1	1/1	0	3	0	0	0	47/3	1
Heaton, J.H.	1938	2	1	0	0	0	0	0	0	2	1
Heaton, P.J.	1977–83	124/12	28	4	1	9/2	2	8/3	2	145/16	33
Heaton, T.	1923–26	59	3	5	0	0	0	0	0	64	3
Hemsley, C.J.	1919–20	7	1	0	0	0	0	0	0	7	1
Henry, A.	1982–87	185/5	25	5	0	12	2	3/1	0	205/6	27
Henry, N.I.	1987–96	264/9	19	21	0	30/4	3	4	0	319/13	22
Herbert, F.	1946	4	0	0	0	0	0	0	0	4	0
Heseltine, W.A.	1989	1	0	0/1	0	0	0	0	0	1/1	0
Hesham, F.	1907–08	34	8	6	1	0	0	0	0	40	9
Hewitson, R.	1907	27	0	4	0	0	0	0	0	31	0
Hey, C.	1926–29	11	1	0	0	0	0	0	0	11	1
Heywood, F.	1905	0	0	5	1	0	0	0	0	5	1
Hibbert, W.	1922	16	4	1	0	0	0	0	0	17	4
Hicks, K.	1971–79	240/2	11	15	0	12	1	17	1	284/2	13
Hill, C.S.	2002	17/1	0	2	0	4	0	2	0	25	1
Hilton, M.G.	1977–80	48/2	2	0/1	0	2	1	5	0	55/3	3
Hilton, W.A.	1934–38	129	4	9	1	0	0	6	0	144	5
Hitchen, T.	1956	3	0	0	0	0	0	0	0	3	0
Hobson, W.	1954–58	170	1	10	0	0	0	0	0	180	1
Hodge, M.J.	1982	4	0	0	0	0	0	0	0	4	0
Hodgson, D.J.H.	1996–97	33/8	4	3	0	0/2	0	0	0	36/10	4
Hodkinson, A.J.	1983–84	4/1	1	0	0	0	0	0	0	4/1	1
Hodkinson, D.	1961	2	0	0	0	0	0	0	0	2	0
Hodson, J.	1905–14	252	1	37	0	0	0	0	0	289	1
Holden, A.I.	1988–89	22	4	2	0	0	0	0	0	24	4
Holden, D.T.J.	2001	20/3	2	1	0	0	0	0	0	21/3	2
Holden, J.S.	1965–66	39/3	5	2/1	0	1	1	0	0	42/4	6
Holden, R.W.	1989–91 & 1993–94	171/18	28	20/1	3	18/3	4	3	1	212/22	36

Player	Played	LEAGUE A	G	FA CUP A	G	FL CUP A	G	OTHERS A	G	TOTAL A	G
Hollis, E.	1912–13	2	0	0	0	0	0	0	0	2	0
Holt, A.	1996–2000	104/20	10	7/4	0	8	0	0	0	119/24	10
Holt, D.	1974–79	141/1	1	4	0	9	0	7	0	161/1	1
Holt, E.	1905	0	0	3	0	0	0	0	0	3	0
Holt, R.	1965	14/1	0	0	0	2	0	0	0	16/1	0
Hoolickin, G.J.	1976–88	209/2	2	7/1	0	23	1	3/2	0	242/5	3
Hoolickin, S.	1969–72	8	0	0	0	0	0	0	0	8	0
Hooper, D.	1919	5	0	0	0	0	0	0	0	5	0
Hooper, F.W.	1919	5	1	0	0	0	0	0	0	5	1
Hope, J.R.	1931	4	0	0	0	0	0	0	0	4	0
Hopkinson, E.	1951	3	0	0	0	0	0	0	0	3	0
Horrocks, H.	1922–23	23	2	0	0	0	0	0	0	23	2
Horsborough, J.J.	1961	1	0	0	0	1	0	0	0	2	0
Horton, L.	1945–47	79	2	8	1	0	0	0	0	87	3
Hotte, M.S.	1997–2001	59/6	0	2/1	0	2/2	0	0	0	63/9	0
Houlahan, H.	1952	6	3	0	0	0	0	0	0	6	3
Howarth, C	2006	2/1	0	0	0	1	0	0	0	3/1	0
Howe, F.	1946	30	20	1	0	0	0	0	0	31	20
Howson, W.	1923	21	5	2	0	0	0	0	0	23	5
Hudson, C.J.	1982–83	16/4	0	1	0	0/1	0	0	0	17/5	0
Hudson, M.A.	2003	15	0	0	0	0	0	1	0	16	0
Hughes, A.J.	1995–97	18/15	1	3/1	0	1/1	0	0	0	22/17	1
Hughes, L.	2007–	15/3	7	3	1	0	0	0	0	18/3	8
Hughes, M.A.	2004–05	55/5	1	7	0	1	0	2/3	0	65/8	1
Hulme, A.	1905	0	0	4	0	0	0	0	0	4	0
Humphries, J.S.	1982–83	7/6	0	0	0	2/1	0	0	0	9/7	0
Hunter, A.	1966–68	83	1	2	0	5	0	0	0	90	1
Hunter, G.C.	1911–12	40	1	6	0	0	0	0	0	46	1
Hurst, J.	1946–50	98	2	9	0	0	0	0	0	107	2
Hurst, J.	1976–80	169/1	2	11	0	11	0	17	0	208/1	2
Hutchinson, J.A.	1948–49	14	3	0	0	0	0	0	0	14	3
Innes, M.	1997–2001	52/21	1	4/2	0	4/3	0	3/1	0	63/27	1
Ironside, I.	1997	1	0	0	0	0	0	0	0	1	0
Irvine, D.	1976	18/3	7	2	0	3/1	1	0	0	23/4	8
Irwin, D.J.	1986–89	166/1	4	13	0	19	3	5	0	203/1	7
Ivill, E.	1924–31	276	2	9	1	0	0	0	0	285	3
Jack, R.A.	2004	5/5	2	0	0	0/1	0	0	0	5/6	2
Jackson, A.	1963–65	22	4	2	1	1	0	0	0	25	5
Jackson, H.	1951–54	10	1	0	0	0	0	0	0	10	1
Jackson, N.E.	1956	2	0	0	0	0	0	0	0	2	0
Jackson, R.	1951–54	29	1	2	0	0	0	0	0	31	1
Jarrett, J.L.M.	2007–	12/3	3	0	0	0	0	0	0	12/3	3
Jarvis, J.B.	1959–62	88	2	12	1	3	0	0	0	103	3
Jeavons, W.H.	1933	3	1	0	0	0	0	0	0	3	1
Jennings, A.	1926	2	0	0	0	0	0	0	0	2	0
Jepson, R.F.	1997	9	4	0	0	0	0	0	0	9	4
Jessop, W.	1947–50	94	16	12	2	0	0	0	0	106	18
Jobson, R.I.	1990–95	188/1	10	13	0	19	1	2	0	222/1	11
John, R.C.	1958–59	32	5	2	0	0	0	0	0	34	5
Johnson, H.	1931–33	37	13	1	0	0	0	0	0	38	13
Johnson, J.	2003–04	31/8	9	1/1	0	2	0	1	0	35/9	9
Johnston, T.B.	1951	5	3	0	0	0	0	0	0	5	3
Johnston, W.C.	1966–68	28/1	6	0	0	3/1	0	0	0	31/2	6
Johnston, W.G.	1932–34	67	8	3	0	0	0	0	0	70	8
Johnstone, R.	1960–64	143	36	12	1	3	0	0	0	158	37
Johnstone, W.	1930–33	68	28	2	0	0	0	0	0	70	28
Jones, A.	1982–85	7/1	0	0	0	0/1	0	0	0	7/2	0
Jones, A.	1935–38	98	30	4	0	0	0	7	2	109	32
Jones, C.	1922–24	56	5	2	0	0	0	0	0	58	5
Jones, C.N.M.	1971	3	1	0	0	0	0	0	0	3	1
Jones, E.	1927–28	7	3	0	0	0	0	0	0	7	3
Jones, E.	1910–11	50	25	4	0	0	0	0	0	54	25
Jones, G.A.	1972–75	63/8	19	7	3	5	3	5	1	80/8	26
Jones, G.B.	1931	2	0	0	0	0	0	0	0	2	0
Jones, J.T.	1948	22	0	4	0	0	0	0	0	26	0
Jones, P.B.	1985–86	32	1	1	0	1	0	1	0	35	1
Jones, P.N.	1999–2000	26/2	3	0	0	3	0	0/1	0	29/3	3
Jones, R.	1920–21	25	0	2	0	0	0	0	0	27	0
Jones, S.	1936	1	0	0	0	0	0	1	0	2	0
Jones, T.	1919	10	2	0	0	0	0	0	0	10	2
Jones, T.	1938	1	0	0	0	0	0	0	0	1	0

Player	Played	LEAGUE A	LEAGUE G	FA CUP A	FA CUP G	FL CUP A	FL CUP G	OTHERS A	OTHERS G	TOTAL A	TOTAL G
Jordan, T.E.	1978–79	2/3	0	0	0	0	0	0	0	2/3	0
Joyce, W.	1967–69	68/3	2	1	0	0	0	0	0	69/3	2
Joynson, G.E.	1912–13	5	0	0	0	0	0	0	0	5	0
Kamudimba Kalala, J.P.	2007–	14/6	0	2	0	2	1	2	0	20/6	1
Kane, P.J.	1990–91	13/8	0	1	0	2	0	1	0	17/8	0
Keedwell, J.H.	1924	16	4	0	0	0	0	0	0	16	4
Keegan, G.A.	1979–82	139/5	5	4	0	11	1	6	0	160/5	6
Keeley, G.M.	1987	10/1	0	0	0	2/1	1	0/1	0	12/3	1
Keeley, J.H.	1991	2	0	0	0	1	0	1	0	4	0
Keizerweerd, O.	1992	0/1	0	0	0	0	0	0	0	0/1	0
Kellard, T.	1927	2	0	0	0	0	0	0	0	2	0
Kelly, A.C.	2007–	0/1	0	0	0	0	0	0	0	0/1	0
Kelly, A.C.P.	1905	0	0	3	2	0	0	0	0	3	2
Kelly, G.A.	1996–2002	224/1	0	19	0	13	0	6	0	262/1	0
Kelly, J.	1987–88	51/1	6	1	0	4	0	1	0	57/1	6
Kelly, N.	1987	0/2	0	0/1	0	0	0	0/1	0	0/4	0
Kemp, G.	1912–19	64	23	8	5	0	0	0	0	72	28
Kennedy, F.	1930	5	0	0	0	0	0	0	0	5	0
Kenny, W.A.	1994	4	0	0	0	0	0	0	0	4	0
Kerr, J.	1954–55	34	4	2	0	0	0	0	0	36	4
Key, L.W.	1993	2	0	0	0	0	0	0	0	2	0
Kilcline, B.	1991	8	0	0	0	2	0	0	0	10	0
Kilkenny, N.M.	2004 & 2007	43/4	5	6	1	1	1	5	1	55/4	8
Killen, C.	2002–05	53/25	17	3/2	4	4/1	1	2	1	62/28	23
King, D.	1954–55	22	7	0	0	0	0	0	0	22	7
King, G.C.	1922	4	1	1	0	0	0	0	0	5	1
King, J.	1926–28	80	12	4	1	0	0	0	0	84	13
King, S.	1929–30	91	0	5	0	0	0	0	0	96	0
Kinnell, G.	1966	12	8	0	0	0	0	0	0	12	8
Kirkpatrick, E.	1925–26	15	4	0	0	0	0	0	0	15	4
Knight, D.S.	2006	2	0	0	0	0	0	0	0	2	0
Knighton, K.	1966–67	45	4	4	0	3	0	0	0	52	4
Koffman, S.J.	1947	3	0	0	0	0	0	0	0	3	0
Kowenicki, R.S.	1979–80	40/2	5	3	0	2	1	2	2	47/2	8
Kyratzoglou, A.B.	1997	0/1	0	0	0	0	0	0	0	0/1	0
Large, F.	1965–66	34	18	3	1	0	0	0	0	37	19
Lawless, A.T.	1956	9	0	0	0	0	0	0	0	9	0
Lawrence, V.	1913	1	0	0	0	0	0	0	0	1	0
Lawson, A	1964–69	128/10	1	6	0	5	0	0	0	139/10	1
Lawton, W.	1945–47	10	0	7	1	0	0	0	0	17	1
Ledger, R.H.	1962–66	221/1	37	12	1	6	0	0	0	239/1	38
Lee, A.	1950	3	1	0	0	0	0	0	0	3	1
Lee, D.J.F.	2004	5/2	0	1	0	0	0	1	0	7/2	0
Lee, R.M.	2004	0	0	0	0	0	0	1	0	1	0
Leedham, F.	1934–36	48	11	4	0	0	0	1	0	53	11
Legzdins, A.	2006	0	0	0	0	0	0	0/1	0	0/1	0
Leigh, T.	1906	0	0	2	0	0	0	0	0	2	0
Lester, H.	1914	1	0	0	0	0	0	0	0	1	0
Lester, M.J.A.	1972	26/1	2	0	0	2	0	0	0	28/1	2
Lewin, D.J.	1953	10	1	0	0	0	0	0	0	10	1
Lewis, J.	1905	0	0	1	0	0	0	0	0	1	0
Liddell, A.M.	2005–07	89/4	21	8	1	3/1	0	5	3	105/5	25
Liddell, J.C.	1960–61	23	10	0	0	1	1	0	0	24	11
Lightfoot, C.I.	2000	3	0	0	0	1	0	0	0	4	0
Linighan, A.	1985–87	87	6	3	0	8	2	4	0	102	8
Lister, H.F.	1960–66	135	81	14	10	4	6	0	0	153	97
Litchfield, P.	1988	3	0	0	0	0	0	0	0	3	0
Littlejohn, A.S.	1997–98	16/5	5	0	0	2	1	0	0	18/5	6
Littlewood, S.C.	1928–30	78	46	3	2	0	0	0	0	81	48
Livermore, D.	2007–	10	1	0	0	0	0	0	0	10	1
Lochhead, A.L.	1973–74	44/1	10	5	1	3	0	0/1	0	52/2	11
Lomax, K.	2003–07	27/13	0	2/1	0	0	0	3/2	0	32/16	0
Lonergan, D	1995	1/1	0	0	0	0	0	0	0	1/1	0
Longmuir, A.M.	1923	22	4	0	0	0	0	0	0	22	4
Lourenco	2002	1/6	1	0	0	1/1	0	1	0	3/7	1
Low, J.D.	2002	19/2	3	2	1	2	0	2	0	25/2	4
Lowe, J.	1928	7	2	0	0	0	0	0	0	7	2
Lowrie, T.	1952–54	79	5	5	0	0	0	0	0	84	5
Lyons, G.	1906	0	0	1	0	0	0	0	0	1	0
McAllister, A.	1905	0	0	5	2	0	0	0	0	5	2
McBride, J.	1983–84	28/8	5	1	0	1	0	0	0	30/8	5

Player	Played	LEAGUE		FA CUP		FL CUP		OTHERS		TOTAL	
		A	G	A	G	A	G	A	G	A	G
McCall, P.	1962–64	108	5	5	0	3	0	0	0	116	5
McCarthy, P.P.	1965	2/1	0	0	0	0	0	0	0	2/1	0
McCarthy, S.C.	1993–97	117/23	42	6/1	1	10	1	1	0	134/24	44
McCormack, F.A.	1949	14	0	2	0	0	0	0	0	16	0
McCormick, P.	1936–38	38	13	3	2	0	0	5	2	46	17
McCready, B.T.	1958	7	0	0	0	0	0	0	0	7	0
McCue, J.W.	1925	1	0	0	0	0	0	0	0	1	0
McCue, J.W.	1960–61	56	0	6	0	2	0	0	0	64	0
McCurley, K.	1960	1	0	0	0	0	0	0	0	1	0
McDonald, G.M.	2006–07	70/8	11	9	2	1/1	0	2/1	0	82/10	13
McDonald, H.L.	1910–11	41	0	3	0	0	0	0	0	44	0
McDonald, N.R.	1991–93	19/5	0	2	0	3	0	0	0	24/5	1
McDonnell, P.A.	1978–82	137	0	4	0	11	0	13	0	165	0
McDonough, D.K.	1980–86	178/5	14	5	0	12	3	0	0	195/5	17
McGarvey, S.T.	1989	2/2	1	2	1	1/1	0	1	0	6/3	2
McGill, J.H.	1959	38	2	2	1	0	0	0	0	40	3
McGinlay, J.	1998	4/3	1	1/1	2	0	0	1	0	6/4	3
McGinn, W.B.	1963–65	37/1	0	4	0	1	0	0	0	42/1	0
McGlen, W.	1952–55	68	3	2	0	0	0	0	0	70	3
McGowan, G.J.	1965	5	1	0	0	0	0	0	0	5	1
McGuire, M.J.	1984–86	65/4	3	3	1	2	0	1	0	71/4	4
McIlroy, J.	1965–66	35/4	1	1	0	2	0	0	0	38/4	1
McIlvenny, R.	1949–54	139	36	8	2	0	0	0	0	147	38
McKennan, P.S.	1951–53	78	28	5	5	0	0	0	0	83	33
McLean, I.J.	1998–99	6	0	0	0	0	0	0	0	6	0
McMahon, I.	1982	2	0	0	0	0	0	0	0	2	0
McManus, B.	1947	35	0	2	0	0	0	0	0	37	0
McNeill, A.	1969–74	154/16	19	9/1	0	5	0	3	1	171/17	20
McNiven, D.J.	1996–99	8/18	2	0	0	1/2	0	0	0	9/20	2
McNiven, S.A.	1994–2001	204/18	4	18/1	1	13/1	0	5/2	0	240/22	5
McShane, H.	1953–54	41	5	1	1	0	0	0	0	42	6
McTavish, J.K.	1910	10	0	0	0	0	0	0	0	10	0
McVitie, G.J.	1972–75	108/5	19	7	2	3/1	0	3	1	121/6	22
Maddison, J.A.B.	1927–28	6	0	1	0	0	0	0	0	7	0
Magee, E.	1967–68	41/4	9	1	0	3	1	0	0	45/4	10
Makin, C.G.	1993–95	93/1	4	11	0	7	0	0	0	111/1	4
Makin, J.	1966–67	6	0	0	0	0	0	0	0	6	0
Mallon, J.G.	1958–59	31	8	2	0	0	0	0	0	33	8
Malpas, E.	1927	3	0	0	0	0	0	0	0	3	0
Mardon, P.J.	1998	12	3	0	0	0	0	0	0	12	3
Marlor, A.	1945	0	0	4	0	0	0	0	0	4	0
Marrison, T.	1911	17	4	0	0	0	0	0	0	17	4
Marsh, J.S.	1959	2	0	0	0	0	0	0	0	2	0
Marshall, A.W.	1920–22	66	3	3	0	0	0	0	0	69	3
Marshall, I.P.	1987–95	165/5	36	14	3	17	0	2/1	1	198/6	40
Marshall, J.H.	1920–23	80	17	4	1	0	0	0	0	84	18
Marshall, W.	1962–63	57	0	3	0	3	0	0	0	63	0
Marsland, G.	1970	1/3	0	0	0	0	0	0	0	1/3	0
Martin, B.	1964	42	4	3	1	1	0	0	0	46	5
Martin, J.C.	1931	11	1	2	0	0	0	0	0	13	1
Martin, W.T.J.	1908–09	7	0	0	0	0	0	0	0	7	0
Matthews, W.H.	1908–25	344	0	24	0	0	0	0	0	368	0
Mawson, C.J.	2004	3/1	0	0	0	1	0	0	0	4/1	0
Mayor, J.	1937	0	0	0	0	0	0	1	0	1	0
Melville, L.	1957	2	0	0	0	0	0	0	0	2	0
Middleton, H.	1923–26	22	0	0	0	0	0	0	0	22	0
Mildenhall, S.J.	2004	6	0	0	0	0	0	0	0	6	0
Miller, S.	1909–12	39	0	2	0	0	0	0	0	41	0
Milligan, G.H.	1935–37	82	2	4	0	0	0	4	0	90	2
Milligan, M.J.J.	1985–93	278/1	23	21	1	30/1	2	5	1	334/2	27
Millward, A.E.	1931	1	0	0	0	0	0	0	0	1	0
Milne, J.B.	1947	13	0	0	0	0	0	0	0	13	0
Miskelly, D.T.	1998–2002	17/3	0	0/1	0	3	0	2	0	22/4	0
Mitchell, J.	1909	4	1	0	0	0	0	0	0	4	1
Mitchell, P.	1965	0/1	0	0	0	0/1	0	0	0	0/2	0
Moffat, H.	1910–14	162	10	20	0	0	0	0	0	182	10
Molango, M.	2006	3/2	1	0	0	0/1	0	0	0	3/3	1
Molyneux, W.S.	1968	8	0	1	0	0	0	0	0	9	0
Montgomery, W.	1909–11	70	26	5	0	0	0	0	0	75	26
Mooney, S.G.	1988	0	0	0	0	0	0	0/1	0	0/1	0
Moore, K.T.	1986	13	1	0	0	0	0	2	0	15	1

Player	Played	LEAGUE		FA CUP		FL CUP		OTHERS		TOTAL	
		A	G	A	G	A	G	A	G	A	G
Moore, N.	1994	5	0	0	0	0	0	0	0	5	0
Morgan, S.J.	1987	1/1	0	0	0	0/1	0	0	0	1/2	0
Morrisey, J.J.	1972	6	1	0	0	1	0	0	0	7	1
Morrow, J.J.	1996	1/1	0	0	0	0	0	0	0	1/1	0
Moss, F.	1929–31	29	0	1	0	0	0	0	0	30	0
Moulden, P.A.J.	1989–92	17/21	4	0	0	2/1	1	0	0	19/22	5
Muir, I.B.	1957	35	0	2	0	0	0	0	0	37	0
Mulvaney, R.	1971–73	88/4	2	7	0	3/1	0	3	0	101/5	2
Mundy, H.J.	1970	3/5	2	0	0	0	0	0	0	3/5	2
Munro, J.F.	1949–52	119	20	9	1	0	0	0	0	128	21
Murphy, E.C.	1956–58	72	0	4	0	0	0	0	0	76	0
Murphy, J.	1934	7	3	0	0	0	0	0	0	7	3
Murphy, W.	1929	2	1	0	0	0	0	0	0	2	1
Murray, K.	1956–57	35	14	1	1	0	0	0	0	36	15
Murray, P.	2001–03	93/2	15	3	0	2	0	4/1	0	102/3	15
Naylor, H.F.	1950	1	0	0	0	0	0	0	0	1	0
Naylor, J.	1922–28 & 1932	238	5	11	1	0	0	0	0	249	6
Naylor, T.W.	1947–58	224	0	14	0	0	0	0	0	238	0
Ndiwa–Lord, K.	2003	3/1	0	0	0	0	0	0	0	3/1	0
Neale, P.	1955–58	117	28	5	3	0	0	0	0	122	31
Newton, L.F.	1907–09	81	45	5	2	0	0	0	0	86	47
Nolan, M.W.	1966	2	0	0	0	0	0	0	0	2	0
Nord, J.G.	1920	3	0	0	0	0	0	0	0	3	0
Nuttall, M.	1980–81	8/5	1	0/1	0	0/1	0	0	0	8/7	1
O'Callaghan, B.R.	1984–85	10	0	0	0	0	0	0	0	10	0
O'Donnell, J.	1954–55	15	3	1	0	0	0	0	0	16	3
O'Donnell, R.M.	2007–	3/1	0	0	0	0	0	0	0	3/1	0
Ogden, C.J.	1971–77	128	0	5	0	10	0	10	0	153	0
Ogden, F.	1947–54	156	0	11	0	0	0	0	0	167	0
O'Halloran, M.V.	2003	2/11	1	0/1	0	0/1	0	1/1	0	3/14	1
Olney, I.D.	1992–95	42/2	13	1	0	2	1	0	0	49/3	13
O'Loughlin, W.J.	1959–60	27	0	2	0	0	0	0	0	29	0
Orlygsson, T.	1995–96	65/11	1	3/1	0	7/1	0	0	0	75/13	1
Ormandy, J.	1946	30	5	1	0	0	0	0	0	31	5
Ormond, W.	1949–53	122	25	5	2	0	0	0	0	127	27
Ormondroyd, I.	1986 & 1996	34/7	9	1	0	0	0	1	0	36/7	9
Ormston, A.	1925 & 1928	43	22	4	2	0	0	0	0	47	24
Outhwaite, G.	1955	4	0	0	0	0	0	0	0	4	0
Over, E.	1957	21	2	0	0	0	0	0	0	21	2
Owen, G.D.	2003 & 2004–05	41/1	1	2/1	0	1	0	0	0	44/2	1
Palmer, R.N.	1980–93	419/47	141	19/5	5	34/5	10	5/2	1	477/59	157
Parker, D.	1983–84	54/3	11	1	0	4	3	0	0	59/3	14
Parkin, B.	1983–84	6	0	0	0	2	0	0	0	8	0
Parkin, S.	2000	3/4	3	0	0	0	0	0	0	3/4	3
Parkinson, H.	1921	3	0	0	0	0	0	0	0	3	0
Parnaby, T.W.	1947	7	1	0	0	0	0	0	0	7	1
Pateman, G.E.	1933	7	4	0	0	0	0	0	0	7	4
Paterson, A.A.	1920	1	0	0	0	0	0	0	0	1	0
Paterson, A.	1937–38	21	1	0	0	0	0	2	0	23	1
Pears, J.	1930–33	92	34	5	0	0	0	0	0	97	34
Pearson, D.T.	1956	25	12	2	1	0	0	0	0	27	13
Pearson, H.	1931–32	38	0	1	0	0	0	0	0	39	0
Pearson, M.	2006	0/1	0	0	0	0	0	0	0	0/1	0
Pederson, T.A.	1993	7/3	0	2/1	0	0	0	0	0	9/4	0
Pemberton, M.C.	1995–96	0/5	0	0	0	0/1	0	0	0	0/6	0
Pennington, J.	1965	23	0	3	1	2	0	0	0	28	1
Pennington, T.E.	1909	1	0	0	0	0	0	0	0	1	0
Philliskirk, A.	1988	3/7	1	0	0	0/2	1	1	0	4/9	2
Philpott, A.	1967–68	28/3	1	1	0	2	0	0	0	31/3	1
Phoenix, P.P.	1957–61	161	27	12	4	5	0	0	0	178	31
Pickering, W.H.	1948–50	78	0	9	0	0	0	0	0	87	0
Pickersgill, T.	1931–32	39	0	1	0	0	0	0	0	40	0
Pilkington, E.	1911–25	269	14	11	1	0	0	0	0	280	15
Pilkington, S.T.	1910	5	0	0	0	0	0	0	0	5	0
Platt, J.R.	1975–80	109	0	9	0	1	0	1/7	0	120/7	0
Player, P.R.I.	1959	2	0	0	0	0	0	0	0	2	0
Pogliacomi, L.A.	2002 & 2006	160	0	13	0	4	0	10	0	187	0
Pointon, N.G.	1992–94	92/3	3	7/1	2	5	0	0	0	104/4	5
Pollitt, M.F.	1997	16	0	0	0	0	0	0	0	16	0

Player	Played	LEAGUE		FA CUP		FL CUP		OTHERS		TOTAL	
		A	G	A	G	A	G	A	G	A	G
Pollock, W.	1947	4	0	0	0	0	0	0	0	4	0
Porter, C.J.	2005–06	52/14	28	6	3	0	0	2/1	0	63/15	31
Porter, W.	1927–34	274	1	10	0	0	0	0	0	284	1
Prenderville, B.	2000–01	16/5	0	1	0	3/1	0	0	0	20/6	0
Price, N.M.	1936–37	73	0	4	0	0	0	4	0	81	0
Prince, J.	1927	1	0	0	0	0	0	0	0	1	0
Purcell, L.	1931	1	0	0	0	0	0	0	0	1	0
Pynegar, A.	1925–28	131	51	7	4	0	0	0	0	138	55
Quinn, M.	1983–85	78/2	34	2	1	4	2	0	0	84/2	37
Quinn, N.P.A.	1967	4	0	0	0	0	0	0	0	4	0
Quixall, A.	1964–65	36	11	2	0	3	1	0	0	41	12
Rachubka, P.S.	2001	16	0	0	0	0	0	1	0	17	0
Rackley, R.W.	1960	19	5	2	0	1	0	0	0	22	5
Radcliffe, M.	1945	0	0	4	0	0	0	0	0	4	0
Ramsay, A.A.	1906	0	0	8	3	0	0	0	0	8	3
Ramsey, D.	1949	2	0	0	0	0	0	0	0	2	0
Ratcliffe, B.	1935–38	156	1	6	0	0	0	7	0	169	1
Redfearn, N.D.	1989–91	56/6	16	7/1	3	3	1	1	0	67/7	20
Redmond, S.	1992–97	195/10	4	10/2	0	20	1	0	0	225/12	5
Reeves, D.E.	2001–02	11/2	3	0	0	0	0	0	0	11/2	3
Reid, J.	1908	5	2	0	0	0	0	0	0	5	2
Reid, P.R.	1996–98	93	6	8	0	4	1	1	0	106	7
Reid, T.J.	1932–34	67	34	4	1	0	0	0	0	71	35
Rhodes, A.C.	1987–89	69	0	1	0	7	0	2	0	79	0
Richards, M.J.	2001	3/2	0	0	0	0	0	1	1	4/2	1
Richardson, J.P.	1935	3	0	0	0	0	0	0	0	3	0
Richardson, L.J.	1994–97	82/6	21	3	1	6	2	0	0	91/6	24
Richardson, L.M.	1996	0/1	0	0	0	0	0	0/1	0	0/2	0
Richardson, S.	1959	22	0	1	0	0	0	0	0	23	0
Rickers, P.S.	1994–2001	242/19	20	17/2	0	13	2	4/1	0	276/22	22
Ricketts, M.B.	2007–	8/1	2	0	0	2	0	1	0	11/1	2
Ridding, W.	1935	1	0	0	0	0	0	0	0	1	0
Ridings, F.	1932–33	2	0	0	0	0	0	0	0	2	0
Ritchie, A.T.	1987–2000	201/42	84	9/4	4	20/2	19	3/1	0	233/49	107
Roach, N.	2000	0/1	0	0	0	0	0	0	0	0/1	0
Robbins, P.	1935–37	80	15	3	0	0	0	4	2	87	17
Roberts, C.	1913–14	72	2	7	0	0	0	0	0	79	2
Robertson, J.	2007	2/1	1	0	0	0	0	0	0	2/1	1
Robins, I.	1969–77	202/18	40	12/1	3	4/2	3	4	0	222/21	46
Robinson, J.	1961	3	0	0	0	0	0	0	0	3	0
Robinson, K.	1958–60	40	4	1	0	0	0	0	0	41	4
Robson, J.C.	1934–35	37	8	4	1	0	0	0	0	41	9
Roca, C.J.	2003	0/7	0	1	0	1	0	0/2	0	2/9	0
Rocastle, C.A.	2006	17/18	2	0/2	0	1	1	1	0	19/20	3
Rollo, J.S.	1960–62	59	0	3	0	0	0	0	0	62	0
Rooke, W.	1905	0	0	4	2	0	0	0	0	4	2
Roque, M.	2006	1/3	0	0	0	0	0	0	0	1/3	0
Roscoe, J.H.	1931	19	8	2	0	0	0	0	0	21	8
Ross, A.	1956	3	0	0	0	0	0	0	0	3	0
Round, E.	1907–08	10	0	0	0	0	0	0	0	10	0
Rowley, H.B.	1932–34	70	13	3	1	0	0	0	0	73	14
Rush, M.J.	1996–97	17/7	3	0/3	0	0	0	0/1	0	17/11	3
Ryan, J.B.	1981–82 & 1985–86	97/3	8	4	0	8	0	0	0	109/3	8
Salley, G.	1911	3	0	0	0	0	0	0	0	3	0
Salt, P.T.	1997–2000	12/10	0	1/1	1	1/3	0	3	1	17/14	2
Sanokho, A.	2004	0/1	0	0	0	0	0	0	0	0/1	0
Sawbridge, J.	1946–47	8	0	0	0	0	0	0	0	8	0
Schofield, F.	1933–35	82	3	0	0	0	0	3	1	85	4
Schofield, G.	1969	1	0	0	0	0	0	0	0	1	0
Schofield, M.	1946	7	0	0	0	0	0	0	0	7	0
Scholes, R.	1924–25	5	0	0	0	0	0	0	0	5	0
Scholfield, J.	1925–26	4	1	0	0	0	0	0	0	4	1
Scott, J.	1961–63	76	0	7	0	3	0	0	0	86	0
Scott, R.	1959	9	1	2	0	0	0	0	0	11	1
Scott, R.	2005	19/2	1	2/1	0	1	0	1	0	23/3	1
Scrine, F.H.	1953–55	78	21	4	1	0	0	0	0	82	22
Seddon, R.C.	1925	1	0	0	0	0	0	0	0	1	0
Serrant, C.	1995–99	84/6	1	6	1	7	0	0	0	97/6	2
Seymour, T.G.	1929–35	127	0	7	0	0	0	3	0	137	0
Shackleton, A.	1961	10	7	1	0	1	0	0	0	12	7

251

Player	Played	LEAGUE A	LEAGUE G	FA CUP A	FA CUP G	FL CUP A	FL CUP G	OTHERS A	OTHERS G	TOTAL A	TOTAL G
Shadbolt, J.A.	1905–08	23	9	16	13	0	0	0	0	39	22
Sharp, A.A.	1934	1	0	0	0	0	0	0	0	1	0
Sharp, G.H.	1957	1	0	0	0	0	0	0	0	1	0
Sharp, G.M.	1991–94	103/6	30	11/1	2	12/1	4	1	0	127/8	36
Sharratt, H.	1955	1	0	0	0	0	0	0	0	1	0
Shaw, G.	1908	10	1	0	0	0	0	0	0	10	1
Shaw, G.D.	1969–77	210/4	91	9	2	5	2	1	0	225/4	95
Shaw, J.	1934	2	0	0	0	0	0	0	0	2	0
Sheffield, L.J.	1967	18	6	0	0	0	0	0	0	18	6
Sheridan, D.S.	2001–03	72/16	3	8	0	4/1	0	8	0	92/17	3
Sheridan, J.J.	1998–2003	132/13	14	14/1	2	2/2	0	1	0	149/16	15
Shimwell, E.	1957	7	0	0	0	0	0	0	0	7	0
Shipman, T.E.R.	1938	40	0	6	0	0	0	1	0	47	0
Short, M.	1970	5	0	0	0	2	0	0	0	7	0
Shufflebotham, J.	1907–08	7	1	0	0	0	0	0	0	7	1
Sievwright, G.E.M.	1963	37	4	3	0	0	0	0	0	40	4
Sinclair, N.J.T.	1978–84	73/2	1	6	0	0	0	0	0	79/2	1
Sinkinson, F.	1937	2	0	0	0	0	0	0	0	2	0
Sinnott, L.	1997–98	25/6	0	1	0	3	0	0	0	29/6	0
Skipper, P.D.	1988	27	1	1	0	2	0	0	0	30	1
Slater, P.	1906	0	0	6	0	0	0	0	0	6	0
Sleeuwenhoek, J.C.	1971	2	0	0	0	1	0	0	0	3	0
Smalley, D.A.	2006–	19/20	2	5	0	1/1	1	0/1	0	25/22	3
Smalley, L.W.	1931–32	20	5	0	0	0	0	0	0	20	5
Smart, A.A.C.	2001	14/7	6	1	0	0	0	2	1	17/7	7
Smelt, T.	1929	2	0	0	0	0	0	0	0	2	0
Smith, G.D.	1985	14/1	0	0	0	0	0	0	0	14/1	0
Smith, I.P.	2000	3/1	0	0	0	1	0	0	0	4/1	0
Smith.J.B.	1960	1	0	0	0	0	0	0	0	1	0
Smith, L.	1949–55	178	3	14	1	0	0	0	0	192	4
Smith, N.H.	1948	1	0	0	0	0	0	0	0	1	0
Smith, R.	1967	0/2	0	0	0	1	0	0	0	1/2	0
Smith, S.J.	1957	4	0	0	0	0	0	0	0	4	0
Smith, T.	2006	0/1	0	0	0	0/1	0	0	0	0/2	0
Smithurst, E.	1919	2	0	0	0	0	0	0	0	2	0
Snodin, G.	1991	8	1	0	0	1	0	0	0	9	1
Snodin, I.	1994–96	55/2	0	1	0	0	0	0	0	56/2	0
Speedie, F.B.	1908	15	6	2	0	0	0	0	0	17	6
Spence, A.N.	1968–69	26/1	12	0	0	1	0	0	0	27/1	13
Spence, D.M.	1922	4	0	0	0	0	0	0	0	4	0
Spence, D.W.	1971–72	5/1	0	0	0	0	0	0	0	5/1	0
Spink, H.	1933–34	20	1	0	0	0	0	0	0	20	1
Spooner, N.M.	1998	2	0	0	0	0	0	0	0	2	0
Spurdle, W.	1947–49 & 1957–62	200	24	18	4	2	0	0	0	220	28
Stafford, H.E.	1928–33	17	0	1	0	0	0	0	0	18	0
Stafford, J.	1905–07	1	0	2	0	0	0	0	0	3	0
Stainrod, S.A.	1978–80	69	21	1	0	3	1	6	4	79	26
Stam, S.	2004–2007	73/11	1	7	0	1	0	1/1	0	82/12	1
Standring, N.	1945	0	0	2	2	0	0	0	0	2	2
Staniforth, A.C.	1922–23	35	7	2	1	0	0	0	0	37	8
Stanton, C.	1927–28 & 1930	18	5	1	1	0	0	0	0	19	6
Starbuck, P.M.	1997	7/2	1	0	0	0	0	0	0	7/2	1
Steel, W.J.	1978–82	101/7	24	6	0	9/1	1	7/1	2	123/9	27
Steele, E.	1932	14	1	0	0	0	0	0	0	14	1
Stenner, A.W.J.	1956	3	0	0	0	0	0	0	0	3	0
Stephenson, R.L.	1957	8	0	0	0	0	0	0	0	8	0
Stevens, D.	1965–66	33	0	5	0	0	0	0	0	38	0
Stewart, R.	1919–20	34	0	1	0	0	0	0	0	35	1
Stock, H.	1948–50	35	10	4	1	0	0	0	0	39	11
Stokes, P.	1908	2	1	0	0	0	0	0	0	2	1
Stringer, E.	1949	1	0	0	0	0	0	0	0	1	0
Stringfellow, P.	1958–60	54	16	1	0	0	0	0	0	55	16
Sugden, R.S.	1998–2000	4/17	1	0	0	1/2	0	1	0	6/19	1
Swailes, C.	2005–06	18/1	0	0	0	0	0	0	0	18/1	0
Swallow, E.	1950	6	0	0	0	0	0	0	0	6	0
Swan.I.	1998	1	0	0/1	0	1	0	0	0	2/1	0
Swan, R.M.	1964–66	64	0	5	0	2	0	0	0	71	0
Swarbrick, J.	1907–08	4	2	0	0	0	0	0	0	4	2
Sweeney, A.	1970–74	37/5	2	2	0	0	0	0	0	39/5	2

Player	Played	LEAGUE		FA CUP		FL CUP		OTHERS		TOTAL	
		A	G	A	G	A	G	A	G	A	G
Swift, F.	1933–34	54	0	1	0	0	0	0	0	55	0
Swinbourne, A.T.A.	1963	4	0	0	0	0	0	0	0	4	0
Tait, J.A.	1999	0/1	0	0	0	0/1	0	0	0	0/2	0
Talbot, G.R.	1934	2	0	0	0	0	0	0	0	2	0
Talbot, R.C.	1935	13	0	0	0	0	0	0	0	13	0
Tannahill, R.	1905	0	0	2	1	0	0	0	0	2	1
Tatton, J.H.	1920–21	67	2	3	0	0	0	0	0	70	2
Taylor, A.	1969	2	0	0	0	0	0	0	0	2	0
Taylor, C.D.	2006–07	91/9	9	8	0	1/1	0	5	0	105/10	9
Taylor, E.H.	1912–21	87	0	4	0	0	0	0	0	91	0
Taylor, G.	1924–28	71	22	3	0	0	0	0	0	74	22
Taylor, G.B.	1963	40	0	3	0	1	0	0	0	44	0
Taylor, J.	1929–31	12	7	1	0	0	0	0	0	13	7
Taylor, J.T.	1938	13	6	2	0	0	0	0	0	15	6
Taylor, P.J.	1982	4	0	0	0	0	0	0	0	4	0
Taylor, S.J.	1977–78	45/2	25	2	1	0	0	8	2	55/2	28
Taylor, W.B.	1958–59	51	0	2	0	0	0	0	0	53	0
Taylor, W.	1920–24	109	1	6	1	0	0	0	0	115	2
Teece, D.A.	1956–58	91	0	5	0	0	0	0	0	96	0
Thom, S.P.	1998	28/6	3	1/1	0	1	0	1	0	31/6	3
Thomas, W.E.	1928–32	22	0	1	0	0	0	0	0	23	0
Thompson, J.	1919	2	0	0	0	0	0	0	0	2	0
Thompson, J.	1953–57	110	19	6	2	0	0	0	0	116	21
Thompson, J.	2007–	7/1	0	0/1	0	2	0	1/1	0	10/3	0
Thompson, N.	1997	8	0	0	0	0	0	0	0	8	0
Thomson, A.C.	1969–70	27/1	0	2	0	0	0	0	0	29/1	0
Tierney, M.P.	2003–06	21/16	0	2/2	0	2/1	0	2/1	0	27/20	0
Tilling, H.K.	1945–47	3	0	2	0	0	0	0	0	5	0
Tipton, M.J.	1997–2001	51/60	15	4/7	1	3/4	0	3/3	1	61/74	17
Tolson, N.	1992–93	0/3	0	0	0	0	0	0	0	0/3	0
Toman, W.	1905	0	0	1	2	0	0	0	0	1	2
Tomlinson, F.A.	1946–50	115	27	9	2	0	0	0	0	124	29
Toms, W.L.	1921	20	5	0	0	0	0	0	0	20	5
Torrance, G.S.	1956	4	0	0	0	0	0	0	0	4	0
Toward, A.V.	1909–13	72	30	6	3	0	0	0	0	78	33
Towers, I.J.	1965–67	94/1	45	6	0	4	0	0	0	104/1	45
Travis, D.	1951 & 1954–56	114	62	4	0	0	0	0	0	118	62
Treacy, R.C.P.	1974	3	1	0	0	0	0	0	0	3	1
Trippier, A.W.	1931	6	1	0	0	0	0	0	0	6	1
Trotman, N.A.	2006–07	16/1	1	3/1	2	0/1	0	1	0	20/3	3
Trotter, W.	1926–27	5	1	0	0	0	0	0	0	5	1
Tummon, O.	1912–14	108	19	13	4	0	0	0	0	121	23
Turner, B.H.	2006	1	0	0	0	0	0	0	0	1	0
Turner, B.	1970	10/1	0	0	0	0	0	0	0	10/1	0
Valentine, A.F.	1938	2	1	0	0	0	0	1	0	3	1
Valentine, C.H.	1976–79	75/7	8	6	1	4/1	0	6	1	91/8	10
Valentine, F.E.	1936	5	0	0	0	0	0	0	0	5	0
Vallance, W.	1938	1	0	0	0	0	0	1	1	2	1
Vernon, S.M.	2002–04	43/32	20	3/2	1	1	0	5/2	6	52/36	27
Vonk, M.C.	1995	5	1	0	0	0	0	0	0	5	1
Waddell, G.B.	1922	1	0	0	0	0	0	0	0	1	0
Wadsworth, A.W.	1949–51	33	8	2	0	0	0	0	0	35	8
Waite, W.J.	1946	4	4	1	0	0	0	0	0	5	4
Walders, D.	1906–11	112	8	17	2	0	0	0	0	129	10
Walders, J.	1906	0	0	7	3	0	0	0	0	7	3
Walker, G.S.	1925	2	0	0	0	0	0	0	0	2	0
Walker, R.S.	2003	1	0	0	0	0	0	0	0	1	0
Walker, S.	1947	1	0	0	0	0	0	0	0	1	0
Walker, T.J.	1953–56 & 1957–58	158	23	6	0	0	0	0	0	164	23
Wall, G.	1919–20	74	12	2	0	0	0	0	0	76	12
Wallace, C.W.	1921–22	47	3	3	0	0	0	0	0	50	3
Walsh, D.G.	1998	0/2	0	0	0	0	0	0	0	0/2	0
Walsh, G.	1993	6	0	0	0	0	0	0	0	6	0
Walsh, K.W.	1949–50	3	0	0	0	0	0	0	0	3	0
Walsh, W.	1933–35	78	49	4	3	0	0	3	3	85	55
Walters, G.A.	1959	13	2	3	1	0	0	0	0	16	3
Walters, J.	1912–19	110	35	7	1	0	0	0	0	117	36
Wann, A.H.	1960	19	0	0	0	0	0	0	0	19	0
Ward, M.W.	1883–84	84	12	3	0	5	0	0	0	92	12

Player	Played	LEAGUE A	LEAGUE G	FA CUP A	FA CUP G	FL CUP A	FL CUP G	OTHERS A	OTHERS G	TOTAL A	TOTAL G
Ward, W.	1907	15	1	0	0	0	0	0	0	15	1
Warhurst, P.	1988–90	60/7	2	5/4	0	8	0	2	0	75/11	2
Warhurst, R.	1960	8	0	0	0	0	0	0	0	8	0
Warne, P.	2005–06	80/6	18	8	3	2	0	4	0	94/6	21
Warner, J.	1951	34	2	1	0	0	0	0	0	35	2
Watson, A.	1948–49	42	0	5	0	0	0	0	0	47	0
Watson, M.S.	2000	1/1	0	0	0	1	0	0	0	2/1	0
Watson, R.H.	1921–28	233	64	9	8	0	0	0	0	242	72
Watts, H.P.	1907–09	12	4	0	0	0	0	0	0	12	4
Wealands, J.A.	1983	10	0	0	0	0	0	0	0	10	0
Webster, S.P.	1994	7	0	0	0	0	0	0	0	7	0
Wellens, R.P.	2005–06	87	8	8	0	2	0	3/1	0	100/1	8
Wellock, M.	1926	5	6	0	0	0	0	0	0	5	6
West, E.	1957–60	117	0	7	0	1	0	0	0	125	0
West, J.	1908	1	0	0	0	0	0	0	0	1	0
West, T.	1945	0	0	4	2	0	0	0	0	4	2
Whaites, A.	1907–08	42	8	4	2	0	0	0	0	46	10
Whelan, R.	1952	1	0	0	0	0	0	0	0	1	0
Whitaker, C.	1962–63	72	29	3	2	1	0	0	0	76	31
White, C.	1924–25	5	0	0	0	0	0	0	0	5	0
White, G.D.	1960	1	0	0	0	0	0	0	0	1	0
Whitehall, S.C.	1998–99	55/21	13	6/1	2	0/3	0	2	0	63/25	15
Whittle, M.	1969–76	307/5	39	17	2	14	0	7	2	345/5	43
Whyte, C.	1934	2	0	0	0	0	0	0	0	2	0
Whyte, J.A.	1950–55	234	0	14	0	0	0	0	0	248	0
Wiggins, J.A.	1936	3	0	0	0	0	0	0	0	3	0
Wijnard, C.	2002	24/1	10	2	1	3	2	1	0	30/1	13
Wilbraham, A.T.	2004	4	2	0	0	0	0	1	0	5	2
Wildman, A.	1905	0	0	1	0	0	0	0	0	1	0
Wilkinson, H.	1923–25	17	0	0	0	0	0	0	0	17	0
Wilkinson, P.	1995	4	1	0	0	0	0	0	0	4	1
Wilkinson, W.M.	2003–04	2/4	0	0	0	0	0	0/1	0	2/5	0
Williams, A.	1961–64	172	9	13	1	5	0	0	0	190	10
Williams, D.	1956	28	0	2	0	0	0	0	0	30	0
Williams, G.A.	1985–90	45/16	12	0	0	7/2	3	4	1	56/18	16
William, J.B.	1951	1	0	0	0	0	0	0	0	1	0
Williamson, T.	1935–46	157	4	12	0	0	0	4	0	173	4
Wilson, C.	1911–12	21	0	1	0	0	0	0	0	22	0
Wilson, D.	1906–20	368	16	37	4	0	0	0	0	405	20
Wilson, J.	1947–48	29	2	2	1	0	0	0	0	31	3
Wilson, R.	1969	25	0	3	0	1	0	0	0	29	0
Winn, A.	2004	0/2	0	0	0	0	0	0	0	0/2	0
Witham, R.	1946	5	0	0	0	0	0	0	0	5	0
Wolfenden, M.	2003–07	7/29	2	2/2	0	0/1	0	0/3	2	9/35	4
Wolstenholme, A.	1907–09 & 1919	52	12	2	0	0	0	0	0	54	12
Wood, I.T.	1965–79	517/7	22	27/1	3	18	1	15/1	0	577/8	26
Wood, N.A.	2006	3/2	0	0	0	1	0	1	0	5/2	0
Wood, N.	1946	1	0	0	0	0	0	0	0	1	0
Wood, W.	1921–22	24	3	0	0	0	0	0	0	24	3
Woodhall, B.H.	1969	3/1	1	0	0	0	0	0	0	3/1	1
Woodcock, E.	1948–49	28	4	0	0	0	0	0	0	28	4
Woodger, G.	1910–13	115	22	15	4	0	0	0	0	130	26
Worrall, F.	1928–30	105	21	2	0	0	0	0	0	107	21
Worthington, F.	1956	10	1	1	0	0	0	0	0	11	1
Wright, D.	1946 & 1951	9	0	0	0	0	0	0	0	9	0
Wright, E.	1938	37	5	2	0	0	0	1	1	40	6
Wright, J.W.	1905–07	3	0	5	0	0	0	0	0	8	0
Wright, T.	1956	7	2	0	0	0	0	0	0	7	2
Wright, T.E.	1986–88 & 1997	120/4	25	4	2	7/1	2	3	0	134/5	29
Wylde, R.J.	1979–82	109/4	51	3	0	9	1	3	2	124/4	54
Wynne, S.	1921–26	145	9	8	1	0	0	0	0	153	10
Yarwood, J.	1922–23	11	0	0	0	0	0	0	0	11	0
Young, A.F.	1974–78	107/15	30	6	4	4	1	12/3	4	129/18	39
Zola–Makongo, C.	2003	21/4	5	1	1	0	0	2	1	24/4	7

ND - #0354 - 270225 - C0 - 260/195/16 - PB - 9781780913001 - Gloss Lamination